Remembering
ROHATYN
and its Environs

First Person Accounts

An 800-year-old Town.
Centuries of Jewish Life.

Compiled and Edited by
Donia Gold Shwarzstein

An earlier version of this work was published in 2015 by Fields Publshing, LLC under a pseudonym.

Included in this volume is an English transation of "The Community of Rohatyn and its Environs," published in 1962 by The Society of Rohatiner in Israel. The right to translate that work was granted to Dora Gold Shwarzstein who is solely responsible for the translation. A version first appeared online in 2001 and in superceded by this edition.

This book documents the 1998 Commemoration Service and the Preservation Project of the gravesites in Rohatyn. Participants in the memorial service provided their eulogies and memoirs at the behest of The Society of Rohatiner in Israel. The Society of Rohatiner in Israel stipulated that the translation and documentation of the Commemoration be published in book form. It is intended to be a lasting possession of the Jewish expatriate families of the Rohatyn area.

ISBN: 978-0-9965999-1-7

The Rohatyn District (Powiat), 1939

1943 Map of Rohatyn, Under German Occupation

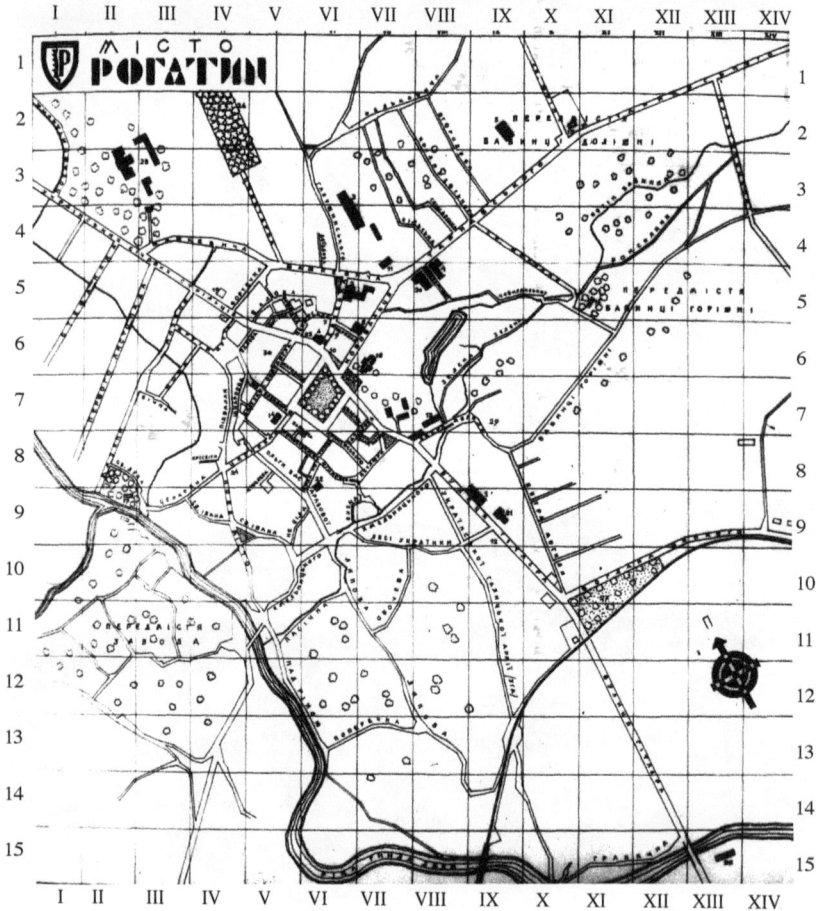

Note: The Jewish ghetto area on this map is blank. In June, 1943, it had been burnt down by the Germans to smoke out people hiding in bunkers.

Map received from municipality in Rohatyn on June 11, 1998. Translated from Ukrainian by Donia Gold Shwarzstein.

Legend of streets and neighborhoods in Rohatyn

1. Babincy-upper, X-7
2. Basarasovoy Olgi, V-8
3. Bazaarova (Market St.), VII-7
4. Bichna, III-7
5. Bozhnicza (Synagogue St.), V-5
6. Tzerkovna (Greek Ortho. Church St.), V-5
7. Khmelnitzkoho Bohdana, VII-9 (29 Listopada/ Artema)
8. Tzvintarna (Cemetery St.), V-4
9. Chernika, VI-6, /Raykha (German Reich St.)/ Timoshenka
10. Dotsdova, VI-4
11. Dookha Sviatoho, II-8 /Pilna
12. Franka Ivana/Ploshcha (Square), VI-7/Rynok (Umschlagplatz on 3/20/42)
13. Fedkovicha, VII-2, /Yasna
14. Fortechna, IV-5
15. Fundush (Pron. Foondoosh)
16. Galushchinskoho, A. Proborska, VI-4
17. ADOLPH HITLER ST., X-9/Pilsudskiego/ Chervonoy Armii
18. Hranichna (Boundary St.), XII-15
19. St. Ivana St., IX-9
20. Yaroslava Osmomisla, V-6/Dolinikanska/St. George Sviatoho Yuria
21. Yaricheskoho Silvestra, VI-8 (Reich St./Par. Komuni)
22. St. Yuri, X-2
23. Karpenna Karoho, V-7 (Korotka)
24. Kobilyanskoi Olgi, VIII-5 (Kilinskoho, Rozy Luxenburg)
25. Konovaltz Yevg., VI-4 (Mickiewicza)
26. Kotlarevskoho Ivan, VIII-3 (Kosharova)
27. Kruty, IV-4 (Stolarska)
28. Kupeleva, V-8
29. Depkoho Bohdana, XI-10 (Pratzkoho, Chapayeva)
30. Lisovi
31. Lipova, VI-10
32. Pershoho Listopada, III-5
33. Mazepy, III-5 (Staromlynska)
34. Mereshiska or Pereshiska
35. Petra Mohili, VIII-7 (Petra Skargi)
36. Nikolaya Sviatoho, IX-4
37. Nad Rikoyu, V-12
38. Ne Tzila, V-9
39. Nova, III-6
40. Nove Misto, IV-9
41. Ohonovskoho Omeliana, V-8 (Einstein/Stakhanova)
42. Ohorodova, VIII-2
43. Ovocheva, VII-10
44. Pasichna, V-2
45. Pekarska, V-6
46. Perenivska
47. Petliuri Simeona, VII-8 (Marayatzka)
48. Pidvallya, IV-7
49. Polerechka, VI-13
50. Pozashpitalna, I-3 (Pozaklasztorna)
51. Prosvity, IV-8 (Karla Livknevta)
52. Putyatinetzka, XIII-2
53. Yurka Rogatintzia, VI-8 (Torgova)
54. Bohdana Rogatinskoho, (V-4 (Herzl, I.Trawna)
55. Roksolyani, XI-4
56. Silska, VIII-4 (Wiejska)
57. Sliysarska, VIII-4
58. Stefanika Vasila, II-4 (Komsomolska)
59. Vashevicha, VI-5
60. Shevchenka, VI-6
61. Shkarpova, IV-7
62. Tarnavskoho Generala, VIII-4 (Mickiewicza)
63. Ukr. Halitzkoy Armii, VIII-9 (Sienkiewicza)
64. Lesi Ukrainski, VII-9 (Kosciuszko)
65. Ukrainskikh Sichovikh Striltziv, I-3 (Slowatzkoho, Chervonoy Armii)
66. Valova
67. Vapniyana, V-7
68. Voozka,VI-9
69. Volodimira Velikoho, V-7 (Kazimierska)
70. Voozka, VI-9
71. Zmkniena, VII-8
72. Zavoda, III-11
73. Zelena, VIII-6

Most important institutions and enterprises:
1. County Administration (Starostwo of Povit), IX-9
2. City Hall (Magistrat), VI-6
3. Ukrainian High School/Seminary, VI-4
4. National School, VIII-8
5. German School, IX-2
6. District Cooperative Union (National Market),VI-4
7. Ukrainebank, VI-6
8. Post Office, VII-7
9. Ukrainian Police, VI-6
10. German Gendarmerie, VI-6
11. Forestry Division, VII-5
12. Zbirna Hromada Rohatyna, IX-9
13. Flour Mill, VIII-7
14. Parish Church, V-7
15. Church of St. George (Yuri), X-2
16. Church of St. Mikolai, XI-5
17. Church of St. Luke, II-9
18. Roman Catholic Church, VII-6
19. Greek Orthodox Parish Office, IV-5
20. House of Culture, VIII-5
21. Movie House (Kino), IX-9
22. CityElectricPower Station, VI-8
23. City Hotel, VI-6
24. Public Bath House, IV-8
25. City Slaughterhouse, VIII-15
26. Miske Kladovishche (Town cemetery), IV-2
27. City Park, XI-10
28. Monastery Hospital-III-3
29. Deutscher Berg (Yerusalem St.), IX-7
30. City Marketplace, V-6

Ed. Note: Three periods of history are recorded in street names, in reverse chronological order: 1939-1943: German, Soviet, Polish.

Contents

Contents

Contents

PART II

Contents

APPENDIX

Foreword

In 1989, the synagogue in which I was raised celebrated its 50th anniversary, and we, the children who had regarded Kew Gardens Synagogue as our religious home, were invited back to join in that celebration. My parents had left the community some 17 years earlier as part of the great migration from New York to Florida, and this was the first time that I had returned to my childhood home. Much was the same, but so much was different.

I came back not as a son but as a father, not as a child but as an adult. The synagogue seemed smaller and less imposing. I was struck by the most mundane of matters. I was startled by how small the bathroom was, how low the urinal, in part because I remembered how proud I was once I as a boy could finally reach that urinal. The streets were the same; even many of the houses looked as they had once looked, but they were not the homes we knew–not our homes. The people who had shaped our community had either died or moved away–all this, in only 17 years.

In 2009, Cornell scientist Professor Robert H. Lieberman produced and directed a film, *Last Stop Kew Gardens*, depicting his generation of Kew Gardens residents, the European or American-born children of parents who had emigrated from Europe just before the war, just in time to avoid the Holocaust. I read the review, ordered the film and watched it immediately. I then sent it by Fed Ex to my sister in Israel, who expressed great interest in seeing the film, and to my utter surprise she did not see it. She waited and waited until she could invite those with whom she had grown up to watch the film with–something that has yet to happen.

These experiences kept coming back to me as I read *Remembering Rohatyn and its Environs,* which Donia Gold Shwarzstein initiated and so lovingly compiled. The book is based on the work that had been done almost a half century ago, in 1962, by the Rohatyner Association in Israel in Hebrew, Yiddish and English, which was entrusted to Shwarzstein, and which she had translated into English–and Part Two, which has never before been published and which she compiled for the very first time for this work. The result is a *Yizkor buch*, a memorial book, homage to a Jewish town and a

Jewish region that was but is no longer and to its many different inhabitants who carried images of that town and that time in their mind and in their memory.

I know that one has no right to compare the evolution of the Kew Gardens city of my youth with the decimation that was the lot of Rohatyn. There is no comparison—there can be no comparison—and yet, we all, even those of us who did not experience The Cataclysm, carry within us memories of a world that was and is no longer, of people who touched us, shaped our lives, gave meaning to our existence, who are no longer. When a world is destroyed, the only tool that we have to bring it to life again is memory, and the urge not to give destruction the final word, the last say, is overwhelming.

Scores of survivors of Rohatyn joined together to offer their insights into this town and its vicinity to make this work a sacred act of collective memory. Some were scholars and historians, philosophers and rabbis, but most were ordinary men and women who were drawn to these acts of remembrance, who had a story to tell, a recollection to share, who were bequeathed a document and felt the overwhelming need to share it with history, to state it for the record. As you read through this book, you will read a work of uneven quality. Some contributors are gifted writers; others wrote with hesitation but with the determination to commit their words to paper and, through this work, to immortality. All were committed to a collective task: to remember, to record for history, to obey the very admonition that was said to have been the final statement of Simon Dubnow, the great Jewish historian who was murdered in the Shoah; "Yidn, shreibt un farshreibt!" ("Jews, write and record!").

The town they remember is the same–there is still a town called Rohatyn, even the streets are the same - but what they remember of the town is so very different. And when they made a pilgrimage back to the town, they understood that one can—and one cannot—return. They experienced the ultimate paradoxical situation of the Jews who visit Poland—the Presence of Absence and the Absence of Presence.

Naturally, religious Jews remember the synagogues and the rabbis. The Hassidim remember their Rebbes, the dancing on Simchas Torah, the joy of worship. The more scholarly remember the learning. Children remember their teachers, some even fondly and with gratitude. The Yiddishists remember the Yiddish they learned and loved. The Hebraists remember the rebirth of a language they now speak routinely to their children and grandchildren.

The Zionists remember their youth movements—right, left and center. They remember the tension within the community, but equally important within their own families over this revolution in Jewish life, which offered hope, but also shattered the seemingly timeless norms of the community.

Those who engaged in business remember the different businesses that kept the economy of the town and its environment afloat. They remember the few who were wealthy and so many who were poor, but they do not remember despondency of the poor. Jewish communities then were more compassionate than we are today—or perhaps the distance between comfort and poverty was short and could be bridged by some bread, soup and produce.

Those who dwelled in neighboring towns where only a few people lived and only a few Jews made their homes recall each of those towns one by one, memory by memory.

The historians describe the history of the town from its inception through its transformation and up until its destruction. Readers knowledgeable in Jewish history will marvel that Sabbatai Zvi is recalled, along with the Frankist messianic movement that strayed so far from Judaism that it led to the conversion of prominent members of the town. Readers will be surprised by the power of these movements, by how disquieting they were to the town's traditions, and by how honest the historians were who recalled this shameful past of Jewish history. Gershom Sholem would be proud. These were religious scandals that threatened to shake the foundations of Rohatyn. Some Jews believed that the Messiah had come. Some Jews converted—sons and daughters of some of the leading families of Rohatyn, together with their parents, even at the initiative of their parents. Even today, among the pious, there is a reluctance to speak of these matters. It was so uncharacteristic of the town, which was proud of its piety.

Just a brief word of the history of this town: Rohatyn is in the Stanislaw district of Poland that is today in the Ukraine. Stainslaw and Lvov [also called Lviv and Lemberg] were the large cities in the region. Jews had lived there for centuries and constituted a substantial but ever-changing segment of the population. Throughout *Remembering Rohatyn and Its Environs* you will read of the diverse relationships between Jews and Ukrainians and Jews and Poles and also of the peculiar position of Jews with regard to the shifting rules of the town. From September 1939 to July 1941, Rohatyn was in the zone of Soviet occupation. The Ribbentrop/Molotov Pact divided Poland, with the Germans taking Western Poland and the Soviet Union occupying Eastern Poland where Rohatyn is found, and thus the Germans did not enter the town until July 2, 1941, eleven days after their attack on the Soviet Union. A ghetto was formed, and a Judenrat was named. Jews from surrounding areas were moved into Rohatyn and with that first deportation into Rohatyn, the ghetto became desperately overcrowded; you will read of a typhoid epidemic which led to death and devastation, the natural result of the difficult conditions. You will also read accounts of survivors of that epidemic.

Those who know the history of ghettos understand that the winters were most difficult. Jews suffered from cold made more acute by starvation and inadequate clothing and shelter. Springtime should have brought natural relief. But the last day of the first winter of ghettoization was March 20, 1942, the day the Germans chose for an *Aktion*. Three thousand five hundred Jews were killed; one in four of them were children. The full thrust of the Holocaust was felt in this town. First there were the mobile killers. Jews were marched to mass graves where they were shot on the edge of open pits near the railroad station where they were buried. In June 1943, the *Aktion* in Rohatyn made the town *Judenrein*; its last Jews were buried in mass graves near the Polish monastery. Both sites are marked by monuments. You will read of escapes, hiding, and even of a few who emerged from those mass graves, having not been fatally injured. Jews were powerless; they were not without initiative.

The Nazis loved to play God. It was not quite satisfying enough to kill the Jews, but one had to defile them and demoralize them. So many survivors recall the *Aktion* of Yom Kippur, when on the most sacred day of the year, when religious Jews believe that their fate is sealed for a New Year and judgment is passed, the Nazis came to execute judgment and they, not God, determined who shall live and who shall die.

The second stage of killing was deportation from Rohatyn to the death camp of Belzec. Beginning on September 2, 1942, one thousand Jews were deported. Refugees were brought into the ghetto in October and November, and on December 8, there was a large deportation of 1,500 Jews to Belzec, where they were killed upon arrival. By June 6, 1943 Rohatyn was *Judenrein*, without Jews. The murder of the few Jews who had managed to escape and hide in the countryside continued until the very last days of the war.

A word about Belzec, which was situated along the rail line between Lublin and Lvov: Belzec was one of the three *Aktion* Reinhard Camps designed solely for the murder of Jews, what the Nazi euphemistically called "The Final Solution to the Jewish Problem." Belzec had a particular mission; it was dedicated to the annihilation of the Jews of Galicia and located within the heart of that well-known Jewish region. Opened in February 1942, the first deportation began that month and then in April and early May the gas chambers were shut down to allow for improvements and expansion. They resumed operation in May and continued to operate between May and

December.

Five hundred thousand Jews were gassed in Belzec; their bodies buried in mass graves on the site. There were two—I repeat, two—known survivors. Only one of whom, Rudolf Reder, lived to give testimony.

Let us pay attention to his testimony–the only words we have of the victims at Belzec.

Arrival:

About noon the train arrived in Belzec. It was a very small station surrounded by small houses… At the Belzec station the train moving from the main line and onto a siding about one kilometer long led straight into the gate of the death camp…

The area between Belzec and the camp was surrounded by SS men. No one was allowed in. Civilian people were shot at if they happened to wander in…

A moment later, "the receiving of the train" began. Dozens of SS men would open the wagons yelling "Los!" [get out]. With whips and their rifle butts, they pushed people out. The doors of the wagon were a meter or more above the ground. Driven out by whips, the people had to jump down: everybody, old and young; many broke their arms and legs falling down. They had to jump down to the ground. The children were mangled in the bedlam. Everybody pouring out—dirty, exhausted, terrified…

The sick, the old, and the tiny children—those who could not walk on their own – were put on stretchers and dumped at the edge of huge dug-out pits – their graves. There the Gestapo man, Irrman, shot them and pushed their bodies into the graves with his rifle butt.

Immediately after the victims were unloaded, they were gathered in the courtyard, surrounded by armed askars, for Irrman to give a speech. The silence was deadly. He stood close to the crowd. Everyone wanted to hear. Suddenly there was hope: "If they talk to us...maybe they want us to live . . . Maybe there will be work...maybe?"

Irrman talked loud and clear: "You are going now to bathe. Later you will be sent to work. That's all."

Everybody was glad, happy that, after all, they will be working. They even applauded.

The men went straight ahead to a building with a sign "Bade und Inhaletionsräun" [bath and inhalation rooms]. The women proceeded 20 meters more to a large barrack about 30 x 15 m to have their heads shaved. They entered quietly, not knowing what to expect. Silence was everywhere.

After a few minutes they were made to line up and made to sit on wooden stools, eight at a time. When eight Jewish barbers entered and silently, like automated figures, started to shave off hair completely to the skin with shaving machines, that's when they realized the truth. They had no doubts then.

Everybody—young and old, children and women–everybody went to certain death. Little girls with long hair were herded into the shaving barracks. Those with short hair went to the barracks with the men.

Suddenly, without even a transition from hope to despair—came the realization that there was no hope. People began to scream—women became hysterical, crazed . . .

I was chosen to be one of the workers. I would stand on the side of the courtyard with my group of gravediggers and looked at my brothers, sister, friends, and acquaintances herded toward death.

The Killing Process:

While the women were rounded up naked and shaved, whipped like cattle into a slaughterhouse, the men were already dying in the gas chambers. It took two hours to shave the women and two hours to murder them. Many SS men using whips and sharp bayonets pushed the women toward the building with the chambers.

Then the askars counted out 750 persons per chamber...

I heard the noise of sliding doors, moaning and screaming, desperate calls in Polish, Yiddish—blood-curdling screams. All that lasted fifteen minutes

Screams of children, women and finally one common continuous horrible scream. All that lasted fifteen minutes.

The machine ran for twenty minutes, and after twenty minutes, there was silence.

The askars pulled open the doors on the opposite sides of the chambers, which led to the outdoors.

We began our assignment.

We dragged bodies of people who minutes ago were alive. We dragged them—using leather straps—to huge prepared mass graves. And the orchestra played—played from morning til night.

The Jews were arriving from everywhere and only Jews.

The storeroom for hair, underwear, and clothing of the victims of the gas chamber was located in a separate, rather small barracks. Hair was collected for ten days.

Baskets filled with gold teeth.

When the barracks were locked for the night and the lights were out, one could hear a whisper of prayers for the dead. The Kaddish, and then there was silence. We did not complain; we were completely resigned.

We moved like automated figures, just one large mass of them. We just mechanically worked through our horrible existence.

Every day we died a little bit together with the transports of people, who for a small moment lived and suffered with delusions.

Only when I heard children calling: "Mommy. Haven't I been good? It's dark." My heart would break. Later we stopped having feelings.

What remains after bearing such total devastation? Memories of what was before; the names of those who were murdered, the stories of their lives and their deaths, but also the biographies of those who escaped the inferno, by emigrating before, escaping during, or rebuilding after.

So much was lost that one reads this book with trepidation, but the final word of Jewish history is not death and destruction, but the remnant that survived, that rebuilt their lives and that dared to face the abyss by remembering.

Generations of Jews from the community of Rohatyn and its environs will be grateful to Donia Gold Shwarzstein so ably assisted by her determined, detailed and dedicated son Meyer, for her diligence and perseverance. Simply put, she brought it all together and thus enabled the descendants of Rohatyn and their children and children's children to know from whence they came, which is so important in deciding where one must go.

Michael Berenbaum
Los Angeles, California

Preface

Just before leaving Rohatyn in 1945, I resolved to keep fresh in memory the images and personal history of the many Jewish people who lived along our main street in order to `bring them to life' in the future. Alas, without occasions for reminiscing, the names of those neighbors and friends who perished became attenuated over time. All I can do now is visualize walking beside their houses along Slowackiego, the route my parents and I took from our home toward the town square and past it to Kolejowka (Koleyoovka) - Rohatyn's chestnut tree-shaded promenade. We would turn left into Kolejowka. There on the Sabbath we strolled and greeted young and older Jewish families, friends and acquaintances.

As one of the lone children surviving in Rohatyn, I was driven by the desire to get in-depth information about my town and yearned to read the 1962 Rohatyn Memorial Book from cover to cover - but the Hebrew was too difficult and the Yiddish too slow. I also wanted to open the book to Rohatyn area descendants who are not fluent in Hebrew or Yiddish. The translation into English of upwards of 300 pages of the Hebrew and Yiddish sections started as my quest and project. I was fortunate that in 1986 Mr. Spiegel and the Society of Rohatiner in Israel granted me permission to have the book translated into English.

The only groups underrepresented in the depiction of pre-1939 Rohatyn in the 1962 Rohatyn Memorial Book are couples in their thirties raising young children who were unable to leave Poland. And missing from the original 1962 Memorial Book are the refugees, who in their flight from Fascist regimes, found a temporary haven in Rohatyn.

The 1962 Rohatyn Memorial Book (Part I) together with the Part II expansion transport us to Rohatyn and its surrounding communities, and to its people, in their heyday - and to their tragedy.

In 1998 I was granted the privilege by the Society of Rohatiner in Israel to expand the 1962 Rohatyn Memorial Book to include the eulogies, poems, and speeches delivered in 1998 at the Yizkor Service in Rohatyn, as well as to include additional memoirs. At Mr. Fishel Kirschen's direction, Chairman of the Society, all these writings were submitted to me. With this book, Part

I and Part II, I am fulfilling my commitment to the Society of Rohatiner in Israel, to those who submitted their writings, to Mr. Jacob Hornstein, the major donor to Rohatyn projects, as well as to those who perished.

Just as so many of their achievements, this book, too, is to the credit of the Society of Rohatiner in Israel, and to the members of the Independent Rohatyner Young Men's Benevolent Association in the United States.

Donia Gold Shwarzstein

Acknowledgments and Notes

Many thanks are due to the most generous Sabina Wind Fox, Z"L, whose contribution to this book is immeasurable. Many thanks to Rosette Faust Halpern for her contribution to this book and for the encouragement that helped sustain this effort. We owe a debt of gratitude to Freda Kamerling Perl, Z"L, whose communication in Ukrainian on behalf of the Israeli Society facilitated the commemoration in 1998 and many related endeavors.

Thanks are due for their work on The Rohatyn Jewish Community, A Town That Perished (Part I), hereinafter the 1962 Memorial Book: to Michael Bohnen for his initial review of the translation from Hebrew, to Julian and Fay Bussgang for their review and editing of the translation of the first 118 pages of the 1962 Memorial Book.

This volume consists of two parts:

Part I is the English translation, spearheaded and overseen by me, of the Memorial Book, published by the Society of Rohatiner in Israel in 1962. To Mr. Yehoshua Spiegel, Z"L, the editor, goes the credit for producing the 1962 Memorial Book. Publishing the translation fulfills my long-standing promise to him. The translation was made possible by monetary contributions of many, the largest of which came from Mr. Jacob Hornstein, Z"L. Messrs. Herman Skolnick and William Halpern, Z"L, endorsed the translation project with enthusiasm. They would have been pleased to see this entire volume completed.

Part II, the so-called Appendix as per Mr. Fishel Kirschen's herein attached letter, consists of speeches/poems/memoirs submitted by the first and second generation of Rohatyner following the 1998 Memorial in Rohatyn. Mr. Kirschen approved all contributions. Many thanks are due to those writers who hailed the project, gladly volunteered their work and photos, and looked forward to the publication of this volume. The publication of this volume was delayed for two reasons: 1) it took a long time to obtain biographies of the deceased contributors of articles to the 1962 Rohatyn Memorial Book, and 2) software technical problems impeded progress.

Translations Part I
We acknowledge with gratitude the work of the Hebrew translator, Rabbi Mordecai Goldzweig, Z"L (MA in History, U. of Chicago), and his partner in this work, Mrs. Hassia Goldzweig, Z"L. They devoted time to researching the history of Hassidism in Eastern Galicia. We thank Mr. Benjamin Weiner for his translation from the Yiddish. Both these translators, Rabbi Goldzweig and Mr. Weiner, were attentive to the appropriate religious and technical terms, the feelings of the author, as well as the flavor of the Hebrew and Yiddish idiom.

Translations Part II
Translations from Polish, Yiddish and German are my work, as well as some minor work in Hebrew. I received the material in hard copy, both type-written and hand-written. I sought expert help in deciphering a couple of handwritten passages in Polish.

Persons' names in the 1962 Memorial Book
Translation into English of names from the Hebrew text, which omits vowels, and from the Yiddish text, which alters the pronunciation of names, posed a problem. We attempted to standardize the spelling of persons' last names – last names of Slavic derivation we spelled closer to the original Slavic; names of German derivation closer to German; however, we left a number of names spelled phonetically, as written by the translators. We merely reduced the number of translators' variants in the spelling of last names in Part I.

The difficulty arose, in particular, with the spelling of first names. Hebrew first names were frequently transformed into Yiddish diminutives or forms of endearment. In the case of Polish, the first names had their own particular informal inflections. We resisted standardizing all those names completely, in order to preserve the specific regional flavor reminiscent of a way of life.

In the case of Hassidic names, the same Hebrew first names appeared in 1962 in many permutations; we hesitated tampering with these. Hassidic family names were kept as originally translated from the Hebrew and Yiddish.

Biographies of contributors of articles
The biographies of deceased writers of memoirs in the 1962 Memorial Book were realized through the efforts of and/or authorship of two members of the Society of Rohatiner in Israel; some were provided by me. Authorship of the biographies is attributed to the respective writer.

Place names, Zionist terms, and German titles

In an effort to standardize place names, by and large Polish versions were chosen. Rohatyn may appear in other sources as Rohatin and Rogatin. An effort was made to be consistent in the use of Zionist organization names and titles. An effort was also made to render the correct translation of German Nazi official titles and administrative units.

The librarians and staff of the YIVO Institute for Jewish Research (YIVO), New York City, were invaluable in providing assistance and access to the following resources:

1. Encyclopedia Le'Chalutzei Hayishuv U'Bonav, Vol V,
2. Mirkevet Hamishne on the Mekhilta of Rabbi Yeshaya by Rabbi David Moshe Avraham.
3. Cartons of files of the two Rohatyn Societies in the United States,
4. Slownik Geograficzny Krolestwa Polskiego i Innych Krajow Slowianskich, Warszawa, Nakladem Wladyslava Walewskiego, Druk "Wieku" NowySwiat Nr. 61, Vol. IX, 1888.

Other resources consulted for place names

Zydowskie Okregi Metrykalne i Zydowskie Gminy Wyznaniowe w Galicji Doby Autonomicznej w Latach 1894-1938, Uniwersytet Jagiellonski, Instytut Historii, Jerzy Michalewich, "Ksiegarnia Akademicka", Krakow 1995, and Gesher Galicia to verify that Red Rus corresponded to our area of Western Ukraine and that Galicia derived its name from the town Halicz. Further resources utilized are noted in the footnotes.

Additions to the List of Martyrs

I've added names of people I knew who perished and weren't in the original list. At the end of this book, there are blank pages in honor of those who perished and as of this printing are as yet not identified. These pages may be used to add names and to add recollections.

Refugees in Rohatyn 1939-1941

One memoir was added in honor of refugees, who made positive contributions to Jewish life in Rohatyn.

Number of Jews murdered

The number of murdered in various mass actions differs somewhat from report to report in the 1962 Memorial Book; they are approximate, but are not greatly divergent from actual numbers killed.

Not translated
Identical Memoirs contained in both the Hebrew/Yiddish and the English sections of the 1962 Memorial Book needed no translation. Original documents in Latin and Polish (Royal Charter & the Disputes) and Elisha Schorr's letters were not translated.

"YB p." references
References YB p. Followed by number (e.g., YB p. 166) at top of Part I translations are a reference to the page number of each article in the original Hebrew/Yiddish 1962 Rohatyn Memorial Book article.

Footnotes
There are several sets of footnotes: numerical footnotes in Part I are from the 1962 Rohatyn Memorial Book. "Tr" stands for translator. Translators' footnotes belong to the named translator. Editor's footnotes (Ed.) refer to Julian and Fay Bussgang and to me. Julian and Fay Bussgang edited Part I through the article Inside Rohatyn by Chuna Yonas, Paris. My editing continued from A Bundle of Memories by Marcus Zin, Acco.

An apology for unintentional omissions or duplications
I apologize for inadvertent errors. I apologize for any omissions in the Index of surnames of Jews. In the Martyrs translation I tried to reproduce all entries, including apparent repetitions in Part I. I did not include Polish and German diacritics.

A special thank you
The participation of my son Meyer Shwarzstein was the decisive step in bringing this work to press. But for his efforts this material would be languishing in Word format in my computer. He undertook to master publication software and joined separate articles of the translation of Part I, as well as the articles of Part II, into this volume. His invaluable suggestions provided an overarching frame for the whole. His dedication and commitment of time to this complex task are without peer. Thanks as well to my daughter Rena, who in her wisdom suggested for the task of Hebrew translator a man eminently qualified for the task. I thank my children for their enduring moral support.

Donia Gold Shwarzstein

A Tribute to My Jewish Rescuers of Rohatyn
March 20, 1942, First Mass Akcja
Umschlagplatz, Rohatyn town square
by Donia Gold Shwarzstein

At the end of 1945, before I turned my back on my town Rohatyn, I looked back to one day burned into memory. I vowed that I would be the voice of the people on the Umschlagplatz. I was one of them. They would speak through me. March 20, 1942, was the day the Jewish people on the Umschlagplatz let me know they were with me.

They were in my mind while I worked on this book.

As one who was very young in 1939, I am not best equipped to write about my town. Moreover, for many decades the story of the Holocaust was unwelcome, therefore in sharing my experiences, I refrained from entering into the painful memories and dwelt instead on the serenity of early childhood. My prewar memories are of an idyll; and they are more about nature than about people.

I am writing now because I must no longer delay acknowledging my debt to the townspeople who perished. Were it not for them, I would not be alive. I must pay tribute to my Jewish rescuers. Yet pain and horror overwhelm speech and words come hard.

One more impetus comes from the request of surviving townspeople to help create a memorial to our Jewish town, in addition to the Yizkor Book written in the 1960's by the expatriate town elders.

Until 1939, the cares of the adult world seldom intruded into mine. Being an only child and living on the outskirts of town, I developed an intimate knowledge of nature and considered flora and fauna among my playmates. My memories include astonishment at discovering a clear brook at the back of our courtyard; the brook peered through tall spindly hedges, its banks covered with forget-me-nots; tracking it uphill led to a gurgling spring which was its source.

It is difficult to fast forward to the scene, which evokes overwhelming pain. The scene is the Umschlagplatz on March 20, 1942.

That scene, the people whose voices will never be heard again, speaks with overpowering authority. Hushed voices rising unexpectedly from beneath the field of crouched compacted bodies, tamped down onto icy ground, a field of 'humanware' at its point of dispatch. The handlers of this 'humanware' intermittently drove the mass to inch forward, closer to the point of no return, to the loading area. Rear rows were drawing precariously close to the forward field of the Rynek (town square), which was already half cleared by the rapid rotation of pickup and delivery trucks carting off its `humanware.'

Having left my grandfather en route, I was alone in the double file march at gunpoint since early morning. Urged on by the adult marchers, "You are small, crouch down, crawl back." I dropped back to the rear of the double file columns heading for the Umschlagplatz, the loading place for the deportees.

The sight of the Umschlagplatz struck me to the core. In repeated attempts to save me, people took risks by calling out my name to guide me to a safer place. Again and again I heard individual voices call out, then a series of voices carried the message "Get up, go!" At last I waveringly stood up, quite dazed; I took a step forward, found myself treading on living bodies, and came to a stop. Though it was strictly forbidden on the Umschlagplatz to move or make any sounds, people urged me to step over them to disregard their anguish in doing so, directing me: "Go to your uncle; tell them you are his daughter …"

This all-out effort inevitably got the attention of the henchmen at the flanks. They began heading in our direction, cutting a swath with their rifles. They were coming frightfully close. But that didn't stop the determination of the people on the ground to rouse me, to get one of theirs from the field! The approaching menace – the Gestapo's threats slicing through the air and through our consciousness, the sound of bullets coming nearer – did nothing to silence my rescuers' exhortations, "Go!" As I accelerated to a run, I didn't see what swift punishment my rescuers brought upon themselves; behind me were the unmistakable blitz of Nazi boots and the thud of bludgeoning rifle butts.

Jewish townspeople who knew me, but whom I did not know, went to their death without a whimper, as they ordered me to step out of their ranks. Many were brutalized or killed on the spot in order to have me whisked from this depot, which led to mass graves just outside of town. All the able-bodied Jewish males of Rohatyn worked at those excavations (rumored by the Nazis to be the foundations for brick factories), until the morning when the first trucks arrived! Caught unawares at dawn, they were the first ones executed. Only a few escaped!

I made my way to my uncle. He had responded to the call for dentists and doctors to step out of the mass of bodies. The local villagers requisitioned from the Gestapo a supply of doctors and dentists for short-term service. It was a temporary stay of execution. My uncle Szymek stepped forward in front of the thinning rows of crouching human bodies. I seized his hand. He didn't react. Spurred on by the people who ordered me to save myself, I shouted to him: "Wojciu, powiedz im ze ja jestem twoja corka!" (Uncle, tell them that I am your daughter.) He didn't grasp the meaning. I held his hand tightly. As the Gestapo waved him out of the Umschlagplatz, I moved with him. The Gestapo shoved me back. Only then did my uncle say in German "This is my daughter." We were marched out of the Umschlagplatz and ordered to stand with our faces to the wall. There were 11 of us lined up against the wall, 10 doctors and dentists, and I, one female child.

Behind us the jackal threats and jeers of the Gestapo, the din of shots, cracking rifle butts, human voices in distress, the whir of motors ... then silence! At dusk the handlers of the `humanware' finished their job.

Eleven of us, our faces to the wall, stood until 5:00 in the evening. As darkness fell, we were ordered to turn around. The Umschlagplatz was empty. Even the gloating local onlookers were gone. The show was over.

Around the Umschlagplatz, frozen blood-soaked corpses had become part of the icy ground, among them the body of a baby suckling at his dead mother's breast. Frozen blood stained the pristine March snow. Three thousand Jews of Rohatyn and the surrounding communities, 600 children, went to their death that day in that infamous Akcja, the first one, of March 1942!

Years later, after surviving my entire family as a young child in light of overwhelming odds, a fragment of the recurring chorus of Bialik's poem (learned in a D.P. Camp) recounting past Jewish ordeals, persistently urged itself on me: "Eem Yesh et Nafshcha Lada'at ..."[1] Why? What impels me to go on? And it is not I who provides the answer. The answer is provided by the extinguished voices of my compatriots on March 20, 1942 in Rohatyn.

"Forget it!" were the compelling words hurled at us after our survival! An impassable wall was erected against exposing the vista of the Holocaust, and those who tried to scale it did it at the risk of isolation. This was a double defeat and double pain, the death of those whom we cherished and the second death through silence. We are impelled to be the vehicle, however deficient, to keep alive the memory of the extinguished Jews who perished in our towns

1   H.N. Bialik, Kol Shirei Bialik, 1921 "Eem Yesh Et Nafshcha Lada'at et hama'ayan mimenu sha'avu achicha hamumatim oz kaze." ["If your soul wants to discover the fountain from which your brethren in times of evil (persecution) drew the strength to leap into the flames ... then go to the House of Study ..."]

and hamlets, and who by their own acts preserved their dignity in the very last moment of their lives!

Could we but project on a screen the images etched in our minds and hearts, and let their acts speak for the unvanquished spirit of the men and women of our home towns! They are the real actors of the drama of resistance to annihilation. They have robbed evil of its victory. In a time when "The individual, or what was left of him, was nullified"[2], his body absent all recognizable form, each rescuer of another's life gave expression to his and her most fully realized personal individuality. By speaking, though that comes hard, we affirm them and life itself.

The Yizkor Book recounts that our town Rohatyn in eastern Galicia, the seat of county administration, a Royal Free Town, nearly 800 years old, with Jewish history stretching from the Middle Ages, lay on the crossroads between Austria, Lithuania, and Russia. It was the administrative center for the towns Bukaczowce, Bursztyn, Bolszowce, Stratyn, and Knihynicze and for 100 villages. Its position on these artery roads made Rohatyn into a business center. Our Jewish town, in which some Jews in earlier times of despair fell prey to the false preaching of Sabbatai Zvi, a town located on the fertile soil where Hassidism, the hope of ordinary men, thrived, was also a place in which Zionism flourished and which produced so many doctors, engineers and lawyers in this century.

Just five children from Rohatyn and environs survived our town's annihilation, two born during the Holocaust. I may be the oldest of the surviving children. I am old enough to have memories, but not old enough to know all that the town encompassed. No relations survived to transmit to me an oral history of the town.

In recent years, surviving Jewish townspeople have sat with me and have put on record an oral history of each Jewish man and woman who was killed, but was not mentioned in the Yizkor Book, so that their names would not perish from the annals of our community's struggle.

This year my town's survivors plan to go back to Rohatyn to put up a monument there. At most, barely a Minyan (communal prayer quorum) may go. I ask, why go? To dedicate a monument, which at best will be neglected, and more than likely may be desecrated? And can we face those scenes where our Jewish towns and villages died and still preserve our health?

At the same time, a number of my town's survivors are passionately engaged in assembling photos and memorabilia to set up a memorial to

2   Aharon Appelfeld, Beyond Despair Three Lectures and Conversations with Philip Roth, Introduction, x, Fromm International Publishing Corp., New York, 1991

give visible witness to the once vibrant Jewish community of Rohatyn and vicinity.[3] In this way those who perished will not be surrendered to final annihilation through oblivion.[4]

As for me, that first sight of the Umschlagplatz has not left me. It is burned into my consciousness.[5]

In spite of my enormous resistance to going to Rohatyn to the Memorial, I had to go. As the date of the Memorial drew near, the pull of the graves was powerful. I knew with my whole being that I had to be there, to be at the graves of my family, at the graves of the playmates who perished, and of all the townspeople interred in the ground in Rohatyn during the Holocaust.

Donia Gold Shwarzstein
New York, New York. October, 2010

---

3   The best-known photo of a klezmer orchestra is that of the Faust Family Kapela of Rohatyn, located at the Jewish Museum, New York.
4   The assembling of photos of people who perished, which I started in 1998 with the help of Israeli townspeople and two second generation members, stopped short. At the outset, I received a few photos.
5   The article, beginning with paragraph two is reprinted by permission of TOGETHER, a semi-annual magazine published by the American Gathering of Holocaust Survivors (August 1996 issue).

The Rohatyn Societies
By Donia Gold Shwarzstein

Society of the Rohatiner in Israel (Irgun Yotzei Rohatyn V'Hasviva B'Yisrael)

This Organization of Survivors of Rohatyn and its vicinity was established in 1949 at the initiative of Zvi Fenster (aka Felker), Herman (aka Zvi) Skolnick, then residing in Israel, together with the efforts of Yehoshua Spiegel, Dr. Sterzer and of many others. Its initial activities were annual commemorations honoring the martyrs of Rohatyn and its surroundings and dispensing of moral and financial support to those in need. This was followed by further actions: 1) in 1960 sacks of earth brought from Rohatyn by Dr. Sterzer were buried in the cemetery in Kiryat Shaul; 2) in 1961 names of Rohatyn area martyrs were inscribed on a scroll and placed in the memorial on Mount Zion; 3) in 1962, under the helm of Yehoshua Spiegel, the Rohatyn Yizkor Book was published.

Rohatyn Societies in the USA (YIVO archives, New York)

1. The Rohatyner Young Men's Society, Inc. was organized as a membership corporation on May 9, 1894, under the laws of the State of New York. In January 1964 the Society revised its constitution and by-laws.

2. The Independent Rohatyner Young Men's Benevolent Association (YMBA), was founded on the East Coast in 1903. As reported in its minutes, the organization made contributions to the UJA Federation of Charities, and the Red Cross. In 1967 it made a contribution to the Israel Emergency Fund, and, at the same time, submitted a petition to President Lyndon Johnson, dated May 22, 1967.

My involvement with the Societies

Having immigrated to the Midwest with my Rohatyn guardian, Herman Auster Z"L, his wife Manya (of Dabrowice, Polesie) and their growing family, my first contacts with the Rohatyn societies weren't until the 1970's on my visits to Israel and New York. I established communication with members and leaders of the Rohatyn Society in both countries and interviewed several Rohatyn survivors in Israel. When I relocated to New

York in the mid-1980s, I was warmly received into the fold by the YMBA, the organized Rohatyn survivor family on the East Coast. By this time a number of members had moved away or passed away, and the YMBA was holding its meetings in members' homes, including mine. Once or twice a year Herman Skolnick, Secretary of the Society, invited the members and their families to a dinner in a Brooklyn restaurant, underwritten by the Society. I look back with pleasure on my days with this Rohatyn Society in the USA.

Starting in 1997, Mr. Skolnick and I became involved in raising funds via correspondence and phone calls for projects initiated by the Society of the Rohatiner in Israel, as well as in helping mobilize the extended US Rohatyn community to attend the 1998 Memorial in Rohatyn.

Encounter at Ratner's, N.Y. with Rohatyner Young Men's Society

In 1997, just after my return from urgent discussions by the Israeli Society of their ambitious Rohatyn cemetery and mass grave projects, I had the privilege of attending a meeting of the 'other' U.S. Rohatyn Society. Mr. Skolnick invited me to help him enlist their help in funding the projects in Rohatyn. I was delighted to discover the uninterrupted existence of this society. It was a sizeable and congenial gathering. We received a warm welcome and a thoughtful hearing. There I also met two ladies, with whom I had contact before, one had published an article about her visit to Lwow, and the other, Phyllis Kramer, was in the vanguard of putting information about Rohatyn on the Internet.

By coincidence, at that meeting I ran into a couple whom I had met on a summer tour. They championed our request; their motion was adopted and we received a pledge of $500.00.

At that meeting, for that brief moment, I was able to touch the reality of my elders, who were there when two vibrant societies existed in New York. It was a privilege and I am still inspired by it and grateful for it.

I was deeply affected by learning that Dr. Lewenter, a highly respected person in Rohatyn, had been president of that society for a number of years. The name Dr. Lewenter brought to mind poignant events, one of which was his son's ordeal in the Rohatyn ghetto, where he perished. (Refer to Biographies)

Ending on a high note – the Israeli Society's Culminating Achievements
A. Achievements in Rohatyn: Memorial, Mass Grave Monuments, Restored Cemeteries.

In 1996 Freda Kamerling Perl came from Israel to New York to prevail upon the YMBA to assist the Israeli Society in raising funds to restore the cemeteries and put monuments on the mass graves in Rohatyn. Four leaders of the Israeli Society went to Rohatyn in 1997 and 1998 and two in 1999. In 1999 in Rohatyn it was my privilege to represent the American contingent and to assist the Israeli leaders Fishel Kirschen and Freda Kamerling Perl in finalizing their work in Rohatyn (to be further monitored by Rabbi Kolesnik and Boris Arsen, since deceased, aka Axelrod, of Ivano Frankivsk). Their efforts culminated in the restoration of the two cemeteries (with tall tablets at the entrance of each), the erection of memorial monuments on the two mass graves, and the epochal Memorial Service held in Rohatyn in 1998.
Following the Memorial in Rohatyn a report about it was given to a gathering of Rohatyn area people at a meeting held in a New Jersey hotel paid for by Mr. Jacob Hornstein. Mr. Hornstein was the greatest booster of and contributor of funds to all 1990's projects.

B. The Publication of this Expanded Yizkor Book

The Society of the Rohatiner in Israel 1) in 1986 at a meeting at the Spiegels gave me authorization to translate the Yizkor Book into English and to publish it in book form; 2) in 2001 they authorized the uploading of the translated Yizkor Book to the Internet, and finally, 3) in 1998 and again in 2001 they mandated that I publish in English this expanded Yizkor Book in book form. They required that this expansion should encompass the eulogies, poems, and speeches delivered at the Memorial in Rohatyn in 1998, plus additional memoirs submitted to me right after the Memorial. This was Mr. Fishel Kirschen's, the Israeli Society's express written mandate for me. The cost of publishing was to be solved by me. This expanded Yizkor Book is my fulfillment of the mandate they gave me. In the final analysis, this too is their achievement. In its last decade the Israeli Society's determination and passion motivated the Rohatyn community worldwide to follow its lead. Its last chapter marked its greatest achievements.
The Society of the Rohatiner in Israel and the Rohatyner Young Men's Society, Inc. have ceased to exist. May the memory of Yehoshua Spiegel, Fishel Kirschen, Freda Kamerling Perl, Herman Skolnick, as well Jacob Hornstein, William Halpern, Kuba Glotzer, Sylvia Lederman, who in recent

years left the ranks of the living, serve as a blessing to their families and the generations of people from our region.

May the memories of all contributors to this book, participants in the Rohatyn Memorial, all members of the Rohatyn societies and of the surrounding communities, who are no longer among the ranks of the living, serve as a blessing to their families and the generations of people from our region.

The Rohatyn Societies

Society of the Rohatiner
IN ISRAEL

4 March 2001

Ms. Donia Shwartzstein
The Organization of former Rohatiners
USA

Dear Ms. Gold-Shwartzstein,

In 1986 we gave you permission (at a meeting at Mr. Spiegel's) to translate into English the *Yizkor Book* of our home town Rohatin. Three years ago, at your request, we gave you permission to publish the English part of the Yizkor Book on the Internet, and two years ago we gave you permission to publish the translation on the Internet. Since you personally undertook the translation project, I'm turning to you now, asking about its progress. We would like to emphasize a few conditions, which are actually obvious, and were pointed out in personal conversations held by us:

1. In publishing it on the Internet, it must be stated that the book is the property of the Organization of former Rohatiners in Israel, written and edited in Israel, by former Rohatiners living here. The financial aspects of publishing the book were completely covered by us. It is inappropriate for someone to publish it, or parts of it in memory of one family or person. I'm sure you can recall the meeting with Joshua Spiegel, in which he described the ordeal he had to go through in obtaining the funds for writing this book.
2. It would also be appropriate to point out that the main three figures involved in the book were Mr. Joshua Spiegel, Mr. Zvi Fenster and for a short while Mr. Yehiel Ben Nun (son of Joel Fisher).
3. We would like to have an appendix added to the Yizkor Book about the perpetuation project we held in Rohatin, including a description of the ceremony and selected parts of the speeches. This task has been given to you in 1998. We would like to have this preserved in book form, so it can be a lasting possession of Rohatyn area families.
4. Furthermore, the actual production of the perpetuation project in 1998 in Rohatin was financially supported by all former Rohatiners known to us from around the world. The main donations came from Mr. Yakov Hornstein of the USA, Mr. Henrick Schnapp from Germany, Mr. Z. Fenster, Mr. Y. Ben Nun, Ms. Leah Shualy from Israel, and Mr. Felix Rohatyn from the USA.

We would be grateful for your quick response.

Mr. F. Kirschen
Chairman of former Rohatiners Organization in Israel

PART I

Translation of
the Yizkor Book

KEHILAT ROHATYN V'HASVIVAH
IR B'KHAYEKHA U'V'KHILYONA

THE COMMUNITY OF

ROHATYN

AND ITS ENVIRONS

THE LIFE AND DESTRUCTION
OF A CITY

EDITOR AND PUBLISHER:
MORDECHAI AMITAI

YIDDISH EDITING: ENGLISH EDITING:

DAVID STOCKFISH   SHMUEL BARI

ORIGINALLY PUBLISHED IN ISRAEL IN 1962
BY THE SOCIETY OF ROHATINER IN ISRAEL.
TRANSLATED BY PERMISSION OF THE
SOCIETY OF ROHATINER IN ISRAEL.

Introductory Remarks

By Yehoshua Spiegel, Tel Aviv

Translated by Rabbi Mordecai Goldzweig - YB pps. 5-6

This book about the town of Rohatyn and its environs presents the historical documents, personal recollections, and testimony carefully preserved by each and every one of the people of our town who has remained alive. Once more, before our eyes, appear the events of the distant past and those that occurred more recently up to the tragic days of destruction of the Jewish community of Rohatyn and its surroundings. There, almost all the Jews perished; only a few remained. I feel that it is my soul's desire to save those memories and the way of life that they portray in this memorial book.

Although hesitations existed at first because of problems regarding financial means and content, the initiators of the project began to act. Thanks to the strong resolution in their hearts, they overcame the difficulties and the indifference of those who had it within their power to ease our task but did not respond. The goal to leave a memorial to our town is what helped us persevere.

We turned to past residents of Rohatyn in the country and abroad with a twofold request—to gather material and money. We became galvanized in the task of writing, and others responded and took an interest, some with written material and others with monetary aid. Every additional response encouraged us to continue. We wish to call attention especially to four past residents of Rohatyn who now live in America and did not content themselves only with their own personal contributions but also added new contributors: Dr. Golda Fisher, Dr. Yitzchak Lewenter, Engineer Dr. Yaakov Faust, and Mr. Sam Henna. May they be blessed and accept the heartfelt thanks of the initiating body and the Association of Immigrants of Rohatyn and its Surroundings in Israel.

We do not deny that gaps exist in the contents of the book, and we may assume that not everything found its full expression here, but the editors of the book did what they could with the material at hand. Undoubtedly, were it not for those who stood aside, we could have had more. You will have to forgive inaccuracies or certain duplications in the articles, as the writers are not professionals. And, after all, 20 years have passed since the time of the Holocaust, and some who wrote had already left Rohatyn 30 to 40 years before. Nevertheless and despite all of these shortcomings, we are still of the opinion that the reader will feel a strong affinity and empathize with the thoughts, feelings, and memories presented here by writers who are stating facts on the pages of this book that are simple and forthright.

The book is divided into four sections:

(1) The early period—from the 16th century until and including World War I

(2) The interim between the two world wars (Times of Peace, Jewish life, Zionism, the development of Chalutziut, etc.)

(3) World War II and the Holocaust

(4) A memorial to the martyrs and a list of their names

Most of the material was written in Hebrew, a part in Yiddish, and a part in English. Testimony about the period of the Holocaust was given in these three languages now spoken by survivors of Rohatyn. We have enhanced this book with a wealth of photographs that were gathered after a great deal of effort. All the sections together accurately reflect the life and destruction of the Jewish community of Rohatyn and its neighboring towns.

In conclusion, we wish to express our heartfelt thanks to the people of our town who lent a hand in this project, whether in content or in spirit, and thanks to them, we now have before us this memorial book. We also take this opportunity to thank those who took part in the creation of this book—the members of the organizing committee and the committee for the preparation of the book– who successfully worked to enable the publication of this book about the Jewish community of Rohatyn and its surroundings. We also wish to express our gratitude to all those who wrote articles, beginning with the historian Dr. N. M. Gelber to the editor and publisher, Mordechai Amitai, who worked primarily with the Hebrew materials; to David Stockfish, the editor for Yiddish; and to Shmuel Bari, the editor for English.

Congratulations! It is our fervent hope that this book will act as a beacon to the coming younger generation to enable it to follow in our path in the future.

Organizing Committee of the Association of Immigrants of Rohatyn and its Surroundings in Israel: Standing from the right: David Blauenstein, Zvi Fenster (Felker), Zvi Skolnick, David Kartin, Yehoshua Spiegel, Yosef Green, Dr. Avraham Sterzer, and Anshel Milstein.

Fire!
By Mordecai Gebirtig

1936 (Hebrew: Ha'Ayarah Bo'eret; Yiddish: Es Brennt!), Translation
by David G. Roskies (by permission of David G. Roskies). Reprinted
from The Literature of Destruction (p. 371), Jewish Responses to
Catastrophe, Jewish Publication Society, 1988 YB p. 7

Fire, brothers, fire!
Our poor town's on fire!
Raging, winds so full of anger
Shatter, scatter, tear asunder
Fanning the flames ever wilder
Everything's on fire!

While you stand there, looking on
With folded hand.
While you stand there, looking on
At the fire brand.

Fire, brothers, fire!
Our poor town's on fire!
The whole town's already devoured
By flaming tongues of force and
power
And the wild wind howls and churns
As our shtetl burns.

While you stand there, looking on ...
Fire, brothers, fire!
The dreaded moment may soon come
When the town with us included
Will be turned to flames and ashes
As after battle a city falls,
With empty, blackened walls.

While you stand there, looking on ...
Fire, brothers, fire!
It all turns to you.
If you love your town,
Take pails, put out the fire,
Quench it with your own blood too.
Show what you can do!

Don't look and stand
With folded hand.
Brothers, don't stand around, put out
the fire!
Our shtetl burns!

From the Desk of the Publisher
By Mordechai Amitai

Translated by Rabbi Mordecai Goldzweig - YB p. 8

The Jewish communities of the Diaspora—an open ledger lay before them. On page after page, they inscribed their histories and the deeds of the Jewish people in exile who, even when transplanted to foreign soil, still preserved their roots well enough to infuse a vibrant life both into the individual and into the community. Their children are occupied in both their day-to-day existence and in the study of the Torah; their synagogues and schools bustle, as do their fairs. Just as they never lose touch with their daily worldly affairs, so do they also turn their hearts to their Heavenly Father and keep Jerusalem before them on a pinnacle during their festive occasions.

The Jewish communities of Poland in Eastern Europe have disappeared, and their record books are also gone. It therefore behooves those who remain to return and gather up the pages of their history and accomplishments—never again to be written on that soil which has been drenched in their blood but to be written here in the Jewish land of redemption—to leave a memorial to those who were exterminated and to pass it on to posterity.

One can say that this memorial book to the community of Rohatyn in Malopolska (southeastern Poland) will pass unnoticed, being inundated, as it were, by the many memorial books that are now being printed and are of no interest to anyone except the survivors of only that community. But this is not true. The essence of a drop of water is the same as that which is found in a whole sea. The story of one community teaches the history of many, in all of Poland, in all of Eastern Europe. Wherever Jews are exiled, the Shechina (spirit of G-d on earth) follows them. Perhaps that place is Rohatyn; perhaps it has another name. It is the same way of life, the same people, the same course of events, the same trends. It is the same story of suppression and revival—the battle for existence, the struggle for emancipation and equal rights, evil decrees and misfortunes at the hands of man and the Almighty, and again awakening and revival. And thus we have the dichotomy—the overtones of destruction on one side and the intimations of redemption on the other, also introduced by suffering.

We find in this book the history of a Jewish community whose beginnings emerge from the midst of the Middle Ages at the mercy of kings and nobility. Yet it continues to gain strength despite its enemies. Standing at the edge of oblivion during World War I, it returned and was regenerated during the period between the two world wars. A rich gallery of figures and personalities—merchants and craftsmen, religious school teachers, rabbis and judges on one side—bartenders and butchers on the other. Admorim (respected leaders) and their followers on one side, nationalist intelligentsia and assimilationists on the other. No national and social movement passed it by—Sabbateans and Frankists, Haskalah and Hassidism, Assimilationism and Zionism. At the pinnacle were the pioneering youth movements, the realization that opened the road to redemption and paved the way for its survivors.

One may well ask, "Where did they find the power to continue to exist? Where did they obtain this viability, during their many gyrations, to return and to reappear in those Jewish communities generation after generation?" To this there is only one answer—belief, faith in all its manifestations. The belief that the Messiah will come although he tarries. Thus it had been sustained among our parents and their parents, especially the belief in deeds that promote redemption, as viewed by the pioneering movements. If there is something to be learned from a memorial book, it is this.

For those who are near, this may be the only memorial to their dear ones and all that was destroyed. For the distant, this is an overwhelming chapter in the history of the Jews in exile. The publisher, who is one of the latter, can only express his happiness at being privileged to aid in this holy work and bring it to its conclusion. If he did it well, and this only the reader can judge, this will be his reward.

A City in Life and in Destruction
And Their Blood Will I Never Cleanse...
By Rabbi Dr. Mordechai Nurok

Translated by Rabbi Mordecai Goldzweig - YB p. 9

It is now almost twenty years after the terrible Holocaust, and the further we move away from it, the closer we are drawn to our noble and holy ones and the desire to perpetuate their memories and present them to the Jewish world in a manner that befits them.

Every Jew has his memorial days, when he reunites with the memories of his dear ones and friends who have passed away. This holds true for average memorial days. At least we know how and when they left us. We ourselves brought them to burial, and we are able to visit their graves and pour out our tears on both happy and sad occasions.

To our sorrow, we are now in a period that is characterized by an entirely different type of memorial, not at all of the usual type. We do not even know when and where their holy souls were taken from them. We do not know where their ashes are spread. To paraphrase what is written in the Torah—"And no one knows their place of burial to the present day." For this reason, the people of Rohatyn took a very important step when they decided to publish this memorial book about their community and its holy martyrs.

Unfortunately, there are many among us, especially among our dear young people, who can be classified as "a generation that did not know Joseph." Therefore, they are relatively unaffected by this terrible calamity, the likes of which our people has not known, even though its history is soaked in blood and tears.

The trial of Eichmann, that German oppressor, which took place in our holy eternal city of Jerusalem, comes under the category of what the Bible terms, "And the redeemers will climb Mount Zion to judge the hill of Esau." The trial has brought about a noticeable change in this trend and helped to instill greater recognition of the evil that was done to us, in the hearts of all who heard what happened. It has also caused a renewal in the search for war criminals who still pass as "democrats" all over the world (included among them is Hans Krieger, the murderer of the Jews of Rohatyn, about whose capture we have only recently heard). The truth is, if we really want to honor the memories of our martyrs, it behooves us to stay away from this murderous people and their culture, for we need to know that it is not only the "Führer" (שר״י—Shri—

The name of the wicked shall rot!) and his whole gang who carry the blame for our misfortune, but the whole German people.

I have had to force myself on two occasions to speak with so called "good Germans." The first time was at the International Parliamentary Convention in Constantinople where I was approached by a former acquaintance, the last chairman of the Reichstag, Paul Laba. The second time was when I met with the head of the socialists of West Germany, Adenauer, who came to Haifa for the meeting of the Socialist International. I demanded of him then that he make an effort to extend the statute of limitations with regard to war criminals. This was of course a form of mitzvah haba-ah be-aveira—doing a meritorious deed via illegal means. I asked these "nice Germans," "Where were you?" Where were those millions of Germans who still voted for the socialists and communists in that last election to the Reichstag in March 1933? They did not raise a finger; they made no proclamations and did not even utter a sound of protest from the Underground.

I have been privileged to initiate the law for establishing Yom Hashoah, Holocaust and Martyrs' Day, as well as the law for bringing the Nazis and their cohorts to justice, the law under which Eichmann was judged. But even that is not enough.

Maintaining a friendly relationship with murderers, whose hands are covered with the blood of Jews, violates the memory of our martyrs whose voices seem to be arising at memorial gatherings and from memorial books saying, "Who asked you to trample my courtyard?" Who needs all of this?

May the memory of our martyrs bring merit to the survivors who were privileged to see with their own eyes the Beginning of the Redemption, the realization of the goals of those who set Zion at the head of their banners.

And we say to the community of Rohatyn as Jonathan said to David, "You are missed because your place is empty." You will not be forgotten because your place in world Judaism cannot be filled!

May their memory be blessed!

The Early Period

History of a Town
History of the Jews of Rohatyn
By Dr. N. M. Gelber

Translated from Hebrew by Rabbi Mordecai Goldzweig,
Edited by Fay and Julian Bussgang.
Polish and German text translated by Donia Gold Shwarzstein.

YB p. 10

A. Historical Background

The town of Rohatyn is situated in Galicia on the shores of the Gnila Lipa River. Its recorded history began as early as the 12th century, and the events therein left their stamp for future generations. There are not many documents available from the earliest periods of its history, but from what there are, the following picture appears. Rohatyn first began as a small village that slowly grew, deriving a good amount of its income from marketing fairs. It does not seem to have constituted a special political entity of its own, in the beginning, but was attached to other areas and was politically affected by what happened in the surrounding areas. It began as a village, and it became a town in the 13th century. From one document we learn that in 1375, King Wladyslaw gave the town of Rohatyn to the Cardinal of Wladyslaw.[1][Ed1]

From this period until about the middle of the 15th century, we do not have any information. Around 1444, the starosta (district administrator) of Rohatyn was Wolsko, who was followed by Mikolaj Paraba of Lubin in 1444.[2]

In the year 1460, the town and its surrounding areas were transferred to the ownership of the Parait family from Chodecz as a pledge for a loan made to King Casimir Jagiellonczyk (Kazimierz IV, 1447–92). During this period, as we learn from various documents, Rohatyn was doing business with Zydaczow.[2a]

The yearly town market fairs became so successful that they interfered with the trade of the city of Lwow and caused it a serious loss of income, whereupon

1 M. Hruszewskij, *Historja Ukrainy-Rus* 5:193.

Ed1 The above citation is apparently a misquote. In 1375 Wladyslaw of Opole was a regent, not yet a king. Also, reference to Rohatyn in M. Hruszewskij (5:428) states that Rohatyn was given at that time to the archbishopric of Halicz, with the right to collect revenues.

2 *Akta grodzkie i ziemskie* (Municipal and land records) 5:124.

2a *Akta grodzkie i ziemskie*, vol. 9, 1906. Reports and documents for years 1481–86.

the voivode (provincial administrator), Andrzej Odrowaz, petitioned the king to abolish the yearly trade fairs in Rohatyn, which were so damaging to the city of Lwow.

On 23 June 1461, King Casimir Jagiellonczyk responded by abolishing not only the Rohatyn fairs but also those of Tysmienica, Trembowla, Gologory, and Jazlowice, which apparently had also contributed to the loss of income to the city of Lwow.[3]

These restrictions applied only to the regional fairs. The local market days were permitted to continue, and by the 16th century, they grew beyond the scope of a local fair.[4]

In the 15th century, we learn that Rohatyn received a singular honor when the Halicz district parliament (sejmik halicki) met there.[Ed2] Until then, it had been meeting in Sadowa Wisznia.[5]

Living among the Slavic inhabitants of the town were also people of German descent. Included among them were Johannes, "the famous citizen" of Rohatyn, procreator of Petrusi, Raphal, and Otto, German brothers[Ed3] who did business with the nobility.[6]

In 1482 a suburb was added on the other side of the entrance to the town near the gate that was termed "*Suburbium Rohatinense*,"[7] a place that would be associated with the history of the Jews for hundreds of years thereafter. At that time, legal matters were still carried out for the town in the courts of Halicz.[8] In 1523 Otto of Chodecz, voivode of the province of Sandomierz and a *starosta* in Red Ruthenia [Ed4], tried to improve the position of the town by granting it a special permit to carry out special fairs known as *sochaczki*[9]

---

3   M. Hruszewskij, *Historja* 6:101; "Anuale forum pro festo Corporis Christi" (Annual market fair for the festival of Corpus Christi [Boze Cialo in Polish]), *Akta grodzkie i ziemskie* 19, no. 1319:235.

4   *Akta grodzkie i ziemskie* 6:64, no. 43. L. Ehrlich, Starostwa w Halickiem (Lwow 1914), 107.

Ed2 Before Lwow developed and became more important, Halicz was the capital of Red Ruthenia. The district of Halicz included the town of Rohatyn and surrounding communities. The name Galicia derives from Halicz (Galicz, in Russian).

5   H. Chodynski, *Sejmiki ziem ruskich w 15-tym wieku* (District parliaments in Russian lands in the 15th century) (Lwow 1906), 119. Red Ruthenia was divided into four districts—Lwow, Przemysl, Halicz, and Sanok.

Ed3 "German brothers" here may mean "cousins" rather than German nationality.

6   *Akta grodzkie i ziemskie* 14:515, no. 2870, 1475, starting from 18 December

7   *Akta grodzkie i ziemskie* 17:464, no. 3809; 19:190, no. 972.

8   *Akta grodzkie i ziemskie* 19:235, no. 1319.

Ed4 "Czerwona Rus," a province that included the area that later became Galicia.

9   Liberum forum generale pro carnibus vendendis (free general market fairs for

every Saturday during the period between Wielkanoc (Easter) and John the Baptist Day (June 24). This permit applied only to the butchers of Rohatyn and only during the three months before the Holiday of the Three Kings. However, after the fairs, cattle belonging to the inhabitants of the area could be brought to Rohatyn to be slaughtered and sold upon payment of a fee to the national treasury of a groschen for each ox or cow and six denars for each sheep or goat.

During that year, a bridge was erected and paved, the use of which required, by order of the voivode of Red Ruthenia, the payment of a toll of two denars for each wagon and one denar for each horse.[10] In 1533, the government transferred the proceeds of this fee to the town.[11] After the death of Otto of Chodecz, the town again became the official property of the king,[12] and the first starosta was Johann Boratynski.[13]

In the year 1535 King Sigismund I applied the Magdeburg law to Rohatyn and thus exempted the town from the payment of a number of taxes (on such items as eggs, cheese, spayed chickens, and oats) and permitted the hewing of wood in the forests. Because of incursions into the town by surrounding enemies that caused great damage, the king granted Rohatyn a special "privilege" in 1539 that permitted it to erect fortifications and a protective wall, the expenditures of which the king subsidized from taxes on liquor and szos (paved roadways). He wrote in the privilege, "Desiring that the town grow and develop, it shall be surrounded by walls, and We permit the erection of a citadel in the center of town, including a town hall with a tower." The expenses for the maintenance of this citadel were to be derived from taxes on the sale of textile remnants (postrzygalnia) and liquor.

---

the sale of meat). The free markets were special fairs at which only meat was sold. They were named for the sochaczki or benches on which the butchers placed the meat. The first permits for these fairs were granted to the town of Kolomyja in the year 1443 at the request of its inhabitants. The income from these fairs was earned by special leaseholders. However, no Jews took part in these fairs. The income from the fairs of Rohatyn added up to about forty florin a year. *Akta grodzkie i ziemskie 5:119, no. 91.*

10   Denar—coin, discontinued in the days of King Mieczyslaw I, that was worth a third of a groschen.

11   Teodor Wierzbowski, Matricularum regnis Poloniae (Public Record of the Kingdom of Poland (Warsaw 1912) 2:287, no. 13716, paragraph 4.

12   Bona nostra Rohatin post obitum Ottae de Chodecz iure optimo ad nos et mensam nostram devoluta essent (following the death of Otto of Chodecz, whose rule was excellent for us, our good Rohatyn deteriorated).

13   *Akta grodzkie i ziemskie* 9:595, no. 3064.

According to a survey in 1572, the town had a population of 115 homeowners, 18 tenants, and 36 citizens who lived on the outskirts, while the new town held 100 homeowners and 11 tenants. In 1578, Rohatyn paid 700 gulden in taxes on liquor.[14] The condition of the inhabitants at this time had deteriorated so much that apparently King Stefan Batory issued an order on 12 December 1576 exempting the town from payment of levies and taxes except for customs at the borders. This directive was sent to all of the customs offices and tax collectors.[15] In reaction to this directive, a quarrel broke out between the customs inspectors of Red Ruthenia and those of the village of Rohatyn, because the people of Red Ruthenia did not wish to recognize the decree of the king and demanded the payment of duties. The issue came before King Stefan Batory on 4 August 1578 in Lwow, and he confirmed that the inhabitants of Rohatyn were required to pay only customs at the border.[16]

During these years, there existed a variety of guilds. Of note are the goldsmiths who received a special charter from King Stefan Batory on 15 June 1575. Among the best known of their works were those created by Bartolomy.[17]

Another attempt by the king to improve conditions in the town was a call by His Majesty to all merchants and travelers not to encroach on the town of Rohatyn.

In the 16th century, the town was attacked by the Tatars. In one of their incursions, they kidnapped Anastasia, the daughter of the local Ruthenian priest Lisowski, who was sold into the harem of Suleiman I. She found favor with him to the point where she became his first wife, taking the name of Roxolana. For a time, she even directed the official policies of Turkey.[18]

In the 17th century, the Cossack bands began their attacks on Poland. In 1615, an intensive battle was waged against them near Rohatyn, and the Hetman (Commander) Zolkiewski succeeded in destroying them as well as capturing their leaders and executing them. In 1616, King Sigismund III permitted the erection of a public bathhouse known as the Babinski Patopek on the Babianka River, and the income from it was transferred to the town for its expenditures.[19] The

14   M. Hruszewskij, *Historja* 6:108.
15   *Akta grodzkie i ziemskie* 5:122, no. 1840–41.
16   *Akta grodzkie i ziemskie* 10:131, no. 1985.
17   Leonard Lepszy, *Zlotnictwo w Polsce* (The goldsmith trade in Poland) (Krakow 1933): 270.
18   *Encyklopedia Orgelbranda* 22:205–6.
19   Balinski-Lipinski, *Starozytna Polska* (Ancient Poland) 2:867.

Chmielniszczyzna (followers of Chmielnicki), a Ukrainian anti-Polish movement, expanded into the Rohatyn area. Ruthenians from there joined them in their military preparations and maneuvers. Together with other Ruthenians from surrounding towns, they took part in military attacks on the manors of the nearby Polish nobility, threatening not to leave one "Polak" alive. The Ruthenians of Rohatyn were filled with a burning hatred toward the Catholic religion, monasteries, and churches.[20]

According to a survey dated 1663, the town had 200 houses in the old town and 31 in the new suburb. The residents complained that the podwodne they were forced to pay was unfair.

Despite its relatively small size, the town had a wide variety of guilds—tailors, weavers, cobblers, butchers, bakers, furriers, belt makers, musicians, blacksmiths, iron mongers, harness makers, and armorers. Tinsmiths, saddle makers, and carriage makers were united into one guild.

In the 1670s the starosta was Sigmund Karol Pszaromski, followed by the nobleman Adam Mikolaj Sieniawski, who carried out many important duties in the community.[20a] For a number of years, he was the president (marszalek) at sessions of the district parliament (sejmik) at Sadowa Wisznia.[21]

In the 17th and 18th centuries, the town became known as a center for the sale of cattle, horses, and agricultural products. To the town were attached the villages of Perenowka, Firlejow, Podgrodzie, Zalipia, and Zawadowka. In the census of the year 1765, the population of the town numbered 539. The starosta was Franciszek Bialinski, and the net income for the district rose to 37,560 gulden per year. At that time, the town belonged to Jozef Bielski.

After the conquest of Galicia by Austria, Rohatyn was transferred to the noblewoman Zofia Lubomirska as partial compensation for her Dobromil manor, which was taken by the Austrian government.[22]

Under the Austrians, the town grew. In 1857, Rohatyn had 5,101 inhabitants. In 1870, 4,510; in 1880, again 5,101; in 1887, 6,548; in 1890, 7,188 and 914 houses; in 1900, 931 houses and 7,201 inhabitants; and in 1910, 7,664 inhabitants. In 1921 the population was reduced to 5,736 because of World War I.

---

20   M. Hruszewskij, *Historja* 6:261.
20a   Obligation of the towns and villages to provide horse-drawn carriages for the king, his court, and the officials who were traveling in the name of the authorities as well as for the armed forces.
21   "Lauda wiszenskie (Proclamations of Wisznia) 1673–1732," *Akta grodzkie i ziemskie*, ed. Antoni Prohaska (Lwow 1914): 151–52, no. 59.
22   Kuropatnicki, *Geografia Galicji*, Lwow, 1780.

In 1885, occupations in the town of Rohatyn included:

Merchants, 51: textiles, 3; shoes, 11; iron, 2; eggs, 1; grain, 13; glass, 1; flour, 12; agricultural products, 4; and wagon grease, 4;

Crafts: furriers, 2; tailors, 1;

Lease holders: millers, 1; bartenders, 1.

In the general area of Rohatyn, there were 1,290 people in different occupations. They included as follows:

Trades, 393 merchants: wine, 11; textiles, 35; spices, 16; wagon grease, 7; salt, 12; handicrafts, 6; flour and cereals, 14; hides, 19; cattle, 8; horses, 5; petroleum, 5; lumber, 8; whiskey, 4; flooring, 1; eggs, 5; iron, 12; fish, 4; grain, 43; fruit, 5; haberdashery, 53; peddlers, 5; money changers, 5; middlemen, 3-4; brokers, 3; retailers, 95.

Craftsmen, 520 workers that included: tailors, 55; furriers, 21; hosiers, 4; weavers, 18; cotton wool makers, 2; rope weaver, 1; soap makers, 7; shoemakers, 58; chimney sweeps, 2; comb makers, 3; charcoal makers, 2; metal forger, 1; stonecutters, 2; carpenters, 26; potters, 21; precious metal smiths, 2; watchmakers, 5; glaziers, 7; tanners, 4; bronze coater, 1; coachmen, 12; belt makers, 4; woodcarvers, 3; bookbinders, 4; butchers, 44; wooden house builders, 25; blacksmiths, 20; iron mongers, 4; insulation, 4; gardeners, 2; millers, 58; mechanics, 2; fence makers, 19; harness makers, 4; wood cutters, 3; musicians, 4; barber-surgeons, 17; builders, 3; painters, 2; bakers, 16.

Leaseholders, Bartenders, Suppliers, Druggists, Factory Owners, 337, including: leaseholders of mills, 49; owners of mills, 40; tavern keepers, 96; leaseholders of inns, 7; owners of blacksmith shops, 2; distillery owners, 13; bartenders, 152; distillers, 2; meat suppliers, 2; partition suppliers, 3; fodder suppliers, 4; milkmen, 4; soda water suppliers, 2; druggists, 4.

In the year 1889, the town of Rohatyn transferred its records to the state archives in Lwow, among them a large number of documents, such as thirteen permits and charters from the years 1438, 1525, 1535, 1539, 1567, 1581, 1603, 1663, 1669, 1676, 1729, 1738, 1796.[23] After World War II, this important historical treasure remained in the hands of the Soviet Union.

B. The Beginning of the Jewish Community

There is no way of knowing when the Jewish community of Rohatyn began, since we do not have any documents attesting to its beginning. We only know that by the end of the 15th century, Jews of Red Ruthenia and

---

23   Stefan Sochaniewicz, Archiwum krajowe aktow grodzkich i ziemskich, Prze-glad naukowy i literacki (National archive of municipal and land records, Scientific and literary review) (Lwow 1912) 40:1039.

other parts of Poland were coming to the market fairs to buy cattle that were, in turn, sold in Silesia and Western Poland. They also bought horses that were brought there from Hungary.[24] We learn from one document, dated 1463, that one of the cattle wholesalers was a Jew by the name of Shimshon from Zydaczow. He bought cattle, oxen, and horses from the landowners of the areas around Rohatyn.

In 1463, an agreement was reached between the Polish nobleman, Johann Skarbok, and the Jewish wholesaler, Shimshon, from Zydaczow. According to this agreement, Skarbok would provide Shimshon with the use of his town, Olchowiec, in the district of Halicz, for the rental fee of 40 marks, and Shimshon would agree to accept 500 head of cattle (peccora quinta) from him to be sold at the next fair in Rohatyn. In the event that the fair did not take place in Rohatyn, Skarbok was to deliver them in Olchowiec[25].

Shimshon also did business on a large scale with other nobility in the Rohatyn area, where he was the major buyer at the Rohatyn fairs in the years 1447–64.

As a result of this, Jews began to settle in Rohatyn. Jews are first mentioned in legal documents of Rohatyn dated in the year 1531.[25a] During the 15th and 16th centuries, their numbers were still quite small, and they did not as yet have an organized community. They were subject to the jurisdiction of the Jewish community of Lwow. The residents of the area were directly tied to the kahal (Jewish community council) of Lwow, or through one of its branches in the district of Halicz. As the town expanded and became a larger marketing center, more Jews were attracted to settle there, since the town needed skilled workers, retailers, and peddlers. In the year 1582 the collection of taxes on liquor in Rohatyn was leased to Mendel Izakowicz for an unknown number of years.[26]

On the other hand, Rohatyn, a crown property, did not grant the right of citizenship to Jews or anyone else who was not a Catholic, in contrast to "free" towns, not officially under royal jurisdiction, whose economic

24   J. Schipper, *Studja nad stosunkami gospodarczymi Zydow w Polsce podczas sredniowiecza* (Studies of economic conditions of Jews in Poland in the Middle Ages) (Lwow 1911): 189.

25   *Akta grodzkie i ziemskie* 12 (Municipal and land records) (Lwow 1887), 450, no. 4461; *Akta ziemskie halickie* 1435–61 (Galician land records).

25a Archiwum Skarbu Warszawa taryfa (Archives of the treasury, Warsaw tariffs) fol 22, quoted by Feldman, Elazar in Oldest Information regarding Jews in Polish Cities in the 14th and 15th centuries. Pages in History (Warsaw 1934): 69. (In Yiddish)

26   *Akta grodzkie i ziemskie* 10:14z, no. 2202.

interests led them to grant Jews rights equal to those of other inhabitants. They even gave Jews the right to vote for members of the town council, as exemplified by Brody, Dukla, Zmigrod and so on.

As a result, Jewish inhabitants in areas like Rohatyn, who were not under the jurisdiction of such towns, did not benefit from the provisions of the Magdeburg law, which provided for the administrative and judicial independence of municipalities. They were deprived of the possibilities of taking part in some of the economic endeavors available, such as the distilling and sale of hard liquor. Since the Jews of Rohatyn lacked a charter, the economic rules that applied to them were different from the rest of the community, with the exception of sales connected with the yearly fairs. Thus, during this period, the number of Jews in the community did not increase in proportion to those living in "free" towns.

Changes in the development of the Jewish community of Rohatyn did not really gain momentum until the year 1633 when King Wladyslaw IV granted it a charter that was continued by King John Casimir (Jan Kazimierz) and restated again by King Michael (Michal) in 1669. This charter laid the foundation for the legal establishment and organization of a Jewish community. In it he states that he, King Michael, reaffirms and validates the charters of earlier origin granted to the Jews by his predecessor, Wladyslaw IV, on 27 March 1633, and continued by John Casimir on 21 May 1663, and on this, the day of his coronation, the 22 November 1669, (he reaffirms) the plan and contents of the privileges previously presented in their magnanimity by his predecessors.[27]

The text states in part, after a prologue written in Latin, that "on the fifth day after the religious holiday Purificationis Beatissimae Virginis Mariae,[27a] there appeared by himself, in the town of Lwow, the Jewish intermediary (Jacob) Selig[28], who presented the signed charter by His Majesty for registration in the archives of Lwow and addressed in His magnanimity the Jews of Rohatyn, the text of which states as follows:

"Polish king Wladyslaw IV (followed by all of his titles) publicly declares that whereas We have accepted in this, the coronation session of the Sejm, all of the laws of our kingdom and of those of the cities, do We, in keeping with the petition of the Jews in Our

---

27 See appendices.

27a feria quinta post festum Purificationis Beatissimae Virginis Mariae. The holiday took place on 2 February; five days afterwards would have been 7 February.

28 Selig was intercessor for the "kehilot (Jewish communities) surrounding Lwow." Majer Balaban, *Zydzi na przelomie 16-go i 17-go wieku* (Jews at the turning-point of the 16th to the 17th Century) (Lwow 1906): 225, 355, 379, 445, 502.

town of Rohatyn, reinstate and recognize all of the privileges, decrees relating to surveys of the houses and lots where they live, the synagogue, the cemetery, all trades, and businesses without distinction as to buying and selling, and the buying and selling of lead and other goods; they are permitted to keep taverns and the varieties of liquor in them, to brew beer and mead, to distill whiskey; they further have the right to sell and buy cattle, meat, whole or in parts, in the rynek (town square), in keeping with their past marketing customs, being equal with the townspeople according to privileges, and without prejudice, as practiced in the town.

"As to the taxes on the Jews, they are to pay city taxes similar to those paid by the townspeople but are not required to pay 'private taxes.' On the other hand, taxes that they have been paying, according to law and earlier customs, are to be maintained.

"His Majesty authorizes all customs and laws that were enjoyed previously to the extent that they are still in use and do not violate the body of the laws as a whole. In addition to this present authorization, We do give our promise that they will continue to remain in effect."

It is stressed in the charter that the Jews of Rohatyn had presented a petition in writing asking that the third day of the week, their traditional market day, be continued and recognized as found in previous documents. The king granted their petition, taking into consideration their right to recuperate from the ravages of enemy incursions and to operate their business affairs to their best advantage.

The charter instituted rules for the legal maintenance of the Jewish economy and insured their rights, permitting them to conduct their business legally. The salient passage here is "rowno z mieszczanami tamecznymi wedlug przywileju i starodawnego zwyczaju" (on a par with the local citizens according to the privilege and long-standing customs). We see that equal rights were ensured to all residents of the town. In contrast to Jews in a number of other towns in Red Ruthenia, they were free of various levies such as the supply of tools; participating in the construction and repair of roads, repair of bridges and town walls; and tributes to officials, the church, and the priests and so on. These special rights derived from the permission given to the Jews to maintain their stores in the center of town and their freedom of trade. These rulings did not cover the socio-legal organization of the Jewish community, since the community of Rohatyn developed in the same fashion as did other Jewish communities in Poland. It is quite possible that by the 17th century, the Jews of Rohatyn had received a charter in this area as well, but there are no definite documents to validate this assumption with certainty.

In practice, the Jewish community of Rohatyn was one of nine communities that were included in the general Jewish community of Lwow prior to the attacks of Chmielnicki. These communities included Bohorodczany, Buczacz, Brody, Zolkiew, Tysmienica, Lesko, Zloczow, and Rohatyn. The officials under the jurisdiction of Lwow included the chief rabbi. As in all other Polish communities there was a va'ad (governing council) consisting of:

(a) 3 - 5 parnassim (leaders) who were responsible to the government and were elected yearly after swearing loyalty to the government of Poland. The election of the parnassim was contingent on their acceptance by the voivode (provincial administrator) because it was a crown town as opposed to a private town, where acceptance of Jewish officials was determined by the owner of the town or his deputy;

(b) 3 - 5 tuvim (notables);

(c) members of executive committees.

The officials of the community were the rabbi (rav), judges (dayanim), the preacher (darshan), the scribe (sofer), and the beadle (shamas). An intercessor (shtadlan) represented the Jewish community before the government when the need arose. Thus we find Selig, the Lwow shtadlan, presenting the charter granted by the king of Poland for entry into the official books of Lwow. Rohatyn, a small town, was unable to maintain its own shtadlan and thus employed the services of Selig from Lwow. Many heavily populated communities kept a doctor, a druggist, a nurse, a midwife, guards, collectors, and messengers in addition to the above. To what extent this existed in Rohatyn, we do not know. Even in Rohatyn, there existed organizations for burial and so forth.

Since Rohatyn in the 17th century had within it a large number of craftsmen in various categories, it also had many trade unions that stood guard to protect their interests within the Christian guilds, the municipality, and within the governing committee of the Jewish community as well.

In 1658, at the request of the Red Ruthenian nobility at the sejmik in Sadowa Wisznia, there were established va'adei gelilot (Jewish district councils) which in the end resulted in the creation of a council for towns surrounding Lwow and eight additional Jewish communities.

In practice, it was the kahal (Jewish council) of the city of Lwow alone that directed all the activities of the regional council, to the point where the parnassim of Lwow had concentrated under their control the enactment of all the activities of the kehilah (Jewish community). They stood guard to protect this hegemony from falling out of their hands and thus excluded the kehilot (Jewish communities) within the eight provincial towns. After the wars during the 17th century and the revolt of Chmielnicki, the kehilah of Lwow sharply decreased in size. In its place, politically, there emerged the provincial towns, which effectively took the leadership away from the parnassim of Lwow in the national Jewish council. The kehilah of Zolkiew, which hitherto had been considered a branch (przykahalek) of the Lwow Jewish community, succeeded, with the aid and support of King Jan Sobieski, the owner of this royal town, to free itself completely from the domination of the Lwow kehilah. It also went on to take control of the regional council, together with the kehilot of Brody, Tarnopol, and Buczacz. This enabled the rabbi of Buczacz to be elected chief rabbi of the whole region. Among the other kehilot that joined it were Rohatyn, Lesko, and Zloczow, whose representatives were included among the heads of the new executive council of the area.

The declining economic conditions of Lwow forced many Jews there to leave the city and settle in the eastern towns of Red Ruthenia. To what extent this affected their coming to Rohatyn is hard to tell. One thing is certain, that due to the continued wholesale exodus of the Jews from Lwow eastward, the city was so weakened that they were unable to fulfill payment of their required head tax that was placed on the small number of Jews remaining there. This fact was brought to the attention of the sejmik of Wisznia on 18 April 1701.[29]

The members of the nobility complained that they were not obtaining their tax money because large numbers of Jews were leaving for Podolia, then under the Turks, where there was no head tax. They therefore asked that the taxes be reapportioned for the existing number of inhabitants. The sejmik approved the request but did not put it into effect until 15 years later in 1716. Eventually, Red Ruthenia and Podolia were given different tax schedules.

In 1664 the kahal members from the nearby towns of Buczacz, Zolkiew, Jaworow, Kolomyja, and Brody attacked the Lwow contingent at the Va'ad Hagalil (district council) meeting in Swierz and forced them to revise their monopoly to include the views of their neighbors that had heretofore been ignored. This brought about the addition to the council of seven more members from the nearby towns. The council, which met in Kulikow in 1720, had 14 members—five members from Zolkiew, three from Brody, one from Bohorodczany, one from Stryj, one from Rohatyn, one from Zloczow, and one from Buczacz.[30] Among the issues that this session dealt with, on 11 Tammuz 5480 (17 July 1720), was the (previous) unseating of the Gaon Rabbi Yehoshua Falk, author of *Pnei Yehoshua*, from his office as

---

29 "Lauda wiszenskie," *Akta grodzkie i ziemskie* 22 (Ed. Prohaska), 364, no. 67.

30 Majer Balaban, Z zagadnien ustrojowych zydostwa polskiego (Selection of issues concerning the organizational structure of Polish Jewry) (Lwow 1932): 6–7.

rabbi in Lwow.[31] This council, which included Rohatyn, unanimously voted to return the Gaon to his office, which had been taken from him and given to Rabbi Chaim ben Leizerel, Rabbi ben Leizerel's having been elected through the intercession of his father-in-law, the purchasing agent for the voivode Jablonowski.[32] The representative from Rohatyn, Zvi Hirsh, took part in this.

C. Economic Conditions

During the 17th century, the area of Halicz and its surrounding towns was prey to violent attacks and invasions by Tatars and Turks. Later, in the time of Chmielnicki, Russians and Cossacks wreaked havoc—destruction, murder, rape and fire—wherever they went, as they did in all of Red Ruthenia. In this Rohatyn was no exception and fared no differently than the other communities in the area. There are no exact recorded figures of the extent of destruction and murder that was committed there, but in general, the effects of the ravages of Tach V'Tat (the tragic years 1648–49) continued to be felt until the middle of the 18th century. What is known is that the damage in Rohatyn was no less than those in the other neighboring areas. This resulted in a great deterioration in the economic condition of the Jews of the area, to the point where on 23 December 1675, even the sejmik of Halicz was impressed and brought up the topic for official discussion with regard to the payment of the head tax by the Jews of Red Ruthenia. It was clear, even to them, that the Jews would no longer be able to pay it. The Ukrainian rebellion against Polish rule erased whole communities that had once supplied taxes that were now sorely missing.[33] This finally resulted in bringing the members of the Halicz parliament (sejmik) to petition the national parliament (Sejm) to absolve the Jews from paying this tax. King Jan Sobieski III took note of this request in his directive of 27 July 1694 when he declared, "The

31 In the decision, the community of Lwow, the opponents of Rabbi Falk, were rebuked for their behavior "in depriving him of his money and property in the amount of 30,000 Polish gulden."

32 The decision was published in the article of Dr. Simchowicz, "Zur Biographie des Rabbi Jakob Josua," (The biography of Rabbi Jakob Josua), Monatschrift zur Geschichte und Wissenschaft des Judentums (Monthly journal of Judaic history and studies) (1910); 616–18. Other signatories: Gershon Natan of Zolkiew, Shimshon Natan of Zolkiew, Yaakov Babad of Brody, Yaakov Aharon of Lesko, Moshe of Bohorodczany, Yehuda Leib of Jazlowice, Moshe Avraham of Zloczow, Mordechai Segal and Klonimos Kalman of Tysmienica, and Aryeh Leib of Buczacz.

33 "...because the whole population perished in Buczacz, Tarnopol, and Podhajce, and throughout the whole voivodeship entire towns perished, there were not enough people to pay the levied sum." Akta grodzkie i ziemskie 24:398, no. 205.

Jews of Red Ruthenia have suffered more than the rest of the Jews from the movement of Polish soldiers through their area plus the incursions of the enemy."

Nevertheless, the Jews were required to contribute their part in paying for the expenses of the war, as provided by the laws of the sejmik of 3 September 1633. This money was used to pay for the salaries of soldiers. Every person without exception had to pay one zloty. In times of general conscription, a tax on lead and gun powder was levied on tenants and tavern owners of the towns and surrounding villages, while the inhabitants had to appear before the army to be drafted in time of attack. And one may very well imagine that in case of invasion, Jews were not exempt from joining the general community in fighting off the enemy; this would include Rohatyn. The economic situation became so bad that people became wild and did what Gentiles do to Jews whenever they are under pressure. Jewish debtors found themselves pulled off the streets and tied up by their creditors without recourse to the courts. This was too much even for the sejmik, and on 11 December 1675, the sejmik at Sadowa Wisznia ordered its representatives to the Sejm to complain about this anarchy rampant at that time and to do something to eliminate such behavior.[34]

There was a similar occurrence of this nature that took place in the 1620s, when a nobleman, a Skopowski from Rohatyn, grabbed one Yaakov and his wife from Rohatyn and threw them into prison. No reason for this was given, and this aroused the ire of the town, which issued an official complaint against this so-called nobleman as part of its role as the defender of its citizens, even if they were Jews.[34a]

On the other hand, by 1639, the sejmik began to clamp down on Jewish sources of income. It wanted to limit competition with the other inhabitants in business and trade and in public leasing.[35] The sejmik further requested of the Sejm, on 6 November 1713, that it forbid Jewish communities from levying taxes on Jewish tenants in the villages on their own initiative without the assent of the voivode of the area. The sejmik claimed that these kehilah taxes, which went for Jewish

---

34 "Great prejudice is directed against the Jewish people living under the protection of the Polish Republic, such that the innocent may be captured on the roads and tied up until they pay for the debtor; therefore, the deputies must try to prevent this. "Lauda wiszenskie," *Akta grodzkie i ziemskie* 23:49, no. 21, 24, 25.

34a Horn, Elzbieta, "Zydzi w ziemi halickiej na przelomie XVI i XVII wieku" (Jews on the soil of Halicz at the turning-point of the 16th to the 17th century), Bulletin of the Jewish Historical Institute (Warsaw 1962) 40:34.

35 *Akta grodzkie i ziemskie* 24:44 (23.6.1632).

community use, were emptying the pockets of the tenants to the point where they were unable to meet their obligations to the owners of the estates.[36]

In addition to the rental of properties, the Jews of Rohatyn engaged in brewing liquor, maintaining taverns, selling beer and wine, peddling, and keeping small shops—which brought in the greater part of their income. At the end of the 17th century and the beginning of the 18th century, we find Jews primarily engaged in the production of liquor—the brewing of beer and the sale of whiskey, mead, and wine—areas that were open to them in keeping with the rulings of 1633. Jews leased the brewery in the suburb of Babince.

As wholesalers, they engaged, to a large measure, in the sale of agricultural products and cattle. As craftsmen they were engaged in a wide variety of occupations—as bakers, tailors, butchers, brewers, and hatters.[37]

Relations between Jewish and non-Jewish workers were correct until around 1663, when the shoemakers' guild complained that Jewish shopkeepers were selling shoes of sheepskin and yellow and red boots in their stores and stalls without notifying it. It felt that this was unfair competition, and therefore, Jews who did so should be required to make a payment of a liter of beeswax for each violation, on pain of confiscation of their goods by the shoemakers' guild. Those who continued to sell black boots should be required to pay the guild ten grzywne on pain of confiscation by the guild.[38]

This was in keeping with the privilege granted to the non-Jewish shoemakers in 1589 and 1633, whereby they could confiscate substandard goods. It also accorded them the right to have first choice in buying leather, effectively enabling them to stifle competition, since the best goods would come from them. However, some Jews continued to ignore these regulations and bought as good a quality of leather as they could obtain as early as they could get it, privilege or no privilege. This aroused the shoemakers' guild to investigate the matter between 1661 and 1664 and resulted in a report that concluded that Jews were indeed buying up first-quality leather ahead of the members of the guild, in violation of prescribed privileges. The guild therefore proclaimed that Jews should not be allowed to continue this practice of engaging in the purchase of leather ahead of their non-Jewish competitors. If Jews were caught violating this ruling, the shoemakers' guild had every right to confiscate their merchandise, since it was manufactured illegally, and the guilds were to have first choice in

---

36 *Akta grodzkie i ziemskie* 22:547, no. 212, § 33.
37 M. Horn, "Rzemieslnicy zydowscy na Rusi Czerwonej" (Jewish craftsmen in Red Ruthenia), Bulletin of the Jewish Historical Institute 34 (Warsaw 1960): 65–67.
38 Balinski-Lipinski, *Starozytna Polska* (Ancient Poland) 2:867–68.

purchases of leather.[38a]

From the instructions of the sejmik of Halicz to its parliamentary delegates in its session of 1712–14, we learn that, based on the list of Jews that paid the chimney tax (podymne), Jews were at that time engaged in the sale of wine, in the brewing and sale of beer, in keeping inns, taverns, stalls and stores, as well as being owners of houses in the town square (domy rynkowe) and of taverns in the surrounding villages.[38b]

The economic condition of the Jews of Rohatyn, in particular, as part of the total picture of what was going on in Red Ruthenia, in general, continued to degenerate during the 18th century. Their tax load, normally heavy before the invasions, became progressively unmanageable following them. While the sejmik agreed that there was reason for this condition and indeed the Jews were under great strain economically, it nevertheless, on 9 December 1710, demanded a levy from the Jews of Halicz of 30,000 zlotys per year. However, it agreed to release the towns of Rohatyn, Bursztyn, and Tluste from this obligation for "certain reasons."[39]

As noted above, the legislators in the district of Halicz—which included Rohatyn—sought especially hard to impose prohibitions and limitations on Jewish commerce, particularly against lessees of government and church-owned real estate. This was backed by the representatives to the sejmik of Halicz, who demanded punishment of those Jews who still held property, on the grounds that they opposed Christianity and therefore had no right to hold Christian property. Those who continued to do so were to be punished.[40] The result was a demand by the sejmik of Halicz, on 20 July 1696, via its representatives, to pass a law in the Sejm of Warsaw to this effect during the time of the interregnum.

This approach dominated the economic policy of the Halicz nobility and was based on the proposition that Jews were "untrustworthy people" (gens perfida), whose only interest was the filling of their own pockets at the expense of the welfare of the republic.[41] In 1718, the nobles of the Halicz sejmik instructed

---

38a "And these Jews, not having the right to purchase leather, buy it ahead of the shoemakers, and afterwards, they extract from the poor shoemaker whatever they want. Thus we declare in this matter that Jews shall not dare do this, and if they buy it up ahead of the shoemakers, then the shoemakers' guild will have the right to... seize it." (In Polish) Elzbieta Horn, "*Zydzi*," 27

38b Akta grodzkie i ziemskie 25: 211, no. 139, §§ 5 (12.IX.1714).

39 "Lauda sejmikowe halickie (Proclamations of the Halicz parliament) 1696–1772," *Akta grodzkie i ziemskie* 25 (Wojciech Hejnosz: Lwow 1935), 133, no. 101.

40 "Lauda," *Akta grodzkie* 25: 6, no. 2.

41 Directive to deputies to the Sejm of 20 January 1710, "Lauda," *Akta grodzkie* 25:114, no. 88.

their representatives to the Sejm in Warsaw to demand an end to the collection of taxes by Jews, Armenians, and the like of customs, national levies, and rental of properties belonging to the nobility. A violation of this should result in the expropriation of the said property.[41a] Even worse was the demand to forbid Jews from exporting salt, horses, oxen, and wine—a large source of income for the Jews of Rohatyn and environs.[41b] They also forbade Jews, by law, from keeping Christian servants.

In addition to attacking the Jewish economy, the gentiles of Halicz directed their hatred at the personal life of the Jewish people and tried to keep them from growing in number. Toward this purpose, the sejmik at the session of 17 September 1736 instructed its delegate to the national Sejm to ask the Sejm assembly in Warsaw to pass a law that would decrease the number of early marriages among Jews. This was to be done by requiring a payment to the government by anyone marrying at an early age of either a certain portion (sortem certum) of their possessions or of their dowry, on threat of a fine.[41c] These economic tribulations were encouraged by the Catholic Church through its anti-Semitic exhortations in church, which fired everyone up against the Jews—as if they needed being fired up.

On 14 August 1752, a complaint was lodged by the sejmik of Halicz in the Sejm that the Jews were greatly upsetting "the Christians and the merchants in their business, thus wrecking our cities and the royal cities. Therefore, they should be prevented from engaging in all forms of trade with the exception of the sale of textiles and liquor (kwaterka—quarter of a liter) and to embody this in law."[41d]

In view of this anti-Semitic approach, it is surprising to find the sejmik stressing the need to ease the full brunt of the pressure on the Jews of Rohatyn with regard to the national head tax—from time to time, although not for an extended period.[42] Similarly, in 1725, the tax on liquor was lowered for Rohatyn because of its poor economic condition, attested to under oath by Jews and other people of the town.[42a]

With regard to the head tax, the Jews of Rohatyn paid 715 zlotys and 12 groschen of the 33,857 zlotys levied on the total population of Red

---

41a "Lauda," *Akta grodzkie* 25:275, no. 168, §§ 33 (13.VIII.1718).

41b "Lauda," *Akta grodzkie* 25:276, no. 160, §§ 48.

41c "Lauda," *Akta grodzkie* 25 (12.IX.1720): 287, no. 174, §§ 34.

41d "Lauda," *Akta grodzkie* 25 (14.VIII.1752): 498, no. 269.

42 "and so Jews on the estates of His Lordship Andrzej Krakowski, i.e., in Rohatyn, Bursztyn, and Tluste, are to be free of this levy." "Lauda," *Akta grodzkie* 25:137, no. 102.

42a "Lauda," *Akta grodzkie* 25:328, no. 189, ¶5

Ruthenia in 1717.[43] This caused an uproar by the Jewish taxpayers, who presented a complaint about the criminally unfair division of the head tax on certain communities by some of the people who were in charge of apportioning the head tax. This caused the sejmik at Sadowa Wisznia to decide on 15 March 1717 that the Jews of the towns and villages should gather together in one place and, in keeping with the numbers there, divide the total sum of the tax among those assembled.[44] Then there would be no discrimination against anyone and no reason to complain.

However, the head tax continued to plague the area, and a complaint was again lodged with the marszalek of the regional sejmik in 1734. It was recorded in the town ledgers to the effect that the tax load was unjust and beyond the ability of the inhabitants to pay, since it did not take into consideration the economic condition of the towns and villages, in general, and that of the individual tax payer, in particular. Taking this complaint into consideration, the sejmik ordered the representatives of the Jews to assemble on 28 April 1734 in Tarnopol in the presence of the secretary general of the Va'ad Arba Aratzos (Council of Four Lands) and the trustee of the Jewish community, Mordechai (Marek) Rabinowitz. They were entrusted to apportion the head tax equally among the Jews of the towns and villages, without doing injustice to the communities from the point of view of the number of towns and villages, taking into consideration their economic condition. The resulting figures were to be recorded by the secretary general of the Jews and entered into the Halicz and Trembowla ledgers.[45] The result was that in 1734, the Jews of Red Ruthenia were required to pay a head tax of 55,590 zlotys.

In 1750, Reb Yitzchak Yisaschar Berish Babad of Brody, the son of Reb Moshe Ze'ev, was appointed "Trustee of the House of Israel" for the Council of Four Lands in place of Isser of Zolkiew, as well as acting parnass (leader) for the area kahal. These appointments caused an uproar among the members of the Jewish district council to such an extent that a number of the communities excommunicated him and accused him of misusing public funds for his own purposes. They also complained about the way in which the head tax was apportioned. In 1756, Rohatyn lodged a similar complaint against him.[45a]

In the 1760s the relationship of the sejmik of Halicz with the Jews

---

43   Ossolineum 279 II 94, Manuscript.
44   Akta grodzkie 22:653, no. 261, paragraph 20.
45   "Lauda," *Akta grodzkie* 25:384, no. 215, Halicz (15.IV.1734), §§4.
45a   Bernardine Archive, Lwow, *Castrum Leopoliense: 574:544, 591.* Besides Rohatyn, in that same year, complaints were also brought by Drohobycz, Dolina, Zolkiew, Pomorzany, Kulikow, and Grodek.

deteriorated even further. In 1764, it instructed its delegates to the national Sejm, during the interregnum and during the session of the coronation, to demand that Jews be forbidden to hold and lease private, national, church, and royal properties; to act as tax collectors, officials, or clerks in tax offices; to sell wine, oxen, and horses; or to sell merchandise from one estate to another and that the nobility be forbidden to place Jews under their protection.[46]

D. The Sabbateans and the Frankists in Rohatyn

The depredations of Chmielnicki and his hordes as well as the others who ravaged Galicia left their mark not only on the Jewish economy but also on its religious views, in two opposing directions. There were those who wanted a Messiah immediately and tried to bring him to redeem them, and those who were willing to play up to the temporal powers that existed at that time in order to improve their lives, even if it meant leaving their religion to accomplish this. The traditional procedures for Jews trying to bring the Messiah has been to pray, study the Torah, and do good deeds. Later, two new elements were added—Cabala mysticism and the Land of Israel, the Holy Land of the Jews. These last two sources were stressed by Rabbi Yehuda Hachasid, an esteemed Cabalist, who succeeded in convincing over 1,000 Jews to try to come to Eretz Yisrael (Land of Israel). Earlier, around the time of Tach V'Tat (the terrible years of 1648–49), the opposite also took place. The charlatan Sabbatai Zvi claimed to use Cabala but was unable to and was later succeeded by Jacob Frank, using the relatively same ploys but with even greater ignorance than his predecessor. Both attracted far too many people on false pretenses of messianic promises.

When Rabbi Yehuda Hachasid left, the drive toward mysticism weakened for lack of an outstanding leader. There were some Cabalists here and there in the Carpathian Mountains who attracted followers, but this was sporadic. On the other hand, at this time, there were Jews who approached the Catholic Church to a lesser or a greater extent, some becoming Catholics officially. This could especially be found among lessees of land. The exact number of these apostates is not known. What is known is that King Jan Sobieski, on the recommendation of the nobility, encouraged these practices by granting the apostates properties and even titles of nobility.

This aroused the jealousy of the sejmik of Halicz, and in its session of 27 July 1696 at Sadowa Wisznia, it accused the Jews of deceiving the country and pocketing a good deal of the money that they received, rather than

46   "Lauda," *Akta grodzkie* 25: 579, no. 307, § 40 (31.I.1764); 615, no. 319 § 42 (20.X.1764).

passing it on to the national treasury. Prominent among those accused were the tax collectors Abers and Barnet from the area of Sambor.[47] These accusations by the sejmik were accepted as valid, and their properties were transferred to Daglan Nowiorski of Czestochowa.

As a result of this decision, the nobility of Red Ruthenia cast doubt on the veracity of the Jewish apostates, while the Jews utilized these events in their war against the Sabbateans and the Frankists.

That brings us to the coming of Jacob Frank to Rohatyn. The movement of Sabbatai Zvi spread in Poland, especially in Podolia, Wolhynia, and the parts of Red Ruthenia that bordered on Podolia. Spearheaded by the missionaries of Sabbatai Zvi, it succeeded in gaining adherents in the towns of Malopolska (southeastern Poland) and Red Ruthenia, including Rohatyn. What it officially presented to their audiences was mysticism perverted to suit its purpose. The same was true in the towns of Zolkiew, Podhajce, Busk, Gliniany, Horodenka, Zbaraz, Zloczow, Tysmienica, and Nadworna.[Tr1]

Among the first residents in Rohatyn to join the Sabbatean movement was the family of Elisha Schorr, which moved quickly into the foremost ranks of the movement due to the large family and effectiveness. Elisha Schorr and his sons were joined by Yehuda Leib, the son of Nota Krysa. Even after Sabbatai Zvi died, there remained a large residue in Red Ruthenia that still believed in the Sabbatean claims. It tried to continue to absorb new members by preaching quietly to individuals, so that the rabbinate would not officially be aware of it.

But Schorr was not the only one by any means engaged in this belief in Sabbatai Zvi. There were others such as Moshe David in Podhajce,[48] who claimed to be a Cabalist and miracle worker, and Krysa, whom we have already mentioned, in Nadworna. These three towns in Red Ruthenia, which border with Podolia, were the strongholds of Sabbateanism in Red Ruthenia. Not only did they have the largest number of adherents but also the greatest number of Sabbatean missionaries who spread the beliefs.

In Rohatyn Elisha Schorr and his sons, Shlomo, Natan (Lipman), and Leib were the principal activists. Elisha Schorr was known as a preacher in Rohatyn. He was a descendent of Rabbi Zalman Naftali Schorr,[49] author of Tevuos Shor, which gave him a facade behind which he could hide, since the

---

47   "Lauda," *Akta grodzkie* 22 (Lwow 1914), no. 100 § 91, no. 120 (151), no. 176 (§ 18).

Tr1   Interestingly enough these towns later became Hassidic strongholds.

48   See Chaim Warszawski, "The Sabbatean Cabalist, Moshe David of Podhajce," in Zion 2 (1942): 73.

49   Rabbi in Lublin, son-in-law of Shaul Wahl, died 1634

family was highly respected. Nobody would dream of what he was up to, and since he was accepted as a religious and learned person, people believed what he said. Those who knew better kept quiet.

Elisha Schorr was also in contact with outlying towns in Podolia through his son-in-law, Hirsch Reb Sabbatai, in Lanckorona, who was married to his daughter, Chaja. Chaja eventually was accepted as a prophetess in the Sabbatean camp and became known officially when the activities of the Sabbateans came to light, during the report given by witnesses to the rabbinate, of her sexual aberrations. These included having sexual relations with her brother-in-law, to whom she even bore children, her brothers, as well as with strangers. In this she did not fall far behind her sister-in-law, the wife of Shlomo, whose own sexual activities became well known in Rohatyn—all in the name of religion, the Sabbatean beliefs.

When Frank appeared on the scene, these Sabbatean centers in Red Ruthenia became Frankist strongholds. The elder Elisha Schorr was among the first to join up with Frank, whom he considered to be the heir to Sabbatai Zvi. Frank had reached the Dniester River on 5 December 1755. From there, he crossed over to Moghilev, then to Korolowka, his birthplace, on to Jezierzany–Kopyczynce, and from there to Busk. From Busk, he went to the German settlement of Dawidow near Lwow and from there directly to Lwow. In Lwow he settled outside of the city wall in a Christian suburb, but apparently he did not enjoy his stay there and quickly left the area, returning to Dawidow. From there, he came to Rohatyn together with his entourage, at which point he was joined by the Schorr family.

Frank himself related in the year 1756, "I was already engaged in special activities in Brzezany, Rohatyn, and Dworow to such an extent that I turned all of their heads. Even among the Polish magnates, I succeeded to the point where they were all completely befuddled. So you see how it goes with them."[50] This gives us some concept of the kind of egomaniac he must have been.

After arriving in Rohatyn, Frank began his sexual orgies similar to those that he had carried out in Lwow. Among the most active in these orgies was the wife of Shlomo Schorr who engaged in these with a will, all with the permission of her husband. She accepted not only the outside believers but also her father-in-law, Elisha Schorr, and her brother-in-law, Lipman Schorr, who up until then had been more circumspect in their behavior. Now they

---

50 *Zbior Slow Panskich w Brnie mowionych* (Collection of the word of G-d spoken in the city of Brno/Brunn), Manuscript in the National Library (Biblioteka Narodowa), Ph 190/1-S, 1: 28 § 14.
Ed5 probably Zbrzyz, possibly Zbaraz.

released all inhibitions "under the influence of Sabbatai Zvi, and even the rabbi from Zbish[Ed5] fell in with them and confessed that he could not forgive himself for his love for the wife of Shlomo." [51]

The prayers of the Frankists were carried out according to the tradition of Sabbatai Zvi before Frank arrived and continued after his arrival with the addition of the name Jacob next to Sabbatai Zvi—Jacob Sabbatai—according to a witness presented to the Satanow rabbinical court. Rabbi Yaakov Emden in his work, *Sefer Shimush*, describes how far these people went in their perversion, in which they created a divinity of Sabbatai Zvi. They termed him "the true creator, king of the universe, the true Messiah, after whom there is no other anywhere in the universe," and so on.[51a] So far did they go in their perversions. It is not surprising therefore that they were capable of anything.

When Frank left Rohatyn with his followers, he went to Podhajce and then Kopyczynce, where they grew substantially in number. In general, he added new followers wherever he went. By the end of January 1756, he reached Lanckorona where he lived at the home of Hirsch (Zvi), the brother of Leib, son of Sabbatai, and his wife Chaja, the daughter of Elisha Schorr, who served as the center of attraction for the orgies.[Tr2]

The Schorr family was very active in the events in Lanckorona. Once their activities were uncovered, they placed themselves together with Frank under the protection of Bishop Dembowski, a rabid anti-Semite, who used them against the Jews. At their instigation, a debate (the first of two) was held between the Frankists and the rabbis in Lanckorona. The protagonists included Elisha Schorr and his son, Shlomo, who together with three more Frankists signed the text of "Accusations and Answers," around which the debate centered. Elisha, Shlomo, and Krysa probably composed its contents. Frank certainly could not have done it. He was a complete ignoramus who knew how to twist words but used the Schorrs as his "rabbis."[52]

In other words, the Frankists completed the full gamut to the other side and dropped their religion. When Dembowski died suddenly in November 1757, the Frankists lost their protector, and they followed their leader, Frank, to Dziurdziow, which was at that time under Turkish rule. Frank had already

---

51   Majer Balaban, *History of the Frankist Movement* (Tel Aviv 1934): 122 (in Hebrew).

51a   Yaakov Emden, *Sefer Shimush*, (Amsterdam 1748): chap. 7: 1

Tr2   As a result of their debaucheries, they were reported by the Jews to the Polish government, which arrested them and transferred them to the rabbinate and the kahal for trial. Afterwards, they were excommunicated, while Frank was banished. (See Dubnow, History of the Jews in Russia and Poland, 1:213.)

52   Majer Balaban, *History*: 139.

become a Moslem, emulating his predecessor, which is not strange since he did not believe in any religion. Even in his early stages of activity he proclaimed that, as he put it, "I came to Poland solely to destroy all law and beliefs."[53]

The outstanding religious opponent of Frank in Rohatyn was Rabbi David Moshe Avraham, the author of *Mirkevet Hamishne*. His descendants were very proud of his war against the Sabbateans and the Frankists. How effective he was in this campaign varies with whom you read. According to the tradition in his family, he is described as "a man of the mighty arm who warred against the band of evildoers and raised the sword of G-d and smote them until they were annihilated." "Were they not the unclean evildoers who adopted the path of that arch evildoer, Sabbatai Zvi, may his name be erased? And the head of this unclean sect was Elisha, may the teeth of the wicked rot, whose nest was in the town of Rohatyn and was known as Elisha of Rohatyn."[54]

The descendants of the family further relate that "when this cursed criminal Frank came to our town to lure Jews in the direction of those who had lost their way, the Gaon and author rose up against them, took a spear in his hand and risked his life in order to beat, attack, and annihilate him. This criminal fooled the ruler of the town and inveigled him into chasing the rabbi and the dayan out of town and he, the author of *Mirkevet Hamishne*, risked his life and did not spare himself from attacking him. And the Almighty was by his side, and this criminal finally dropped his religion and then all the evil was turned on him, and he could no longer lead any Jew astray."[55] The fact is, however, that Rabbi Adam's campaign against Frank did not stop Schorr's family from continuing with the Frankists as part of their upper echelon.

Schorr and his family were the most prominent personalities of the Frankist movement during the debate of Lwow in 1759 and after. Frank himself said that when he lived in Dziurdziow, he was always told to go to Rohatyn, on the border of Poland, and he would immediately go there "in order to fulfill the command of his Lord with love."[56]

---

53 Manuscript Photo 190, 1:62, ¶129.
54 Words of Rabbi Ze'ev Wolf Salat, presiding rabbi of the rabbinical court in Lwow, in his recommendation of the work of Rabbi David Moshe Avraham (Adam)—Mirkevet Hamishne—a broad commentary on the Mechilta. The manuscript of the work, which was printed only in 1895, was in his hands. He handed it to his teacher, the rabbi of Lwow, Rabbi Yosef Shaul Nathanson. Nathanson had heard a great deal about the activity of Adam from his uncle, Rabbi Avraham Shlomo, who served as rabbi of Rohatyn after Adam.
55 Preface to *Mirkevet Hamishne*.
56 Manuscript Photograph 290, 323.

Shlomo Schorr and Krysa headed the Frankist faction of the debate. They also carried out the arbitration between the priest Pikulski and the Frankists and signed the petition presented to Primate Lubienski on 16 May 1759. This document was also passed on to the Polish king, Augustus III. It included a petition to have their group settled in the towns of Busk and Gliniany. Although the reasons for the debate began with the relationship between the Christians and the Frankists, after the death of Bishop Dembowski, the protective umbrella that had been placed over them was removed.

The rabbis had attempted to open the eyes of the authorities to the fact that the Frankists were not really Christians. Therefore, they requested that one side of their face be completely shaven, resulting in their abuse by many people and causing some of them to run away to Turkey. Among those who ran away was the elder Elisha Schorr of Rohatyn. At that point, the decree was passed officially to persecute them and shave off their beards. But here, too, they received no respite, because the Jews informed the Turks of their perverted ways, and then the Turks oppressed them and took everything away from them. Elisha Schorr was mercilessly beaten and died there, ignominiously, at the end of 1757, "bereft of everything."[57]

When Frank saw the treatment of his group by the Turks, he decided that they had better leave Turkey. He told his followers to return to Poland, become apostates, and petition Bishop Lubienski of Lwow to accept them into the Catholic religion because they wanted to "leave the religion of the Talmudists." This is the background to the infamous debate about the Talmud in Lwow, and that is when Shlomo Schorr and Krysa went to Lwow to quietly arrange the (second) debate there, in retaliation against the Jews for their troubles.[Tr3]

The debate caused troubles not only for the Jews of Halicz, among themselves because of the anarchy that it had introduced there, but also for Jews all over Poland because it muddied the relationship of the Polish people with the Jews. This became obvious in the decision of the 16 March 1761 sejmik at Sadowa, Wisznia, in which they petitioned the Sejm in Warsaw to take extraordinary measures against the Jews. This was based on the results of the debate of Lwow in 1759 which, they claimed, proved conclusively that the Jews do not follow the Torah of Moses and degrade Catholic religious beliefs; their sole purpose is to "undermine our homeland."

---

57   Yavetz (Rabbi Yaakov Emden), *Sefer Shimush*, 80.
Tr3 This debate was composed of seven theses, six of which dealt with the Messianic belief and basic Christian dogma. In the seventh, they claimed that "the Talmud considers the use of Christian blood obligatory." After the second debate, no radical action was taken by the Church, but there was a reaction among the people.

To prevent this, they asked, via the delegates of the Halicz sejmik to the national Sejm, to pass a law forbidding the Jews of Poland and Lithuania the use of their Hebrew religious books and to command them to hand these said books over to the Polish authorities for destruction. In addition, it shall be forbidden to them the use of the Hebrew language in print, which shall be replaced by the Polish language or Latin. To this purpose, it is necessary to close all Jewish printing presses and schools. Furthermore, their prayers shall only be offered in Polish or in Latin and only in front of two priests, and they that resist these commandments should be severely punished.[57a] This was the proposal. How much of this was actually officially accepted by the Sejm of Warsaw is not known.

The leading troublemakers who helped to bring about these problems were Frank and his associates, foremost of whom was the Schorr family. Frank knew how to utilize their capabilities for his nefarious purposes and sent them ahead of him as his messengers to spread the Frankist propaganda. However, in the end, Shlomo Schorr, one of Frank's biggest promoters, brought serious trouble upon Frank and his group, including himself, the result of which was that they were hauled up before the ecclesiastical courts of Warsaw to account for their beliefs.

This came about as follows. Schorr and five of the Frankists who had become apostates were staying in Lwow. The priest Gaudenty Pikulski in Lwow, Schorr's teacher of the Christian religion, was treated to wonder stories about Frank. In the process, Schorr told Pikulski that not only was Frank a miracle worker, but also he believed him to be the reincarnation of Jesus. As proof of this, he pointed to the fact that Frank had marks on his forehead that were related to the tortures of Jesus.

The Church had been suspicious of the Frankists in view of their behavior, and it decided to investigate what lay behind their conversion, in view of the fact that what they claimed officially and what they really believed did not correlate. Pikulski[Tr4] contacted the Papal Nuncio Serra in Warsaw. Frank was arrested in Warsaw on January 1760. He was interrogated, and then the true beliefs of the Frankists came out in the open. He was therefore tried before an ecclesiastical court that sentenced him and some of his followers to imprisonment in the fortress of Czestochowa. Interestingly, Frank could

---

57a "Lauda ziemskie, wiszenskie, lwowskie, przemyskie i sanockie," ed. Anton Prohaska, Akta grodzkie 23 (Lwow 1928): 415, no. 162 § 12. Full version in appendices.
Tr4 According to Dubnow and also Balaban (History of the Frankist Movement), the administrator of the diocese was Mikulski.
Ed6 The Schorrs changed their family name to Wolowski and took Christian first names.

not talk his way out of this and had to wait until the Russians freed him 13 years later, perhaps because too many of his followers had made too many incriminating statements during their interrogations. Among those in prison with Frank was Jan Wolowski (Schorr).[Ed6] Shlomo Schorr apparently succeeded in being released before Frank.

From 12 September 1759 to 15 November 1760, which was after the debate of Lwow, 48 Frankists from Rohatyn apostatized and became Christians, as did 47 in Lwow and one in Warsaw. Among the first to convert from Rohatyn was Eliyahu, age 73, the son of Leib and Feige, also Ze'ev Wolf, the son of Shlomo, who took the name of Andrzej. The family members of Schorr who became apostates included Shlomo, his wife and children (Joseph, Jan, Feliks, Michal, Ludwik, Henryk, and Tomasz), their wives and children, and also their relative, Jan Kanti Rafal Wolowski of Satanow. Shlomo Schorr, henceforth Franciszek Wolowski, and his brothers, Natan and Michal Nota, became the "apostles" of Frank and traveled to St. Petersburg on his behalf.

In the year 1768, a group of women from Rohatyn joined the group of Franciszek and Pawel Wolowski. In that year, the Wolowskis sent letters to the Jews of Moravia, Bohemia, and Podolia with a call to accept "the religion of Edom, because only that can save the Jews." We find the Wolowski children as activists and messengers as well as the "sages" among the group. They composed the leaflets and signed the appeals to the Jewish communities. Later, after Frank's release, when he had settled in Brunn (Brno), we find a deputation that included Shlomo-Franciszek and Jan and Michal Wolowski being sent to Warsaw by Frank. In December, Frank sent Jan and Ludwik Wolowski with two others to Constantinople.[58] Michael Wolowski stayed with Frank in Vienna. In Offenbach, Lukasz Franciszek Wolowski approached Chava, the daughter of Frank, with intentions of matrimony, and she turned him down. Jan, Michal, and Joseph Wolowski raised money in Warsaw and in Turkey on behalf of Frank.

The same letter that was sent to the Jews of Tatria was printed in 1914 by Dr. M. Wishnitzer in the publications of the Academy of Scientific Studies under the name, "A Letter from the Frankists, Year 1800." In 1921, the letter to the Jews of Hungary was published by Dr. A. Brauer, "Hashiloach," Jerusalem, Volume 22:38, Pamphlet 5-6.

When the Schorrs stopped practicing Judaism, they gained fame of a more constructive nature, although not Jewish. The son of Shlomo, Franciszek Lukasz, became secretary to King Stanislaw August Poniatowski. In 1761, he was made a nobleman with a "red ribbon." The sons of Franciszek were:

---

58   Kraushaar, Al., *Frank i Frankisci* (Frank and the Frankists) 2: 11, 20, 33, 53, 91.

1) Jan Kanti (1803–64)[59] became a well-known lawyer and later secretary of state of Poland and the author of the civil code of Poland. In 1839, he was made a nobleman and received a medal from Czar Nicholas I. In 1861, he became the head of the Department of Justice and a professor and deacon of the Faculty of Law at Warsaw University. He was the author of professional books on studies in law and founded the scientific quarterly *Biblioteka Warszawska*.

(2) Teodor became an officer in the Polish army and, in 1839, received the same honors as his brother.

(3) The same was true of the third brother, Feliks Franciszek.[60]

The great grandson of Elisha, Franciszek (1776-1844), became a member of the Sejm in 1818 and from 1830–31.[61] He and his sons, Ludwik and Casimir, were prominent among the Polish émigrés in Paris and had no small effect on their political direction.

Ludwik (1810–76) was a well-known economist. In the Polish-Russian war of 1831 he was an artillery officer and then became secretary of the Polish national delegation in Paris. After the Polish revolt, he remained in Paris. From 1834 on, he published a monthly magazine dealing with issues in law together with his brother-in-law, Leo Faucher (who was also of Jewish descent). From 1839 on, he served as a professor. Between 1848 and 1875, he also played an active part in political life in France. Casimir excelled as an officer in several battles in the War of 1831.

The Wolowski family was one of the most diverse of all of the Frankists, with many branches. In the beginning of the 19th century, it included tens of male members who were heads of families. They were also the most able of the members of the cult. Many were outstanding in international relations, economics, and Polish literature.[62] In the beginning,

---

59 He was the only one of the Frankists who was not ashamed of his Jewish ancestry and was even proud of it. Once, when a professor ridiculed his Jewish roots, he answered that he was proud to have been part of a Jewish family that had in it learned rabbis such as the author of Tevuos Shor, and he emphasized that all his talents stemmed solely from his Jewish origin. He viewed his opponent with scorn as one whose ancestors were most likely murderous lowly knights. (Ignaz Bernstein, "Brief an Adolf Jelinek," printed in Jüdisches Literaturblatt 27 [1882]: 107). Bernstein also notes that in Poland the Frankists were called "Mechesy," which he thought was the abbreviation of Mikat Senor Santo, from the Cult of Senor Santo. Frank was known to his followers as Senor Santo (Ha'adon hakadosh—Holy Lord).

62 Itemized listing in Teodor Jeske-Choinski, Neofici Polscy (Polish neophytes) (Warsaw 1904): 100–103. Mateusz Mieses, *Polacy Chrzescijanie pochodzenia zydowskiego* (Polish Christians of Jewish Descent) (Warsaw 1938), 2: 257–85.

A letter in red ink written by the sons of Elisha Schorr of Rohatyn, Franciszek Wolowski (Shlomo), Michal Wolowski (Natan Nota), and Jedrzej Dembowski (Yeruham, the son of Hanania Litman from Czernikosnice) to Beit Israel (the House of Israel) dispersed among the Saxon states.

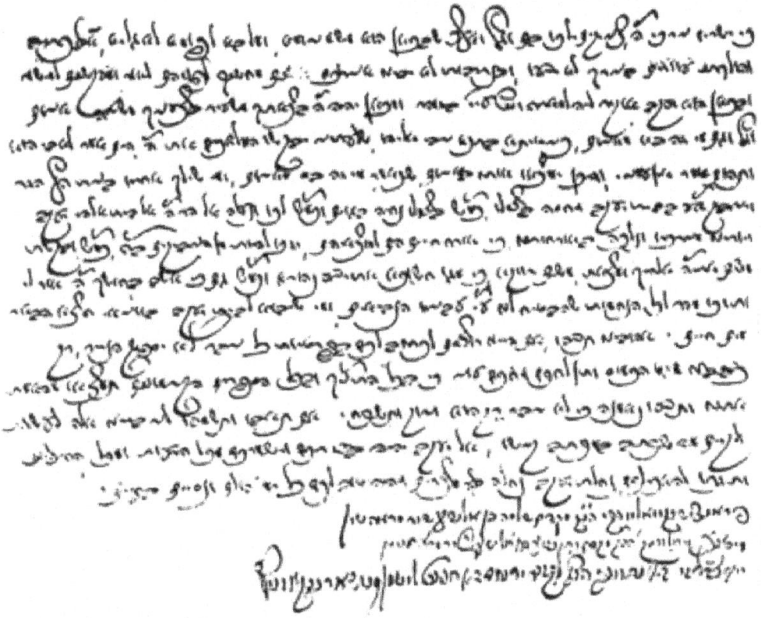

they followed the spirit and teachings of Jacob Frank, but from around 1830, they began to break away and ceased marrying only Frankists of Jewish descent, intermarrying instead with Polish nobility. The Wolowskis were among the first families to make a determined effort to break away from the Frankist tradition and to intermarry with Catholic families, in order to forget that they were descendants of Elisha Schorr of Rohatyn, the "prophet" of Jacob Frank. In Rohatyn itself, once the Frankists converted to Christianity in 1759, the Sabbateans and Frankists dropped out of the Rohatyn scene.

E. The Rabbis – The Census of 1765

The following were the rabbis of Rohatyn during the period of Polish independence who are known to us:

At the beginning of the 18th century, the rabbi in Rohatyn was Rabbi Avraham Leibers, the son of Reb Zalman Leibers, the parnass (leader) of the Lwow Jewish community, a great-grandson of Rabbi Yosef ben Mordechai Ginzburg, rabbi of Ostrog and author of *Leket Yosef* (Prague, 1789).[62a] In the middle of the 18th century, the rabbi was Rabbi David Moshe Avraham, known by the shortened version of his name, Rabbi Adam.[63] He is famous not

62a   Annals of the Ginzburg Family (St. Petersburg 1890): 224; M. Biber, Recalling

only as a great scholar but also as a brave warrior against the Frankism that had infested Rohatyn, abetted by the Schorr family. Rabbi Adam is described as one who displayed bravery and spiritual drive "and battled with a mighty arm against the band of evil-doers" headed by Elisha Schorr.[Ed7]

This did not deter the Frankists from presenting false reports about the rabbi to the authorities of the area and demanding his expulsion from the town of Rohatyn. His descendants and the members of the family of the rabbi of Lwow, Rabbi Yosef Nathanson (Shaul), have recorded the difficulties that Rabbi Adam had to overcome in his battle with the Frankist followers.

As a rabbi, Adam excelled as one who possessed a deep knowledge and sense of fairness. In the year 1745, he is recorded as having given his endorsement of *Milei D'Avot* (Words of the Fathers) printed in Lwow in the year 1746.[64] He exchanged correspondence with the great rabbis of his day, and his responsa (comments) were printed in their works. He wrote *Mirkevet Hamishne*,[65] which received a letter of endorsement by the rabbi of Lwow, Rabbi Chaim HaCohen Rappaport, and by Rabbi Yitzchak Landau, first rabbi of Zolkiew and later rabbi of Cracow.

The manuscript never reached the printing press during his lifetime and lay hidden for 150 years with his family. It came to light when his granddaughter, Teme, the wife of Yechezkiel Goldschlag, visited the Belzer Rebbe, who ordered it to be printed when he learned that she was the granddaughter of Rabbi Moshe David Avraham. He told her that she and the other grandchildren had a duty to print their grandfather's work.

Accordingly, headed by Reb Moshe Nagelberg, the grandchildren carried out the directive of the Belzer Rebbe and printed the book. In addition to Reb Moshe Nagelberg, his sons, Yudel and Itche Nagelberg, his son-in-law, Ephraim

---

the Great Men of Ostrog, Berdichev (1907), 89. (in Hebrew)

63   About him: The Introductions to his work, *Mirkevet Hamishne* (Lwow, 5655/1895) and the article by Rabbi Reuven Margulies on the identification of Rabbi Adam in Mishor, (5711/1951): 64:13–15. Listed in: Rahmers, *Jüdisches Literaturblatt* (1885), no. 38.

Ed7   See note 66 for an elaboration of this statement.

64   Leopold Loewenstein, Index approbationum (Index of endorsement) (Frankfurt a/M 1923): 46, no. 802.

65   Text of frontispiece appearing below on page 74: "*Mirkevet Hamishne*." A wide-ranging commentary on the Mechilta of Rabbi Yishmael as presented by Rabbi Hai Gaon, The Holy Light, Holy One of God, Crown of Torah, Our Teacher and Rabbi, Rabbi David Moshe Avraham Z"L, descendant of Troyes, Chief Rabbi of the Holy Community of Rohatyn. Published in Lemberg by the Esteemed Rabbi Yechezkel Goldschlag (may his light shine) on the Press of the Esteemed Mrs. Pessil Balaban (long may she live), 5655 [1895].

Struhl, and Yechezkiel Goldschlag and his wife, Teme, took part in this project. The work appeared in print in Lwow in the year 1895, introduced by the letters of endorsement of Rabbi Yosef Shaul Nathanson, author of *Shaul Ve'Meshiv*, rabbi of Lwow, and Rabbi Ze'ev (Wolf) Salat, who kept the manuscript of *Mirkevet Hamishne* in his possession.[66] According to Rabbi Margulies, in his article cited previously, Rabbi Adam also wrote *Tiferet Adam* and various other religious works that remained in manuscript form. The exact years of his birth and death are not recorded.[67]

---

66   Rabbi Salat writes about the author who signed his name, "The Little" [an accepted form of modesty] David Moshe Avraham, the son of my father and teacher, our teacher and rabbi, Rabbi Tzadok, Z"L, a descendant of Troyes: "This great scholar and Godly man, our holy teacher and rabbi, Z"L, the chief rabbi of Rohatyn, was a man who warred with a mighty arm against the band of evil doers and raised his sword, the sword of the Lord, and beat them to the ground, these evil unholy ones who held to the ways of that evil Zvi, may his name be erased. And at their head stood the evil and unclean Elisha (Schorr), may his name be erased, who then nested in the town of Rohatyn. He was known as Elisha of Rohatyn, as is known to anyone who reads that zealous book by Rabbi Yavetz in Lwow (Rabbi Yaakov Emden, Z"L, 29 Marheshvan, 5651 (1891)."

Rabbi Salat also had a letter from Rabbi Yehoshua of Belz in which he heaped praise upon the rabbi of Rohatyn. The Belzer Rebbe said that he had seen two more works by the Gaon and author, Z"L, in manuscript form, and it would be a mitzvah for whoever finds them to bring them to press. However, the manuscripts were not found and were not printed.

67   The descendants of the author relate in their preface to his book that following his battle with the Frankists, the Besht (Ba'al Shem Tov), came to see him: "Our forefathers related that our teacher, the holy Besht, may he be remembered for eternal life, came in person and notified him that he was delegated by the heavens to inform him that they were holding to his credit the goodness and the beauty of his zeal in fighting the battle of the Lord of Hosts, similar to the zeal shown by Pinchas, the son of Elazar, the son of Aharon the Cohen, where the Torah says, 'Behold I give him my Pact of Peace.'"

Also in the preface, the publisher of the book (a member of the Nagelberg family) states in his introduction, "I heard from our grandparents who had been informed by their parents that the Besht came to visit Rabbi Adam prior to the time that 'the Ark of the Lord,' the author, was taken to the heavens. He came to visit him to serve him the 'service of scholars', and the Besht told the Rabbi, the author, 'My teacher, bless me,' and Rabbi Adam placed his two hands on him and blessed him, and while on his way back, the Besht, Z"L, said, 'It appears that the rabbi has passed away, for I saw there a heavenly company going out to meet him. And I heard that the great men of his day called him Rabbi Adam.'

If this meeting of the Besht with Rav Adam does not belong to the realm of legend, we can derive from this that Rabbi Adam passed away between the years

45

Rabbi Adam passed away in Rohatyn and left an extensive family that lived in Rohatyn as well. He was followed by Rabbi Avraham Shlomo, the uncle of Rabbi Yosef Shaul Nathanson.[68] We do not know how long he served as rabbi, but we know that he was the rabbi in 1765, because he signed the census document of the Jewish community of Rohatyn in the name of the kehilah at that time.

Rabbi Adam was followed by Rabbi Yitzchak ben Aharon (Icko Aronowicz), who gave his approbation in 1766 to the *Ohel Moed*— comments on the portion of the Talmud dealing with holidays written by Rabbi Yosef Yaski, the rabbi of Ulanow, and printed in the year 1767 in Frankfurt-an der-Oder.[68a]

As we know, the Jews of Podkamien and Stratyn were considered as branches of the Jewish community of Rohatyn. Therefore, they were part of the general census of Rohatyn on 14 February 1765 that included the surrounding villages and hamlets.

The national committee enumerated in the town of Rohatyn 742 adults and children and 55 children under the age of one. In the two towns of Podkamien and Stratyn, there were 200 adults and children and 25 infants under age one. In the 40 hamlets attached to the Rohatyn community, there were 295 adults and children and 30 infants under the age of one, making a total of 1,237 adults and children and 110 infants under the age of one.[69] In total, there were 797 people in Rohatyn together with all the children, and when we add the 550 people in the hamlets attached to Rohatyn, we have a total population of 1,347 people.

The following are the villages where Jews lived:

Town	Adults & children	Infants under 1	Town	Adults & children	Infants under 1
Podgrodzie	7	1	Lipica Dolna	5	1
Ruda	5	1	Šistelniki	10	--
Kleszczowna	8	1	Szumlany	19	1

1759 and 1760, since the Besht, as we know, passed away in 1760.

68   Rabbi Uri Salat states in his introduction, "Rabbi Nathanson has told us that his uncle, the great Avraham Shlomo, Z"L, was rabbi of the holy community of Rohatyn after the rabbi, the author, may he be remembered for eternal life, and that he spoke of awesome matters that the rabbi saw through divine inspiration."

68a Leopold Loewenstein, Index, 82, no. 1473

69   Podkamien numbered 117 adults and children and 13 infants, together 130 people. Stratyn had 83 adults and children and 12 infants, together 95 people.

Firlejow	6	--	Slawentyn	29	3
Korzelica	7	--	Sarnki	7	1
Hulkow	5	--	Zolczow	12	--
Janczyn	8	1	Danilcze	4	1
Potok	5	--	Czesniki	13	2
Czercze	11	1	Lopuszna	5	--
Soloniec	5	1	Dusanow	5	1
Wierzbolowce	3	--	Kutce	4	1
Putiatynce	6	1	Zalipie	2	1
Luczynce	9	2	Psary	2	--
Babuchow	5	--	Doliniany	4	--
Koniuszki	9	--	Dehowa	4	--
Ujazd	2	1	Zalanow	7	--
Obelnica	5	--	Dziczki*	7	1
Kunaszow	4	--	Bienkowce*	11	
Zelibory	3	1	Fraga	4	1
Lipica Gorna	3	1	Dubryniow**	22	4

* Annexed to Podkamien   ** Annexed to Stratyn

Dr. M. Balaban, Spis Zydow i Karaitow ziemi halickiej i powiatow trembowelskiego i kolomyjskiego w r. 1765 (Census of Jews and Karaites in the Halicz region and in the districts of Trembowla and Kolomyja in 1765) (Cracow 1909): 10–11.

We have no details on the breakdown of occupations of the Jews in Rohatyn during this time. From the census that was made of the Jewish towns of Jazlowice and Zaleszczyki for the year 1772, two towns that are similar to Rohatyn in their makeup, we can, by comparing them, make a breakdown of the occupations of the Jews of Rohatyn—which were, as a matter of fact, no different from the others. According to the census there were:[70]

Occupations	Jazlowice (pop 968) Employed	Zaleszczyki (pop 859) Employed
Silk Merchants	2	1
Storekeepers	10	25
Town Bartenders	27	25
Barber-Surgeon	1	--
Goldsmiths	2	--
Coppersmith	1	--
Tailors	11	17

---

70   Aged or Sick on Pension: Avraham Yaacov Braver, "Joseph II and the Jews of Galicia," *Hasholeach* 23, no. 2: 147–48.

Bakers	3	3
Butchers	2	6
Tavern Lessees	26	--
Other Lessees	7	7
Middlemen	2	--
Servants	19	25
Bath keepers	--	2
Aged or Sick on Pension	14	2
Unemployed	46	36

From these numbers, we learn that from the Jewish community of 968 people in Jazlowice, there were only 60 families where the head of the family had a trade. There were also 14 aged and sick, 46 unemployed, and 19 men and 14 women who worked in housekeeping and maintenance. Similar figures were to be found in Zaleszczyki. Of 859 people, there were 79 regularly employed, 25 men and 10 women working in homes. There were also 2 people listed as sick, and 36 listed as unemployed. We may assume that the same figures more or less existed in Rohatyn with one difference—the number of trades.

During the last years of Polish independence, starting in 1763, Rohatyn was forced to endure the invasions and passages of foreign soldiers, especially those from Russia and later from the invading troops of the Confederation. This ended only when Poland ceded all of the Halicz district to Austria after the first division of Poland in 1773.

F. Under Austrian Domination

Rohatyn was included in the district of Zloczow, which was headed by Starosta Tannhauser. Zloczow was raised to the rank of district capital; this correlated with the beginning of the development of the district. In contrast to the typical Austrian bureaucrats common in Galicia who stressed pan-Germanism, Tannhauser was a Polish sympathizer and was more interested in stressing the development of a stable economy. He saw to it that taxes were eased and looked for ways to improve the socioeconomic condition of the population. In the first years of the Austrian conquest, the conditions of the Jews of Rohatyn were difficult because of the new conditions introduced by the Austrian government that differed from those that had existed under Poland. During the first four years, the organization of the Jewish kehilah remained substantially the same as it had been under Poland. However, after the proclamation of the ordinances concerning Jews

(Judenordnung) of the Empress Maria Theresa on 16 July 1776, the ordinances of Joseph II of May 1785, and the tolerance ordinances of 7 May 1789, a new permanent organization of Jewish affairs was established in Galicia that brought about decisive changes in the community life of the Jews.

The Jewish community (kehilah) was organized according to the ordinances mentioned. At the head of the committee in Rohatyn, as in all other medium size and small communities, there was a community council (va'ad kahal), composed of chosen heads with very limited powers, that was required to obey and to submit to all the demands of the district authority (Kreisamt). The kehilah was responsible for collecting all of the taxes that were levied on the Jews, for providing soldiers to the army, and so on.

According to the Jewish ordinances of the year 1776, the community council was composed of six members. According to the rulings of Joseph II, the council was reduced from six members to three, except for Lwow and Brody, which had seven members. The right to vote "actively" was given to heads of families who paid a Sabbath candle tax of seven or more candles during a full year before elections, and the right of "passive" voting applied to heads of families who lived in Rohatyn, had a good name, knew how to read and write German, and paid a Sabbath candle tax of 10 Sabbath candles during a full year before elections.

In addition to heads of the community, heads of the burial society (chevra kadisha), beadles, managers of the hospital, and auditors were elected. The officials of the community included a secretary (scribe), a caretaker, cantors, beadles, ritual slaughterers (shochtim), and gravediggers. The direction of religious matters was placed in the hands of a rabbi who was elected for three years by the electors of the community. This state of affairs lasted until the period between 25 August 1783 and 23 May 1784 at which time the central government in Vienna no longer recognized the jurisdiction of the Jewish communities and the rabbinical courts. After the regulations of 1785, the Office of Community Rabbi (Rav Hakahal) was abolished, and only the appointment of teachers of religion (Religionsweiser) and cantors was permitted. Every district was given its own district rabbi (Kreisrabbiner), and in Rohatyn, there was officially only a teacher of religion who held all jurisdictional powers.

According to the regulations of 7 May 1789, the leaders of the Jewish communities received their salaries from community funds deducted from taxes. This resulted in a rush for these positions, as they were a sure source of constant income. The desire to receive the honor of being head of a Jewish community (parnass) was understandably strong right from the beginning of the establishment of Jewish autonomy in Poland, as this was the most prestigious office among the Jews there.

Even in Rohatyn, a great deal of activity took place during the elections of the Jewish kehilah. These were accompanied by conflict, complaints, and secret accusations against candidates who were accused of levying taxes illegally. It was claimed that they placed the main burden of taxation on the weakest class of the population while sparing themselves and their families.[70a] This resulted in not a few explosive reactions as well as false accusations to the authorities, based on fictitious concoctions of their imagination. Every Jew required to pay taxes had a tax ledger (Steuerbuechel) that served as his passport of membership in the community. If his ledger were taken from him because of any differences with the kahal (council) or any other violation, his name was erased from the official roster of the members of the kehilah. More than once, these so-called violations were fabricated by the heads of the kehilah in order to ostracize someone whom they did not want or like for any reason.

Such things were recurrent in Rohatyn during the years 1781–94 and during the 1820s,[71] as we can see from the records in the archives.

The salary paid to the rabbi of Rohatyn was 86 florin per year plus the free use of the house in which he lived during his tenure.[72] Rohatyn under Poland was a possession of the crown, in contrast to the other towns of eastern Red Ruthenia that had established Jewish communities. This facilitated the sale of whose property by the Austrian government. Indeed, a short time after the Austrian conquest, it began to sell Polish royal property, which included towns, and by 1783, it had sold 5,000,000 florin worth of property. In this way, the ruling government tried to promote the development of towns. The residents saw this action as a sure means for the removal of Jews, or at least a reduction of their numbers. However, after investigating this project, the Austrian government concluded that such a move would accomplish just the reverse of what it was intended for and wreck the towns, since other than Jews, there was no established sound economic factor that could maintain the economy; Jews were the essential economic pipeline of the towns.

The Austrian government also recognized that there was an element of cruelty in their suggestion and stated, "It would appear that this contains

---

70a Protokolle Galicien (Official records of Galicia), Archives of the Ministry of Internal Affairs, Vienna, IV T 2, Carton 2601.

71 Protokolle Galicien, Archives of the Ministry of Internal Affairs, Vienna.

72 Michael Stoeger, *Darstellung der gesetzlichen Verfassung der galizischen Judenschaft 1* (Description of the legal code of Galician Jewry 1) (Lemberg/Lwow 1833), 85.

within it an element of cruelty even if the circumstances would seem to make it necessary, unless they are willing to forego the improvement of the towns."[73]

At the beginning of the conquest, Rohatyn was included as part of the district of Zloczow and administered by the chief official Tannhauser, a man who was interested in the welfare of the inhabitants. He was an able administrator who put in effort to ensure that all taxes were paid on time, and indeed, in his district, this was the case.

He recognized the contributions of the Jews to the economy and opposed their being driven out, either from his district or from the properties that they were renting, because such an act would cause an economic vacuum. Later in the 80's, Rohatyn was transferred to the district of Brzezany.

Taxes and Other Payments

In 1774, the Austrian government raised the head tax in Poland from 30 kreuzer to one gulden. This tax was made part of the Jewish Ordinances of 1776, under the name of a tolerance tax (Toleranzsteuer), rather than a head tax, in the sum of four gulden per family. In addition to this, it levied an income tax in the sum of four gulden per Jewish family and a marriage fee, levied according to the wealth of the family. Taxes were first apportioned by the Austrians according to communities. This apportionment of taxes was divided among the communities, which in turn divided it among their members.

Then, in the year 1784, Joseph II of Austria abolished the income and property taxes and replaced them with the following:

I   A national real estate tax (Landes-Domestical Beitrag) in the sum of one gulden per family. This tax was strictly enforced by officials especially chosen for this purpose by the government.

II   The existing marriage fee was replaced by a marriage tax that was divided into three categories:

(1) Craftsmen and salaried workers, who paid three ducats upon the birth of the first son, six ducats on the birth of a second son and twelve ducats on the birth of a third son if their annual income did not exceed 100 gulden. If their income was estimated at over 100 gulden per year, they paid twice as much.

(2) Public employees, who paid 12 ducats after the birth of the first son and 24 ducats after the birth of the second son.

(3) Those who engaged in commerce and related occupations and

73   "This certainly seems very harsh, but the circumstances make it necessary; otherwise we must abandon the idea of improving the cities." (in German)

those who earned as much as 400 gulden paid 20, 40, and 80 ducats. Jews engaged in agriculture were completely freed from paying this tax.

III   A tax was imposed on kosher meat the amount of which varied with the type of meat being sold.

IV   In 1789, Jews engaging in agriculture were exempt from paying the tolerance tax. Even before Joseph II's regulations of 1789, the following taxes were to be found on the books:

Opening a new synagogue required one payment.

Opening a new Jewish cemetery required a payment of 200 gulden upon its opening and 100 gulden every year thereafter.

A census fee of 50 gulden per year.

In 1797, the real estate tax was abolished and replaced by the Sabbath candle tax and a supplementary tax (Erganzungssteuer). When not enough taxes were realized from the property tax and kosher meat tax, the difference was covered via a supplementary tax.

A special tax (Extrasteuer) was levied on Jews in place of the income tax that was collected from Christians.

Every Jew and Jewess was required to pay the candle tax with the exception of (a) those whose sole income was derived from agriculture (b) soldiers and their wives (c) widows of soldiers (d) unmarried children living with their parents, guardians, relatives, or friends and (e) helpers in a store or business, apprentices, house cleaners and helpers, bachelors, and widowers.

The above were the special Jewish taxes (Judensteuer), but Jews also had to pay the taxes that were incumbent upon all inhabitants as well—a storage tax, a land tax, municipal and community taxes.

With the enactment of the kosher meat tax, which was tied up with exorbitant profits, strife broke out in all of the communities. Collection of these taxes was the official monopolistic prerogative of tax collectors who were granted powers to determine the size of the kosher meat tax at their discretion and to limit the right of slaughtering meat to certain butchers, resulting in the raising of the price of kosher meat. Since these butchers worked hand in hand with the tax collectors, the customer had no way of knowing what the price of meat would be at any given time. The butcher could always claim that the rise in price was due to the rise in taxes, which were subject to sudden change. This situation aroused the ire of the Jewish population, especially of the poorer families, who were being incited by the butchers who had been refused the right to sell kosher meat, thus wrecking their livelihood. This problem existed in all communities and engendered hatred and bitterness among the Jews of the community.

In addition to the relatively large amounts of money to be paid in taxes, there were also the methods employed in collecting the taxes that aroused the anger of the people in no small measure. Thus, when people fell behind in their payments, confiscation might be carried out by soldiers on horseback and police who seized private belongings and furniture without pity. Then too, there was the element of graft related to such matters. Most tax collectors were parnassim who received the full ire of the community, thus deflecting it from the government that had levied the exorbitant taxes.

According to figures arrived at by the commissioner of the district of Zloczow in the year 1806, each Jewish family paid the following for basic Jewish taxes alone:

Candle tax: 6 florin per year
Meat tax: up to 15 florin per year
Tolerance tax: 4 florin per year
Special tax: 5 florin per year

Adding up to a total of 28 florin per year.[74] This situation caused problems for the head of every family.

The town of Rohatyn had the help of a clerk, officially called the Judischer Amtsschreiber, a non-Jew working for the Jewish community (Judendirektion). This position was filled between 1 November 1779 and 1 May 1785 by Johann Silva, who received 200 florin a year. Before this appointment, he was a sergeant in the quartermaster corps of the infantry. When Jewish autonomy was eliminated in May 1785, he was retired without pension because he was appointed investigator for the district of Brzezany. In addition, there was a clerk who worked on a daily basis.[75]

In addition to the usual load of taxes that Jews of Galicia, including Rohatyn, bore, they were also required to clear up their old debts dating from the time of Jewish autonomy in Poland. These included the debts of the central agencies, such as the Council of Four Lands and the District Council, as well as the different Jewish communities.

This demand for the liquidation of the debts of Jewish organizations dated back to 1764 when Jews were still under Polish rule, at which time this task of settling the debts of the Jews was assigned to a committee of the treasury. On 22 April 1766, this liquidation committee provided, in a special report, that Jews must pay three gulden per capita in order to liquidate the debts of the Jewish councils. When it received no satisfactory reply to its request, it

---

74   Report of the head of the district of Zloczow (14 August 1806), Teki Schneidra (Schneider files), National Archives of the History of Israel, Microfilm H.M. 7905.
75   Teki Schneidra Personal (Schneider personal files), Microfilm H.M. 7905, Stand no. 26, National Archives of the History of Israel.

repeated this demand in an official notice on 21 March 1767. In it, the council pointed out that with the passage of time, the debt had increased, due to the addition of interest and fines accrued because of delinquency in payments.[76] Special note was taken of the debts of the communities of Red Ruthenia that had not forwarded their payments. In the meantime, the first partition of Poland took place, and Rohatyn, as part of Red Ruthenia, was ceded to Austria with the debts being left unpaid. These unpaid debts included money owed to churches and monasteries and Jewish institutions as well as private individuals.

After the partition of Poland, the victorious powers agreed that the outstanding debts of the areas belonging to them would be paid. In Galicia, the Austrian government appointed a special committee for the liquidation of debts (Liquidationskommission), which included the provincial advisor Ernst von Kartum, Joseph Baum von Appelshofen, advisor to the department of accounts, and Joseph Milbauer.

The committee was ordered to decide on the amount owed, by whom and to whom, to organize detailed lists of these names, and suggest procedures of payment by the Jewish organizations. Creditors were required to present detailed lists of the debts incurred prior to 12 June 1772 to the district offices, in four months, if they were in the country, and in six months, if they were out of the country. Creditors were promised that they could expect to receive the full payment of their loans any time after 1 August 1785 plus an additional interest of 5 percent.[77]

In its meeting of 26 July 1786, the department of accounts presented the committee for the liquidation of debts with a full list of Jewish debts and debtors, including their relevant documents. These combined debts amounted to 602,285 florin. In order to ease payment, the government decided that the Jewish communities should transfer to the debt fund the korowka, i.e., the levy of one kreuzer that was added to the price of kosher meat.

From these lists, we learn that the Jewish community of Rohatyn owed the local church 125 gulden, the Dominican monastery 1,250 gulden, and Firlejow 300 florin, for a debt that dated back to March 1735, and a second debt of 75 florin to the same Firlejow, also dating from 1735.[78]

---

76   Israel Halprin, *Notebook of the Council of Four Lands* (Jerusalem 1945): 77–83 (in Hebrew).

77   Hofdekret vom 26.VI.1785 (Court decree from 26.VI.1785).

78   "Passiva der Jüdischen Gemeinden" (Real estate of the Jewish communities), Teki Schneidra (Schneider files) Microfilm H.M. 7096, Polish State Archive in Cracow,
National Archives of the History of Israel.

In addition to these sums, Rohatyn had to take part in the payment of 34,654 Polish gulden to pay off the debts of the kehilot of Red Ruthenia to Yaakov Zelikowicz and Tzadok Meirowicz. After a lengthy and continual arbitration between them and the directorate of the Jewish communities of Galicia (Judendirektion), via the mediation of the government, the two parties came to a compromise on 28 January 1781, whereby the debt would be lowered to 14,500 florin, the payment of which would be apportioned among the different communities.[79] The portion to be paid by Rohatyn amounted to 63 florin and 10 kreuzer[80] to be paid over a period of five years.[81] In addition to the taxes and elimination of debt, Jews were required to participate in war loans during the period of 1794–99.

In 1784, conditions became worse when the government issued an edict that anyone derelict in his payments for a period of over three quarters of a year could be officially declared a Jewish pauper (Betteljude) and could be expelled at any time from his town or even Galicia as a whole.

This engendered fears and suspicions among Jews, since there could always be found Jews and non-Jews willing to falsely accuse other Jews of harboring paupers in their homes or of having quiet marriages without paying the marriage tax. To prevent these slanders, Jews had to pay hush money (Denuntiationsgelder). In Rohatyn there circulated, as we learn from the pages of the archives, informers and even clerks who were engaged in informing to obtain this easy money. People were forced to pay this bribery to "keep the dogs from barking and wagging their tongues."

The Jewish economic situation became so bad, that in the year 1789, the office of the district of Brzezany ordered the expulsion of 1,050 families from the district, including Rohatyn. The government in Vienna viewed this as overbearing and passed a directive on 9 March 1789 that expulsion for non-payment of taxes should be eliminated from the Jewish statutes, and this was brought up for discussion before the Austrian government.[82]

In the year 1782 the Department of Occupational Status (Wydzial

79   Teki Schneidra, Microfilm H.M. 7096.
80   Teki Schneidra, Microfilm H.M. 7096.
81   Staatsratsakten, Wiener Staatarchiv (Privy Council documents, Vienna State Archive), 1789, no. 1835.
82   "This is a reminder that the expulsion of the Jews is being deferred by the new ordinance concerning Jews who are in arrears in respect to the three-quarter yearly tax, so that the Brzezany district authorities can be notified not to insist on the removal of the considerable number of 1,050 families that find themselves in this situation, and under the present circumstances, in any event, the remaining ones should be drafted into the military and, if need be, assigned to service with the military transport corps." (in German) Protokolle Galizien, 3 March 1789.

Stanowy) of Galicia suggested that the Jews be removed from all leasing of property. The central government in Vienna utilized this initiative of the department to order the removal of Jews from leased properties and from engaging in brewing.[83] Indeed, in the district of Brzezany, many Jews in small villages were in fact removed from their properties. In addition to forbidding Jews from leasing taverns, in 1785, Jews were also forbidden to take part in the leasing and management of estates, fields that were not worked by Jews, mills, and houses in cities that were originally intended for German settlers. They could not collect fees for markets and stalls or district taxes, emblems of estates, money for the clergy, taxes on tobacco, export of salt, leasing of beer breweries, producing lumber for housing, or for surveying, wagons, or tolls. This order strongly affected the Jews of Rohatyn, since no small number of them were engaged directly or indirectly in these areas of the economy. It was emphasized that within three years, by the end of 1787, Jews must relinquish these properties to Christians.[84]

In reaction, the Jewish community of Lwow joined other communities of Eastern Galicia in a combined attempt to influence the powers of Lwow and even Vienna to rescind these edicts, but to no avail. On their side, the Jewish communities attempted, between 1785 and 1793, to put into effect a joint policy that would protect their economic interests and limit as much as possible the areas of endeavor that were being forbidden or limited to them. These defense measures attracted the attention of the Christians who sought to prevent the Jews from putting them into effect, and to this purpose, employed agencies of the district and national government. The result was that in 1794 a court commission (Hofcommission) in Vienna recommended that an explicit prohibition be made against Jewish communities holding combined assemblies.[85] There were differences at this time between Rohatyn

---

83   W. Tokarz, *Galicja w poczatkach ery Jozefinskiej w swietle ankiety urzedowej* z r. 1783 (Galicia at the beginning of the [Kaizer Franz] Joseph era based on government files from 1783) (Cracow 1909): 500.

84   Galizien Judenwesen, Leibmaut, Pachtungen (Galicia Jewish affairs, personal customs, leaseholds) IV T 11 (1785–87): carton no. 2657, Interior Ministry Archive in Vienna.

85   Galizien Judenwesen... IV T 11 (1793–1800): carton 2659, no. 1295 ad no. 85 ex Maio 1794. "The Jews should not under any pretext be allowed to convene a general assembly of a number of community councils (kahals) without the prior knowledge of the local authorities in question and of the gubernia (province) and without the approval and permission of the local authorities and the presence of a Royal Commissioner. Minutes of the deliberations should be taken, and the summary together with the conclusion submitted for royal confirmation."

and its outlying communities regarding the payment of taxes and the like.

The census of 1788 reveals very little about the condition of the Jews in the district of Brzezany, including the town of Rohatyn. We learn that there were in Brzezany at that time ten communities with a total of 2,757 Jewish families. This included 2,700 men, 2,685 women, 1,100 boys and 993 girls above the age of twelve, 2,137 young boys and 2,108 young girls below the age of twelve, 719 servants, 819 maids, 112 poor men, and 245 poor women, making a subtotal of 6,758 men and 6,845 women, in total, 13,603 people. Of the 2,757 families, the taxpayers on Level A numbered 278, Level B, 32, and Level C, 1,568, with 879 paupers.[86]

In the 1791 census, there were 2,514 families, which included 2,801 men, 2,490 women, 878 boys and 737 girls above the age of twelve, 944 boys and 1,905 girls below the age of twelve, 372 servants, 489 maids, 146 poor men, and 304 poor women, making a subtotal of 5,841 males and 5,925 females and a total of 11,766. During this year, of 2,514 tax paying families, there were 1,793 on Level A, 266 on Level B, forty-six on Level C, and 409 paupers.

In the four years following 1788, the number of Jews decreased from 13,603 to 11,766, i.e., a reduction of 1,837, and the number of paupers dropped from 889 to 409. As to the economic composition, there is only one list from 1780, which shows that in Rohatyn there were 401 Jews engaged in business (Jüdische Handelsleute).[87] The business composition did not indicate any change. Most of them were merchants, retailers, traders, and peddlers; a number were engaged in brewing beer and distilling liquor. Still others were craftsmen working as tailors, furriers, hat makers, butchers, and bakers.

*

Educational institutions, which had hitherto been under Jewish supervision, were, by the ruling of Maria Theresa, transferred completely to the supervision of the government, something that caused opposition and displeasure on the part of the Jews. The government, for its part, was interested in drawing Jewish children into public schools, which were open to them as of 1782. Since Jews did not wish to utilize these "rights," the Jewish communities were legally required on 27 May 1785 to establish their own general public school system—also to no avail.

The Jews paid no attention to these rulings and angered the authorities, who severely castigated them. Placing upon the Jews the blame for the "backwardness" of their children, they demanded that children up to thirteen

---

86   Galizien Judenwesen... IV T 11 (1786–92): carton 2658.
87   Teki Schneidra, H.M. 7099.

be enrolled in a secular school.[88] Each Jewish community was required to establish a German-style elementary school to correct the "Jewish approach" to learning. To achieve these goals, the government stipulated that no Jew would be permitted to get married without written proof that he had learned German at school or at home.

Herz Homburg, (1749–1841), a student of Moses Mendelsohn, was appointed in 1806 as head of this Jewish educational system in Galicia. In 1788, 48 Jewish schools were established in Galicia, including one in Rohatyn—a school for youths taught by Shlomo Kornfeld at a yearly salary of 200 florin.[89] This school was maintained until the closing of the whole system of Jewish schools in 1806. The system failed because of the negative attitude of the Jews who, despite wheedling, punishments, and fines, refused to send their children to the (state) schools because of their fear that attendance there would lead them to apostasy.

Another goal of Joseph II to improve Jewish life in Galicia was to move Jews into agriculture. By contrast, this did not meet with much opposition, because in 1785 the new laws had caused thousands of Jewish families to lose their source of income. To those willing to enter the field of agriculture, the government promised to lower the tolerance tax by 50 percent. In 1785, Joseph II ordered the establishment of a Jewish agricultural community in Galicia. In the spring of 1786, the first Jewish colony, called Dabrowka, was founded near Nowy Sacz, and in it there were close to 20 families.[90]

After that, another colony was founded near Bolechow that was named "Neu Babylon" (Babilon Nowy). In Brzezany, this affected 69 families, 12 of whom came from Rohatyn. By 1793 this allotment was completely filled by the communities as follows: Brzezany, 10 families; Kozowa, 5 families; Podhajce, 9 families; Bursztyn, 7 families; Chodorow, 3 families; Rozdol, 5 families; Strzeliska, 4 families; Bobrka, 8 families; Przemyslany, 6 families, and Rohatyn, 12 families. These families, settled by 1803 on 49 parcels of land, were composed of 98 men, 83 women, and, below the age of eighteen, 91 boys and 80 girls. The settlers received 66 houses, 66 barns and silos, 124 horses, 88 oxen, 147 cows, and 66 pieces of agricultural equipment.

The 12 families from Rohatyn were settled on six parcels of land and included 14 men, 16 women, and, below the age of eighteen, 16 boys and 12 girls. They were supplied with 12 houses, 12 pieces of agricultural equipment, 12 barns and silos, 24 horses, 8 oxen, and

---

88 "All the Jewish children who do not yet observe the ceremony of binding phylacteries."

89 Galizien Judenwesen. IV T 11 (1788): carton 2658.

90 By the year 1815 there were no longer any Jewish farmers there.

22 cows.[91] In the year 1822, an agricultural census in the district of Brzezany revealed that out of the 69 families that had entered farming, 40 of them had actually become farmers—24 at the expense of the community and 16 at their own expense.

The heavy tax load upon the Jews of Rohatyn caused them great suffering. Especially oppressive was the candle tax, which afflicted every family. The tax collectors generated ill will, resulting in altercations between themselves and the people. In 1798 Rohatyn, together with other communities in the district of Brzezany, presented complaints about the inhumanity of the candle tax collectors.[92] The government rejected these complaints and even punished the writer, who happened to be the Christian clerk of the district by the name of Heinrich Hepp. Thus the 18th century ended with the Jews of Rohatyn at an economic low without any prospect for improvement.

In the beginning of the 19th century, taxes rose, accompanied by oppression from the collectors. They made unrealistic assessments and applied pressure to pay quickly and remove earlier debts without any consideration of the severe economic conditions that the Jews were enduring. Then, too, because of the many wars in the first decade of the 19th century, Jews had to pay heavy war loans. Together with other communities, Rohatyn presented its objections, which reached Kaiser Franz I. These appeals were ignored; they received no answer, and the tax collectors were given a free hand. The important thing was to bring in money, and the government did not care what methods were employed to obtain it. In addition to the war loans, there were other taxes that were paid directly to the government. These included a property tax, a housing tax, a personal tax, income tax[93], and a supplementary tax[94] to make up for what the meat and candle taxes did not provide—in total some 52 different types of taxes and payments.

In 1810, a census was taken of the Jews of Galicia. In Brzezany there

---

91   "Summarischer Ausweis ueber den Fortgang der Jüdischen Anssiedlung in den Koenigreichen Galizien und Lodomerien bis letzten Octobris 1804" (Summary documentation of the progress of Jewish settlement in the royal lands of Galicia and Lodomeria until the end of October 1804), Galizien Judenwesen. IV T 11, (v. 4.11.1804): 201 e.a. 1805.

92   "Akta: Lichterzuendpachtung" (Termination of lease for candle tax collection), *Protokolle Galizien* 1798 (February 1798): 11.

93   Beginning 1 November 1824 the tax was collected according to the general principles applying to Christians, separately, however, from the taxes of the Christians.

94   Abolished in 1829.

94a Galizien Judenwesen. IV T 1, 1811–28, carton 2582.

were at that time 2,457 families with 10,933 people—5,395 men and 5,538 women. As compared to 1788, this was a decrease of 300 families. The census of 1792 showed 2,514 families, resulting in a decrease of 243 families, and a further loss of 57 families between 1792 and 1810. In Rohatyn itself the census of 1810 showed a population of 282 Jewish families, in which there were 595 men and 621 women—a total of 1,216 people.[94a] However, by 1819 the downward trend was reversed, and the district of Brzezany had 2,539 families, showing an increase of 82 families as compared with the population of 1810.[95]

In 1810, when the Jews of Rohatyn were again given permission to lease breweries, the town in turn again complained to the authorities in Lwow in an attempt to prevent this. However, this time the central government sided with the Jews and reprimanded the authorities in Lwow, saying that from now on the Jews in the towns would either have to be accorded equality in leasing breweries or they would all be removed from brewing.[96]

In the year 1819, conflicts developed between the Jews of Rohatyn and the tax collector, Marcus Kreizler, who collected bridge tolls, legal payment on weights and measures, and rentals for the use of town grazing land. Kreizler was a resident of Rohatyn who made these collections on behalf of Citizen Tomasz Sobienski. With the aid of a soldier on horseback and a policeman on foot, he would receive various pledges from Jews and squeeze money out of them for his own benefit. The Jews presented a complaint to Czetsch, the commissar of the district, during one of his visits. They claimed that not only was Kreizler taking money legally for the government, but he also took money for himself that should have been going to Sobienski. In view of this complaint, the administration of the district of Brzezany sentenced Kreizler to 10 lashes. This decision was authorized by the central government of Vienna.[97]

During this period, a question arose concerning the wearing of traditional Jewish clothing. According to the decrees of King Joseph, Section 47, the Jews of Galicia were required by 1794 to discontinue wearing their traditional garb that separated them from other inhabitants. Only rabbis were permitted to wear traditional Jewish clothing. The Jews did not pay any attention to this, and on 20 May 1790 the government abrogated this decree. Between 1816 and 1821 the central government of Vienna again tried to institute laws forbidding Jews from wearing their traditional dress. These laws applied to all the Jews of Galicia. Baron Hauer suggested that they

95 "Conscription," Galizien Judenwesen. IV T 8, carton 2632, no. 4357.
96 Galizien Judenwesen. IV T 11, 13 ex February 1810, carton 2657.
97 Galizien Judenwesen. IV T 11, ad 8 April 1819, carton 2662.

institute a new ruling that explicitly forbade the wearing of Jewish style clothing since it was not of the accepted conventional mode. Thus, the central government should be required to take steps forcing the Jews of Galicia, with the exception of rabbis and those engaged in religious occupations, to change their mode of dress in keeping with accepted European styles.

On 17 May 1821, the Viennese government notified the authorities in Lwow that this matter was linked with the announcement of Jewish laws that would improve their condition. When the Jews heard of these machinations, groups arose to oppose them. Led by the community of Stryj, they rose to take action in this matter and to appear in person before the government in Vienna to oppose the demands of the district authorities. All the communities of Galicia presented a joint written request that Jews be permitted to retain their traditional form of dress.

Rohatyn was among those joining this appeal and, in April 1821, also sent a petition of its own to the district authorities. It requested that this matter be removed from the agenda since the Jewish population was still very poor and lacked the funds to buy the proper cloth needed to produce German-style clothing (Deutsche Kleider). Also, the Jewish stores selling cloth were still filled with their stock of woven goods, intended for Jewish clothing, which would not be sold for quite some time.

The only ones who approved of the governmental demands were members of the Haskalah (Enlightenment) of Brody, Tarnopol, and Lwow. They pushed for the enactment of these demands, since they thought it would hasten the Europeanization of the Jews of Galicia. The merchants, furriers, and cloth manufacturers among the gentiles of Austria followed suit and also presented their own petitions. The government of Vienna sent a reply to each petition of April 1821, stating that the objections to the change in dress were not valid. The proof of this was that taxes from the sale of meat among the Jews of Moravia were not lessened despite the fact that they had changed their way of dress. In any case, these recommendations of the district authority of Galicia never took hold. The problem of Jewish dress was removed from the agenda, and things calmed down.[98]

In 1827, a change took place from an economic point of view. The retail liquor trade, which was forbidden elsewhere to Jews, was permitted in Rohatyn. The official reason was that these rights were controlled by the local authorities, and more than once in the past, they had leased this privilege to Jews.

During this time, the head of the Jewish community was Benjamin Wunderlich, who was not well accepted by the members of his

98   Galizien Judenwesen... IV T 11, carton 2583.

community. More than one complaint was presented against him, especially in such matters as management of community funds and appointing new parnassim of the kehilah.[99] The Jews also complained about the collector of the candle tax from Brzezany, Aharon Klar, who mercilessly oppressed the inhabitants of Rohatyn and carried out seizures and attachment of properties at will.[100]

*

During the 1830s the Hassidic movement developed in the district of Brzezany. Those who were active in this included the Grand Rabbis (Rebbes) Yitzchak Meir of Przemyslany (known as Meir'l of Przemyslany), Yehuda Hirsch Brandwein of Stratyn (the Stratyner Rebbe), and Yitzchak Yehuda of Baranowka, who gathered many followers in Rohatyn. By contrast, we do not precisely know to what degree the Haskalah movement made inroads into Rohatyn and to what degree its influence was felt. We do know that during the 30s and 40s the Maskilim (proponents of Haskalah) were active in politics and worked toward the improvement of the political and economic condition of the Jews of Galicia as well as removing the special Jewish taxes. In the Haskalah circles of Brody, Tarnopol, Stanislawow, Lwow, and Tysmienica, they spoke about the need for establishing schools in the cities and the towns,[101] but Rohatyn was still far away from this goal. In 1847 there was a gathering in Lwow at the initiative of the Lwow kehilah, headed by members who had already achieved a high level of secular education. They met together with the heads of the Jewish communities to discuss their common problems and decided to forward a petition to the central government in which they described their economic conditions. This petition was sent only by the large communities, and it is not clear whether Rohatyn took part in this meeting.

The Jews of Rohatyn were not as affected by the events of 1848 as were the communities of Lwow, Tarnopol, Brody, Zolkiew, Tysmienica, and Stanislawow. Rohatyn did send an elected representative to the June 1848 parliament in Vienna; his name was Sabrin Smarowski, a prominent landowner. We do not know to what degree the Jews contributed to his election. The constitution of April 1848 did not bring equal rights to the Jews, as they had hoped it might, and did not solve the Jewish problems, as the Jewish intelligentsia thought it would. The Galician Jewish interest was

99 Galizien Judenwesen... IV T 10 (1822): carton 2646, 3915/158.
100 Galizien Judenwesen... IV T. 10 (October 1826): carton 2646.
101 "Stimmen aus Galizien (Voices from Galicia)," Busch, Osterreichisches Zentralorgan für Glaubensfreiheit, Cultur Geschichte und Litteratur der Juden (Austrian Central Organ for Freedom of Religion, *Cultural History and Literature of Jews*) (Vienna 1848): 235.

primarily directed toward the elimination of two taxes that were exceedingly oppressive and despised by them—the kosher meat tax and the candle tax—which were collected by the people who paid the highest bid for the job. The constitution of April 1848 did not specifically eliminate these taxes. However, because Section 25 provided equality for all inhabitants with regard to serving in the army and paying taxes, the Jews interpreted this to mean that they, too, could benefit from these laws. The members of the Galician government did not agree, and the district of Brzezany publicly announced that "false rumors are being spread to the effect that the meat and candle taxes have been abrogated. It should therefore be known that this is not the case, and the authorities are still required to collect these taxes."

The Jews did not heed this warning, however, and were at loggerheads with the tax collectors. In the end, on 5 October 1848, the parliament voted 243 to 207 to abrogate all Jewish taxes, and in this way, the Jews were formally acknowledged by the government as equal citizens with equal rights. This emancipation did not last very long, only until 1851. In 1850, when Jews were permitted to acquire real estate, they presented petitions to the government asking permission to purchase property. This included the Jews of Rohatyn who forwarded a number of petitions requesting permission to purchase real estate. However, it was only in 1866 that two Jews, the merchants Goldschlag and Weidenfeld, were granted this right.[102]

In contrast to the other areas where we know that a great struggle took place between the pious Hassidim on one side and the intelligentsia on the other, in Rohatyn, either prior to 1848 or after it, this was not the case. The Maskilim were unable to make a dent in the way of life of the Jews there; they were completely rejected.

In the first half of the 19th century, the Hassidism of Rabbi Yehuda Zvi Hirsch Brandwein of Stratyn took strong root in Rohatyn. Rabbi Yehuda was the disciple of Rabbi Uri of Strzeliska, termed the Saraf (burning angel), who had been a student of Rabbi Shlomo of Karlin. Rabbi Yehuda was one of the famous rebbes (Admorim) in the first half of the 19th century and had a great influence on the masses of Jews in the towns of Eastern Galicia. He was noted for his remedies and cures for diseases and for women with difficulty in bearing children. This was true to such a point that he attracted the attention of the Austrian government, which conducted an investigation of his practices. His opposition stemmed primarily from the Maskilim of Tarnopol who went out of their way to complain to the government about his wonder-working remedies and amulets. They claimed that the Hassidim were

---

102 Goldschlag, IV T, Besitz (Property) (1866): no. 3751/5054, Archives of the Ministry of Interior in Vienna.

being duped and extorted.

Rabbi Yehuda was followed by his oldest son, Rabbi Avraham, who inherited his position as rebbe. He in turn was followed by Rabbi Nahum, in 1865, who became the rebbe at the early age of 18. Rabbi Nahum moved from Stratyn to Bursztyn, where he was the rebbe until 1914. Most of his Hassidim lived either in Bursztyn or Rohatyn or in the surrounding towns. There they established small synagogues (Burshtyner kloizen) whose congregants followed the Stratyn customs. In addition to the Stratyn brand of Hassidism, there were also Hassidic groups affiliated with Belz, Czortkow, Bojanow, and Husiatyn.

G. 1848 - 1914

The second half of the 19th century marked the beginning of an increase in the number of Jews. As a result of the spiritual and cultural ferment of the times, which came about as a result of the Revolution of 1848, new slogans appeared in the Jewish towns and villages of Galicia, carried by a relatively small percentage of the Maskilim intelligentsia. Rohatyn, too, albeit later, experienced this phenomenon. With the passage of time, political conditions developed in which the leadership of the communities passed to power-seeking individuals. These individuals made it their business to serve the interests of the rulers of the area at the expense of the important needs of the Jews. Until 1876 the Jewish Galician leaders were centrist-German in political outlook. Later, however, they turned for many decades to support the Poles during elections and helped to bring in the Jewish vote in national political matters.

At this time, Galicia became one of the main centers of Hassidism, including all its factions. The courts of the rebbes and especially the court of the Belzer rebbe became strong supporters of the Polish faction in the Austrian parliament. His followers were ordered to vote for the Polish nominees. In this way, the common political platform brought about a cooperation between Polish assimilationists and rabbinic Hassidim, both of whom accelerated the political subordination of the Jews to Polish policy.

On the other hand, these phenomena in Galicia awakened Jewish nationalism a number of years before the appearance of the Herzl Zionist movement and opened a new chapter in the political battle of the Jews of Galicia. This process could also be found in the Jewish community of Rohatyn but slightly later than in other towns. At the head of the community stood leaders of the old school. The size of the intelligentsia there was still too small to have any effect in gaining control of the community, and matters continued to run in much the same fashion as they had before, which brought about conflict with the authorities.

In the 1850s the government accused the kehilah of Rohatyn of illegal conduct. This arose as a result of the difficult economic condition and great deficits when the community could not cover its budget via the usual taxes.[103] It thus placed special taxes on staples such as salt, flour, kitchen utensils, and even lubrication for wagon wheels. Anyone who engaged in the sale of these products was required to pay a certain amount to the community treasury. The government suddenly rose to the defense of the "poor Jews" and declared that these taxes were illegal. It said that the officials should be punished for oppressing the weakest elements of the population by raising prices on basic necessities. Vienna ordered immediate steps to be taken by the Galician governors to eliminate these practices.[104]

After receiving permission in 1859 to reside and purchase land in the small towns, Jews began to settle in the villages surrounding Rohatyn, as brewers, lessees of estates, and farmers. The wealthy invested money in buying estates that were in turn managed by Jewish supervisors.

In the year 1857, Rohatyn had 5,101 inhabitants of whom about 3,000 were Jews. They were engaged primarily in business—the sale of agricultural products (such as flour and milk), clothing, fur, shoes, woven goods, and groceries and the operation of taverns, inns, and restaurants. Crafts included primarily tailors and furriers.[105]

In the year 1868, Jews were granted equal rights, including the right to

---

103   (Image and text (in German), p. 52 of Yizkor Book.) In 1849, there was a shortage of banknotes in Rohatyn and the surrounding area. To ease the monetary distress, the municipality and the Jewish community issued money orders that were used for a certain period as a means of payment. (This is an example of a money order issued in 1849.)

104   Galizien Judenwesen... IV Vol. 11 23472/682 - In a notice of 11 November 1854 to its officials in Galicia, the Interior Ministry said, "However, what can least be tolerated are levies that involve a thoroughly illegal burden on commerce, indirectly involve other co-religionists in the expenses of the Jewish religious community, and are partly put to uses that may thwart the effectiveness of existing governmental provisions. Therefore, the administration is requested to examine this matter urgently and to revoke those taxes that have been introduced without authorization and unlawfully, and, in cases where the established sources of income are found to be insufficient, to cover necessary expenses of the local authorities and initiate legal hearings on this basis."

105   Avraham Mendel Mohar, *Shvilei Olam* (Pathways of the World), (Lwow 1865): 156, section 3. [This paragraph occurs a few paragraphs later in the Yizkor Book (and is marked as footnote 106) but chronologically belongs here. Tr]

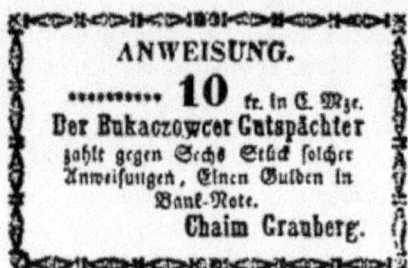

ANWEISUNG.

•••••••••• **10** fr. in C. Mze.

Der Bukaczowcer Gutspächter

zahlt gegen Sechs Stück solcher
Anweisungen, Einen Gulden in
Bank-Note.

Chaim Grauberg.

1849 המחאת־תשלום משנת

Remittance/Cheque
10 Franks in Austrian Currency
Bukaczowcer Land Leaseholder
Paid Against 6 Orders/Demands
One Gulden in Banknotes
Chaim Grauberg

participate in town councils. Thus, in keeping with the law of towns, the town council of Rohatyn was composed of 30 members, divided among 18 Polish Catholics, 6 Greek Catholic Ruthenians (later called Ukrainians), and 6 Jews.

Under the influence of the equal rights laws, there arose among the Maskilim of Galicia a movement to eliminate the kehilot (organized communities) or at least to limit their powers. It wished to place them under town supervision and to take these powers into its own hands, together with all the funds that were now being held by the communities. This movement was a reaction to the control of many kehilot by the ultraorthodox. In this they were backed by the Poles who were interested in integrating Jews with Poles, primarily for political reasons. The Poles wanted to strengthen their position against the Ruthenians, especially since the Ruthenians had begun to demand the right to determine policy in Galicia. These demands were also supported by the municipalities in order to weaken the power of self-rule by the Jewish community organizations and place them under their domination.

The movement first arose among the groups of Maskilim in Cracow that were then joined by similar groups in Tarnow. Together they turned to the central government in Vienna and petitioned it to eliminate the independence of the kehilot.

The Viennese government opposed this request to intermingle the Jewish communities with the towns, because it realized that behind it lay the desire to promote the Polonization of the Jews of Galicia. This was contrary to the policy held by the Austrian national government, which was interested in Germanizing the Jews. In addition to the political aspect, the heads of the government pointed to the legal factor found in Paragraph 15 of the Basic Laws of 21 December 1867. The law stated, "The organization and administration of all internal affairs of churches and religious communities recognized by law shall be carried out by their own community organizations and remain under their control and administration, including their foundations and trusts that are related to religious, educational, and charity needs."[106] Therefore, it was very clear from the start that these requests would be met by a strong negative reply.

It is interesting to note that this movement found appeal and backing in Rohatyn where the Jewish representatives—Ostern, Leib Weidman, Shmuel Holder, and Marcus Nagelberg—were seated in the town council. Judging by the wording of the Ostern suggestion that we will cite, we can deduce that it was motivated by a strong antagonistic movement against the leaders of the kehilah. Ostern, the sponsor of the proposal, and the members of the town council were all Maskilim who saw that the kehilah lay in the hands of leaders who were irresponsible and careless with the assets of the community. Wishing to remove these community leaders from their position, they therefore requested that the administration of the community be brought under town control.

On 20 February 1868, at the session of the town council, Ostern, the Jewish member, presented the following proposal: "The Rohatyn Jewish community has under its control a large amount of capital derived from a variety of contributions, pledges, and collections that are in the hands of its leaders who do not present managerial reports to the town, and no one knows what they are doing. The synagogue, whose structure was begun years ago, is still waiting to be completed. At this rate, this holy structure will collapse. Despite the fact that large sums are constantly being collected for graves, the cemetery still lacks a fence. The bathhouse, for which three hundred florin are collected annually, is ready to collapse. There is no registry of Torah scrolls and megillot, which are in the hands of the beadle of the synagogue who has no supervision. According to Section 93 of the town ordinance, the town has the right to supervise special matters concerning the Jewish community. Therefore, I suggest that the town council should decide that from now on the administration of affairs, that heretofore have been in the hands of the heads of the Jewish community, be placed under the strict supervision of the town. Towards this purpose, a supervisory committee of three councilmen should be chosen, whose task it would be to supervise the operation of the affairs of the community in all of its aspects. These would include the signing of all

---

106   "Uber die allgemeinen Rechte der Statsbuerger fuer die im Reichsrate vertretenen Koenigreiche und Laender" (About the general rights of citizens in the kingdom and lands represented in the parliament), "Staatsgrundgesetz v. 21.12.1867" (State Constitution of 21 December 1867), Regierungsblatt (Government document), no. 142. [This appears as footnote 105 in the Yizkor Book. Tr]

documents and legal papers, the receiving of accounts and the registration of property, and, from time to time, presenting a report to the town council on its activities and undesirable impressions."

The proposal of Ostern was unanimously accepted, and a committee was immediately chosen that included three Jews—Leib Weidman, Shmuel Holder, and Marcus Nagelberg.[107]

The mayor of the town, Ambrose Mruczynski, passed the decision of 20 February 1868, on to the hands of the chief official of the district, who declared that this decision stood in contradiction to the existing laws and forbade the town to carry it out. The town council appealed the decision of the district official on 9 September 1868 before the commission on Galicia, which also turned down this proposal. The town then turned to the Ministry of the Interior in Vienna. The Ministry of the Interior viewed this decision as another attempt similar to the decisions of the cities of Cracow and Tarnow "to take out of the hands of the Jewish community the supervision of religious Jewish affairs, which it is legally required to carry out, and pass these powers on to the committee of the town council. This decision, whose purpose is to eliminate an organization recognized by law, directly contradicts Section 15 of the fundamental laws as well as the town ordinances of Galicia."[108] On 19 November 1869, the Ministry of the Interior upheld the decision of the commission to reject the proposal of the town council.

Having been turned down by the central government, the town authorities were helpless to make any basic changes, and matters remained as they had been until the 1870s when a new administration, composed of younger and educated members capable of initiative, was appointed.

In the years 1866 - 68, the chief rabbi of Rohatyn was Rabbi Eliezar Horowitz (1820 - 68), the son of the rabbi of Stanislawow (Rabbi Meshulam Yisaschar Horowitz), who was raised in the house of his grandfather, the Gaon, Reb Aryeh Leybisch. Before his appointment, the rabbi of Rohatyn was the rabbi of Maryampol, 1850–56. Contrary to the ways of his father, Rabbi Meshulam Yisaschar, who refused to recognize the Admorim (the Rebbe leaders) and did not permit them to exert any influence in community matters in Stanislawow, Rabbi Eliezar became attracted to Hassidism and traveled to the Tzaddik, Rabbi Yehuda Zvi of Rozdol. He copied the works of his grandfather on the Torah and organized them according to the portions of the week under the name of *Pnei Aryeh* (Face of the Lion), to which he added his own addenda, entitled *Ateret Zekenim* (Crown of the Elders) (Przemysl,

107   Galizien Judenwesen... IV T 10 ZL 14499 ea/1868, 1841 ea 1869. Interior Ministry Archive in Vienna.
108   108 Galizien Judenwesen... IV T 10 14499/1041, 1869.

1874). After that, Rabbi Meir Yehuda Leib, the son of Reb Shmuel Glass, previously rabbi in Pomorzany, was appointed rabbi. He remained rabbi in Rohatyn until he passed away in 1894.

In 1896 Rabbi Natan Lewin was appointed rabbi. He was born in Brody to a family of famous rabbis and was the student and later son-in-law of the rabbi of Lwow, Rabbi Yitzchak Schmelkes. He was learned in both secular and religious subjects and successfully matriculated as an extern at the gimnazjum (high school) of Brody. After the passing of Rabbi Meir Kristianfoler, Brody did not hold any further elections of rabbis until after the victory of the Haskalah in the community elections. In the new elections, there were five candidates, all natives of Brody—Rabbi Avraham Binyamin Kluger, the son of the preacher, Rabbi Eliezar Landau, Rabbi Moshe Reinhold, Rabbi Yitzchak Chajes, and Rabbi Natan Lewin. They chose Rabbi Yitzchak Chajes, the son of the rabbi of Zolkiew, Rabbi Zvi Hirsh Chajes.

Two years later, in 1896, Rabbi Natan Lewin became the rabbi of Rohatyn. He was, as we have said, a man of wide education and nationalistic views. He did not become involved in the differences between the Hassidim and the Mitnagdim (those who objected to Hassidic views). He urged the establishment of Jewish schools and a Jewish gimnazjum because he viewed a well-rounded education as the solution to and defense against the assimilation of youth. He objected to the desires of the Admorim to separate the communities similar to what was occurring in Hungary and saw a unified kehilah as the only national religious institution that would serve the interest of all Jews.

During his rabbinical term in Rohatyn—until 1905—he took part in the congress of the Jewish communities of 1 May 1900, and initiated an intensive drive to expand and improve Jewish education in Rohatyn. In 1903, he participated in the first general rabbinic congress, which assembled on August 13 in Cracow. In 1905 Rabbi Lewin was appointed rabbi of Rzeszow.

Pressed by the Zionist movement that was striving to dislodge the administration of Jewish communities from the control of the traditional conservative families, a congress was held on 1 May 1900, in Lwow after a break of 22 years. The previous congress of kehilot had last taken place in Lwow in 1878 and was initiated by the organization Shomer Yisrael (Protector of the Jews), which was promoting at that time the rejuvenation of community life. Rohatyn did not take part in the first meeting and contented itself with sending a congratulatory telegram.

As for the second gathering, Rohatyn sent its rabbi, Rabbi Natan Lewin, as a delegate. The meeting was attended by 70 representatives, 40 of whom came from the smaller communities; 30 representatives were from Lwow alone. 29 representatives, including Rabbi Natan Lewin, united to form the Zionist club, which succeeded in obtaining representation in the leadership of the congress. They elected Rabbi Natan Lewin, who had been taking part in the proceedings, as their representative. During the debate, he sharply attacked the corrupt methods of community organization that had become the main obstruction to development of public life in Jewish Galicia. He made a strong impression on the delegates during this address when he presented the need for opening a Hebrew gimnazjum.

Lewin stressed that "the necessity for a Hebrew gimnazjum is strongly felt by us. If with regard to secular studies there may not be a great difference between one school and another, from the religious point of view, we need to worry about our children becoming assimilated as a result of their contact with the outside world. In any case, we can no longer leave the sad conditions as they are now. Do we want a school in which the study of Hebrew predominates and Jewish studies do not exist, like 'those souls who walk around naked'?[Tr5] The Jewish student must first and foremost be an exemplary Jew who respects his people, his Torah, and his nationality. How sad is the picture that exists now, in which Jewish students are so poorly educated that they celebrate our holidays while at the same time violating the laws of the Sabbath and the Holy Days. Since, at this point, we have a long way to go before we can erect a special gimnazjum, because that would result in too many hardships and be difficult to put into operation, we will therefore have to content ourselves, at this point, with something small and attempt, where it is appropriate, to incorporate a suitable curriculum in every gimnazjum that would enable Jewish students to withstand the pressure to violate Shabbat and Yom Tov."[109]

When the spokesman for the assimilationists, Dr. Bernhard Goldman, demanded that the official language of the community organization be Polish, and Dr. Gotlieb attacked the Zionists, claiming that rabbis are anti-Zionist, Rabbi Lewin replied, "We Orthodox rabbis are all Zionists even if we do not always take part in Zionist activities. For how is it possible for an Orthodox rabbi who constantly thinks of Zion and constantly pours out his soul in prayers for the return to Zion not to be a Zionist? Not Zionists? We are waiting with baited breath to return to our land. It is our heart's desire to which all of our poets have dedicated their most inspired works in the holy tongue. Here they saw their visions that have maintained us for generations. Every lump of earth in our land is holy to us, and we are all tied to it body and soul—and we are not Zionists?" (During the speech Dr. Caro

---

Tr5   'devoid of adequate religious knowledge'

109   "Assembly of the Delegates of the Communities of Galicia," Hamagid May 17 (Cracow 1900): 19-20:216.

interrupted with the objection that this address implied that only Orthodox rabbis are ardent Zionists. Progressive rabbis are also very attached to Zion.)

"However," continued Rabbi Lewin, "the time has not yet come to put into effect the use of Hebrew in community matters. On the other hand, to use Polish would result in a great disadvantage to the Jewish community, since most of the people, especially the rabbis, who should be in the forefront of community affairs, do not know Polish adequately and would therefore be unable to function properly. They would be regarded as outsiders, sitting with folded hands, because they would be unable to take part in the community assemblies." Rabbi Lewin therefore requested that matters be left as they were, wherein each group managed its affairs in the language it found most comfortable.[110]

Most of the proposals that dealt with the creation of a permanent representation of the communities—ranging from a renewal of the Council of Four Lands to an increase in the productivity of the Jewish masses in order to improve their economic condition—were accepted under the pressure of the Zionists. In the end, a permanent committee for the congress of the communities was established, consisting of 60 members, including 4 Zionists—Dr. Kornheiser, Adolph Stand, Hillel Badian, and Rabbi Natan Lewin.

*

During the 1890s, the Jewish intelligentsia and secularists became more nationalistic. Shalom Meltzer (1871–1909), a very religious man, was among the first Zionists of the town. He organized and activated the intelligentsia who had previously been affected by Zionist ideals. He founded the Zionist organization "Bnai Zion," as well as a branch of the Austrian group in Vienna, "Zion," whose goal was to repopulate the land of Israel. The Bnai Zion group offered lectures and courses in the study of Hebrew literature and Jewish history on a regular basis. These Zionist Hebrew activities found a home in the house of Shalom Meltzer, who, together with his family, made it a point to speak Hebrew in the home. It was because of his religious background that he was able to attract religious people to the Zionist movement, while regarding with understanding people of other points of view. This enabled him to be well accepted by members of the secular intelligentsia, who joined him in the Zionist movement.

As early as two years after the establishment of the Tarnow branch of "Ahavat Zion," Rohatyn made the largest contribution of any of the towns of Galicia, 200 florin. After the appearance of the pamphlet Der

---

110   Hamagid June 7 (Cracow 1900), 23:262.

Judenstaat (The Jewish State) by Theodor Herzl, the Zionist organization of Rohatyn became among the first to decide, at a meeting, to notify Dr. Herzl of its affinity with his ideas. These were expressed in "his pamphlet that was written in the Jewish spirit and in which was propounded a Godly and elevated plan to establish an independent Jewish state. This has met with enormous response and is accepted with great enthusiasm among all sectors of the people."

Thanks to this plan, it was stressed in the decision, "We now know what we want and what we have to do. You have presented us in a clear and definite fashion with a true, elevated goal, and we must do all that is in our power to realize it." However, they went on to say that these Zionist hopes were based on the proposition that he, Dr. Herzl, would take upon himself "to be the captain of our ship that is shaking on the waves of dangerous political oceans and will raise the fallen flag of our people that will gather the masses about him with enthusiasm." The contents of this decision were relayed to Dr. Herzl in a letter dated 22 April 1896, two months after the publication of Der Judenstaat.[111] In response to their letter, the Zionists of Rohatyn received the following reply, dated 27 May 1896, which stated: "Honorable Sirs, Having only recently returned from my journeys, I was unable to answer your letter of encouragement and acceptance of my views until now. I thank you wholeheartedly for your kind words, and I hope that when the time comes and the proclamation is announced in our ranks, that we will all march together, united and willingly. I am still working and fighting almost entirely alone through my own efforts, and I am planning on promoting matters through a society that I will create in London called the 'Society of Jews.' The efforts of one man alone do not suffice to awaken the stragglers, and the stragglers are mostly those who do not lack for anything. However, we must be strong in spirit and not stray from the great purpose that lies before us. Your devoted, Theodor Herzl."[112]

Beginning with the year 1894, Rohatyn was represented at all national gatherings of the Zionist movement of Galicia as well as at the general meeting of the "Chevrat Yishuv Eretz Yisrael Zion: (Society for the Settlement of Eretz Yisrael and Zion) and "Ahavat Zion" (Love of Zion) in Tarnow.

Shalom Meltzer was the representative of the Zionist association and took part in debates at the assemblies. At the national congress that took place on 26–27 December 1897 in Lwow, he was elected to the national committee and took an active part in its procedures. Ahavat Zion was founded in Rohatyn as a

---

111   The Herzl Archive, Central Zionist Archive.
112   Printed by Yisrael Weinlaz in Haolam, 1937, 36:643.

branch of the organization in Tarnow and was headed for several years by Alter Weidmann, with Ephraim Sternhal as his deputy. Other members included the physician Dr. Siegfried Scharf, Manish Schenker, Hirsch Yoseph Haber, Moshe Damm, Naftali Schumer, Eliezer Igra, Avigdor Edelsberg, and Avraham Zlatkis, while Shalom Meltzer basically managed the Zionist activity behind the scenes.

In 1896, Ephraim Sternhal, Alter Weidmann, Yitzchak Nagelberg, Dr. S. Scharf, Daniel Damm, and Shalom Meltzer were elected to the local committee. In the contest that took place between the leadership of Ahavat Zion in Tarnow, headed by Dr. Avraham Zaltz, and the Action Committee of the World Zionist Organization, Shalom Meltzer attempted to mediate and reach a compromise. At the general assembly of 19–20 May 1897 in Tarnow, Meltzer and Ephraim Sternhal were elected representatives of Rohatyn to the Tarnow Ahavat Zion convention.

The representatives of Rohatyn—Meltzer and Zlatkis—played an important role in the national Zionist convention that took place on 26 - 27 June 1898, in Stanislawow. This convention dealt with the question of taking a unified stand by the Zionists of Galicia regarding problems that were on the agenda of the Second Zionist Congress. In the convention, Meltzer opposed the goals of the group headed by Rosenhock of Kolomyja—to sever their relationship with the national committee of Lwow and form a central organization of their own because they felt that the Lwow committee opposed political Zionism. The representatives of Rohatyn strongly backed the national organization led by the committee in Lwow, and Meltzer was elected to this national committee.

In 1898, the Bnai Zion organization of Rohatyn numbered 100 members, headed by Alter Weidmann. In the fund raising campaign for the Treasury for Settlement (JCT), which took place between March 1899 and 28 April 1899, 112 shares, at one pound sterling per share, were sold in Rohatyn as compared with 7,210 shares in all of Galicia.

With the selection of Rabbi Natan Lewin as Rabbi of Rohatyn, intensive activity began in the field of education. He represented the community of Rohatyn at the assembly day, which convened on 1 May 1900, in Lwow.

Between the years 1900 and 1905, the Bnai Zion organization was headed by A. Weidmann, and many political and social activities were carried out. Shalom Meltzer was among those who laid the foundation for the Mizrachi organization, which came into being at the convention of Pressburg in August 1904. He was elected to the central executive committee as the representative of Galicia, but he refused the mandate and remained with the national Zionist organization. In 1909 the Zionist organization of Rohatyn suffered a great loss with the passing of Shalom Meltzer.

Leibel Toives of Rohatyn was among the 63 representatives elected in Galicia to the Zionist Congress of Vienna in 1913. In the year 1905, the Zionists became an important active factor in community leadership. Their impressive activities, led by Shalom Meltzer, resulted in the establishment of a Hebrew school that year through the community council. This was the first Hebrew school of its kind in Galicia. With the appointment of Raphael Soferman as principal of the school, a noticeable change came about in Hebrew cultural life among the Jews. Teachers included Lichtman, Berkowitz, Zvi Scharfstein, Carmi, and Sobel. The number of students reached 176. Raphael Soferman (1879–1956), an outstanding personality, was one of the first modern Hebrew teachers who instilled new energy into the nationalistic activities and was the driving force of the Hebraic Zionist movement of Galicia. Under his initiative, the Hebrew Teachers Union was founded, and its main headquarters were in Rohatyn. In 1911, Soferman went to Brody, and the new school principal was Jacob Prost. The years 1910–14 were characterized by a high degree of Jewish nationalistic life that left its stamp and color on the entire Jewish population of Rohatyn.

*

The Jewish community continued to grow. In 1880, Rohatyn numbered 5,101 inhabitants, of whom 3,035 were Jews (59.5%).[113] In 1890 the town had 914 homes and 7,188 residents, of whom 3,503 were Jews (48.8% of the population).[114] In the year 1900, Rohatyn had 931 houses and 7,201 residents, of whom 3,217 were Jews (about 44.7% of the population).[115] In 1910, in the last count under the Austrian rule, there were 7,664 inhabitants, of whom 3,254 were Jews (about 42.4% of the population).[116] With the increase in the town's population, the number of Jews also increased. However, as a result of the large increase in the number of inhabitants of the town, the proportion of Jews fell from 59.5% in 1880 to 42% in 1910. In 1880, among 89 surrounding villages in the Rohatyn district, there were 2,397 Jews

---

113   Bohdan Wasiutynski: Ludnosc zydowska w Polsce w wiekach XIX i XX (The Jewish population of Poland in the 19th and 20th centuries) (Warszawa 1930): 123.

114   1,086 Poles (15.1%), 2,576 Ruthenians (35.8%), 23 others (0.3%). Stanislaw Gruinski, Materialy do kwestyi zydowskiej w Galicyi. (Material pertaining to the Jewish question in Galicia)(Lwow 1910): 15.

115   1,206 Poles (16.7%), 2,678 Ruthenians (37.2%), 100 others (1.4%). Stanislaw Gruinski, Materialy.

116   1,530 Poles (20%), 2,863 Ruthenians (37.4%), 17 others (0.2%). In the first census taken by newly independent Poland in 1921, there were 5,736 inhabitants; of these, 2,233 were Jews (38.9%). Stanislaw Gruinski, Materialy.

(approximately 19% of the total population). In 1890 the number of Jews in these villages numbered 2,434 (about 17.2% of the total population), while in 1900 this number fell to 2,070 (about 15.4% of the population).

In 1880, in the total district of Rohatyn, including the town of Rohatyn, there were 72,491 non-Jewish residents and 12,569 Jewish residents. Of this number the Christians residing in towns and villages numbered 10,331 (13.6% of their total number), while the number of Jews was 9,561 (76.1% of the total Jewish population in the district). In 1890 there were 81,743 Christian residents, of whom 12,810 lived in towns and villages (15.7%), and 14,149 Jews, of whom 10,609 lived in towns and villages (75% of the total Jewish population in the district). In 1900 there were 94,799 Christian residents, of whom 14,368 lived in towns and villages (15.2%), and 13,472 Jews, of whom 10,305 lived in the towns and villages (76.5% of the total Jewish population).[117]

At the end of the 19th and the beginning of the 20th centuries, there were in the town "learned" families such as the Nagelberg family, the grandchildren of David Moshe Avraham (Rav Adam); Holder, Ostern, Goldschlag, Alter Weidmann, Ephraim Sternhal (one of the wealthy members of the community); and, of course, Shalom Meltzer (one of the first Zionists of Galicia). They all held top-level positions in the Jewish community.

For decades, until 1904, Chaim Holder stood at the head of the Jewish community, followed by Alter Weidmann. Weidmann instituted many changes in the community and initiated the building of the large synagogue that was famous for its artistic murals. After that came Dr. Pinchas Scharf, who held the position until the day of his death. Lastly, Shlomo Amarant followed and remained in this position until the Holocaust.

Between the years 1904 and 1910, Alter Weidmann was assisted by his deputy, Ephraim Sternhal. The executive department (Kultusvorstand) was staffed by Dr. Siegfried Schaff, Avraham Zlatkis, Motel Kreizler, and Z. Weidmann. In the council (Kultusrat) were Yonah Rappaport, Daniel Damm, Sender Margolis, Shalom Meltzer, Yaakov Fisch, and Yaakov Lewenter. The community budget amounted to 14,400 crowns.

The officials who participated in the last community council of the Austrian regime were Alter Weidmann, chairman, and Ephraim Sternhal, vice-chairman. The executive members were Dr. Siegfried Schaff, Avraham Zlatkis, and Motel Kreizler. The members of the board included Yonah Rappaport, Daniel Damm, Sender Margolis, Avraham Koenigsberg, Yaakov Fisch, Zadik Zeidman, and Yaakov Lewenter.

No new rabbi was appointed after Rabbi Natan Lewin left. The rabbinical

117   Stanislaw Gruinski, Materialy: 23.

tasks were performed by the dayanim rabbis, Shmuel Henna and Avraham David Spiegel. In the general schools, religion was taught by Hirsch Schwartz. The community budget rose to 20,000 crowns, which was covered by the community taxes paid by 620 taxpayers. This was in addition to revenues permitted by law, such as the tax on kosher meat, payments for the bathhouse and cemetery, etc. The community recorder of births, weddings, and deaths was at that time Yisrael Ostern.

The Jewish elected representatives to the municipality included Ephraim Sternhal, Alter Weidmann, Shalom Meltzer, Yerachmiel Schwartz, the attorney Dr. Goldschlag (who also functioned as deputy mayor), and Rabbi Avraham David Spiegel. In addition to the chevra kadisha the following committees were active in the town:

1) Association of Merchants: Presided over by Fischel Banner. Members of the committee included Yitzchak Doller, Yeshaya Singer, Akiva Wagschal, Yechezkel Weiler, Yoel Granowitter and Aharon Weinstock;

2) The Diligent Hands Craftsmen Association: Presided over by Chaim Skolnick;

3) Maot Chitim: Money for Passover officially collected by the community;

4) Kimcha D'Pis'cha: Money for Passover, collected for the poor by individuals;

5) Community charity organization: directed by Shimon Teichman;

6) Dorshei Tov: Seekers of Goodness;

7) Rodfei Zedek: Pursuers of Justice;

8) Women's Society (Frauenverein): presided over by Helena Ostern.

In 1906 the I.C.A. Loan Society was founded. In 1907 it had 168 members, and by 1908 it had 385 members. During 1907 it granted 155 loans valued at 29,050 crowns; in 1908 it granted 346 loans amounting to 71,425 crowns. The administrative cost for 1907 amounted to 600 crowns, and in 1908 it came to 1,222 crowns. From the day it was founded until 31 December 1908, 501 loans were distributed, totaling 100,475 crowns, 65,336, of which were returned by that time. Loans of between 50–600 crowns were granted to merchants, retailers, and craftsmen.[118] In addition to this loan association, 39 other loan associations existed in Rohatyn, 15 of which were Christian and 24, Jewish.

One of the great accomplishments at this time was the founding of the Hebrew school under the sponsorship of the organization called "Safa

---

118   Stanislaw Gruinski, Materialy: tablica XLVI, 73.

Translation of the election ballot at the top of p. 62 of the Yizkor Book :

Election ballot
Being entitled to vote for one representative to the state parliament from District 29,
I give my vote to:
DR. WLADYSLAW DULEBA.

Brura"—clear speech. There was also a small yeshiva run by Reb Avraham Grünberg.

The Jewish community played an important role in the election campaign to the Austrian parliament. In 1907, the Viennese parliament passed a law eliminating the system of constituencies, and suffrage was granted to all citizens of the empire. This act aroused new hopes and possibilities among the Jews in Galicia. In the Zionist camp, preparations on a large scale began for the elections that took place between 17 and 27 May 1907. Election publicity was organized throughout Galicia that was also geared toward realizing Zionist ideals. Wherever there was a Jewish community, candidates were nominated. Gatherings were held, speeches were made; preachers and rabbis and just ordinary Jews aroused the masses from their political lethargy and brought into the darkened streets of Galicia light, national hope, and political clarification. Rohatyn belonged to the 29th election district, which encompassed the municipal areas of Brzezany, Rohatyn, Chodorow, and Brzozdowce. The Zionist organization of the district nominated the well-known Zionist leader Rabbi Dr. Shmuel

PROTEST
against the election of
Dr. Wladyslaw Dulemba.

A picture of the terrorism and crimes
committed in favor of
Dr. Wladyslaw Dulemba
in connection with the elections to the
Austrian parliament from the 29th
Electoral Circuit in the district towns
of Brzezany, Rohatyn, Chodorow,
Brzozdowce, etc.

=== At the same time we ===

Appeal to civilized Europe

Issued by the United Ruthenian
(Ukrainian)- Social Democrats,
Ruthenian (Ukrainian) town– and
Jewish–National Election
Committees in Brzezany.

Publisher

Richard Timm's Family Press, Vienna
II, Darwin Street (etc.).

YB p.63: Poster (in German)
featuring a picture of Dr. S.
Rappaport

Rappaport. The Polish choice for nominee to the Austrian parliament was Dr. Wladyslaw Duleba (or Dulemba), who was nominated by dint of terror, bribery, and fraud. He had been the representative for the district in 1902. Duleba was backed by assimilationists but also received aid from the court of the Admor of Belz. The Admor ordered his Hassidim not to vote for the Zionist, Rabbi Dr. Shmuel Rappaport, but to vote for the Pole Dr. Duleba who, as it was known, was one of the leaders of the National Democrats (Endecy).

The Jewish national election committee of Rohatyn was headed by Dr. Katz, Dr. Moritz Fichmann, Marcus Weiler, A. H. Holder, and Dr. Oswald Klugman. Right from the beginning, the Poles, with the backing of the Austrian government, waged a tyrannical election campaign that became worse on Election Day. The campaigners for Dr. Duleba paid 5 crowns for each vote. The Jews were not given ballot slips, and the head of the district, as well as the mayor, distributed ballots with the name of Dr. Duleba—all this with the backing of the Austrian government. On Election Day, the police stood in front of the election hall, and anyone who did not present a ballot with the name of Dr. Duleba was not permitted to enter.

Despite the terror, stealing of ballots, and bribe money, Duleba was unable to obtain a majority in the first round and was forced to run again, against Dr. Rappaport. In the second round, which took place 31 May, the Ruthenians decided to vote for Dr. Rappaport. On Election Day the terror was increased even more. Contrary to election laws, government officials together with the head of the district and the mayor openly carried out acts of bribery and deceit with threats of pogroms against the Jews. Ballots marked Dr. Rappaport were stolen out of the ballot box, and in this way, Dr. Rappaport lost, and Duleba was elected. The election committees of the Zionists and Ruthenians presented an appeal to the parliament contesting the election—however, to no avail.[119] The Polish club, backers of the members of the national government, saw to it that the election of their candidate, Dr. Duleba, would be accepted. In the elections of 1911 the Jewish nominee for Rohatyn was the lawyer Dr. Horowitz of Stanislawow, and his campaign was waged by the Austrian member of parliament Ernest Breiter, a Gentile who was pro-Zionist, and again, the Jews lost.

By the end of the 19th and the beginning of the 20th century, Rohatyn

---

119   Protest against the election of Dr. Wladyslaw Duleba. A picture of the terrorism and crimes committed in favor of Dr. Duleba in connection with the elections to the Austrian parliament in the 29th electoral district of Brzezany, Rohatyn, Chodorow, and Brzozdowce in Galicia. At the same time, an appeal to civilized Europe (in German) (Vienna 1907). See printed proclamation on following page.

possessed a class of intelligentsia with academic training. Among doctors these included Dr. Siegfried Schaff and Dr. Moritz Stein, and among lawyers, there were Dr. Moritz Lipiner, Dr. Yosef Weidmann, Dr. Pinchas Scharf, Dr. Herman Zahnhauser, Dr. Ferdinand Katz, Dr. Shmuel Schoder, Dr. Oswald Klugman, and Dr. Moritz Fichmann.

*

After the outbreak of the war on 31 July 1914, many Jews fled to Austria where they were gathered in evacuation camps in the towns of Moravia, Bohemia, and Austria. An especially large number gathered in Vienna. In August the Russians entered Rohatyn. They burned the Jewish quarter and arrested 570 Jews. Rohatyn became the headquarters for supplies under the command of the cruel officer Purbana. Esther Schorr and Sarah Butfeld were executed on the excuse that they had sold soap two kopeks above the prescribed amount. Before being forced to leave the town, after a siege of the town for six months, the Russians tried to convince the Polish and Ruthenian inhabitants to move to Russia - however, to no avail. They assembled all the Jewish inhabitants and deported all the males - 570 men - to Russia, including very old people between the ages of 70 and 95 and children between the ages of 10 and 13.[120] One woman was exiled in place of her husband who was in hiding. In June 1915, the town was recaptured by the Austrians, who found a few Jews left. The refugees did not return at that time, and the town was not rebuilt. However, by the end of 1917 and the beginning of 1918, people began to return and rebuild their homes. Life slowly returned to what it had been before the war.

At the end of World War I, political changes began to take place. The Ukrainians set up the Western Republic of Ukraine in eastern Galicia. Then a war broke out between Poland and Ukraine in which the Jewish leaders declared their neutrality and refused to take part in the dispute. To protect their interests, all the Jewish parties united to create a national Jewish committee for all the communities. Community councils were eliminated and national committees were elected in which all parties were represented.

The Jewish community of Rohatyn had many problems under the Ukrainian regime. There was a Jewish population of 3,000, of whom 2,000

120   The names of the elderly are as follows: Yisrael Gotlieb, 85; Berel Eigen, 78; Meir Staltzer, 94; Shmuel Braun, 90; Moshe Faust, 70; Wolf Schwartz, 72; Moshe Stok, 85; Lazar Michael Putzter, 70; Yitzchak Spiegel, 65; Eliahu Aharon Klareneter, 65; Aharon Barenfeld, 70; Isaac Schrafer, 70; Yehoshua Kalman Fox, 65; Simcha Natan Rotraub, 50; Yona Rappaport, 75; Simcha Toffler, 80; Shalom Weiler, 73. Children: Mendel Blochsberg, 12, Yisrael Putzter, 13, Yehuda Hirschenhaut, 10. The woman was Janette Rotraub. Jewish War Archive (Vienna 1915).

(66%) were in need of monetary aid as compared to 150 (15%) before World War I. There were 2,100 (70%) without any means of support. Shops and crafts were paralyzed because of the anti-Jewish policies of the Ukrainian regime and its ineptness in government and economics. As a result, Jews were unable to find any source of income. In addition, there were pressing shortages of food and basic necessities. Persecution, attacks by soldiers, robbery, and thievery were the outstanding characteristics of daily life for Jews at that time. The Jewish committee of Stanislawow made every effort to obtain redress from the Ukrainians, but to no avail, because the town authorities paid no attention to the demands of the committee and did exactly as they pleased. Nevertheless, despite all the difficulties, schools and cultural institutions functioned. In June 1919, the Poles broke through the Ukrainian front and conquered all of eastern Galicia, thus beginning a new chapter in the Polish exile.

Surrounding Towns

Bukaczowce: Bukaczowce is first mentioned in documents dating from 1438. In 1489 it received the rank of a town. In 1515 the town paid three and one half grazovna tax on liquor. From 1489 on, the town, together with Chodorow, was owned by the noble family Zarwinski. In the year 1578 the town had six craftsmen and paid a liquor tax of 28 florin. No one knows when Jews first settled there.

In the census of 1765 there were 289 Jews listed in the town and 72 Jews in the surrounding villages, making a total of 361 Jews.

In the year 1880 the town grew to 2,085 inhabitants, of whom 1,115 were Jews (53.5%).

In 1890 there were 260 buildings with 2,459 inhabitants, of whom 1,216 were Jews (49.5%). In 1900 there were 288 buildings with exactly the same number of inhabitants and the same number of Jews.

In 1921 the town had a population of 2,251 inhabitants, of whom 649 were Jews (8.8%).

Prior to 1914 there were 230 taxpayers in the Jewish community organization headed by Yona Bick and his deputy, Meir Schorr. The executive department consisted of Zev Bronzweig, Leib Steinberg, Marc Scher, Chaim Dickman, Avraham Bregman, Anshel Wilf, Shlomo Gelber, Alexander Willig, Beresh Axelrod, Moshe Dickman, Shlomo Hoftman, Heinrich Horne, and Benedet Yupiter. The rabbi was Ephraim Chamaides; the teacher of religion in the general schools was Yeshaye Schwartzberg.

Stratyn: Until the 17th century, Stratyn had the official rank of a village. In 1671, King Michael agreed to the request of the owner of the village, Gabriel

Sylinski, to grant Stratyn the status of a town, with the right of holding three yearly market fairs and a market day every first and sixth day of the week. In 1675, the Tatars attacked and were severely defeated by the Polish commander, Ataneus Miaczynski.

As of the year 1671, there existed Nowy Stratyn, the town, and Stary Stratyn, the village.

In 1765, the census counted 95 Jews, which included 83 adults and 12 children. The Jewish community increased 50% by the second half of the 19th century.

By 1880 the town had 143 houses and 840 inhabitants, which included 192 Ruthenians, 19 Poles, and 593 Jews (73.8% of the population).

In the year 1890 there were 99 houses, 768 inhabitants, of whom 552 were Jewish (71.9%).

In 1900 there were 97 houses, 694 inhabitants, of whom 413 were Jewish (59.5%).

In 1921 the population fell to 373 inhabitants, of whom 151 were Jews (41.6%).

Stratyn was famous for being the seat of the Stratyn Hassidic court of the Brandwein rabbinical family. In the beginning of the 19th century Rabbi Yehudah Zvi Hirsch Brandwein of Stratyn — a student of Rabbi Uri of Strzeliska, known as the Saraf (burning angel), who was the student of Rabbi Shlomo of Karlin— founded the Stratyn Hassidic dynasty. Rabbi Yehuda Zvi Brandwein, who lived during the first half of the 19th century, was one of the most influential and well-known Admorim in the towns of eastern Galicia. He was noted for his remedies and cures (segulot) for diseases and for women with difficulties in bearing children. He was bitterly opposed by the Maskilim of Tarnopol, who accused him, before the Austrian government, of taking money from his followers under false pretenses, by giving amulets that he claimed had the power of curing diseases and other ailments. In their campaign, they used the letter that Rabbi Yehuda Zvi Hirsch wrote to his Hassid, Yitzchak Chaim Moishes in Gologory, in which he suggested "remedies" to cure his sick wife. The Austrian government conducted investigations against him in this matter.

His position as Admor was inherited by his eldest son, Rabbi Avraham, whose brother, Rabbi Eliezer (Reb Laiserel), became the Admor in Jezupol. He had two sons—Rabbi Uri, who inherited his father's position in Jezupol, and Rabbi Nachum, who became the rabbi of Stratyn in the year 1865 at the age of 18. After a few years he moved to Bursztyn and was the Admor there until 1914. He was a Cabalist and a very erudite man who published four books on Cabala—*Imrey Tov*, *Imrey Chaim*, *Imrey Brachah*, and *Imrey*

Ratzon. He established a stately court in Bursztyn where a large number of "residents" lived at his expense. There were many "Stratyner Hassidim" in the surrounding towns of Bursztyn, Rohatyn, Bukaczowce, Bolszowce, and Nadworna. After his passing in 1915, the Stratyn court was divided up into two courts—one headed by his son, Eliezer, and the other, by his son-in-law, Rabbi Isaac of Podhajce. The son of Rabbi Eliezer, Rabbi Moshe, renewed his grandfather's court in Bursztyn in 1935. He was killed together with his wife and children during the Holocaust.

Bolszowce: Bolszowce is first mentioned in documents dating from 1436. In 1578 it became the property of the Szeniewski family, which owned it until 1624. In the year 1624, it became a town with the right of holding markets. The marketing fairs for oxen were especially well known. In the 19th century the town was owned by Kornel Kaszczonowicz, a well-known Polish statesman, who was a member of the Sejm of Galicia as well as a member of the Austrian parliament.

In 1765, there were 178 Jews in Bolszowce, of whom 166 were adults and 12 were children.

In 1880, it had a total population of 2,932 inhabitants, of whom 1,760 were Jews (58% of the population).

In 1890, the town contained 364 houses and 3,481 inhabitants, of whom 2,058 were Jews (59.1% of the population).

In 1900, the town contained 415 houses with 3,938 inhabitants, of whom 2,256 were Jews (57.3% of the population).

In 1910, the town had grown to 4,029 inhabitants, of whom 2,438 were Jews (52.7% of the population).

By the year 1921, the population had fallen to 2,186 inhabitants, of whom 825 were Jews (37.7% of the population).[Ed8]

Ed8 No source is given for the data about the surrounding towns. Presumably it comes from Bohdan Wasiutynski: Ludnosc zydowska or Stanislaw Gruinski, Materialy.

Royal Charter for the Jews of Rohatyn

YB p. 68

Michael Dei gratia rex Poloniae, magnus dux Lithuaniae, Russiae, Prusiae, Masoviae, Samogitiae, Kiioviae, Volhyniae, Livoniae, Smolensciae, Severiae Czerniechoviaeque. Significamus praesentibus literis nostris quorum interest universis et singulis productas nobis fuisse literas pargameneas manu serenissimi Joannis Casimiri subscriptas sigillo regni communitas, sanas, salvas et illaesas omnique vitio et suspicionis nota carentes, continentes in se confirmacionem privilegiorum Judaeorum Rohatynensjum supplicatumpue nobis, ut easdem literas ex benignitate nostra regia approbare, confirmare et innovare dignaremur, tenoris sequentis: Ioannes Casimirus Dei gratia rex. Poloniae, magnus dux Lithuaniae, Russiae, Prussiae, Masoviae, Samogitiae, Livoniae, Volyniae, Kiioviae, Smolensciae, Czerniechoviaeque, necnon Sueccorum Gottorum Vandalorumque haereditarius rex. Significamus praesentibus literis nostris quorum interest universis et singulis. Reproductas nobis esse nomine infidelium ludaeorum oppidi Rohatyn literas infrascriptas papiraceas videlicet extractum privilegii certi serenissimi divae memoriae Vladislai IV fratris et praedecessoris nostri desideratissimi, eisdem infidelibus ludaeis benigne largiti et ad acta castrensia capitanealia Leopoliensia oblati et suscepti authenticum et suspicioni non obnoxium tenoris sequentis: Actum in castro inferiori Leopoliensi feria quinta post festum Purificationis Beatissimae Virginis Mariae proxima anno Domini millesimo sexcentesimo trigesimo quarto. Ad officium et acta praesentia castrensia capitanealia Leopoliensia personaliter veniens perfidus Zelig synagogus ludaeorum Leopoliensium obtulit eidem officio privilegium sacrae regiae maiestatis infrascriptum ratione (sic) ludaeis Rohatinensibus benigniter concessum, authenticum, manu propria eiusdem sacrae regiae maiestatis subscriptum, petens illud ab eodem officio suscipi per oblatam, quod et obtinuit, cuius privilegii tenor sequitur talis: Władysław Czwarty z łaski Bożej król polski, wielki, xiąże litewski, ruski, pruski, mazowiecki, żmudzki, inflantski, szwedzki, gottski, wandalski, dziedziczny król, obrany wielki car moskiewski. Oznajmuję wszem wobec i każdemu zosobna komu to wiedzieć należy teraźniejszym listem naszym. Aczkolwiek prawa wszytkie rzeczypospolitej naszej i miastom w niej będącym na sejmie koronaciej królewskiej naszej approbowaliśmy, jednak i teraz Żydom miasta naszego Rohatyna, na pokorną prośbę ich wszystkie przywileja, dekreta, lustracje domów, gruntów, w której mieszkają bużnicę i kierchowa, handle i pożywienie wszelakie, nic niewyjmując, kupowania i przedawania, tak ołowiu jako i innych wszelakich towarów, szynki wszelakiego napoju, warzenia piwa, miodu robienia, palenia gorzałki, reczników wolne przedawania i kupowania bydła i mięsa tak całkiem jako sztukami na rynku, na starym dawnym miejscu, a wszystko nie nieexcypując, równo z mieszczanami tamecznymi według przywileju i starodawnego zwyczaju. Podatki miejskie także równo z mieszczanami dawać niemają ale podług praw i zwyczajów dawnych zachowani być mają. Które to wszytkie zwyczaje i prawa im dawno należące teraźniejszym listem naszym, jeżeli są w ich w używaniu i nie przeciwko prawu pospolitemu aprobujemy i obowiązujemy, potwierdzamy, chcąc aby od każdego wcale zachowane zostały i moc wieczną miały. Na co dla lepszej wiary ręką swą list ten podpisawszy pieczęć koronną przycisnąć rozkazaliśmy. Dan w Warszawie, dnia marca XXVII roku Pańskiego M D C XXXIII. panowania naszych królestw polskiego i szwedzkiego roku pierwszego. Vladislaus rex. Marcus Skibicki. Post cusius ingrossationem exemplar originale eidem offerenti ab officio praesenti est resitutum. Martinus Borkowski vicecapitaneus Leopoliensis (L. S.). Ex actis castrensibus Leopoliaensibus extractum correxit Stasiorowski. Atque supplicatum est nobis nomine eorundem Judaeorum oppidi nostri Rohatyn videlicet a tota synagoga, ut praeinsertas privilegii literas tum renovare tum etiam approbare et confirmare authoritate nostra regia dignaremur. Cui supplicationi uti iustae morem gerentes easdem literas privilegii serenissimi fratris nostri defuncti renovamus et simul in omnibus punctis, clausulis et conditionibus descriptis approbamus et confirmamus volentes easdem in quantum iuri communi non contrariae ususque illarum habetur, ius et robur suum perpetuum habere debere. In cuius rei fidem praesentes manu nostra subscriptas sigillo regni communiri iussimus. Datum Leopoli die XXI mensis Maii anno Domini MDCLXIII regnorum nostrorum Poloniae et Sueciae XV Ioannes Casimirus rex. Stephanus Hankiewicz secretarius sacrae regiae maiestatis. Naostatek ponieważ wniesiona do nas jest supplika od niewiernych Żydów rohatyńskich, abyśmy im targi, które zawsze w dzień wtorkowy zdawna w Rohatynie bywały, na co i dokumenta z metryki pokazać gotowi, reassumowali i tenże dzień wtorkowy targowy uczynili. Tedy przychylając się ku słusznej tychże niewiernych Żydów prośbie a do tego widząc jako i od nieprzyjaciela przez te czasy w tamtych krajach zniszczeni, żeby się tedy ratować jako najprędzej i handle swoje z większym pożytkiem prowadzić mogli, wzwyż mianowany dzień targowy, jako dawno był, reassumujemy i naznaczamy. Nos itaque Michael rex praefatae supplicacioni ac ipsius aequitati benigne annuentes praeinsertas literas in omnibus earum punctis, clausulis, articulis approbandum et confirmandum esse. duximus, uti quidem approbaums et confirmamus praesentibus literis nostris decernentes easdem vim et robur perpetuae firmitatis obtinere debere, in quantum iuris est et usus earum ratio habetur. In cuius rei fidem praesentes manu nostra subscriptas sigillo regni communiri iussimus. Datum Cracoviae in comitiis felicis coronationis nostrae die XXII mensis Novembris anno Domini MCLXIX regni nostri anno primo. Michael rex.

Kronika pow. Rohatyńskiego t. VI nr. 1. p. 7—8. : ב נדפס

Order of the Sejmik in Sadowa Wisznia

Following the dispute of the Jews with the Frankists in Lwow in 1759

YB p. 70

Ponieważ z dysputy publicznej ne Lwowie roku 1759 między Żydami talmudzistami i kontratalmudzistami odprawianej, Żydzi talmudzistowie oczywistami dowodami (jako sufficientissime książką przez J. Mci Księdza Pikulskiego Zakonu O. O. św. Franciszka regularnej obserwacji prowincji ruskiej „teologa titulo" „Złość żydowska" — w roku, przeszłym tysiącznym siedemsetnym sześćdziesiątym we Lwowie do druku podana informuje, zostają od kontratalmudzistów dostatecznie przekonani, iż zamiast obserwy prawa mojżeszowego w wierze swojej talmudami się rządzą pod pretextem nabożeństwa wiarę naszą świętą katolicka, tudzież Syna Boskiego Odkupiciela narodu ludzkiego i Matkę Najświętszą Protektorkę wszystkich nas prawdziwych katolików (Horret animus cogitare lingua loqui) ustawicznie bluźnią, przeto aby Zelantów wiary katolickiej na wygubienie siebie ciż bluźniercy nie pobudzili, a per consequens wewnętrznego zamieszania nie byli okazyą, albo też za tę disymulacyą, i protekcyą w państwie naszym katolickim takowych bluźnierców i ustawicznych szarpańców honoru Boskiego, Bóg w Trójcy Świętej jedyny, sprawiedliwym sądem oprócz pogróżek w terazniejszym czasie praktykowanych (na ojczyzny naszej zniszczenie) sowitej nie zapłacił kary, więc od avertenda utraque immumentia pericula. J. W. posłowie zelo religionis amore. Zbawiciela swego Syna Boskiego i Matki jego ostatniej grzeszących ucieczki instabunt do najjaśniejszego majestatu, conferent cum ordinibus, proponentque medium takowe: primo aby Żydzi w Koronie i w kś. litewskiem zostający we wszystkich dyecezyach znajdujące się księgi swoje wszystkie hebrajskim albo żydowskim stylem drukowane, czyli też pisane ad loci ordinarios lub ich officiales in spation roku komportowali i tam do spalenia deponowali; secundo aby ci Żydzi talmudzistowie ani ksiąg ani pisania

87

jakiegośkolwiek stylu hebrajskiego między sobą nie zażywali, lecz polskiego i łacińskiego stylu lub języka w potrzebach swoich używali; tertio aby wszystkie drukarnie i szkoły do ćwiczenia stylu i języka hebrajskiego oraz żydowskiego, zakazane i skasowane zostały, jeżeli zaś do nabożeństwa podług opisu prawa Mojżeszowego byle bez bluźnierstwa na religią katolicką i majestat Boski ksiąg i pisania stylem polskim lub łacińskim predentowali, to ich szczególna pretensya abrogari nie powinna; quarto, gdy w bożnicach swoich czyli to w święta i szabasy, czyli w dni powszedne nabożeństwa swoje polskim jednak językiem albo łacińskim odprawować będą, aby bluźnierstwa warowali się, zawsze dwóch księży czyli to z kościoła albo też z magistratu miasta onego dwa delegowani attentowali, za którą attendencyą, abyśmy uniknęli cenzury szukania privati lucri attendentes nie pretentować ani też dobrowolnej offerencyi, akceptować nie mają. A gdyby któremukolwiek z pomienionych, któremu artykułowi talmudzistowie Żydzi sprzeciwili się i wypełnić kiedykolwiek iunctim et partitim nie chcieli albo z nich jedna jakowa osoba sprzeciwiła się, paenam colli subire powinien, o co forum ziemstwa lub grodu proprii territorii ad instantiam cuiusvis zelantis, prascisa quavis appellatione naznaczywszy.

(Akta grodzkie i ziemskie z archiwum Bernadyńskiego we Lwowie, t. XXIII Lauda sejmikowe, wiszeńskie, lwowskie, przemyskie i sanockie 1731—1772. Wydał: Antoni Prochaska, Lwów 1928 r. p. 416—417 §§ 12).

Collected Sources on Rohatyn during the Time of the Sabbatean Movement

Collected and Adapted by Yehoshua Spiegel, Tel Aviv

Translated by Rabbi Mordecai Goldzweig - YB p.72

A. Shimon Dubnow, History of the Eternal People, Vol 3, Chapter 53, "Mystics and Hidden Sabbateans"

Among the Messianic sects, there arose the desire to put an end to Jewish suffering no matter what this would entail, even to the point of reaching a compromise between Judaism and Christianity, similar to the compromise made by the Turkish Sabbateans with Islam. In the wake of these desires, the Frankist movement arose (1672–1699). The man who succeeded in gathering around him these desperate straying individuals who were prepared to leave the Jewish community was two-faced—one face turned toward Judaism and the other toward Christianity. He was born into a background of opposition to the traditional rabbinic approach.[Tr1] As opposed to the disciplined observance of the Talmud, he propounded the sanctity of the Zohar, in which he claimed were to be found anthropomorphic sources for the godliness of the Messiah and the worship of the "Shechina." He replaced asceticism with release of the sexual appetite, terming it "a mitzvah" and part of religious fervor. As a result, after a few months of this type of behavior, he came to the attention of the rabbis. On Sivan 5516 (1756), the Va'ad Arba Aratzos (Council of Four Lands) in Brody placed an edict of excommunication on the whole cult, distancing and separating them from the Jewish community and proclaiming their wives and daughters "harlots" and their sons and daughters "utter bastards." The text of the excommunication was signed by Rabbi Chaim Rappaport of Lwow and 13 other rabbis and was made public under the name of Cherev Piphiot (Double Edged Sword). It was sent to all the Jewish communities, where the excommunication was proclaimed publicly in the synagogues, in the traditional fashion, to the sounding of the shofar and the extinguishing of candles.[1]

Tr1 His father, Leib, was dismissed from his position as sexton for teaching Sabbatean dogma.

1   It stands to reason that Rabbi Avraham David Moshe, the man of Troyes, Chief Rabbi of Rohatyn, was one of those who signed. This I gathered from the introductions to his work Mirkevet Hamishne on the Mechilta of Rabbi Ishmael, as one who at that time pursued and condemned Sabbatai Zvi and his followers and "put a spear in the body

The Debate in Kaminetz—20 June 1757

The participating members of the sect who took part in the debate included the leaders from Galicia—Leib Krysa from Nadworna, Elisha Schorr and his son, Shlomo, from Rohatyn, and 15 other people from Podolia and Galicia.

The Debate in Lwow—17 July 1759[Ed1]

The debate began on 17 July 1759 and took place in the large Catholic cathedral of Lwow before an assembly of churchmen and dignitaries. The Jews, loyal to the Talmud, sent as their representatives 40 rabbis and sages, headed by the chief rabbi of Lwow, Rabbi Chaim Rappaport. Representing the Frankists were, again, Jacob Frank and his close advisers—Leib Krysa of Nadworna and Shlomo Schorr of Rohatyn. Krysa and Schorr were the main speakers for the sect, since their leader, Frank, was not sufficiently fluent in Polish... (After the debate many Frankists converted to Christianity.) In Lwow alone, between 1759-60, 514 Frankists became Christians, men and women, led by the leaders of the group from Galici— Leib Krysa and Shlomo Schorr. (The latter came to be known as Franciszek Wolowski.)

B. History of the Jews, (H. Graetz), Volume 6, Page 110

"Among these Frankists who opposed the Talmud were rabbis and preachers—Yehuda Leib Krysa, a rabbi from Nadworna, and Rabbi Nachman ben Shmuel Levi of Busk. Most prominent among the Polish Sabbateans or Frankists was Elisha Schorr of Rohatyn, an elderly man of distinguished lineage. His son and his daughter, Chaya, who supposedly knew the Zohar by heart and was considered to be a prophetess, nevertheless, behaved in a very loose manner. His grandchildren and his sons-in-law had already become complete converts to Sabbateanism to the point where they jeered at rabbinic Judaism on the slightest pretext."

In the year 1800, the leaders of the sect, the brothers Wolowski (previously Schorr of Rohatyn), disseminated a manifesto to the Jewish communities of Podolia and Volhynia to the effect that one should not reject "the Edomite beliefs," because only they would enable the Jews to continue to exist. However, these declarations were seized by the Russian government, which

---

of Elisha Schorr of Rohatyn," one of the preachers of the above Messianic movement. All of this I will better clarify in a separate chapter, "Our Town of Rohatyn."
Ed1 For details about the trial and the Frankists, see Gelber's chapter "A History of the Jews of Rohatyn."

suspected this so-called Edomite sect of being in reality a secret society of revolutionaries and sent them to St. Petersburg for investigation.

C. Introduction to Mirkevet Hamishne

"This is the history of the first Adam, the great Adam, among the giants, our grandfather, a true Gaon and tzaddik and example to this generation, the rabbi and teacher, David Moshe Avraham, the man of Troyes—Ashkenazi, Z"L, whose honorable abode and light appeared in our town, the holy community of Rohatyn. "For there the place of the lawgiver was hidden (Deuteronomy 33:21),"[Tr2] i.e., for he was buried in Rohatyn and where the tree took root there are to be found its fruits, his great-grandchildren and grandchildren, May the Lord bless them. Known far and wide as a Gaon and tzaddik who ruled powerfully here and disputed with the giants of his day in a number of responsa. Among these great men who gave letters of approval to this book, *Mirkevet Hamishne*, are the Gaon, paragon of his generation, our rabbi and teacher, Rabbi Chaim HaCohen Rappaport, chief rabbi of Lwow, who reads [from the Torah] first; and after him, the Levi, the Gaon and paragon of his day, our teacher, Rabbi Yitzchak Landau, Z"L, who, at the time when he was chief rabbi of Zolkiew and later became chief rabbi and justice of Cracow and its environs, agreed with him to fulfill the will of the tzaddik and to publish the masterpiece.

"He (Rabbi Adam) passed on to eternal life and was unable to fulfill his desires, leaving behind him many works, as the author writes in his introduction. Their light was hidden for approximately one hundred and fifty years—these dear works—one here, one there, and many years have passed, and no one thought to spread this beam of light.

"And since the author, the Gaon, Z"L, was taken from us so many years ago, we decided that it is proper to tell our brothers of this generation something of the greatness of the author, that the Gaon, Z"L, was zealous for his G-d and brought forgiveness to the Children of Israel. He was zealous with zeal for the Lord of Hosts when there arose that evil offspring of the cursed sect, and the last of them, after they fell at the debate before the nobility of the holy Jewish community of Lwow, may the teeth of the wicked rot. To separate the unclean from the pure paragon of the generation, our teacher and rabbi, Chaim HaCohen Rappaport, together with the paragon of the generation, our teacher .

Tr2   A comparison between Moshe Rabbeinu and Rabbi Adam, one of whose names was Moshe. Rashi explains that the Tribe of Gad decided to settle in Trans-Jordan because they knew that Moshe Rabbeinu would be buried in their territory, and their love for him was so great that they did not want to leave him.

and rabbi, Nota Ashkenazi, chief rabbi of Rozdol. "The accursed criminal came to our town to entice Jews to the heart of the errant, but the Gaon, the author, Z"L, arose to do battle against this evil and took his spear in his hand, endangering his life for the purpose of beating and chasing him to the end. This criminal succeeded in deceiving the governor of the town and in bringing him to his rescue and causing him to drive the chief rabbi out of town. He, the rabbi, took his life in his hands and did not protect himself while attacking him and pushing him out with all his might, in order to prevent Jews from being deluded into following him. The Creator came to his aid, and this accursed criminal abjured his faith, becoming the means for ending the evil. No longer would he be able to cause any Jews to leave the fold. Our grandfather told us that their parents told them that the Holy Ba'al Shem Tov, Z"L, came to him in person to inform him that he was sent as a messenger by the Heavens to impart to him their appreciation and approbation of his zeal on behalf of the Lord of Hosts. It is similar to what was written by Moshe Rabbeinu, Z"L, who states at the time that Pinchas, the son of Elazar, the son of Aharon, the Cohen, was zealous for the Lord. It is written, "Therefore, say unto him, Behold I present to him my covenant of peace." Rashi, Z"L, explains, "Similar to when a person shows his appreciation and friendship to one who has done him a kindness." His greatness, wisdom, and piety are still being related, just as it was told by their ancestors."

ספר

מרכבת המשנה

ביאור רחב על המכילתא דר' ישמעאל מרב האי גאון בוצינא
קדישא קדוש אלהים כש"ת מוהרי"ר דוד משה אברהם זללה"ה
איש מרויש אשכנזי זללה"ה האב"ד דק'ק ראהאטין :

לעמבערג

הוצא לבית הדפוס עי חרבני הנניד פיחר"ר יחזקאל נאלרשלאג ני'
בדפוס של הנגידה מרת פעסיל באלאבאן חיי'
בשנת תרנ"ה לפ"ק,

Lemberg
Druck von
Pessel Balaban
1894

Marke weth Hamischna
Nachdruck verboten.

p. 74, YB. Title page of the only existing book by the Gaon, Rabbi David Moshe Avraham, Justice of the Holy Community of Rohatyn, which was completed in 5500 (1740) and printed in 5655 (1895) in Lwow. [From this we learn that 150 years passed before this work was printed in 5655 (1895) in Lwow. According to this, the book was originally written over 200 years ago. Author's note.]

Reb Yudel Finds a Husband for His Daughter in Rohatyn

Excerpts from "The Bridal Canopy" by S.Y. Agnon

Translated by Rabbi Mordecai Goldzweig - YB p. 75

In short, Reb Yudel was staying in Brzezany, living like one of the manna eaters[Tr1] until it was time for him to leave. From Brzezany, they turned southwest, that is to say toward Lemberg (Lwow), because the places between Brzezany and Lemberg abound in riches far more than other places. And they arrived in a village called Kushan; it was Thursday, and Reb Yudel wanted to remain there for Shabbos because he was accustomed during all of his travels to remain in the same place from Thursday to Motzei Shabbos (when Shabbos ends) "in order to add from the mundane to the holy," i.e., he was curtailing his weekday activities before Shabbos required it. But since he could not find a mikveh there to immerse himself in honor of Shabbos, he was forced to arise and travel to another place. In short, he left Kushan and went to the "holy community" of Rohatyn.

The sun stood in the heavens and colored the face of the earth, and, although the winds from the mountain tops quietly blew and brought the smell of snow, one did not feel the cold.

And Reb Yudel said, "Reb Nota, when we reach the town, take me to a place of lodging" to which he (Nota) responded, "And where else would I take you if not to a lodging where you are provided with a table and a bed and some money?" He (Reb Yudel) answered, "I will explain what I mean. Normally, when we come into a town, you drop me off at the Beis Medresh (House of Study) and you go off to feed your horses. But now, what I would like you to do is bring me to an inn." So he said to him, "And why is this town so different from all other towns, that 'your honor' requests to go to an inn? Innkeepers want money, and, if you do not pay them for your food and lodgings, they collect what is owed to them by taking your belongings and throwing you out." He answered, "Please Nota, please don't force me to tell you what came to my mind. I was thinking that I would like to eat a piece of bread of my own. It is true that I have 200 gulden, and according to the laws of the Torah, I am forbidden to touch charity money. So bring me to an inn and stop asking questions." Nota grabbed his head and screamed, "Heavens, is Reb Yudel going crazy? Everyone feels obligated to feed Reb Yudel, and Reb Yudel feels obligated to throw out his money! And what about his wife and

---

Tr1 He did not have to make any exertions to obtain his daily needs; it all came from Heaven.

children? What will become of them? But, oh well, what's the sense of arguing with him? In any case, he ends up doing exactly the opposite of anything he makes up his mind to do." When they arrived in Rohatyn, Reb Yudel repeated, "Bring me to an inn." When Nota heard this, he said to himself, "Nota will do what he is asked, and we will see what comes of it."

In short, Reb Yudel installed himself at the inn and sat and studied Torah. The innkeeper asked Nota, "Who is this man?" And Nota answered, "If you knew who this is you would crawl on your belly before him." So he went away, his curiosity half unsatisfied. He was terribly anxious to know who this guest was. So something inside told him, "Stand by the door, place your eye to the keyhole and peep into his room to see what he is doing, quickly open the door and enter." And he followed his heart. . . All day he stood bent over in front of the doorway, peeping into the keyhole until his back became hunched, and then he suddenly entered. And what was Reb Yudel doing? He was used to hiding his learning in the Torah and, if a person is in the habit of hiding his ways, he will continue to do so especially in an inn. The innkeeper said to his wife, "This is very strange. A man sits in an inn, spends money like a rich man and does not leave his room to go out and do business."

His wife said, "You're telling me something new? Just what you are wondering, I have been wondering, too." Suddenly she cried out, "Be quiet!" He said, "Why are you screaming so loud?" So she said, "I'll tell you why. He has a grown daughter in his house and wants to marry her off." And who told this woman that Reb Yudel was looking for a match for his daughter? Except that Reb Yudel's face had that look of a man who is weighed down with the problem of daughters, because people in this condition are betrayed by this look on their faces. In short, they decided to notify the shadchan (matchmaker).

The shadchan came, entered Reb Yudel's room, sighed deeply and said, "May the Creator help you." Reb Yudel raised his eyes from the Gemara and answered, "May you also be helped by the Creator." The shadchan said, "Blessed is the one who is here," and Reb Yudel answered, "Blessed is the one who has come." So he gave him Shalom and received Shalom. The shadchan took a chair, sat down in front of him and took out a snuff box. He opened the box, gave him a full pinch of snuff and started to speak to him in a down-to-earth fashion and said, "By the way, since I happened to come in, may I incidentally ask his honor what caused his honor to trouble himself to come here?" Reb Yudel quoted the citation from Tractate Chulin 7, "A man does not lift his finger below unless it is so decreed above." "And if I came here it is because the Creator so decided." The shadchan said, "Since the Creator invited us to meet in the same place perhaps something will come of this to our mutual benefit." So the Hassid Reb Yudel asked, "What do you mean?" The shadchan put his right hand on his head and rubbed with all five fingers into his hair. "And if I were to propose a match for your honor, what then?" the shadchan continued and smiled. Reb Yudel answered, "Blessed is He who reminds us of things forgotten. I too have been traveling because of my daughter who has reached the age of marriage." So the shadchan said, "What is your honor looking for, that is, what type of bridegroom does your honor want?" Reb Yudel answered, "You asked a good question. After all, in the end a person has to have the fear of G-d, and if the Holy One were to present me with a religious young man who can learn a page of Gemara, I would give him my daughter." The shadchan asked Reb Yudel, "What is your honor's name?" He said to him, "My name is Yudel". So he said to him, "And from where does your honor come?" He replied, "I am from Brody." "And what is your honor's family name?" "The name of my family is Nathan-Son." When the shadchan heard the name Yudel Nathan-Son he became very impressed because Reb Yudel Nathan-Son was a very rich man, and his good name wafted like balsam all over the country.

The shadchan said to himself, "I will go to Vovi Schorr who is a very rich man, whose son is looking for a bride, and I will notify him that Reb Yudel Nathan-Son came here and is looking for a groom for his daughter." The shadchan then received permission from Reb Yudel and went to Reb Vovi Schorr.

When Reb Vovi heard this he arose and said, "I am offering twelve thousand gulden." The shadchan took to his feet and returned to Reb Yudel and said, "I am now coming from the home of Reb Vovi Schorr. The outstanding young man, Mr. Sheftel, that is the son of Reb Vovi, has reached the "Perek ha-ish mekadesh."[Tr2] And your honor's daughter has also reached the stage of "besula nisat."[Tr3] In short, I only mean to ask how much dowry your honor is presenting." Reb Yudel replied, "Whatever the father of the groom is offering, I offer for my daughter."

In short, in less than an hour, the shadchan returned to Reb Yudel with a marvelous looking young man, handsome, very learned, immersed in piety and pampered since he was a child with the knowledge and wisdom of the Torah. Reb Yudel tested him and found him to be full of old wisdom, e.g., the Torah. He became greatly attached to him immediately. It went so far that he called him "my son," and this attachment reached the point where he found him worthy of

---

Tr2 The second chapter of Tractate Kedushin which deals with betrothals.

Tr3 Besula niseit l'yom ha-r'vi'i – A maiden is married on the fourth day etc., e.g. the first words in Tractate Ketubot which deals primarily with marriage contracts.

marrying his daughter.

By the time the stars came out, they wrote the engagement contract, broke plates and made merry with food and drink—songs and praises to the Lord.

(Ecclesiastes 3) "'Everything has its time...,' as King Solomon wrote," said Reb Yudel. "I enjoy my stay in Rohatyn far more than my jostling on the road, but the time has come to return to Brody and tell my daughter, Pessele, that I have found her a husband. I haven't told her anything yet."

Yet Reb Yudel continued to remain in Rohatyn, to eat, drink and learn and debate on topics in the Torah until he saw that his money was running out and decided to return; he paid his expenditures and took leave of his future in-law, Reb Sheftel, and all of his other friends, and left Rohatyn. He who did not see the happiness of the two future in-laws when they parted never saw a happy parting of in-laws. Reb Yudel was happy to be on the way back to Brody and was happy that his in-law lived in Rohatyn.

But why was Reb Vovi happy? There is a reason for this. All the time that Reb Yudel was staying in Rohatyn, Reb Vovi was afraid that Reb Yudel might hear things that he shouldn't, such as—that the ancestors of Reb Vovi were followers of Sabbatai Zvi, may his name be erased. They said about the great-grandfather of Reb Vovi (in other words, about one hundred years before), that on Tishah B'Av, he used to go down to a cellar to eat half a small cherry, at which time he would say, "If Sabbatai Zvi is the true messiah, I am fulfilling the requirement for the meal,"[Tr4] and if Sabbatai Zvi is not the messiah, it is as if he has not eaten anything, since what he ate is less than the size of an olive. Because of half cherries such as these, families were uprooted, and Satan was still dancing. And the problems still existed, because it was difficult for Reb Vovi to find brides for his sons, because his enemies used to poke fun at him saying, "Did you see that Sabbatean whose grandfather ate on Tishah B'Av?" and Reb Vovi was afraid that they would bring his shortcomings to the attention of his forthcoming in-laws. But he did not realize that this was a match made in heaven, and even if all the jealous people in the world would get together, they could not have broken up the match.

Tr4 If Sabbatai Zvi is the messiah, then he would be permitted to eat on Tishah B'Av.

The Hassidut of Stratyn
By Yehoshua Spiegel, Tel Aviv

Translated by Rabbi Mordecai Goldzweig - YB p.78

There lies before me a thin book that contains 88 pages in all in a format of one sixteenth of a full newspaper sheet. It has a black binding with the title engraved in letters of gold—Sefer Degel Machane Yehuda. On the inside of the page this title is repeated with the addition of the sentence, "And in it, opened before you, are three books of the rabbi and Tzaddik, Rabbi Yehuda Zvi, Z"L, and his Holy Children, Z"L."

The whole book is printed in Rashi script and was published by the brothers Eliezer and Chaim Brandwein, the grandsons of the holy rabbi, our teacher and rabbi, Yehuda Zvi of Stratyn. It was printed in Jerusalem in the year 5717 (1957). This book was obtainable then at M. D. Blum of Meah Shearim, Jerusalem, as recorded in the frontispiece. I, however, received this book from Rabbi Yehuda Zvi Brandwein, Shlita, one of the descendents of the Admor (Hassidic leader) Rabbi, Avramtsche of Stratyn, Z"L. It is stamped with his seal, "the Admor of Stratyn." In this introduction, I will attempt to present something of the background lineage of Rabbi Brandwein.

Rabbi Avramtsche had four daughters and no sons. The first one, Bluma,[Trl] was the wife of Rabbi Uri of Rohatyn. The second one, Ester, was the wife of Rabbi Aaron of Felsztyn, near Sambor. The third one, Leah, was the wife of Rabbi Berish of Dolina, and the fourth one became the wife of Rabbi Pinchas of Brzezany. Rabbi Yehuda Zvi Brandwein of Israel is the grandson of Rabbi Aaron of Felsztyn, a continuation of the line of the family of Rabbi Avramtsche Brandwein. The others are considered to be part of the family of Rabbi Uri Langner. The following were the sons of Rabbi Uri of Rohatyn: Rabbi Yitzchak Isaac Langner, who went to Bobrka, Rabbi Avraham Langner, who went to Knihynicze, Rabbi Yisrael Langner, who went to Brody, Rabbi Moshe Langner, who went to Kosow and in our town there was Rabbi Shlomo Langner, whose children were Yehuda Zvi, Toibe, Uri, Avraham, and Yisrael, may their souls rest in peace.

At my request, Rabbi Brandwein permitted me to use this book in obtaining the following information, which according to the publisher

Trl *Encyclopedia L'Chochmei Galicia* by Rabbi Meir Wunder, Vol. 1, Pps. 593–94, states that Bluma was the wife of Pinchas Brandwein of Brzezany, and Sarah, the wife of Rabbi Uri Langner of Rohatyn.

ספר

רגל

מחנה יהודה

וכו

שלושה ספרים נפתחים

מהרב הצדיק

דבי יהודה צבי זצ"ל

מסטרעטין

ומבניו הק זי"ע

עיה"ק
ירושלים
תובב"א

This is the Gate Through Which the Righteous Enter
Blessed Is G-D

The Book

Degel Machane Yehuda

And In It Opened before You Are Three Books
of the Rabbi and Tzaddik

Rabbi Yehuda Zvi, Z"L,
Of Stratyn

And His Holy Children, May Their Merits Protect Us

The Holy City of
Jerusalem
May It Speedily Be Rebuilt

Title page of the book Degel Machane Yehuda. Added to this book as an appendix was the booklet "Remedies and Cures of Rabbi Yehuda," enumerating remedies for various ailments that were thought to have had some value even by standards of conventional medicine.

99

contains "articles that are pleasant and sweeter than honey, written by his holy children, Z"L."

The publisher continues, "And now to you, sirs, do I call; take this blessing into your home at full price, and I pray for you and for your family that through the merit of these tzaddikim, you will be helped from the Source of Blessings and Great Success, and may the Almighty fulfill all your heart's desires for good."

The worship of the Creator contains within it the use of different texts of prayers that are said through pleading, are written poetically, and involve different forms of behavior, bearing, and the like. There is the Ashkenazi text of prayer, which differs from the Sephardi version, which is again different from the Yemenite version, and there is even extant a Karaite version of prayer and its like. Similarly, customs differ at weddings, circumcisions, and funeral services. Even among Hassidim, there are large and small differences based on customs, texts, and versions attributed to this or that rebbe.

The book Degel Machane Yehuda details the customs of Stratyn for the whole year. The rabbis of Stratyn were considered to be miracle workers like other tzaddikim of their generations, such as the Ruzhiner, the Zydaczower, the Czortkower, the Belzer, and others. Even people who were not so religious were accustomed to come to them in their time of need to ask for their help. When a tzaddik passed away, his Hassidim remained devoted to his sons and other descendents. The Degel Machane Yehuda tells about two of these children, tales and stories that were passed on by word of mouth. I cannot completely ignore them as some of them do have a grain of historical truth within them.

The following are a few of these stories:

The Holy Rebbe, Rabbi Shmelke of Nickelsburg, Z"L, went on a trip for a worthy cause, and by Shabbos he had gotten as far as the town of Zawalow. The Holy Rabbi Shmuel Zanvill, Z"L, the chief rabbi of Zawalow, received him in keeping with his exalted stature, but the people of the town did not. When the Holy Rebbe Shmelke decided to leave, he called the chief rabbi and said to him, "Tell me what blessing you would like."

And the rabbi asked to be blessed with a son who will be a tzaddik and a Gaon like the Rebbe, and indeed, there was a son born who filled the house with light, later to become the Holy Rabbi, Yehuda Zvi of Stratyn, Z"L, student of the Holy Rabbi of Strzeliska, Z"L.

Now we know the origin of our teacher, the first Rabbi of Stratyn, Rabbi Yehuda Zvi, who he was and whose son he was.

Our tale begins when he was still a young man, and the people of

Stratyn were in need of a rabbi. They sent a committee to the town of Zawalow to request of the rabbi, the father of Rabbi Yehuda, to permit his son to become the rabbi of their town, but the young man was not willing to accept this position. He was, however, willing to be the town shochet (ritual slaughterer) and returned with them in this capacity.

It soon became known in Stratyn that chickens ran after him to be slaughtered, while cattle crouched down and extended their necks to be slaughtered. In one instance there was an ox that was very wild and gored anyone who came close to him. This ox escaped from his owner, and no one was able to catch him. People therefore advised the owner to have this ox slaughtered by the new shochet of the town, and when the shochet appeared with his slaughtering knife, the ox immediately crouched down and extended his neck to be slaughtered.

The Rabbi of Strzeliska once said, "When Mashiach ben David arrives and all of the tzaddikim come out to receive him, the Ba'al Shem Tov with his students and the Holy Magid, the Rebbe Reb Ber, with his students, I shall come with my student, Reb Yehuda Zvi, and I will have nothing to be ashamed of."

It is related that after the demise of the holy Stratyner, Z"L, a number of Hassidim came to the Ruzhiner to spend Shabbos. After Shabbos the Ruzhiner said, "It is no great marvel that these Hassidim behave as they do, having had such a rebbe, but it is also no great marvel that their rebbe was as elevated as he was, having Hassidim of this stature." And when the Holy Ruzhiner used to refer to the Stratyner, he would call him "my heartfelt friend."

Once when the Holy Ruzhiner met with the Holy Reb Yehuda Zvi, they sat facing each other while important people stood behind them, and the Holy Ruzhiner ordered them to leave the room, permitting no one else to hear what was being said. When the Holy Reb Yehuda Zvi returned to his lodgings, the Holy Ruzhiner sent him one of the tefillin straps of his arm, while Reb Yehuda Zvi sent the Ruzhiner the tefillin strap of his arm.

One time on learning that there was a Hassid from Stratyn travelling to the Admor of Lublin, he sent a kvitel and a pidyon nefesh[Tr2] with him. When the Hassid arrived in Lublin and delivered the kvitel, the Lubliner said, "He shines, he shines all over the world. Tell him in my name to immediately stop being a shochet. Thousands of Jews are waiting impatiently for his prayers to help them in their spiritual elevation, and there is one celestial hall where the prayers of a shochet are not permitted. When you return home, tell him in my name that

---

Tr2 A "kvitel"—special note asking the blessings of the Admor for a request; "pidyon nefesh"—a ransom of the soul, a sum of money sent to the rebbe.

I order him to stop being a shochet." When the Hassid returned, he passed this message on to Rabbi Yehuda Zvi, and this is how he eventually became the Stratyner Rebbe.

It is well known that Rabbi Yehuda Zvi had a book of remedies and cures, and many times he literally saved people's lives through these remedies, but what is not so clear is where he obtained this information. Some say that he obtained it from his holy teacher, the Admor of Strzeliska, Z"L, who in turn learned it from his rebbe, Rabbi Shlomo of Karlin, Z"L, and the Holy Rabbi of Strzeliska said to him, "I never wanted to make use of them for private reasons of my own, but you have my permission to make use of this book."

The Holy Rabbi Meir of Przemyslany, Z"L, called him the "Stratyner Chacham" (Sage of Stratyn). One Purim he sent him a Megilla (scroll) that he himself had written. (This Megilla is now in the possession of the esteemed Rabbi Eliezer Melech, a grandson of Rabbi Yehuda Zvi.) Part of the text of this story is missing, but one gathers that a decree had been written driving the Jews out of the small villages. Rabbi Yehuda Zvi became aware of this and appealed this decision to the Celestial High Court, claiming that it was an unjust act and all that the Gentiles really wanted was to rob the Jews of their property. The Megilla is symbolic of Purim and what occurred then.... The Celestial Court decided to accept Rabbi Yehuda Zvi's appeal, and in the end the Jews were not driven out. (Degel Machane Yehuda, Chapter 36). To this the Holy Rabbi Meir remarked, "Didn't I say that he was a wise man?"

Before he passed away, the Holy Rabbi Zvi of Zydaczow, Z"L, used to sigh and cry and then say, "The reason why I am so upset is because I will have to leave the world, and I do not know of any tzaddik who has the power to aid Jewish souls and arouse pity on them." Later he said, "Now I was informed from heaven that the Holy Rabbi Yehuda Zvi of Stratyn is able to correct the deficiencies of Jewish souls and to bring blessings on them."

The Holy Rabbi Shalom of Belz once told his saintly rebbetzin as follows, "The Stratyner Rabbi was a marvel. I can give truthful testimony to the fact that for three years before his passing, only his body was in this world; his spirit was already in the heavens."

The Rav Gaon of Buczacz upon hearing that Rabbi Yehuda Zvi had come to town went to receive him; when he came close to him, he stood up on a chair and said the blessing Shehechayanu (prayer for new occasions), pronouncing the Holy Names.

There was a man who was caretaker of a river with fish. Once he caught a fish, cut off its tail, and threw it back into the river. For several months thereafter he was unable to catch a single fish. He would spread out his net but did not succeed in catching even one fish. After a few months of this, he went to Rabbi Yehuda Zvi and wanted to know if he had done something wrong at the river. He had completely forgotten about what he had done to one of the fish and could, therefore, not understand why he was being punished and said so to the rabbi. The rabbi asked him whether he had not done something wrong. Finally he reminded himself of what happened, and he related it to the rabbi. The rabbi advised him to spread out his nets on a certain side, because that was where all the fish were congregated, because after he had cut off the fish's tail and embarrassed him, he asked the other fish to hide him. The rabbi ended up by saying, "From this we can learn how careful you have to be when dealing with people." It was known that the Stratyner knew the language of the birds and the speech of the trees and was once asked by one of his friends where he learned how to do this. Who taught it to him? He replied, "If one attaches himself to klipot (this is a concept from Kabbalah), he understands their speech. Certainly then someone who attaches himself to the Creator, who is the source of all life, will certainly understand it. This is not such a big thing."

The Holy Rabbi Yehuda Zvi went up to the heavens on Tuesday, 11 Iyar 5604 (30 April 1844). Approximately 21 years later, when his son, the Holy Rabbi Eliezer of Jezupol, Z"L, passed away in the year 5625 (1865), they dug his grave next to that of his father, Z"L. In the process, a board that was covering the grave of Rabbi Yehuda Zvi fell off, and everyone could see Rabbi Yehuda Zvi lying in his grave, in the shrouds in which he was buried that were as white as they had been on the day that he was buried, while his face looked as if he were sleeping. The Rabbi of Rohatyn who came to eulogize Rabbi Eliezer said, "Now what can the apikursim (non-believers) say to this? It is over twenty years, and you can see clearly that he looks as if he went to sleep yesterday." It was a marvelous sight, that is, it caught the attention of everyone around. May his merit protect us all.

Rabbi Yehuda Zvi had four sons. The first son worshipped the Creator quietly and did not become a rabbi. He became a merchant instead and passed away in his younger years in 5598 (1838). His second son was a holy man. This was our teacher and rabbi, Rabbi Avraham (Avramtche), Z"L, who filled his father's position as Admor in Stratyn to whom thousands of Hassidim and religious people flocked in order to be in his proximity, for he truly worshipped the Almighty in holiness and purity. And what is the work of worship if not prayer? When he prayed, it was with the pouring out of his whole being with great emotion, reminding one of the style of prayer practiced by the Holy Rabbi of Strzeliska, Z"L. He brought succor to the needy and solved their seemingly insurmountable problems when they came to him as a place of last resort. His face was like that of an angel. To this, the

Rabbi of Sacz (Nowy Sacz), Z"L, gave witness in his book Divrei Chaim, Hoshen Mishpat, Siman 32, new edition, in which he wrote, "His face brings fear of the Lord."

When his father, Rabbi Yehuda Zvi, became very ill, he went to the Holy Rabbi of Ruzhin with a pidyon in order to save his father with his prayers. When Rabbi Avraham left, the Ruzhiner said, "It's marvelous! That someone so young should answer to the point so well," and Rabbi Avraham said that at that time he was given ordination to be an Admor by the Ruzhiner. His father (Rabbi Yehuda Zvi) used to say, that if he had not come to the world for any other purpose but to bring down the soul of Rabbi Avraham, the Holy Rabbi Avreimenu, this would have sufficed.

Rabbi Avraham had many Hassidim among whom there were a number of scholars who sat and learned all year and engaged in Torah and worship. Among them there was a young man, an orphan, who sat and learned with a great deal of hatmada (zest) and was an unusually great scholar. When he reached the age of "Ha-ish Mekadesh," the time for him to take a wife, the Rebbe called him over and asked him why he was not fulfilling the commandments of the rabbis—"marriage at 18 years." The young man answered him, "Obviously, because I am very poor." The Rebbe then ordered him to look for a wife and accept the first offer that was presented to him.

The young man went out to fulfill the command of his Rebbe and came to the home of a rich man and owner of a concession who had an unmarried daughter. At the time, there were many people in his house coming and going, but the owner himself was not home. The young man walked over to the oven to warm himself, and people asked him where he was going. He innocently answered—to look for a wife. When they heard this, it occurred to them that this young man could provide them with some fun and told him, "We have a good match for you, the daughter of the owner of this house." The young man innocently answered, "Call her and ask her whether she would be willing to marry me." They called her, and joining in the fun, she replied that she was willing. They then wrote a Tna'im (engagement contract). After this they asked him, "Maybe you would like to get married now?" And he answered, "If the bride is willing, so am I." And so it was. He himself wrote the Ketubah, and the people there carried out the ceremony of the Huppah. A complete legal marriage ceremony had taken place.

In all of this time, the young man was serious, and the people there were having a good time at his expense, while he personally was not aware of it. Then everyone wished him mazel tov and a happy marriage. Having had their fun, the people wanted to go home and go to sleep. They told the young man to get out because they wanted to close the door, to which the young man replied, "Very well, give me my wife, and I will leave, but if you don't, I won't leave." When the people there saw that he was truly serious and would not leave of his own free will, they threw him out by force. And he continued to scream, "Give me my wife!"

In the meantime, the owner returned home and asked what all the noise was about. When they told him what had happened, he was devastated because he realized that his daughter was officially married. He then called the young man and asked him to please release his daughter and give her a divorce. But the young man innocently replied, "Why should I give her a divorce? She is a very pretty girl, of fine character and the daughter of a talmid chacham (a learned man). One is exhorted to take the daughter of a learned man for his wife. If you were to give me anything in the world, I would not release her." The rich man asked him, "Who sent you here?" and the young man replied, "The Admor of Stratyn ordered me to do so, and this is what I did." The rich man replied, "In that case, I am coming with you to the Admor and whatever he decides we will do." The young man answered, "Fine."

When they reached the grounds of the residence of the Holy Admor, the rich man in a desperate effort offered the young man 1,000 rubles if he would divorce his daughter. However, the father of the bride did not have 1,000 rubles with him at that time. So he took out 200 rubles and went with him to buy him a suit of clothes worthy of a rich man. After a month, he gave him 200 rubles and promised to give him the remaining 800 in another month.

Then the rich man came to the home of the Rebbe with his daughter, gave the money to the holy rebbe and asked him to put an end to this affair quietly. The Rebbe answered, "I have a very good match worthy of you and your daughter, a very highly learned young man of very fine character, good looking, and the descendent of a distinguished family. He also has 1,000 rubles to cover the dowry."

The rich man answered that he would be interested in seeing this young man, and if he indeed finds favor with him, he will agree to the match. The Rebbe called in the young man, but he was not recognized as he was dressed like a rich man. He spoke with the young man and determined that he was truly a very learned person, while his daughter, too, was attracted and agreed to marry him.

Then the Rebbe asked him again and again if he was willing to accept this young man as his son-in-law, and he always replied in the positive. The Rebbe then said, "Very well, you may take possession of your wares. This is the young man who came to you and married your daughter. I saw that this match was officially made in heaven where it was announced, "Bat Ploni L'Ploni." (This woman will be married to this man.) However, since this young man was a poor orphan, and your honor would probably not be willing to take such a young man into your family, it was decreed that you must die, and all of your wealth must go to waste, while your daughter must marry him anyway in the end. When I heard this heavenly decree, I sided with you and promised to see to it that the match would be carried out. I did what I could. Now the choice is yours. You can accept the young man and everything will be all right, but if you don't, then you will die." The rich man predictably accepted the young man and gave him his daughter. From then on everything went along smoothly.

Rabbi Avramtche rose to the heavens in a storm (reminiscent of Elijah the Prophet) on 3 Tevet 5625 (January 1865), leaving four daughters who married four rabbis. His first son-in-law was Rabbi Uri (Langner) of Rohatyn (who took over his position in Stratyn in 5625 (1865) when Rabbi Avramtche passed away). He was an outstanding scholar and personality and rose to the heavens on Lag B'Omer 5649 (1889).

Rabbi Uri of Rohatyn, Z"L, left children after him—the famous and Holy Admor Rabbi Yehuda Zvi, Z"L, the chief rabbi of the town of Stratyn, who took over his father's position. Hundreds of Hassidim flocked to him. He had an excellent voice and served as rabbi for eighteen years, passing away on 14 Iyar 5667 (1907) and was buried in Rohatyn. The second son was Rabbi Yitzchak Aharon, a very pious Jew who passed away at an early age on 26 Tammuz. His third son was the Holy Rabbi Yisrael of Brody.

The Holy Rabbi Berish of Dolina, Z"L, left after him a son, the Holy Rabbi Yehuda Zvi and he passed away 12 Iyar 5670 (1910).

It is possible that, as a copyist, I have proportionately devoted a little too much time to the genealogy of those whose connections were with our town of Rohatyn, Stratyn, and the general area. Perhaps it is proper to add here the fine descendents whom we knew in our day who walked on our streets, some erect and some bowed, each one according to his personality but all of them alike in their dress. The same black hat with large brim, the double-breasted Capote (frock) of silk, white stockings, low shoes un-laced. The younger ones wore a wide black tie that covered their chest completely under the white collar of the shirt. Their parents did not need this because their beards came down and covered their sensitive faces. This was why people used to say, partially in jest, that the beards fulfill the statement "Melo Kol Ha-aretz K'vodo" (the land was filled with their dignity). It is also no great wonder that the name Yehuda Zvi, that great tree, was repeated over and over among this family of rabbis, i.e., Rabbi Yehuda Zvi of Stratyn or Rabbi Uri, after him, the Admor of Rohatyn who was also named after the Saraf (the burning angel), Rabbi Uri of Strzeliska. I remember that families in our town who were Stratyner Hassidim for numerous generations named many of their children after the rabbis. One such name immediately comes to my mind—my friend Yehuda Zvi, the younger son of Reb Avraham Messing, Z"L.

I also remember that on the yahrzeit of Rabbi Uri of Rohatyn (on Lag B'Omer), when we children went to a school called Czerwona Szkola (Red School) and could see through the windows the hill leading to the graveyard, we would wait for the recess bell and then run after that wonderful parade of rabbis, rebbes, and learned Jews from the town and its surroundings. We used to join them and walk up to the graves of the tzaddikim. The singers stood near the eastern wall, and the sweet voice of Rabbi Elimelech of Lwow could be heard holding forth singing, "Bar Yohai, Bar Yohai."

Life in the City

Rohatyn

By Rabbi Yitzchak Weisblum, Haifa

Translated by Rabbi Mordecai Goldzweig - YB p. 84

R ohatyn is one of the small towns of Galicia that does not usually appear on a world map but left its lasting impression on the Jewish map of Galicia in the hearts of Torah, Judaism, and Hassidism. It is not the size of an area that brings about important decisions but the amount of influence that a place exerts and the distinguished personalities who live within it and honor it with their presence. This applies to Rohatyn. It earned its fame through the great people who lived in it. One of the most outstanding of these was the holy Gaon, Rabbi David Moshe Avraham, the son of Reb Tzadok Ashkenazi, Z"L, the dayan (chief justice) of Rohatyn and the author of Mirkevet Hamishne, who passed away in Rohatyn on 18 Heshvan 5510 (October 30, 1749). According to tradition, he used to be visited by the Ba'al Shem Tov, Z"L, and even received his blessing.

It was a privilege and an honor for a rabbi to live in a place where his predecessors were great men. Such greatness was a drawing factor in attracting rabbis who chose this place over a larger one. Rohatyn was a town that excelled over others because of its great rabbis and dayanim. The last of those who presided over the religious court was our teacher and rabbi, Avraham David Spiegel, Z"L (may his blood be avenged by the Almighty), who was murdered by the butchers (may their names be erased).

Rabbi Avraham David Spiegel was a native of the town of Rohatyn, born in 5645 (1885), a descendent of the Gaon, Rabbi Avraham David Moshe, the author of the *Mirkevet Hamishne*, who blended within his personality a wide variety of superior qualities. As a chief justice, he was strong and strict on one hand and meek and gentle on the other. A great man in Torah, it automatically follows that he possessed wide understanding and comprehension, a strong feeling of pity for others, as well as a pleasant demeanor toward people. He was ordained as a rabbi in his youth by the greatest rabbis of the day in Galicia. This included the Gaon, the Marsham of Brzezany (Moreinu Rabbi Shalom Mordechai HaCohen Schwadron), a famous posek (rabbinical religious authority) of his day, Z"L, and the Gaon, Rabbi Meir Arik, Z"L, chief dayan of Tarnow, as well as other rabbis. The extent of his greatness may be judged by the Shelot U'Tshuvot (responsa) he exchanged with the great rabbis of the day. These included Rabbi David Halevi Horowitz, Z"L, chief rabbi of Stanislawow, who recorded his questions together with his response, indicating that he was communicating with an important rabbi.[1]* Because of his greatness and the charm of his personality, he served as Av Beit Din (chief justice of the rabbinical court) of Rohatyn for over thirty years, as well as many additional years as acting chief justice, until Rabbi Mordechai Lippe Teumim, Z"L, was officially accepted as chief justice, may his blood be avenged.

The Hassidism of Stratyn that established its residence in Rohatyn through the Admor, our teacher and rabbi, Rabbi Uri, Z"L, the son-in-law of the Holy Admor, Rabbi Avramtche of Stratyn, Z"L, placed its stamp on the people of the area. This approach of forgiveness and simplicity was also the way of the great Rabbi Spiegel, Z"L, who gave up his position in favor of Rav Teumim, even though he could easily have continued as acting rabbi and prevented the acceptance of anyone else. This action, reflecting his noble

p. 85, YB: This picture was taken January, 1938 in the courtroom of Rabbi Spiegel, Z"L, also showing his library. First row, standing to the right: Chayche, Yente, Reizel, Chana-Taube, Yuta, Yehoshua, Rabbi Avraham David Spiegel, Ryfke, Rebbetzin Chaya, and Yaakov Meshulam. Rabbi Spiegel is shown holding Yalkut Shimoni, the book he constantly studied.

personality and meekness, renders him as a true heir of the B'nai Beteira (the sons of Beteira—Shmaya and Avtalyon) who gave up their presidency of the Sanhedrin (High Court) to Hillel Hazaken (1st century BCE and early 1st century ACE). Rabbi Yehuda Hanassi said about him, "There were three who personified meekness, my father (Rabbi Shimon ben Gamliel), the sons of Beteira, and Jonathan, the son of Shaul (Bava Metzia Chap. 5) (It was written at the end of Tractate Sota of the Jerusalem Talmud about Rabbi Yehuda Hanassi, that when he passed away "there came to an end meekness and the fear of sin in the world.") Where his greatness lay, there was his meekness. This memory of Rabbi Avraham David Spiegel is engraved in the hearts of all of the people of Rohatyn as one who shaped the character of the town and the living spirit that existed within it that was lost when the town was lost, thereby closing the grave of this elevated community. May they rest in peace.

∽

The Rohatyn Way
By Dr. Isaac Lewenter, New York

Translated by Binyamin Weiner - YB p. 86

1

Rohatyn was actually once a little shtetl. Back in the Polish days, letters were addressed to us as follows: "Rohatyn by Firlejow." Jews called it Perlew. Later, Firlejow became one of the villages surrounding Rohatyn.

Rohatyn stood at a crossroads that went on in one direction toward Lwow and Stanislawow, and, in the other direction, toward Tarnopol and Stryj. This facilitated the development of trade and transport in our shtetl. When they built the train station in Rohatyn, it became a passage point between Tarnopol and Stryj.

Jewish life in Rohatyn dates almost from the earliest years of Polish history. Jews lived in Rohatyn for over 900 years. In the old cemeteries, one could find gravestones seven to 900 years old. Rohatyn was also associated in Jewish history with a number of its inhabitants who were followers of the Sabbatai Zvi movement (hence we were called by the nickname "Shabbetzvinikes") and Frankists.

These are my words of introduction to the actual description I will offer of Jewish Rohatyn prior to the destruction of the Third Temple. I will use no historical material in my exposition of this topic. These will be personal memories.

2

Rohatyn was considered a "Jewish city." Close to 4,000 Jews lived there. In the time of World War II, around 10,000 Jewish souls thronged together in Rohatyn as people fled Hitler's advancing soldiers. Of this number, very few survived. Nearly the entire Jewish community of Rohatyn was murdered by the Germans and their local assistants, the Poles and the Ukrainians.

Prior to World War I, life in Rohatyn, from a Jewish standpoint, was quite interesting. A Zionist movement was organized very early on, and many of its leaders became known, not just within our shtetl but also outside its borders (Shalom Meltzer and Sender Margolis among others). We had many Hassidim, as well, who did not constitute an anti-Zionist force but were simply honest and faithful followers of the Rebbe.

The hall of the Zionist league was a gathering place for older and younger

Zionists alike. There, we spent long hours "politicking," playing chess, and participating in a host of other activities. I had the pleasure of defeating the old chess players, Avrum Zlatkis and Yaakov Fish.

3

I remember the rabbi of Rohatyn (and later Rzeszow) well—Rabbi Natan Lewin. He was a learned Jew with a fine, stately beard. He was esteemed and highly thought of by all. When he walked in the street, he was met with great respect. His face shone with such a special light that not just Jews but Christians, too, would give way as he passed. His sermons, full of Jewish and worldly knowledge, were renowned. It was said that people did not walk to his sermons, they ran to them. He gave them every Shabbos "after table."

On the birthday of the Kaiser and other state holidays, the rabbi would deliver his witty, German "speeches" that would astound the fancy-dressed local officials in attendance and fill them with wonder at the rabbi's oratorical skill.

When I was still a little child, my grandfather used to take me with him to the rabbi's table. I would listen carefully to his clever words about Torah, without understanding a thing...

As I remember, the rabbi did not stay long in our city because Rohatyn was too poor to support his family. After his departure, the city remained without a rabbi for a long time. Meanwhile, the office was occupied by the dayan (judge), Reb Kave Schein, a man entirely the opposite of the rabbi. Whereas the rabbi was steeped in Jewish and worldly knowledge, and on top of that was a handsome man who commanded the attention of everyone he met, the dayan was an introverted man, small in stature, his understanding limited to matters of halacha and other points of Jewish law. He was, however, honesty and piety personified. For this reason, he was held in high esteem.

In his old age, the dayan no longer had the strength to carry out his duties, and in 1904, his place was taken by Rabbi Meir Henne from Strzeliska. Rabbi Henne was an old-fashioned Jew, with all of the attendant virtues. He knew how to study and was esteemed for his piety and kindness.

After a time, a "local boy" from Rohatyn was chosen to serve as dayan. This was the "young dayan," Reb Avrum-Dovid Spiegel, whose family was well known in Rohatyn. His brother, Neftali, returned from America and struggled bitterly his entire life to make a living. He was popular in the shtetl because of the wonderful cloth work he used to do for the gimnazjum (high school), embroidering curtains for the holy ark and decorative mantles for the Torah scrolls. Generally, he was an expert in piecework. The second brother, Pinchas, was a clever and handsome man, a devoted Zionist, and my good friend. He also eked out his existence bitterly until the final years.

Even though Reb Avrum-Dovid Spiegel was a "local boy" from Rohatyn itself, the administration of the community did not provide for his livelihood. When his children grew up, they were obliged to provide for themselves. One of his children, Yehoshua, now lives in the state of Israel, and, as I understand it, the yoke of putting together our Yizkor book lies mainly on his shoulders.

p. 88 YB: "The red public school."

4

Rohatyn was generally regarded by inhabitants and outsiders alike as a progressive town. It contained two gimnazja—one, Ukrainian, and the other, Polish. Many Jewish children studied in these schools. In Austrian times, no educational restrictions were placed on Jewish children. These were first instituted when Poland achieved independence.

The Ukrainian gimnazjum, a private school, was founded in 1907, and the Polish (state) school, in 1912. Most Jewish children went to the Polish school, although the instruction there was useless. It was maintained by the civil authorities. There were also some Jewish boys and girls who attended the Ukrainian gimnazjum.

Most of the Jewish population of Rohatyn made their living in small trade. They bought eggs, butter, cheese, chickens, geese, and ducks from the local farmers and sold them to other Jews. A fair was held every Wednesday.

In our shtetl, there were a few merchants with bigger trade. They would bring their goods from Lwow, Stanislawow, Vienna, and Budapest. These were the shtetl magnates, the gentry, who dealt with rich Jews and local landowners.

p. 89 YB: "The Ukrainian gimnazjum."

There was also, as in every other Polish-Jewish shtetl, a significant class of Jewish craftsmen—shoemakers, tailors, carpenters and the like. The shtetl also possessed a few Jewish clerks, a small number of lawyers, three Jewish doctors (Dr. Stein, Dr. Schaff, and Dr. Mehlman) and a few Jewish schoolmistresses. I must also mention the local religious teacher, the tiny Schwartz (we used to call him "Schwartzenyu"). He had one outstanding quality; he did not teach too much to the children, simply because he did not know very much himself. No child ever received a "two" in religion from him, and therefore no child ever needed to be held back for a second year in the same class.

Jewish children also studied Hebrew. This subject was taught in two places—the cheder (Jewish elementary school) and the Hebrew school. In cheder, the youngest children started off with the "children's teacher." As they grew, they advanced to the study of Chumash and "Chumash with Rashi" until they worked their way up to the study of Gemara with Tosafot, and Tanach.

5

Such was the path I took. My "children's teacher" was Rabbi Hirsh Fang. Baruch, the rabbi's eldest son, and Leib, a relative of the rabbi's, served as his "assistants." Their job was to drag the children to cheder. Not every child wanted to go with them, and many bitter tears were spilled.

We did not learn a great deal in cheder. After a year or two, we more or less knew the alphabet. Children began attending when they were barely three years old. We were told that from the earliest ages a Jew must take upon himself the yoke of Torah.

Etia, the rabbi's wife, was as good as the day and as poor as the night. As we lived next door, the rabbi's children often received their board in our house, eating together with us. As the rabbi had, keine hora (no evil eye should harm them), many children, Etia could often be found pouring out her bitter heart to my mother. The two women would cry and hope for better times.

Later, their whole family went away to America.

My "Chumash with Rashi" teacher was Judah-Ber, nicknamed "the kitten." He often whipped us with his bamboo stick; yet we all still loved him. Our study was not at the highest of levels. It is worthwhile taking this opportunity to relate the following incident:

On a certain Sunday, we were learning the weekly Torah portion— Vayisrotsitsu (and they struggled together) habonim (the children, Jacob and Esau) bikirbah (in her belly). This was sung to the appropriate tune. We were all five years old and could by no means understand how children could struggle together in their mother's belly...so we asked the teacher. And we got the answer, "Rascals! Don't ask!"

He had a hard time making a living, as well. Every Thursday evening we went to his house to review the Sabbath Torah portion. As he came in to listen to us, his wife would always whisper: "Nu, Judah-Ber, give me something to make Sabbath."

The rabbi, however, had nothing to give, as many of his students had not paid their fees. He answered simply, "I don't have anything." She began to curse him. He answered her curses as follows: "Why do you curse? You have with me the greatest pleasure a person can have!" Her curses grew louder and stronger; it is a bit of good luck that none of them came true. In the very middle of cursing, she would ask him the question, "So tell me, great breadwinner, what is this pleasure that I have with you?"

The rabbi answered her, "The greatest pleasure a person can have when they itch—is to scratch themselves! So, do I not let you scratch?" The rabbi's wife was not to blame; she worked herself to the bone.

Besides this rabbi, I also had another "Chumash with Rashi" teacher. He was called Nachum Melamed. He had three fine sons and two daughters. The sons were already grown, and two of them later immigrated to Israel.

Nasan and the "Finch" (I still remember his nickname) were Gemara teachers, but I never studied with them. I went away to Stanislawow and prepared for worldly studies.

The Jewish population of Rohatyn had the good fortune, before World War I, to have good Hebrew teachers, among them Soferman, Scharfstein, Spiegel, and Ahnd. Many youngsters, between the ages of ten and fourteen, studied the language and used it, as well.

6

Every Jew from Rohatyn would certainly remember the "family band of musicians," the Faust family. They were the talk of the town—Moshe, Dovid, Itzik-Hersh, Mordecai-Shmuel, and Yaakov. Moshe, the father, was the conductor, Dovid, the fiddler, Itzik-Hersh, the flautist, Mordecai-Shmuel, a multi-instrumentalist and clarinet player, and the little ruffian, Yekel, the trumpet player and drummer.

Weddings in Rohatyn reverberated throughout the surrounding countryside. The canopy was set up beside the large synagogue, and the bride and groom were led there amidst a grand parade. The band led the way. The music rang through the streets and raised a great crowd. Children ran ahead and had a great time chasing after the band. It was lively and cheerful in the shtetl.

7

A different spirit pervaded the so-called "propinacja" (tavern). This was the place for all the drunks, where they sat all day as long as it was open. There was no end to the drinking that went on there. When the doors to the tavern were closed, the drunks left for home. They often fell down and took a nap on the street. Passersby would smile—and go on their way.

8

My father once told me a story about a Jew who lay down to sleep

Friday night and slept for thirty-six hours straight. Early Sunday morning, he finally awoke and was convinced it was the Sabbath morning. He put on his Sabbath clothes, his long black coat and fur-trimmed hat, and went to the house of prayer. Along the way, he greeted everyone he passed with a "Good Shabbos." People answered him, "Good morning." Nobody brought the error to his attention. The first thing he saw upon entering the house of prayer was the entire congregation putting on phylacteries.

9

In the village of Podgrodzie, next to Rohatyn, there lived a fine Jew. He had only one fault—though he never brought any horses into strangers' stalls, he was in the habit of stealing them away. It was difficult to catch him. He managed to alter the stolen horses to such a degree that it was impossible to identify them. He made them younger, changed their color, stuck teeth in their mouths. How he did all of this remained his secret.

Once, however, he slipped up and was consequently brought before the court. He went calmly to his trial, singing a hassidic melody…

He enlightened the judge as follows: "I was strolling peacefully when I came upon a ditch. I realized that I would have to jump over it. So what does G-d do? A horse was lying in the ditch. When I jumped, the horse rose up, and against my will, I landed on his back and was carried far far away. I had no way of knowing whose horse it was…"

10

In the year 1914, life in the shtetl proceeded as in normal times. Jews rose in the early morning to worship at the house of prayer. The less religious were satisfied with coming only on the Sabbath and holidays. People traveled to fairs in other towns, and our own fair in Rohatyn was still held every Wednesday. Weddings took place as well as births, festive occasions, and misfortunes. Everything in the shtetl flowed in the usual channels as if nothing were taking place in the world at all. Nobody anticipated the catastrophe that was creeping upon us.

At the start of the summer of 1914, the army reserves were mobilized. The newspapers brought no good news.

When the Austrian Archduke Franz-Ferdinand was assassinated in Sarajevo, everyone knew it would lead to the outbreak of war. Yet people still comforted themselves with "maybe" and "perhaps."

After the war broke out, a great misfortune befell our shtetl. A division of Austrian infantry put up in Rohatyn. The fully equipped soldiers settled in to rest, following a difficult march. An entire regiment bivouacked in the middle of the marketplace.

All of a sudden, there was the sound of gunfire. Nobody knew where it came from or who had fired. It was probably the provocation of informers or spies. The soldiers answered by shooting blindly in all directions. It was a miracle that nobody was injured.

Yet panic took hold of the shtetl. On the second day, nearly the entire population fled, taking with it only small packs. They believed that they would soon return—and so left everything behind. Later, it became evident that the running would be without cease; that the wandering had just begun. They were forced to flee to Vienna and even further into Austria.

We went to Stryj, toward which the Russians were rapidly advancing.

After a few weeks away, we were able to return to Rohatyn. Unfortunately, our home was no more. After the Russians ransacked everything the Jews had left behind, they set fire to the houses. They were assisted in this task by our Ukrainian neighbors. Of the whole city, only a few back streets remained. The Jewish bath still stood, as well, and there the young rabbi, Avrum-Dovid Spiegel, had gathered the remaining Jews together.

Nearly the entire large Beit Midrash (house of prayer and study) still stood, as well. The Russians had tried to set it on fire, but only a few floorboards had burned. The building remained intact. The Jews said that we had my old uncle, Alter, to thank for that, the "jester," who was a righteous man in his generation and had bequeathed to the house of prayer the beautiful holy ark and all of the Torah scrolls.

Materially, life was very hard. The remaining Jews of Rohatyn, together with those who had come in from the surrounding countryside, made their living through great hardship. They engaged in small trade. A few craftsmen managed to find work. The overwhelming majority fed themselves by calling in loans that their honest Christian neighbors returned.

11

In these ways, people coped with the new situation. The winter of 1914 - 15 passed. Spring came. In May, the German-Austrian offensive in western Galicia began. The Russian Army was defeated and fled east. As the Galician Jews were known to be Austrian patriots, they were deported to Russia by the retreating army.

Rohatyn was no exception. On a certain evening, the Russians dragged the entire male Jewish population of Rohatyn out of their homes, assembled them in the center of town and thereafter marched them to Podwysokie. The first night there was spent sleeping under the open sky. In the morning, the

p. 95 YB: A group of Rohatyn Jews (men only) during the Russian captivity. From top right: unknown, unknown, Mendel Rotenberg, Shmuel Weissbraun, unknown, Monish Schechter, Aharon Schechter, Benzion Weissbraun, Nahum Mantenberg, Shaul Teichmann, Moshe Weissbraun, unknown, Wolf Steinmetz, Yehoshua Otner, Selig Nagelberg, Wolki Allerhand, Dr. Yitschok Lewenter, Neftali Rosenstein, unknown, unknown, Moshe Schechter, Neftali Spiegel, Bertsi Weissbraun, Selig Holz, Weissbraun, Zushe Holz, Meir Maor, Yosef Hammer, unknown, unknown, Nahum Milstein, Yehoshua Lipshitz, Yosef Mark, Rokeach Mivutshats, Yosef Widhoff, unknown, Alter Durst (Dorst), Yudel-Michel Sofers, Moshe Freiwald, unknown, Alter Lewenter, unknown, unknown, Yehoshua Stryjer, Volvel Weissbraun, Yehuda bar Zilber, Avraham Roten, Alter Faust, Urtsi Horowitz, Nehemiah Reich, Avraham Zeif, Noach Milstein, Dovid Weissbraun, Elisha Teichmann, Avraham-Yosef Ehrenberg, Kalman-Yoel Lipshitz, Uri Lipshitz, unknown, Yechezkel Henne, unknown, Lipshitz, Ehrenberg, unknown, Natan Wald, Shaul Pantzer, Yosef Wald, Itsi Spiegel, Chuna Wachman, Pinia Spiegel, unknown,
Nachman-Yeshia Wachman, Dovid Einshtum, Moshe Lewenter, Noach Leyner, Moshe Mitman, unknown, Yaakov Leiter, Avraham Lichtgarn, Yaakov Barban, Yantsi Leiter, Mendel Bernstein, Iser Glotzer, Wolf Freiwald, Hori Pater, unknown, Meir Lewenter, Dovid Wald, Leyb Widhoff, Nuni Eichenstein, Moshe Faust, Moshe Freiwald, Itsik Bokser, Leyzer Bokser, Meir Glotzer, Boris Teichmann, Hirsh Hochwald, unknown.

long march began and continued until we reached Kiev.

In Kiev, a special Jewish brotherhood committee attended to all of our essentials. There were also Jewish families who took us into their homes, guaranteeing to the Russian authorities, even though they did not know us, that we would not flee. After a few days in Kiev, we were loaded onto a wagon and taken to the Pez-ner province in the state of Chembar. Material life was not difficult there, but we were completely cut off from our families; we did not know anything about our wives, sisters, and little children who had remained behind. We longed for them greatly.

Only three Russian-Jewish families lived in Chembar proper. One was a pharmacist, another, a large manufacturer, and the third, an engineer, who, by the way, was a provisional railway man and worked on the laying of the local train tracks. I personally spent long hours in intimate conversation with them, discussing the situation of Jews in Russia and Austria. For all of us, everything that we reported to each other was fresh and new. We therefore felt that brother and brother could speak to each other about one and the same matter.

12

At the end of 1915, we were sent back to Galicia. We went as far as Tarnopol, as this was the last city remaining in Russian hands. We stayed there for almost two years, until the summer of 1917, when the Germans occupied it.

In Tarnopol, it was every man for himself. There was no joint Rohatyn committee to look after the group. Everyone sought out his own means by which to live through this terrible time.

Tarnopol was liberated after the first revolution in Russia. Kerensky had come to Tarnopol and delivered a speech on freedom and the justice of Socialism.

When we returned, full of longing, to our region in Austria, we found it pervaded by a strange spirit. The air was full of the nervous anticipation of something overwhelming. It was no longer the same land for which we had longed and yearned.

I cannot write about Rohatyn during that time, as I was among those sent away to Przeworsk. From there we went to Lwow. I could not join my family, as my mother and the smaller children were in Austrian Silesia. In the meantime, I grew sick and was therefore released from the army for six months. This gave me the opportunity to renew my study of medicine in Lwow.

13

In 1918, it was felt that defeat was imminent. Our armies were far from their borders, deep in Russia or in France. The general impression was of an oncoming catastrophe.

An influenza epidemic broke out in the city, claiming as many casualties as had fallen at the front. At the end of 1918, I also fell sick. After a short time spent in a hospital bed, I recovered. In November, we were told that the Ukrainians had taken Lwow.

I remember that Friday when, still weak, barely able to stand on my feet, I went out into the street to gather news. The Ukrainian militia had taken over the rule of the city. Relations were tranquil. Early the next morning, a few incidents broke out between the Ukrainians and the Poles, and on the third of November, the battle between these two armies began.

A Jewish militia was organized on the Ukrainian side. It remained neutral in this struggle and had as its one and only objective protecting the lives and property of the Jewish population.

As the battle between the Ukrainians and Poles raged in Lwow, the rest of the province was quiet. Rohatyn, too, felt the tranquility. It lay in a region occupied by the Ukrainians. This new power evinced loyalty toward the Jewish population.

Meanwhile, combat between the two sides continued in Lwow. On 21 November 1918, a two-day cease-fire was declared. A thousand people took advantage of the occasion to leave the city. I took the opportunity, as well, and returned to Rohatyn where life flowed peacefully. The divided families were once more reunited. This occurred while the Austrians were still in the town. Throughout 1917–18, Jews returned to Rohatyn and resettled in their old homes.

In May and June of 1919, the Ukrainians were defeated, and the Poles occupied Galicia, including Rohatyn. The Jews, as usual, were victims of this shift in power. Before the Ukrainians left, they plundered the Jewish population. Many fell in this attack against the Jews. Persecution of Jews began as soon as the Poles arrived. I personally had to flee Rohatyn, because in Lwow I had given a speech against the pogroms, and therefore a warrant had been issued for my arrest.

14

I was away from Rohatyn until 1922. Many people were missing from the shtetl when I returned. Many had perished on the battlefields, and many, with the passage of time, had died natural or unnatural deaths.

In the meantime, life had normalized for the Jewish community of Rohatyn. A younger generation had arisen, full of the energy and will to put an end to the abject life of Jewish exile in which we were subject to constant danger. Jewish youths organized into various pioneer movements in order to immigrate to the land of Israel and build a new life. Many of them actually reached Israel, where they live to this day, together with their families.

15

I will record a few general features of Jewish communal life in Rohatyn in the period between the two world wars.

The great majority of Poles were predisposed toward anti-Semitism. It was in their blood. Parents taught their children that Jews were to blame for everything because Jews had crucified Jesus. They were convinced that Jews were swindlers whose only concern was how they might manipulate the Poles. This attitude had its consequent impact on their day-to-day dealings with Jewish citizens, even though the Polish constitution was among the most liberal.

In the first years of the Polish Republic's existence, when Pilsudski and his socialist memories were still alive, when the Poles were not yet drunk with the power they had acquired, Jews were treated liberally by the state. A Polish Nationalist party did exist, however, that was anti-Semitic through and through. It maintained that Poland had too many Jews, who, therefore, had to leave the land and go to Palestine. This party called unceasingly for a Polish boycott of Jews and made it its business to harass Jews in whatever way possible.

The Jewish representatives in the Polish Sejm (parliament) struggled continually with the Sejm for the rights of the Jewish minority. In civil life, however, as in economics, this did little help.

Trouble had already begun for the Jews of Rohatyn in the 20s when Pilsudski took power and established the well-known "sanacja" (BBWR—Nonpartisan Block for Cooperation with the Government). Although this party was a conglomeration of various elements, it was uniform in its anti-Semitism. It sought to remove Jews from their economic status and, if possible, throw them out of Poland proper.

The Jews of Western Galicia had an additional problem—local Ukrainian nationalism. The Ukrainian element, a more virulent faction, exhibited a more brutal form of anti-Semitism, striving to cut off Jews at the root. They began setting up cooperative organizations that undermined the economic foundation of many Jewish families. Many of these families were therefore forced to leave their dwelling and set off across the sea.

Jews in our region suffered from both sides, from Poles and from Ukrainians. Anti-Jewish pogroms also occurred from time to time.

In those years, Jewish life was ceaselessly inundated with "zoological", anti-Semitic propaganda. This was printed in two languages, though of one and the same content. The Polish "Swoj do Swego" (each to his own, i.e., buy from your own) was translated verbatim into Ukrainian. The economic boycott took on more severe forms that served to increase the already substantial level of Jewish poverty.

Two cooperatives were organized in Rohatyn, one, Polish, and the other, Ukrainian. Each sapped the livelihood of many Jewish families. This led to emigration. There were many Jews, however, who could not afford to leave and thus remained in their place, suffering want and hunger.

Still, parents who could barely get through the day never stopped considering how they might provide their children with an education. Meanwhile, the Polish authorities did all they could to deny Jewish children access to middle and high schools.

In the thirties, the Polish government began taking lessons from Hitler in how to make life miserable for Jews. Ritual slaughter laws dried up business for the twenty Jewish butchers of Rohatyn. They had the right to sell only kosher meat and were obliged to throw out all of their non-kosher stock. This was a blow not just to the Jewish butchers but also to the Jewish cattle dealers, slaughterers, and deliverers who lost their livelihood. A Jew who wanted to deal in dairy products had to obtain a concession, for which he had to pay heavily. Therefore, very few concessions were issued. For such a business, one needed to have three rooms and a special facility, which cost quite a lot. Everything had to be certified by the authorities. In our shtetl alone, this affected one hundred families who lost their livelihood. This was the real intent of these anti-Jewish laws.

The fact that we were forced to open a communal kitchen is indicative of the extent to which the material situation of Rohatyn had deteriorated.

At the initiative of my wife, a women's committee was convened and took responsibility for the organization and upkeep of the kitchen. It was located in the building of the Jewish bath. The kitchen provided meals not just to the truly poor Jews but also to those who had recently become impoverished.

I must acknowledge, with thanks and praise, the dear Jewish girls who contributed so much toward fulfilling the purpose of the kitchen. Every day they carried food to the homes of those families who did not come to the kitchen. For this, the holy memory of Zofia Kleinwachs should be recalled. She lived through the years of occupation, and after liberation immigrated to America where she died young. Lora Mark, the daughter of Joseph Mark, who now lives in America, should also be remembered. These two girls used to carry food to the homes of those too ashamed to come to the kitchen.

16

In this manner, a significant Jewish community lived and evolved—

until the catastrophe came. In July of 1939, I traveled as a tourist from Poland to America to attend the World's Fair. We did not then anticipate that tragedy was approaching. The official organs of the Polish state boasted about the potential power of their army. Poland flirted for a long time with the Nazi leaders, until these leaders realized that they no longer needed Polish help.

From then on I was severed from Poland and from my beloved Rohatyn. All of my nearest and dearest perished there, and my heart still grieves for them. The holy images of those I knew, and with whom I traveled the long road of joint struggle for a Jewish life, hover before my eyes.

May their memory be honored!

p. 100 YB: Beside the brickyard, in front of the area of the train station, to the left, lie our dear ones, the thirty-three hundred victims of the first "action." The two who stand together with bowed heads are Ulki Schwartz, who lives to this day in Bursztyn, and the son of Selig Nagelberg (a leather merchant)

CSO

A City In Life And In Destruction
Our City Rohatyn
By Yehoshua Spiegel, Tel Aviv

Translated by Rabbi Mordecai Goldzweig - YB p. 101

Introduction

I lived in Rohatyn twenty-five years before I immigrated to Israel. During this time I came to know Rohatyn from the perspective of a resident. I received additional information from the elders of the town especially from my father, the rabbi, Z"L. Other residents of Rohatyn who were my neighbors will write about the things that they knew and that were close to their hearts—the more the better.

p. 101 YB, Wald, Lunka Teichman, Rosenstein, Yechiel Fischer, Yosef Weich, Suzi Ehrenberg, Yosef Weiss, Rozia Reiss, Nuncia Willig, Chana Gold, Sarah Reiss, Unknown, Klara Cytryn, Unknown, Weissbraun, Zilber. A group of Jewish students of the Polish high school in our city Rohatyn.

It is natural that names and events that are linked to childhood and the growing years will elicit a great deal of emotion from survivors of a town, wherever they may be, as it reminds them of those times and places. These threads of the past tie them to those who are no longer alive and whose memories are as close and dear to them as their own lives—family, relatives, and friends. But even those who did not live in Rohatyn will still find a replica of their own town here—the same life, the same traditions, and the same stereotypes. Perhaps the names are different. Still, we are talking about those who continued to spin the age old threads while guarding the values of their people that have been carried down to the present day.

Situated as they were in a sea of ignorance, among gentiles, Jews displayed a wide knowledge and deep understanding of the ways of the world and of the individual. Quite a few giants of spirit rose from within their midst.

The Town

The Rohatyn that I knew was for the most part populated by Jews. The mailmen used to joke that "the streets are ours but the houses are yours." Relatively few Ukrainians and Poles lived within the town itself. Ukrainians populated the one hundred and fifty villages and hamlets, big and small, that surrounded our town, whereas only a few of the Jews lived in the villages. The closest villages around the town included Babince, Putiatynce, Zaluze, Wierzbolowce, Podhajce, and Perenowka. Perenowka—who did not go walking to Perenowka and its forests? I remember how my father, the rabbi, Z"L, used to go walking there with his students and stop there to teach them their lesson in Talmud. On the way they would pass in front of a spring whose waters were recommended by Rabbi Meir of Przemyslany as a cure for eye diseases. People believed in its remedial powers and came to drink from its waters. Among our neighbors were the towns of Stratyn, Bukaczowce, Bursztyn, Podkamien, and Knihynicze. Especially well known was a village called Czercze, which had a clinic for the treatment of rheumatism. Another village, Potok Psary, had a limestone quarry with lime that went directly from the quarry to a furnace, from which it was shipped to the cities and towns of Poland.

Rohatyn is situated in Eastern Galicia between Lwow and Stanislawow, with which it was in contact for both culture and business. If you wanted to go to Lwow, you took the train through Chodorow and then the bus through Przemyslany—and to Stanislawow, by train through Chodorow and by bus through Halicz. This town, Halicz (Galicz), which was at one time the capital of the area, gave its name to the whole surrounding district—Galicia.

There were at that time approximately ten thousand people in Rohatyn. A road went through the center of town dividing it into two parts. It had a mountain pressing in on either side with the names of Mount Putiatynce and Devil Mountain.[1] Rohatyn rests on the shores of the Gnila Lipa River, which looks

---

1   Menashe Unger writes in a Yiddish newspaper in an article entitled "Fun Eibiken Kval" (From the Eternal Source), "Rohatyn hot men gerufen 'Shabse Tzvinekes'" (Rohatyners were called followers of Sabbatai Zvi.) In the back of the town there is

like its name (rotten linden tree), with many forests along its shores. These supplied wood for fuel and industry. The town had three elementary schools— Polish, Ukrainian, and Jewish. The first high school built in Rohatyn was Ukrainian, but the Jews attended it since they did not have one of their own. When the Poles built their high school, the greater part of the Jewish student body transferred to it.

Occupations

Most of the Jews of the town earned their livelihood in business. Weekly market fairs were held on Wednesdays. They also engaged in crafts and brokerage, and there were doctors and lawyers among them as well. The town candy factory belonged to Reb Ephraim Kanfer and his family. Two printing shops there belonged to Jews—Chaim Skolnick and his family and Szymon Teichman and his family, Z"L. Chaim Skolnick was chairman of the Association of Craftsmen, a Jew of importance in business and industry and a lover of cantors. Any chazan who appeared in our town could find a place to stay and eat, as well as other help, in his home. Now, only his son, Zvi, has survived and lives in Israel. He is a sergeant in the police department and active in affairs relating to the people of Rohatyn in Israel. The second shop belonged to Mr. Szymon Teichman and his family, Z"L. Here I learned printing. He was the chairman of the charity organization Gemilas Chesed in Rohatyn and active in other public affairs of our town. His two daughters, Bluma and Leah Teichman, now live in Israel, and his son, Mordechai, a doctor, now lives in the US The soda factory in our town was owned by Mr. Schumer, Z"L. The American-style flour mill belonged to Reb Uri Messing, Z"L, and it was there that my uncle, Reb Yosef Klarnet, Z"L, worked as a bookkeeper. Reb Uri was active in community affairs, especially those dealing with religion. Bakeries were owned by Dudke Horn, Z"L, Gira, Reb Meir "Kumizbeker" (as he was known), Z"L, and Reb Alter Faust, Z"L, a religious Jew, active in doing good deeds and helping the needy in the community. In addition there were the home bakeries.

Various Torah Scholars

In Rohatyn as in other Polish towns, there were to be found a fine

---

situated on flat land a mountain termed "Chortova Hora or Czortowa Gora." The Jewish legend explaining this goes as follows: Sabbatai Zvi flew with the power of the Divine Name, carrying the mountain, and when the rooster crowed after midnight, it was placed on the flatland. From this story we learn that there were in Rohatyn many adherents of Sabbatai Zvi. We even know the names of those adherents."

assortment of Torah scholars such as Reb Mordechai Pikower, Reb Zalman Piktinitzer, Reb Chaim Jupiter (from Czesniki), a true talmid chacham (scholar), ordained and G-d fearing, versed in the mystic and revealed Torah knowledge. Even when he lived in a village, he dug out a mikveh (ritual bath) in his yard so that he might be able to immerse himself at anytime that he found it necessary. There was Reb Elisha Aharon Klarnet, Reb Yosef HaCohen Laks, Reb Moshe Leib Kowler, Reb Tuwia Shochet, Reb Avraham Hirsch Koenigsberg, Reb Chaim Hirsch Weissberg, Reb Nachman Szaja Wachman, Reb Azriel Gan, and Reb Yisrael Gleicher, all Z"L. May they all rest in peace.

Shochtim

The town shochtim (ritual slaughterers) included Reb Moshe Schechter, of keen mind and well versed in Torah, a man who was both very religious and wise, yet knowledgeable in worldly affairs and a composer of melodies. His wife's name was Sarah. Four of their sons are alive, two in Israel, two in other countries. His brother, Mordechai, was a ba'al tefilah (leader of services) during the holidays and serenaded his neighbors on Shabbat and Yom Tov with zemirot (hymns) for the occasion, his children joining in. His wife's name was Esther. There was also Reb Leib Shochet and Reb Tuwia Shochet. The latter was the supervisor of the shochtim and among other duties examined their ritual slaughtering knives. He was a pious Jew filled with Torah. May they all find themselves in a bright Gan Eden (Garden of Eden).

The Rebbes

There were two Hassidic rebbes in Rohatyn, Rabbi Eliezer Langer and Rabbi Shlomo Brandwein, Z"L. Rabbi Eliezer Langer, Z"L, was the essence of wholeness and was loved by everyone. He possessed a sharp mind and was a great scholar as well as being dignified looking and very refined. Rabbi Shlomo Brandwein was an excellent ba'al tefilah with a Stratyner background, very dignified in his appearance. The two rebbes were related to each other.

Hassidim

Jews who lived in Rohatyn and the surrounding area were Stratyner Hassidim as a result of their physical proximity to the town of Stratyn, famous in the world of Hassidism.

The first Rebbe of Stratyn was the "Strelisker," Rebbe Uri of Strzeliska, known among Hassidim as the seraph (angel of fire). He was immediately followed by his student, Rabbi Yehuda Zvi, Z"L, who was the true founder of the present-day Stratyner dynasty of Hassidism. When Stratyner Hassidim repeated

Rebbe Yehuda's "Toiras" (Torah dissertations), they introduced them with the words, "Der Alter Rebbe, Rebbe Yehuda Hirsch hut gesugt..." (The Elder Rabbi, Rebbe Yehuda Hirsch, has said.) He was followed by his son, Rebbe Avrumche, Z"L. After him, the rabbinic dynasty was presided over by his son-in-law, Rebbe Uriale Rohatyner, who was in turn followed by his son, Rebbe Yehuda Zvi, Z"L. Both of them were buried in Rohatyn. The last mentioned rebbe marked the end of Stratyner Hassidim in Rohatyn, even though their descendants were still to be found in the other towns of Galicia and even in the U.S. One of the characteristics of Stratyner Hassidism was the stress on dvekus (strong emotion) in prayer. They used to sing their prayers with melodies that tugged at the heartstrings and which have enriched religious Jewish culture in general. (Some of the melodies were put down on paper by the composer Mr. Stoczewski after hearing them from me, the author.)

p. 104 YB: Owner of printing house, Szymon Teichman, with his wife, Sarah.

Owner of printing house, Chaim Skolnick, Z"L.

The Stratyner melody for "Sefirat HaOmer" (Counting of the Omer) left a strong and lasting impression on all who heard it. And even now, everyone who comes from Rohatyn and still remembers this melody uses it when singing the brachot (blessings) for Counting of the Omer—and only for that. On Lag B'Omer, the yahrzeit (anniversary of death) of the Rebbe Uriale of Rohatyn, Hassidim would gather around his grave—rabbis, Admorim, and just ordinary Jews, including women and children. They would offer their prayers and leave their pitkaot (notes of request) in the cracks of his gravestone. Even non-Jews used to stand in awe near the gate when they heard the closing ceremony—the singing of Bar Yochai—sung with good taste by the assembled forming a choir. Perhaps it would be proper to keep these melodies that were sung by the Hassidim of our town for future generations, or by Rebbe Yosef HaCohen Laks, Z"L, or by the shochtim, and transfer them to a recording—as long as there is still someone who remembers them and thus carries out the saying "but the song always lingers on."

But back to the customs of Stratyn. On the night of Shvii shel Pesach (the seventh day of Pesach), it was customary to meet at the home of Rebbe Eliezer L., Z"L, to commemorate the crossing of the Red Sea with song and dance. Water was poured on the feet of the dancers so that they would feel that they were "actually crossing the sea on dry land," in order to fulfill what is written, "Bechol Dor VaDor Chayav HaAdom Lirot et Atzmo keilu hu yatza miMitzrayim" (Pesach Haggadah). (In every generation a person is required to visualize himself as if he were actually leaving Egypt.)

On the last night of Chanukah (known as Zot Chanukah) the Hassidim used to gather by the rebbe for a festive meal, and the rebbe would deliver his words of Torah, which were preceded by a sigh and the words, "Der Zohar HaKadosh sugt... (The Holy Zohar says...) Divrei Chachamim b'nachat nishmaim (Words of the Sages are heard best quietly)." And I still recall a crumb of his teaching: When the Torah (Exodus 30:13) refers to the half shekel, contributed by each man as part of the census, why does it use the unusual term "machtzit" (spelled mem, chet, tsadi, yud, tav) for the word "half" rather than the usual term "chatzi"? Because the middle letter of the word machtzit is tzaddik, suggesting that a person must be close to a righteous person (also known as a tzaddik). For a person who is close to a tzaddik will merit the two letters which surround the letter tzaddik, that is chet and yud, which spell "chai," meaning life, as in the phrase (Leviticus 18:5) "v'chai bahem" (and you shall live by them). However he who distances himself from the tzaddik brings upon himself, God forbid, the combination of the two outer letters, that is mem and tav, which spell "met," meaning death. And the discerning person will understand the meaning of this.

Keepers of Tradition

After World War I, Hassidim began to change the style of their dress from the long robes to more modern garb. They stopped praying all the time with the Admorim and attended the established synagogues to pray. Instead of wearing a shtreimel (fur-trimmed hat) on Shabbat, they might put on a black hat. Instead of dressing in a bekeshe, the silk robe of the Hassidim, they might wear something shorter of woven cloth and put on a tie and shoes with laces. However, they did not stop studying the Torah or the Talmud, the Mishnayot, or the Chumash with Mephorshim (Commentaries). You could still hear them

p. 105 YB: Ruins of the Main Synagogue after World War I

Synagogue of Reb Nataniel Sofer

p. 106 YB: The Main House of Study

from afar studying and praying in the filled synagogues and study halls.

Houses of Prayer

And these are the synagogues that remained after World War I—and after a fire—and were used by our town until the time of the Shoah: There was the Beit HaKnesset HaGadol (the main synagogue) with two wings, each housing a separate synagogue, the Schneider Shulechel (the tailors' small shul), and the Schuster Shulechel (the cobblers' small shul). The large Beis Medresh (House of Study) had remained intact after World War I. It had been erected by Reb Alter Weidman and Reb Yakov HaCohen Lewenter. I remember the name of the latter, because it was to be found on the memorial plaque that was mounted on the northern wall of the Beis Medresh. (Not far from this plaque on the mizrach vant, the eastern wall, to the left of the Aron HaKodesh, the Holy Ark, where his son Reb Alter Lewenter, Z"L, continued to pray.)[2]

Reb Alter Lewenter was the father of Dr. Yitzchak Lewenter (Yibadel B'Chaim, may he be set aside for life). It is interesting to note that a short time before the war broke out, Dr. Lewenter and his wife, Cyla, took a trip to the U.S. but were unable to return. The war broke out, and our town was pillaged. Its Jewish inhabi-tants were murdered, including the doctor's only son, Maciek,

135

along with the rest of his family. May this memorial book to which they contributed and for which they collected funds be of some solace to them. May they enjoy a long life. This large Beis Medresh was the only religious building that survived World War I. The rest were destroyed. And then there comes to my mind Reb Yosef Zilber, the bathhouse caretaker. He was completely devoted to his work and also was the usual ba'al tefilah for mincha (services) in the Beit HaKnesset HaGadol. May his memory be blessed.

It was to this Beis Medresh that everyone came to pray after the fire; it was a place of breathtaking beauty, decorated with paintings of the Chayot HaKodesh—the Celestial Animals—and the symbolic drawings of each of the Twelve Tribes, all painted in oil. Reb Joel Granowiter, Z"L, was the gabbai (sexton) there. Reb Avraham Messing used to "tear the world apart" when he pronounced the words, "Yachid Chai HaOlamim" (of Baruch She-Amar), according to the melody of Stratyn, and used to complete the "Echad" (of Sh'ma Yisrael) with a special melody accompanied by his friend, the Hassid, Reb Yehuda Sofer, Z"L, in his hoarse voice, shaking his head up and down and to the sides so as to teach you that the spirit of the Lord permeates in all directions of the universe.

On the other side of the bathhouse, a shed was erected to be used for prayers that was called "Barak" (barrack), where the candles were lit in candle holders that still were made of clay. Here, the younger children were taught by Reb Moshe Gershon, "der Langer" (the long). (He received this name because he was very tall and very thin.) Reb Artzie (Aaron), the principal of the cheder (religious Hebrew school), a full-fledged scholar in his own right, used to teach the older students Gemara and Tosafot (Talmud and Commentaries) in the alcove there. Reb Artzie later left for America.

As new synagogues were built, the old shed was torn down. Not far from there, a small place of prayer was opened in a cellar termed "Im Keller" (in the cellar). The founders of this minyan (prayer group) were Reb Yankel Yona Schneekraut and Reb Natan (Nushi) Chaimowicz, Z"L. A small Beis Medresh was built later. (By the way, they sometimes used to call people who prayed in this Beis Medresh "Shabse Tzvinekes" in jest, because some claimed that in the past the adherents to Sabbatai Zvi had once met in this cellar.)

Then there was the small kloiz (prayer house) of Reb Nataniel, Z"L (I think he was a sofer), the Czortkower Kloiz, the Stratyner Kloiz, and the two rebbes of our town each had his own kloiz. An empty lot near the home of Yossel Fidelbogen, Z"L, was intended to become the place where a Zydaczower prayer house was to be built, but this never came to fruition.

By contrast, the Poles and the Ukrainians each had only one church in addition to the chapels at their cemeteries. On the other hand, when it came to other communal buildings, the Poles had a community center called the "Sokol," the Ukrainians had their "Proshvite," while a Jewish community center was not built until later.

The Rabbis

Among the rabbis who practiced in our town a special place is reserved for the Holy Gaon, our teacher, Rabbi Avraham David Moshe, or David Moshe Avraham, whose initials were A'D'M—the author of Mirkevet Hamishne on the Mechilta of Rabbi Yishmael,[3] a world renowned scholar. Because of him the reputation of our city spread to the Jewish communities throughout the world. In their letters of approbation of the book, in the forward, the rabbis describe the Gaon as follows: "A true genius, holy and marvelous, whose name enlightens. Rabbi David Moshe Avraham was the chief dayan (judge) of Rohatyn." To tell the praises of this genius is superfluous. But this I will tell you, my brothers—that which I heard from our grandfathers, which their forefathers told them—that the Ba'al Shem Tov visited Rabbi Adam prior to his demise when this G-dly man went up to the heavens. He came to visit him and to attend him in the fashion that one attends a great scholar, and the Ba'al Shem Tov told the rabbi, the author, "Rabbi, Bless Me," and the rabbi put his two hands on the Besht's head and blessed him. On his way home the Besht said to his student, "It appears that the rabbi has now passed away, for I saw the heavenly company coming towards him." And I heard that the great rabbis of his generation called him "Rabbi Adam." The story was told in our town that Rabbi Adam commanded orally, with his holy mouth, before he passed away, that no one should be buried next to his grave, and, if they did not fulfill his instructions, then the flour mill would burn down, the water wheels would go up in flames, and his tombstone would split. One or two generations later a talmid chacham passed away, and they violated the will of the Gaon, Rabbi Adam, Z"L. The talmid chacham was buried next to the grave of Rabbi Adam, Z"L, and his warning came to pass. The mill became a blazing inferno, and his gravestone split.

When I was still in Rohatyn, I remembered that the community and rabbis set aside a day to repair his tomb and support it with metal posts on both sides. All the Jews of the town came to his grave to ask for his

---

3 First printed by his grandchildren and their families in the year 1895 in Lwow with the backing of the modest Mrs. Tema Goldschlag, Z"L, who was known for the fine comportment of her family and noted for her good deeds in our town. This book was presented as a gift to the Rambam Library of Tel Aviv by Mr. Zvi Nagelberg of Lwow.

forgiveness and recite Tehillim (psalms).

It was customary for anyone who came to the cemetery to pass by his grave and spend some time there as a segula—a protective measure. I did the same after visiting the grave of my mother, the Rabbanit Chana Tova, daughter of Reb Elisha Aharon Klarnet, Z"L, in keeping with the instructions of my father, Rabbi Avraham David ben Reb Yitzchak Spiegel, who was a descendant of Rabbi Adam.

The successor to the holy Rabbi Adam was the holy Rabbi Avraham Shlomo (the uncle of Rabbi Shaul Yosef Nathanson) and after him came the pious Rabbi Elisha Aharon, Z"L.[Tr1] Among the rabbis of note in later generations were Rabbi Eliazer Horowitz, the author of the book Sefer D'var Halacha (Book of the Word of Law), the son of Rabbi Meshulam, known as "Ish Horowitz." He was followed by Rabbi Meir Glass; after that there was Rabbi Nosson Lewin (father of Reb Aharon Lewin, of Rzeszow, and of Rabbi Yecheskel Lewin, the Reform rabbi of Lwow, both born in Rohatyn). He was followed by Rabbi Yaakov "Kavi" Schein. (My father was his student for many years.) After that, Rabbi Meir Shmuel Henna of Strzeliska, Z"L, known as the "Old Dayan" (he was my teacher), a man who was very astute, very learned in the Talmud and religious laws, a person who kept to himself and was very careful of his behavior, as if he were not part of this world. (Not so long ago his son Yehoshua Henna came to Israel from the United States.)[4]

My father, Rabbi Avraham David Spiegel, Z"L, served the town for thirty-some years. He was a native of Rohatyn, born in 1885. At first he studied with his father, my grandfather, Reb Yitzchak Spiegel (an acknowledged scholar in his own right), until he was about eighteen years old. Then he went to study with Rabbi Yaakov Kavi, Z"L, and afterwards, he was ordained as rabbi by

---

4   Our thanks to him for his own contribution and the money he raised from others for this book.

Tr1   There is a difference of opinion as to who succeeded Rabbi Adam. In the book of HaRav Zvi Halevi Horowitz, Chief Rabbi of Dresden for many years, LeToldot HaKehilot B'Polin (Towards an Understanding of the Jewish Communities of Poland) ed. Yitzchak Rafael, Mosad HaRav Cook (Jerusalem), from manuscripts that had escaped destruction during WWII, page 509, we find that the successor was Rabbi Yitzchak, his (Rabbi Adam's) son. This is verified in his introduction to the book, Ohel Moed (Tent of Meeting), Frankfurt an der Oder, 1756. Other rabbis in Rohatyn included Rabbi Yehuda Leib of Cracow, known as Rabbi Leybisch Jolles, the rabbi before Rabbi Adam; Rabbi Adam was followed by his son, who was followed by Rabbi Yosef Halevi Landau; after that, Avraham Shlomo Halpern, the son of the renowned Rabbi, Yechiel Michal Halpern of Brzezany, the one to whom the author apparently was referring.

the renowned Rabbi Meir Arak of Tarnow and by Rabbi Shalom Mordechai HaCohen, the chief rabbi of Brzezany. In 1910, at the age of twenty-five, my father became rabbi of Rohatyn.

Before I left for Eretz Yisrael, my father had finished writing his book, The Mesorah (Tradition). He was incisive and scholarly, an excellent speaker and an excellent teacher, whether it was in Halacha or Talmud. He had a dignified appearance and would lead the prayers during the High Holy Days in his clear and distinct fashion. In addition to this, he was a man of action and did many things for the town of Rohatyn. A few years before the Shoah, Rabbi Mordechai Lippa Teumim, Z"L, served as the rabbi in Rohatyn.

Age of the Zionists

The first of the early Zionists whom I came to know was Mr. Zvi Latterman who lived near Zaluze. His son-in-law, Yisrael Fried, was a well known athlete. Latterman was a maskil, "enlightened one," and an open promoter of Zionism in Rohatyn. For this he suffered more than one towel thrown at him in the Beis Medresh or in the kloiz of Rabbi Nataniel, Z"L, by the Hassidic opposition, or, in general, by those who opposed Zionism. However, he, Zvi Latterman, never tired of urging Jews to return to Israel. His younger followers included Pinchas Spiegel (my uncle) and Elchanan Wachman, his friend. They founded the first Zionist group in our town under the name of "Eretz Yisrael Verein" (Society for Israel) and later united with Hitachdut, where many young people were indoctrinated into Zionism. From time to time they delivered lectures in the Verein and presented general information on the developments in the Land and made collections for Israel. In fact, the names of Elchanan Wachman and Pinchas Spiegel are inscribed in the Golden Book of KKL (Keren Kayemet L'Yisrael—the Jewish National Fund). The founding of HaChalutz, an early pioneering group, began the active process of return to Israel, and the young people in it joined the hachshara (preparation) for emigration to Israel.

As in other towns of Poland, the first youth group established in our town was called HaShomer, Zionist Youth Scouts, which eventually became HaShomer HaTzair. Later were formed such Zionist groups as HaNoar HaTzioni, Brit Trumpeldor and later still Gordonia and Mizrachi. In this way young people of our town began to prepare for aliyah (emigration to Israel), and some actually emigrated.

The General Zionists were composed mostly of middle-aged and even older people, including very important citizens of the town such as Yaakov Seidler, Lippa Mandel, Akiva Wagschal, Elisha Teichman, Dr. Zlatkis, Dr. Goldschlag, Izzie Doller, Pinnie Spiegel, Szymon Teichman, and attorney Szmuel Spiegel.

This is how I remember Rohatyn, my town, to which I am linked by so many memories, both sad and happy. Here I was born and here I grew up. The wounds caused by World War I had not yet healed, and the early harbingers of improvement were just beginning to appear as a result of the hard work of the Jews (one Jew, Dr. Goldschlag, Z"L, even became Vice Mayor of Rohatyn)—when that evil hand was brandished, the hand of the murderers, the bloody Nazi murderers. The town was destroyed. Our nearest and dearest were murdered. We could not imagine such a blood bath—so terrible a storm that passed over the towns of Poland and among them, our town. Who would have thought that the tree would be so completely uprooted? Twenty years have passed since that terrible and bitter day when the scythe was raised against the inhabitants of our town; yet the pain burns, and the wound pours blood as if it all had just happened yesterday. Their memory will never leave us.

An Elegy to the Martyrs of Rohatyn and its Environs

The cruel tide of that time swept away the Jews of our town, the innocent and the righteous, during the storm of the total destruction that Jews endured from the evil decrees of 1942–43. Our dear ones were scattered, humiliated, oppressed, and brutally murdered. The grandeur of the aged, the greatness of the wise, the joy of childhood, the exuberance of youth—all wiped out in the deluge of blood and fire by the unclean hands of the demons of our generation. In place of a Jewish community, alive and vibrant, there remains a void, empty and defiled...

In this book we are memorializing the history of the community during the passage of its generations, its organizations and institutions, its personalities and activists to the last ones—all of whom were erased from the Book of Life. We will tell about a life that was effervescent, dreams that were woven, experiences and longings of many generations, those years of the town of Rohatyn and her children that maintained the traditional and ethnic way of life in the Polish land of exile.

p. 110 YB: Library of the "Eretz Yisrael Verein" (Society for Israel). Standing to the right: Mucia Modlinger. Seated: Halpern and Dudke Beidof. Standing: Lipa Freiwald, Chaim Eisen, Yosef Mantenberg and behind them, Yehuda Bratspeiss. (photo courtesy Dale Friedman)

Pinchas Spiegel and Chuna Wachman, Z"L.

p. 111 YB: The "Deborah" group of HaShomer HaTzair in Rohatyn 1918: Upper row from the right: Braincia Teichman, Esther Grad, Sarah Baraban, Unknown, Raiza Leiter, Salka Wald, Czarna Schneekraut, Braina Stryjer, Rachel Lieder, Leah Katz.

*p. 112 YB: Top from the right: Michal Kizel, Yehoshua Bader, Yuzia Freiwald,
Widow Schorr, Mordechai Kizel, Weissberg, the wife of Yonia (a Christian),
Benjamin Melman (Schorr) and his son Moshe, Raiza Leiter, the daughter of
Melman, and her husband, Dr. Pasweg. Seated from the right: Esther Schorr
with her two granddaughters, Nechemia Grinzeid with his wife, Grinzeid's son,
the groom with his bride (of the Schorr family from the United States), at his
side, the wife of B. Melman with their grandchildren next to her; the son-in-law
of Grinzeid, his wife standing next to him, and the daughter of Yonia and Benny
Grinzeid.*

Inside Rohatyn
By Chuna Yonas, Paris

Translated by Binyamin Weiner - YB p. 113

Parties, Societies, Institutions

A Zionist society, known as the "Land of Israel League," existed in Rohatyn prior to World War I. In 1917 a group initiative, led by Chana Wabman, Pinia Spiegel, and Meir Lewenter, revived the League, which was then headquartered in the house of Buzio Bomze. The organization had two hundred fifty members. Many shtetl boys and girls attended League meetings. A number of young people joined both the academic association and the Zionist organization HaShomer.

Nor were we backward when it came to the matter of education. There was a Hebrew school. A Talmud Torah also existed before World War I. There were many houses of study, one large school, and three small schoolrooms. Our large Beit Midrash (house of prayer/study) was particularly fine, with its beautiful decorative paintings. The building of the Beit Midrash was across from the old house of study. The Stratyner synagogue, behind Yudel-Mechel Sofer's house, was not far away, and across from that, the little Czortkower synagogue, between Selig Nagelberg's and Baumrind's houses. There was also Reb Nathaniel's synagogue.

The local butcher shop was not far from Reb Nathaniel's synagogue. An artisan's guild also existed in our shtetl, headed by Michal Katz.

The large and beautiful Zionist library run by the Zionist organization should not be forgotten. It was a tradition that every Shabbos afternoon a different person would read aloud from some writer's works. (One reader, Fischel Weiler, now lives in Tel-Aviv.)

We had good prayer leaders. It is enough to mention Yehonoson Rappaport, who in addition taught a chapter of Gemara every Friday night; Mordecai-Shmuel Horszowski; Reb Yosef Laks, the Kohen; the famous cantor and composer Moshe Zushes, Z"L, and Efraim Sternhal, who led prayers in the Stratyner synagogue.

All kinds of Jews of different parentage and station lived in Rohatyn—rich, poor, tradesmen, craftsmen, butchers, doctors, lawyers, unaccomplished intellectuals, Hassidim, misnagdim (opponents of Hassidism), hackney drivers, porters, village traders, and peddlers. We were not lacking in poor people. In a word, Rohatyn was no different from any of the surrounding Jewish shtetls in Galicia.

Jewish children studied Torah fervently in cheder. The cheder in wintertime is especially etched in my memory. We would return home in the evening, each child bearing a lantern, with a lit wick inside. Our pride in possessing a lantern was great.

Performing Tashlich (casting bread crumbs on water as if casting away sins) on Rosh Hashanah was a beautiful custom. I especially remember Chaim Teichman who used to return singing to the synagogue where he would dance on the tables.

Before World War I, the Zionist youth leaders organized a mandolin orchestra that played every year on 18 August beneath the windows of the local commissioners, mayors, and other important people.

Let us remember those who stood out in the life of Rohatyn, such as our neighbors Aaron Winkler and Moshe Leder. The latter was a leather dealer and the owner of two houses. I remember him as an old man, sitting by the gate with his long-stem pipe. I also recall Shmuel Einstoss, whom we called "Shmuel, the merchant," Eli Glazer, and Avrum Ziff. We lived with Avrum Ziff. I grew up with my grandmother, Etel Banner. Yehoshua Ziff and his two sons-in-law, one, a schoolteacher, and the other, a coachman, lived in the same house. The Withoff family, who later moved to Lemberg (Lwow), also lived there, as did Shmelke Rokach, who made ornamental collars for prayer shawls, and Yankel Brieftraeger, with his wife Lajcie, "the grandmother."

In general, Rohatyn was considered an enlightened shtetl. It contained Hassidim and misnagdim. The latter had greater influence. They waged an unceasing struggle for influence over the local community. Alter Weidmann was the head of the enlightened faction, and Efraim Sternfeld, of the religious one.

Rebbes and Rabbis

There were four camps of Jews in the shtetl, each one backing its own candidate for rabbi. This was in the time of the Russo-Japanese War, when the old rabbi of Rohatyn, Rabbi Natan Lewin, left the shtetl for Rzeszow. Following his departure, there were many disputes concerning the candidates seeking to occupy the position of the shtetl's new rabbi.

As I recall, the first dayan (judge) appointed in this period was the Strelisker Rabbi Meir-Shmuel Henne. After him, we had "one of our own" as rabbi, someone from Rohatyn. In his youth, he had worked for a lawyer as a scribe. In those days, the typewriter had not yet made its way into Rohatyn, and the fine handwriting of the future Rabbi Spiegel served the lawyer well. Together with his old friend, Szymon Teichman, he worked for the attorney Lipiner who was greatly pleased with his employees. It happened once that the lawyer returned from court to find his scribe, Spiegel, sitting in the office, and peeping out from beneath his shirt, were the four fringes of his ritual undergarment. Lipiner told him, "You will have to make a decision; devote yourself to working for me or become a rabbi. Because sitting in my office with your fringes hanging out - this will not do." Clearly, the young Spiegel chose the path of Torah and left the lawyer's office. For a year, this incident served the shtetl as a topic of discussion.

Rabbi Avrum-Dovid Spiegel was more worldly than pious and therefore had many followers in Rohatyn. During his term, there was also another dayan in the shtetl, Rabbi Meir Henne, who represented the more pious Jews. He was known as the Strelisker Dayan. He spoke no foreign languages. On 18 August, Franz-Joseph's birthday, when they were obliged to greet the local commissioner, the two dayanim went together, but Rabbi Spiegel did all the talking, as he spoke Polish, Ukrainian, and German.

Our first Hungarian rabbi was the Grand Rabbi Eliezer Langner, son-in-law of the Stratyner rebbe. Later, we had the son of the Stratyner rebbe, Yehudeh-Tzvi, may his memory be blessed among us, the Grand Rabbi Shlomo Langner.

Many Jews were arrested in 1915. The two dayanim were set free. They appealed to the local commandant, Pogrebny, to use his influence to free those Jews held by the authorities. The commandant began speaking to the older dayan, the Strelisker Dayan, Rabbi Meir-Shmuel Henne. As the older dayan could not understand him, however, he had no choice but to address the younger dayan, Rabbi Avrum-Dovid Spiegel.

Elections for the Austrian Parliament

In 1907 or 1908, elections were held to the Austrian Parliament. It could easily have led to soldiers firing on the turbulent crowd. The ballot boxes were located in the Jewish communal office, the headquarters of the Jewish parties, in the Beit Midrash (house of prayer). There were three Jewish candidates—Breiter, a socialist, Dr. Reitzes from Zloczow, who was elected to represent Zloczow proper, and Rappaport, a lawyer from Lwow. All three were unable, by any means, to find lodging for the night in Rohatyn. Late at night, a Ukrainian lawyer, Babyuk, took them in, and they stayed over with him. It turned out that the local hotels had received an order from the commissioner not to rent a room to them. They also had a hard time obtaining meals.

There was a Polish candidate, a certain Kowalewski, in whose election the authorities were interested. The Jews would not vote for him, however, preferring the Zionist candidate, Dr. Rappaport. Therefore, all kinds of tricks were employed. As the Polish candidate was led from the train station amidst a grand parade, the Jewish candidates were left on their own. Dr. Breiter and Dr. Reitzes had both also arrived at this time and had to wander through the shtetl on their own, having nowhere to go. The local commissioner arranged all of this.

In the middle of the election, the commissioner interrupted the voting. A few Poles were stationed by the ballot box to carry out the orders of the authorities. Hired Ukrainians searched every voter, making sure that they didn't have any additional ballots.

Dr. Reitzes, who was then already an elected deputy in Parliament, struggled energetically against these maneuvers. He rushed from the Zionist party's headquarters to the election headquarters and strongly protested before the commissioner against the violation of voters' rights. I remember, as if it were today, the way he addressed the commissioner in the informal second person, which made quite a strong impression. The Zionist youth weren't caught sleeping either and they guarded, as well as they could, against the searching of voters. A militia encircled the building in which the ballot box was located. The commissioner would not let Dr. Reitzes into the building even though he was a deputy. In addition, he gave an order to the officer of the army unit that was stationed beside the building to disperse the crowd by force. Of course, the first to flee were the little Jewish children, among whom I was to be found. And after us—went the Jews who wanted to cast their votes.

Deportation to Russia

When the Russian Army took Rohatyn, in 1915, all Jews were driven out of the shtetl. In the middle of the night, all of the men were roused from their beds and sent away deep into Russia, to the province of Pezner. On Wednesday, the arrested Jews were driven into the local school in Babince. After sunset, we were lined up in rows, counted and ordered to march to Podwysokie. There we spent the night in an open field. In the early morning, we were once again lined up and counted and then marched still further, to Brzezany. Along the way, we were severely beaten. The first to receive a beating was Mendel Rotenberg. At midday, we came to Brzezany. We had to make our way on foot. We were led into the local army barracks. At dusk, we were again ordered to go. We noticed then that Velvel Weissbraun's eldest son, Moshe, had also been arrested. By then, we had no strength left. I was the youngest of those sent away.

Just before our arrest, 22 community leaders, prominent men of the town, were rounded up. The Russians demanded from them a list of all the Jews in the area. Yankel Leiter found himself at the head of this group. They refused to carry out the order of the Russian authorities. Jews were therefore taken from their beds. That is how 500 Jews were arrested in all, of whom only 350 survived. Upwards of 150 died on the roads of Russia. A cholera epidemic had broken out among us.

The Town Intelligentsia

Rohatyn was also a town in which an intelligentsia sprang from the native Jewish population—lawyers (Dr. Scharf and Dr. Weidmann) and doctors (Dr. Stein, Dr. Lewenter, Dr. Hekel Weinstock, and Dr. Chaika Kiesler). Meir Lewenter, the elder brother of Dr. Yitzchak Lewenter, both outspoken Zionists, was a contributor to the Lemberg Tageblatt. There were many other strong intellectuals active in many realms of local life—the physician Dr. Stein, who was the town doctor, the local lawyer, Dr. Kleinberg, a leader of the leftist "Poalei Zion" (Workers of Zion) and also Dr. Alter, who, as a lawyer, undertook political defenses in the court of Rohatyn.

Time, which has run on since I left my shtetl in 1920, has done its work. I do not remember very much. Also, my efforts to survive under the German occupation of France sapped my strength. Twice the Germans had me in their hands, and each time, I managed to escape. From Paris I went to Grenoble where I joined the resistance movement and fought against the German occupation.

A Bundle of Memories
By Marcus Zin, Acco

Translated by Binyamin Weiner - YB p. 118

In the Jewish world, Rohatyn was known for its rabbis. Great learned men would have paid us to choose them as our rabbi. This high office was occupied by Rabbi Meir Gloz and Rabbi Natan Lewin, who later became a rabbi in Rzeszow. Rabbi Natan Lewin was the father of Rabbi Ortsi (Aaron) Lewin, who, apart from being a rabbi, was also a deputy in the Polish Sejm (parliament). Rabbi Lewin's second son, Rabbi Yecheskiel Lewin, was the chief rabbi for the Lwow (Lemberg) district. In addition, Rohatyn had Rabbi Yaakov Kovi-Schein, dayan and righteous teacher; later there was the old dayan, Rabbi Shmuel Henne, or, as we called him, the Strelisker rabbi[Ed1] (rabbi from the Strzeliska dynasty), and last but not least, Rabbi Avrum-Dovid Spiegel[Tr1] (even in his later years, he was still called "the young dayan"). Rabbi Spiegel also represented the Jewish population before the secular authorities.

I remember certain events that were characteristic of "the young dayan." After the synagogue burnt down in 1915, he not only collected money to rebuild it but also rolled up his sleeves and helped clear away the half-burnt bricks from the wreck in order to begin transforming the ruins into a new building. His example inspired others, and many Jews helped in the rebuilding of the synagogue. The city valued the rabbi's achievement greatly and awarded him a permanent seat of honor in the synagogue behind the lectern by the eastern wall ... He was consequently given this honor in every holy place.

Rabbi Spiegel also gave ritual sanction to, and therefore was the inventor of, a way of keeping the ritual bath warm, even on the Sabbath. This ritual bath was renowned for its cleanliness, and even the impious used to use it, especially on early winter mornings. The surrounding shtetls later followed the example.

To the account of Rabbi Spiegel's achievements and initiatives must be added the establishment of the Talmud Torah, which provided a Jewish education to numerous children of Rohatyn and the study of the "daily page" of Talmud,

Ed1   Rabbinic dynasty which was established in Strzelisko, a small town/village in Lwow Voivodeship, close to Rohatyn.

Tr1   Yiddish form of name Rabbi Avraham David Spiegel.

which he led. He served in deed and counsel with a warm word and substantial assistance over the course of his thirty years in the office.

After our Rabbi Avrum-Dovid Spiegel, Rabbi Mordecai Lipa Teumim held the position in the remaining few years before the war.

Among the Hassidic rebbes in our city was Rabbi Eliezerel—a man possessing all of the virtues and one who didn't mix in city matters—he was beloved by all the Jews. Later, Rabbi Shloimele of the Stratyner[Ed2] (Stratyn) dynasty came to Rohatyn.

***

The Zionist movement in our city was organized and led by Elchanan Wachman, Pinchas Spiegel, Akiva Wagschal, Hersh Laterman, Lipa Mandel and others. They instilled in the youth a desire to go to the land of Israel. The leaders of the Zionist organization suffered considerably at the hands of the Austrian government, but this did not stop them from undertaking their work.

***

After the outbreak of World War I, in 1914, when the Czar's army came to the city, Rohatyn was burned down. In 1915, all of the Jewish men in the city were deported to Russia. Only Rabbi Spiegel was left behind. He became the father of every child in the city. He knew when to tell the mothers that their children had to begin putting on phylacteries, and he prepared the children to do so. I myself was one of those children …

In 1918, the Austro-Hungarian monarchy collapsed. The Ukrainians took power, then the Poles, later the Bolsheviks, and finally it was Poland again. For Jews, those times offered nothing but pain and suffering. Elchanan Wachman, the well-known Zionist activist, was severely beaten by the Hallerczyki[Ed3]. The blows left him permanently impaired; he saw everything double… He went from the world at a young age.

In 1921, the city was rebuilt and life normalized. At that time, many unions were organized, political and professional, as well as aid societies, Zionist organizations, Hitachdut, Yad HaRotzim, artisan guilds and others.

The Jewish landowners in Disanow (or Dysanow) permitted the Jewish youth to practice farming (Hachshara) so that they could later immigrate to the Land of Israel as pioneers. The Russians had burned the city's two houses of study, the synagogue, and the large Beit Midrash (House of Study) with

---

Ed2   See article Hassidut of Stratyn, Yehoshua P. Spiegel.

Ed3   Encyclopedia Judaica, p. 1200, "Haller's Army (Blue Army), force of Polish volunteers organized in France during the last year of World War I, responsible for the murder of Jews and anti-Jewish pogroms in Galicia and the Ukraine."

its rich history. They had twice tried to set fire to this house of study, but the fire had not caught. People said that it was an act of G-d, and it stands to this day. So does the historic 600-year-old cemetery with the common grave from Chmielnicki's time.

***

In 1939, with the outbreak of World War II, many refugees came to Rohatyn. The city gave much assistance to the unfortunates. A committee was formed consisting of Pinia Spiegel, Dr. Goldschlag, who was vice-mayor, Akiva Wagschal, Lipa Mandel, Yisroel Gleicher, Dr. Zlatkis and our beloved Rabbi Avrum-Dovid Spiegel. They made sure the refugees had food to eat and a place to sleep.

In 1941, the war between Germany and Russia broke out. On Rosh Hashanah, Hitler's murderers entered our city and began annihilating the Jewish population.

*p. 119 YB: The clearing of the ruins of the Great Synagogue and its
restoration, after World War I. Pictured from the right: Yankel Leiter, Dudel Wald,
Yosef Fidelbogen, Nachman Fidelbogen with his grandson in his arms, Moshe
Schein (with the wheelbarrow,) Berish Hirsh, Volvel Weissbraun, Yoel Granowiter,
Abba Kartin, Reuven Brodbar, unknown, and two youths.*

*p. 120 YB: The small, Russian Beis Medresh (Beit HaMidrash -study-house)
after World War I.*

Tones (Sounds) of Home

By Dr. Natan Spiegel, Jerusalem

Translated by Binyamin Weiner - YB p. 121

According to historians, Rohatyn was not a big city when compared with the others in its region. In 1912, Rohatyn had over 7,000 inhabitants, half of them Jewish. In 1941, there were 12,000, approximately 6,000 of them Jews. The murderous Nazis destroyed nearly the entire population.

But Rohatyn was more to me than the mere statistical number of its inhabitants. It was where my parents, family, and friends lived and perished. There I attended traditional cheder and school. There I experienced my first joys and sorrows. There I spent the years of my childhood and youth.

The material conditions of my upbringing were poor: a small and aged one-story house with a wooden floor, the walls of the hallways covered with mildew. It is no wonder then that under these circumstances I contracted a kidney disease, and my sister, three years my junior, had a sickness that affected her sight. My brothers, Muah and Sami, years older than I, were exceptional for their good vision.

Despite these poor conditions, I have preserved fond memories of childhood. This was no doubt due to the positive atmosphere that pervaded our house.

My father, may he rest in peace, a wise man with a good heart, was an expert embroiderer, and bore the responsibility of providing for his family and seeing to the education of his children.

Our mother was a "Jewish mother" in the very spirit of the ideal. Though her health was always poor, she looked after the well being of her children and husband. We loved her very much and rejoiced in the wonderful mutual affection that bound her to our father, a warm and heartfelt love that was never clouded by the shadow of misunderstanding.

From my earliest childhood, I attended a traditional cheder. Despite its academic flaws, I still recall it lovingly as a

> "small room, narrow and warm,
> a fire within its stove,
> where the rabbi teaches aleph-beis
> to his little children."[Tr1]

Tr1   This is an excerpt of the Yiddish song "Oyfn Prepitschok."

153

One of my teachers was Nahum Milstein. I remember him affectionately. His son Anshel was a dear childhood friend of mine. Anshel lives here in Israel now, in Ramat Gan.

I was especially gladdened when our big brother came to cheder to take us, that is, my brother Sami and me, to the cinema. My father, as I recall, put up a whole crown to finance these expeditions. Three tickets cost 45 pennies, and whatever remained was devoted to the purchase of "shtulbriki," "milkeh-soshard" (a heler got you one piece), and balls of chocolate (liberkneidlech). Such joy! Such delight!

In 1912, when I was seven years old, I began attending a Polish elementary school, in addition to the cheder. Ms. Tsirler, an excellent teacher, who later became the wife of Dr. Milgrum, the regional doctor, taught me there. She was a prominent woman, who employed a modern method of instruction, a rarity in those days.

I still hold on to the memories of a special possession, whose light made my heart tremble when I was still in elementary school. At the end of my second year of studies, I received a small book as a reward for my diligence. Two birds were drawn on the cover and the book itself contained several poems. Whenever I read them I was moved to tears. One song, for instance, went like this:

> "Do not pursue the butterfly.
> That which passes in an instant
> Think it gone—
> This is the secret of a peaceful life:
> Do not pursue the butterfly."

I held this book among my greatest treasures, and I lost it in World War II. I recall that during this same span of years our city passed frequently from hand to hand. Once we fell into Austrian hands, once into the hands of the Germans, and once into Russian hands. We were often compelled to hide in the basement, in times of shooting, when soldiers passed through our houses to plunder and desecrate.

During the Russian retreat, most of the Jewish houses were set on fire. Earlier, the Jews had fled to the outskirts of the city, and all night we watched as a pillar of fire played above the rooftops.

At dawn, full of worry, we rushed to see if by chance our house had not burned. And truly, wondrously, our little old house had been saved from the tongues of flame.

In 1916, during another retreat, the Russians carried all of the older males of the city away with them. A short time after the coming of the Austrians (or Germans) our family went to Moravia.

There I worked for a rich farmer in the village of Dambuzce (Dambooztze), though I was all of eleven years old. Among other things, I would feed and water eight cows, clean the barn, and work in the field. There is one incident that was burrowed deep into my mind and remains etched there to this day. Once, I traveled with my boss in a wagon full of manure, of which I was the driver. All of a sudden, the reins "became confused" (tangled) and the cattle (that were used in Moravia to plow) veered from the road into the field we were passing. The boss, his eyes full of rage, shouted at me, "Jew!"

After our return to Rohatyn, the turbulence of two new wars engulfed us: the war between the Poles and the Ukrainians, and the war between Poland and the Soviet Union. And, of course, Jews were persecuted on both sides. The Poles and Ukrainians would shave the beards of pious Jews, beat them, and brutalize them. A Polish officer accused my brother of treachery, because he had fastened a telephone apparatus to his rooftop, through which he had established contact with the Bolsheviks. This meant certain death, but, miraculously, my brother was saved.

At the end of 1918, I was studying in the local Polish gimnazjum. Once, my Russian language teacher heard me chatting with my friends in Yiddish. The next day, this teacher mocked and abused me for nearly an entire hour, in order to expose me to scorn and ridicule for having "stammered in the tongue of my people"—in Yiddish.

During my years in high school I gave private lessons for a fee, in order to support my parents and lighten the load they carried in providing for the household. In 1925, after passing the matriculation exam, I began studying at the university in Lwow (Lemberg), in a humanities program. Due to the students' anti-Semitic riots, I was more than once afraid to walk between the walls of the university, because of the beatings they gave us.

After completing my degree, I received a teaching position at the city gimnazjum in Kalusz (pronounced Kaloosh). Out of a faculty of twelve there were only three Jews. We were hired by yearly contract, and each year we worried afresh over whether or not these would be renewed by the authorities, and over which Jewish teacher would lose his job.

After the outbreak of World War II, I continued working in the education administration of Kalusz, though now under the authority of the Soviets. In 1940, I was in Rohatyn for the last time. My mother was already sick and bedridden. My father clung to her with devotion and warmheartedness. Poverty and destitution ruled the house. Their only consolation was the marriage of my sister Clara to a respectable man in Stanislawow.

In the same period of time, I saw my immediate family and relations for the last time: my brother Shmuel, a lawyer in Rohatyn, who for years had stood at the head of the local Zionist organization; his wife Felicia and their lovely and intelligent two year-old daughter; my uncle Rabbi Avrum-Dovid Spiegel, a man distinguished for his kindness, righteousness, and wisdom, and also his family; my uncle Pinchas Spiegel, who devoted all the days of his life to the Zionist cause, and his family; my aunt Golda, beloved of all, and her family (her son Chaim now lives with his family on Kibbutz HaMapil).

With the outbreak of World War II, I fled with a friend to Russia. On my way there, I stopped in Stanislawow to say goodbye to my sister Clara. She and her husband did not want to leave behind our elderly parents, who were not strong enough to withstand the hardships of moving from place to place. Soon after, all of my family went to their graves, together with the rest of Polish Jewry, killed by the murderous Nazis.

In 1944, I sent a letter from Russia to the city of Rohatyn, inquiring after the fate of my family. I received a letter on the 16th of December, 1944, with the following response: "The city council of the Labor Ministry in the city of Rohatyn informs you in response to your inquiry that of the family of DR. SPIEGEL, SHMUEL, not one is still living. The Germans murdered all of them on 20 March 1942.

Signed: Vice-Chairman of the City Council Stolarczuk."

In 1946, we returned, my friend and I, to Poland, and from there we immigrated to Israel in 1957. Here, we awoke to a new life, and I believe with a full faith that sooner or later the verse will be fulfilled: "They will return from the land of the enemy...the children will return to dwell within their borders."

A City of Torah
By Leybisch Zukerkandel, New York

Translated by Binyamin Weiner - YB p. 124

W e were three brothers: Itsik, who was the eldest, my younger brother Aron and myself. Our father, a learned Jew, was also knowledgeable in worldly matters. He was an expert in the Polish language and had a wonderful handwriting. He used these skills in the service of anyone who sought his help, writing petitions to Polish institutions and attending to matters affecting the Jews. He was always immersed in communal business. Even in his later years, when he moved to Lwow (Lemberg), his tobacco and newspaper shop served as an inn for traders from Rohatyn, who would heed his words of advice and maintain their connection with this dear friend.

p. 124 YB: Moishe Zukerkandel and his wife Blumah, with their children: Yitzchok, Leybisch (in America), Batiah (in Israel), and Aron.

Our father paid strict attention to our Jewish education, just as every Jewish parent of the time did for his children. It began with Moshe-Gershon the melamed (schoolteacher), and continued with Urtsi Menahel, the Gemara melamed (teacher of Gemara, i.e. of recorded Jewish oral law and rabbinic discussions). When we grew older, we were delivered into the faithful hands of the "young dayan," Rabbi Spiegel, my father's old friend. We were among the chosen few who merited learning

157

from him, and it must be emphasized that the rabbi taught us without the expectation of reward. His students included the distinguished Eliyahu Mesing (the son of Avrom Mesing), my brother Yitzchok, may he rest in peace, and myself, the present writer.

I will never forget my period of study with Rabbi Spiegel: his patriarchal demeanor, his gentle and majestic face, his appearance on State birthdays, and the way he would interrupt his lessons in order to address some question that had arisen regarding a matter of meat and milk. Nor will I forget his clear and lucid explanation of the laws concerning kosher and treif (non-kosher).

In the winter we arose at four in the morning, and walked with a lantern in our hands (not every boy was lucky enough to have his own lantern) to study at the beis midrash (house of prayer and study.) There it was a special privilege to receive a candle from the gabbai (synagogue officer) to serve as light for three or four boys.

But all of this - these memories that still bring a smile to the lips - now belongs, much to our sorrow, to the past. To those of us, however, who were fortunate enough to see how this town stood out and to know how it still serves as an inspiration—to us Rohatyn still remains a town of enlightened men and of the study of Torah.

What a loss are those who are gone! The German murderers destroyed not only one third of the Jewish people, but also one third of its spirit and one-third of its hope for complete redemption.

But "the Glory of Israel will not fail." We were worthy enough to see with our own eyes the founding of the state of Israel, and we will hope that, despite all of our enemies, Israel will yet flower and flourish, and that there the mourners of the nation of Israel will be comforted for their terrible Shoah (Holocaust). Amen. May it be so.

Rohatyn: The Town and Its Character
By Uri Mishur

Translated by Binyamin Weiner - YB p. 125

I myself am not a son of Rohatyn, but of one born in Rohatyn. I am referring to my father and teacher Reb Avrom son of Reb Uri Todfeler, may the Lord avenge his blood, whose family flourished in Rohatyn.

I often recall my visits to the city, which occurred yearly in my childhood, when I was on vacation from my studies. I would stay with my uncle and aunt, and their family: Kubler, Beigel and Averbuch.

I arrived in the city on the train that crossed the bridge on the river Gniła Lipa. The Jews lived in the center of town, and in the very center of the center itself there was an aqueduct, with the river water flowing through it. I have known many cities and towns in Poland, but in none of them have I seen a system of supplying water similar to the one in Rohatyn.

I too came to Rohatyn to draw its water, that is to say its Torah, for there is no water but Torah, from the wells of Torah and Hassidut (piety) that were our great Rebbe and teacher Rabbi Shloimeleh, Z"L, and his son Yehudeh Tsvi, Z"L. The latter taught us chapters of Gemara. How great was his passion during lessons in the Likutei Amarim of the Ba'al Tanya (Rabbi Shneur Zalman of Liadi) on the Divine Essence: "Oy, oy, the wicked men, the heretics ask, 'Where is God?' Oy gevalt, how shall we answer them? 'There is no place where He is not!' All the wicked men, all the heretics ask, 'What is God?' How shall we answer them? 'There is no thought that can imprison Him!'"

I also studied with my uncle, Reb Moshe-Leyb Kubler, may the Lord avenge his blood. He was always cheerful, never complaining for lack of anything, and he accepted both good and bad fortune with equanimity. Indeed, during the time I spent with him his material conditions were truly good. He paid little attention to business and much to the study of Torah. He always prayed in the shul (synagogue) of our grand Rebbe and teacher Rabbi Eliezerel, Z"L, where he was also the regular Torah reader (at prayer service). Every day, after finishing the morning prayer, he came home to eat breakfast and then returned immediately to the "shtibel," (small house of study) to study his regular lesson of Torah: the weekly portion along with the interpretation of Ibn-Ezra, whom my uncle considered superior to all of the other commentators.

On Fridays, he released me from my studies, because, as the reader, it was his responsibility to prepare the Torah chanting. He was strict about every single note, not lengthening when he should shorten, and not shortening when he should lengthen.

p. 125 YB: The bridge on the river Gniła Lipa.

A Completely Sacred Sabbath

These were Jews who lived by (the teaching of) Torah and service, "service" meaning the service of the heart. And what is the service of the heart? It is prayer.

And these were Jewish merchants, immersed in business day and night, who still fulfilled their Jewish obligations at all times through acts of loving-kindness and charity, even in business matters and even when serving their Gentile customers.

My cousin, Reb Chaim Kubler, may the Lord avenge his blood, was one of them. He was always occupied with his business, but was nonetheless devoted to the charitable relief of poor wayfarers, who would wander from village to village and city to city, gathering alms. In Rohatyn, they did not have to pass from doorway to doorway, instead they received a special, biweekly or monthly stipend, financed by my cousin. Every poor wayfarer received a stipend according to his turn, as recorded in a register. My cousin undertook this project out of goodness, and not in expectation of reward. He kept his door open all the time in order to provide relief for those in need, never fixing only certain hours for receiving the poor.

These people, and many like them, devoted their entire being and existence to the performance of good deeds, and they fulfilled their obligations in simplicity and sincerity. Woe onto us that they were killed before their time to die had come. May the Lord avenge their blood.

p. 126 YB: Binyomin (his son), Malkeh (his wife), and Henni (his daughter).

Chaim Kubler as an Austrian soldier.

p. 127 YB: They were four friends—standing, from the right, are: Yosef Bir, Chombe Mandel, Yitschok Krig (alive, and living in Netanya); seated: Yechezkel Otner. It is said of the last that he rose up against the oppressors in our city, and they shot him.

Public Life in Rohatyn

By Dr. Natan Meltzer

Translated by Binyamin Weiner - YB p. 128

I remember Rohatyn as a town rich in public life, which, for me, was centered on the Bnai Zion association. This group met in Mendel Bernstein's house. There I read the newspapers, learned to play chess, and debated both the Zionist issues on the agenda and matters regarding the Jewish world in general.

Herzl died during the time that I spent there, and we were all deeply distressed by this tremendous loss. I still remember the special edition brought out by the newspaper "Di Velt."[Ed1] It was set against a black background and contained a letter from Herzl's widow Julia. We were like fatherless orphans, and for months the burden of this loss lay upon us, without relief.

The Jewish community of Rohatyn, led by Alter Weidmann, was among the first in Galicia to establish a modern Hebrew school. The esteemed pedagogue Raphael Soferman, Z"L, served as its principal.

In addition to Zionist activity, there was also a great deal of interest focused on the elections for the Austrian parliament. There were three candidates for the Rohatyn-Brzezany district: Dr. Shmuel Rappaport, of the Jewish nationalist party, Dr. Nebokovsky, of the Ukrainian party, and Wladyslaw Duleba (or Dulemba),[Ed2] of the "Voice of Poland" party. None of the candidates received a sufficient margin of votes in the first round of the elections. In the second round, Dr. Rappaport, despite his slim chances, was still struggling against the Polish candidate.

Some of the important Jewish merchants of the community were Sender Margolis, Jacob Fish, Shalom Meltzer, and Alter Weidman (the aforementioned community chairman.) The Jewish representatives of the town participated in a body with the Ukrainian representatives, in addressing all local problems.

My father, Shalom Meltzer, Z"L (the son of Dovid Meltzer the Kohen, who immigrated to Israel and settled in Safed), was one of the

---

Ed1 In Yiddish: The World.
Ed2 See History of the Jews of Rohatyn, Dr. N. M. Gelber, 1848-1914.

founding members of the Zionist Association Bnai Zion. He was elected to the communal board and the city council, and served as a liaison with the Zionist Center in Lwow, which was led by Dr. Adolf Stand (Shtand). He was also a business representative for the "Carmel" company (wine produced in Palestine/Israel).

p. 128 YB: Shalom Meltzer, Z"L.

A City in Life and in Destruction

In Honor of Moshe Lewenter, Z"L

By Yosef Green, Tel Aviv

Translated by Rabbi Mordecai Goldzweig - YB p. 129

We had been friends from childhood, tied body and soul. We went to grammar school and gimnazjum together. Our studies were interrupted by the Russians who rounded up all of the Jewish males during World War I when they left our town, and still we were not separated. We were together in Ponza[Ed1] until we received permission to return to our homes. On the way back we were held up for two years in Tarnopol until it was conquered by the Austrians. In Tarnopol we studied in the "Polish" gimnazjum (under the supervision of the Russians) until we were released by the Austrian army when they conquered the city. Two months later we were drafted into the army at Lwow. This time we were separated; Lewenter was sent to Przemysl[Ed2] and I was sent to Bielsko[Ed3]. The separation was difficult for both of us. We felt that this would be the end to our friendship. Shortly afterwards I was informed that my friend, the most wonderful of people, became sick in Przemyslany and died of pneumonia. His memory will never leave my heart.

Ed1   One of four Pontine Islands near Rome, Italy.

Ed2   W. Galicia, southeastern Poland.

Ed3   Since 1950 Bielsko Biala, S. Poland, German: Bielitz.

Fragments

In 1918 Pinchas Spiegel, Chana Wachman, Z"L, and I, the writer of these lines, opened a hospital in Rohatyn to save the lives of the Jewish soldiers who were returning from the war and had contracted the plague. Thanks to this place we succeeded in saving many of them.

After World War I, aided by the late Dr. Goldschlag, we established the Histadrut Poalei Zion (Zionist Labor Organization) in Rohatyn. We acted as counselors to the youth, who engaged in lively and invigorating activities. We founded a football (soccer) club as well as a wonderful dramatic group, of which I am presenting one picture. This drama club enriched the cultural life of the town.

p. 129 YB: "The Jewish Escapee" – Directed by Yosef Green

Precious Images

By Leah Zuch, Tel Aviv

Translated by Rabbi Mordecai Goldzweig - YB p. 130

Rohatyn together with its dear Jews was destroyed during World War II, but the beloved images of our holy martyrs still rise up before our eyes and it is hard to forget them.

Yes, this is the town covered with greenery where our ancestors had lived for generations. I can still picture my grandmother, Dvorele Moshele (Wagschal), lovely and gentle returning from the synagogue in her scarf and fine silk clothes – how proud I was of her.

I remember the Purim se'uda (festive meal) in my parents' home. That evening many children of the town would come to us in their costumes. Especially noticeable were the groups of students who portrayed historical figures including those of the Megilla. Others came from Zionist youth groups wearing blue and white sashes emblazoned with the Star of David. These were joined by four klezmorim (lively musicians) from the Faust family who played the typical Jewish songs and ended their musical performance with Hatikvah. The faces of my father, Akiva Wagschal, and my mother, Tzirel, would shine with joy upon every display of Zionism in the town. My father, who was a Zionist in heart and soul, was one of the founders of the Hebrew School of Rohatyn and was also privileged to visit Israel.

After World War I we were among the approximately 30 university students considered to be the "Golden Youth" of Rohatyn (not in today's sense). However, none of our knowledge or personal qualities helped us obtain a teaching position in the local gimnazjum—only because we were Jewish. Those were the days of the infamous quota system.

I still remember the libel case staged against Steiger[Ed1] who was falsely accused of attempting to assassinate the president of the state. We of Rohatyn were particularly interested in this trial, since Steiger was the son-in-law of a Rohatyn townsman, the husband of Jozka (Yoozka) Mark. If we had only been wise enough to pay attention to the warning signals of those days…

Ed1   Steiger Trial, trial held in 1924-25 in Lwow against the Jew Stanislaw Steiger on the trumped-up charge that he had conspired to assassinate the Polish President. " … Steiger's acquittal on Dec. 20, 1925." Encyclopedia Judaica, Ed. Michael Berenbaum and Fred Skolnik. Vol. 19, 2nd ed. Detroit: Macmillan Reference USA, 2007. p. 174

Nonetheless, on "The Third of May," the national holiday of Poland, we Jews would watch the celebrating throng of "The Sokols" (The Falcons), i.e. Cadets marching and singing "Poland Has Not Perished.[Ed2]" They were joined by the school children who marched with them in the parade. At that point attorney Dr. Alter would call out: "Next year in Jerusalem." How unfortunate it was that he as well as thousands of other Jews of Rohatyn were not privileged to reach this goal.

And so it is that our souls mourn...

p. 130 YB: Two student groups in Rohatyn:

Unidentified person, Dr. Avraham Sterzer, Salka Zuch, Unknown, Yulik Skolnick, Busko Sharer, Manka Fuld, Grina Foist and Ludwig Mondschein.

Ludwig Katz, Salka Zuch, Ze'ev Halprin, Unknown, Izzie Sharer, Shiko Pantzer.

Ed2   Polish National Anthem.

My Home that is Gone
By Chaya Weisberg-Weinreich

Translated by Rabbi Mordecai Goldzweig - YB p. 131

p. 131 YB: The Ukrainian house, the house of A. Kartin. Opposite: The house of Noach Becker; To the Left: The house of Moshe Preiss which is attached to the house of Yisrael Zilber with a passage between them. At the far edge of Max Zilber's store you can see the cleared area of the market place.

M y home that is gone…
It is generally on days of rest that I think about the town of Rohatyn that was destroyed and is now totally gone.

Our little house faced Tserkovna[Ed1] Street. This street led from the marketplace to the bath house reaching the Gnila Lipa river. This was the only place where we could enjoy ourselves during the summer, tanning in the

---

Ed1   In Ukrainian: Church Street (Tserkva is a Greek Orthodox church).

sun and swimming in its cold waters to our delight. The treetops of the forests appeared from across the river and in the months of January and February, they were covered in white, attracting both young and old.

We had many neighbors near our house. Even now I remember the Godstein family, the Winter family, Gitel Weiler and her two daughters Sheva and Rozia, the Fried (with her son) and Yisrael-Leib Gotlieb (the grocery man) and his family. They lived peacefully undisturbed by the noise on the street emanating from the workshops and lumber yards of Alter Faust-Allerhand or Liebling.

The town could easily be identified as Jewish by the many beards and curly peot (side-locks) that were to be seen there. However, there were also many expressions of vibrant nationalism to be found within the Jewish community. Hundreds of young people were members of youth groups such as HaShomer HaTzair, HaNoar HaTzioni, Gordonia, Hitachdut, Betar and Chalutz, to which I belonged.

The war of annihilation by the German murderers came and put an end to all plans of Jewish existence. And my heart aches within me…

Inside the Center

Jewish and non-Jewish Businesses around the Rynek before World War II

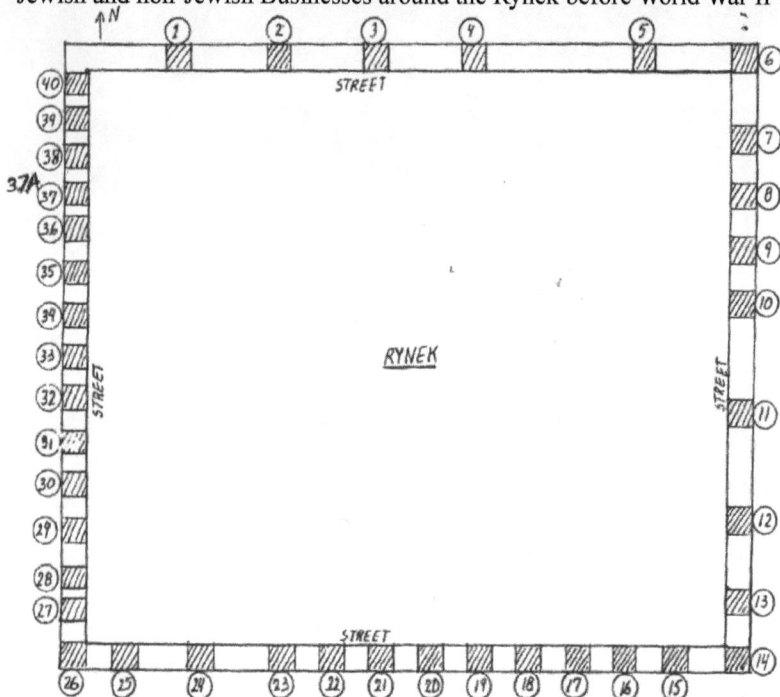

Prepared by Jack Glotzer, Arranged by Alexander Walzer, August, 1999

1. Zlatkis (lawyer)
2. Kerchner-Kleinwachs Wholesale Grocery
3. Gimnazjum (located somewhat off the rynek)
4. Horn's Saloon (szynk)
5. Catholic Church
6. Dollar Saloon (szynk)
7. Podchorcer Textiles (sklep blawatny)
8. Rothenberg Textile (sklep blawatny)
9. Sharer Textile (sklep blawatny)
10. Landau Saloon (szynk)
11. Kizel Eggs (wholesale)
12. Holder Saloon (szynk)
13. Brick Textile (sklep blawatny)
14. Rosenstein Booth (kjosek) for newspapers
15. Mayer Glotzer Butcher Store (Jack Glotzer's father's store)
16. Rosenkranz Textiles
17. Braunstein Kitchen Supply Store (dishes, pots, pans)
18. Schaps
19. Kerchner's Grocery
20. Fischer Shoe Store
21. Gustein Haberdashery (men's clothing)
22. Szyje Glotzer Butcher Store
23. Winter Clothing Store
24. Top's Saloon
25. Horn's Bakery*
26. Fruchter Saloon
27. Bromberg Handyman
28. Bohnen Plumbing Store (sklep zelazny)
29. Kleinwachs Grocery
30. Rosenberg Restaurant
31. H. Reiss Hardware
32. Fiol Barber
33. Mark Drugstore
34. Kreizler Tobacco Store
35. Kreizler Book Store (ksiegarnia)
36. Grad Textiles
37. Lipszyc Gasoline & Oil
37a. Gitel Rajszer (Reischer) Galanteria
38. Kirschen Saloon
39. Silver Candy Store
40. Price Shoe Store
   * Note: Horn's Bakery is #26 and Fruchter Saloon is #25

Within the Town

By Yehoshua Spiegel, Tel Aviv

Translated by Binyamin Weiner - YB p. 132

The Rohatyn Fair

Wednesday was market day in our town. It was known in the entire area as the day on which all manner of merchants, shopkeepers, artisans, and thousands of others from towns and villages in the district, gathered in Rohatyn. It all began on Tuesday night, with the preparation of market stalls, called "shteles," and special tents. Of course, this did not proceed without tremendous fights over who had a prior claim to the more strategic positions. The buyers and sellers were for the most part farmers, who never came to town on any other day of the week. But on Wednesday, market day, they came en masse, until it was difficult to pass through the sidewalks and streets, for all the press and tumult.

Everyone was a merchant on market day, even the schoolteachers, who would take off from work in order to help their wives hawk the daily wares. Those who did not speak the language of the "uncircumcised" got their points across through winks and sign language, and the clowns of the town always found much to laugh at.

Now we see a wagon, driven by a middle-aged farmer, his rough-skinned wife beside him and on her knees two great baskets of butter and cheese, and an even larger basket of eggs. Four sacks of grain rest in the wagon, and in back an enormous pig, over two hundred kilograms, is bound. The farmer whips his two fine horses. The wagon nears the first houses of the town. Coming out of a granary, Yechezkel Bratshpis shouts to the farmer:

"Shoda, drive on!"

"How much will you pay for the wheat?" asks the farmer, without stopping his wagon.

"Thirty-three."

"How about forty-four?"

"A few more groschen," shouts Yechezkel, "you won't get more in town. Stop and come in a minute."

But the farmer does not listen, whipping his horse on quickly, and muttering: "Viyo! Ah, ah! I'll go to little Israel Zilber, one of our

173

Jews…"

But he gets no further, finding himself suddenly surrounded by all kinds of merchants. They handle his butter, cheese, and eggs. They ask the price, and they haggle and bargain. Again the farmer raises his whip and drives the horses on, despite the merchants. But they climb into the wagon, tempt the farmer with their ready money, and do not let up until he finally tires and gives in to them.

Farmers and their wives, as well as miserably poor Jews, wander in on foot selling their wares as they go. Here market poultry is sold. Buyers grab the chickens by their wings, stroke them, and blow through their plumage. Feathers fly as the farmer's wife snatches a turkey away, not pleased with the offered price. They will go to the fair and figure out the going rate.

The marketplace fills with animals: cows, bulls, pigs, goats, and horses. Neighing and mooing mixes with the shouting of the farmers.

Here comes a farmer leading a young horse. Somebody slaps it and it takes off running, forcing the farmer to chase after it. He runs, only to find a "connoisseur" sitting on its back, wanting to buy. The only problem is the price: the buyer wants to close the sale with a "handshake," but the seller is unmoved and will not lower the price. Finally, a mediator intervenes, and with a "compromise" the deal is done. A long line of healthy looking calves comes plodding along from another direction.

There are potatoes, greens, radishes, green onions, fruit just plucked from the tree, and dried fruit as well. The clanging of metal tools is heard in another corner: plowshares, scythes, axes, hammers, and saws. Farmers test the scythes, judging the quality of metal by the tone it makes when struck, and again the two sides haggle over the price. The same is true for the wide variety of pots and pans to be found in the marketplace, from earthenware to aluminum to brass frying pans. Buyers try them with their fingers and raise them up to check for holes. In front of the Polish church, cheap little rings and ornaments are sold to farmers. In another place, leather straps are sold for whips. Beside the well is a table laden with furs and skins. The neighboring stall is offering woven, ready-made suits, called "tzayg," similar to our khaki suits.

A Jew, tall as Og, king of Bashan, with a black curly coiffure, stands on a chair and calls out, without stopping: "My friends, everything must go!" His fingers sift through combs, mirrors, and other "finds," and the farmers stretch out their hands and buy whatever comes into them. Next to that is a table of eyeglasses and shoes. A gentile finds a pair here, a pair there, and the second seller lowers the price so as to win a customer.

The sun tends westward. The day draws to a close and with it the fair. Most people go off to taverns and parties, to taste the "bitter drop" and get drunk. Later on, the first swayers and staggerers will be seen by the roadside. Often quarrels broke out between drunks and ended in bloodshed. Sometimes knives were drawn, forcing the police to intervene and take the quarrelers to jail.

Coachmen

They walked among us, strong men of great height, known by name: Nahum Fingerhut, a man with open eyes; Dovid Fuchs (Sini) who was once stabbed, but returned to strength and continued in his hard labor; Zalman and his brothers—Dudzi, Vebi, Dovidl, and Neftali (they also had a sister, named Brani); Alter Fiakernik, a man beset by daughters; and other "charioteers," all of whom maintained the "transportation system" of our town, in winter and summer, carrying passengers to and from the train station.

This was a very unique society, which guarded its professional interests jealously. If from time to time, a fight broke out among them, over a "pilfered" fare, or a "ride" that one had "stolen" from another, thereby cheapening the going rate, it was normally resolved with a handshake over a glass of brandy.

They used to sit on their platforms and from the heights of their coaches and cabs look out over the proceedings of the town. A Jewish spark continued to glow in their hearts, and if ever a fight broke out on market day between Jews and gentiles, they knew how to land blows with their sinewy hands and were ready to strike fear and panic into gentile hearts, for having dared to assail Jewish honor.

The Bathhouse

The benefit to health of immersion in a bath was an accepted fact among Jews and gentiles alike, and both visited the bathhouse frequently. As can be seen in the photograph, our bathhouse still stands in its place.

But this building was not only used for bathing. On weekdays, apart from Thursdays and Fridays, its hall was used as a Hebrew school, a place of assembly, a site for public lectures, weddings, and the various parties of the Zionist youth organizations.

It must be noted that even by today's standards this was a modern bathhouse. Its separate bathing compartments were each equipped with hot and cold running water. The "sweat room" was a large hall with many concrete benches, one above the other. The veterans of the sauna would stretch out on the highest shelves and enjoy the steam that rose when water was poured on the red-hot rocks.

p. 134 YB: Marketplace and coaches.

p. 135 YB: From the right: Polish house, Polish middle-school, house of Boitsuk, house of Zlatkis, Ukrainian house.

p. 135 YB: The marketplace: The first house, with the balcony, belonged to the Bronstein family, and the second to the Schnaps family.

p. 136 YB: Formerly the community hall on Shevtsenko Street, now a movie theater.

p. 136 YB: Formerly the Rohatyn post office (the house of Tsukhuzer). Behind, on the right side, are the windows of the registrar, the teacher Mrs. Shwartz.

p. 137 YB: Bathhouse with steam room on Tserkovna street, in front of the houses of Tzvi Reiss and Baruch Weinreich, Z"L. On the right side, where the three open windows are, there was, years ago, a Hebrew school and an assembly hall.

Jewish beverage vendors would pass among the sweating and reclining clientele, distributing cold drinks to all who asked. Skilled bath attendants would circulate in the bathhouse, one gentile among them, earning a living on those two days of the week, Thursday night and the following Friday.

Women bathed only on Thursdays, at the hours set by Yosef Zilber, the superintendent.

Of the three mikvehs (ritual baths) there were two cold-water ones located in the general bathhouse. The third (called "di kashere mikveh"— "the kosher mikveh") was heated on cold days.

This enterprise was established thanks to Reb Alter Weidman, Z"L, (the head of the community) before World War I. After the war, Rabbi Avraham-David Spiegel returned and invested a great deal of energy and initiative in the bathhouse, making its large proceeds into a source of revenue for the community.

Military Service (Shtelers, conscripts)

Twenty-one year olds, whose turn had come to report to the army, knew beforehand under what conditions they would be found fit to serve, and to which companies they would be assigned. Many sought to evade military service at all cost, each for his own reason: some of them so as not to waste two years in the barracks, or in order to prevent an interruption of studies, others so as not to hurt their business. More than anyone else, those observant of religious obligations, sought to be released, firstly because they abhorred the work of spilling blood, and secondly so as not to take time away from the study of Torah and so as not, God forbid, to be corrupted by forbidden food.

p. 138 YB: A group of Jewish conscripts from Rohatyn. The two standing, from the right: Feffer, Uri Drucks. The three sitting, from the right: Zvi Schwartz, Zvi Zunnenstein (Dr. Zvi Zohar,) and Zev Barban (an actor in the "Ohel" troupe).

During World War I, Jewish young men would even inflict wounds on themselves, so as to be deemed unfit for the army. Even in my time, they would put themselves through all kinds of tortures so as to lower their weight and be released on this account.

Some weeks before the time appointed for reporting, they would gather at a late hour and march through the night (after a hard day of labor, or other occupation) from one end of the city to the other. This was a social experience, whose nature was determined by the mentality of the participants, which changed from year to year. If it was cold outside, they would drop into one of the Jewish taverns and warm their hearts with brandy or other drink. And woe to the barkeeper who made fun of them and refused to satisfy their thirst.

p. 139 YB: Zvi Blank (a Polish soldier). The image of the family of Moshele Blank is evident in its son.

"Secret gifts" and protekcja (protektzia) worked much better than these tortures. The young men would bribe their way out of the "physical," when a doctor from a regional city was appointed by command of the military examiners. Eliyahu Mesing, Yehuda Mesing, Michael Zucker, and others like them, Z"L, escaped service in this way.

But we had no cause to be ashamed of those who were taken into the army. Who does not recall those dear boys upon their return home on leave? They stood straight and tall, powerful and broad-shouldered, their faces flushed with health, when they appeared in public with their parents at prayer services. There were those who rose in the ranks, merited high posts, and also received awards for distinguished service. There were none like the Jewish soldiers for devotion during the Polish war for independence. But in the days of Przytyk[Ed1] and Prystorowa[Ed2], the era of boycotts on Jewish stores, onslaughts on Jewish centers, this passion faded, and the conscripts began to ask themselves if it was still worthwhile to fight for this Poland.

The Jewish Orchestra of our City

There was not a person in our city who did not know the musicians of our orchestra. And in none of the other towns was there such a unique group as this father and his four sons—the well-known members of the Faust family.

p. 140 YB: Seated in the center: Moshe Faust, Wolf Zimbler (Shwartz). Standing from the left: Mordechai-Shmuel Faust, Mendel Bass, Yankel Faust, Alter Marshalnik, Itsik-Hersh Faust, and David Faust.

After the father's death, the four sons carried on. David Faust, the eldest, was the fiddle player, and also used to call the tune at everybody's wedding. The second son, Itsik-Hersh, a small and delicate man, played the flute; his

---

Ed1   Pogrom in the Polish town of Przytyk on March 9, 1936.
Ed2   Janina Prystor, member of Sanacja, in February 1936 introduced in the Polish Sejm the bill banning ritual slaughter.

lips seemed to have been molded to fit his instrument. The third, Yaakov Faust, stout and powerful, was the trumpeter, and as his cheeks were always puffed up from trumpeting, he was a quiet man, with an endearing smile. When he had time between festivities, he earned a living selling "tzayg" suits (similar to our khaki suits). The fourth, Mordechai-Shmuel, a young, bearded, bespectacled man with a cultivated demeanor, could read music; he directed and led the orchestra on his instrument—the clarinet. He earned his living on the side by giving private music lessons. He pounced on every new and modern melody and incorporated it into the program of his orchestra; he fit his melody to the taste of each individual. In short, it may be said of them (from Psalm 119): "Thy statutes have been my song in the house of my pilgrimage."

The Butchers

The butchers in our city were concentrated in an area not far from Reb Nataniel's synagogue. Like those of their generation, most of them were very pious, both on the inside and on the outside. They included: Reb Yitschok Hersh, Reb Nushi Chaimbuts, Reb Avraham-Chaim Eisen, Reb Yaakov-Yonah Schneekraut, three brothers together with their large families, Reb Kalman Glotzer, Reb Reuven Glotzer, and Reb Yisrael Glotzer, and others. Their trades were inherited by their offspring. Some continue in the profession to this day. Two sons of the Schneekraut family are in America, Yehoshua Glotzer is in Argentina, and David Blaustein is in Israel. Even Reb Zushe Springer and his wife Rachel can be counted among those who handed down their business. Being childless, they adopted Shlomo Zisser, who continues to practice his skill in Netanya.

Representatives from the board of rabbis often came to visit the aforementioned butcher shops, to check on their kashrut (adherence to Jewish dietary law).

Matzah was baked in the shop of the butcher Reb Avraham-Chaim, and on most Shabbat eves (Fridays) the cholent was placed in his oven. In his final years he was somewhat paralyzed, but his sons kept up the tradition, until one by one they left our city and immigrated to America. If I am not mistaken, Chaim Eisen, and perhaps even young David, tall as a cypress, can also be found in America.

I remember an event having to do with Reb Nushi Chaimbuts, after he was found liable in some matter of religious law. Being learned, and of the opinion that he was not guilty, he let fall from his lips an improper comment against my father, the rabbi, Z"L. From then on, over the course of a whole year, he ceased coming to our house almost entirely, contrary to his custom. On the eve of Yom Kippur, the day of forgiveness of sins, he appeared at our house, at the Turtledove house, and asked for my father, Z"L. He was told that my father had gone to the mikveh. He waited, and when he heard my father's steps on the stairs, he took off his shoes and fell on his face at my father's feet, crying bitterly and asking my father's forgiveness. Of course, my father, Z"L, would not accept this self-abnegation, and commanded him to rise, and so forth. The event made an indelible impression on us, the children.

Often the butchers would come to the rabbi's house to ask questions, such as for instance, about laws concerning lungs and stomachs in which holes have been found, and the like. There was good a reason that these questions evoked such emotion in the poor butchers. Money would be lost if slaughtered meat were judged to be unclean. There was, as there is today, suspicion cast on the shochet (ritual slaughterer)—perhaps the fault lay in his lack of proficiency in his art. He would hold up the lung of a cow, inflate it, listen for any air expiring through the hole, check the hole itself, and so on.

"Rabbi, do you know how much this cow costs?" they argued. It seemed that the butchers knew something of the laws of Israel themselves, and in case of doubt, they pleaded for a lenient ruling. In such cases, there was no reason to envy the religious officials, rabbi and shochet alike.

The Slaughterhouse

Four men walked around the slaughter room, keeping watch: Tuvya the shochet, faithful overseer of the butchering knives, who received compensation for the slaughter; Reb Moshe the shochet; his brother Reb Motsi the shochet; and with them Reb Leyb the shochet.

Two tall concrete tubs stood at the entrance to the slaughter room. There were iron bars with hooks upon them, from which hung chickens, tied by their legs with rope, their necks dripping blood. The room was stained deep red. There was constant noise and tumult, beginning on Wednesday evening, at its height on Thursday, and even more intense on the eve of Yom Kippur. But this tumult did not prevent the shochet Reb Tuvya from sitting in his adjoining room and studying Torah with great diligence ...

And then came the German Messenger of Death and slaughtered ...

May the memory of these pious meat-handlers be blessed forever in the hearts of all survivors of Rohatyn. Woe unto the evil one who murdered those men and spilled innocent blood...

p. 142 YB: In the center: Moshe Schechter, the shochet, his wife Sarah, and their grandchild between them. On the right: Monish and Pearl. On the left: Aharon and Leah. Above from the right: Rachel, Bracha, and Blima. The children below: Shlomo and Zvi.

The Melamdim (teachers) of Our City

Our parents were of the opinion that the only good thing for a Jewish boy to do was to study in cheder. This well-known system of education was in the hands of the melamdim (religious instructors), who did not make our childhood overly pleasant, and seldom spared the rod. But some of the students gave them no great pleasure either. They would take revenge on their teachers, gluing their beards to the table as they dozed, and other such pranks. But after having to learn all morning in a different school, under a different authority, how could the heart of a Jewish boy yearn for the cheder in the hours of the afternoon? It is no wonder that the most heartening news of the day came when the melamed announced that it was time to go home. Yet despite all this, these melamdim still managed to implant Torah in our hearts, as it is said: "I gained wisdom from all my instructors." May God remember them for good!

I will list those among the melamdim whose images are etched in my memory:

The first: Yehuda Ber, Z"L, who taught in the women's section of the large Beit Midrash. He was a widower. His son was known to all of us as Itsikl "the dancer." This "rabbi" served to the end of his days in this office, and most of the Jews of Rohatyn studied with him.

The second: Moshe-Gershon (the tall) At first he taught in a hut beside the "bath-house" and later in the neighborhood of the shochtim. He was a sickly man, also widowed, and burdened with children. He was well-versed in his trade, though not clear in his manner of instruction. He was one of the Hassidim of Reb Eliezerl, Z"L.

The third: Reb Nahum Milstein. He also taught in the large Beit Midrash, in the women's section, and afterwards in his own house, opposite the house of Natan Skolnick (the carpenter). He was steeped in Torah, was the regular Torah reader at the Chesed Elyon[Ed3] and was a grammarian as well. He taught Chumash (the five books of the Torah) according to commentaries of Rashi and Ibn Ezra and was strict about purity of speech. He was devoted to Zionism, to the revival of the Hebrew language, and such issues. Though blind in one eye, he watched over his students with seven ... His daughter Perl was married to Yaakov Straulicht (Shtrolicht). Two of their sons survived—Zvi Milstein and Anshel Milstein, who has taken root here with us, the survivors of Rohatyn in Israel.

The fourth: Noach Milstein, the brother of Nahum, taught in the large Beit Midrash. He had few students. He was survived only by two daughters who, following the death of their children, went to America.

The fifth: Reb Michal the blind, a meek and small man, was married to Malkah, his second wife. Gedalia, the eldest son of his first marriage, broke away from his father and settled in Przemysl. Reb Michal remained with his other two children, Moshe and Tovah.

This Reb Michal had a sharp mind; he made his students advance. I still recall a certain midrash (Torah commentary) that we would review with the traditional melody: And when Nebuzadin drives the Jews into exile, they will pass by the tomb of Rachel weeping, and mother Rachel will rise up from the grave and weep with them and beseech God, as it is written: "Rochel mivacho al boneyha" "Rachel weeps over her children." And the Holy One, blessed be He, will answer: "There is reward for your deed, the children will return to dwell within their borders..."

The sixth: Reb Nechamya (Nehemiah) Roich (Rauch), the lame, was the son of Reb Mordechai Roich, Z"L. He was a widower. All his life, as far as I can recall, he lived with his father, Reb Mordechai, and his son, Reb Orich Roich. Nechamya taught in his house, in the courtyard of Dr.

Ed3   Name of the synagogue.

Yuzi (Juzio) Weidmann (attorney). He was not as learned in Torah as his father but, with the help of his father and son, he knew enough to teach Chumash with Rashi. He was also a Torah reader and prayer leader in the shoemakers' synagogue, and on the High Holidays he went out to the countryside to serve as a leader of the Shacharit (morning) and musaf (additional) prayer services. Despite his disability, he was a violent man. Uri Roich was already able to teach according to more progressive and intellectual methods.

The seventh: Reb Shlomo Wohl (formerly Fiakernik) a preliminary-melamed, taught in the large Beit Midrash. He vented his spleen on his students, treating them with such a strong hand that parents would be compelled to deliver their children from his hands. He was a powerful man, straight and severe, though what little he knew of Torah came from his brother, the tall Reb Moshe Gershon...

The eighth: Reb Shmuel Unterman, a melamed and shamash (synagogue caretaker) in the synagogue of Reb Nataniel and his wife Yuta. Before that, he had taught in the apartment of Mrs. Malkah Landau, Z"L, where his two children, Sorel and Tziporah, were also born. He was a straight and simple Jew and a guardian of tradition. He was made shamash because he could not earn a living as a melamed after his hearing was damaged by disease.

❦

A Person I Was Fond Of
By Avraham Cohen

Translated by Rabbi Mordecai Goldzweig - YB p. 144

My cheder teacher was called Gershon HaMelamed (Gershon, the teacher). His pupils called him Gershon the Straw. Reb Moshe Gershon's house was located on a side street that had no pavement, was sunken into the ground and was made of clay. It had tiny glass windows, most of them broken, with wooden shutters made of unfinished boards hanging clumsily on rusty hinges. Attached to the front of the house was a kind of low railing where the family sat on summer evenings. From the outside the house looked sad and abandoned. However, when a person came close, he could see that the inside was brimming with life. In the large single room, with an earthen floor, we would sit around a dilapidated table - approximately 20 small children - and repeat the words of Reb Gershon out loud. He would sit at the head of the table and follow what we were saying with eyes half closed. We called him Gershon the Straw because he was tall and thin. His thin yellowish beard and hair shook at the slightest breeze. He had a wife and an only daughter of marriageable age. Despite the large number of pupils, he earned a very meager livelihood, and the signs of poverty could be seen in his worn coat, his wife's patched sweater, and particularly in his aging daughter who sat at home with no chance of marriage. Despite all this, Reb Gershon did not become angry. He accepted his fate. "If this is the will of the Creator," he would say, "it is forbidden to complain."

He was very strict about studies, and woe to any child who did not know the weekly portion of the Torah by Wednesday, for how would he be able to appear before the dayan with his pupils? (The custom was to have the pupil go every Sabbath afternoon to the Dayan Rabbi Avraham David Spiegel, Z"L, and be tested there, and every boy who did well would receive as a prize "a pinch on the cheek" and some special Sabbath fruit.)

One Tuesday Reb Gershon turned to me and asked me to read the weekly portion of the Torah with the Targum (the Aramaic commentary on the Torah by Onkeles). But what was I to do? I hadn't learned anything during the preceding two days for the very simple reason that we had all decided to enjoy the winter weather and play with snowballs. Reb Gershon said this was a pastime for urchins and there was no greater sin than to waste time and not learn Torah. In order to get us back into class, he had to make use of his long stick. In theory we gave in but not in practice. Each boy put a snowball in his pocket, and since we learned by candlelight, each boy took some of the snow and put it on the candle nearest to him. The candles soon began to go out one by one, and the Rebbe had no means at hand of replacing them. In view of this, I did not pass the test, and I did not know the portion of the week. I received the combined punishment due both me and my friends so that "they all would know and be forewarned" (against future misbehavior). However, neither Reb Gershon nor I realized the serious consequences of the beating that would land me in bed for a week. What's more, even my mother justified Reb Gershon's behavior. After I had been lying in bed for five days, I was surprised to see Reb Gershon arrive at our house. In his unique way, he began to calm the situation indirectly by saying to my mother, "This time he has learned his lesson; he will behave differently from now on." I felt guilty, and tears came to my eyes. I could see in Reb Gershon's eyes that he too felt guilty and regretted what he had done. I was sorry for the grief I had caused him but did not know how to express my feelings. Within me there was a desire to make it up to him for this visit, and at that moment I knew that I truly admired him.

My mother broke the ice by taking out her purse and paying Reb Gershon for the week that I was absent from cheder saying, "We were all mischievous when we were young; there is still hope for making a Jew out of him."

p. 145 YB: Chaim Weiler, Shalom Banner, Yehuda Brachfiss, Lipa Freiwald, Naftali Gera.

189

Secular Life

Daily Life
Work and the Workers after World War I - Jewish Artisans
By Anshel Milstein, Ramat Yitzchak

Translated by Rabbi Mordecai Goldzweig - YB p. 146

The socioeconomic composition common to most Jewish towns of Poland and Galicia after World War I was also typical of our town Rohatyn. The greater part of the Jewish community completely forgot the rabbinic admonition to love work and, on the whole, turned to small business - peddling, brokerage, and storekeeping. Out of approximately 2,000 Jewish families, no more than between 30 to 40 engaged in crafts (trades) of any kind. Those who did, continued in the crafts in which their parents had been engaged, such as tailors, shoemakers, hat makers, furriers, dressmakers, barbers, bookbinders, and the like. It is true that with time new crafts and craftsmen were added, such as tinsmiths, blacksmiths, builders, watchmakers and others. Even one primitive smelting plant, owned by Leichtermacher, appeared in Rohatyn (so that, all in all, there was a relatively wide range of crafts in a town of this size). This was not the only primitive workshop in the town. Most of the workshops were like that. There was no new machinery or modern equipment to be found in the town; nor was hired help prevalent. Only the builder Koenig needed hired help. You could earn a living but you could not become rich. There was just enough to maintain a simple, quiet, subdued, traditional home, and only this could be obtained by working - a worker's life was not paradise. People pressed down upon workers as much as possible.

A Jew who wanted to declare himself an independent professional craftsman had to pass muster before a committee of examiners of established workers, after an apprenticeship of four years. The board of examiners was composed mostly of non-Jews, but it also included three Jews, Shabsi Friedman, Mordechai Lilien and Yehuda Shames; the latter being known as Yudel the Carpenter. It was a great honor to be a member of the board of examiners and yet it was Shabsi Friedman, a Jew, who was the presiding examiner. He was a Jew who was very exacting in his profession and devoted a great deal of his time to examining students. He owned a fine metals workshop, which did repair work of such items as sewing machines and scales, upon which he affixed the official seal for the local authorities. At times he might hire a few apprentices to help him in his work. These included Moshe

Katz, Shmuel Ehrenberg and Litman Lev. The board of examiners, more than once, was under pressure of gentile workers to fail a Jew who appeared before them, in order to prevent further competition in their field. I was lucky. I don't know why, but I was accepted as an apprentice in the repair shop for agricultural equipment that was owned by the Gentile Schwab. He had 12 gentiles working for him, and I was the only Jew. They accepted me on a one month's trial basis and continued to keep me four years more, until 1924, when I left Rohatyn. This gentile insisted that I should be tested by no one but himself, and this was not because he was afraid that I might work for someone else, as no Jewish boy was permitted to enter a non-Jewish workshop to learn a trade. The Jewish applicant could accomplish this only through Jews. The products of Jewish shops were sold to farmers in the area; farmers were their main customers and source of income. Many were the tinsmiths, tailors, carpenters and builders who made their living by dealing with nearby non-Jewish farms.

Tailors: Heinech Freiwald and his sons, Yisrael Leib Green, Wolf Lev, Nachman Fidelbogen and his son Yosef, Shmuel Schulster with his sons, Nissan Fried, the Tahler family, S. Loifer, Yisrael Zin, Leybisch Friedman and his son, and others.

Barbers: Max Korfierst, Nachum Buchser, Leizer Buchser, Matisyahu Broinstein and others.

Cobblers: Mechal Katz and his sons, Shmuel Schuler, Hirsch Mandel, Putzter and sons, David Itche Zin and his son Yisrael and others.

Carpenters: Yudel (Yehuda) Shames and his son Michael, Mordechai Lilien (the owner of the carpentry shop for building) who worked together with his son Butchie, who now lives in the United States. From time to time he also hired workers. The sons of Reb Moshe Gershon who was an acknowledged Zionist and member of the Poalei Zion; the brothers Hass (furniture); Yitzchak and Shmuel Mohl.

Shoemakers: Baruch Weinreich and his sons Mechel and Bezalel.

Builders: David Koenig, Yeshayahu Hoftman and Shmuel.

Watchmakers: Avraham Roda, Yaakov Zeidler, Zvi Axelrod, Bergstreit and others.

Bakers: Horn, Tzelniker, Gera, Sofer and others.

Printers: Chaim Skolnick and Shimon Teichman.

Painters: Lichtgarn and Hass.

Tinsmiths: Avraham Blassenheim, Zalman Kirschenboim, Ignaz Grinsboim and others.

Photographer: Nushie Wald.

Candle factory: Meir Mauer.

Seltzer factory: Zlatkis brothers, Naftali Schumer.
Beer bottling plant: Akiva Wagschal and the lawyer Shmuel Spiegel.
Hatmaking: Mrs. Schumer, the sister of Yonah Nemet; the Zeider family.
Kiln: Alter Faust.
Candy Factory: Ephraim Kanfer and family.
Bag Factory: Shmuel Kertzner and family.

The Jews of the town earned a living mostly from retail sales, brokerage, peddling and storekeeping. Trades involving manual labor did not attract people, not even the youth, and only a relatively few people adopted them and continued to stay with them. Most of the youth followed the path of their parents, and in time took their place behind the counter of the little store, the other side of the stand (stall) in the market place, the shoe stores, notions, textiles and hardware stores.

There were people who wondered about what I did - "Anshel, the son of Reb Nachum the melamed (teacher of young children) learning a trade that requires working with his hands?" - unlike the rest of those my age in the town. They forgot about the changes that were taking place in the world and did not notice the new winds that were beginning to blow in our town, the winds from the Land of Israel after the Balfour Declaration to which the eyes of the youth were raised.

This spirit also expressed itself through organizations that were formed. Many of the workers joined the Poalei Zion party. Generally, their new members were young workers but there were also older people who tied their future to Israel. The Poalei Zion was founded in Rohatyn in the year 1920 and was headed by Dr. Goldschlag, with Yosef Green as secretary. When I joined, I was appointed treasurer of the branch until 1924, at which time I left Rohatyn. It is proper to relate that the Poalei Zion was the largest and most popular Jewish labor party in Poland – the "Bund" did not take root in Rohatyn. What happened was that those who had previously belonged to the "Bund" went over to the Poalei Zion. Part of the older workers belonged to the "General Zionists."

The older workers found their social outlets in the Tailors' and Cobblers' Synagogues, none of which was very large. Here they found release from the everyday activities, to which they were tied all week long. They tried to find some degree of spiritual elevation during Shalosh Se'udot (the third meal of the Sabbath, which traditionally has special spiritual powers). Here they sang and heard someone giving a short discourse dealing with the weekly portion of the Torah; they drank a small glass of whiskey at the end of the Havdalah ceremony and took part in the festivities of Simchat Torah. Here they took part in Bar Mitzvah inductions, and learned a portion of Mishne in honor of some friend who had passed away. In addition to meeting their spiritual needs, they helped each other with their material needs by means of a variety of charities; some help was given secretly. They visited the sick and helped young couples begin their married life; they also fulfilled other commandments governing the relations between man and his fellow man, that have been the traditional inheritance of the Jewish people for generations.

All this was buried in the grave of the Holocaust, which befell the Jews. May their souls know eternal rest in the knowledge of the renewal of Jewish life in the Land of Israel.

p. 148 YB: Family of Yisrael-Leib Green, Z"L. First row standing from the right: Feige, Altche, Esther, Leah, Itamar Loifer, Yisrael-Leib, Gitel, Yosef and his daughter Ruth, Shmuel, Shalom and David.

p. 149 YB: Family of Nachum Milstein, May he rest in peace. From upper right: Feivish and Sarah Zonenschein, Uri and Devorah Schreiber, Benzion and Sala Milstein, Pearl Milstein, Nachum and Alta Milstein, Anshel Milstein.

The families of: Shmuel Blech, Shimon Teichman, Gavriel Nusshofer and Ze'ev Steinmetz. Some of the children: Moshe and Aryeh Blech and daughters. Blima and Lunka Teichman live in Israel.

p. 150 YB: Shmuel Weiler and his wife, Meyer Weiler and his wife, with two daughters, and Chaim Weiler.

p. 150 YB: Family of Shlomo and Esther Reichbach in center of photo; from top right, Rachel Leder and Chaya Leder, Hoogie Reichbach, Chaya Bratspis, Sarah Reichbach, Genia Haber (from Zalipia), Fani, Manka Faust, Chaya Bader, Sarah Zimmerman, the children: Malka Reichbach, Feige Bratspis, Yitzhak Haber, Shaindel Bratspis, Yaakov Bader, Nushi Haber, Tzvi Bader. [Ed] Also in photo are Tonia Faust and Helena Faust, third and fourth from left in the bottom row.

p. 151 YB: From right to left, standing; Shimon Ehrlich, Brane Gotlieb, Elisha Mark (brother of Elimelech); Seated; Elimelech Mark and his wife Tzirl-Dvora; Avraham Top, Sartzi and the children.

p. 151 YB: Bezalel, Esther, Adela and Michel Weinreich.

The Printing Trade in Our Town
By Yoseph Yuzef, Pardess Hanna

Translated by Rabbi Mordecai Goldzweig - YB p. 152

Our town Rohatyn was essentially a poor town that suffered from a shortage of industry. It was therefore to the credit of the two printing concerns owned by Chaim Skolnick and Shimon Teichman, who lived in the town, that they employed close to 16 Jewish workers and apprentices (some of whom continued to practice their trade in Israel). These included Yehoshua Spiegel, Yerachmiel Wind and Yosef Yuzef. Printing shops were among the few places where young Jews could learn a trade.

Sanitary conditions and social benefits in the factories of the towns in eastern Poland were limited and poor. An 8-hour working day may be the accepted norm now but it was not even dreamt of then. We won't talk about social benefits and salaries consonant with experience, etc. However let it be stressed, to the credit of the printing trade, that they were the first to begin the struggle for attaining social benefits. This resulted in their obtaining an 8-hour workday for their workers while some of the workers even received health insurance at the expense of the owners of the press. These struggles waged by the workers of the printing trade indirectly affected the working conditions at other small plants in Rohatyn. Moreover, their influence was felt beyond the area of their own trade and extended to national Jewish education.

In Eastern Galicia, the population was composed of several nationalities—Jewish, Polish and Ukrainian. The official language in use was Polish, but printers were required to serve the general population, and each national group insisted that its material be printed in its language. The Jews felt the same way and insisted that their national life be presented in their own tongue and that invitations and announcements to assemblies were to be printed solely in Yiddish or Hebrew. This was made possible only because of the existence of a Jewish-owned press and their owners.

From time to time a book might appear written in Ukrainian or Polish by a local writer. The printing press of Chaim Skolnick, the largest in our town, also served the governmental agencies of the town and its environs. Because of this, business increased and more workers were employed. This aroused the unconcealed envy of the Poles as they watched these profitable businesses expand, and they did their best to establish a Polish press in Rohatyn that would compete with the Jewish press. They even succeeded in establishing one small press, but it offered no competition to the Jewish printers who had at their disposal the use of large machines and a wealth of printing type.

When the Soviets entered the town, the printing trade lost its Jewish identity. All three printing presses of the town were united into one, with all the type being removed by the Soviets and taken out of town. These were replaced by Ukrainian letters. The Soviets then began to make preparations for a daily newspaper to be printed in the Ukrainian language under the title "The Red Star."

Here it is proper to remember two workers—Zvi Blumenreich and Shlomo Skolnick, who were among the pioneers of the printing industry in Rohatyn, and who were brutally murdered by the Nazis.

❦

Jewish Merchants Among the Gentiles
By David and Esther Blaustein

Translated by Rabbi Mordecai Goldzweig - YB p. 153

Our town Rohatyn was located on the fertile soil of the Ukraine, which is noted for its wealth of produce in field, garden and barn. The silos of the farmers were filled with grain and varieties of fruit. Surrounding the Jewish town were the villages of the gentiles and the manors of the nobility. Economic ties and business connected the Jews of Rohatyn with the surrounding farmers; the relationships between them were correct. They supported each other economically. No anti-Semitism was felt from the farmers until just before World War II. Jews rented farms, land and flour mills from the gentiles and bought cattle and agricultural products from them, while the farmers obtained clothes, shoes, cloth, furniture and equipment for the farms from the Jewish merchants and craftsmen.

Rohatyn was surrounded by a thick dark forest, the dimensions of which could not be fully encompassed. It had many paths trod by many generations of young and old; the paths led from the side streets of the town towards the green forests. Here young people found escape from prying eyes and gossips, when their love was in full bloom. Jewish adults, who all week long were immersed in their business activities, also came there together with their wives and children on Shabbat (Sabbath), in order to rest in the shade of the trees and enjoy the quiet of the forest.

(Afterwards, the paths became sad, and the young lovers seeking privacy, disappeared. Different people began to inhabit the woods then. Those were the Jewish partisans. There they found shelter from the Nazi invaders, who had set fire to the Jewish homes, and, aided by the Ukrainians, sent their children to the crematoria. But the forest remained faithful and protected the Jewish partisans. It was from here that they attacked and hit against the oppressors.)

However, prior to the Nazis, the forest was a happy place; it was the source of sustenance for many Jewish families. Many Jews of Rohatyn were engaged in the export of trees and in the lumber business. These included Alter Faust and his brother, Moshe Leib; Uri Kartin and Yosef Altman. Avraham Yitzchak Goldschlag and Eliezer Boim (Baum) used to buy from the noblemen sections of the forest, which they cleared, and then they shipped the trees to Austria and other countries, either by freight train or on barges along the Dniester River. Those who were not in the export trade usually had warehouses of lumber, which consisted of boards, planks, beams, etc. These included Alter Faust, Wolf Allerhant, Nachman-Shaye Wachman, Pin'e Spiegel, Yudel Rosenzweig, Liebling and others. They used to buy beams or planks of wood in the sawmills, in order to sell them for building homes or making furniture; the furniture then was sold to the Jews of the town and to the farmers from the surrounding areas. They also supplied firewood in winter. This was sold by merchants such as Meir Wald, the brothers Moshe Leib and Uri Kartin and Alter Faust, etc.

Forest and lumber were not the only source of business for the Jews of the town. They also engaged in renting land and manorial farms ("fulwark"). Elias Kanarik rented the Zalanow estate from the Nobleman Schacht. The estate spread over 1,500 acres of land and had within it a livestock inventory of 60 cows, 30 horses, 32 oxen, etc. He employed about 15 regular and seasonal workers. Zvi Breitbart did the same thing; he leased the "Nastashchin" estate which spread over an area of approximately 400-500 acres of land. Avrumche Adler maintained an estate of between 500-600 acres of land, while Goldhaber and Porush leased only agricultural land. Jews also managed flour mills. Fishel Baner and Bussgang leased the flour mills from the Poritz (Nobleman) Tichoshevitz (Tychoszewicz) who owned "Putiatynce." The flour mill of the Nobleman of Rohatyn was leased by the brothers-in-law Messing and Nota Gutenplan, who from time to time hired many workers. Usually they ground flour and corn for the surrounding farmers and for the Jews of the town, who sold flour.

There were also grain merchants in Rohatyn. These included Yisrael Zilber, Noach Becker, Yosef Widerker (Viderker), Avramtche Roch, Yechezkel Bratshpiss, Yankel Bratshpiss, Henie Mirels Garten, Velvel Ze'ev Weisbraun and his sons and others. Among these Fishel Band was the largest exporter of grain; his business reached as far as Lwow and Warsaw. Sometimes they bought the grain while it was still on the ground at a lower price, but then they would give the seller a down payment on the whole crop. It was known that the Ukrainian farmers were always short of cash and the Jewish merchant came out the winner in this type of transaction.

Another type of product that the Jews bought from the gentiles was cattle. They too were a commodity that could be exported. The exporters of cattle were the three brothers Glotzer – Kalman, Reuven and Yisrael. They sent their merchandise to Katowice (Katovitz) and Myslowice in Upper Silesia, Poland. Every week two to three carloads of cattle left for those cities. They also sent cattle from the Rohatyn area to Vienna. The brothers Schneekraut were big cattle merchants, but they earned their reputation and good name for their good hearts and their concern for the people around them. They never spared their own effort, nor their ability to intercede with the nobleman, with whom they had good business relations, in order to help a Jew in his time of trouble. They used their connections with the gentiles for the benefit of the Jews who turned to them for help. Their hands were always open to anyone who was in need of help in the form of a loan or a quiet donation.

The cattle merchants were successful in their efforts. Their businesses flourished and the same was true of the butchers of the town, of which there were 12. Within their shops could be found either kosher or treif meat; the meat was sold to a gentile or to the most religious Jew, to each according to his faith. But it never happened that a Jewish butcher would fool a Jew and sell him treif meat as kosher meat, because the ties between the butcher and the customers were based on full trust. The most religious Jew never had reason to have the slightest suspicion about the honesty of the butchers. Of course, these two types of meat were kept far apart one from the other. Every Thursday morning the town dayan, Rabbi Avraham David Spiegel, together with Reb Tuvia Shochet, investigated the butcher shops for their kashrut to make sure that there was no treif meat there; they made sure that their constituents would not, G-d forbid, G-d forbid, inadvertently transgress by eating treif. Of course, as the Shabbat drew nearer, the income of the butchers increased, as compared with the rest of the week, for which Jew would deny himself a piece of meat on this important day? But even in the middle of the week Jews of Rohatyn enjoyed eating meat. Of all the butchers that I mentioned before, Meir and Isser Glotzer (with whom I used to be friends), Yehoshua Glotzer and Moshe Eisen, and a few others, were those of the newer generation, who followed the path of their parents and became independent butchers. They maintained a family-like relationship among themselves. We were one big family.

Butchers, like all other tradesmen, required a license in order to engage in their trade without being bothered by the government. In order to accomplish this, they had to pass examinations before the master butchers. Therefore, Yisrael Glotzer, the Jewish representative to the butcher's cech (guild), used to ease the way with his friends in the cech at a table loaded with goodies at the tavern of Abba Kartin, because with the help of a bottle of free whiskey the heart of even the most obstreperous gentile could be melted. And since we are talking about meat for Shabbat, we must mention the names of Ze'ev Steinmetz and his family and Yehoshua-Falik Straulicht, who supplied the Jews of the town with fish all week long, and especially before Shabbat. As our sages have said, "There is no pleasure during the Shabbos without a meal of spinach, large fish and garlic heads." These large fish were supplied by Ze'ev Steinmetz from his fish ponds.

But, of course, Jews never contented themselves with just a good meal in honor of the Shabbat Queen. They dressed up in festive clothes and shiny clean shoes. A young lady, who reached marriageable age, would be particularly careful about her appearance when people talked about her with regard to shiduchim (arranging a match). She might then order shoes from Slonim[Ed1] where you could find elegant styles in keeping with those of "Lwow and Paris." The fulfillment of this desire was made possible by Yoel Fisher and Moshe Preiss and their brothers, who went to the trouble of stocking a light and dainty shoe that would not, G-d forbid, pinch their toes. However, working people who had the problem of earning a living wage, were not so choosy. They made do with less elegant shoes that were strong. They were called "boikes." They had a thick leather sole with an inner lining and were laced up with long shoelaces. With such shoes you could be certain to walk securely anywhere you wanted to go, and they could be obtained at the shop of Netaniel Schein. Shoe leather was bought from leather merchants, the biggest of whom were Yehoshua Streier (or Stryjer) and Reb Avraham Hirsh Koenigsberg and his children Shiltche and Yechezkel. They bought hides from the butchers, shipped them to Stanislawow and other towns, and in return imported finished leather for the leather retailers of the town. These were Azriel Gan, Shmuel Mordechai Kasten, Mordechai Weiler, Mendel Weiler, Zelig Nagelberg, Alter Lewenter, Fruchter and others.

Wednesday was market day. The Ukrainian farmers came from all over to make their purchases and sell their wares. Afterwards they took care of their personal needs for clothing and shoes. The Ukrainian farmer did not know anything about a ready made shoe. He bought leather and made his own boots. The Jewish retailer would measure his feet and cut him a piece of leather to his size. The same was true for his wife. And then the retailer would send the couple to a clothing store or a store selling cloth (a dry goods store). There were many "shnit gesheften" (yard good stores) in Rohatyn. This is one area of trade that has been traditional among Jews for many generations, and just to mention a few who engaged in this business, they were: Shaul Gratt, Lippe Mandel, Mandel Rothenberg, Moshe Leib Kovler, Chaim Kovler, Bunim Ohrbach, Avraham Yosef Ehrenberg, the Klarnet family, Wolf Gold, Michel Zucker, Pinchas Rosenberg, Esther Holtz, her sons-in-law and sons, Elisha Teichman, Akiva Wagschal, Rafael Baumrind, Meir Weiler, A. Lustig, Shloime Shaye

---

Ed1   City in Belarus.

Straulicht (Shtrolicht), and many more. The farmers were not choosy. For their wives, they bought whatever the women wanted. After all, even a farm woman in the most forsaken village still wanted a nice red shawl, a flowery skirt or a colorful dress and the like, just as her sisters in Paris. On the other hand, the men from the farms required much less. They were content with a pair of pants, a jacket, or even a suit made of linen; in this they could feel good when they went to church on Sunday. This was provided for by Nachman Granowiter, Zushe Holtz and others. Sometimes the farmer insisted on his own price and thought that the Jewish merchant was overcharging him. The storekeeper might then place a zloty in one of the jacket pockets that he was fitting. When the farmer found the money in his pocket while trying on the jacket, he ceased to worry and accepted the purchase without being fussy about size or quality of the merchandise. (Money spoke loudest to these people who had very little money.) He reasoned, that if he found one zloty in the jacket, who knows what else might be hidden there ... This was not a common practice, and one should not compare this to what these murderers and ravagers did to the Jews. It was just a bit of small town trickery...

Nor did things always go smoothly among the Jews themselves. More than once arguments would break out among the Jewish storekeepers because of competition - storekeepers running after a customer, who was being yanked this way and that way. This one pulled him into this store and that one pulled him into that store, until the sleeves got torn because of the tugging. In the end, this could end up in the customer covering the heads of both competitors with juicy oaths. But they did not run from the glasses of whiskey that Jews presented them. The most prominent of those who engaged in this practice were Yehoshua Horn and his sons, Yonah and Dudke, who were owners of a tavern. They took care of the feelings of the gentiles, especially on Sundays, Saturday nights, or on long, cold, winter nights. If his spirit soured, the gentile would turn his eyes and heart to the liquid that warms the blood and mixes up the brain. But it wasn't only the gentiles who made use of the good services of Yehoshua Horn. He knew well that, even our brothers, the Jews, do not run away from the "bitter drop," if only a few times a year - on such occasions as Simchas Torah, Purim, a wedding or a brit. He did not rely on Jewish heavy drinkers. From them he would not make any profit. Many times people came to the taverns and inns owned by Jews; there they would complete transactions over a glass of whiskey and a piece of roast goose. However, most of the people who came there were gentiles – Poles or Ukrainians – who during market day could not resist entering the taverns of Malia Landau,

Abba Kartin, Buny Kirschen, Tzvi Holder or Shloime Landau.

Motel Kreizler supplied Jews with tobacco to smoke[Ed2], or snuff[Ed3], while learning a page of Gemara – and even when they were not learning - on weekdays, Shabbos or Holy Days. His relative Shloime Kreizler saw to the improvement of the spirit of the Jews of Rohatyn by supplying them with siddurim (daily prayer books) and machzorim (prayer books for festivals) for festive and high holy days, but he also carried general reading books and newspapers, as well as office supplies. Textbooks and readers in great abundance could be found in the store of Chaim Skolnick, who also had the printing press and supplied forms for the city and national government offices. There were also more prosaic stores, which sold equipment and iron for building, such as that of Hirsch Zvi Reiss, one of the wealthy men of the town, and Moshe Bunin, and Feivel Horshovsky and others.

There were Jews in Rohatyn who chose the vocation of "Tuvia the Milkman." Many were the Jewish wagons that wended their way from the town along the dirt paths of the villages to bring milk from there in order to convert it into butter, cheese, and cream. There were two dairies in town—that of Yaakov Eichel and Hirsch Presser. They processed milk and its products and sold them to Jews, or they shipped them out of town. Hirsch Weiner bought his products from them and shipped them to Warsaw and Vilna. Chaim Hirsch Weisberg engaged in the shipping of eggs to Germany, while Yaakov Leib Shor (a descendent of the Shor that had followed Jacob Frank) was one of the big egg exporters. We also have to mention Shmuel Blech and his sons, who also engaged in the export of eggs. They all hired skilled and unskilled workers. The milk suppliers were Isaac Freiwald, Shloime Mandel Reichbach, Hodjie Eichel Hoichberg, Rachel Zieder and others. There were also wholesale grocers such as Shmuel Kleinwachs, Yisrael Gleicher and Zvi Kertzner. There were retail grocers, such as Ephraim Kanfer, Yisrael Leib Gotlieb and the salt supplier, Yechezkel Weiler. We must also mention the housewares and kitchen utensils store of Moshe Shneikrom. Some of these stores had three to four helpers.

With the establishment of the electric power station in Rohatyn (before that they used gas and kerosene for public lighting and private buildings), they needed light bulbs and various accessories. These could be bought at the wholesaler and retailer Zelig Gorton. Windows and mirrors could be gotten wholesale and retail by Gavriel Nashofer, who was also a glazier.

Ed2   Religious Jews and traditional Jews did not smoke on the Sabbath or the holidays. These were the overwhelming majority.

Ed3   Older men could be seen taking a whiff of snuff.

The town storekeepers with their varied professions and skills may not have become rich in their business, but they were able to earn a living, and they did not need to turn to outsiders for relief and assistance. However, this did not last forever and, when the anti-Semitic movements began to grow, especially in the years before the outbreak of World War II, their conditions deteriorated. Poles and Ukrainians pushed them out of their businesses, and they were deprived of their sustenance. This was especially felt in the field of agriculture and milk products. In the 1930s the Ukrainians began to organize soyuzim (cooperatives) for dairy products and eggs. These cooperatives bought all the farmers' products, especially eggs, milk and grain products. Then they began to process milk products. Little by little, the merchants and Jewish suppliers were deprived of their source of income and could not enter the small towns. Their homes and equipment were burned. Thus the work of "Tuvia the Milkman" came to an end. Only the Jewish experts, such as egg packers, were kept by the cooperatives for a while, until they learned to do the job themselves, and then the Jews were thrown out like a pot that is not needed.

The town and national authorities began putting pressure on the Jews, and the tax authorities bore down on them with all their might. The chief tax assessor used to go through the town feeling out the Jewish financial position, also making use of informers, and paid no attention to the economic condition, which was becoming worse and worse. The belt was tightened around the neck of the Jews. But all of these evil decrees and pressures that were heaped upon the heads of the Jews were nothing compared to the tragedies that were waiting for them when the war broke out; then the Jewish community went up in flames, and its children were brought to slaughter. May these pages serve as a memorial light to their pure spirits, and may their souls be gathered together in the treasury of life.

Academic Professions

By Grina Sterzer (nee Foist/Faust)

Translated by Rabbi Mordecai Goldzweig - YB p. 158

Our town was proud of its intellectuals – its golden youth and the members of the academic professions, and all the surrounding towns were envious. This was thanks to the two gimnazja – Polish and Ukrainian - where the children received their education, and this is where they received the foundation for higher education at the universities. During the last years before World War II, Rohatyn had its own professionals – doctors, dentists, lawyers, engineers, high school teachers, clerks, and merchants with higher education. The youth of Rohatyn continued their education in all the universities of Poland and Europe and dispersed all over the country in order to practice their profession. Many of the teachers of gimnazja in Poland came from the youth of Rohatyn.

At this point, it is appropriate to commemorate those who are no longer alive:

Lawyers: Dr. Yosef Widman, Dr. Shmuel Sherf, Dr. Ludwig Schauder, Dr. Leon Katz, Henrik Katz, Ludwig Katz, Dr. Freiwald, Dr. Tzekhauser, Dr. Samy Spiegel, Mgr. Fishel Kreizler, Mgr. Pinye Mauer, Mgr. Yaakov Mondschein, Mgr. Sheike Pantzer, Mgr. Buni Pantzer, Dr. Leon Baraban, Mgr. Anshel Kaufman, Mgr. Rothroiber (Rothrauber), Mgr. Michel Weich, and others.

Doctors: Dr. Osias Tzenner, Dr. Chaike Kreizler, Dr. Lena Schumer, Dr. Michal Gold, Dr. Berel Manhart, Dr. Yoel Blumenreich, Dr. Yehuda Pasweg, Dr. Itta Weissbraun, Dr. Yosef Teichman, Dr. Nuncia Willig.

Secondary school teachers: The elderly teacher of religion, Herman Schwartz; Max Peled (Feld), Urtzie Gottwort, Aryeh Gottwort, Chayke Mauer-Gottwort, Shmuel Zeidler, Lunka Zeidler, Isidore (Izydor) Mondschein, Rozia Mondschein, Tulche Lev, Chana Baum, Bronia Bomze, Munio Kartin, Yosef Pantzer, Tonka Lewenter, Pinye Lewenter, Dov Serle, Dov Salka and Ita Mandel.

Pharmacists: Marcus Lewenter, the elderly pharmacist Wagner, Lustig.

Merchants with higher education: Turkel; Bomze; Hochberg, Yaakov Kartin, Yehuda Skolnick, a Polish army officer.

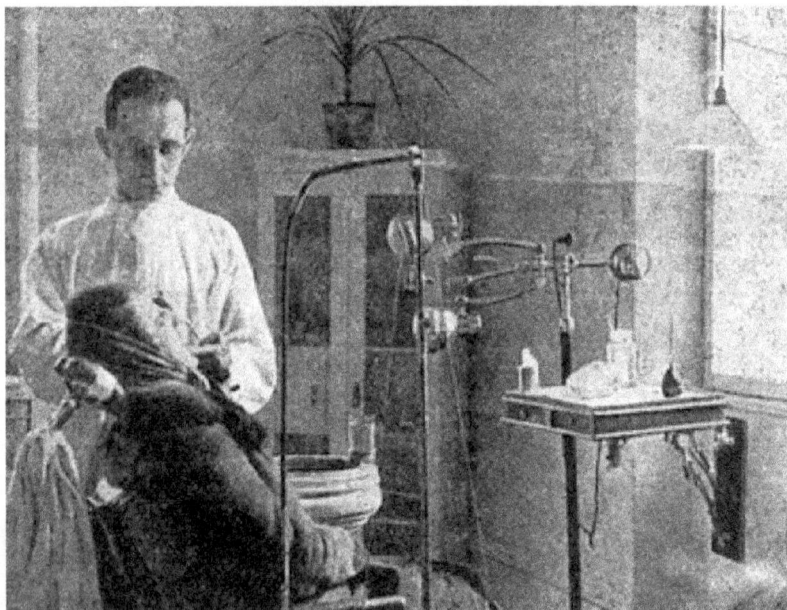

p. 158 YB: Yosef Teichman – Dentist (son of Elisha Teichman, Z"L).

Attempts at Drama
By Zev Barban[Ed1], Tel Aviv

Translated by Rabbi Mordecai Goldzweig - YB p. 159

p. 159 YB: The production of "King Lear", December, 1920 - Chaim Drooks, Avra-ham Top, David Prageh, Fishel Weiler, Unknown, Gutwort, Yaakov Faust, Shaul Pantzer, Hinda Baum, Tova Barban, Dr. Leybisch Zlaks, Yitzchak Bernstein, Tonke Horn, Reize Leiter, David Rosenstein, Devorah Hauser (Hoizer). [From the Jacob Faust [Photograph Collection, courtesy of Alex Feller.]

Rohatyn, the town in which I was born and spent my childhood, was one of several hundred towns in Galicia, immersed in a struggle for existence. Its worries were about sources of income and work, while the echoes of previous social and religious uproars were still being felt in the town. It was therefore not yet interested in developing the dramatic arts and it therefore never established any amateur dramatic companies. Only on infrequent occasions was it fortunate enough to be visited by one of the

Ed1 "In 1925 joined the founders of the Dramatic Studio and the Ohel Theatre Troupe. He became a permanent member and performed leading roles." "Zev Barban," Encyclopedia Le'Chalutzei HaYishuv U'Bonav (Encyclopedia of Pioneer Settlers and Builders) by David Tidhar, Vol. V, p. 2096-2097, Tel Aviv 1952, 1956 edition

traveling companies. One such occasion that has stayed in my memory from childhood was when a group of traveling actors appeared on stage in the town one evening in the Jewish play, "Der Wilder Mentch" (The Wild Man). The plot of the play escapes me, but I remember down to the present day one of the songs that were sung in it. This is the popular song "Tzu fun a shtein bin ich geboiren, tzu hot mich mein mame gehat." (Was I born to a rock or did my mother give birth to me?)

These rare visits by the drama companies in the town would arouse a great deal of interest among the inhabitants and become an exciting event for them. Even as a child I could not miss seeing a single play. We would receive our tickets through my father, Reb Yaakov Barban, Z"L, who was a mail carrier, thus enabling us to obtain the tickets.

As I began to grow up, these plays aroused my imagination more and more, and in a relatively short time I and my friends organized a dramatic club in the "Otrakvistit" gimnazjum, where the "star" was someone we now know as Dr. Tzvi Zohar and where I would appear on stage playing the flute. (Incidentally, this flute has played an important part in my life, and I appeared with it in 1925 in the first performance of the Ohel Theatre in the play "Neshef Paratz."[Tr1] The club did not last very long because World War I soon broke out and Rohatyn and its youth were swept into the bloody storm. It was only after the war that attempts were made again to organize dramatic clubs among the students.

These were frightening times for the Jews of Galicia - days of pogroms by the gangs of Petlura[Ed2], the Hallerczyki and the military regime. Yet in the midst of this torrent of blood, Jews enjoyed a certain amount of internal autonomy. This was because the battling parties, the Ukrainians and the Poles, both needed the Jews on their side and this was the time when "dramatic" groups began to be organized in our town. It was something new among the youth. Amateur groups were organized by Dr. B. Zlatkis, and they presented a number of plays. The same thing happened among the workers of our town who organized actors' groups, where I presented the play "Der Beitler Altz Millionaire" (The Beggar as Millionaire). This play was quite successful.

This led to our presenting the play by Gordon, "G-tt Mentch und Teivel" (G-d, Man and Devil). The devil was played by my good friend Max Fuld and it even received favorable reviews from the Lemberger Tageblatt (The

---

Tr1   The title may translate to "The Party that Broke Up."

Ed2   Simon Petlura, Ukrainian Nationalist Leader. In 1919 his followers were responsible for pogroms in which at least sixty thousand Jews were murdered (in the cities of Proskurov, Lvov, and others). See The Holocaust, p.22, Martin Gilbert. The Red Cross estimated that 120,000 Jews were slaughtered.

Lwow Daily), which considered me to be a good director but found some weaknesses in the play. (However, in 1934 when I presented the same play again in Lwow (Lemberg) with the Ohel[Ed3] company, the reviews were much better and I felt much better…)

When we visited Poland in 1934 with the Ohel group, I felt the need to see Rohatyn again; my wife, Dvora Kastelanitz, and I spent about seven days there. During that time, she appeared in a dramatic reading at the "Sokol" hall before the Jews of the town and the Zionist youth groups, but I was very disappointed to learn that the youth had not heard any Hebrew spoken and would not understand what was being said. Therefore, my wife was forced to introduce her play with an explanation in Yiddish for each portion of the play as well as her readings. Though this was an evening of readings and drama, it was also a case of "shnayim targum ve'echud mikre" (two times translation and one time text)[Tr2]. Nevertheless, the evening was considered to be a great success since the Jews were very thirsty to hear something live from Israel.

p. 161 YB: Souvenir of the play "Seder Night" performed by town actors: Top right: Leib Faust, Mordechai Stryjer, Moshe Eisen, Shlomo Mark, Dudke Praga (Frage), Reuven Kreizler, Yehoshua and Esther Schulster, Bella Taller, Dziuniek Bernstein, Feige Zider, Yosef Green.

Ed3 HaOhel Theatre was founded in 1925 in Israel.
Tr2 A play on words on the requirement to read the text of the weekly portion of the Torah twice and the Aramaic commentary once – meaning that communicating with the audience was difficult.

p. 160 YB: Dr. Max Fuld, high school teacher, sharp minded, a brilliant mathematician, lost his position because of illness and remained in Rohatyn until World War II. He was shot in bed by the Nazis on March 20, 1942. The only survivors of his family are two sisters, Tzila Knosov and her daughter and Manke Fuld in Australia.

Dr. Yaakov Kupferman, Lunke Zeidler, Ze'ev Barban –the first leaders of HaShomer HaTzair of Rohatyn, 1919.

Seated to the left: Leitche Barban, two grandchildren of her daughter Golda who is standing at her side; Meir Glotzer with Kiva on his knees; Golda and her husband Adolph Rappoport, Toiva Glotzer (Barban).

214

Portraits

The Personalities of our Town
By Naftali Schein, Ramat Gan

Translated by Rabbi Mordecai Goldzweig - YB p. 162

Rabbi Yaakov "Kavi" Schein, Z"L

My grandfather Rabbi Yaakov "Kavi" Schein, Z"L, a full-fledged scholar in Torah and Poskim (religious legal decisions), served as dayan and teacher before Rabbi Avraham David Spiegel, Z"L. He had many students who followed his path in Torah and Halacha, and even cited his halachic decisions, many of which I still have in my possession. Included among his students were my father Reb Yitzchak Schein, Z"L, and Rabbi Avraham David Spiegel, Z"L (later the rabbi of the town).

p. 162 YB: Handwriting and signature of Our Rabbi the Dayan, Rabbi Yaakov "Kavi" Schein, Z"L.

By means of this publication, I have been given an opportunity to preserve a representative example for the former residents of Rohatyn of a document by Rabbi Yaakov "Kavi" Schein, Z"L, establishing a partnership that was written and signed in his clear script. He passed away in 1906. It therefore stands to reason that his brilliant student, our townsman Rabbi A. D. Spiegel, Z"L, would follow in his halachic

217

footsteps. After all, grandfather was his teacher down to the time when he was ordained by the great rabbis, Rabbi Meir Arik, Chief Dayan of Tarnow, and the Great Gaon Rabbi Shalom Mordechai, Chief Dayan of Brzezany.

It was because of the encouragement that Rabbi Spiegel received from my father, Reb Yitzchak Schein, Z"L, that he persisted in his rabbinic studies, which qualified him to occupy the position of my dear grandfather, of Blessed Memory, and thus my father was able to realize the dream, by which his friend and the student of Rabbi "Kavi" would fill the position of Rabbi "Kavi."

At this point it behooves us to remember his descendents who were put to death and slaughtered. These included his daughters, Mrs. Chana Jupiter and her husband Reb David Jupiter, their daughter Soshe Kaveh (their son died before the war), Manye, Leah and Avraham. I also wish to commemorate other close members of my family: my dear father Reb Yitzchak Schein, my dear mother Rivke Schein, my sister Manye Schein, my two brothers Moshe and Kavi Schein—may their souls rest in peace—as well as my uncle Reb Yehuda Zvi Weiss (the Reader of the Torah in the Main Synagogue and scholar in his own right), Leah, Elsa, Rivke, Meir (who died right before Rosh Hashana 5718 (1958) in London – leaving a wife and daughter), Nachum and Joseph Weiss. May they all be eternally remembered and rest in peace.

p. 163 YB: Two of the sons and daughter, daughter-in-law and father-in-law of Reb Yehuda Tzvi Weiss, Z"L. In the second row, on the right: Moshe Schein, grandson of Rabbi Yaakov "Kavi" Schein, Z"L.

Pessia Holler, Manye Jupiter and Leah Holler – the grandchildren of Reb Chaim Jupiter; Yafa Reichbach and her friend.

Rabbi Avraham David Spiegel, Z"L
By Rabbi Alter Meir, Tel Aviv

Translated by Rabbi Mordecai Goldzweig - YB p. 164

O ur sages, Z"L, state that when one is a talmid chacham (a serious student of the Torah) and his son learns the Torah, and his grandson does the same, then "the Torah returns to its inn," i.e., the Torah remains within the family.

There was a great gap in time between Rabbi Spiegel and his ancestor four generations removed, the Gaon, Tzaddik and author of the Mirkevet Hamishne,[Ed1] Rabbi "Adam," Z"L. The rabbinic line in between was interrupted and the descendants of the Gaon and Tzaddik, to whom the Besht came in order to fulfill the requirement of "shimush talmid chacham" (serving a sage), did not maintain the rabbinic line, preferring to remain simple "ba'alei batim" (respectable and learned members of the community). This was so until the appearance of the Rabbi of Rohatyn, Rabbi Avraham David Spiegel, who placed an "olah (sacrifice) on the altar" of public religious service, devoting himself completely to his calling and setting up his rabbinate at the level at which it had been during the time of his holy grandfather, Z"L, the author of the *Mirkevet Hamishne*.

In addition to his greatness in Torah, he was very exacting in his personal

Ed1 See History of Rohatyn by Dr. N.M. Gelber, footnote No. 65

behavior, a Hassid, as befits the descendants of the [author of] *Mirkevet Hamishne*, and he therefore merited seeing his eldest son, Rabbi Yisrael, Z"L, may his blood be avenged, being ordained a rabbi. He received his smichot (ordinations) from Rabbi Steinberg of Przemyslany, Rabbi Tziff of Lwow, and Rabbi Horowitz, the Chief Dayan of Stanislawow. His diligence in the study of the Torah was a model among the rabbis of Galicia and, when he visited the Admor of Czortkow on the holy days, he was greatly honored by the assembly and the Admor. He stood out with his fine manners and proper bearing, never displaying his great

Yisrael Spiegel, Z"L

knowledge ostentatiously or parading his pride in his family and its standing. He and his family perished in the Holocaust except for one son, Yehoshua Spiegel, who joined a chalutz youth group and immigrated to Israel. His life, literally, was saved by Israel.

The great people of the time of the author of *Mirkevet Hamishne* called him Rabbi "Adam," because of his name, Avraham David Moshe, the abbreviation of which is A.D.M. However, as can be seen from his introduction to his book, he also refers to himself as "Adam," and these are his words[Tr1]:

"The first of His works from of old (compare Proverbs 8:22), a delight each day (Proverbs 8:30) when He established the foundations of the universe and the earth (Proverbs 8:29); then He did see it and declare it (Job 28:27)—in text, in numbers and in story (Sefer Yetzira 1:1)—He established it and searched it out (Job 28:27), and he brought her to Adam. (Genesis 2:22) "For this is the whole man [= Adam]" (Ecclesiastes 12:13) [which the Talmud interprets to mean that] the whole world was created as an accompaniment for this man [who keeps the commandments] (Talmud Brachot 6B) – Is

---

Tr1   The reader will have to bear with us, if what he now will read appears to be unintelligible. It is not intended to be anything different. All that the author is trying to present are words of a certain nature. The accent of the introduction is on the word "ADAM", i.e. MAN, which is mentioned twice, telling us that we are in contact with ADAM-Avraham David Moshe.

there any among them to declare that this is the Torah? (See Talmud Avodah Zara 2b)."[Tr2]

He waged an ever-increasing battle against those who followed Jacob Frank (Shri -The name of the wicked shall rot!), overcame them and drove them out of Rohatyn. This high level of zealousness also applied to his grandson, who was zealous for the Creator - to keep every custom, every tag, i.e., every iota of tradition ("tag" is the term for the required decorations of the letters in the Torah). Under his direction, the town served as an example to the rest of the world. "May his memory be inscribed forever together with those of all the holy men and women who were murdered, slaughtered and strangled"[Ed2] for the sanctity of Israel and the Land.

p. 165 YB: Reb Itche Spiegel and his family who were taken into captivity by the Russians in World War I, and they are from the right: Pinye Spiegel, Zushe Holtz, Naftali Spiegel, next to him the grand-daughter Ryfke Roter (the wife of Yehoshua Landau), Reb Itche (Yitzchak) Spiegel and the oldest son of Naftali, Moshe Spiegel, who is presently in the U.S.

Tr2 As can be seen, this is a metaphoric text, which relies on a variety of religious sources for quotations, a not uncommon procedure, which leaves the impressions that the author, who terms himself Adam, desires, as indicated by the repetition of the name Adam in the text. For the rest, his message seems to be that he considers his book to be a very important contribution in the study of Torah, the text of which he was born to write, and he seems to conclude his message by asking people to read his work. (All parenthetical material in citation inserted by translator.)

Ed2 Reference to the Yizkor (Memorial) Service for the martyred dead.

The Young Dayan[Tr1]
By Ben (son of) Avraham-David, Tel Aviv

Translated by Rabbi Mordecai Goldzweig - YB p. 166

During World War I, the town was burned down. All the men were either taken to the front, or to prison, or they ran away and went into hiding. We should also add that there was an outbreak of the plague in the town. My father was almost the only male left in town. Our house was not overlooked by the plague, and it took my oldest brother, Moshe. My father was forced to attend to his own son's burial because the town was left without a gravedigger. The funeral was attended only by women, who listened to the pearls that came out of my father's mouth when he brought his son to burial in a wheelbarrow.

The war dragged on for a long time and left its effects. One of those effects was that my father, the Rabbi, was drafted into the Austrian army. While in Vienna, my father went to see the Czortkower Rebbe, the holy Rabbi Yisrael, the son of Rabbi David Moshe Friedman, Z"L, in order to obtain his advice on whether to desert from the army or not. The Rebbe suggested that he exchange his uniform for a silk capote, with which he [my father] complied successfully. Before leaving Vienna he saw the Rebbe again and gave him a "kvitel," in which were included all of his children. When the Rebbe came to my name he stopped and said, "Der Eibershter zol helfen" - May it be the will of the One Above that Yehoshua Pinchas remain well." On the way back my father stopped in Stryj. Since their official rabbi was drafted, the community implored my father to remain as its rabbi until their rabbi returned, and so it came about that a long friendship was established between the two rabbis. From Stryj my father came home to Rohatyn, and the first thing that he heard was that his son Yehoshua Pinchas had returned, as if from the grave. My father asked me when this took place - when did I receive this special dispensation - and it turned out that it occurred on the same day my father was visiting the Czortkower Rebbe in Vienna.

There is no question in my mind that this miracle gave added impetus to my father to become a Czortkower hassid, even though his father, my grandfather, Reb Itche Spiegel, was a Boyaner hassid (also of the Ruzhiner dynasty).

Tr1 Rabbi Avraham David Spiegel, as opposed to Rabbi Shmuel Henne who was known as "The Old Dayan"

He used to visit very often the Rebbe, who would come yearly from Vienna to Czortkow for Shavuos. Once he took me along so that the Rebbe could bless me before my bar-mitzvah.

On returning to our charred town, he faced a difficult task. He had to raise the town from the rubble. The central synagogue had to be rebuilt, since the walls were all that remained of the old one. He instituted lessons in Torah, established a "Talmud Torah" for poor children, opened a subsidized kitchen and taught many children of meager means. He also instituted in our town Daf Yomi, a program initiated by Rabbi Meir Shapiro of Lublin.[Ed1] He ordained many shochtim, gave money to Maot Chitim and Kimcha D'Pis'cha for Pesach (Passover); he saw to it that the flour mill and ovens were cleansed, made kosher and ready for baking matzos; he lectured on Shabbos Shuva[Tr2,] on Shabbos [Parshas] Bereishis (Reading from beginning of Genesis, initiating the annual cycle of reading of the Five Books of Moses).[Tr3] On the 3rd of May, Polish Constitution Day, he gave his speech in Polish; and so on and so forth.

Father, father – my teacher, my rabbi – words fail me to describe you. You were beloved by all your children for your pleasant manner and delicate approach to every young person. There isn't a Shabbos or Holy Day, or simply a joyous occasion, that I do not remember your face appearing in the middle of our large family to celebrate and entertain in the proper fashion – an example to all who saw us.

"Shalosh Se'udos" (The Third Meal of the Shabbos)

Shalosh Se'udos – you went home after the prayers of Mincha together with your children and friends. The sun was setting. You washed your hands and sat down to the table. My father, the rabbi, would serve everyone his portion and then begin to sing, "Az b'yom ha-shevi-i nachtoh." Then he would sing "Askina Seudosa" according to the Stratyn melody, after which he would ask those assembled to join in the singing of one of the zemiros. Mr. Welke Allerhand would sing "Dror Yikra." Reb Naftali Spiegel (my father's brother) would sing "Tzur Mishelo." My brother would sing, "Yom zeh m'chubad," and I sang "Kel Mis-tater." When I reached the portion supplicating for redemption, my father would join me with greater emotion and repeat the

---

Ed1 "When Rabbi Meir Shapiro, the rabbi of Lublin between the two World Wars, initiated the program for Jews all over the world to study the same daf yomi, he explained the significance of this undertaking by paraphrasing Rabbi Akiva: A daf is the instrument of our survival in the stormy seas of today." Herman Wouk, Daf Yomi, http://www.ohr.org.il/web/yomi.htm#Wouk

Tr2 On the importance of repentance.

Tr3 On the importance of learning the Torah.

words over and over until you could feel that tomorrow the prayer would be answered, and then it all came to a stop and was over. The house lights came back on, the Shabbos came to an end; we departed with a "Gutte Voch," and returned to the dark weekdays. If the close of Shabbos was like this, can you imagine what the Shabbos and the Holy Days were like…

But the Life of Job Did Not Stop

I was about seven years old when, as I remember, the Bolsheviks occupied Rohatyn. At that time, we lived in Turtletaub's house that remained standing after the war and now was housing several tens of people: Shimon and Tzipora Windreich and their children; Reb Alter Faust and his family; Avraham Yosef Ehrenberg and his family; Moshe Hochman with his family—they came later to Israel (he is no longer alive); Rabbi Tzvi Katzman and my father and his family – May they all rest in peace.

Our town Rohatyn was still showing the ravages of the last war. It had not yet taken stock of its losses both in people and property, when the Bolsheviks burst in with a threat that, if by a certain day they did not receive a supply of tobacco, the rest of the town would go up in flames. The town was still charred from the previous fires. Panic seized the town - more evil times. The refugees had just returned from Vienna and other places of refuge, and behold, one problem leaves and another arrives in its place. The heads of the community came to my father, and it was decided that they would turn for help to the residents already groaning under the effects of the times. The decision was that the demand would be fulfilled and tobacco would be brought directly to the rabbi. My father dressed in his rabbinic robes and gathered up all of the children. Together we dragged the tobacco. My father walked at the head to the home of Yulik Weidman in Babince. Upon approaching, my father hid his long beard in his coat for fear they might cut it off, as had already happened to him once before during World War I. We came and stationed ourselves in front of the gate. The area was covered with Bolsheviks lying on the grass barefoot and in tatters; they did not seem to possess anything other than rifles and bayonets. The gatekeeper looked at us in surprise –a large assembly of young children dragging sacks – and asked my father in Ukrainian, "Where are you going?" "We brought the tobacco to the commander," was the answer. The gate was opened wide and the soldiers became happy. "Enter! Come in!" The commander received my father graciously, gave him a chair next to his, pulled out my father's beard and stroked it. "Wonderful, wonderful. Thank you for the tobacco." At the end he concluded by saying, "It's true that I frightened you so that you would fulfill my request, but I definitely did not intend to burn down this town. I am a Jew just like you, and my heart is with you." And so they separated politely. This pleasant surprise was a topic for repeated discussion among all the Jews of the town.

We had no sooner recovered from the first surprise, and a second surprise of a very different nature took place. My mother died. Her name was Chana Toibe, Z"L, the daughter of Reb Elisha Aharon Klarnet—a wholesale dealer of flour in his day, a full-fledged scholar and a G-d -fearing man—and the pride of his family. And then my father's youngest child, my brother Tzvi, passed away (he was named after my grandfather on my father's side, Reb Hirsh Liebreich, Z"L, who lived a long life, 92 years - ramrod straight and healthy to his last day).

My father was then forced to marry again. This time, he married Chaytche (Chaya), my stepmother, the daughter of Rabbi Moshe Reuven Ginzburg, the rabbi of Chodorow, Z"L, and the granddaughter of the illustrious Rabbi Yitzchak Meshulam, the Chief Rabbi of Lwow. Then six more children were born, one of whom died during the period of quiet, and my father rebuilt his home and family. He filled his courtroom with books, and his library made a fine impression on people who saw it, but this put him in debt over his head, while he at the same time had the expenses of raising nine young children.

The children grew up and arranged their lives according to their own views. My brother Yisrael, brilliant in halacha, was ordained a rabbi. My sister Chaytche wanted to go to Israel; she started to make preparations to do so (something that at the time was very difficult to accomplish legally, and therefore she planned to go illegally). My father forbade her to go illegally. I made plans to go to Israel, and for this reason I learned printing. This appealed to my father, for in his eyes it fulfilled the principle that a person should teach his children a trade. As a result of this trade, I am still tied to the Hebrew word. In February, 1938, I immigrated to Israel, and during the period of peace, and again under the Russian occupation, I was still able to send a shipment of etrogim. If my father, Z"L, had remained alive, he would have discerned in this the finger of G-d – in that I alone of all the members of our family should remain alive, could only have been a result of the blessing of the Czortkower Rebbe. But then there were my brothers and sisters who were younger than I - my sister Yuta, Z"L, my brother Yaakov Meshulam (named after the Chief Rabbi of Lwow, Rabbi Yaakov Meshulam, Z"L), a learned student of the Torah, with a keen mind, my four sisters, Yente, Chana-Toibe, Reizel, Vitze-Ryfke – all of them met an untimely death. May their souls be gathered together in the treasury of life and their memories be blessed forever.[Ed2]

Ed2 Phrase from the Memorial Service (Yizkor).

And I bereaved remain bereaved. (Genesis 43, 14)

Yitzchak (Izzie) and Tussia Spiegel, the children of Malche and Pinye Spiegel.

Rabbi Avraham David Spiegel with his youngest son Yaakov Meshulam returning from the mikveh.

Attorney Shmuel Spiegel with Paula (Schwartz).

Yuta, Chaytche, Yisrael and Yehoshua Spiegel

Two Letters of Rabbi Avraham David Spiegel to his Son Yehoshua Spiegel

By Avraham David Spiegel

Translated by Rabbi Mordecai Goldzweig - YB p. 170

With the Aid of the Almighty;

The Second Day of the Week of the Portion of the Torah, "These are the words which the Almighty commanded to perform …" (Va'Yakhel, Exodus 35, 1), 20 Adar.

Filled with blessings of the Almighty… And Abraham is still standing before the Almighty to pour out his words…standing and praying for his sons and daughters to merit "raising the glory" with satisfaction and honor…and David commanded Yehoshua Pinchas his son on the day of his emigration to the Holy Land saying,

My dearest son! Behold you leave today to travel to the Land of the Deer (poetic term for Israel). Please remember your Creator and accept the responsibility of the Worship of the Heavenly Kingdom. Be sure to remember what I am commanding you today, to follow the proper path and the way of the righteous. Be careful to guard yourself and be very careful to guard your soul, that your heart will not, G-d forbid, be led astray from following the straight path. Remember your mother, the Rebbetzin, the lady Chana Toive, Z"L, who gave her life to raise you for the sole purpose of following the Torah and doing good deeds. And when you will take it upon yourself to guard the Torah and the commandments and to carry out the commandment "in all your ways know Him," you will enable her soul to rise (to the upper spiritual spheres) and commend you to The One Who Rests In The Heavens, and the Creator will then command a blessing of life that is true life upon you, and you will become strong and mature, rise upward and succeed wherever you turn and merit bringing and receiving good tidings. From your father who prays and sighs from the wounds of time, but looks forward to Heavenly pity and deliverance in the near future - a complete deliverance in which we will all soon merit going up to Zion in song.

From the one who loves you greatly and closes with all blessings and the blessing, "May the angels be commanded to guard you in all your ways."

Rabbi and dayan –
Avraham David Spiegel

(Seal of office: A.D. Spiegel, Rabbi … in Rohatyn)

*p. 170 YB: On the day I left for Israel, 20 Adar 5698 (February 1938) –
My father the rabbi, Z"L, accompanied me to the train station and handed
me a letter of farewell in his beautiful handwriting and rich style of
Hebrew. (Note: This is the first letter presented on the previous page.)*

229

Blessed Be the Name, The Day Before the Holy Shabbos Portion of the Torah (Pinchas, Numbers 26, 55), "According to the names of the tribes of their fathers shall they inherit"... 5698, Our Community Rohatyn, May it be rebuilt.

My beloved and dear son, the joy of my life, complete with virtues and fine traits, Yehoshua Pinchas, May His light shine, and to my future daughter-in-law, the esteemed young woman, Miss Hadassa, Tichye (May she be inscribed for life) - complete with virtues and fine traits, from a fine family.

I hereby agree in consonance with my dear and honored soon-to-be relative of elevated family and of learned background, his honor Rabbi Avraham Barad, May His light shine, to set your wedding day, in a good and successful time, at the home of your uncle, the very distinguished Rabbi Y. A. Birnbaum of Haifa, the 6th day of the week, on the Torah portion, (VaEtchanan) which says, "... that we will be careful to keep all of these commandments" on the 15th of the month of Menachem Av, May it come to us for good.

Behold, I hereby welcome you with heartfelt blessings. May it be the will of the Creator that the marriage take place at a good and successful time. And you my children, take to heart what is written in the portion of the Torah, "according to the names of their fathers shall they inherit," that as you enter your marriage, accept upon yourselves the responsibility of the Torah and the fine details of its commandments as forever practiced by your illustrious ancestors, Z"L, and especially you, my dear son, please remember how many prayers your mother, the Rebbetzin, prayed when you were a child that she would be worthy of having children who followed the proper path, and [she] is still standing before the Creator in Gan Eden (Garden of Eden) where she rests and pours forth her prayers before the Creator that at least this be her consolation for the loss of her best years, that her dear son who is marrying a daughter of a talmid chacham will take upon himself to follow all the fine details of the Torah and tradition. Therefore, make all efforts to eat kosher food, not to violate the Shabbos and the Yom Tov (Holy Days) and to immerse in a kosher mikveh as is customary among religious Jewish women. And you, Hadassa, should make a point of reading the *Korban Mincha* siddur in the section called Maayan Tahor and other similar books. Everything you need to know about this matter is clearly and logically to be found there. And if you follow this path properly, you will receive what is written in the portion of the week (Deuteronomy 5, 25) at the time of your marriage, which states, "that we will be careful to keep all of these commandments," "according to the names of the tribes of their fathers"—which means, that you should take upon yourselves the responsibility of the Torah and the commandments according to the custom of your fathers and the custom of our holy and pure ancestors; then will you inherit in the end. Then you will inherit everything that is good, you will have a happy marriage and you will be blessed from the Source of All Blessings in everything, from everything, with everything for many long years to come; the marital union will be successful; your banner will rise; you will build a home faithful to the Creator and His Torah; and you will merit seeing fine generations that will bring joy to you, to your parents and to the whole family forever.

So says your father who blesses you with the blessing of Mazel Tov from the depths of his heart and concludes with much love and eternal love.

Our Rabbi and Teacher, Rabbi Mordechai Lipa Teumim, Z"L, may his blood be avenged
(The author's name in the book is unclear)

Translated by Rabbi Mordecai Goldzweig - YB p. 172

For about 25 years, a generation, there was no official chief rabbi in Rohatyn – not since Rabbi Aharon Levin, Z"L, left to assume the position of Rabbi of Rzeszow. Just as a widow who loses her illustrious husband cannot easily find a second his equal and whose pride will not permit her to take just anyone, so too did the Jewish community of Rohatyn have difficulty in finding an acceptable new rabbi. Of course, Rohatyn did not lose everything. It had two dayanim (Judge of the rabbinical tribunal, arbiter): Rabbi Meir Shmuel Henna, Z"L, known as the "Old Dayan", and Rabbi Avraham David Spiegel, Z"L, known as the "Young Dayan," who provided for most of its religious needs so that the lack of an official presiding chief rabbi was not particularly felt. The activities of the "Young Dayan" were especially significant. Nevertheless, since the community had grown and replenished itself after the destruction of World War I, the Jewish Community Council decided in 1932 to reinstate the glory of the rabbinate, and when the candidacy of Rabbi Teumim for this position was presented, it was seriously considered.

Why was he such an attractive candidate? Was it his name? His ancestry? There were no mean considerations - rabbis reaching back to the author of the "Pri Megadim" on "Orach Chaim" and "Yoreh Deah" on his father's side, and on his mother's side, Rabbi Yeshaye Horowitz, the Holy Sheloh. This alone was enough lineage that would suffice to elevate the standing of the community both to the outside world and for its own self-esteem - a worthy compensation for its fallen prestige.

However, that alone did not decide the selection of Rabbi Teumim, Z"L, as town rabbi. His sermon before a large crowd of admirers, including his extended family, made a very fine impression. There was a young rabbi, a second candidate, who spoke after him, but only succeeded in emphasizing Rabbi Teumim's superior qualities. However, even this was not the deciding factor in the choice that was made.

He had a charismatic personality and a noble appearance comparable to an elegant etrog. A round full face was encircled by a short full blond beard. His appearance and speech reflected the certainty he felt about his purpose

232

in life, and his high forehead reflected the weightiness of his thought. He accompanied his speech with a winning smile and expressive graceful movement of his hands. He would look directly into your eyes and with his penetrating glance break down any barrier within your heart. His speech was a bit breathless, yet he loved to talk and smile warmly and lovingly. If he felt that he had won you over to his views on the holy Torah or his ideas on the secular subjects that he was presenting, he would smile broadly or laugh heartily if breathlessly, gently take your hand and draw you close to him. However, once he stood up to leave, these mannerisms would disappear and he would walk away dignified and tall, with steps that were slow and majestic, reflecting in his bearing Jewish internal and external authority.

When he dressed in a spodek (a round fur hat with a velvet center), bekeshe (light black coat) and shining boots, he reflected in his appearance a touch of the Polish aristocracy that had long since passed, combined with the spirits of the generations of rabbinic leadership that went back to the Holy Sheloh and even further. On the other hand, when on Shabbos he drew his tallis over his head covered by a kippa or walked out in his shtreimel, he seemed to have r moved this outside glory and reflected inner greatness, as did the High Priest when he exchanged his golden garments for the white - wholly reflecting his inner personality.

It was his inner personality—rich, deep and broad—that was particularly attractive. There are people who make you aware of their greatness unexpectedly—and thus capture your heart, while there are others whose greatness you become aware of intuitively but cannot comprehend, and in order to verify your beliefs, you draw close and quietly acquire some of their light and warmth. When this occurs, you become aware of the fact that your earlier impressions were correct and in this way your soul is captured. Rabbi Teumim was charismatic in both senses; the more you demanded from his greatness, the more it surprised you.

He was only 27 years old when he competed for the position of rabbi of the community in 1932, against his two competitors who were older than he. However, in view of his reputation, the townspeople streamed to the synagogue to hear him speak. These included many who were not of the kind that frequented a synagogue; and it was this first sermon that sealed the decision. His sharp talmudic argument, expressed clearly, with quiet self confidence, caused raised eyebrows among the scholars, but left them with a feeling of satisfaction. This was what they had hoped for, but they were surprised when it actually appeared before them. (Later some of these scholars were proud to acknowledge the fact that they had not been able to follow all of what had been said.) However, this same broad knowledge, which expressed itself in the subject and structure of the sermon, also appeared in his use of scientific concepts and foreign expressions, surprising the academics in the audience by their unexpected accuracy. His later sermons continued to justify our expectations, and we would leave the synagogue after a sermon proud of his greatness and pleasantly surprised by the constant new ways in which it was revealed to us.

All that he taught was G-d's Torah and the Torah was all that he taught. In his learned discourses on Shabbos HaGadol (the Shabbat before Pesach) and in the chastisements of Shabbos Shuva (the Shabbat before Yom Kippur), in the study of Talmud and in the explanations of the Torah, in religious law and story, and even in day-to-day conversation on philosophical or political matters, or on ceremonial national occasions, when he spoke in brilliant Polish and expressed a wealth of ideas which even penetrated the closed hearts of the Polish officials – in every way he lifted you into the aristocratic sphere from which he drew inspiration for his daily activities. His stability in the stormy reality in which we found ourselves was broader and more enlightening because it was based in the bright heavens of our eternal Torah, holy optimism, which guides towards security on earth. The Torah which he studied and in which he was immersed became a total part of his being. This was felt in every word he uttered.

He was not a Zionist, but nationalistic feelings were part of his religious thought. There were those who thought that this was because of his hassidic family background. Others felt that this was part of the neutral attitude cultivated historically by the rabbinate of Galicia. And there were those who felt that this was a sign of personal greatness which was not restrained by social convention. Shortly after he was accepted as rabbi, Reb Yosef Laks (the luminary of our community, who was renowned for his discourses, poetry and prayer, and who had spoken before the Community Council not long before that in favor of the Mizrachi) made a remark that, "A rabbi does not have to be a Zionist!" although he might be one, and he had no obligation to explicitly declare himself a Zionist, whatever his feelings on the subject might be – the feeling was that he was referring to our rabbi, that is to say that the rabbi should be judged on his own merits. If there had been any hesitations among the Zionists who comprised a majority of the community as to the choice of rabbi before the election, they were clearly shown to have been dissipated when they voted for him enthusiastically (even against his competitor who was a declared Zionist). After the election, the Zionists continued to accept him as their rabbi, just as the various Hassidim had accepted him as their rabbi.

Moreover, members of the intelligentsia who had strayed from tradition, could also view him as their rabbi. This is illustrated by a story that is told about a lawyer who smoked in public on Shabbat. When his son became engaged and the engagement contract was being drawn up, he acquiesced to the modest request of the father of the bride that he stop smoking in public on Shabbat, only out of respect for the rabbi who had said that this was his wish as well. Even non-Jewish intelligentsia, priests, judges and other academics stood in respect before him and listened carefully to his words when he spoke in their circles – they too could find a way to call him "rabbi."

Not only was he great but he was simple and modest. The dayan, Rabbi Spiegel, who was much older than he, and had been acting rabbi before him, served under him and was treated with friendship and great respect. The two honored Admorim (Rebbes), Rabbi Eliezerel and Rabbi Shloimele were treated with veneration. In general, he behaved respectfully toward every person in our town. His home was a gathering place for sages and notables of the community, but it was also open wide to every townsman, and the flow of guests to his home became a new custom in the community. Just as the town was proud of its rabbi, so the rabbi was proud of his town. This can be shown by the fact that when he was offered a position as rabbi of Stryj, a much larger town, which was able to offer a higher salary, he preferred to remain in our community, where his predecessors "were rabbis of more worthy lineage and great renown in Torah." His salary was modest and even that could not always be paid at one time because of the constant shortage of money in the communal treasury. The Rebbetzin sometimes had the undignified task of returning again and again to collect parts of the rabbi's salary. The rabbi himself refused to accept money. The first time that someone offered him a gift in honor of a family occasion, as was customary, he explained that this was an unwitting offense to the Torah, although he personally was not offended, and it would be better if the gift were given to a charity fund to which they both agreed.

His words expressed his great love for all Jews and feeling of obligation towards them. They were not mere empty sayings, but carefully and deeply thought out. One that I cannot forget took place when the new cemetery was opened that was located at a long distance from the town. The community had been forced by Gentile trickery to close the old cemetery, which was closer, and there were those who suggested discontinuing the custom of carrying the litter on the shoulders, as practiced in the large cities. He said, "If it is difficult to carry a litter, then it will be difficult to die!" and they did not discontinue the custom. The cemetery was inaugurated with the burial of remnants of Torah scrolls that had been destroyed in World War I and that had been waiting for burial at the proper time. The rabbi was greatly upset during the proceedings and he called out to his "Holy Flock" in heavy tones lamenting the fate of the destroyed Torah scrolls, as well and his own fate to be the one to bury them. "If I had known that I was destined to bury the Torah, I would not have presented myself to be the rabbi of your congregation." His purpose he felt was to increase and magnify Torah and not to bury it, G-d forbid.

The second shock was greater than the first. After seven years of fruitful activity in the town, World War II broke out with the contaminated witches' dance that completely uprooted all holiness. The defiled fingernails of Nazi bestiality, as well as its Ukrainian incarnation, had nothing to do with anything human. They trampled all that was holy and pure in our community as well as the saintly ones—those who symbolized holiness. When he saw the abominable deeds of the collaborators among our brethren, G-d forbid, his spirit broke completely. The last words he uttered that were heard by survivors were: "If G-d wills me to live after this Holocaust, I will never again be a rabbi."

And there was no other rabbi...
May their souls be gathered together in the treasury of life.

From the Letters of Rabbi Teumim

Translated by Rabbi Mordecai Goldzweig - YB p. 176

To a Former Inhabitant of our City   Rohatyn, Weds, Portion of the Torah
                                       Va'era, 25 Shevat, 5695 (Jan, 1935)

On this occasion it gives me great pleasure to express my congratulations and heartfelt wishes to you on your receiving a doctorate from Heidelberg College. May you rise and succeed in these endeavors on the altar of Torah scholarship. Your seat of honor will be established with the banner of achievement in the most important place in town, the place of Torah and recognition, and seeing this your parents will be happy.

Can I hide from you my friend that I have always held you in high esteem and now I would like you to do something for me. We have decided to celebrate the 800th anniversary of the birth of the Rambam,[Ed1] Z"L. Therefore, towards this goal we chose a committee that would arrange all details of the celebration according to subject matter. Due to the fact that we are lacking in literary background and competent lecturers, we are facing many difficulties and impediments in formulating our plans. Therefore, we would be interested and happy to have you appear before us in person, because you have amassed a great amount of Jewish knowledge. However, since ability and wishes sometimes conflict with each other, we would therefore appreciate your sending us a copy of an interesting lecture on the topic of the jubilee that you have written as a religious philosopher, or as a teacher, or on topics dealing with ethics or the like. Do I need to suggest topics to you? Think the matter over carefully and I will rely on your judgment. Unless I am mistaken, there should be no problem in this since you have all the literary material necessary and I am quite certain that your lecture will be presented on a high level as is becoming a man who combines both Torah and knowledge within himself. This will find high favor in the eyes of your father, who is a member of the celebration committee, and in the eyes of the Creator Above.

Mordechai Lippa Teumim, Chairman of the Committee
Needless to say the text of your lecture must be strictly in keeping with high religious standards.

Ed1   Rabbi Moses ben Maimon (Moses Maimonides, 1135-1204).

ממכתבי הרב תאומים

לאחד מיוצאי עירנו

ראהאטין יום ד', פ' וארא, כ"ה שבט תרצ"ה

בהזדמנות זו, ינעם לי מאוד להביע לך את ברכתי ואיחולי הלבביים
לרגל הכתרתך בתור דר. מהמכללה בהיידלברג; עלה והצלח בדרכך זה על
במתי ההשכלה התורנית, וכסא כבודך יכון בקרן בקרן־בן־שמן על גופי
מרומו קרת, לתורה ולתעודה; ועיני הוריך רואות ושמחות.

המכסה אני מאוהבי כי תמיד תהלתך בפי, ועל שלי עתה באתי; הן
החלטנו לחוגג חגיגת יובל זכרון הרמב"ם ז"ל לרגל השמונה מאות שנים
משנת הולדתו, ולמטרה זו בחרנו בועד החגיגה שעליו לסדר את כל עניני
החגיגה למקצועותיהם; ולא אכחד תחת עטי כי מחוסר ספרות ומרציאים
מומחים, יש לנו מעצורים והתחתיים על דרכנו זה, ומה מאוד היינו שבעי־
רצון ומתענינים לקראת הרצאתך פא"פ כי כבר מצאה ידך עשרת מונים
במדעי היהדות אך יען כי היכולת עושקת את הרצון תאבה נא להמציא
לנו הרצאה מעינית אודות נושא היובל, — מפי כתבך — בתור פילוסוף
אלקי, או בתור מורה, או על מושגינו המוסריים, וכהנה. מה לי לפרוט עליך
נושאים; תשקול הדבר במאזני פלס שכלך ועל בינתך אשען. אם אין
דמיוני כוזב לי לא יבצר זאת מאתך בהיות לך החומר הספרותי הנדרש
לזה, ותקותי רעננה כי הרצאתך תעמוד על הגובה הראוי, כיאות לאיש
אשר התורה והחכמה אצלו יתלכדו ולא יתפרדו. ויעלה זאת לריח ניחוח
לפני אביך חבר ועד־החגיגה, ולפני שוחר טובתך וח"ה מעלה

מרדכי ליפא תאומים — יו"ר הועד

למותר להדגיש לך כי טופס ההרצאה מוכרח להיות על טהרת הקודש הנ"ל

In Memoriam to Yosef HaCohen Laks, Z"L

By Yehoshua P. Spiegel

Translated by Rabbi Mordecai Goldzweig - YB p. 177

Who was worthy to be in his presence
Who heard his voice and saw his person
How could one forget him
His sweet voice that reverberated in prayer
When he sang his musical compositions
And when he noted his deep comments on the margins of Talmudic volumes
And in his business dealings his knowledge floated
His writing ability could be discerned from letters to his colleagues
And his signature testified to his writing
That expressed friendship in the effectiveness of his poetry:

To a former resident of our town[1]

I will sing to my friend in my name and yours
And at the beginning of the verse set your eyes
Please see the joy of my heart
For a wise man is greater than a prophet
And a student such as you brings joy to his teacher
And in my eyes is filled with favor.

My heart rejoices in your raised prestige
And my bones rejoice in the happiness of your parents
The Primal Cause was in your behalf
Honor is placed upon your head.

You are worthy of honor and greatness
You my dear friend a man of excellence
The rays of your splendor will shine as fine porcelain
Your fate is to grow tall as the date palm and cedar
Turn and listen and receive my blessing
For it stems from the depths of my heart

---

1   In Hebrew (following page) the initial letters of the next three stanzas form an acrostic of the name Yosef Laks HaCohen.

May He Who Resides in the Heavens bring success to your path
Satisfaction and pleasure will sate your ancestors.

Yosef HaCohen Laks (Signature)

י. ם. ש.

לזכרו של יוסף הכהן לאקס ז״ל

אשר זכה להיות בקרבתו / לשמוע קולו ולראות דמותו / איכה יוכל
לשכוח אותו / קולו הערב המהדהד מתפילתו / בהנעימו זמירות שכלותו /
וברשמו בשולי מסכתות חריפותו / משיחו ושיגו צפתה השכלתו / ומאגרותיו
לעמיתיו ניכרת כתיבתו / ועל כתב ידו תעיד החיימתו / יביע ידידות בכוח
שירתו :

לאחד מיוצאי עירנו

אשירה ל.ד.ד. בשמ. ובשמ.ך
ובראשי חרוזים חתן עינ.ך
הבט נא בשמחת לבב.
כי חכם עד.ף מנביא
ותלמיד כמוך חביב רבן
ויקר בע.נ. כרב החן

יגל לב. בהרמת קרנך
ויתגלנה עצמות. בשמחת הוריך
סבת הסבות היה בעזרך
פאר וכבוד ניתן בראשך

לך יאתה יקר וגדולה
אתה אהובי איש סגלה
קרני הודך יזרחו כחרס
סופך להתגדל כתמר וכארז

הסב ושמע וקבל ברכתי
כי נובעת מעומק לבחי
השוכן בשמים יצליח דרכך
נחת ועונג ישבעו אבותיך.

Reb Yosef Yehuda ben
Reb Michel Sofer (Blattner), Z"L

By Yehoshua P. Spiegel

Translated by Rabbi Mordecai Goldzweig - YB p. 178

Reb Yehuda "Sofer" was a poor man who was born in Rohatyn, a hassid of the Bursztyner [Rebbe] (from the Stratyn dynasty), and a father of five daughters, who followed the well-known Reb Michel Sofer (scribe) and continued in his path. He was unable to support himself at his profession because many scribes, such as he, were forced to travel with their holy wares from town to town and were his serious competitors. Then too his customers had become fewer and fewer. As a result, his wife, Freia, had to join him in earning a livelihood by baking her special homemade bread that certain people liked, and he was forced to join her in this task, thereby reducing the time in the exercise of his regular profession. Gradually his hands became heavier and he could no longer continue as a full time Sofer (scribe), about whom it is written, "With his soul he brings his bread." However, he did not drop his profession completely, and the townsmen used to invite "Reb Yudel Sofer" to check their tefillin and mezuzot. When his daughters grew up they helped to augment the income of the house. Unfortunately, when the time finally came to have a little satisfaction from them, when they got married and bore children, the terrible war came and put an end to everything. He was killed by the German murderers, together with his wife Freia, his son-in-law Aaron Gutman, Brunia and Motel, their grandchildren, and his married daughter Sarah with her two daughters, Tovah and Chava. Two married daughters, Esther and Gitel, are now in our country, together with their children - the grandchildren of Reb Yosef Yehuda ben Michel Sofer.

*p. 178 YB: Yosef-Yehuda ben Michel (Sofer) and his family: Gitel and Moshe
Mandelberg, Chava Blattner.*

*p. 178 YB: Mordechai (Motel) Gutman (grandson), Esther Blaustein (Blattner), Tova
Blattner and David Blaustein.*

Yerachmiel Schwartz, Z"L
By Yehoshua P. Spiegel

Translated by Rabbi Mordecai Goldzweig - YB p. 179

Yerachmiel Schwartz was a maskil (member of the Enlightenment movement), that is, he spoke accurate Polish and had ties with the town authorities. Nevertheless, he could boast, "I live with the non-Jews, but I keep the Jewish commandments." He was quite a rich man from his sales of liquor, and he had a monopoly on the sale of mead. I still remember when on the Seventh Day of Pesach if there was a lack of liquor at the gatherings by the Rebbe Reb Eliezerel some of us boys would go to the house of Yerachmiel Schwartz, Z"L, to obtain what was lacking. He personally would come out into the yard, step into a structure that served as a small winery to the north of the Sokol and draw from whatever came in hand. He would also present a "l'chaim" to the boys smiling all the while his sweet smile that would spread across his Viennese white "kaiser" beard. His home was traditional, and he was blessed with refined children who mingled with Jewish scholars and eventually married into their families. Yerachmiel Schwartz, Z"L, was not a person who waited for people to come to him. On the contrary, he would take the initiative and joined those who were trying to help the community. He was one of the builders of the Czortkower Kloiz, a member of the town council as well as of the Jewish community council and an honorary member of the official judiciary. He served in these three capacities until the day he died. May his memory be blessed.

One of his descendants, his eldest daughter Ronia, survived and is now living in Israel. Her only son, Dr. Ezra Zohar, is a physician in the Israel Defense Forces.

Yaakov Leiter and his Wife Sarah, Z"L
By Yehoshua P. Spiegel

Translated by Rabbi Mordecai Goldzweig - YB p. 180

Is it possible to forget this couple, Yaakov and Sarah "who were beloved and pleasant in their lifetime and in their death were not parted." [Tr1] They do not allow themselves to be forgotten. A youthful rhythm always beat within them, even in small day-to-day matters. This Jew who lived far from the Main Synagogue, in the neighborhood known as "the new town," was accustomed to appear every day early in the morning, in order to prepare whatever was needed for the worshippers at the Main Synagogue.

Yahrzeit[Tr2]

He remembered and carefully noted every yahrzeit that had to be kept and reminded people of its date. He saw to it that in the synagogue liquor and pastries were prepared for the occasion; he would always set some aside in the closed section of the reader's table, thus helping out anyone who had a yahrzeit, but for some reason might not have been able to prepare for it. I am not exaggerating when I say that the aroma coming from the reader's table when Reb Yaakov Leiter, Z"L, opened its door, tempted the lovers of liquor to draw closer to the person having a yahrzeit. At that time there was still no printing press in Rohatyn (Reb Chaim Skolnick, of Blessed Memory, opened his small press next to David Jupiter, Z"L, in 1922). And who could print notices and announcements that had to be written? Reb Yaakov Leiter would print them in Assyrian script, the print of Torah scribes. His cleanliness and the cleanliness of his home were exemplary, and were symbolic of his inner self, neat and clean outwardly and inwardly.

He was a man who loved to talk, and he spoke rapidly. If anyone made an announcement before kiddush Friday night, or before reading the Torah

---

Tr1 Probably from the weekly Sabbath morning service which contains a petition to the Av HaRakhamim (Merciful Father) to remember the Jews of Worms, Germany, 1096, who refused to convert to Christianity at the time of the Crusades and were murdered. The petition reads: "the holy communities who offered their lives for the sanctification of G-d's name. They were beloved and pleasant in their lives, and not parted [from Judaism] in their deaths."

Tr2 Annual anniversary date of death of loved one

Shabbos morning, only those who stood nearby could hear what was said, and they would explain to the others that "mimachenmodia" (we are making an announcement), which sounded like one word but was meant to be the phrase "mir machen modia (moyde)" etc.

p. 181 YB: Yaakov and his wife Sarah, in their old age, standing at the gate in Gan Shmuel.

He wore a Deitsche Kapel (a German, i.e., a modern hat) and his curly silver peyot (sidelocks) waved in the wind like "little bottles." His suit of lustrous material was made to order; he wore short boots. You could depend on his watch like on the clock in the train station. I remember when we used to take a break on Yom Kippur between the prayers of Mincha and Ne'ila, which was the last opportunity to chat about the topics of the day, such as opinions about the various ba'alei tefilah (the beginning chazan, the chazan for shacharit and the chazan for musaf) and the latest events. When it started to get dark, they used to call out, "Her Leiter, s'iz shpeit?" (Mr. Leiter, is it becoming late?) But Mr. Leiter would continue to talk. He would pull out his chain and gold watch and announce with finality: "We still have two minutes."

After one minute, he would walk over in his exact steps to the hall. Everyone knew that it was his watch that would decide, and there was no argument about it. If the chazan for Ne'ila appeared to be extending his melodies far too long, he [Yaakov Leiter] would place his watch in front of the chazan and urge him to complete the prayers at the proper moment with the words "L'shona ha-bo-oh b'Yerushalayim" (Next year in Jerusalem).

There was no happy occasion in which he did not take part as one of the officials of the synagogue – as the shammes of the community. He would call out: "so-and-so, the son of so-and-so, has become engaged to so-and-so, the daughter of so-and-so"; and when the time of the wedding came, the poles of the huppah were waiting in his hands. He encouraged and carefully advised the parents of the bride and groom as to the proper procedures and the fine points to be followed at the huppah. He was the master of ceremonies at the huppah and called out the names of those who were given the honor of making the various blessings. He brought the Ketubah (marriage contract) and accompanied the rabbis home after the ceremony. At a brit (circumcision) he would carefully watch the mohel, and if something in his opinion seemed to be improper, he would quote the passage of the Sacrifice of Isaac, "Do not stretch out your hand against the lad nor do anything to him."

I am reminded of a joke (that Leiter told) – Reb Yosef HaCohen Laks, of Blessed Memory, was a well-known ba'al tefilah (non-professional cantor) who was very popular in the community for his pleasant and strong voice, and also because he was very learned and possessed a "keen mind" in his studies. When he studied the Talmud, or while he was teaching the Talmud and came to a fine point, he more than once stopped to write a commentary in the margins with his particular interpretation of the passage they were studying.

When he finished the prayers on Yom Kippur, a discussion would ensue in which there were differences of opinion as to who was the better chazan and the "authorities" would express their views. Some would say that Reb Moshe-Zushe, Z"L, (a composer and chazan of Rohatyn) was the better chazan. Others would say it was Reb Mordechai-Shmuel Horszovsky, Z"L, and still others liked Reb Yonatan Rappaport, or someone else. Then Reb Yaakov Leiter would conclude: "As far as I am concerned, Reb Yossel is a difficult ba'al tefilah and why? Because it is difficult to pick him up when he falls to the floor in the "Avodah" (the description of the role of High Priest on Yom Kippur during the Musaf prayers)."

After the High Holidays – no one could replace him at plaiting palm leaves to house the myrtle and willow twigs. He was unequalled in this skill. And who would receive the etrogim from Israel? He did. He would recognize his friends' special merit with the blessing "upon the taking of a palm branch," when he personally took out the choice etrog.

Reb Yaakov and his wife were privileged in their later years to settle in the Land of Israel and to enjoy the fruit of our land. They made a fresh start in Kibbutz Gan Shmuel, where a new task awaited them: Reb Yaakov would print the names of the cows in the barn and his wife Sarah, Z"L, would do embroidery and knit.

About such as they, it is said: "Beloved and pleasant in their lifetime and in their death they were not parted." They are buried in the cemetery of Kibbutz Gan Shmuel. May their souls be gathered together in the treasury of life.

The Long Moshe (Moshe Roher, Z"L)
By Yehoshua P. Spiegel

Translated by Rabbi Mordecai Goldzweig - YB p. 182

He was tall with a long white beard, dressed in traditional hassidic garb. Religious and honest was he all of his life. I don't remember his wife's name anymore. She must have died young but she did have children – all of them living out of the country – and as soon as he received a letter from them, he would tell everyone in the synagogue about it.

He was always cheerful and his face always expressed goodness. We boys from the Beis Medresh (House of Study) came to know him in his later years and we did not know what his occupation was before. I remember him as the drummer in the Faust band. His fingers would beat out the rhythm nimbly at weddings and other happy occasions where his drum would provide much joy.

He prayed in the new small synagogue where he used to present everyone with a good whiff of snuff tobacco. As soon as he heard that someone wanted to recite a chapter of Tehillim (Psalms), he would immediately express his willingness to join in the mitzvah (good deed). His hand would reach into the breast pocket of his jacket and take out his glasses with the thick dark rims and golden handles and he would mumble, "What did I tell you, Shi'ele (little Yehoshua), happy is the man who did not go (the first phrase in Chap. 1 of Psalms) [Tr1]... the man who doesn't go and doesn't ride off, has no regrets, right?"

"Long Moshe" did not go in the ways of the wicked. He was a good Jew.

Tr1   Long (tall) Moshe probably meant, "who has not left [the world or the country]" – a reference perhaps to his children who all left the country.

❦

Some of the Personalities of our Town
By Yehoshua P. Spiegel

Translated by Rabbi Mordecai Goldzweig - YB p. 183

R eb Yudel Weidhof, Z"L, was an ordained rabbi, who was among those who restored our city in the 1870s. He was a man who excelled in giving donations secretly. His store was well known throughout Galicia as a place that engaged in the import and export of sugar, tea, coffee, etc. There was a time when his son Yaakov Weidhof was one of the biggest merchants in Rohatyn. Yaakov was killed in the Holocaust together with his youngest son who was 31 years old when he died. His son Yitzchak is an engineer with Mekorot (Israel Water Company).

Avramche Horowitz, Z"L, lived on the way toward to the monastery. He was a loud and bitter Jew who sold lime. Due to his occupation, his face was always pale, shriveled, and wrinkled; the hair of his short beard appeared plucked because of this. Only once did I ever see his face light up. Reb Avramche, Z"L, was childless, and his wife was barren. When they grew older, they decided to donate a "Sefer Torah" to the small synagogue, in which they prayed, and in this way establish an everlasting memorial to themselves. When the writing of the Torah was completed, it was carried in a grand procession through the town to the new synagogue, accompanied by a band with dancing and singing of "Give honor to the Torah." Avramche Horowitz and his wife, Z"L, were honored by having him carry the Torah. For the first time, I saw his face light up with joy and become young again.

May his memory be blessed.

Reb Ze'ev Steinmetz, Z"L, was thick-bearded and heavy. He would hold a box of snuff in one hand and a heavy cane in the other. His concern was to provide the inhabitants of Rohatyn with fish for Shabbat. He had difficulty in supporting his family— lovely sons and daughters, most of whom succeeded in reaching the United States; he and two of his daughters were killed. May their souls be gathered together in the treasury of life.

His partner in the fish business, Yehoshua-Falik Straulicht (Shtrolicht), a Jew who was tall and heavyset, not only engaged in sales, but also cared for the deceased. He was an engraver of tombstones, and in this capacity he was an assistant to Kopel Teich and his son Hirsh. This was a profitable business, since in the end everyone is in need of a gravestone. We also wish to remember their family: Yaakov and Uri Straulicht (Shtrolicht), Z"L.

Akiva Wagschal and Elisha Teichman were very close friends and partners from the beginning. Akiva, a gabbai (synagogue manager), had all the problems of the synagogue on his shoulders. He was the one who prepared the barrel of beer for Simchas Torah at the rabbi's home and cheered everyone with his pleasant smile. He succeeded in visiting Israel during his lifetime, when he went to see his two daughters who had settled there. The older one, Mrs. Zuch, who is living here with her husband, is constantly active in the organization of the former inhabitants of Rohatyn. In this she is so like her mother, Tzirel Wagschal, Z"L, a capable woman, who devoted herself to the Zionist activities sponsored by WIZO in Rohatyn. The younger daughter Salke recently passed away.

His partner, Elisha, used to finger his mustache while humming the melodies of Reb Moshe-Zushe. He was a ba'al tefilah in the main synagogue every Shabbat. They and their families were refined people. They were killed in the Holocaust. May they rest in peace.

Reb Mordechai Kreizler was well to do, knowledgeable in Torah and in general subjects; he was tall and dignified in appearance. He engaged in the sale of all kinds of tobacco. His son Shlomo had a stationery store that had a board on its front door on which the daily newspapers were displayed. Many of the inhabitants of Rohatyn would crowd around the board and its newspapers in order to read the daily news; and his shop became a meeting place for those who were involved in communal matters and came up with ideas.

His second son continued his education, and his daughter Chayke Kreizler became a doctor in our town. She was a good-hearted woman.

Their memories have been kept in the hearts of all the former inhabitants of Rohatyn.

May their souls be gathered together in the treasury of life.

Lipa Mandel was a cloth merchant. He was well to do, a General Zionist, and the Reader in the main synagogue. While vocalizing his readings of the Torah, he would glance up at times at the ladies' balcony. He was a good parlor speaker, educated, a maskil, but traditional in (religious) practices. He had a respectable position in the town; he and his family were active in Zionist fund raising. May their memories forever remain.

Reb Yoel Fisher was a nice Jew, sensitive and active in all public affairs in our town. He was an enthusiastic Zionist, but was careful to keep Jewish tradition. He was the Reader in the new synagogue and was strict in following the "Ta'amei Hamikra" (notation) when he read the Torah. He supported himself by selling shoes. He was fair minded and a man of ideals, who tried to get along with people. Incidentally, his son, Dr. Ben-Nun, lives in Israel and is a member of the Hebrew Language Committee, while his sister, Dr. Golda Fisher, recently visited Israel.[1]*

p. 184 YB: Reb Yoel Fisher, Ania (his daughter) and Esther (his wife).

---

1   * She will attend the blessing of this book; she donated to and raised money for its publication.

Raphael Soferman, Z"L
The First Hebrew Teacher of Rohatyn
As told by his wife Matilda Soferman

Translated by Rabbi Mordecai Goldzweig - YB p. 185

The plaques engraved with the names of Raphael and Matilda Soferman still remain in their places. There is quiet all around, and the apartment seems to be mourning Soferman, the educator who passed away.

I called - and there was Matilda, the wife of the deceased, standing before me in person. She invited me in without knowing who I was and without asking what brought me there. Before me stood a woman of about 80 years old. Her face bespoke dignity, and she addressed me in a polished Hebrew.

"Yes, what did you want?" I answered, "I am sorry to trouble you. I came with a twofold task – one, to evoke the memories of your husband as the first Hebrew teacher in Rohatyn and two, to describe the town itself in those days. We wish to memorialize them in the Yizkor Book of Rohatyn and its surrounding areas. We would be very interested in sharing your memories with the survivors of the town in Israel and the Diaspora." "Gladly, I will try," Matilda answered and immediately came to the point, and this is the essence of what she said:

"We arrived in Rohatyn in 1906, where my deceased husband, Raphael Soferman, became the first Hebrew teacher in the first Hebrew school in Rohatyn. The school opened with only two classes and an enrollment of 100 students in all. My husband taught there 4 1/2 years, and I taught about half a year – less. In this school, students reached a high level of achievement not only in Hebrew but also in Bible, History, Grammar and Literature as well.

"In time it also presented plays of national and Zionist content that were spoken in Hebrew. You mustn't forget that the Zionists were already a majority in the community. The members of the Jewish community council were Shalom Meltzer, Sender Margolis, Yerachmiel Schwartz, Alter Weidman, and others. Rohatyn had a Zionist union, HaTechia whose outstanding participants included: Chuna Wachman, Pinye Spiegel, the son of Rudy the watchmaker (I can't remember his name), Doler (Dolar), Drucks, Wagschal, Mandel, Zlatkis, Leiter and others.

"Most of the people of that generation were very religious, but you could already feel the effect of the generation of maskilim arising and becoming stronger. The youth went to Polish school in the morning and in the afternoon to the Jewish school, maintained by the community that had Zionist leanings and from whom the Hebrew teacher received his salary. Those who wanted to complete their high school education had to go to Lwow, Stanislawow, Stryj or Sambor.

"Soferman's helper was the teacher Reiter (Z"L)[Ed1], and when they added another class, they added another teacher, Rosenbaum. The teacher Hirsch was once a student in that school (and now lives in the U.S.).

"The deserters from the army who escaped from Russia and crossed the border illegally came to live in our town, where they learned Hebrew very well and became teachers. After Rohatyn, we went to Brody, where we stayed for 1 1/2 years. We came to Israel in 1912. Then

*p. 186 YB: Raphael Soferman
(the first Hebrew teacher).*

my husband founded a Hebrew school in Safed where he was the principal for two years. Afterward, the family moved to Jerusalem, where my husband became a teacher in the Seminary for Kindergarten Teachers and in a Girls' School. Four years later, we moved to Tel Aviv, where he became a teacher of history and Tanach in the upper grades of the Herzliya Gimnazjum. He taught there until he reached the age of 70, when he retired."

His oldest daughter, Dr. Sharona Soferman-Binyamini, is now a teacher of history and Tanach in the Herzliya Gimnazjum. His son, Dr. Nadav Soferman, became a well-known gynecologist in Tel Aviv. Another son, Amnon Soferman, is a cartographer.

Dr. Gelber commemorated the deceased educator Soferman in his book *Mothers of Israel*, and there you will find his picture. Dr. Gelber also commemorated him in his *Book of Brody*. Soferman passed away of cancer on 13 Iyar 5716 (1956) at the age of 77. May his memory be blessed!

Yehoshua P. Spiegel

Ed1   Zichrono le'Vracha, i.e. Z"L

p. 187 YB: Kindergarten in Rohatyn.

The Hebrew teacher Edelstein with his students in the Hebrew school of Rohatyn.

The Hebrew school in Rohatyn, with the teacher, Edelstein, featured in the center. (photo courtesy Dale Friedman)

Summer camp 1931 - in the center of the picture is Naftali Lev wearing a tie.

The Tarbut Hebrew School, 1936. The teacher Leah Teichman and her assistant Chava Blotner.

The Tarbut Kindergarten in Rohatyn, 1936. The teacher, Leah Ring (Teichman) and her assistant Chava Blotner.

Looking to Zion

Memories of the HaShomer HaTzair Movement in Rohatyn

By Leah Ring (Teichman)

Translated by Binyamin Weiner - YB p. 191

I was only a little girl, and I could not understand why the students, friends of my brother Motyo and my sister Blimah, came to our house night after night to sing and converse. My parents did not know the topics of their discussions, and perhaps even closed their ears deliberately.

These were the first meetings of the HaShomer movement, which was illegal and had no hall in which to hold its activities.

The gimnazjum authorities investigated these activities assiduously. I remember how a mysterious figure appeared in our yard one winter evening, came up to the lit window and, after a while, went away. The next day everything was cleared up. One by one, everyone who had attended the meeting was called into the office of the gimnazjum principal, Lambert, for the sin of belonging to the Zionist organization HaShomer. Of course, my brother and sister came home late from school that day. The lots were cast and the decree issued: all of the boys and girls who had participated in the meeting were expelled from the gimnazjum.

After certain influential parents intervened and accepted responsibility, and with the help of a great deal of money, which went toward the establishment of the gimnazjum library, then in its inception, the punishment was nullified.

A few years later, we began to see groups of Shomrim in full uniform, hiking around on the outskirts of town. A Hebrew song was on their lips, as well as many words of Hebrew speech. Publicity events were organized, related to various festivals and occurrences in the Land of Israel.

Most of our actions were based upon a clear world view. We believed absolutely in our clandestine and socialist-oriented Zionism. It gave us the strength to stand strong in the face of the many humiliations suffered by our HaShomer chapter.

Throughout the year, we would assemble on Wednesdays in our Shomer lokal (our meetinghouse), which was usually located in the poor Jewish neighborhoods, where the craftsmen, market vendors, and day laborers lived. (This was where the Rohatyn ghetto was later established.) These neighborhoods, far away from the gentile quarters,

p. 192 YB: The 'Aryeh' club of HaShomer HaTzair, Rohatyn, 1919. From the top right: Tzvi Milstein, Zushe Brik, Yesheya Freiwald, Izi Holtz, Nusi Reiss, unidentified person, Itzi Holtz, Samush Zeidler. (photo courtesy Dale Friedman)

became thickly muddy whenever it rained. They answered our need to be hidden from gentile eyes, and the investigation of the school authorities.

Here, without anxiety, we could sing the Hebrew songs that came to us from Israel, and dance and rejoice without fear. We were among "our people."

The locals were certainly suspicious of us, these children, boys and girls keeping company "without supervision." More than once the door opened suddenly, and a prying neighborhood man or woman would stare at us with inquiring eyes.

They did not understand that the raucousness that rang out from the lokal issued out of the purity and innocence of our youth. Only a few members of the chapter were fortunate enough to receive their parents' patient support. Most fought fiercely with their parents, and their participation in the chapter was for the most part secretive.

Many in the large adult Zionist circles were sympathetic toward HaShomer HaTzair. Most of the community, however, was wary of the leftist Zionist youth movements and did not hesitate to describe them as "Bolsheviks." Those who took responsibility for our group before the Polish authorities were called "Opieka Organizacji Związek Młodzieży Żydowskiej Haszomer Hacair." The class separatism that was endemic to every Jewish city did not skip Rohatyn, and it was a matter of great surprise that

p. 192 YB: HaShomer HaTzair of Rohatyn in costume for a Purim play to benefit Keren Kayemet L'Yisrael.

"respectable children" could possibly mix in one basket with the children of the poor and the craftsmen. In the case of parents such as mine, who resigned themselves to it, there was always some "respectable man or woman" who took the time to remind them that they should not be so resigned: "The Shomrim are communists, Bolsheviks, and they shame the upper classes."

My parents were Zionists (especially my father), but they were constantly troubled by the thought that their children were going to leave them, their property, and their possessions, and immigrate to Israel where they would be poor farmers. Our debates were bitter and drawn out. Often we managed to persuade them to our opinion, but then they would be overcome by their feelings of love and pride and begin the debate anew.

I confess that the heat of our youthful bitterness pressed us on to radical action, fleeing the house, for instance, to attend summer encampments and assemblies. Mother shed her tears of despair, and I and others like me, though we believed in stifling our emotions in order to dedicate ourselves to the achievement of our goal, we cried and cried in our sorrow at the way we were expected to behave.

The image of my parents on the occasion of my immigration to Israel is etched in the depths of my soul. My father and mother stand in the station, all alone on the platform beside the train that will carry me away from them.

Tears are choked in our throats. When will we see each other again?

But my mother, who was widowed before the Shoah, declared repeatedly in every letter she wrote me how happy she was, how she thanked God that her children were in the Land of Israel. Over time she forgot all of the blows we had struck against her "respectable" motherly pride and blessed the youthful restlessness that before had pained her so.

We dreamed modestly of the kibbutz. We could not possibly have imagined the modern kibbutzim of today, with their well-organized agriculture, societies, training programs, joint ventures, and so forth. Our youthful experiences accumulated in the course of a romantic scouting life, of nights spent beside the bonfire on nighttime excursions. In organized discussions, we immersed ourselves in the study of Zionist issues, news of Israel, aspects of the labor movement, and socialism. At summer encampments we would race to stand in line to receive our meager portions of food. Our budget was limited, and often the full payment of four or five participants went to cover an additional ten.

Transportation to these encampments was, for the most part, very primitive. We traveled in black wagons, driven by farmers. Most years, preparation for the encampment consisted of drawing a collection from a variety of sources, including from individual and group donations, publicity events, and contributions from our few sympathizers.

For two weeks every year, we would gather in the bosom of our rich natural surroundings, the forests and the cool streams, together with other youth of the district, including HaShomer chapters from a number of cities: Rohatyn, Brzezany, Podhajce, Narajow, and Tarnopol.

I do not recall any periods of apathy or cynicism breaking out among the young members of the pioneer movement of our city, although relatively few remained with the kibbutz movement following their immigration to Israel. Those who continued to call the kibbutz home, now remain active in its affairs, and still dwell within its boundaries. Our children live with us, and there is even a generation of grandchildren on the kibbutz, whose grandparents came out of Rohatyn.

I have pleasant memories of my Hebrew education in Rohatyn. The authorities of the Polish gimnazjum explicitly forbade us to study Hebrew, but not a single Zionist in Rohatyn submitted, and for many years we were concerned with finding Hebrew teachers for ourselves. As for me, I went to Hebrew classes secretly, in the evening, hidden from the eyes of my gentile classmates.

We were affiliated with the Tarbut association in Poland, and it supplied us with the teachers that we needed. Later, it sent an official to

Rohatyn to establish a Hebrew nursery school and kindergarten.

In closing, I offer this short anecdote:

In March of 1959, Sheva Weiler, who was visiting Israel from the United States, stayed in my home on kibbutz Ayn-HaMifrats. In her youth she had been a leader in the Rohatyn chapter of HaShomer HaTzair. This was her first visit to an Israeli kibbutz. Everything was a startling discovery, and it all made her very happy, but the high point was when she encountered a friend in the dining hall whom she had known from the HaShomer encampments. He had been responsible for the cooking, and was in the habit of adding a repeta, that is, a little extra, to her portion of food. She ran across the length of the dining hall, and, full of emotion, shouted, "Do you remember me? You used to give me repeta! Repeta!"

A small occurrence, but much more significant than it seems. This same Sheva passed through the seven levels of Hell that was the Shoah, but her happy memories of childhood, of the Shomrim encampments and the passion of the young people who participated in them, have not left her to this day. The same is true of all who were fortunate enough to be a part of this organization at some time.

In our city, HaShomer HaTzair lasted, despite resistance from the very beginning, from the twenties, until the Soviet occupation, when its members fled on foot to Vilna. There they joined up with the local Shomrim chapter, and its leader (Chaim Alon).

p. 194 YB: Uncaptioned picture of the Rohatyn HaShomer HaTzair chapter

p. 195 YB: Field-work day, Shomrim of Rohatyn, 8/12/1919. Standing from the left: Uri Kartin (the leader,) Kuva Dam, unknown, Enge Schumer, Bronka Hornstein, Zev Baraban, Dr. Yankev Kupferman, Attorney Shmuel Spiegel, Jack Faust, Grine Faust, Manye Kartin, Bokser Zusha, Meltsi Holtz, Chayke Maor, Ruzke Hoder (Hader), Junik Bumze, Huchbarg Feybush, Devora Leyner.

The HaShomer HaTzair Chapter

By Yehoshua P. Spiegel, Tel Aviv

Translated by Binyamin Weiner - YB p. 196

There are some who remember the organization in the days when it was still called HaShomer. I am speaking here of a later period. Our forebears were the daughters of Yaakov Leiter, Bracha and Miriam, who now live on the HaShomer HaTzair kibbutz. Reyze Stryjer also managed to make it to Israel after the Shoah, and died there. Her son Buni lives on the kibbutz as well.

I recall the founders of the HaShomer HaTzair chapter in our city as Zev Altman, Bluma Teichman, and Shimshon Liebling. After these first few made aliyah (immigrated to Israel), their places were taken by Lea Teichman, Michoel Noitler, Aryeh Teichman, Tsvi Bratsfis (or Bratshpis), Kalman Katz, and Clara Grienfeld. They too went to Israel in their time, and can be found on the HaShomer HaTzair kibbutz. The only one missing is dear Tsvi Bratsfis, whom we affectionately nicknamed "Barbaz." He put an end to his life, because of a false love.

Next comes the third generation (according to time of immigration): Yehoshua Spiegel, Avraham (Bumek) Cohen, Etka Goldhaber, Chaim Alon, and Yeshayahu Klomberg. We even carried on in secret through a fourth generation: Elimelech Bratsfis, Klara Schuler, Rachel Straulicht (Shtrolicht), Chave Blotner, Gershon Goldhaber, and many, many more.

p. 196 YB: The Chavatselet group of HaShomer HaTzair, in 1919. From the right, first top row: Kinzler, Kupferman, Lipshitz, Baum, Weiss, Schumer. In the middle, the leader of the troop, Itka Mandel. Below from the right: Lonka Bomze, Baum, and Malka Schwartz.

265

What role did our chapter not fulfill in the city? Due to the chapter, we learned Hebrew, awakened our passion for Zionism and labor, circumnavigated the city on hikes, and held discussions in the bosom of nature. We argued and debated over books, sang songs in Hebrew, Yiddish, and Polish, and engaged in sporting and scouting activities.

Most of the time, we would cross the bridge over the river Gniła Lipa, march past Yosef Altman's house straight to the field, Łąka (meadow) not far from the brickyard of Mr. Alter Faust, Z"L. Often we competed for the field with the other youth organizations, but we never relinquished our right to it.

Even our adversaries knew to appreciate HaShomer HaTzair, and we did not lack adversaries, whether from among the other strands of Zionism, the religious and traditional authorities, or those who simply opposed anything new. Over time we made it evident that our cause was an earnest one. We began to participate in summer encampments, and to travel to assemblies and administrative meetings—which meant spending money or missing classes or work. It must be remembered that most of the participants in our chapter assisted their parents in supporting the household, help that their parents could not do without. On this basis, bitter arguments often broke out between children and their families, and not everyone could weather them. With time, as increasingly we began to despair of leading a normal life in the exile of Poland, opposition weakened. But the appointed season had passed, and World War II was already looming on the horizon.

We used the chapter as a beacon and a refuge from all of the bothers and obstacles of the outside world. In it we sought solutions to all of the questions that troubled us. We received knowledge and wisdom in the chapter. After a workday, we would crowd into the chapter auditorium, entering group by group from different corners. The group leader would lecture us on a certain topic: Zionism, the history of the Jewish nation, news from Israel, kibbutzim. Or he would open up a discussion on a literary matter that was central to our concerns, or offer a friendly clarification. In the older groups, it was the custom to distribute reading material, and every member, according to his turn and topic, had to make a presentation, and was thus trained for later responsibilities in facilitating educational activities and leading new groups.

On Fridays, we held nights of song and dance. We rejoiced in every new Israeli song, and did not merely learn their words and tune, but saw before our very eyes the nature and landscapes that they depicted. We also sang Yiddish songs, which expressed the social problems of the nation in exile. We went away to summer encampments, where we were far from the noise of the city and free from every yoke and limitation. These were not easy to organize. We assembled the means in what time we had, gathering food in the chapter facilities, and soliciting donations from men of means to cover the expenses of those in need. A chosen few among us were privileged to participate in leadership encampments. I remember the leadership encampment in Maksimeyts, where we were fortunate enough to spend a month with dear emissaries from Israel. Thanks to them and their students, who afterwards returned to their cities, we were able to double our ranks.

We saw ourselves as trailblazers for the many that made aliyah after us, but sorrowfully the Rohatyn chapter was not to reap the fruit which was meant for it, as only a few were able to immigrate to Israel before the Shoah… Most remained to suffer at the hands of the enemy, may his memory be blotted out. Only two were saved: Tsvi Straulicht (Shtrolicht) and Aryeh Rozman, who were abroad.

p. 198 YB: The Porachat group of HaShomer HaTzair in Rohatyn (4/2/1925). In the center, group leader Shaul Bader. From above right: Shlomo Rotroiber, Shmuel Teichman, Moshe Mett, Avigdor Hamburg, Michael Kizel, Eliyahu Katz, David Kartin, and Leybisch Blech.

p. 198 YB: The HaShomer HaTzair chapter in Rohatyn, at the departure of Yehoshua Spiegel for training.

HaNoar HaTzioni
By Dov Kirschen, Haifa

Translated by Binyamin Weiner - YB p. 199

HaNoar HaTzioni ("Zionist Youth") was one of the Zionist and pioneer organizations that played the biggest role in shaping the character of the young Jewish generation in Rohatyn.

The movement began to organize in 1928, through the initiative of a group of students in the Polish gimnazjum. In those days, most Jewish children studied in this gimnazjum because there were no other possibilities for Jewish boys and girls in the city. There were no vocational or professional schools, or any other kind, and the Jewish youths were locked out of most occupations. Without any other choices, they were forced to attend this particular school.

But the state directorship of the gimnazjum sought the "Polonization" of all city dwellers, especially the school children, through the imposition of many restrictions on the students. For instance, it was forbidden to speak Yiddish in the street, forbidden to participate in Jewish communal life, strictly forbidden to participate in any Zionist youth activities, and so forth. In response to this situation, the Jewish students sought an appropriate framework for themselves, illegal in the eyes of the gimnazjum administration, where they could live Jewish lives, read Jewish books, hear news from the land of Israel, sing Hebrew songs, give expression to their Jewish and Zionist sentiments, and all this for several hours a week.

A group of twenty young people organized and met for "discussions" beside the well on the road to Perenowka. On winter days, most often on Saturdays, they rented a room in a secret place, where they held their activities.

Similar groups organized at the same time in other cities. Soon these various groups banded together into a new youth movement, consisting mostly of high school students, with its headquarters in Lwow. The ideology was general Zionism, without additional leftist, rightist, or religious identification. This movement offered a place to young men and women, who saw a future as pioneers in the land of Israel, and also to those who then thought they would remain as activists for the Zionist cause in the cities of the exile.

The Rohatyn branch grew significantly after news arrived of the events in Israel in 1928: the slaughters in Hebron and Safed, and the activities of the Haganah in Jerusalem, Chulda, and other places. A great Zionist fervor grabbed hold of every sphere of Jewish youth activities in the city. Most of them signed up for immediate immigration to Israel, in order to participate in the defense of the settlement, and masses of them became members of pioneer youth movements. And so HaNoar HaTzioni brought together large numbers of boys and girls of different ages, who organized into groups and troops, the older ones beginning preparation for aliyah.

We were as busy as ants in our chapter. We held meetings, discussions, lectures, games, holiday parties, excursions to the surrounding forests, and summer encampments. We learned Hebrew, Jewish history, and about the various strands of the Zionist movement. We worked on behalf of the Jewish National Fund. All of these activities had the educational purpose of preparing us for our future lives in the land of Israel. Members of the movement found in the "nest" (as we called the hall where we gathered) everything they lacked or could not find in the school or in their parents' houses. It was always happy there. They sang their beloved national songs, danced the hora with great enthusiasm, built bonfires, heard lectures from their leaders on the state of the world, especially the Jewish world, and received answers to all the questions that troubled them, and even to personal problems.

It is hard to describe the great dedication of the leaders of HaNoar HaTzioni. They devoted every free moment to the movement's activities, in order to win the souls of the Jewish children, and to provide a Jewish, Zionist, and scouting corrective to their general education. The results were excellent. Most of the members of HaNoar HaTzioni eventually immigrated to Israel, where they can now be found in every city and settlement in the land.

But the members of HaNoar HaTzioni in Rohatyn were not restricted to the confines of the "nest." Over time, the sphere of their activities widened. Emissaries went out from Rohatyn to all the cities and villages in the area, and brought the movement's ideology to the Jewish youth, thereby founding new branches in Brzezany, Przemyslany, Podhajce, Bursztyn, Bukaczowce, Wojnilow,[Ed1] and other places. Thus, the "nest" in Rohatyn was transformed into a regional center for the movement, and its members became leaders in the regional branches.

Rohatyn members often also served as leaders in far away cities, lecturers at summer encampments, and heads of training centers. One member served a long time as the movement's national director in Galicia.

The older members of HaNoar HaTzioni were actually involved in

Ed1   Wojnilow (Winnilow in YB is incorrect).

all kinds of communal activities in the city and exerted an important influence on every matter that had to do with Zionism. In various elections, they devoted all of their energy to the campaign of the Zionist candidates. They were especially active in the elections to the Polish parliament and the Zionist Congresses. As a centrist Zionist movement, standing between the rightist and leftist factions, HaNoar HaTzioni served as bridge builders in the city, between "enemy" camps so to speak. We should also recall the activities of the "Histadrut HaKeren Kayemet Li-Noar," ("Jewish National Fund Youth Association"), which was founded in Rohatyn for the most part by members of HaNoar HaTzioni, who generally occupied the leadership role over a leftist and rightist membership, drawn from every Jewish youth organization in the city.

"Histadrut HaKeren Kayemet Li-Noar" was a special Rohatyn creation. In no other place was such an association established. It had three objectives: 1) to carry out all of the activities of the Jewish National Fund in Rohatyn, including collecting money, organizing "flower days," emptying the donation boxes, and so forth; 2) to gather new donations from every Jewish young man or woman in the city; 3) to attract the attention of all city-dwellers to the Zionist ideology, through lectures, discussions, and publicity events.

There were also the public farewell evenings, which were held for members of HaNoar HaTzioni on the eve of their departures for Israel. These were organized in the great hall of the communal board, or in the halls of the Ukrainian Gimnazjum. These parties always drew a big crowd of people, who made use of the opportunity to express their respect for those who had done so much for the Jewish community of Rohatyn, and who stood as an example to all the youth in the city. Israeli singing and dancing went on until the wee hours, and in the morning "the entire city" accompanied the emigrant to the train station.

These were the activities of HaNoar HaTzioni in Rohatyn. It was a seething cauldron of youth, full of lofty aspirations and strong enough to achieve the goals of its ideology. It is hard to make oneself believe that all of this is no more.

p. 201 YB: Members of Stam-Tsioni and HaNoar HaTzioni of Rohatyn—a meeting of two generations.

p.200 YB:HaNoar HaTzioni of Rohatyn, on the immigration of B. Kirschen to Israel.

p. 201 YB: HaNoar HaTzioni of Rohatyn, June 1930. (photo courtesy Dale Friedman)

The Chalutz Association in Rohatyn
By Yitschak Bomze

Translated by Binyamin Weiner - YB p. 202

The Chalutz ("Pioneers") branch in our city was founded as a division of the national association of Galicia. The founders were Bulke Kupferman, who was also a member of the training and immigration boards, and myself, the writer of these lines.

We began our activities by organizing training squads and Hebrew classes, and our members sought out occupational training. A friend and I worked in Shabbatai Fishman's locksmith shop.

Our first major training activities took place in 1924, when we worked in Alter Faust's field. Over the course of three weeks, over twenty members participated.

In 1924, we founded a daughter organization, called HaChalutz HaTzair (The Young Pioneer) a general youth pioneer movement, led by Shaul Bader and Max Hochberg.

In 1925, I was privileged to receive the first certificate issued to our branch, and immigrated to Israel as the first official Chalutz from our city.

The Stam Chalutz (General Pioneers) association was organized in Galicia as a sister movement to "HaShomer HaTzair," and even established its kibbutz in Israel under the auspices of "HaKibbutz HaArtsi." Even Rohatyn was not without this association.

p. 202 YB: The organization Stam HaChalutz functioned in Galicia as a sister organization of HaShomer HaTzair. It also established collectives in Israel in the framework of the Kibbutz HaArtzi. Also in Rohatyn it was not absent.

272

Gordonia in Rohatyn

By Yehoshua P. Spiegel

Translated by Binyamin Weiner - YB p. 203

p. 203 YB: Members of Gordonia beside the well in Czercze.

Gordonia[Tr1] was the last youth movement founded in our city. Among its founders were Avraham Hirsh, Tsvi Brodbar, Yitschak Levanon, Yaakov Geller, and others. Hitachdut ("Unity"), its sister association, first supported the group.

Among the remnants of Gordonia privileged to fulfill their goals through immigration to Israel were Yitschak Levanon (who now lives in Mishmar HaSharon) and Yosef Yuzef, who continues his printing trade in Pardes-Chana.

Hitachdut was worthy enough to see its members play a prominent role

---

Tr1   Gordonia was a Zionist pioneering youth movement, based largely on the ideology of A. D. Gordon. Its stated principles were the "building up of the homeland, education of members in humanistic values, the creation of a working nation, the renaissance of Hebrew culture, and self-labor (avodah atsmit)." For articles on Gordon and Gordonia, see *Encyclopedia Judaica*, Jerusalem (1972), Volume 7, pps. 790-794, and pps. 805-6.

on the local Zionist board. Among its most important achievements was the establishment of the Israel Library Union, a cultural meeting place for all the Zionists in Rohatyn. Those active in Hitachdut included Tsvi Halpern, Yitschak Holtz, Shaul Bader, and others. The founders of the library included Chuna Wachman, Pinchas Spiegel, Meir Lewenter, and others.

p. 204 YB: The Gordonia chapter in Rohatyn.

Betar

By David Kartin, Tel Aviv

Translated by Binyamin Weiner - YB p. 204

The Rohatyn chapter of Betar, founded in 1929, was one of the biggest in the region. Its founders were Izio Sharer, Pinia Mauer, Izio Bernstein, Vilush (Wiluś) Weiland, Shmuel Teichman, and Uri Kanfer.

Before long, the chapter numbered nearly 100 members, divided into twelve groups (ranks). The older members, when their time had come, joined the Tzohar (Revisionist Zionists).

A few years later, "Brit HaChayal" ("The Soldier's Pact") was founded in Rohatyn, led by Yulek (Julek) Skolnick (an officer in the Polish army). This organization gave its members, some 100 Jewish youths, military training, to prepare them for their future role in Israel. In addition, in Lwow, Brzezany, and elsewhere, it provided vocational training to its members. The Revisionist movement in Rohatyn drew from every class of youth, without regard to social origin: laborers, students, merchants, artisans, and so forth. Everyone held fast to the doctrine of Jabotinsky, Z"L.

p. 204 YB: The elders of Betar: Simcha Faust, Meir Weisbraun, Meir Reiss, Shmuel Kartin (Teichman), Yisroel Weinstock, Shmuel Acht, Moshe Bussgang, Tsvi Freiwald, Shmuel Teichman, and Motchke Zilber.

Cultural activity was centered on the study of Jewish literature and Jewish and world history. This activity was conducted in groups and through biweekly general assemblies, during which we listened to lectures on various topics. Members of Betar were especially diligent in their use of the Hebrew language, and when walking in the street, their lovely manner of speaking made a pleasant impression on gentiles as well as Jews. Their appearances during readiness drills struck confusion into the hearts of the enemies of Israel.

p. 205 YB: The daughters of Betar: Regina Bergstreit, Etka Shar, Henia Bussgang, Malka Baumrind, and Leah Skolnick.

p. 205 YB: Yulek (Julek) Skolnick (son of Chaim Skolnick).

p. 205 YB: Pinia Mauer (son of Meir).

We excelled in sports as well, and our members trained in various sporting clubs. Our teams went through several name changes: Z.K.S., Betar, and later Maccabee. Yosef Kartin was the captain. We were not only occupied with sports, but also with many preparatory activities, including the pioneer training that had been set up in Rohatyn proper. Twenty pioneers immigrated to Israel: Chanina Feldblum, his sister Adela Feldblum, Tsvi Freiwald, David Kartin, Feyga Hochberg, Uri Kanfer, Etka Kizel, Yechezkel Etner, and others.

After the Shoah, the following came to Israel with their families: Simcha Faust, Shmuel Acht, and Moshe Bussgang. Yulek Skolnick, Z"L, perished during the Shoah in a bunker.

Kuba Dam was prominent among the members of the Revisionist movement in Rohatyn. He took a position in the national office and was afterwards a member of the Revisionist world executive body, and there is truth to what is said about his being Jabotinsky's right-hand man. Today he lives in Buenos Aires, Argentina.

We, who remain, mourn all of the members of the movement who perished in the Shoah, and were never able to witness the fulfillment of their dream.

p. 206 YB: Simcha Faust, Zushe Top, Tsvi Freiwald, Shmuel Teichman, Michael Kizel, Eli Katz, Uri Kanfer, and Muni Halpern.

p. 206 YB: Revisionist gathering in Rohatyn.

CP

The Youth of the Town
By Tzvi Skolnick, Tel Aviv

Translated by Binyamin Weiner - YB p. 207

A boy's day was full to overflowing. School, sports, youth groups, and first dates with girls filled our lives, and so we never contemplated the blood storm on the horizon. Until the last days, our lives coursed along regularly, with school taking the primary place. But fortune did not shine her face upon every young person. Not everyone crossed the threshold of the gimnazjum, because tuition was high and many parents could not afford to cover it. There were two secondary[Ed1] schools in Rohatyn, one Ukrainian, and the other Polish. Jews did not attend the Ukrainian school, because the language of instruction was Ukrainian, and because no Jew was fortunate enough to receive the matriculation certificate sold by the Polish education bureau. The Jewish youth, therefore, turned to the Polish gimnazjum, named for the priest Piotr Skarga.

p. 207 YB: Sixth grade of the state high school—1926.
Ed1 Gimnazjum/gimnazja.

278

p. 208 YB: Prof. Schlesinger with Jewish gimnazjum students in Rohatyn.

The gimnazjum was located in a broad, four-story building, equipped with laboratories, sports facilities, and various machines. This gimnazjum, in contrast to the Ukrainian one, was full of privileged students. The education bureau sold the matriculation certificates. It was coeducational, boys and girls studying together, Poles alongside Jews. But not every Jewish boy or girl was accepted into the school, even if they were able to meet the demanded fee, because the gimnazjum enforced a quota system for minority children, in accordance with the percentage of the general population they represented. Even for the Jewish student who overcame this obstacle, completion of studies was uncertain. The education bureau did its best to fail Jewish students on exams, even though they were among the most distinguished students.

In order to minimize the influence of Jewish students in the Polish universities, a quota system was employed. In addition, Jewish students did not receive any scholarships. There was no thought of releasing students from their studies on Shabbat or holidays. They were only free on Rosh Hashanah and Yom Kippur. No anti-Semitism was experienced from the students directly, though no close friendships were formed either. All students wore the school uniform, bearing the number of the school, 593, on a special insignia. This was at the order of the education bureau, in order to facilitate the supervision of students outside the walls of the school. A gimnazjum student was forbidden to be in any public place, cinema, theater, or street after nine in the evening, and anyone caught out after that hour was in for punishment at the hands of the administration.

p. 209 YB: In the first row above, from the right: Tsia Stein, Salka Wagschall, Etia Leiter, Gotwort, Reyze Leiter; Leah Rosenstein, Salka Brunholtz (or Bernholtz), Pepka Schleicher, Maltsi Dam, Tsipa Teichmann, Beidof, Felicia Schumer, Leah Wagschall. The teachers: Frost (with the beard); Rosenbaum. Leyner Bulke, Bracha Leiter, Miriam Breitfeld. Sitting from the right: Chaya Hoffman and Clara Stolzberg.

At this public school, the Jewish students were provided with instruction in Jewish religion and history. The teacher was Yitschak Schlesinger (now in Israel), who also taught mathematics and zoology, and who represented his Jewish students before the administration, until he transferred to the gimnazjum in Zloczow. Shtekel from Dubromil took his place.

Students in our gimnazjum, like students throughout Poland at the time, were organized into pre-military training corps (similar to our youth battalions), and no one was excused. Many weeks, several hours of general instruction were given over to training activities. At the gimnazjum, there were also sport, dance, and drama clubs, in which Jews participated alongside Christians.

In later years, before the war broke out, when anti-Semitic winds began to blow through Poland, a melancholy spirit pervaded the atmosphere of the gimnazjum as well. A new principal came, whose deep-seated anti-Semitic inclinations were sensed by the students with foreboding. Many dropped out mid-course, and those who graduated and had their certificates in hand, found the gates of the universities locked to them. Those students who wanted to pursue their higher education were forced to turn to universities outside of Poland. Few of the gimnazjum graduates were able to do this, and most turned their eyes to the land of Israel.

p. 210 YB: Z.K.S. in Rohatyn, with Coach Pantzer—the soccer squad in Rohatyn.

The community provided our Jewish "spiritual nourishment," what we would call today our "Jewish consciousness." It organized an evening Hebrew school ("Hebreishe shule") where the Jewish youth could acquire knowledge of Judaism, literature, Jewish history, Tanach (Hebrew Bible), and Talmud. These evening classes were very successful, and were a great help to every student and young person who sought to learn about the history of his nation and the treasures of its culture. The community planned to build an assembly hall for the Jews of the town, and even constructed its frame, but then war broke out and this skeleton passed into the hands of the conquerors, who finished it and made it into a general assembly hall.

But youth does not live by book alone, then as now. As in Tel Aviv so in Rohatyn—the young people were preoccupied with sports, specifically soccer. And Rohatyn was proud to have a soccer team that won its fame throughout the region: the Ż.K.S. (Żydowski Klub Sportowy), organized under the auspices of the Betar youth movement. The living spirits of the club were Yulek Skolnick, Z"L, and Yozef Kartin, long may he live. Above all, the team was devoted to soccer, and even met with success and

281

satisfying victories. It competed against Polish and Ukrainian teams. I still remember the game against a Ukrainian team in the village of Podhajce, which they won eight to one. After the game, the Jews of the village lavished the players of Ż.K.S. with adoration, appreciating the team for having defended the honor of the Jewish people. Living among hostile gentiles, it was rare for the Jews to have an opportunity to humble their anti-Semitic neighbors, and so the village Jews derived great satisfaction from this soccer game. The players themselves were very devoted to their team, and even personal honor and ambition were not considered when the team faced defeat. An example of this was the behavior of Yozef Kartin, who was angry with his team for a long time (I no longer remember why), but when he saw that they were in danger of losing a match he took the field and led his team to victory. He was the captain of the team, and his teammates on the soccer squad were Hershko Leder, Dolek Faust, Simcha Faust, Yaakov Faust, Yaakov Oster (or Auster), Chaim Blaustein, Moshe Erlich, and others.

p. 211 YB: Marcel Lewenter, only son of Tsila and Dr. Yitschak Lewenter.

p. 211 YB: Max Zilber. One of the elder members of Betar in Rohatyn.

The clubhouse was open every day, and young people of every class met their friends there. Even the students, who were forbidden, as already mentioned, to leave their houses in the evening, and were forbidden to join any organizations, found here, under the pretense of sport, the opportunity to meet freely and without worry. Youth from all strands and factions of the town belonged to the soccer team, and political tensions were never a factor. Even though the clubhouse was under the auspices of Betar, an atmosphere of pure sport pervaded it. Everyone there strove to elevate the proud spirit of Jewish youth, to increase their own self-esteem, and to engage vigorously in the physical culture that had been so foreign to Jews throughout the years of exile.

The clubhouse was active until the outbreak of war, when, with the entry of the Red Army, it was transformed into a youth center for all of Rohatyn.

p. 211 YB: Lipa Freiwald, active in the "Erets Yisrael Verein" library. (Son of Sheva and Chinoch Freiwald.)

p. 211 YB: Dudok Faust. Born: May 1921, Rohatyn. Died in Russia in 1943, in the camp of Aktiovinsk.

p. 212 YB: Yosef Weiss, Golda Fisher, Y. Wald, Baumrind, N. Rosenstein.

283

p. 212 YB: Chaim Holtz and Carla Schuler with a group from HaShomer HaTzair.

p. 212 YB: The group Hitachdut with leaders of HaShomer HaTzair in Rohatyn.

Lamentation

The Community of Rohatyn Destroyed

By Rachel and Moshe NasHofer, Haifa

Translated by Binyamin Weiner - YB p. 213

The war broke out in September of 1939, and the Red Army took control of eastern Galicia. The normal, quiet life ceased for the Jews, though as of yet no one had been beaten or killed...

In June of 1941, Hitler's soldiers fell upon the Soviet Union, and on July 2nd they entered Rohatyn. It is impossible to describe the fear and panic that took hold of the Jewish populace.

The next day, July 3rd, the Ukrainian militia was formed, which afflicted the Jews even more cruelly than the Germans did. On July 6, 1941, they played out their first blood sport. They arranged themselves in two rows on the city field, and forced the Jews to lie prostrate before them, for some time, as they struck them brutally with iron poles.

Right away, in the first few days of the occupation, a great hunger began, because the Gentiles stopped selling necessary food to the Jews.

On July 12th, a burning summer day, the murderous Gestapo assembled all of the Jews in the synagogue, and locked them in for several hours, forcing them to lie on the floor and pray for Hitler's victory.

The real trouble began on August 1, 1941, when eastern Galicia came under control of the General Government (Generalgouvernement). Rohatyn became the regional city. The Regional Commander Asbach, was among the worst of the murderers. Orders were immediately issued which later led to the complete annihilation of the Jewish community.

1. A "Jewish quarter" was established, in which the Jews lived in overcrowded conditions.

2. All refugees from Poland hiding in the town had to leave immediately.

3. The Jews had to pay a penalty of 1,000,000 rubles.

4. A "Jewish Council," and "Jewish police force" were formed.

The decrees took effect immediately. Jews had to wear Stars of David on their arms. A Jewish labor board was also formed, which had to provide Jews for hard labor, especially for the hewing of stones.

In November, Rohatyn went from regional city to sub-district, attached to the district of Stanislawow. The murderer Asbach moved to Brzezany.

We believed that things would improve slightly, but it soon became clear that we should hope for no changes. In December of 1941, a new state advisor appeared and instituted a "fur operation." Every Jew possessing furs or pieces of fur had to hand them over on penalty of death.

That winter was among the harshest and coldest, and the Jews, exhausted by hunger, had to work outside, nearly naked, hewing stones.

Till then the Jews had only suffered persecution and had not yet been the victims of mass murders.

On March 8,[Ed1] in the morning, shots were heard in the city, and it was immediately known that the murderers of the Gestapo had come, a special battalion assigned specifically to the destruction of the Jews. With the help of the Ukrainian militia, they shot some 3,600 Jews (1,000 of them refugees),[Ed2] a number of whom had stayed on in the city.

Jewish blood flowed in streams two kilometers long. On the second day, the earth still shook, because some victims had been buried alive, and shouts were even heard from the graves. Two Jewish girls managed to get out of the graves alive, but they died two days later. That day others went to their death, but heroically, of their own free will: Dr. Zlatkis, Dr. Goldschlag, and Flank, Stryjer's son-in-law. [Ed3] On the 21st, hundreds of Jewish corpses still lay in the street, among them mothers with little children in their arms.

On May 1, 1942, a new Judenrat was formed, the dead members replaced with new ones. The perimeter of the ghetto was reduced, despite the arrival of all the Jews of Knihynicze. It is impossible to describe the want that arose there. Hunger was rampant and a typhus epidemic broke out. Day to day, ten to fifteen Jews died of hunger and sickness.

A new page was turned in the catalogue of Jewish martyrdom. They began transporting men to the camps, and the men never returned. To our great sorrow, the Jewish Council, and specifically the Jewish police,[Ed4] played a part in this deportation – this was a very nasty task.

On September 21st, Shabbat fell on Yom Kippur. This was the second of the tragic days for the community of Rohatyn. Savage Gestapo murderers from Tarnopol came early in the morning and carried out an akcja with the help of the Jewish police. Eight hundred Jews were assembled in the field beside the Talmud-Torah and transported to Belzec, where they died by gas and were incinerated in the crematorium. Among the 800 were 300 from Rohatyn, the rest being from Knihynicze. In the course of this akcja 25 men were shot on the spot.

Ed1   Typographical error in text. The date was March 20, 1942.
Ed2   Parentheses in original text.
Ed3   Members of the Judenrat.
Ed4   In German: Jüdische Ordnungspolizei.

In October of 1942, all of the Jews of Bursztyn, Bolszowce, and Bukaczowce were driven into the Rohatyn ghetto. The overcrowding was intensified, and on many days hunger and typhus claimed 40 to 50 victims. As in other cities, a diabolical game now began: Jews with the right documents had a better chance of living than those with other documents. The persecuted and afflicted Jews now began to think about how they could ransom their "lives."

On December 8, 1942, another akcja was carried out in Rohatyn. In this one local murderers (non-Jews) took part, and men from the Jewish police also participated.[Ed5] The results were as follows: all the sick from the Jewish hospital in the ghetto, numbering some 200 according to their doctors and attendants, and an additional 1,250 were transported to Belzec, where they perished in the gas chamber. The people were transported naked, through the punishing cold.

There now ensued a daily hunting of Jews, whose numbers kept dwindling - if they were not shot on the spot, they were cruelly tortured by the Ukrainian beasts.

In January of 1943 the size of the ghetto was further reduced, though it still contained 1000 people (a few hundred from Rohatyn and the rest out of town). The ghetto was locked and there was no getting out. Even for work, transportation was only in groups. Most were no longer suited for labor, and so the Germans and Ukrainians were used. The Jews suffered through the tortures of the winter, and the spring of 1943 came. Most sought hiding places underground, and prepared fortified bunkers for themselves.[1] But

---

Ed5 Expression of outrage and pain at Jewish Police having to carry out the enforced task of apprehending people.

1 [Tr The following extended footnote appears here in the original text:]
On Jewish Resistance in the Rohatyn Ghetto as Attested to by the Murderers Themselves The Report of General Katzman (according to the article of A. Eisenbach in "The New Life" 28-309).
Prime sources of information on the history of Jewish self-defense in the ghetto and the form that it took are the published report of Meyer Straap on the Warsaw ghetto uprising, and the report of SS Grupenfuhrer Katzman, who was officer-in-charge of Galicia. This second report was made to Katzman's superior, Krieger, and it contains important details concerning actions taken against ghetto rebellions and partisans. Among other things, the report depicts in detail three bunkers in Rohatyn, called by their builders "Stalingrad-Bunker," "Sevastopol," and "Leningrad." The "Stalingrad" bunker, for example, was thirty meters long, and was covered by a two-meter-deep layer of earth. It was built very artfully, with electricity, three-level bunk beds, and a sufficient stockpile of rations to feed sixty people for a long time. Katzman discovered the bunker thanks to an informer, but when his soldiers began

often enough, the bunker was discovered and its occupants destroyed.

The last act in the tragedy of Rohatyn Jewry opened on June 1st, 1943, when village after village was "cleansed" of Jews. Rohatyn's turn came on June 6, 1943. It was a Sunday, the first day of Shavuot. At 2:30 in the afternoon, armed groups of Gestapo soldiers and Ukrainians surrounded the ghetto and began setting fire to the houses. When the fire did not catch, they would throw grenades.

People were driven naked to the pits that the Ukrainians had prepared the day before near the new cemetery (on the way to Perenowka, beside the monastery). On the way there, they were beaten cruelly, and beside the pits they had to wait their turn to be shot.

This lasted three days. On the second and third days, the Jews were forced to dig their own graves, and whoever did not strip off their clothes fast enough be- *p. 215 YB: Aliza Blech.* fore death was tortured cruelly, shot in the legs or even thrown living into the graves. Children were generally not shot at all, but thrown living into the pits.

On the third day, silence prevailed. There was no one left to shout. The flames still rose in the ghetto. The fanning of a light wind kept them from going out.

Thus, in such a tragic manner, ended a large Jewish community that was 700 years old. Eight thousand were the martyrs of Rohatyn and its environs, cast into three mass graves, or dusting the earth of Belzec with their ashes.

Some tens of Jews found refuge in the forest. Others fled or were exiled to the Soviet Union [in 1941], where they lived until liberation.

God of vengeance! Do not remain silent for yourself or our blood.

---

to break in, the fighters opened fire. The fighters gave no answer to the soldiers' warning, and the bunker was blown up.

From Tales of Those Days
By Ana Schweller-Kornbluh, Tel Aviv

Translated by Binyamin Weiner - YB p. 216

The Story of a Night

"What time is it?" I asked.

My husband looked at the watch that was still in his pocket, and whispered, "Three."

I was shocked. "So late!" Soon the sun would rise, and we would find ourselves in the middle of a field, without a hiding place. Around us were wide-open spaces, forests, and hills. Where should we go? All night we had walked on and on, without finding the right road to the village where the merchant lived, who had once promised to help us.

Yesterday we waited impatiently for nightfall, thinking we would soon find the village. We lay down in a grove and waited, my family and I. Then there were still five of us. We shivered from the cold. My father Moshe lay in the middle. We wanted to warm him, to prevent the cold wind from blowing on him. My husband Yosef lay on one side, and looked out over the expanse with sorrowful eyes. On the other side lay my sister Malwina, her son David, thin and pale, beside her. I closed the circle.

This was our third day without food, but we were not hungry. We did not even have any water, but this too was unimportant. All that mattered was that night come, the darkness of night, and the still of night—night, our dearest friend.

We were frightened time after time. Who was that up on the hill? Perhaps gentile children had come to the grove to gather nuts? No, it was only birds flying by, oblivious to the fear they had stirred in us.

Finally, night fell. The stars came out, and the moon showed its face. But this too was dangerous. The light of the moon was liable to disclose us. But no, nature was on our side: clouds covered the moon.

Slowly, slowly we rose from our place and moved on in our desired direction. We walked on, hour after hour. We were already so tired, and still we had not reached our destination. We crossed fields and forests, great wide-open areas, and more fields, and more forest. Where were we?

All of a sudden it dawned on us: we went the wrong way! And what now?

291

We stood a whole hour deliberating.

Suddenly our little boy lay down on the grass and lay his walking stick beside him. "I won't walk any further. I can't. My strength is gone. Go if you still can. I will stay here." His mother lay down beside him and pleaded, "Go, go on without us. I will stay with the boy."

I could not raise my voice, but I begged angrily, "Get up! Come on! I won't go on without you. You must walk. Dawn is coming. They will find us and kill us!"

"And what if I want to die?" said the boy. "Leave me. I'm staying here!" I did not cease to tug at him. "We will take you by force!"

"We will rest five minutes," this in the quiet voice of my father. "Yes, Father. We will rest and afterwards go on," I said, and likewise lay down on the grass. How nice it was to lie down! I thought of the people lying in their homes, on their beds, in restful quiet. Would we ever again live like human beings? We had no hope that we would.

Silently, I contemplated my responsibility. I was the one burdened with moving this group onwards. I initiated our flight from the ghetto, in the face of an "akcja," and our wandering along this road. It was up to me to find the village. What should I do now? How could I find the right path?

I rose, and pleaded, "Get up. Time is pressing." Everyone arose, even the boy and his mother. We went on together. How happy I was! Even under those circumstances there were moments of happiness.

I ran some paces ahead, looking for some kind of path, some kind of way, and then returned to my family, dragging on behind me. I drew away from them frequently, and then came near again. And here before us was a wood, with a little narrow path leading through the middle of it. This must certainly be the path that leads to our merchant. We walked as quickly as our strength would allow. I was the first to arrive at the edge of the woods, but, to my great dismay, the path stopped. I went out into the clearing, but no sign of a village could be seen.

I stood in the middle of the clearing and wondered where to turn. Who would help us? I looked to the moon. The clouds were parting, and the moon poured out its light on the world.

Suddenly I thought of dogs. Dogs bark at the moon, and if one dog starts to bark, other dogs will follow. If we were near a village there would certainly be dogs around and in the same instant I began to bark, at first in a small dog's thin voice, and then mightily, like a big dog.

I did not stop barking for some time, though my family surrounded me and began hugging and kissing me, caressing me and whispering loving words. Panicked, they held me fast, without knowing what to do with me.

I understood: they thought my mind had given out.

"Don't worry about me," I snapped angrily, "I am quite sane." And I told them what I was doing, and began barking again, beautifully, in a mighty voice full of force and power.

The dogs answered. It was as if they understood me. How good the dogs were! In those times dogs were better than men…

We went in the direction of the barking dogs. The village we had been searching for all night was not far away.

We passed through another grove, and there before us on a hill stood the solitary house of the merchant, a good man, as far as we knew. The stars paled in the sky, and the sun rose.

A Loaf of Bread

Does anyone really know the value of a loaf of bread?

Whenever I see bread thrown away—slices, quarters, half-loaves of bread lying in the garbage can—I am obliged to think back to a single loaf that caused me great trouble. Sometimes I want to plead with the people throwing out bread not to do it, not to throw it away!

In those days, when I was hungry, a single loaf of bread restored me to life.

I suffered from hunger and insomnia. One night, at long last, I dozed off.

My mother's voice shook me out of my sleep. She was crying. Years have passed since my mother cried in her sleep in the Polish ghetto. Years have passed, and I have not forgotten that night.

"Mother, why are you crying?" I asked her, stroking her hand, "Don't cry, Mother."

Mother awoke. She sighed deeply and answered, "It's nothing. It was a dream. Was I crying?"

I saw her face in the moonlight that pierced through the window. She tried to smile, but the tears still flowed from her eyes.

"What did you dream of, Mother?" I asked. "Tell me."

"I dreamed," she told me, "that winter had come, that the ground had frozen and it was impossible to dig out the money that we hid. And we don't even have a slice of bread."

I laughed softly. "Mother, that's not a problem. Don't worry, everything will work itself out. Sleep soundly."

I returned to my corner, but did not shut an eye. I resolved then to go to the house where my parents lived before coming to the ghetto, to steal into the flower garden where we hid the money, and to get it out from beneath the bushes and bring it into the ghetto. And then we would buy bread. Before dawn, I had already planned out how I would recover the silver and gold that could, I thought, save our lives.

In the morning, when the members of my family gathered together—everyone slept in a different corner—I began putting my plan into action. First of all I had to lie to them, because I knew that if I told the truth they would not let me go. They would not agree to my going to dig in the garden at night; would not let me go on such a dangerous mission.

Lightly, I told them that I would go to the village, to our former maid, who had kept all of our clothes, and bring back bread. They were against the idea. A storm broke out. "It is better to die of hunger," they said, "than at the hands of murderers."

That very day we ate nothing. We "drank" our breakfast, our meal for the whole day: a broth of boiled water and sugar beet, with a little honey.

"Die of hunger? No! No! I want to live, to live along with you. And in order to live I will go!" They did not agree. I was forced to plead, to struggle, to pretend that I was not afraid, that for me it was just a little stroll. And in the end, against their will, I disguised myself in the clothes of a village woman, and went.

With great effort, I left the ghetto. There, in the city, among free people, I felt so wretched, so solitary, that I yearned for the ghetto, for those wretched like me, for the Jews.

I walked slowly. I tried to follow the pace of the villagers, and was very happy when I finally arrived outside the city. When I came to the main road, I widened my gait and began to contemplate the work that lay ahead of me: I had to wait for night to fall, in a field beside my parents' house, to steal into the garden, to dig beneath the bushes... I did not dare think any further. I would buy bread. This was my dream, the dream that gave me strength and courage.

And now I felt that someone was watching me. I looked to the left, and my sight went dark. A Ukrainian policeman was approaching me. How I panicked! My heart beat like a hammer? Could he also hear the beating of my heart?

"Why are you smiling?" he asked me, "and where are you going? You're probably hurrying because tomorrow is a holiday."

I did not know there was a smile on my lips. This smile saved me. Jews had by then forgotten how to smile.

"Yes," I stammered, "I'm hurrying because I have housework to do. Tomorrow is a holiday. I like holidays." He walked beside me. I tricked him into thinking I was one of them. People looked at me, and not a single one of them suspected that the policeman himself was walking beside a Jewish woman.

When we came to the crossroads I was supposed to go right, but at that very minute I changed my plan and kept on walking beside him. I looked at his ruddy face and spoke of village matters. As long as I was walking beside him I was sure that no one would recognize me. When we parted ways and he was gone I was near the village where our former maid lived.

I walked the path to the village and soon saw her house. People were working in the fields. How I envied them. Not only them, but also every bird that flew through the air. "If only I were a bird!"

I arrived and went in. The first thing I saw in the room was the bread. The table was covered with bread, loaves and loaves, one beside the other, fresh and moist and glowing. And what an aroma! It was the aroma of luxury.

The maid was not at home. Her mother was shocked to see me, as if she were seeing a ghost. "What are you doing here?" she asked me. I asked her to give me some of our clothes. "It's cold. The winter is coming," I told her. She left the room.

Beside the table sat a relative of theirs, staring at me through evil eyes. When I looked into his eyes, it was as if an electric current passed through my body. I understood that I had to get out of there.

The mistress of the house returned. In her hand was a pair of sky-blue shoes of mine, which were not to her taste. "How can you wear these?" she said, "They're just toys."

Without a word I took the shoes and made to leave the house. "See you," I said, and against my will stole another look at the bread. And now the woman went to the table, chose the smallest loaf, and put it in my basket.

I left the house and hurried away. I ran through the field and could not calm down until I reached the main road and saw that the bad man was not running after me.

Now I thought of the bread. I glanced into the basket several times, as if thinking, God forbid, the bread had disappeared. Hunger, to which I had grown accustomed and even lived with in peace, now began to argue with me.

"Why," said the hunger angrily, "do you only look at the bread? You have a whole loaf. Tear of at least a little peace."

My head hurt. I had difficulty breathing. My whole body felt weak. "It must be hunger," I thought, "For all of this, I will eat a piece of bread." I took a piece and began to eat. What a wonderful taste!

"I'll take another piece," and I took it, and another, and another.

"In exchange for my sky-blue shoes," I dreamed, "I'll get more bread, and besides, the day after tomorrow, I'll go get our money." There was also gold there, clocks, and precious stones that my grandmother got from her parents and in-laws. I remembered the stories associated with these jewels.

"In two days, I will go," I thought, "the day after the holiday. Of course, on a holiday eve it would be impossible to dig at night, because everyone is out strolling. They could catch me, and then... And to that end it's good that today will be rainy and everyone will stay indoors, and the night will be dark, and a heavy darkness will cover everything, and no one will go outside."

With all of these arguments I sought to justify my change in plans.

And so I thought and ate, and walked and ate, until I looked into my basket and could not believe my eyes: the bread was gone. I had eaten the entire loaf. The bread was warm and fresh and glowing. "What have I done?" I said out loud to myself. I called myself all kinds of nasty names. I could not believe what I had done. "What will I bring home?"

I saw my family before me, pale with blue lips. How miserable I was then? I cried loudly, like a little girl. Only when people approached me could I overcome my tears. I turned aside, into a cabbage field beside the road. I had a sack, in which I had wanted to carry our treasures, and now, in the field, I stole cabbages and sugar beets, stuffed them in the sack, raised it on my back, and returned to the road.

It was late. The sun set. I had to hurry. The sack was very heavy and I dragged it on with difficulty. The beets pressed down like stones. It seemed to me as if the road would never end. And now I heard bells ringing. It was the eve of a holiday and the church bells were ringing.

I was near the city, near the ghetto, and the bells were ringing for peace.

After a full hour I finally saw the city. The sight was blurred in my moist eyes. I did not know if they were wet from sweat or tears.

When I entered the ghetto—which was not an easy thing to do—I had already begun to think with a heavy heart of the road awaiting me the day after tomorrow.

I looked up at the sky and begged the clouds, "Please, let there be rain."

And all this for bread...

Who Is Knocking on the Door?

Someone was knocking on the door. Even so, I did not panic. Who could be knocking on the door so late?

It was already after midnight. The first night after the awful day, a day I would never forget...

It was winter in Poland, in the time of the World War and the pogroms ("akcjas") in our city of Rohatyn. The murderers had captured me in the morning and marched me before them with sub-machine guns in their hands. Beside me the elderly prayed and the children cried, and the murderers mocked us and laughed.

All at once I jumped away and began running. I do not know how far I ran. When I fell to the ground I was in a field far from the city. I lay down and looked around me. Snow covered the world like a white blanket. Sun rays flooded the area with their radiance. Only the howling wind told of our tragedy.

I thought of my family. Where were they? Perhaps they had been able to hide. When would night fall?

The day passed, as everything passes in this world. The sun set, and darkness enveloped the city. I left the field and sneaked like a thief into the ghetto. Those still living wandered like shadows, searching for their families. I too searched, running from alley to alley, asking, "Has anyone seen my dear ones?"

One man had seen my dear mother.

And so I sat that night, after midnight, alone in our room, surrounded by the stillness and quiet. Those who had hidden in cellars or other places had already returned home, but no one returned to me.

I gave up all hope. I sat alone, broken and infinitely miserable. What were my thoughts then? It is difficult to say.

Was someone knocking? No, it must have been my head that was pounding so.

I lit a candle that I found on the table, and slowly went toward the door. I opened it. My husband stood before me.

Pepka Kleinwachs
By Yehoshua P. Spiegel

Translated by Binyamin Weiner - YB p. 221

It seemed to Pepka Kleinwachs that she had found life and security when she arrived in the bosom of her American family, after six years under the Nazis in Poland and Germany.

In 1939, the Germans invaded Poland. Pepka's mother, her two sisters, and her two brothers, all of them registered as Jews, were killed by the invaders. But a Polish youth gave Pepka an Aryan identity card he had found on the body of a Polish girl. Pepka presented the identity certificate as her own and was transported, along with many thousands of Poles, as a slave laborer to that despised Germany.

p. 221 YB: Pepka Kleinwachs, Z"L.

For four years, Pepka worked as a maid for a Nazi family, all the while trembling that the Nazis might discover she was Jewish. Finally the Allied army came, and she went to Paris. From there she contacted her uncles in America, who immediately arranged for her to join the family.

"All her troubles are over," said her happy family as they led the beautiful girl with the dark eyes to her new home, for not in vain had she spent six years in the Nazi hell.

A short time after her arrival in America, she was struck down by a malignant disease, which claimed her as an additional victim of the Shoah. May her memory be blessed.

Rohatyn During the Occupation Years
By Aryeh and Cyla Blech

Translated by Binyamin Weiner - YB p. 222

1 Tr1

The outbreak of World War II, in September of 1939, was felt in our shtetl immediately with the influx of a large wave of refugees from western Poland. As Rohatyn lay near the Rumanian border, the number of refugees was estimated to be 8,000-10,000.[Ed1] Clearly, this tide of people may have brought revitalization and economic increase, but at the same time, it initiated the descent into a typical wartime regimen with its chaos and disorder. The balance that had previously existed was disrupted, and everyone felt as though horrible days were coming.

The German-Soviet pact had, by mutual consent, held Hitler's soldiers on the far side of the Bug River, and the Red Army marched on Rohatyn. With slow but sure steps, they began the Sovietization of everyday life. Trade was nationalized, which caused great disquiet among the Jewish population. The deportation of Shaul Grad to Siberia, the first sacrifice to the "new winds" beginning to blow through the town, made a different, and stronger impression.

The Jewish community had the hard task of caring for the homeless families that the fates of war had brought to Rohatyn. Almost every family in town gave up a room for the refugees. Workplaces were created for them. The general opinion was that we should help them, and that together we would push through the bitter days of war.

All of a sudden—a sensation: everyone who wanted to could register to return to where he had come from. The refugees, who wanted to be reunited with their severed families, their lost wives and children or their far-away grandparents, flooded the registration office and expressed their desire to return. It turned out, however, according to

Tr1 Sections mis-numbered in the original—skips from 4 to 6.
Ed1 In 1940 Rumania was a satellite of Germany. "On August 10 the Rumanian government passed racial laws,…" "In Rumania, the introduction of these laws coincided with an outburst of anti-Jewish violence, …" The Holocaust, Martin Gilbert, Publ. Henry Holt and Co., Inc.,1985 p. 123.

witnesses, that the matter of registration was nothing more than a trap for the unfortunate refugees who were marked as opponents of the Soviet regime and followers of Germany. The proof—they wanted to return to the Germans...

On a certain night, all of the "enemy elements" were dragged from their beds. They were allowed to take with them only their absolute necessities and were driven away to the train station. There, they were loaded into freight wagons, fifty people to a wagon. The transports went away to Siberia and other regions deep inside Russia.

2

On a hot June day in 1941, we heard the powerful detonation of bombs exploding in the surrounding area. It soon became clear that Germany had declared war on the Soviet Union and that the retreat lines in our area were being bombed. Panic in the town was without measure, and the Jewish population became distraught. Whoever was able fled east to Russia. Unfortunately, their number was not very large. The German Wehrmacht (the regular German army) occupied Rohatyn.

This was the beginning of Hell for the Jews of Rohatyn. The first to demonstrate their animal instincts and anti-Semitic sentiments were the Ukrainians. Their dirty work consisted of denigrating Jews, extorting money, jewels and food from them, and further, beating them, delivering blows without mercy and without any reason other than for sadistic pleasure. When the SS later undertook their anti-Jewish work, they found willing and devoted helpers in the Ukrainians.

Once, all of the finest householders of the town, along with its spiritual leaders, including Rabbi Avraham David Spiegel, Rabbi M. L. Teumim, Eliezer Langner, Izi Doler (Dolar), Lipa Mandel and others, were forcibly assembled in the large synagogue. Two SS thugs, together with local Ukrainians, tied the Jews with their hands above their heads and dealt them murderous blows with rubber truncheons. At the same time, the remaining Jews were driven together. They were forced to pass through the "fire," between two armed rows of Ukrainians who dealt out cruel blows to the unfortunate Jews. Many Jews were severely injured and were left invalids.

This did not satisfy the murderers. They also demanded tribute money. The sum had to be assembled in a short time; otherwise, they threatened to burn all of the Jews of Rohatyn. The chairman of the community, Amarant, began to gather together the ransom, and his action was crowned with success.

3

In 1941, a ghetto was created in Rohatyn. The area stretching from the Russian church to the Gniła Lipa river, on one side, and to the house of Alter Faust, Z"L, on the other side, was declared the Jewish dwelling quarter. Thirteen thousand Jews were crowded together in this narrow space. This meant ten people to a room. The ghetto was entirely isolated from the outside world, and this resulted in a scarcity of food. Hunger, sickness and, above all else, typhus left their mark in the ghetto. Every day there were deaths from malnutrition and from lack of medical aid. Thirty to forty Jews died daily in the ghetto [from these conditions], or fell at the hands of the murderous Germans and Ukrainians.

The nightmare intensified up to the point of the first deportation akcja. Meanwhile, following the pattern of other cities in occupied Poland, the Germans had created a Judenrat (Jewish Council), consisting of Dr. Goldschlag, Shlomo Kreizler, Chaim Skolnick, Lipa Mandel, Pinchas Spiegel and Yonah Horn. The Judenrat appointed a Jewish Ordnungsdienst (police), and together they undertook fulfilling the German demands to establish labor groups, pay tribute, collect furs for the Nazi Army on the front and the like.[Ed2]

Once, the Judenrat received an order to assemble 150 laborers who, under the guidance of two engineers, had to dig two large graves on Putiatyńce mountain by the brick factory, each twenty meters long, fifteen meters wide and three meters deep. The Jews in Rohatyn had a reasonable basis for suspecting that they were actually being forced to dig their own graves. A few weeks earlier, there had been a rumor that 20,000 Jews had been killed in this manner in Stanislawow. What could they do? Who would tell them the truth?

As Mr. Amarant was on friendly terms with the Landeskommissar (Land/County Commissioner), he was given the task of determining the real intention behind the digging of these graves. At the price of five kilos of gold, the commissioner pretended to reveal the secret—the graves were to be used as oil reservoirs by the German Army.[Ed3]

4

On the twentieth of March 1942, at six in the morning, the ghetto was aroused by bands of armed Germans and Ukrainians, especially assembled

---

Ed2   Unarmed Jewish police (Jüdischer Ordnungsdienst) for keeping order in ghetto
Ed3   Various rumors were spawned by the Nazis in Rohatyn to divert attention from their intent.

to kill Jews. They stormed into the apartments and ordered the inhabitants to evacuate immediately. Elderly and sick people, pregnant women and children were shot on the spot. Also, those who did not carry out orders quickly enough received a bullet from those frenzied murderers. The assassins ran through the ghetto like wild animals, bringing death and devastation. Those not killed immediately were assembled in the town square, a mass of 3,000. They were commanded to form precise rows, head to head and back to back, to the exact millimeter. If a head nodded or a back shivered, a shot was heard, and the row of Jews grew thinner and thinner. In this way, the unfortunates were kept out in the freezing weather. The flowing blood coagulated. Though the people were frozen stiff, they were forbidden to move at all. The murderers stood around with pointed rifles, looking for a chance to shorten a human life. They also allowed themselves a number of sadistic acts and, meanwhile, photographed many of their atrocities.

At around eleven in the afternoon, SS General Miller came to the town square, and on his order, the unfortunate Jews were loaded onto the waiting freight trucks.[Ed4] The beaten and frozen people were unable to climb into the wagons on their own power, and so began the throwing of the tormented Jews into the vehicles.

The column of vehicles carrying the people drove to the graves where other SS men and Ukrainians were waiting. First, the pockets of the unfortunates were emptied and everything of value was taken away. Then they were ordered to get into the graves that they themselves had dug several days earlier. There, on their knees, they had to wait for death, which came very quickly from machine-guns and rifle volleys. Then the mass graves were covered up, even though, by this time, the souls of some had not yet ascended.

In this way, 3,000 Jews were killed, in the town square, in the ghetto and on Putiatyńce mountain.

On the morning after the first akcja, the ghetto presented a shocking picture; on the streets, in the houses, on the stairways and in the rooms lay frozen, bloody corpses. A dark nightmare hovered over the Jewish quarter. Those still living were trembling over what their eyes had seen during and after the destruction. In order to prevent epidemics, they were compelled to form forced labor squads and go through the ghetto collecting the remains and expunging the traces of the bloody harvest. For a whole day, the bodies were driven through the streets. It was said that 1,200 corpses had been collected in the ghetto.

At night, there was another nightmare that froze the blood in living veins. Nearly fifty Jews, whom the bullets had not killed, and who had lain in the

Ed4 See p.57 in original English section of this Rohatyn Yizkor Book.

piled layers of the murdered on the mountain, had, on their own power, though wounded and in utter exhaustion, climbed out of the two mass graves. Covered in the blood of their open wounds, they barely managed to drag themselves back to the ghetto, accomplishing the four kilometers on foot while racked with horrible suffering. One girl, her feet shot through, crawled home on her knees, to her still living father. But this same father later had to take her in a wagon back to the common grave of the Jews of Rohatyn.

A state of chaos and disorder reigned in the town for three weeks following the akcja. The Germans, however, had their plans, and, therefore, they found it necessary to hold onto their power in the ghetto, with the help of Jews. They issued an ultimatum to Amarant to assemble a new Judenrat as quickly as possible to represent the remaining Jews.

With the liquidation of the Jewish population in the surrounding towns, Bursztyn, Knihynicze and Bukaczowce, the remnants from these towns came to Rohatyn, which complicated the situation greatly and created various problems. A new Judenrat with new "responsibilities" was established. It consisted of Dr. Amarant, Dr. Rosenstein, Prof. Gutwarg, Beigel and others, whose names I no longer recall. A Jewish police force was also created, led by Meierke Weisbraun that played a tragic role in the ghetto. Their task was to insure that the isolation from the outside world was severe, to prevent the ghetto dwellers from coming into contact with the Christian population while escorting bands of laborers to their work and returning them to the ghetto. These functions and assignments had the objective of assisting the Germans in their vile undertaking.

5

Certainly, "normalized" life in the ghetto did not pass without smaller akcja's, severe overcrowding and that harsh regime that men sentenced to death live out behind sealed walls. The Jewish police carried out the orders of the German authorities diligently. Once, in this way, seventy children were delivered up for liquidation. The Jews were forced to obey an order to provide a young work force to a series of camps. The desperate Judenrat held that it would be better if their authority and their militia carried out the matter, instead of the brutal and bloodthirsty Ukrainians who would tear children away from still-living parents. Having no way out, the Judenrat delivered up orphans…

Hunger raged in the ghetto in full force. Even the kitchen organized by the Judenrat did not have enough to allay the need. In the ghetto, one would see many people, swollen with hunger, falling down in the street. The situation of the refugees was even worse.

The second mass deportation was carried out on Yom Kippur, in 1942. In his cunning and perfidy, Hitler chose to kill Jews on Jewish holidays. This time, the sacrificial victims were taken to the train station where 200 to 300 people were shut into each freight car that had earlier been emptied of pulverized lime. They were taken to the death camp of Belzec. Around forty Jews were able to jump from the wagons, and those that returned to Rohatyn told how, before the train even arrived at Belzec, many died of suffocation, a few lost their minds and others lost their lives jumping from the moving train.

In December of 1942, there was another deportation, this time to Auschwitz. New sacrifices to the German death machine were dragged from the depressed, tormented, demoralized and blood-splattered ghetto. Over 1,000 Jews, Jews of Rohatyn and refugees, were transported in dreadful conditions to the annihilation camps.

6

The nearly empty ghetto and the persecutions, hunger and sickness spread demoralization and despair. Those who remained felt their situation to be hopeless. Their motto was therefore, "Survive another day!" In the ghetto, there were no prospects and no future apart from the concrete and actual danger called - death.

Meanwhile, rumors came to Rohatyn of vicious liquidations in the surrounding towns and settlements. The regional cities of Chodorow and Przemyslany were already considered Judenrein (free of Jews). The Akcjas in those places were still being carried out in the form of raids against surviving Jews who were hiding out in bunkers, fields, and forests. They were picked out tracked down one at a time and in groups. Ukrainians and Poles took the primary place in this hunt for living people.

If any sort of stronghold was discussed in those dark times, it was the woods. The rumors of armed partisans in the woods also met with a thankful response in Rohatyn. There were, at that time, between 400 and 500 Jews of Rohatyn and another 1,500 refugees in the ghetto.

The premonition of an ever-nearing end so dominated everyone that even the Judenrat and the Jewish police understood the only way out of this situation was - armed struggle. At a secret meeting, on May 15, 1943, it was decided to buy arms and to make it possible for certain armed groups to go out to the forest. If there had then been suitable men in the town with the necessary qualifications of moral strength, then the plan would not have been doomed to failure. Unfortunately, not everyone in the first group that went out to the forest was able to hold out through the period of trials of rugged survival and severe disappointment, and they returned to the ghetto to the, so to speak, normal existence. Instead of leading others away with them from the accursed ghetto, these first ones returned, thinking that when the moment of present danger arrived, they would be able to flee.

There was proof that the Germans knew about the secret preparations and plans of the Jewish police. It was exactly on a Sunday (on the sixth of June 1943), the entire Jewish police was gathered together and shot. Their bodies were mutilated and afterwards hung openly by the electric power plant, as a warning and deterrent. Soon after that, a move was made to annihilate the last remaining Jews of the ghetto. Again, the remnants of Rohatyn Jewry were put through cruel sufferings, shot on the spot or transported to the death camps.

During that last liquidation akcja of the Rohatyn Ghetto, around 500 Jews were able to escape and reach either the villages or the forest. But without weapons and without money, harried and pursued, they could not hold out very long, especially as hatred, with a thousand eyes, lurked all around, helping to murder the saved. Those fleeing Hitler's fire fell in the Ukrainian water and perished in the stormy waves of hate and anti-Jewish enmity. Between fifty and sixty Jews from Rohatyn and its surrounding areas were able to procure arms and hold out for a longer time in the forest.

*

The pen cannot pass further over the paper. It is difficult to refresh in memory those days of terror and horror when Jewish life was worthless, and beasts, in the images of men, ordained and executed an absolute death sentence on an entire people. Rohatyn Jewry offered up her portion on the altar of the murder of the Jewish people, a sacrifice to racial hatred and the enmity of nations.

The Destruction of Rohatyn
By Tsvi Wohl

Translated by Binyamin Weiner - YB p. 234

The author of this work, a Rohatyner, a teacher by profession, was in the
ghetto from 1941 until 1943. Afterwards, he was in the woods until the time
of the liberation (July 24, 1944).

The Ukrainians Began It

Ten days after the outbreak of the German-Soviet war, the first Germans
appeared in our city. The local Ukrainians took power and soon outdid
themselves in the persecution of Jews. The priest, Teleshshuk
(Teleszczuk), stood at the head of the new civil authority.

On the first Sabbath, the Ukrainians organized a large akcja against
the Jews. Ukrainian militiamen dragged everyone into the Beit
Midrash, all the while delivering murderous blows. The elite of the Jewish
community were led with ropes around their throats. In this way, about
500 Jews were brought together and shut inside. The intention was to
burn them alive. Only men were in the house of study. Women and
children were not touched. The women went to plead with Police
Commandant Baczynski for mercy. He answered that if they were to fill the
little study house with goods, he would let everyone go free.

Hundreds of women and children actually filled the study house with
foodstuffs, manufactured goods and leather, and the Jews were freed.

On the next morning, thousands of farmers came rushing in from the
surrounding villages in order to beat and plunder the local Jews. Thanks to
German intervention, this did not escalate into a pogrom. The situation came
to an end with some scores of Jews badly beaten.

The farmers proceeded to vent their anger on the village Jews. As if on
orders, all of the Jews were chased out of the villages. They came into the
city, beaten up, telling of the horrible things that the local farmers, their
long-time neighbors, had done to them. The majority of village Jews did not
come to Rohatyn, as they had been murdered on the spot.

In the village of Dziczki, the local farmers murdered the Mantel family
in a horrible manner. They were killed with a scythe and buried in a stable.
It seems that the murderers were not satisfied; they were not able to split
up their plunder between them, and so they later dug up their victims and

searched their clothing for gold and money. They found nothing, but they left the dead bodies unburied, on a pile of manure.

A month later, the German authorities received notice regarding money stolen from Mordecai Mantel. The murderers were arrested, the money was confiscated, and they were set free. No investigation into the murder was made.

Armbands and Tributes

By order of the priest, Teleshchuk (Teleszczuk), the Jews had to wear armbands, bearing a Star of David with the inscription "Jude." Afterwards, the order came to establish a ghetto. The worst section of the city, with its run-down shacks and narrow rooms, was selected. The entire Jewish population (more than 5,000 souls) was forcibly crammed into this area. The entire action was carried out in the span of a day. Attention was given that the Jews take with them only small packages. After a year, the ghetto was completely closed off. Entering and leaving were not permitted.

From the first days, we felt the bitter yoke of forced labor. In the beginning, it took place in a chaotic manner. Every Ukrainian grabbed whatever Jews his heart desired and forced them to work for him. Later, this activity was organized. Every day, several hundred Jews went out to labor.

The whole yoke of labor, from the very beginning of the ghetto to its liquidation, fell on the shoulders of the poorer Jews. Those Jews who were able to do so sent hired workers to take their places in the forced labor gangs. Even though many fell down dead from the hard labor, there were always plenty of volunteers to be hired and to serve in order to live through the bitter times, so great was their need. Every day, enough Jews remained who were unable to earn money for bread even in this manner.[Ed1]

The actual German authority in Rohatyn was established a month later. Regional Commander (Kreishauptman) Asbach had his seat in Brzezany. A certain Kachel was established as Land Commissioner (Landeskommissar). This was a man of small stature, ugly appearance and even uglier expression. It was his habit to appear in the ghetto, in a coach plundered from the Jews and decked out in stolen Jewish clothing. He also used to appear in an SS officer's uniform. We fulfilled all of his orders straight away. His first decree was the tribute of a million zlotys, to be delivered within the span of fourteen days.

Ed1 Prior acquaintanceship with some local Gentile people was the most effective way to survive. People in the daily labor gang outside the ghetto could make secret contact with Gentiles. In the struggle to survive, to obtain food and escape from the ghetto, that was more valuable than hiring a substitute for labor..

This decree filled us with fear. Fortunately, we were permitted to pay this tribute in old Polish money and in Russian rubles. The Judenrat assembled the demanded sum assiduously from the surrounding shtetls (towns) as well as from ours. The imposed tribute was paid on time.

Resistance to the Hooligans

We were completely isolated from the outside world. After the holidays, we received news that a tremendous pogrom had been carried out in Stanislawow on Hoshanah Rabbah. Ten thousand Jews had been murdered. Although the news was true, no one wanted to believe it. The Jews sought out various explanations to justify such a massacre.

On the first day of Chanukah, a group of armed gendarmes entered the ghetto and arrested ten prominent Jews. The next morning, an order was issued —Jews had to give over all furs in their possession.

Later on, during a new action, some furs were found in the homes of a few Jews. These Jews, Wolf Sieder (Zider) and Chanah Shateiler, were killed.

Afterwards, a band of SS men fell upon the ghetto and carried out a food akcja. All of the food to be found was taken from every Jewish dwelling.

In the winter months of 1941-1942, the ghetto survived several Ukrainian ambushes. Late at night, well-harnessed sleighs would ride through the ghetto with three or four young hooligans on each one. They grabbed whatever Jews happened to be going by and rode away with them. The kidnapped Jews were stripped naked on the outskirts of town, their clothes were taken away and then they were set free back in the ghetto.

It is worth telling of these attacks carried out by the local Ukrainians. Once, a band of "intelligentsia," led by the local Ukrainian anti-Semite Striyskiy, fell upon the Jewish lawyer Katz, beat him and robbed him. Fortunately, a group of young Jews were in the area, and they came and broke the bones of the attackers. It sickened the Ukrainian elite that Jews should dare to oppose their evil actions. The Ukrainian committee sent a petition to Governor General (Generalgouverneur) Frank in Krakow, asking for permission to put to death the Jewish community of Rohatyn. This petition was signed by Dr. Melnik, the Priest Kudrik and Vice Starosta Khritzyshyn, among others.

This petition, of course, prevailed and led to the great destruction of Rohatyn Jewry in March of 1942.

The Destruction

In the middle of February 1942, the digging of anti-tank pits began not far from the city. Every day, around 200 men were driven out to work in the lime hills on these ditches. The work was hard, but it was undertaken with joy, as we saw in it the nearing of Hitler's defeat.

The work consisted in preparing two gigantic pits—forty meters long, twenty meters wide and very, very deep. We wished onto the Germans that these "tank defenses" would serve them as graves. We never even considered that we were digging our own mass graves, graves for all of the Jews in the city. This work went on until the twentieth of March, 1942.

This was a lovely day, though very cold. Friday, at five in the morning, 100 men went out to dig the "tank defenses." Others waited by the building of the Judenrat. Suddenly, cars full of Gestapo men entered the ghetto along with a mass of civilians. They dispersed in every direction within the ghetto. At the same time, the local Ukrainian militia appeared and surrounded the entire ghetto, along with the Criminal Police[Ed2] and other armed Ukrainians. The ghetto was still sleeping. The entire armed band split up into smaller groups and began dragging the ghetto dwellers toward the town square.

The Gestapo had already paraded the assembled members of the Judenrat and arranged them in rows together with those who needed to go to work. If a Jew offered any resistance, he was shot on the spot.

Hearing the first shot, the Jews ran in all directions. Thereupon, the Gestapo opened heavy fire on the fleeing people. With this, the intention of the Germans became clear. The slaughter had begun.

The first shot fired roused me from my bed. I ran to the window and saw Germans leading two Jewish girls. The girls were shot, and they fell dead. I quickly slipped out of my room and went into a shack, a kind of sukkah. The Germans soon approached our house and began shouting, "Alle Juden heraus! Aufstellen sich familiensweise! Richtung—Ringplatz! Los! Los!" (All Jews out! Line up by families! Direction—Town square! Forward! Forward!) The akcja was in full swing.

Jews, running to the Judenrat, tried to flee the ghetto on the bridge over the Gnila Lipa. Only a few were successful. Armed men stood at all points of exit. Hundreds fell dead or wounded. Some Jews hid in outhouses and in wooden churches that stood nearby the ghetto, and many ran back into the ghetto.

Ukrainians from the surrounding villages gathered together in order to have a look at our destruction and also to help the Germans with their extermination work. From the sukkah, where I lay hidden, I saw how the Ukrainians grabbed the dead and wounded by the arms and legs and threw them into the water,

---

Ed2   Kriminalpolizei (Kripo): The German (non-uniformed) detective forces. Together with the Gestapo, they formed the Sicherheitspolizei. In 1939 the Kripo became Department V of the Central Office for Reich Security (RSHA).

accompanying their actions with wild laughter. These scoundrels chased after all the hidden Jews and brought them back to the assembly point.

Suddenly, in the midst of this bloody commotion, a woman came running in from outside the ghetto. It was Adele Brik. It seemed as if she had no idea what had been going on. She had not stayed in the ghetto the night before. The Ukrainian Militiaman Dzhera shot her right in the face. She became severely distraught. In this state, she ran through the streets for a long time, flapping her arms as a bird does his wings and crying lamentably, "Mama, mama!" until she fell as a corpse to the pavement.

The Ukrainian woman Zelenenka, who lived by the river, did not concern her conscience with a single Jew. When the woman Brik fell, Zelenenka sent her young daughter to strip the corpse of its boots. After she removed the first boot, the girl became frightened. Her mother encouraged her, "Besisia, Lyuba, vona vuzhe zdochlah." (Don't be afraid, darling, this one is already dead.)

All of the Jews were assembled in the center of town and ordered to lie with their faces to the ground. The Gestapo officers walked across their backs with whips in hand. At the tip of these whips were leaden bullets, and one blow on the head from one of these was enough to kill a man. Many remained, lying dead on the town square. The freight cars began transporting Jews to the graves.

The road from the center of town to the graves was littered with hundreds of corpses of people who had been shot, crushed, or frozen by the cold weather. Many had been snatched from their beds and so had not had time to dress.

Arriving at the graves, Jews were placed in groups of five on a little bridge above the graves and shot. Many lightly and heavily wounded people fell into the graves. The subsequent sacrifices were thrown on top of them. A few, still alive after the shooting, crawled out from under the mountain of dead bodies and out of the graves. Sadly, few of them were able to run away.

The slaughter went on until evening. Around 4,000 Jews were killed.

The Gestapo selected twenty Jews to clean the streets. In the morning, Jews were forced to cover the graves. This work went on for several weeks, because the soil covering the slain kept sinking. It seemed as though the earth was seething and boiling in flowing blood.

A Rohatyn Girl's Road through Hell

Story by Sylvia Lederman (formerly Sheva Weiler)

Recorded by Jacob Kener, Z"L[1]
Translated by Donia Gold Shwarzstein - YB p. 239

In the summer of 1941, when the Germans so treacherously and criminally attacked the Russians, they entered Rohatyn. The local Jews, as well as the Jewish refugees from the West, 1939-1941, did not manage to escape. For them now began a life of terror, persecution, murder, hunger, and agony. The brutal German might showed its claws against the Jewish population – the local Ukrainians and Poles assisted in the anti-Jewish policies.

On March 20, 1942, early at 7:00 in the morning, a large number of German Storm Troopers fell upon the town and unleashed a massacre of the Jewish population. The SS stormed into the town with a wild murderous rage; they shot on the spot everyone they encountered - man, woman and child. Accompanied by the Ukrainian police, they fell upon Jewish homes, dragged the frightened Jews from their hiding places and shot them all. In one single day about 3,000 people perished.

Alone at home, Sheva Weiler was awakened from her sleep by the shots, and when she noticed through the window what was going on in the street, she quickly grabbed a coat, threw it over her robe, fled from the house and hid in an outhouse out back. But she quickly realized that this was not a safe place, so she got out and ran by way of many side streets, gardens, and fields to the outskirts of town. While running, she heard Ukrainian schoolboys, who at that same time were going to school, say:

"Look here, a Jewish woman is running away, it has to be reported to the Germans!" Hearing those words, she began to run with greater impetus, until she reached a peasant hut far outside of town, beside a wood. Rushing to

---

1 In the Tel Aviv "NeiVelt," starting August 1949, appeared a series of articles by Jacob Kener, under the title "Heroic Deeds by Unknown Heroes." Among these was published the story of the Rohatyn girl Sheva Weiler (now in New York). The publishers of the book have decided to reprint this piece and are therefore grateful to Sheva Weiler Lederman for her submission of several improvements and corrections, which were incorporated. These changes do not diminish the substance of her story told to J. Kener in New York, when she arrived there in 1946. Sheva Weiler was 19 years old when World War II broke out. She was born and lived in Rohatyn. There she was employed in a Jewish business of Shlomo Kreizler.

get inside the little house, she slipped, fell, lay exhausted, worn out – close to fainting. Just at this very moment, the peasant woman returned from the stable, where she brought fodder for the cow; seeing the exhausted girl stretched out in the snow, she called her husband to come out; both of them took her into the house, where they revived her and gave her a glass of milk to drink.

The good peasant woman clutched her cross and kept repeating to her husband that at night she had dreamt that a young woman dressed in white came to her and asked for help. It can't be anything else, the girl is an angel sent by G-d, and therefore they have to help her. She is sure that this girl will bring her luck; the cow will now give more milk, the chickens will lay many eggs, and in the summer they will have a plentiful harvest on the small plot of land.

The farmer went into town to look for work, and the woman went to the shed to get some kindling wood. At that very moment, Sheva saw through the window Ukrainian policemen approaching. Quickly like a cat, she climbed above the built-in oven, pressed herself deep into the corner behind the chimney, so she would not be seen.

The peasant woman soon returned carrying wood in her hands; with her came in several policemen, who began searching and questioning her whether there was by her an escaped Jewish woman. The peasant woman didn't know that Sheva was hidden above the oven; she thought that she was gone. Therefore, she was sure that this was only an angel, whom she saw in her dream. So she crossed herself again; she assured the policemen that there was no one in her house. In the meantime, she put some wood into the fire - it became unbearably hot above the oven. The policemen said that they would still search the stable, cellar, below the roof, and in the barn loft. They warned, if they find the Jewish woman, they will shoot her and put the peasant woman in jail.

Sheva sat above the oven, veritably roasting in the heat - terror struck, her teeth chattered. The peasant woman kept crossing herself, until the policemen returned and sternly ordered her that should the Jewish female show up, she should detain her and immediately report to the police. For this she will receive from the Germans a pound of sugar and a pack of tobacco …

Only after the policemen left and the peasant woman went back to the shed, did Sheva crawl down from above the oven. Since the peasant wasn't home and Sheva was hot, she took off her coat and remained sitting in her slip, as she had no dress.

In the meantime, the peasant woman came in and seeing her sitting in white, the woman became certain that this was the very angel she dreamed about at night…The peasant woman again began crossing herself, grabbed Sheva's hands, began kissing them and begging her that she intercede with G-d and ask that her cow give more milk and the chickens lay many eggs.

The peasant woman radiated with joy … an amazing thing, an angel in her house … Sheva explained to her, little by little, who she was, what was going on in town, how she fled from there, and she begged her not to tell anyone, just to permit her to hide by her until the next morning – and for this she will pray for her to G-d. The peasant woman gave her a dress to put on, some food and let her stay till the next morning. In the morning the peasant went into town to find out if it was already peaceful. When he came back with the news that the SS left the town, Sheva put on a peasant head scarf, and toward evening, as it was getting dark, she returned to town, sneaking around side streets. The town was full of corpses lying in the streets – but she found her sister and mother alive. The mother hid in a wood shed, while her sister lay hidden in an outhouse, inside the toilet. Only when the Germans left town, after killing 3,000 souls, only then did the mother leave the wood shed. When the mother walked around the courtyard looking for her children, she heard calls for help from her older daughter. The mother then called people to help; they pulled the daughter out of the toilet.

Both the mother and her older sister were certain that Sheva was among the corpses. This certainty, as well as their own dread, put them in a deep state of shock, so that when in the evening Sheva returned, they continued to sit like turned to stone …

*

After the shattering March 20, 1942, akcja which the Germans wreaked upon the Jews of Rohatyn, the approximately 1,800 souls who remained alive—among whom were Sheva and her family – had a few quiet months. This quiet however lasted only until Yom Kippur, which fell on September 21, 1942. The Germans suddenly surrounded the town [ghetto]. They dragged all the Jews from the synagogues and study houses, where they had gathered for holy day prayers. They loaded the Jews into trucks to deport them to the gas chambers of Belzec; those Jews who begged to be let go were shot on the spot.

A very small number of Jewish women and girls remained alive then. Among those who miraculously remained alive were Sheva, her sister and her mother Gitel, who for 24 hours lay hidden in a well-concealed bunker. The following morning, when they crawled out of hiding, her widowed mother said to Sheva: "My child, I see that we are lost, take some money, try to rescue yourself, run away to the gentiles. You know how to speak

Ukrainian well, get a document with the name of a Ukrainian acquaintance and run where your eyes will lead you." At the time there were two strangers in town, a Jew and a Pole; they lived in a secret cellar, and for money, they produced Aryan documents.

Sheva Weiler brought her documents with her photograph to them; these "pros" with a chemical process "washed out" her name and in its place put a fictitious Ukrainian name. Armed with this document, Sheva Weiler put her faith in G-d to find means for her to get away from Rohatyn. Walking in the street with her heart pounding, she ran into a Ukrainian by the name Krupka, whom she knew in the days when she worked in a bookstore.

p. 243 YB: German work pass for foreign workers, photo and stamp. Document under a Polish name: Hanka Buczek.

p. 243 YB: Photo of Sheva Weiler taken in the ghetto, November 1942 for an identity document under the name of Hanka Buczek.

Sheva confided in him, and Krupka, who under the Soviet Regime was the town's Administrator of Cooperatives, told her that now he worked for the Germans in Brody as a provisions officer. His wife and child were already in Brody. He came with a truck to move his furniture, and he was ready to take her to Brody as a governess to his son.

Sheva immediately agreed to that; they made up that at midnight they would meet on the outskirts of town. They met. Krupka told her to crawl into an empty wardrobe to assure her arrival in Brody. Several times on the way, German patrols stopped the truck and checked Krupka's identity papers. It never occurred to them to examine the old furniture, and so Sheva arrived in Brody undisturbed on November 21, 1942. When Krupka opened the wardrobe and told her to crawl out, she couldn't move, she was frozen from the November cold. Krupka had to pull her out and carry her into the house.

Sheva lay sick with typhus by the family Krupka a whole month. The entire time she was sick Krupka's wife took care of her like her own mother. Due to the high fever, throughout her illness Sheva spoke Yiddish and talked about the dangers which affected her. But thanks to the efforts of the Krupka family, she ultimately got well and began to occupy herself with the upbringing of their son.

Sheva thought that all her troubles were behind her and that she could peacefully live in Brody till the end of the war. But in May 1943 began new troubles, new dangers and new terrible wanderings.

*

Sheva's Ukrainian document was not good. The "pros" who had altered her document thought up a name that was dangerous. This troubled Krupka. The name Bandorowska sounded too much like the name Bandera, a well-known Ukrainian nationalist. Acting from Berlin before the war, Bandera had established a terrorist organization of Galician Ukrainians opposed to the Polish government. His followers called themselves Banderowcy (Banderovtsy). From the outset they were firebrand supporters of Hitler. During the Nazi occupation they switched positions; they began conducting secret conspiratorial activities against the Hitlerites. Krupka himself was a leader of the Banderowcy; the Banderowcy held secret deliberations in his house. All of a sudden Krupka became afraid of having a governess for his son by the name Bandorowska. For this reason he demanded that she have herself photographed and that she take out new identity papers in the Brody Municipality under the name of a Polish girl, her acquaintance, a former maid of the Kreizler's, Hanka Buczek. When Sheva was about to leave Rohatyn, Hanka Buczek gave her her birth certificate.

At the photographer's atelier, Sheva accidentally ran into Nekhaika, a Ukrainian woman from her town. During the Soviet time, she had worked in a food store not far from the KultMag (bookshop) where Sheva worked. In Brody this woman was the lover of a German chef of the Sonderdienst. She confronted Sheva in a nasty way, "Sheva, what are you doing here? You should at once run away from Brody, because if you don't, I will denounce you to the Germans!"

Sheva saw dark, her feet began to tremble; she nearly fainted. She was barely able to control herself. She immediately fled from the photographer and returned to the Krupkas taking side streets. She told them about her encounter at the photographer's. This happened May 19, 1943 - and on May 20th, Sheva fled to Lwow under the name Hanka Buczek.

*

In the train compartment into which Sheva entered, by happenstance, sat a Ukrainian Militiaman with a rifle over his shoulder. He was traveling to Lwow on some kind of assignment. Next to him was an empty seat. Seeing a pretty Ukrainian girl (Sheva wore a traditional Ukrainian folk outfit), he invited her to sit down next to him. She accepted, and a friendly conversation developed between them. So when the train started and the German military began their document control, it didn't even occur to them to ask the "Ukrainian" girl for her documents – especially since she sat in the company of a Ukrainian policeman.

The following morning, the same policeman led her from the train station to where all exits were occupied by German military checkpoints; he then put her in the streetcar, which she took to the home of a pensioned elderly high school professor.

And in this manner, Sheva was once again rescued from the German paws—but the road of hell did not yet end for her. Actually, her real troubles started in Lwow. Every day new troubles lay in wait for her. Many a time she stood at the edge of the abyss – but she did not lose herself in any situation. She always kept herself brave, and this saved her in every perilous situation. When Sheva Weiler arrived in the Lwow home of the elderly Professor Galitshuk, he and his wife (a sister of Mrs. Krupka) received her in a friendly manner. At the same time, they told her categorically that she would not be able to stay by them more than a few days. Sheva was in despair, she didn't know what to do. The retired high school professor advised her that she report as a Ukrainian to the German Employment Office, where they recruited Ukrainian girls for field or domestic work in Germany. If she got accepted there, she would be able to survive in Germany until the end of the war. She told Professor Galitshuk that "her" birth certificate was at the Brody Municipality - the Ukrainian schoolmate's birth certificate, which she intended to use to obtain a secure Aryan document.

Within two weeks' time, Mrs. Krupka indeed sent her from Brody the necessary document.

With the new document, Sheva set out to the camp located on Janowska Street. There she stood in line. A stranger came up to her and said to her in Polish that she should go with him because he had something very important to tell her. Sheva was sure that she was already lost, but she steadied herself, and she responded in Ukrainian, "What do you want from me? Who are you?" The stranger told her between four eyes that he was actually a Pole from Kalisz. His name was Tadeusz Czewochowski. He was a prisoner of war and was working here as a doctor. He warned her not to report for work to the Germans. Soon will come the Ukrainian Secret Police and they were sure to pull her out of the line, just as they did this every day with other disguised Jewish girls, whom they then shot on the spot. He advised her to run from the camp, because this week there was no transport to Germany (this was June, the eve of Shavuot). During this time the police would identify her. In those days started the liquidation (extermination) of the Lwow ghetto. Sheva thought that the stranger was also from the police and wanted to get out of her that she was Jewish. She explained to him that she didn't want to leave the camp, that she wanted to wait for the transport. Dr. Czewochowski then led her out to a side road and told her to run away for her own safety. Only when she explained to him that she had no place to run did he find for her a hiding place in the camp, where she was able to wait out ten days.

As she was standing in line, ready to appear before the Commission, two Ukrainian policemen went up to her. They pulled her out of the line and declared that she was under arrest.

On the way to the Criminal Police, she asked them why they were arresting her and what did they want from her. The Secret Agent answered that they suspected that she was Jewish and that the Chief of the Criminal Police would investigate who she was. Finally the agent of the Criminal Police turned her over to the authority of an armed policeman, saying "Take her to Kriyenkevitsh; I'm going back to look for more Zhydovkis (Jewish females)."

When Sheva Weiler heard the name of the Head of Police, she remembered that she had heard that name many times in the Krupka house. She heard there that Kriyenkevitsh held a high position in the Criminal Police in Lwow, because the "Banderowcy" practiced tactics to assume high positions both under the Soviet and the Hitler regime; in this way they were privy to all the state secrets ...

Sheva resolved to use all the information she possessed and thereby save herself.

Later during the investigation, when the Police Chief Kriyenkevitsh ordered her to open her suitcase and he found there two pajamas and the silk nightgown, which the Krupkas had packed for her, he began to yell at her in anger: "You shameless impudent, whom do you want to deceive that you are a Catholic Ukrainian. Tell me, what Ukrainian has silk nightgowns and pajamas? Better confess with whose help you got forged documents, then your punishment will be less, for if you don't confess now, you will be shot today."

The hardened Sheva had now also not given herself away; she answered the police chief with a deceptive calmness: "Hear me out, Mr. Kriyenkevitsh!" As soon as he heard that she called him by name, he became as white as the wall, and he interrupted her. He sent the policeman out of the room and ordered him to wait in the anteroom. When they were left alone, he asked where she learned his name. She answered that she knew that he had a connection to the Banderowcy. If he delivered her to the Germans, she would be forced to give them all the names of the Banderowcy, who were being sought by the Gestapo.

The police chief now became friendly toward her. But he kept her under arrest for three days, and during that time he communicated with the Krupkas und the Galitshuks. After that they set her free. Happy and smiling, Sheva returned to the Janowska Street, under the "protection" of a policeman; soon she indeed entered the German Employment Office. In the office, she pretended that she did not understand any German. She was assigned to a transport which was due to set off for Stuttgart.

But at first she had to undergo a medical examination. How great was her surprise when she came face to face with the stranger - the Pole – who earlier warned her … The doctor looked at her with surprise, with a questioning look, to which she said: "I have told you earlier that I am a Ukrainian and I am going to my fiancé."

"May you have good luck!" The Pole wished her well. He signed the certificate stating that she was completely healthy.

Getting into the train compartment, she was sure that she was rid of all her troubles, when suddenly she caught sight of a young Ukrainian girl from her own town, with whom she once went to school. She nearly gave up her ghost out of fear … but before the girl noticed her, Sheva quickly left the compartment. She ran to the last compartment, where she sat like a deaf mute, with a beating heart, until the train – via Cracow and Vienna – brought her to Stuttgart.

In Vienna, all the women were transferred to the Employment Office. They assigned her work in a restaurant, where Ukrainian women and men worked. Later she had to reside in a camp filled with Polish and Ukrainian women. This was dangerous for Sheva. Besides, there she was persecuted by the group leader, who was a member of the Criminal Police. Therefore she asked the Employment Office that she be assigned elsewhere. After they offered her several places, she chose Stuttgart. Three days later she left Vienna.

Traveling several days through Germany, the train made frequent stops, and at all stops officials from the local Employment Offices distributed on all platforms food for the travelers. Sheva preferred going hungry, instead of going down, to avoid having someone recognize her. In this way she arrived in Stuttgart in peace. There she was assigned to manual labor in the local hospital. Nuns worked there as nurses and aides – therefore this place was safer. There Sheva toiled until the French liberated that area from the Hitler regime.

After her liberation, she posted announcements that she was looking for acquaintances from Rohatyn. Her announcement was answered by Max Altman, Z"L, Golda Fisher, Buszke Brik, and Klara Messing. They also sent food packages and clothing, for which she is grateful to this day. The Rohatyn townsman Dr. Yitzhak Lewenter also responded. Before the war, when she was employed at Kreizler's bookshop, she daily delivered a newspaper to his house. Before long she came to New York, actually with the visa provided by the very Dr. Lewenter. She spent the first period at the Lewenters. Mrs. Lewenter and Dr. Lewenter received her like their own child and helped her get settled in New York.

p. 249 YB: Dr. Yitzhak Lewenter.

p. 249 YB: Bronek Schmorak, Miysho Deutsch, Kuba Faust, Karol Faust, Maciek Kreizler.

319

From Hiding Place to Hiding Place
By Regina Hader Rock

Translation edited by Donia Gold Shwarzstein - YB p. 250

[Ed. Note: Marvin Rock had this article translated as tribute to his mother, Regina Hader Rock. The author of this account was educated and raised in Podkamien. She and her family were exiled to Rohatyn and survived the liquidation of the ghetto in Rohatyn. She was among the few survivors who returned to Rohatyn after the war. She aided in discovering, arresting and prosecuting the local Poles and Ukrainian collaborators who assisted the Germans in annihilating the Jews of Rohatyn.]

From Podkamien to Rohatyn

The Germans entered our town on June 28, 1941. During the first week the one hundred Jewish families of Podkamien were ordered to move to Rohatyn, about eighteen kilometers from Podkamien. We harnessed our horses and buggies and moved to our new location; several families took up residence in one house.

On the first day in Rohatyn, the Ukrainians drove us into a large synagogue; they searched every person in brutal fashion and seized all our valuables. They beat us brutally. They forced the Rebbe of Rohatyn, Reb Eliezer'l, to crawl on all fours, and several healthy Ukrainians rode on his body. This was done in the synagogue in the presence of the town's Jews. At that very same time, Ukrainians looted Jewish homes.

There were about ten thousand Jews in Rohatyn. Six thousand were townspeople; the others were from adjacent towns, refugees from the western portion of Galicia. It seems likely that the Ukrainians undertook the above actions on their own, independently, as the Germans forbade such measures when they heard about them.

The Rise and Fall of the Rohatyn Ghetto

In the fall of 1941 the ghetto was established; the Jews were crowded into several small streets. The crowding was really tight. The hunger was real, especially among the refugees. Our family was not that hungry, since a Christian employed me as a seamstress and I had the opportunity to supply my parents and family with food.

In February 1942, the Germans ordered us to dig two huge pits not far from

Rohatyn. We didn't know why; only later did we realize the purpose of these pits. On March 26th, the SS and the Ukrainians sent 3,000 Jews to the pits, including the elderly, children, and pregnant women.[Ed1] This pogrom lasted all day; people were slaughtered with knives and axes; blood flowed freely in the streets of Rohatyn. Several hundred Jews were ordered to stand still, their heads bowed, in Lenin Plaza[Ed2] for six hours. Many froze to death there; the rest were shot near the two pits.

Our ghetto was not fully sealed. Thus, many Jews had the chance to escape that day and hide in the surrounding areas. On that tragic day I was working as a seamstress for a Christian friend in Podkamien. I soon found out what had happened in Rohatyn and hid in the cellar, as the police in Podkamien knew where I was. Thus, I was saved from certain death.

The next day I went to the ghetto in Rohatyn and found the streets littered with hundreds of dead bodies. I recognized my father because of his clothing. Samuel Leib Karp told me that my mother, brother, and sister were shot near the pits. He also told me where my parents had concealed some valuable items.

After a period of time, as things calmed down in the ghetto, Jews started returning. They were required to swear that their apartments were theirs before moving back in. I was scared to go back to Podkamien and remained in this now much smaller ghetto in Rohatyn.

Several weeks later, I became friends with a young man, Anshel Dorfman from Lipica near Brzezany. He was a soldier in the Red Army and had been a German prisoner of war, but he managed to regain his freedom. One time the Judenrat got an order from the Germans to supply one thousand Jews. These Jews were all transferred to Belzec (a death camp) and killed. This akcja (roundup and massacre) chiefly affected the elderly and poor who were dependent on the Judenrat and the Jewish community for sustenance.

Two months later another action took place, this time aimed at children. Children were forcibly removed from their parents and deported to Belzec to their deaths. Every few days there were inductions into forced labor. These people were sent to forced labor camps. We had bunkers in our houses where we hid during these actions.

At the end of October 1942, we learned that the Germans were planning a major action. We fled to Podkamien, where we hid in a well-concealed cellar in a Christian home for six months. On December 8, 1942, the action really did happen, and two thousand Jews from Rohatyn were deported to the

---

Ed1   Actual date: March 20, 1942, actual number: 3,600. See page 51 in English section of the Yizkor Book.

Ed2   Name of town square during Soviet occupation, 1939-41.

Belzec death camp. Afterwards we decided to leave our bunker and return to Rohatyn. Another similar action occurred at the end of December of 1942 when another 2,000 Jews were deported. By a miracle, my boyfriend and I were hiding in a bunker and avoided this action.

Jewish police from Tarnopol came to Rohatyn and behaved as badly as the Germans.[Ed3]

On June 6, 1943 the ghetto was liquidated. We heard rumors to this effect earlier, and many Jews had prearranged suitable hiding places with Christian friends. However, this action started suddenly; no one really survived. My boyfriend stood guard duty all night. In the morning he heard a shot that was the signal for the start of the action. He woke me, and almost naked we ran to the river. The Germans shot after us. We went into the water and crossed the water. We managed to hide in a field for a whole day while hearing constant shooting. We assumed that the ghetto was being liquidated; yet we hoped that we could return to our home after the action.

We had on us several hundred Deutsche marks. We left our valuables and had no contacts or friends. My boyfriend also had nothing, as he had been a prisoner of war. Our only hope was to return to the ghetto and find our hidden valuables.

At night we heard explosions and saw flames from grenade explosions; the ghetto was in flames. We realized that we had nowhere to return to. Tired, frozen, and wet, we set out on our way. Even though we knew the area, we got lost. Finally, at dawn we arrived in Podkamien to seek shelter.

Back in Podkamien

I was well liked in Podkamien; yet I was not sure if anyone would take me in. We sneaked into a loft in a stable where we stayed seven days and nights, almost without any food. Our only food was a daily egg a hen lay not far from our hiding place.

The barn belonged to a well-known farmer, Piotr Jozefin. We knew this farmer killed Jews who escaped from the ghetto. Therefore, we were scared that Jozefin would do the same to us; yet, after seven days of hunger we took a chance. At midnight we knocked at his door and after much crying, pleading, and begging, he took pity on us and gave us some bread and potatoes. This literally saved our lives. He told us to leave, as he could not hide us. He gave us some food for the road. He really was desperate to be rid

---

Ed3 The outrage is understandable, given the desperate situation of the Jews, but the Jewish police in the ghettos were not armed and were essentially powerless. Note the Tarnopol Gestapo was notorious for gratuitous, inventive sadism. For Rohatyn Jewish police, refer to pages 516, 517, 523 in Judenrat by Isaiah Trunk.

of us. We pretended to leave but soon came back to the barn, where we hid for another ten days.

Thereafter we again knocked on his window and told him that we were hiding in the forest and begged for food. He gave us bread, potatoes, and a bottle of water. He told us that two militiamen lived at his place so it was dangerous to be there. After that we left his barn and hid in an adjacent building for fourteen days.

Meanwhile, life in Podkamien normalized. Jews were no longer being sought in bunkers, and the murders ceased. So at night, we sought out a Ukrainian farmer, Ivan Daio, and without his knowledge, we broke into his potato cellar. We lived there for two weeks, living off chicken feed. One day his wife discovered me as I was about to remove a plate of chicken feed. She told us to leave; my tears didn't help. She urged us to hide in the cornfields. She gave us half a kilogram of bread, a little whiskey, and three buds of garlic.

The fields were not safe; we went back to the same farmer's farm and hid in an area of straw and haystacks for five days. Then we went to another Polish farmer, Jan Bielinski. He knew us for many years, so we hoped he would let us stay in his hay barn. Soon, the very next day, our host's son noticed us. He saw that the chain was unlocked from the outside. Right away he told his parents, who came up to us and told us that just the day before there was talk in the town that there were Jews at his place. Therefore, he asked that we leave at once.

We cried in front of them, we kissed their feet and promised to give them our house. . .and the farmer said to us that since the third house from his was uninhabited, he thought that it would be best for us to hide there and that he would see to it that we had food.

In an Empty House

The first four days he supplied us with food as we had arranged. On the fifth day he no longer came, and for four days we had no food. We found some stalks to eat. I decided to go to Jan to find out what happened and tried to disguise myself, wearing my boyfriend's hat. Jan told me that he had been in Lemberg (Lwow) and many Christians were shot for hiding Jews; thus he, too, was scared to bring us food. He didn't like my male disguise, as partisans were being sought by the Germans. Yet, he gave me food and arranged that I could come to him every other day for food. As we were talking, his son-in-law arrived; we were at a loss as to what to do. I pretended to be a forest beggar asking for food. He screamed at me, and I hastened off, carrying the food he gave me.

So it was for two months, as every two days he gave us food, and sometimes we got food from Ivan Daio who lived nearby. One day, the sister of Jan discovered us in the barn as she attempted to remove the hay. She was scared. I called her by her name, as we knew each other. She ran away and told another farmer about us, and, regardless of how it looked, she soon came back with milk for us and ran away immediately.

I was scared that she would give us away, so I dressed up as a man to see her. Her name was Zofia Maksymowicz. At night I knocked at her window; my appearance scared her, and she refused to come to the window. I then went to Jan and told him what happened, and he promised to talk to her. The next day he told me that she was now living with him, as she was scared of us.

My boyfriend went to see her to urge her to keep our presence a secret, but she didn't want to talk to him either. But she eventually promised to keep our secret. She also told my boyfriend who the farmer was who gave us the milk. I soon went to him and thanked him and asked him to keep our secret. His name was Pagoda. While I was there, I heard someone knocking at the window. I rushed out. Later I learned that this was my cousin who was hiding as a Christian; he, too, was knocking, seeking food.

We arranged that Ivan would tell Zofia that we left to go into the forest and that we would not knock on his window, but that he would bring us food. A month later, Zofia and her sister, the owner of the house, Tekla Fedirka, found us in the barn. They were scared of us and left without hay. We were at a loss, for Tekla's husband was a real murderer (by trade he was a smith); if she told him about us, it would be the end of us. Meanwhile a month passed; she had not informed on us to her husband.

One time while waiting for food, my cousin, Alek Fenster (twenty-two years old), suddenly appeared. I learned from him that he, his mother, and sister had been in hiding for eight days in a bunker in Rohatyn, while the ghetto was being destroyed. Later, they left the bunker; his mother and sister were too weak to travel, so he went on his own.

I asked him why he came, and he said to get food. I criticized him for trying to "take away" our food; but he said he had given this farmer a valuable item, whereby he promised to give Alek food. But Alek soon left.

On the 15th of August 1942, a Volksdeutsche (person of German origin living in Poland) company of German soldiers arrived in Podkamien. The fight was enormous. The farmers fled to the forests. At the same time Alek came back because he could no longer stay with his farmer. Our farmer told us to get out because the Germans would search all the buildings. We were in a dilemma— here at least we had some food and shelter. What should we do? What would become of us?

In Cellars, Lofts, Sheds, and Pits

At nightfall we left; we walked a kilometer and hid in an empty potato pit. The floor was wet, so we stood all night, not having anywhere to sit down. The next day we saw the farmer's wife gathering potatoes. We knew she would soon find us, so my boyfriend left to hide someplace else. My cousin and I knew her, and we stayed on, hoping she would give us some food.

After much pleading she gave us bread, kasha, and garlic. We thanked her and told her we were in the forest. Her name was Franka Banarin. She was the lover of the local priest, a notorious anti-Semite who warned the farmers against harboring Jews.

The potato pit was really no place for us. Alek said he had left some possessions in one of his hideouts, an abandoned Jewish home. If they were still there, it would indicate that no one came there, and it was safe.

However the possessions were not there; thus it was not a safe place. Nevertheless, we slept there that night. Alek left to find a new shelter, but he didn't come back. I now recalled that a certain Dżegala Kazszik had told me that if we wanted to leave the ghetto, we could come to him, and he would hide us. We started out for his place, meanwhile hiding in a loft under hay.

After staying there a few days, we realized someone else was staying there, too, as the farmer brought him food also. We soon saw my cousin, Alek, to my shock and amazement. We now, too, appeared before the farmer, and he brought us food but said he really couldn't hide three Jews—one Jew at most was his limit.

We stayed there another day, but he told us that we couldn't stay any longer. Having no place to stay, we went back to the attic of an empty Jewish house and hid there for two weeks, living off plants and shrubs.

After fourteen days the Germans left, we went back to our old hideout, and we had food from both of our farmers (Bielinski and Ivanin), enough for both of us not to starve. One night I was out searching for cucumbers in a nearby garden when I heard the owner unlock the gate to our hideout. My boyfriend jumped out and hid in the garden. After he left, we went back there. I soon noticed that from my dresses that were drying there, there were things missing. Thus, the owner knew we were there, so we had to leave, as this man was a fierce anti-Semite.

We lay in a cabbage patch, and soon rain poured over us, drenched us. A boy noticed us and called his parents. They came, and we pleaded with them to help us. They did not know us; yet they brought us food and allowed us to tear some cabbage but told us to leave the garden.

After two weeks, a man by the name Tatanczuk came to the loft. He didn't notice us, but we now knew he probably wanted to use the loft. In fact, one day he came back with wagon loads of hay. We left, and when we came back, the loft was full of hay. We were there until November 1943, but as the hay became less and less, we were concerned about being discovered. We soon built a phony wall in the loft made from hay where we could hide; and my cousin decided to confront the farmer to see what he knew about us.

The farmer didn't know that we had been hiding in the loft; he even urged my cousin to use the loft as a hideout, but my cousin told him that for now we were in the woods. We decided to remain in the loft. The next day, the farmer came to the loft, called Alek by name, but we did not respond, and the farmer soon left.

At the end of December, the farmer came again, shouting and screaming. Alek came out; the farmer asked Alek as to who else was there, and I soon appeared. After our making monetary promises to him, the farmer agreed to assist us and would bring food from time to time. At first he kept his promise, then he stopped. Then we got scared that we would be caught as criminals. Ten days later he came again with some food. He told us he was Vice-Chairman of the local Banderowcy and had killed many Poles; while he was in the "field" he could not come to us.

He was very cynical about murder, but our promises of giving him our homes served us well. He helped us, brought us food and even newspapers, and even more important than food, the good news that the Russian war effort was very successful. For this we kissed his hands.

Arrest and Escape

On January 10, 1944, the extreme frost literally broke bones; worse yet, I had to search for food in this frost. I was not dressed properly, and the path was dangerous. Many times I would have rather gone hungry than take the risk to search for food on these dangerous paths.

On January 26, 1944, my cousin and I went to look for food. We neglected to close the door to our hideout. My boyfriend was too weak to do so. Soon the Banderowcy arrived, saw the door, beat up my boyfriend and forced him to admit that he had two partners in this hideout. He was taken to the militia, and soon the militia returned to our hideout to ambush us.

I was returning with bread and cabbage, potatoes, and some milk, and my cousin was also returning with some food. Usually I filled a bottle with drinking water, but on this day I was too weak, so I asked Alek to do so. As I was approaching our hideout, I was seized by the Banderowcy. They asked me, "Who gave you the food?" and beat me very badly. All three of my tormentors were known to me. I started screaming, hoping to warn my boyfriend and cousin. One of my captors, Bilczow, hit me with the milk can, breaking two of my teeth, and he stuffed my mouth. I soon named two of the farmers I hated the most as having been my benefactors!!

My screaming worked, as my cousin escaped. They took me to the militia and on the way asked me if I had hidden gold, indicating that they were ready to spare my life if I would tell them where. I told them that my boyfriend knew this information and if I were taken to him, I'd give them all the gold. After torturing me, they threw me into a dark chamber, where to my shock I soon found my boyfriend. After we related to each other what had happened, we looked for ways to escape.

I lifted myself to the window and saw two Polish guards. I asked them to help us, but they said that they could not. Their replacements, two relatively mild-mannered Ukrainians, gave me some matches. We lit them and noticed an opening in our cell. We dug and dug and finally created an exit by removing piles of bricks, etc. My boyfriend decided to escape first, which necessitated jumping down some four meters. He left his shoes with me so as not to alert the guards. He was undetected and escaped.

I jumped next but was noticed by the guards. They shot after us, but we were saved by the darkness. The militia was alerted and chased us. The snow covered our tracks but at times gave us away, too. We managed to escape. Soon I arrived in a small hamlet, but my boyfriend was not with me. He lost his glasses and could not find his way. I went to a well-known Christian woman who gave me milk and told me to go away so as not to bring disaster on her home.

I lay down in a pile of hay, tired and depressed. I soon noticed the militiamen, and they followed my tracks to the Christian woman . . . .

Retracing the same snow tracks, I left for the potato cellar of my friendly farmer who used to give me food, and they could not follow me. The mistress of the house came to me and told me to leave and get out as fast as possible.

The Death of My Boyfriend

This happened at 10:00 a.m. If I left now, then everyone would know who I was. I was bloodied, dirty, my dress was torn; I hadn't changed my blouse in fourteen months. A child could tell that I was a fugitive.

Lying in the hay, I could see what was happening in the yard. The farmer and his son came from the forest with an axe, searching for me, but they didn't find me. They stuck the hay but in the dark still didn't locate me, and

I soon fled. I made my way to another farmer's not far from there and hid in a potato cellar. The dog started barking, and the farmer came running; he didn't find me. Before dawn, I left again for my previous place, to the farmer who wanted to kill me, hoping he would save me, as I hadn't given him away despite being tortured earlier by the militia.

However, the gate was blocked, as he seemed to be ready to prevent my return. I hid in some hay; a neighbor noticed me and told me, not looking at me, that my boyfriend was shot yesterday and buried. He left some bread; I was too distressed to eat and cried all day. When it got dark, the farmer's son came and told me his mother wanted to see me in the barn; she told me I could stay there and gave me some milk, speaking nicely to me.

I became suspicious of their friendliness and told them I would leave. They brought me bread, a dress, and some of my possessions I had left with them. They urged me to stay. I went into the barn but refused to be locked in, as was their wish. From the open barn door, I saw the farmer go to his neighbor; I crawled in on all fours and heard their conversation: "I can't do it; you can do it, and she will only leave before dawn." I fled to the farmer Jan Bielinski and hid in the hay barn in a wall of hay.

At night I heard footsteps and recognized the two farmers; one had an axe with him. I quickly jumped down and escaped. I hid in a large pile of hay belonging to a poor farmer and stayed there. Soon a dog came and started tearing at the hay.

I once again saw death facing me, but the dog soon left. I lay like this for six days and ate the bread I had with me. I ate three bites, three times a day. On the seventh day, I took a risk to get a drink of water at the well; I found a pot, but to my chagrin it had holes in it. Each time I lowered the pot, it came up empty, retaining only a few droplets of water. I hid myself another two days, my mouth dry, hungry, and in pain from the loss of my two teeth. I was in poor condition. After two days without water, I went to the well again; this time the farmer saw me and shouted at me; I forgot about the water and hid in the hay again.

In a Doghouse

My situation was now intolerable. I was determined to surrender to the militia and let them shoot me. One thing just stopped me—I was almost naked, as my clothing was completely torn. I was ashamed of my nakedness, even in front of the militiamen. I now was determined to find a new dress.

I decided to go to my classmate, Danusia, now a teacher, the daughter of a wealthy farmer, and ask her to give me an old dress. In the ghetto, I thought of hiding with these people of fine character but now after a loss of hope, all I wanted was a dress.

By various means and "non-means," I got to their home, which was locked. I knew that only the mother and daughter would help me—maybe—but not the father. He too had joined the Banderowcy and was no better than the rest of the gang. I hid in some hay near a broken window, but soon a dog started barking; the father came out, and I fled. I noticed a doghouse; it was wet and dirty there. The dog wanted to go in, but I prevented him. He didn't bark but stared at me wide-eyed, as if to wonder—what has become of humans, wanting to live in a doghouse? He stared and soon departed.

I soon noticed the mother come out of the house. I called to her in a low voice. She was amazed to see a human in a doghouse. I told her all that had occurred to me, that I had been on the verge of death. She allowed me to stay, brought me several pierogi (filled dumplings), milk, mashed potatoes, and water. More than the food, she offered hope by telling me that in two weeks things would change for the better.

I realized it was foolish to think that I could survive. Surely, the father's teenage son of seventeen would have seen me or will see me and give me away. Meanwhile, I lay in a crouched position in the doghouse; it was dirty and filthy.

That day, the mother didn't return. I thought she regretted her help. The next day she said she had guests and could not come. She brought me hot soup, some bread, and potatoes. She brought the food open, so as to pretend she was bringing food for the dog. The hot pot warmed my feet; at night she brought me soup and bread.

After two weeks in the doghouse, the dog no longer came, as he was no longer the resident of this "house." Crazy as it sounds, in the two weeks in the doghouse, I felt I was getting fat because of the three meals I was getting.

Only the mother and daughter of this family knew about me. She (the daughter) visited me once, telling me that if the father and brother did not become aware of me, I could survive the war.

Again in a Potato Cellar and Loft

I was in the doghouse for four weeks; with tears I implored the mother to allow me to move to the potato cellar. I allowed the dog back in, and I crawled out on all fours, out of the doghouse. I couldn't stand, so I crawled into the potato cellar and lay there. I felt good stretching my limbs. Only the mother came for the potatoes, so I was safe.

The next day the mother told me that perhaps her husband or nephew would come to the cellar, so we had to create a "bunker" to hide in the cellar. I dug this bunker myself in the cellar. I had a problem with my physical needs, but the mother brought me a special pot for this purpose. And in the course of two weeks she treated me like a nurse treats an ill person. In the doghouse, I had removed my waste with hay and straw.

The cellar was warm; my feet hurt because they had previously been frozen; I had suffered from frostbite. I had back pains, I couldn't even think of standing or walking. My Christian friend brought me butter and spread it on my feet. After two weeks my feet healed, and I was able to walk and stand. There were lice in the cellar, and I couldn't sleep. My guardian brought me dried fruit to nourish me.

On 25 February 1944, at night I heard wild noises. In the morning, my guardian told me that the Ukrainians had made a pogrom on their neighbors, the Poles. With knives and axes, they killed sixty Poles, all men. Her brother was a Pole (her husband, a Ukrainian), and he fled, so the Banderowcy would certainly come here to search for him.

I hid again in the doghouse. It snowed that day, so the hut was covered by snow. The Banderowcy did come but did not suspect anyone of hiding in the doghouse because of the snow. I got food once a day when it was very dark.

The village was turbulent as the Ukrainians sought the fugitive Poles and killed and robbed mercilessly. The screams of the Poles were unbearable. Living in the doghouse, I had feelings of revenge, as the Poles had killed Jews. Let them now get a taste of their own medicine. At the same time, I realized that many Jews who had been hidden by Poles must have been hunted down in this latest action. I started to think about my fate.

On 10 March 1944, my former Ukrainian farmer told my present guardian that he thought I was still alive. Another neighbor heard this, Janka Kardat—she was the girlfriend of the militiaman who knocked out my teeth. She wanted to kill me so that I would not take revenge against her boyfriend.

She searched all over for me, including my present guardian's yard. But the owner's wife demanded to know what Janka was doing on her property. At first she said she was seeking a lost hen, but then she said, "Shmuel Leib Karp is hidden at the local priest's, and the Ukrainians were searching for him all night. People also say that Rivka Hader is hidden here, but because you pay off the Banderowcy, they don't search earnestly." When she later told me this story, I assured her that if I were caught, I would not implicate her for hiding me. This put her mind at rest.

The next morning I told her that I could no longer remain there, as the snow was leaking in from the roof. I begged to be hidden somewhere else. I was soon transferred to the barn and hidden in the hay, as the daughter stood guard during this transfer. I felt glad and happy about my new "residence."

The next day I saw the husband come to clean the doghouse. I couldn't believe my good fortune and the miracle that happened to me. Had I still been there, I would have been caught. Seeing G-d's miracle, I decided to take a vow to fast every Monday and Thursday while I was in hiding as a way of showing my gratitude to G-d. I told my guardian of this vow and told her not to bring me food on these days. I fulfilled my vow faithfully and completely.

The farmer woman brought the food to me, and I would take it to the loft. At the same time, the Ukrainians burned seventy Polish homes. One can understand my fright, seeing all the "light" in the dark night.

The next day, the farmer woman told me she was worried; her brother's (the Pole's) home adjacent to hers would be burned, and I would be found out, and she would be killed for hiding Jews. I assured her that I would rather be burned than be discovered and give her away. This reassured her. She had a daughter and a son-in-law, a Pole. During the anti-Polish riots, he managed to escape. He soon found out about my hiding place, too. The daughter now had more feeling for my plight, as her husband, too, was in hiding.

During Easter she brought me good food and told me that the news about the war was good. When the Russians arrive, her husband would return. She told me that the Russians had freed four villages in the Tarnopol region.

I need not say that these news stories gave me hope. I later heard the priest's servant tell my guardian that the Russians gave a "concert" near Tarnopol. The sun shone brightly. Eight days I waited for the liberators; on the ninth day my guardian informed me that the Tarnopol battles were tough and who knows how long they would last. She told me to go to Tarnopol. I was in no physical shape for the one-hundred-kilometer trip, and besides, how was I to get through the front lines? I cried and begged for mercy. I remained in the loft, and once again I doubted that I would survive the war.

Back to Being a Seamstress

My guardian told me she had no field workers, as no one wanted to work for money that was worthless. I told her I would be ready to sew for the workers as their pay. Since her husband was a tailor, it would be presumed that he himself did the work. She soon brought me the stuff and implements, and I was at work in the loft. I felt that I was now honestly eating and boarding: I was paying my benefactor back.

At the end of April, the German troops started marching to the front. One unit stopped in our hamlet; they stayed in the villagers' homes. My guardian had three German "guests," one lieutenant and two ordinary soldiers; I saw them from the loft. Their uniforms and faces scared me. The Germans made minor attacks in the area, and the prisoners were sent to work. Many farmers joined me in hiding. Several members of my guardian's family even hid in the same loft as I. However, they soon departed without discovering me.

After a month, the Germans left, and I was hopeful again. Even when the Germans were in town, I helped by knitting. On 14 June 1944, the Banderowcy, sensing the imminent arrival of the Russians, set fire to the last Polish house, the one that belonged to the brother of the woman helping me. Now I was very hot, instead of very cold, as this house was next to where I was hiding. Soon the yard was filled with people trying to put out the fire.

They poured water from the roof. I was in great danger of being discovered. I jumped off the loft, my guardian came to my rescue, wrapping me in a cloth and hiding me in the weedy area of the yard. I lay there twelve hours from midnight to noon. Finally my guardian told me I could return to the loft, and she watched over my return. However, the food situation worsened, as my guardian brought me only several pieces of bread once a day.

Liberation Draws Near

On July 5, 1944, the retreating Germans advised the civilians and my guardian to leave, as the Russians were drawing near and a major fight would result in civilian casualties. On July 8th, the Soviets started bombarding our village. My guardian and her children fled to the woods. Only her husband remained to guard their property.

She promised to bring me food, but the bombardment was so sudden that she fled without leaving food. She told me to stay out of her husband's way, but hearing of liberation, who thought of food at all?

I was frightened of the master, as he was a thief who hid his loot in the loft. Several times I had to jump from the loft and hide in the garden. Lying on the ground of the garden, I saw him come to collect berries. I crawled out of the garden, back to the loft. He must have noticed something, as he soon came looking in the loft but found nothing. The bombardment reached a crescendo on July 13th. Reflectors lit the sky and ground as the Soviets were after the Germans trying to halt their retreat and kill them. This indeed had the desired effect.

Scared of the bombs, I hid in a cellar for a night. In the morning I heard the Russian language. With great enthusiasm I left the cellar and very carefully looked about. I saw the grizzly Russian soldiers, only slightly resembling humans. These were the Russian frontline troops. I was scared of them and didn't approach them.

My guardian came back and gave me food. At night I went back to the loft and slept. In the morning, she told me that the Russians took her horse. I proposed going to the Russians and telling them that she had saved my life and to return the horse. She was scared and said no, as she didn't want her husband to know and was scared of revenge by the Banderowcy. I remained in the loft three days while the Russian army kept marching and advancing.

On the 12th, she urged me to join the Russians so that in case of a retreat, I could go back with them. This was good advice; she made it possible for me, therefore, to get bathed for the first time in sixteen months. This made me happy, as I felt better about myself being clean. I said goodbye to my rescuer and cried. I kissed her hands for a long time and promised never to forget her kindness.

Revenge

I was scared as soon as I started to walk. I was not accustomed to walking, nor did I know where to go. Finally, I saw two Russians; I ran in their direction shouting, "I am Jewish, I am Jewish." At first, they were frightened, then they calmed down and looked at me, astonished, not understanding what I wanted. Soon more Russians came; they told me they had to march on and could not help me. I refused to leave, demanding to join them, since my life was in danger, as I was the only Jew here. A wagon came, and I was told to sit and that they were going to Chodorow.

On the way, the wagon stopped, and the officers went into an abandoned house and ordered me in. They soon started to accost me. I realized my troubles were hardly over. I begged them to leave me alone, as I had suffered in the war. I cried and cried. Finally, the order came to march, and G-d rescued me from them.

Not having anywhere to go, I decided to go back to the loft. Using side roads I made it back half alive and dropped in my old "lodging place." You can imagine the look on my guardian's face when she saw me there after two days. I invented a story that a Russian captain ordered me back and to stay put. I asked her to let me stay, and having little choice, she agreed.

I was convinced that I was the only Jew in the region. I asked myself what to do, where to go. I was there five days. Finally I decided to go to Rohatyn.

At midnight on July 22nd, I set out for Rohatyn. I soon realized that I was in no shape for the trip. I heard a car approaching. I waved it down. Several Russians sat in the car. I told them I was a Jewish woman and during the German occupation I survived in hiding. They took me to Rohatyn. There I was told that in the house of a certain Amarant there were several Jews. There I met the following people:

Yissocher Hauser, my boyfriend's brother-in-law, with his two children; they were from Lipica. They had been hiding in the woods. They looked more like animals than people. Sara Hauser from Lipica with three children; they looked like the other family. Mrs. Libke Haber and ten-year-old son, from Rohatyn. Mrs. Reizhe Stryjer from Rohatyn. Rachel Bal from Lipica.[Ed4] Bernard Kessler from Lipica. Moshe Blech with his ten-year-old son Bumek, from Rohatyn. Leybisch Blech and his wife Cyla Blech from Rohatyn. Schnitzer (Sznycer) from Rohatyn, brother-in-law of Moshe Kreizler; Hesio Altbauer from Rohatyn; the Schweller family from Lipica, six people. Shmuel Acht, Dr. Sterzer and wife, Grina, and son Menashe; Ciucia (Tzutzia) Tenenbaum; Dr. Hodisch and his wife, from Tłumacz, Paulina Mark from Rohatyn, and others. Pepka Kleinwachs, who later went to America and died there; Motye Modlinger died in an accident in Berlin in 1946.[Ed5]

They all looked like skeletons. I kissed them all, and we told each other our tragic tales. On the second day, we got a hot fatty soup from the Russians and got stomach aches. On the fourth day, we encountered Czech soldiers and Jewish officers who brought us the "best." They stayed with us several days and acted like real brothers. I then became aware that my cousin had surrendered to the Ukrainian militia on 25 July 1944. He could not bear the hunger and was shot by them.

I discovered the fate of Hirsch Kamerling, born 1913 in Zolczow. He died fighting in Stalingrad in 1942; Schlome Kamerling, born 1924 in Zolczow, finished a Red Army officer's school and was seriously wounded on the Kharkov-Kursk front and recuperated in a hospital. In January, 1945 he was recalled to the army; his brother Zev got a letter from him, but he has never been heard of since. I was the only one of my town to survive. My cousin's brother, P. L. Furchsters, also survived, but in captivity in Budapest.

After three months in the town, regaining strength, I first went to the NKVD (Russian Secret Police, now known as the KGB) to take revenge on those who had killed our brothers and sisters and fellow Jews. I worked with the NKVD and turned over fifty farmers, also Dr. Melnik of Rohatyn, all who collaborated with the Nazis and the Gestapo. He received 20 years in jail. Many of the others were shot.

Then I went to Lemberg (Lwow), where I married Yonah Rock. Together we went to Cracow, thereafter to Bytom (Silesia, Poland); then we secretly crossed the border to Germany, and we stayed in a displaced persons camp in

---

Ed4   Actual name was not Rachel Bal but Rachel Rahl.

Ed5   The correct name was Chaim Srul (Yisroel) Modlinger.

Ed6   One of many refugee camps in West Germany for Jewish survivors of the Holocaust.

Eschwege,[Ed6] Germany, for three years. My son, Moshe (Marvin) Rock, was born there. We arrived in America, New York City, in February 1949.

p. 275 YB: Park in Rohatyn, Sep. 30, 1935. From right; Bushko Sharer, Shiko Pantzer, Izi Bernstein (standing); Yulek Skolnick (officer); Yosef Kartin, Munio Kimmel.

p. 275 YB: June 16, 1930. Liga Obrony Przeciw Lotniczej i Przeciwgazowej (Polish League of Anti-air and Anti-gas) maneuvers in Rohatyn.

p. 275 YB: House and garden of Shimon Teichman, standing right, his wife Sartzi, and his young daughter Lonka.

p. 274 YB: Market near the Ukrainian Church, Moshe Bohnen's house, part of Shmuel Kleinwachs' house.

p. 276 YB: Gnila Lipa River, 1938, and the nearby houses.

p. 276 YB: Gnila Lipa, 1935. Paddlers: Weingarten, Ania Fisher, Manya Mandel, Moshe Mett, Golda Fisher, Moshe Granowiter.

The Story of One Bunker
By Yehoshua P. Spiegel

Translated by Binyamin Weiner - YB p. 321

During the Shoah, one of the bunkers in our city was set up in the district town hall, in the same building that housed the Gestapo command center. A Ukrainian named Brudovay (Broodovay) from the village of Putiatynce, who was the watchman, helped set up the bunker in the cellar of the building, where the council archives were kept. Thirteen Jews were housed there: Yehoshua Glotzer and his two daughters, Lusia and Rozia; Avraham Haber, his wife Libtsie, and their son Yisrael; Reize Stryjer and her son Yosi; Rachel and her brother Moshe-Yosef Bal, and her cousin Bernard Kessler; Sarah Rokach, and Chanina Sonnenschein.

p. 321 YB: Yosi Stryjer

The Ukrainian also concerned himself with the provision of food for those hiding in the shelter. But once he could not see to this for many days, and the hidden came to know the wretchedness of hunger. The first victim of hunger was Avrumtsi Haber, who was buried in the shelter itself.

There was no choice but to venture out of the shelter a few times, to look for food. Chanina Sonnenschein (Zonnenschein) was the first to be caught. The Nazis demanded that he reveal the hiding-place, and when he refused, they killed him. He was 18-years-old when he fell. The second, Moshe-Yosef Bal, went out for the same reason and was likewise caught and killed when he refused to reveal the location of the shelter. He was 17 when he died. After them, it was Yosi Stryjer's turn. He managed to obtain a small amount of food but was caught coming back to the bunker, and suffered terribly till his soul took flight. He was not more than 15. May the Lord avenge their blood.

As the upper floors of the building grew too cramped for the Nazis (who had opened a hospital there, in addition to the command center), they requested the use of the cellar. But the influence of this same Ukrainian, Brudovay, protected the nine remaining Jews. He managed to convince the Nazis that it was not possible to destroy the archive cabinet (which hid the entrance to the bunker) because it concealed rare documents. Miraculously, the Nazis were persuaded to forgo their plan. This gentile should be well remembered. The glimmer of G-d had not been extinguished in his heart, one of the few among many…

p. 322 YB: Aryeh Pasvek, Leah Holder, Pinya Lewenter, Klara Messing, Salka Willig, Pinya Maor, Pepka Schumer, Moshe Granowiter, Naftali Lev (in the center), Dvora Bussgang, Moshe Mett, unidentified woman.

p. 322 YB: Yakov Leinwand and his wife Bluma (Spiegel), daughter Elza, and the twins (from Przemislany).

p. 323 YB: Hochberg family, Z"L, David Hochberg with his wife, Hoogie, (bottom) Yakov Eichel and his two daughters.

p. 323 YB: Standing from left: Bruno Alter, Y. Barban, Azriel Granowiter. Seated from left: Gertek Goldschlag, Izio Spiegel, Marcel Lewenter.

p. 324 YB: Four brothers Holtz, beside the fence of the Polish church; Zelko, Heshko, Izio; the oldest among them, Chaim Alon, lives on Kibbutz HaMa'apil.

p. 324 YB: WIZO conference of Rohatyn women in the house of Shimon Teichman.

Surrounding Towns

Jewish Centers around Rohatyn (Rogatin)

By Joseph Millner, Paris

Translated by Binyamin Weiner - YB p. 325

The saintly Dr. Majer Balaban - of whom it can assuredly be said that another like him has not arisen in the study of history of Jewish cities and towns in Galicia - more than 50 years ago, offered interesting facts regarding Jews in Rohatyn. He based his information on a census taken in 1765 (i.e. 200 years ago), according to which Rohatyn was then a community of 797 Jews, in an entire region of up to 1,347 Jews! When we consider the demographic figures for those times (using the *Petersburg Jewish Encyclopedia*, published in Russian and edited by Dr. Y. L. Katzenelson and Baron David Ginzburg, Volume V, pages 77 and 115), we can say that this represented a significant number. Rohatyn could (and certainly did!) exert its influence over the smaller localities in its vicinity. In that era, Rohatyn had two smaller communities under its governance: Podkamien (128 Jews) and Stratyn (453 Jews.)

Historically, Rohatyn played an important role in the era of the false messiahs. Sabbatai Zvi, for example, found in Rohatyn a breeding ground for disciples, and there this false messiah had passionate followers. This atmosphere was exploited by Jacob Frank, who had a real mainstay in Rohatyn. This was the situation in the beginning of the 18th century. These movements were so strong, that the Polish King, August III, had to take them into account, and decreed three cities to be "Frankist zones:" Busk, Gliniani, and Rohatyn.

Around the time of the Enlightenment, Rohatyn once again became a "center." A school for "worldly" learning and the study of Hebrew opened there.

In 1912, on the eve of World War I, Rohatyn was a town of 7000 inhabitants, 3217 of them Jews! It is known that the yearly Jewish communal budget reached the sum of 20,000 crowns.

The large Jewish centers near Rohatyn were:

Bursztyn: a shtetl (town) that provided a well-known surname, which has been carried by Jewish families to many places. Two hundred years ago, there were already 453 Jews in Bursztyn. It can be said with certainty that when Hitler's agents of destruction came to the town, it held around 5,000 Jews. It

345

is interesting to note that from 1908 onward there was, in a single Bursztyn house, a school for 160 students, built with the money of Baron Hirsch.

Bukaczowce: 361 Jews in 1765, and 1,216 Jews in 1909. In 1909, 236 Jews paid the communal tax.

Bołszowce: A considerable Jewish community. The number of Jews in Bolszowce, about sixty years ago, is listed in several sources (erroneously) as 2,256.

Feyge and Yisroel Krig, Z"L.

p. 326 YB: Naftali Lev and his daughter.

p. 326 YB: Sarah Baner with her son Chaim, Z"L, Her daughter Cyla (pictured) now lives in Argentina.

Tzion Mett.   *Michael and Chaya Leder.*   *Soshi and Berel Krig.*

Bursztyn
By Yehoshua Pinchas Klarnet

YB p. 327
Translated by Binyamin Weiner , 327-331 and Rabbi M. Goldzweig, 331-335

In memory of the Ehrlich, Kessler, and Aronberg families, and of Yoel Ginzburg, Z"L.

From the publisher:

Bursztyn was one of the towns in the region known as the Rohatyn district (powiat), which included Stratyn, Podkamien, and Knihynicze. Strong ties existed between Bursztyn and Rohatyn. In civic matters, the population of Bursztyn was subject to the authorities in Rohatyn. The Hassidim of the two towns intermingled in the Rohatyn "court." The fair in Rohatyn was a serious meeting place for Jews from all over the region, a place where trading relationships and solid partnerships were formed. (For example, Shimon Meltzer's father, from Bursztyn, was a partner in the "American Mill" in Rohatyn.) Rohatyn had two high schools, one Polish and the other Ukrainian, which the youth of Bursztyn attended. This led to contact and fast friendship between the young Jews of the two towns. The two towns assisted each other in staging Zionist activities, in both the first and second generations of the movement.

In addition, Jews of the two towns were united through bonds of marriage, and members of the same family could be found in both places.

The same cruel fate befell the towns of Bursztyn and Rohatyn. In the time of the Shoah, Bursztyn Jews were first transported to the Rohatyn ghetto, where they were destroyed or sent to the death camps. Thus, it can be said of Bursztyn and Rohatyn: "United in death as in life."

Many are moved along with me to pick up the pen and dedicate pages of testimony to the town of Bursztyn, for the sake of our book of remembrance Only 16 kilometers separated this town from the district town of Rohatyn. It is therefore no wonder that relationships, sometimes intimate, were forged between the Jews of the two towns: trading partnerships, marriage bonds, agricultural collaborations, and joint youth activities. Jewish students attended high school in Rohatyn, and the two towns were even connected by a single river, the "Gnila Lipa."

Hassidism took root in Bursztyn in the early 19th century, under the influence of Reb Yehuda-Zvi-Hirsch Brandwein, from Stratyn. Grand Rebbe Nahum, who sat on his throne till 1914, was a learned man and a kabbalist. He published four books on the cabbalah: *Imrey Tov, Imrey Chaim, Imrey Bracha*, and *Imrey*

Ratson.[Tr1] He set up a magnificent "court" in Bursztyn, and his many followers came from all over, bearing contributions for the upkeep of the Bursztyn community. In 1914, during a period when many were vacationing in the mountains, a fire broke out in Bursztyn and consumed half of the city, including the Rebbe's court. Consequently, Reb Nahum relocated to Stanislawow, where he died in 1915, leaving an only son, Eliezer, and four daughters. This son took his father's place in Stanislawow. In 1935, Reb Moshe, son of the above-mentioned Reb Eliezer, reestablished his grandfather's court in Bursztyn, and was the Grand Rebbe till he perished with his wife and three children, in the time of the Shoah. Reb Moisheleh's (diminutive, from Hebrew Moshe) leadership was renowned, and he had many followers. The Nazis seized and tortured him, and he died in 1942, in Stanislawow.

Slowly but surely, an aspiration toward enlightenment and the education of children penetrated into Bursztyn, according to the spirit of the times. In 1898, apparently through the intervention and leadership of the intelligent and cultivated academician Dr. David Maltz, a Jewish school for young people opened in Bursztyn. It was established with the assistance of the "Baron Hirsch Fund." The founding of this school aroused the opposition of the Hassidim and the pious. Nonetheless, they had no choice but to accept it. Adult courses were held in the evenings, attended by fifty-two people. The school grew to the point that it required its own building, which was purchased in 1904 by the "Baron Hirsch Fund." In 1906, sewing courses for young women were established under the auspices of the "Baroness Klara Hirsch Jubilee Fund," led by Mrs. Fogel. In the first year, fourteen young women studied sewing and tailoring. In 1914, the school building passed into the hands of the community, and was transformed into a cultural center, named for Y. L. Peretz, complete with its own popular library. In 1905, the "Ika" loan society was founded. In addition, a "cooperative bank" also began to operate, and the two were in business till the outbreak of World War I. In 1918, they merged under the name "Cooperative Loan Society."

The founding of the Zionist association "Chovevey Zion," by Bunem Shapiro, ushered in a period of energetic national life. Zionist-Jewish personalities began to assemble in Bursztyn following the arrival of the attorney Dr. David Maltz. He was the educator of a group of Zionist students led by Dr. Avraham Kurk. Together with others, including Dr. Yehoshua Thon, he founded the "Zion" society in Lwow, which was the cornerstone for Zionist activity in Galicia, a number of years before the emergence of Dr. Theodor Herzl. He was counted among the Zionist writers

Tr1   Good Words, Words of Life, Words of Blessing, Words of the Will.

of quality. In 1909, a Hebrew school was founded, with a teacher and nine students. During World War I, Dr. Wolf Schmorak, brother of the well-known Dr. Schmorak, settled in Bursztyn as an attorney.

The livelihoods of the Bursztyn Jews were similar to those practiced in Rohatyn. The overall character of the city was actually quite Jewish. Even the postman, Reb Ephraim Schneider, wore a beard and sidelocks.

Most of the Bursztyn Jews were Hassidim. Even though the grand rabbis of the Brandwein family "ruled" Bursztyn, most of its Jews were actually Belz or Czortkow Hassidim. Zelig Hammer sat at the head of the communal board.

Dr. M. Haber adds:

The Jews of Bursztyn were quiet people, but by no means cowards. In times of danger they were always ready to rise to the defense of their lives and honor. In the days of Prince Jablonowski (pron. Yablonovski), a fight broke out between the Tatars and the Jews. The fiery Tatars, together with the Poles and Ukrainians, ran about town streets like wild men, shattering windows. The Jewish workmen went out to meet them immediately, butchers with their knives and hatchets in hand, and the Tatars beat a hasty retreat. The courage of the Bursztyn Jews fell upon them like blows. For the first time, the rioters felt that danger was upon them, and they fled in a panic. The town escaped without injury. Meanwhile, officers had arrived from Rohatyn, and the winds soon died down.

In 1917-18, after the end of World War I, battles raged on in the Bursztyn region between the Ukrainians, Poles, and Bolsheviks. The Jews, of course, were left dangling in the wind, victims of robbery and murder, women raped before the eyes of their husbands and children.

Harder than all others were the blows of the men of Petlura. Even General Haller's band could not best them. If not for the assistance of the Joint, the Jews would have faced certain destruction. The Joint set up a public kitchen and cabins for the homeless.

M. Nachvolger adds:

Who can forget the Hebrew teachers: Sobel, the girl from Boryslav, Shorets, Shtroweiss, and others? Each of them individually, and all of them together, devoted their time, even after the fixed lesson hours, to kindling the Zionist spark and love of the homeland in the souls of the youth. The Zionist spiritual centers were the "Poalei Zion Union" (right wing), Betar, and HaNoar HaTzioni. Hundreds of young men and women were members. Youth activities and debates on Zionist issues were held in the "Union" hall. The young people received instruction in Zionism, literature, and communal life and would attend the lectures and theatrical performances that came to town. In 1925, Chaim Ginzburg, son of the instructor, founded the Gordonia association.

Y. Fenster adds:

In 1908, elections were held for seats in the Austrian parliament. The Zionist movement participated in the campaign. Adolf Shtand, the Zionist leader, came to speak in Bursztyn, although the authorities, siding with the Polish candidate, had forbidden him from speaking in the synagogue. But the Zionist youth rose up and threw open the doors to the synagogue, and Dr. Shtand strode in before them and delivered a stirring address on the Zionist cause.

Monye Cohen adds:

When the teachings of Jabotinsky (pron. Zhabotinsky) began to make inroads into the cities and towns of Galicia, his movements also came to Bursztyn. On Shavuot in 1927, the founding committee of Betar was established. Its delegates participated in all of the regional and national meetings. Members of the cell also played roles in the central leadership of Betar. Gershon Gintzberg (the dayan's son, who parted ways with Gordonia) was a district officer in Lwow, and afterwards in Lwow and Cracow. Betar was active until World War II. [The son of Reb Yoel Gintzberg, Gershon was imprisoned by the Russians in 1940, in a jail in Lwow. In 1941, before the Nazis overran Lwow, as the Russians were fleeing the city, this well-known jail was set on fire, and the soul of Gershon Gintzberg, Z"L, was carried upward on these flames. –Yehoshua Spiegel.]

In the first days of the war, as the Germans drew near, and the Ukrainians began to menace the Jews with plunder and murder, the commanders of Betar joined forces with the Polish youth of the city, and together they formed a self-defense force. In this hour of tension, the Jewish youth gained the opportunity to protect their people from the onslaught of robbery and killing.

Lusha (Lusia) Freifeld (Rozen) adds:

I recall one friend of mine, a Christian girl named Renya (Pol. Renia) Gwodowic (pron. Gvodovitz), by whom my life was saved from the caprice of the Nazis. She hid me in her home. Perhaps this can be slight consolation, that in this great sea of suffering and torment, in those days of destruction and annihilation, there were a treasured few among the gentiles who risked their lives to save Jews from the Nazi inferno.

Pinchas Gelernter recounts:

Dov-Ber Gelernter was exceptionally learned in Torah, Talmud, and rabbinic judgments. He had the authority to teach, but chose not to make Torah a tool for his own service. He was a Zionist all of his days. He was a dear friend of the attorney Dr. David Maltz, who was one of the earliest Zionist leaders in Galicia, a gifted speaker and shrewd publicist, an intimate acquaintance of Natan Birenboim (Birenbaum), and a follower of Herzl. Reb Dov-Berish (Dov-Ber) Gelernter and Dr. David Maltz were friendly with Reb Sholem Meltzer, one of the early founders of the Mizrachi organization, and a driving force behind the Hebrew school and the "Safa Brura" organization in Rohatyn.

Mordechai Nachvolger (or Nachvelger) adds further:

HaNoar HaTzioni was founded in Bursztyn in 1928. 164 cadets passed through its program. This organization strove to be the next link in the chain that began with the regional branch of "Poalei Zion," which had sent the town's first pioneers to Israel in the third era of aliyah (Sarah Kessler and Bina Briter). On the eve of Sarah Kessler's departure for Israel, they held a party that went on well past midnight. [By the way, she is a relative of the Klarnet family. She is involved in the Survivors of Bursztyn organization, and continues to be an active socialist. –Yehoshua Pinchas Klarnet.] HaNoar HaTzioni in Bursztyn received aid and encouragement from Yehuda Hader and Dov Kirschen, members of the Rohatyn branch.

Dr. Lipa Shomer, the town doctor of Bursztyn, testifies:

On September 17, 1939, there was no discrimination practiced toward any segment of the population. In contrast, the Ukrainians started inciting against the Jews, and began informing on them to the Soviet authorities. At that time, bad tidings had already reached us from central Poland, pertaining to the suffering of the Jews under Hitler's conquering army. Twenty Six Hundred Jews were then living in Bursztyn. At the same time, the authorities had jailed the young Jewish leaders of the Zionist youth movements. Those arrested and imprisoned were transported to Lwow, where they were executed alongside the Ukrainian nationalists, or sent to Siberia. For the time being, the authorities did me no harm, because, as a doctor, I was necessary to them.

The situation changed on June 22, 1941, the day war broke out between Germany and Russia. The Red Army fled in a panic. At the city limits, they abandoned their battle with the advancing German army, and blew up the bridges. A certain number of local Jews, mostly from among those who had found positions in the Soviet administration, joined the Russian retreat.

Then the many troubles and sorrows began to fall upon the Jews, inflicted by the Ukrainians as well as the Germans, and as an eyewitness Dr. Shomer will describe them:[Tr2]

The best men of the city, among them Rabbi Hertz Landau and Reb Yoel Gintzberg, an old and honored teacher, were beaten and maimed in the town office. One of the Ukrainians came up to the old dayan, shaved off his white beard and threw the hairs in his face. As he was doing so, he said to the old man, "Leprous Jew, the time has come to be rid of all of you, and to pay you back what you have coming." The old dayan's eyes filled with tears, but he did not say a word in response. As we left the room, we saw the Ukrainians tying ropes around the necks of the rabbi and the dayan, and fastening them to the iron lattice of the window. I begged the German sub-lieutenant not to allow them to be tortured. The German commanded me to go, saying, "The rabbis will not be tortured to death." Meanwhile, the respected Ukrainians of the town, among them judges, lawyers, and regular townspeople, had assembled to riot against the Jews. The next day I went to see the rabbi and the dayan. I found them both in their quarters, lying on their beds bruised and wounded, wrapped in tallis and tefillin. I examined their wounds and showed them mine.

In the beginning of August 1941, the order came down to establish a "Jewish Council" (Judenrat) of eight people. I was numbered among them, and was made chairman against my will. The body also included the attorney Phillip Tobias, Mina Tobias, Yehuda-Hirsch Fishman, and others. We received word from the Judenrat in Rohatyn that the German authorities had ordered three representatives from every town in the region to appear before the Rohatyn council. There Shlomo Amarant read an order from the German authorities that a compensatory tax of eight to ten million rubles was being levied on the Jews, as it were, for the damages that we owed.

Our lives hung before our eyes. People lived twenty to a room. Jews were permitted to walk only in the middle of the road. The people, swollen with hunger, were terrible to behold, and the children with spindly legs and bellies inflated by starvation. As a doctor, I had permission to go outside the Jewish zone, but I continued to wear the light-blue-and-white band bearing the Star

Tr2   Narrative voice in this passage is unclear. It seems to alternate, without clear demarcation, between a third-person and Dr. Shomer himself.

352

of David on my arm, according to the law.

The Germans demanded that the Judenrat supply them with quotas of Jews for labor. These were brought to the railroad station in groups of 120, pressed into railcars and sent on their way. Many of the deportees died of suffocation in the overcrowded wagons, or perished of hunger and thirst. They were transported to Belzec, where they were murdered in the crematorium.

On October 15th, the Germans ordered all Jews to relocate to Bukaczowce. Only thirty Jews remained in Bursztyn, working on the roads. Two doctors were among them, Dr. Shmuel Katz and myself, as well as the head of the Judenrat, Phillip Tobias, and two of his friends. A month later, the Gestapo came to the camp and transported all thirty Jews to the ghetto in Rohatyn. We fled into the forest to hide. On July 9th, 1943 [actually June 6, 1943], we heard loud gunfire. The Germans were liquidating the Rohatyn ghetto, shooting all of the Jews that they found. We built bunkers in the forest and hid in them, changing our location often, so as not to fall into a trap. We endured hunger and thirst, slept in damp places, and ate lice, till farmers that we knew began bringing us things to eat. For the most part, these were members of the Christian Baptist sect living around the village of Czarow (Czahrow). We hid in this manner until May of 1944, when the Russians came and drove out the Germans.

Yaakov Feldman continues the account:

On Yom Kippur, 1942, the akcja began in Rohatyn, where very few Jews were still living. It was announced in Bursztyn that two railcar loads of Jews would be transported to their deaths. I will never forget that Yom Kippur. Reb Yoel Gintzberg, Z"L, the religious instructor of the town, requested the people nonetheless to pray as a community on the holy day. The dayan prayed all day through his tears and sobbing, calling out to the assembly to accept the judgment without fear, to walk with heads held high to meet the bitterness of death. It was amazing that this man, suffering the effects of torture and hunger, had the force and courage to preach these words of consolation.

The Germans entered the city on the day after Yom Kippur and began shooting at Jews in the street. Most were seized and transported to Rohatyn. The members of the Judenrat knew that the action was coming, and had hidden their wives and children. Soon Bursztyn too was emptied of its Jews, who were taken to Bukaczowce, where they were loaded into railway cars and transported to the death camp of Belzec. Reb Yoel the Dayan was shot to death in Bukaczowce, as he was passing among the Jews, offering words of comfort and reciting the deathbed confession with them. The remaining Jews of the region were driven into the Rohatyn ghetto, among them many Jews from Bursztyn. One of them was Shlomo Mendelberg, who, when we were being separated, said to me, "I know that I am going to meet death. How strange it is that I came back from the Land of Israel to fall at the hands of these murderers."

The Rohatyn ghetto was liquidated in June of 1943. Even after Bursztyn was "Jew free (Judenrein)" there remained a few isolated Jews in the area, hiding with farmers or in the forest. Mundze Fishman, Wolf Ostrover, and Loti Bronstein dug for themselves a bunker in the stables of the prince's palace. They had a revolver and a number of bullets. Rafel, the lame cobbler who guarded the courtyard, helped them and found them a little food. One week, the Ukrainian police fell upon the bunker, by order of the Germans. The bunker was well concealed, but the son of Fed Boban (or Fedya Bovan), the chimney sweep, had informed the Germans of its existence. The officers called on those hidden to come out of the surrounded bunker. When Mundze realized there was no escape, he came out with the revolver in his hand and shot the German commander, injuring him severely. His shots also hit and wounded the officer firing the machine gun. Mundze and Loti fell as casualties. Wolf grabbed the gun, went back down into the bunker, and came out the other side. The murderers pursued him, and Wolf Ostrover fought like a hero. He hit another Ukrainian policeman, not far from Dr. Schmorak's house. Wounded and losing blood, he still managed to fire on his pursuers. He fell outside the city, hit by Fed's son.

Honor to their memories! Their heroic deaths kindled a ray of light in the darkness of the Shoah and the destruction of our town.

Our Revenge - We, a group of Jews in the forest, decided to take revenge against our oppressors. We disguised ourselves in farmers' clothing and came into the town at night. We then captured the night watchman and forced him to go with us to Fed's house, ordered him to knock on Fed's door and call him to come out. Once Fed came out, we grabbed him and killed him on the spot. His wife followed him, and she too received what was due her. Unfortunately we did not catch their murderous son. Later we found out that he had been hiding in the chimney. We were indeed very sorry for this. Those who took part in this foray included Kalman, the son of Sarah the baker, and two Jews from Bukaczowce.

Kalman the son of Sarah the baker - Kalman had begun fighting the Nazis with live ammunition when there was still a ghetto in Rohatyn. He and a group of Jews attacked Germans on the way to Knihynicze. Some of the Germans were indeed killed, but they were numerous, and the four of our attacking group were killed and their bodies were returned to the Jews for burial. Kalman had been included with the bodies. However, the Jews noticed that Kalman was still alive, but he had a very serious injury to his head, and they buried someone else in his place. There was no shortage of bodies to be buried. Kalman eventually recovered from his wounds and again ran away to the forest, where he stayed for a long time. However, as the time of liberation from the Nazis approached, the Germans sent Kalmucks - Russian prisoners from the army of Vlasov,[Ed1] who had gone over to the German side - with orders to kill the Jews who were wandering in the forests. By that time the Jews had acquired some weapons and stood up well against the murderous attacks on them. In one of those attacks Kalman died a hero's death, gun in hand. All honor to his venerable name!

A Miracle - Long before the destruction of the Jews of Bursztyn we learned about the Germans' evil plans to destroy all the Jews of Galicia. Successive trains filled with Jews passed through the train stations of Bursztyn on the way to the crematorium camps. One time 11 Jews jumped off the trains, were caught and brought into town. At that time there was a German stationed there who had a hobby of shooting helpless people. He was particularly cruel to children and it was he who received these 11 Jews as his targets. First he shot nine of them and there remained a mother and her seven-year-old child. The murderer ordered the child to turn around and face him as he took out his pistol to shoot him. Then a remarkable thing happened. The boy faced the German with an innocent smile on his face. The murderer was stunned and remained standing as if he had been turned to stone, his gun falling from his hand. This murderer, who had killed hundreds of people, many of them children, this animal in the form of a human, who never before had shown pity to any child who may have crawled before him and begged for his life, was completely overcome by the smile of an innocent child and he fell in a dead faint. When he was revived, he ordered the Ukrainian policeman Schtick, the one who had shot the first ten Jews of Bursztyn, to bring the child to the Judenrat making him accountable for the boy's life. This German lay in the Tanka Moskeviten house for many days and would command that the boy be brought to him from time to time because he felt better when the boy was there. When the Jews of Bursztyn were killed, the boy and his mother disappeared and no one knows what happened to them.

Ilana Mischler Schmorak tells this story about Ze'ev Schmorak. She recalls his initiative and Zionist dedication all of his life until the period of the Holocaust. When the important members of the community suggested that he preside over the Judenrat, he refused to accept the position,

---

Ed1   A. Vlasov (1900-1946), Encyclopedia of the Holocaust, MacMillan Co., 1990, Ed. I. Gutman Vol. 4, p. 1579.

explaining that only a criminal could be capable of cooperating with the Nazis. On October, 1942 he, his wife, his mother and the rest of his community were driven out of town to Bukaczowce and from there to the concentration camp in Belzec. A short while afterwards, his daughter also died, as did his brother Dr. Schmorak, a staunch Zionist, who was murdered during the first weeks of the German conquest. May the Almighty avenge their deaths.

Fenster relates hearing from Yaakov Feldman that at one time the German murderers gathered up hundreds of Jews in Rohatyn and informed them that at a given time bread would be distributed to the children, and hundreds of children gathered there; the bestial murderers shot them all to death. Once a German spy came to us and pretended to be friendly to the Jews. When we saw that we had fallen into his trap, we grabbed him, stabbed him to death and buried him on the spot.

Y. Shmulevitz, New York, as heard from Yaakov Glotzer: Together with my wife and three children, I came on the 22nd of October, 1942 to Rohatyn, where the remainder of the Jews of Rohatyn, Bursztyn, Bukaczowce, Knihynicze and Zurow were in hiding. While we were in our room where we were hiding, a Jew by the name of Skolnick, a printer who lived in our proximity, came to me and warned us, "Prepare yourselves. You may be killed at any moment." Knowing that every week the Judenrat of Rohatyn was required to present the Germans with 100 Jews to be shot in their own basement, we began digging a tunnel that night lead from the side of our room to the river Gnila Lipa. Working only at night, the process took three weeks. While we were in the house, we constantly heard the groans of Yisrael Schtander of Stratyn, who was hiding in the attic and was dying of thirst, and we were unable to do anything for him. When we reached the forest where the partisans were stationed, I was given a rifle and I took part in their activities. At night we went out to the farmers of the villages to get food.

The partisans started their attacks by breaking into the police station of Bursztyn and taking nine rifles. Then the Jewish partisans went out of the forests into the roads that led to Bukaczowce and fell upon German drivers, whom they shot, taking their rifles and boots. In this way they collected weapons, clothes, and food.

He also heard a similar story from Paula Tichover: "When we came to the ghetto of Rohatyn, someone from Rohatyn by the name of Shmuel Acht accepted us into his room. After eight days, the akcja began. Shmuel Acht had prepared a bunker before this, and about 20 people hid there. I used to sneak out of the ghetto to bring wood. A Jewish policeman caught me, took away the wood and beat me, but G-d punished him. When the ghetto was liquidated, he hid in the attic of a farmer and there he rotted to death.

By contrast, she praises a Ukrainian farmer Mikołaj Maćkio (Yiddish Matskie) who enabled them to stay alive. She describes life in the forests. One time the Germans came with their dogs that led them by scent to the bunker, which was empty. When a German bent down to look into the bunker Mordechai Blumenfeld shot him with his rifle. The other Germans were frightened and retreated from the forest. They became angry with the Ukrainian militia for not informing them that the partisans had weapons. Upon leaving, the Germans shot Mordechai in the arm and leg. We were able to treat the arm but not his leg and he limped. Mordechai was shot and killed during another attack by the partisans in a different place. May he rest in peace!

Miriam Ginzburg Allerhand recalls the stories of her father-in-law Rabbi Yoel Ginzburg, about his son and her husband, Chaim, who worked as a reporter for the Nowy Dziennik[Ed2] and the HaOlam[Ed3] in London. He was also a teacher of Greek, Latin and Hebrew in the Jewish high school of Cracow (Krakow) and he received from Dr. Yehoshua Thon,[Ed4] Z"L, a citation for excellence, which is displayed in the book of Bursztyn. She relates how they spoke Hebrew to their son Amram from the day he was born.

By means of an Aryan document under the name of Marja Yowserewsky, she succeeded in escaping to Warsaw. She had a miracle, that when the Germans were beating her with a pistol, her child broke out in uncontrollable tears and one of the Germans said to the other, "I can't shoot this child. He reminds me too much of my own children at home," and left them alive.

Yosef Schwartz of New York cites, among other things, the worthy behavior toward Jews of certain gentiles, among them a priest, who supplied Jews with food in the area of Tarnopol.

While they were hiding in the grain fields, Russian soldiers came there and took them to headquarters on suspicion of spying. The interrogator was a Jew from Kiev. "When I started to tell him what we went through and what others are likely to go through, he broke into tears like a child. When it became dark, they wanted to return us to town, but the commanding officer, a Jew, ordered us to remain in the room. He then accompanied us to Brzezany where we met

Ed2 "The New Daily", first Zionist Polish-language journal. It appeared daily in Cracow from the end of 1918. 1972 Encyclopedia Judaica,, Vol. 12, p. 1245.

Ed3 HaOlam, the central organ of the World Zionist Organization, published as a weekly from 1907 to 1950 (except for short intervals). "HaOlam was the Hebrew counterpart of Die Welt ...". 1972 Encyclopedia Judaica, Vol. 7, pps. 1315-1316.

Ed4 Thon, Osias (Jeshua;1870-1936), rabbi, early Zionist, and Polish Jewish leader." 1972 Encyclopedia Judaica, Vol. 15, pp 1121-1122.

other Jews who had succeeded in running away."

Bella Ehrenberg Zinger recounts that the inhabitants of Bukaczowce and the Poles and Ukrainians of the village of Czarow did not usually bother Jews, except in some specific instances. There were some who actively helped Jews. "For instance, Marja Lubinic (Loubinitz) and her son Ped hid me and my first husband Mordechai Blumenfeld for a period of between four to five months. From there we went to the forests, where we built a bunker and joined other escapees. Mordechai, who was born in Czarow, was the chief organizer of the rescues. He took revenge on the Banderowcy, the Ukrainians who grabbed Jews when they left their bunkers and delivered them to Rohatyn. On the other hand, the farmers of Koniuszki and Obelnica were big terrorists."

Shmuel Shapira of New York - He remembers the teacher, Rabbi Yoel Ginzburg, and his three children - Zimmel, Chaim and Gershon - all three of whom influenced Jewish religious and national life in the area. Two of them, Zimmel and Chaim, were teachers in Hebrew high schools. He (Rabbi Yoel) was very pious, an enthusiastic Zionist, and a member of the Mizrachi.[Ed5] It is interesting to note that Rabbi Yoel enjoyed speaking with Mina Tobias, the leader of the awakening youth. These two personalities brought light to the town during the dark period of the Holocaust. Mina Tobias was appointed head of the Judenrat, but when the Germans wanted him to cooperate, he resigned.

Yosef Schwartz relates that, on one winter night in the year 1915, a Russian officer entered the Beit HaMidrash. He was tall and strong, with a gray beard and very dignified. The congregants were frightened and rose from their seats, but the officer began to speak to them in Yiddish and shook hands with all of them. He looked at the open Gemara volumes on the book stands (shtenders), then took out a small notebook and turned to Reb Leybisch Kletiffer with questions. How many Jews left the town? How many remained? How do they support themselves? Before he left he said, "If the Russians try to bother you, come to me. My name is Shloime Rapaport and I live on the grounds of Count Jablonowski (Yablonowsky)." This was S. An-ski.[Ed6]

Yisrael Fenster in explaining Mina Tobias' outlook on life, tells the following story. During World War I, he (Mina Tobias) became acquainted with a learned Russian Jewish prisoner, who was knowledgeable in

Ed5   Encyclopedia Judaica, Vol. 12, 1972, Keter Publishing, Jerusalem, Israel, p. 175 (Mercaz Ruchani, spiritual center), religious Zionist movement, whose aim was expressed in its motto: "The Land of Israel for the people of Israel for according to the Torah of Israel" (coined by Rabbi Meir Berlin-Bar Ilan).

Ed6   Pseudonym of Solomon Zainwil Rapaport, Yiddish playwright (see: Dybbuk)

Yiddish and modern Hebrew literature, and had become an aide at that time to the then-Austrian officer M. Tobias. This prisoner began to read with his officer a variety of Yiddish and Hebrew literature that included Bialik, Peretz, Mendele, Sholem Aleichem. The reading sessions with this Russian Jew had a notably strong effect on Tobias. Thus, during the years 1918 to 1920, when there were altercation between the Poles and the Ukrainians and battles between the Poles and the Russians, the town passed from hand to hand, and the honor of Jews in the town was non-existent, Tobias happened to see a Polish officer trying to cut off the beard of a passing Jew. Tobias stopped him and said to the hooligan, "I am also an officer." The Polish officer slapped him in the face. Mina Tobias told this to the army authorities and resigned as Polish officer, with all the privileges this meant. The Polish army authorities were highly insulted. The survivors of Bursztyn relate that he wa quick to discern the wicked trickery of the Nazis and refused to cooperate with them and act as head of the Judenrat. Because of this he was sent to the ghetto of Rohatyn and died there.

The missing people of the forests of Katyn—In 1943, in the midst of the flames of World War II, the world was very upset by the announcement of the discovery of the mass grave of thousands of Polish officers who were murdered in the forests of Katyn. It turns out, however, that among those murdered were many Jews, including three people from Bursztyn.

The story of the Sefer Torah—Pinchas Haber, the son-in-law of Avrumtsie from Bohorodczany, brought a Sefer Torah with him when he settled in Bursztyn and put it into the Stratyner kloiz (Stratyn small synagogue) where he prayed. When the murderers began to cause riots in town, Pinchas hid the Sefer Torah and no one knew where it was. When Bursztyn was liberated by the Russians in 1944, the Jews who had been in hiding returned to their town to weep over its destruction. One time an old Ukrainian lady came to Yaakov Feldman and said to him that she had a secret that concerned him. She related that at the end of 1941 Pinchas Haber and Mordechai Bernstein gave her a Sefer Torah to hide. They knew this old lady, whom they called Stepanke or Stefanka), and trusted her. She belonged to Sabbath Observers[Ed7] and would probably care for it. She took the Sefer Torah from them and set up a special "bunker" where she placed it in straw to protect it against dampness. The old lady gave him a hat to cover his head and he went with her. The Sefer Torah was still in its hiding place, as she had said, and she handed it to Yaakov Feld-man, the husband of Dazi, the daughter of the above-named Pinchas Haber. After years of wandering, Dazi and Yankel Feldman came to Israel in 1948 and brought with them the Sefer Torah that was rescued.

Ed7   Shomrei Shabbat (Subbotniki) , Encyclopedia Ha-Ivrit, 1972, Vol. 24, p. 734.

Bukaczowce (Bukatshevitz)
By Chedveh Weisman

Translated by Binyamin Weiner - YB p. 336

This essay is based on answers to the questionnaire of the Central Historical Commission of the Central Committee for Liberated Jews in the American Zone (compiled May 12, 1947).

Bukaczowce (or Bukatshevitz, as the Jews used to call it) had 500 years of Jewish history. Before World War II, around 1,000 Jews lived there. Their main occupations were business and handicrafts. There was a Kahal (local communal board), various parties and organizations, two houses of study (synagogues), a library, a progressive school, and a cemetery, where a mausoleum of the local Rabbi Avrumtshe Zinger was found.[Tr1]

From the outbreak of World War II (Sept. 1, 1939) until the Nazis marched into our shtetl (July 1, 1941), life was relatively tranquil. The first anti-Jewish decrees included the wearing of a distinguishing sign on the right arm, and a curfew was instituted after seven o'clock in the evening.

The Ukrainians took advantage of the opportunity to beat and rob. The Jews were seized for forced labor where they beat them murderously. All of the eminent men of the shtetl were held captive as surety: Moshe Grinberg, Moshe Schifer, Dovid Schifer, Shmerl David, Stern and others. The Jews were ordered to hand over all of their jewelry, fur, pelts, silver and gold. Those later found holding on to any of these requisitioned goods were shot.

The first akcja occurred on Yom Kippur 1942. Around 100 Jews were transported in cars to an undisclosed destination from which they never returned.

Twice in January of 1943, Jewish boys and girls were seized and transported to the concentration camp in Brzezany, where they were shot. Our Jewish community was destroyed in the same month. Later, the remaining Jews were driven into the Rohatyn ghetto, where they perished on June 6th, 1943, Hallowing G-d's Holy Name (in Hebrew: Al Kiddush Hashem). Our Jewish community was destroyed in January, 1943.

The non-Jewish population of the town behaved very badly toward the Jews during the occupation years. Often they were even worse than the

---

Tr1 Culturally well-versed Rabbi Zinger, according to statement by translator Rabbi M. Goldzweig.

Germans and it was impossible to offer any organized resistance against them.

Approximately 20 Jews survived by hiding out in the forests, by hiding with Christians, or by "being on the Aryan side."[Ed1] Many escaped to Russia. [Ed2]

Yaakov-Shimon Schifer, well known for being active in the Agudah, perished on the first day of the Hebrew month of Iyar, 1942, at the age of 62. The Ukrainians beat him murderously, on orders of the local Judenrat leader Emil Kraus. He died the next day from the beatings. At around that time, Rav Kafeides (60 years old) and Rav Schwartz also perished.

Ed1 Generally that term meant "passing" as non-Jews, with or without Aryan identity papers.
Ed2 By joining the Soviet retreat in 1941.

Bukaczowce

By Leon Gewanter

Translated by Binyamin Weiner - YB p. 337

B efore the war, Bukaczowce numbered some 1,000 Jewish souls, most of them merchants, peddlers, and butchers. The murder of the Jews began with the coming of the Germans. The Ukrainians killed entire families and threw their corpses into the Dniester. The first "akcja" was directed against the sick and crippled, some 200 in number, who were transported to an unknown destination. A similar "akcja" was carried out in Rohatyn. After the first "akcja," a carpenter friend of ours, an able and inventive man, built us a shelter (bunker) in the cellar. This shelter was concealed by shelves stacked with bottles and jars. The hiding place was behind the shelves.

My father, who was a veterinarian, was taken with the other doctors to a camp. This was a consequence of the testimony of an informer, who said my father was still practicing his profession, though it was forbidden to do so. Father returned to us after two months, thanks to the efforts of a German who knew us.

Before the "akcja," Jews had been transported to Bukaczowce from Bursztyn, and they swelled the local population of Jews. Before the Germans came to carry out an "akcja," the Jewish police would warn us, and we would hide in our bunker for a day or a day and a half, until the hunt had ended. Many Jews were seized in the "akcja," most of them Jews who had been brought from Bursztyn. Members of the Jewish police acted honorably, not handing over any Jew to the Germans, and even helping as far as they could.

After this, my father found a hiding place with a Gentile named Stocki, who lived in a secluded place. My parents, my brother, and I hid there, along with two other Jews who were horse traders. After a month the winds [of persecution] died down, and we returned to Bukaczowce. My father managed to find work, but not for very long. When we wanted to go back to the farmer who had hidden us, he no longer wanted to take us in, and so we turned to Rohatyn.

There we suffered a catastrophe. Someone informed on my father, saying that he had not handed over his veterinary equipment. The Germans appeared and took my parents and brother away. At the time, I happened to be visiting neighbors, and so was saved. But the Gestapo found a photograph from which they became aware that I also belonged to this family. They searched for me, and even threatened the Judenrat that if I were not turned over into their hands they would kill 300 Jews in my place. But all the time I was hiding with the carpenter who had built us the first shelter.

My parents were shot.

Every day we lay waiting for the liquidation, and throughout the week of the "akcja" we stayed in the bunker. There were sixteen of us. After a week, we left the bunker and went our separate ways. I went with the carpenter's family but left them because I wanted to return to Bukaczowce to get a few things. All of this took place during the Christian Pentecost, when there were many people out roving in the fields.

I hid in a grain field and a deep sleep fell upon me. I was hungry, weak, and filthy. Someone found me while I slept and took me for dead. A Ukrainian farmer came upon me. He recognized me from the days when my father used to visit the farmers, when I would accompany my father in his work. The farmer took me to his cottage, fed me, and washed me. I went at night to the Polish farmer who had our possessions. I stayed with him for a few months, in an attic, until they began taking farmers away to work in Germany. People began rising up and fleeing. My benefactor also fled with his family to another village, but could not take me with him because I had no papers and everyone in the area knew me. I banded together with other Jews, and we went to the forest. In the forest there were many well-camouflaged bunkers. Five Jews had rifles. The Germans and Ukrainians were afraid to penetrate the forest. Only two people knew of our hiding place, a Pole and a Ukrainian. The Pole would warn us if we were in danger. But once the Ukrainian got drunk and began to prattle. The Germans dressed him in a soldier's uniform and commanded him to go with them and show them the hiding place. But in the meantime the farmer had sobered up, and he took them to bunkers that the Jews had already left.

The Jews would raid German storehouses at night, and take away necessary foodstuffs. We lacked nothing, except that it was hard for us to wash our sheets and we were covered with lice. Often the Germans placed blockades against us, but they were afraid to penetrate the thick forest.

With the advance of the front, we began digging holes in the forest and filling them with guns. Gathering food grew more and more difficult. When the Germans began blowing up railway lines, we knew that the Russians were drawing near, and we began crossing the Germans lines on the Dniester and Świrz.

There we found many Poles seeking refuge from the Ukrainians. The Banderowcy were killing Jews and Poles alike. There on the banks of the river I received the oncoming Soviet army with open arms.

Zurow and Bukaczowce

By Leon Schreier

Translated by Binyamin Weiner - YB p. 339

(A testimony)

I lived in Zurow from childhood. My father and forefathers lived there too. The Germans entered Zurow at the end of June 1941 and already on the day after the occupation, all Jews, both male and female, ages ten and up, by decree were forced to wear on their left arm armbands bearing the Star of David.

I lived in Zurow until April of 1942. Then the Ukrainian national militia gave the Jews 24 hours to leave the village, and by force barred them from taking more than 25 kilos of possessions per person.

The Jewish population, some 100 people, for the most part worked the land, owning farmsteads, equipment, and cattle. But they were forced to abandon all of this and were uprooted to the nearby town of Bukaczowce, in the Rohatyn district. While still in Zurow, we were privileged to experience the pleasure of the Ukrainian militia's strong arm. They banned trade with four Jewish shopkeepers and forced us to work on the roads and on nearby farms. In Zurow, most earned their livelihood through farming, and a few through artisan crafts. But from April of 1942 onward there was not a single Jew in Zurow.

Bukaczowce

I lived in Bukaczowce from April of 1942 until October of the same year. In peacetime, the town's Jewish population numbered about 1,300, out of 3000 total inhabitants. But now the Jewish population itself swelled to 3,000, with the addition of Jews from the surrounding villages and towns: Zurow, Knihynicze, Podmichałowce, Wasiuczyn, Hrehorow, Lukowce, Wiszniow, Kozary, Czerniow, Poswierz, Tenetniki, Czahrow, Kolokolin, and Martynow. The Jews of these villages and towns were driven out to Bukaczowce. In addition, Jews from the west were transported to Bukaczowce. All of us dwelled alongside the local Jews.

Every Jew 15 or older, male and female, had to go out daily to work on local farms, five to eight kilometers from the place where we lived. We went on foot. As payment for our work we received forty grams of bread a day, and sometimes 100 grams. Many Jews died of hunger. The first victims were Jews uprooted from the surrounding towns and villages. My wife, our two little children and I lived on the potatoes I was able to steal in the field, or the oats I stole from the feed of the horses I was tending and stuffed into my sack. At home, I dried them and ground up the kernels, and we baked them into wafers. Others of us gathered potato skins when working on the farms, and cooked them together with chickpeas.

The local Jews of Bukaczowce were better off, because they still had their own apartments and could sell their remaining clothing for the necessities of life. As a consequence of hunger, flagging strength, and the in human living conditions, a typhus epidemic broke out which claimed several hundred victims in the month of September. Fifteen people were crammed into a single room, an attic, or a manger. There was no hospital. The sick lay among the well in the apartments, without any means of quarantine whatsoever.

On Yom Kippur of the Jewish year 5703 (1942) the Gestapo came from Rohatyn, and with the help of the Ukrainian militia carried out a deportation. We were praying at the time, not in the synagogue, as the Germans had turned it into a granary. When we saw from afar the car full of Gestapo officers, we knew right away that a great catastrophe was about to occur. The young fled and sought cover in the bunkers that we had previously prepared in fields or barns. The Gestapo shot at those who fled and killed scores of them. Others were caught and taken to one of the buildings next to the Judenrat. My father, an elderly man 84 years old, and my brother-in-law and his three little children were removed from the house of prayer and seized by the Germans. In all, 300 Jews were seized and taken in groups to the station, to Rohatyn. In Rohatyn, 200 Jews or more were loaded into each railway car and transported to their destruction, probably to Belzec. On this Yom Kippur, the Germans also carried out a "selekcja" in other towns in the Rohatyn district: Rohatyn itself, Bursztyn, and Bukaczowce. Jews from these towns were transported to Rohatyn, and from there—to destruction.

Three days after the catastrophe, my friend Yisrael David returned. He had been captured by the Germans and numbered among the large toll of Jews who had perished along the way, in the packed cars sealed shut with boards, without any breathable air. The whole transport went west, but he managed to pry loose one of the boards, escape from the car, and return on foot to Bukaczowce.

The next day, the Jews went out again to work, despite the calamity and terror that were upon them. Someone had been taken from almost every family, but they had to work nonetheless. After a few weeks, another "akcja" (action, i.e., roundup and mass killing and/or mass deportation) took place, this time on Sunday and Monday. The Gestapo placed blockades on all roads leading to the town, and with the help of the Ukrainian militia, began the hunt. They went from house to house, looking in cellars and attics, and concentrated all the Jews in the marketplace, from which they were transported to the train station. They were loaded into railway cars facing west, to be carried to Belzec—to destruction. My friend Hersh Jupiter (pron. Yupiter) escaped from this transport. A tinsmith by trade, he had a set of pliers in his pocket, and with their help he pulled off a board from the wagon and jumped out with his brother, in the vicinity of Chodorow.

My children and I hid in the attic of good friends. My wife was captured and carried away with the rest of the transport, because she was unable to escape with us. I saw her through a slit in the closed shutters as she asked the Gestapo men for permission to take a coat, but they responded with blows from the butt of a rifle.

After this "akcja," only members of the Judenrat and Jewish police remained in Bukaczowce, as well as a few hundred people hiding in bunkers. The Jewish police let us know that the "akcja" was ending, and that in three days the Jews would have to leave the town and go to Rohatyn. We left Bukaczowce, taking with us only a few articles of clothing. It was forbidden to take furniture. Bukaczowce was now "Judenrein" ("Cleansed of Jews"). "Akcjas" took place throughout the district of Rohatyn, and those who survived came to Rohatyn itself.

We lived in the Rohatyn ghetto. It was impossible to leave it except for work, and this was done only under the escort of the Jewish police. A great distress prevailed in the ghetto, along with hunger, overcrowding, and typhus epidemics. The Gestapo would often visit the ghetto. They would enter homes, and if a sick person were found within he was shot in his bed. They also broke into the hospital and killed the sick together with their attendants. Many times the Gestapo came suddenly and demanded a few score Jews. The Jews delivered up to them were taken to the Judenrat and shot. Each time, the focus of the actions was broadened, to include children, the elderly, the sick, and those who could not work. After such an "akcja" the Judenrat was still forced to prepare a banquet for the Gestapo, and pay them ransom money. But abductions to the work camps in Tarnopol and to the stone quarries continued.

Three days before Shavuot, in the Jewish year 5703 (1943), the "final akcja" in the Rohatyn ghetto began. The action lasted several days, from Sunday to Wednesday. On Sunday, the Gestapo, helped by the Ukrainian militia, broke into the ghetto, seized members of the Jewish police, and shot them. After this, the Jews were transported group by group out of the city, where they were commanded to dig their own graves before being shot by the Germans. I hid with my children in a bunker we had dug over the course of a few months. David Shifer, whom the Germans forced to cover the mass graves, told me about the events of the "akcja." He himself was able to hide in the forest.

A few thousand Jews fell in this "akcja." All were killed in that place. At dawn on Thursday, when the shots had ceased, I fled with my children from the ghetto to the village where we hid.

Katowice, Poland, on June 18, 1946

p. 341 YB: Moshe-Leib Messing, Mincie Steinmetz, Sheindel Kleinwachs, unknown woman.

Knihynicze

By Aryeh Rebish, Tel Aviv

Translated by Binyamin Weiner - YB p. 342

To the west of Rohatyn lay a little shtetl called Knihynicze. Jesters called it Canaan. Three hundred Jewish families lived there, concentrated around the so-called Ringplatz and its surrounding streets. The other dwellers in the shtetl were Ukrainians.

Knihynicze possessed its own Jewish communal board, rabbi, dayan, ritual slaughterers and other religious officials. Jews were employed in trade. They dealt with the non-Jews and so earned their livelihood. There were no reputable local schools, and this influenced the cultural level of the shtetl. The few boys and girls who received a real education didn't know what to do with themselves in the generally lowly shtetl. Jewish parents sent their children to learn in the cheder or in the Talmud Torah. The education of the growing children was entirely restricted to this. There were therefore, in our shtetl, many people steeped in religious learning.

According to the stories of the older Jewish residents, Jews had lived in the shtetl for over 400 years. There, they survived several military invasions. The old people used to boast of the former splendor of the shtetl. In the time of the Polish-Turkish wars, when the fighting came to our area, the Polish general's headquarters was located in a village fifteen kilometers from Knihynicze.

There were eminent rabbis in Knihynicze such as the righteous Monastritsher rabbi and Rabbi Weiss, later a rabbi in Tschernowitz (Chernivtsi).

Jews used to dress in their traditional long black coats. They grew beards and sidelocks and observed the 613 commandments. They dealt in grain of inferior quality. They had to rinse the grain in water in order to clean it. This was done in the little river Świrz, which ran through the shtetl. It was hard work, but only after they had finished washing the dirty wheat could they receive their appropriate due. Jews worked at this all day and so earned their livelihood, but after the work was done, they sat in the Beit Midrash (house of study) over a page of Gemara.

Stories were often told of the great dispute surrounding the selection of Rabbi Yosef Shaul Natansohn as the shtetl's rabbi. Learned Jews opposed him. Their reason for doing so was not given. Years later,

p. 343 YB: Branch of Torah V'Avodah in Knihynicze.

p. 343 YB: Shmuel Ravitch (Rawicz) - Head of Bukaczowce Community, his son-in-law Yitzhak Albauer, Leybisch, Yitzhak, Martzes (children) Yaakov Tabak, Reizel Altbauer.

Rabbi Natansohn was chosen to be chief rabbi of Lemberg. Certain prominent householders of Lemberg (Lwow) came to escort him to his new residence. The entire retinue, led by the rabbi, rode through Knihynicze. Coming to the little river where the Jews in their long black coats, beards and sidelocks were washing their wheat, the rabbi held up his entourage and addressed them as follows: "Do you see these field-worker Jews? They didn't want to choose me as their rabbi…"

Of the old-time rabbis, it is worth recalling Rabbi Ber. He was thought to have been one of the students of the Ba'al Shem-Tov. In my childhood, I saw this rabbi's gravestone, dating back over 150 years. It was said that before he died, Rabbi Ber had declared that when, G-d forbid, the Jewish community of Knihynicze experienced a time of trouble, they should come with their pleas to his grave. He would struggle in heaven on behalf of his people.

There had also been in our shtetl a Rabbi Yehudah (Yidel), who was reputed to have been a secret saint.[Ed1] He accepted neither fees nor petitions. A tent was put up over his grave. In his lifetime, this rabbi was so beloved by the Jews that the Knihynicze Society in America is called by his name.

At the beginning of this century, Rabbi Avrumtshe Langner,[Ed2] the son of the Stratyner rebbe, was appointed Rabbi of Knihynicze, and as dayan, Rabbi Dovid Halevi Kimsel. The dayan was a respectable young man and a good prayer leader, known in the rabbinical world for his Responsa. He was the author of many religious books, most of which were unpublished. When I studied with him, he would often show me letters from other rabbis who sent him questions on a number of matters. Once, when I was with him, I saw a letter from a rabbi in Kleinmehrn[Ed3] this is how far away Rabbi Kimsel was known. His grandson, Rabbi Hanoch Henech, was, because of me, appointed dayan of Knihynicze on the eve of my departure for the land of Israel.

My grandfather, Yitzhak Tabak, Z"L, who was born in 1828, recounted that in olden times, there were military barracks in Knihynicze where a regiment of Hungarians was stationed. In the time of the 1848 revolution, when the Hungarian leader Kossuth raised the flag of revolution against the Austrian monarchy, the Hungarian regiment left Knihynicze on a certain night and went away to Hungary. As is known, the Russian Czar offered to help Kaiser Franz-Josef put down the revolution. Franz-Josef accepted this help, and the Russian Army marched through Knihynicze on their way to Hungary. Jews were filled with fear of the Cossacks who were marching through town and could have caused great trouble. The Jews of Knihynicze turned to the

---

Ed1   A secret saint, also one of the Lamed Vav.

Ed2   See article on Stratyn.

Ed3   Kleinmehrn, literally Little Moravia.

liberal Austrian government and asked that the Russian Army march through Knihynicze by night and not during the day. In this way, our community was saved from Cossack plunder. The dayan, Rabbi Berel, also told me about this event about which he had read in the annals of the shtetl. These annals were destroyed during World War I.

The real trouble for the Jews began with the outbreak of World War I. A few Jewish families, including mine, saved themselves by fleeing to Austrian Bohemia. Most Jews remained, however, and suffered great hardship at the hands of the Russians and, more to the point, at the hands of the local Ukrainian population. When the Russian Army left Knihynicze, in 1915, they deported the entire male population of the shtetl, including Rabbi Berel, into the depths of Russia. The women and children remained in the shtetl, untouched. The yoke of earning a livelihood now fell upon the women. The shtetl was nearly empty. Even worse was the situation of the children, as at this point, there weren't even any cheders. Children grew up without supervision and without education. This generation of youth didn't know a letter from a hole in the ground.

We returned in the beginning of 1918. The Austrian monarchy had fallen. The Western Ukrainian Republic was established in our area, and our troubles grew greater. We suffered a lot at the hands of the Ukrainian soldiers who openly robbed and plundered the Jews, taking all they could. On top of this, the Ukrainians organized their own cooperatives in competition with the Jewish businesses. Strong propaganda was circulated, instructing the non-Jewish population not to buy from Jews.

It was then clear to us that Jews had no future in Knihynicze. A group of young men and women decided to establish a Zionist organization in order to instill in the local Jewish youth the spirit of Zionism and to prepare them to immigrate to the land of Israel.

Our efforts met with many hardships. The Jewish youth, as was said before, were almost completely without education. It was difficult to lead them in enlightening cultural activities. With great patience, however, we managed to break through the silent wall and establish a respectable Zionist organization, particularly after the end of the Polish-Ukrainian and Polish-Bolshevik wars. During that time, the Bolsheviks were in our shtetl three times, but in the end, they were forced to abandon it completely.

We then established a good Hebrew school, with a teacher from Histadrut HaMorim Ha'Ivriim B'Galicia (Organization of Hebrew Teachers in Galicia). We prepared ourselves to go up to the land of Israel.[Ed4] Of course,

Ed4   Going up to the land of Israel (aliyah) is the customary phrase used in moving to or immigrating to Israel.

there was some commotion, especially on the part of our parents, who could not agree with the notion of not waiting for the days of the Messiah but going right then and there to Israel to build the land...

The first meeting of our newly established Zionist organization was held in the woman's section of the Beit Midrash. The Hassidim tried to frighten me, screaming that I would bring misfortune upon the shtetl. My father, Z"L, was the chairman of the Jewish communal board and an official of the great synagogue.

At that time, more than twenty young men and women went to Israel. They took root in the land and raised families there. Those who couldn't make it to Israel went to Argentina and other lands. Thus, some Jews were snatched away from the danger of being murdered. Of the hundreds of Jewish families left in Knihynicze, almost none were saved. The Germans and their helpers, the local Ukrainians, murdered them all.

p. 346 YB: Society of Mizrachi Girls in Knihynicze.

In the Village Settlement Podkamien

By Zvi Fenster (Felker)

Translated by Binyamin Weiner - YB p. 347

It has been thirty years since I left Podkamien, where I was born and lived until the age of ten. Between 1930 and 1941, I visited Podkamien frequently, but I was not a resident.

Podkamien lies around 10 kilometers to the southwest of Rohatyn, about halfway along the road from Strzeliska Nowe. The village of Czercze is to the east [Ed1], to the west is Bienkowce and Fraga. Zalanow is to the north [of Rohatyn]; about seven kilometers southwest of Zalanow is the train station Pomonieta Psary.

Before World War I, there were at least 100 Jewish families in the village. Most of them left and were scattered, some to other cities and towns in the region, and others to America.

In 1930, Podkamien was home to about twenty Jewish families. Two or three of them left the village after 1930.

Most of the population in the village, apart from the Jews, were Ukrainian, with a few Poles. There were also some German families, holdovers from the Austrian era who had taken root in the village. Most of the Poles had been settled there in the twenties, in separate enclaves, by the Polish government, which was trying to impart a Polish character to the village. A drawn-out war, complete with acts of hostility, was waged in the village between the Poles and the Ukrainians. At the end of the twenties, the violence took on a more serious aspect, and I recall a period in which twenty Ukrainian homes were set on fire by Polish nationalists.

The Jewish populace hardly took part in the communal life of the village, except for the indirect influence of one or two Jews in favor in the court of the Count. The Count actually spent most of his time abroad, but his property manager and the priests, in effect, were the governors of the village, despite the so-called "elections" for the municipal institutions.

Most of the non-Jewish residents were farmers of their own land. Some, however had either no land at all, or small plots that could not provide sufficient livelihoods, and so they hired themselves out to work in the fields of others.

Ed1   Podkamien and Czercze are actually northwest of Rohatyn.

The non-Jewish populace were reserved in their treatment of the Jews. I remember very few public acts of violence or hostility against the Jews occurring in those years, but the Ukrainian children and youths pursued and oppressed the Jewish children. A great fear would befall me whenever I had to pass the house of a Ukrainian boy who was bigger than I. In the thirties, with the opening of cooperatives in the village, a covert economic war against the Jews began.

The Jews who remained in the village were for the most part those who could not immigrate to other lands; they were mostly the elderly and some who were disabled, and others closely related to those who had to stay. Three Jewish families lived off agriculture, owning fertile parcels of land, upon which the Gentiles cast jealous glares.

Two Jewish families eked out a meager living from their village general stores. A third established ties with the Count's court and was therefore considered wealthy, and so they felt the sting of the local cooperatives directed against them.

There were two barkeepers in the village, one of them also maintained an inn; non-Jews met there to consider the municipal and economic matters of the village over glasses of brandy. One of the two taverns closed at the end of the twenties, when its owner, a widow and her two children, immigrated to Canada.

There was also a kosher butcher shop in the village.

Most of the retail trade was based on selling to the local populace on credit. Once a week or once in two weeks the store owners went to the city and brought back goods for sale. After passing them on to their local customers, many mornings they would go out among the villagers with their baskets and collected eggs, hens, and so forth, as payment for the goods they had given out. Once or twice a week, when the peddlers and merchants came from Rohatyn, the store owners would turn over [to them] the produce they gathered.

At the beginning of the thirties Podkamien still had a shochet, who went through the surrounding villages, visiting Jewish families - as far as ten kilometers away – to slaughter fowl and cattle, sometimes at special invitation. In general, he had the most work on the eve of Yom Kippur, when Jews from all around would bring him their kapparot (expiatory sacrifices) for slaughter. This shochet also taught the children Chumash (Torah) with the Rashi commentary. As I recall, he left after a year or two, for lack of a livelihood.

The first stage of Jewish education, the aleph-bet, was provided for the Jewish children by a preliminary religious teacher, but at the start of the twenties a number of families also brought in a Hebrew and general studies teacher.

A public school with four grades was also established in the village. The few Jewish children also attended it. The level of education was very low, and a graduate of all four grades could read with difficulty. The percentage of students who dropped out before finishing all four grades was high, because there was a shortage of manpower in the farming families, and the children served as shepherds of cattle and geese. Two or three times a week, priests would come into the class to give religious instruction, and I remember that always after such an instructive lesson I took a beating from the Ukrainian children, together with curses: "Jew, you killed our lord."

Jewish life in the village centered around the synagogue. This synagogue stood in the center of the village, next to the village council building and a large public square. It possessed four Torah scrolls.

In the period that I remember, there were no public prayer services on regular weekdays, but only on Shabbat, holidays, and festivals. Only on memorial days (yahrzeit) would a minyan (quorum) assemble for prayer. In contrast to this, the synagogue was full to capacity on holidays, when Jews from the neighboring villages of Dehova, Psary, and Zalanow came to pray with the community. When a holiday fell on Shabbat, the Jews would come with their families and stay over, so as not to transgress the "Shabbat limitations."[Tr1] On Yom Kippur they would remain in the synagogue, spending all their time on the recitation of Psalms. On other holidays they would stay as guests in the homes of local Jews. For "Days of Awe" (High Holy Days) they might leave Podkamien and go to the court of the Stretiner (Stratyn) Rebbe or to Rohatyn and spend the holidays there.

To this day, the Torah reading of Reb Mordechai Willig, Z"L, still resounds in my ears. He was the customary reader on every Shabbat of the year; he would walk the village roads from his house to the synagogue and back decked out in his tallit (prayer shawl) because of the prohibition against carrying anything on Shabbat. He would spend Rosh Hashana and Yom Kippur with the Stretiner Rebbe and hear the Torah reading there.

The stirring words of Reb Shlomo Titel before shofar blowing on Rosh Hashana, and before ne'ila (the concluding prayer) on Yom Kippur brought tears to the eyes of everyone praying in the synagogue. This learned old man was the spiritual leader of the regional Jews and was regularly called upon to blow the shofar and to lead musaf (the additional service) on Rosh Hashana and Yom Kippur.

Tr1   Distance one is permitted to walk on Shabbat beyond village or town limits.

When the Archbishop passed through the village in the twenties, it was Reb Titel who went out to greet him with a Torah scroll in his hands. And in those years, when on Simchat Torah the Jews still went dancing out onto the village roads, he went out, together with Mordechai Willig, at the head of all the Jews.

Reb Moshe Fenster, a shofar blower, who led shacharit (morning prayer) on Rosh Hashana and Yom Kippur, used to gather all the youths almost every summer Shabbat and instruct them in a chapter of Pirkei Avot ("Ethics of the Fathers") or a page of Gemara.

And Zvi Axelrod, who stood and recited pesukay d'zimra (preliminary morning prayers) for an hour and a half on Rosh Hashana and Yom Kippur, must be remembered. He could be seen on every summer Shabbat going out to survey the fields.

With the coming of the Germans in 1941, all the Jews of Podkamien were transported to the Rohatyn ghetto. As far as I know, only two or three Podkamien Jews survived, the rest perishing alongside the Jews of Rohatyn and its surrounding communities.

May their souls be bound together in eternal life, and may their memory last forever.

The Jews of Czesniki (Yid. Chesnik)
By Yaakov Palgi, Kiryat-Chaim

Translated by Binyamin Weiner - YB p. 350

The village of Czesniki lies seven kilometers from Rohatyn, along the road that runs eastward from Rohatyn to Brzezany.

Between the two World Wars, Czesniki was a fairly wealthy Ukrainian village. Many of its inhabitants read the newspapers and sent their children to high school in Rohatyn, and even on to higher education.

Czesniki did not differ from the other villages in the area. I do not know its history, but I remember the stories that the old farmers used to tell about their liberation from serfdom to the landlords ("pańszczyzna," as it is said in the foreign tongue). A Jew named Reb Moshe, who dwelled in the village for many years, growing wealthy and living to a ripe old age, worked hard for their emancipation. At a propitious time, he purchased a large tract of forest and cattle-grazing ground from the landlord, for the sake of the villagers. These grounds were transferred to the village council, and every village farmer had the right to graze on them. Every winter, the farmer's family would also receive firewood. The old men also said that the landowner had wanted to sell this Jew the land for a cheaper price and on better conditions, provided he would not hand it over to the village council and the farmers. But this simple Jew saw that emancipating and improving the condition of the farmers was a noble cause, and he did all that was in his power to bring it about.

The old villagers told this story when they gathered in the tavern and reminisced about their hard lives during the era of serfdom, and the emancipation brought about by Reb Moshe. This same Reb Moshe strove to build up his family in Czesniki, and there is some truth to the belief that all of the Jews of the village, totaling some 75 families, are his descendants.

In those days, the accepted practice for rich village Jews was to find grooms for their daughters in the yeshivas (academies of Jewish learning). When their daughters reached maturity, the Jews of Czesniki did likewise. After inspecting the yeshivas, they would bring home a young student, well formed and steeped in Jewish learning, and display him before the elders of the family, testing his strength in Torah. If all went well, they made the match. Reb Chaim Jupiter (pron. Yupiter) was one such groom.

377

The young couple settled in Czesniki. Their house stood beside the main road, on a lovely hill surrounded by a garden, with plum and apple trees. On the other side of the road was an even larger garden, with a fountain in the middle that Reb Chaim Jupiter transformed into a mikveh (ritual bath).

During the summer, Jews would throng there every day, to immerse their bodies before shacharit (the morning prayer), and sometimes they would even go there in the winter.

I remember only a few specifics of this wonderful man's life.

After World War I, between 70 and 75 Jewish families lived in Czesniki. They were very concerned with the upbringing of their children. On Shabbos (Sabbath), the parents would gather up their "jewels," and take them to uncle Reb Chaim tsum farheren, that is, to have their children's Torah knowledge tested. Many feared these examinations, though this was actually a baseless fear, as Reb Chaim was a dear man who loved to joke with the children and make them laugh.

After the Jew from Czesniki died, his Torah scroll was bequeathed, not to his sons, but to his son-in-law, the learned Reb Chaim, whose knowledge of Torah was great, and in whose home all of the men of the family used to pray every Shabbos evening and day. I still remember how all of the men used to wait in the prayer room for Reb Chaim to emerge from his study, where he sat learning all night. Sometimes we would wait a long time, while we were very hungry, and when the door finally opened and he appeared we would rejoice, and ready ourselves to pray. But he, following his own schedule, would cross the room and descend to the garden, where he would enter the mikveh and prepare to immerse himself. We, the little children, would run after him, in order to see what he was doing down there. Once in the winter, in the middle of a great frost, we all caught fever watching as he stripped off his clothes beside the fountain and jumped into the water, immersed himself, and came out. The service began only after he had dressed and returned to the house of prayer. When the shemoneh esrei (silent meditation) was through, and everyone had gone on their way, he stayed standing as straight as a pillar, without moving from his place. Once, when I was feeling bold, I asked my father why uncle stood for so long, when the other men all hurried through their prayers. My father, Z"L, answered that my uncle was communing with the Master of the Universe.

Reb Chaim was good natured, clever, and learned in Torah. In his later years he swore off eating meat entirely. He moved to Rohatyn, where he lived with Rabbi Eliezer (Reb Eliezer'l), and studied day and night. It was pleasant to visit him, and discuss the issues of the day. He was well versed in matters of state, and he showed an understanding of the reasons for aliyah (immigration to Israel) and the building of the State of Israel.

Before I made aliyah, I went to say goodbye to him. He asked me to come to the beis medresh (house of prayer and study) of Our Master and Teacher Rabbi Eliezer Langer, and he set aside time for me during shaleshudes (the traditional third meal eaten on Shabbos). He brought me in to see Rabbi Eliezer, where I received my uncle's blessing that I be a "good Jew." He explained to Rabbi Eliezer that I was going to the Land of Israel. I felt that my uncle was proud of this.

The life of this dear Jew ended when he was over ninety years old, under very tragic circumstances. He was lying on his bed, wrapped in his tallis and tefillin (prayer shawl and phylacteries), when a German Nazi came into the room and saw him. Thus, his worthy soul left this world. May his memory be blessed.

***

At the other end of the village, which was built in a triangle, stood two fine houses, their metal roofs gleaming (in contrast to the farmers' houses, which were covered with roofs of straw). These houses could be seen from afar by travelers on the road from Rohatyn, and in times of war, soldiers, or simply bandits, would come straight to them. Two brothers lived in these houses, sons of the Jew from Czesniki. The elder was Reb Yitschok, and the younger Reb Chaim Schafel. Each was blessed with sons and daughters. They were landowners and also successful merchants. The elder, Reb Yitschok, spent most of his time working in the field—a real farmer. He was not really steeped in Torah like his brother-in-law, Reb Chaim Jupiter, but he had a Jewish heart, and was a straight and simple God-fearing man.

Opposite the house of Reb Yitschok lived his younger brother, Reb Chaim. All his life, Reb Chaim was involved in the communal affairs of the village. He was richer than his brother, his fields bigger, and his business dealings greater. He was always very active in elections for the village council. In his old age, when he was sick and could no longer stand as a candidate for the village council, he appealed to his son Reb Michoel to run, so that the reigns of government might be kept within the family. But at that time the Jews were no longer interested in mixing with village matters, an attitude shared by Reb Michoel. Anti-Semitism was already making its mark.

Once, the village council infringed on the rights of one of Reb Chaim's sons, refusing to permit him to chop firewood from the village forest, as was his right according to the regulations. Reb Chaim Schafel summoned the village "voyt" (headman), and did not speak to him at length, but only struck his staff against the floor and asked that the matter be resolved—and the matter was resolved. These were the three Jewish elders of the village of

379

Czesniki.

During World War I, the village passed from hand to hand. When the Ukrainians left and the Poles came, we thought that the days of the Messiah had come, and at last we would live in peace. But one Shabbos evening, two Polish soldiers came to Reb Yitschok's house, and stole absolutely everything from him, including the challahs (ritual breads) for Shabbos. Reb Yitschok approached the thieves, and asked them to return one of the challahs, so that he could bless it during the Shabbos evening meal. One soldier took out his dagger and stabbed Reb Yitschok to death. Reb Yitschok still managed to get outside. He sank to the ground, and his pure soul left this world. May his memory be blessed.

But this was nothing to the suffering we endured at the hands of the Ukrainians. Our family lived at the other end of the village, by the house of the landowner Milinski. We had neighbors, who, for a good reward, let us know that "Tomorrow the Cossacks will certainly ride through the village," and we attempted to flee to the forest. As they did not inform us until the last minute, we were unable to escape. We ran to our nearest neighbors, to our "close friends" as it were, and begged them to hide us in their bunkers. They refused, and we continued to run and to beg for shelter, until one neighbor had mercy on us, and took us in for the night. The next morning, our grandfather, Reb Moishe Teichman, went out of the bunker, wrapped himself in his tallis, walked out among the ditches, and began to pray. A Ukrainian soldier appeared, and when he saw my grandfather with his white beard, Reb Moishe Teichman, Z"L, he took his sickle in hand, with the intention of slaughtering my grandfather. We heard everything, and, woefully, our neighbor would not permit my mother to go out and try to save her father. To our great joy, an angel appeared, in the form of the same gentile who had sheltered us in his bunker, and protected us through the night. By promising the soldier a sufficient sum, he saved my grandfather's life.

Another time, a Ukrainian soldier from a neighboring village, named Hertz, came to us. Even though my father knew him and his family, he took everything away from our house on horse-drawn wagons, with the help of a second soldier, then locked the doors, and began searching for silver and gold. We were forced to disrobe, and we stood for hours with our hands raised, as they emptied the house. When he had finished, he informed us that he was going outside to throw a grenade into the little room where we were gathered. It is impossible to describe the wailing and the crying. My grandfather, Reb Moishele, approached the gentile and asked that he permit us to recite the "vidui" (the traditional deathbed prayer). The gentile assented, so we sat there, pressed together against the table, my grandfather, my father, and my uncle Reb Avromtsi, and began to pray with broken hearts. How we children trembled with fear, and cried and wailed. Suddenly my mother's sister Rivtsi (then 17 or 18 years old) went to the window, opened it, and jumped out. We, all of the little ones, jumped out after her and began to run through the fields to the forest, and then to our gentile, Tsimbl, who had built the bunker for us. We did not know what had happened to those who remained.

The soldier saw us running, and, thinking that we were running to the officer who lived in the landowner's house, made off hurriedly with all of the goods he had plundered. That night the whole family came to the bunker of the righteous gentile, Tsimbl.

After World War I, the situation of the Czesniki Jews deteriorated. Absence of livelihood, persecution at the hands of the Ukrainian populace, a general boycott, and a lack of opportunity all led the young generation to look toward the road. Some sought their livelihood in other places, primarily Rohatyn, some immigrated to North and South America, and others took the road to Communism. We suffered much, but we still believed that the days of our redemption were coming. There were others, younger still, who stuck to the path of Zionism, to the ideal of making aliyah as pioneers. One of them managed to triumph over the difficulties that stood in his way, and over the pressure of his family, and immigrated to Israel, to participate in the building of the homeland.

He was the only one who managed to get to Israel prior to the Shoah. Two brothers, grandsons of Chaim Jupiter, Z"L, served in the Red Army during the war, and so were saved.

This article is consecrated to the memory of my dear parents, and all of my family who suffered and fell at the hands of the Nazi oppressors.

p. 354 YB: In the village of Czesniki, in April 1935.

381

p. 351 YB: Moshe Teichman and his Wife.

Michael and Estel Schafel.

Moni Jupiter, Yitka Schafel.

Miriam and Reuven Schafel

The Kreizler children

Buntsie Schafel and his wife Leah

Lipica Gorna

By Yisroel Chetzroni, K'far Meserik

Translated by Binyamin Weiner - YB p. 355

L ipica Gorna—for all appearances a village like any other in the anti-Semitic Ukraine. It contains some 1,200 inhabitants, most of them children growing up without education or supervision, abject and poor in material substance and spirit, and as stuffed full of superstitious beliefs as a pomegranate is with seeds. The "Holy Father," the priest, is the only authority figure in the village, financing himself through the registration of the living and the dead and keeping evil spirits at bay, sprinkling his devotees with "holy water" and taking a poor gentile's last chicken as payment.

There is not a single doctor in the village, nor a pharmacy or nurse. A handful of Jews is scattered among the Ukrainians, and about thirty Polish families are closed into a completely separate neighborhood. Like them, we too are hated by the Ruthenians. From the only Orthodox Christian church, which stands on a tall hill in the center of the village, there pours forth a flood of Jew-hatred and calls for vengeance in the name of the crucified Messiah. And the constant danger of the blood libel and destruction hovers over the heads of the Jews.

World War I is over, and Poland comes back to life. The Jews return from their bitter wanderings, downtrodden, poor, and lean. On returning, they discover their property plundered and their houses burned, and their claims of ownership over houses and goods are met with hostility.

The Ukrainians will not be moved. They see the Jewish property as their spoil for the sake of their warriors, their valiant compatriots, and the previous owners having no claim at all. What do they care about the plight of mothers expending all their strength to nurse their babies? Hunger and fear press upon us. We are all tattered beggars, with no one to help us, and nowhere to turn.

The Polish police try to defend us, following the intervention of the Voivode (provincial governor) of Stanislawow, and the Starostwo (office of district elder) of Rohatyn. The head of the village council, Simko Procik, a Ruthenian, also tries to help us, using his great influence over the villagers.

The whole village is surrounded to the east by forest. At the center of the village are fields of corn and wheat. And in the very center is the rich

383

and fertile land owned jointly by a convert named Karel Prycko, and Cerbinski, a Jew-hater from birth, a member of the Polish nobility, and a boor and ignoramus who looses dogs on any Jew that asks for his assistance.

The intervention of the Police and the Starostwo from Rohatyn is helpful, and thirty Jewish families return to their homes and attempt to resume their normal lives, and as much as possible, to reestablish relationships with their Ukrainian neighbors. Houses and fields are returned to every Jew able to prove his ownership of the property, but moveable property is not returned. The Jews are happy that at least they have roofs over their heads.

Of the thirty families, five immigrate to America, and the other twenty-five, some 150 souls of all ages and three generations, stay in their places.

The elderly believe in the coming of the Messiah and the days of Redemption. "I believe in the coming of the Messiah...I will await his coming every day." But the young generation is consumed with despair and disappointment. Their faces darken for lack of knowing where to turn. The nickname "Sliuk" ("hick" in the foreign tongue) pursues them. The townspeople make fun of them and try to convince them to transplant themselves to the urban Jewish centers. But love of their parents prevails upon them, and they remain in their place, helping to reconstruct the family's life and provide a livelihood sufficient for all its members. The small children reacquaint themselves with the free life in the bosom of nature, and faith in their parents erases all worry from their hearts.

Rivers traverse the village, one, the Narajowka, responsible for more than a few floods and horrible scenes. Two flour mills stand on the riverbanks, about a kilometer apart, acquired from the country squire Cerbinski by Reb Moshe Itsi Dorfman. In the course of time, a ramshackle hut has been transformed into a two-story stone building. The second mill, bordering the two villages of Lipica Gorna and Lipica Dolna, belongs to Moshe Schweller.

The Ukrainians bring their grain to the mill and pay the fee in grain because they cannot pay cash. The Jews prove their generosity, and win friends among the gentiles. Reb Eliezer Dorfman renovates his big house, which contains a bread bakery and a primitive oil press. He opens a textile store in his big and generous house. Reb Eliezer Dorfman, a pure soul, turns his warm house into a place of prayer, and is adamant about releasing his clerks on Shabbat, festivals, and holidays, without exception. His wife, Mrs. Matala (Mitla), Z"L, a simple and God-fearing woman, receives all comers with kindness, like a good, compassionate mother.

Reb Yankev Leib Freidan organizes communal prayers, and his voice rises up above the others: "Oh come, let us sing unto the Lord; Let us joyfully acclaim the Rock of our salvation;" or, "Garb thee in raiment beseeming thy worth," though his clothes are worn and tattered. The soul strives for spirituality and Torah, and shared sorrow is half a comfort.

The aforementioned squire (the landowner) Karel Prycko employs Reb Yankel Leib Friedan, an honest and simple God-fearing man, as the manager of his property. Reb Yankel Leib Friedan is an able farmer, confident in his own skill, who has proven his ability to manage the estate, yet never for an instant forgets the plight of his troubled brethren. He disseminates Torah to the multitude, organizing a communal printing press, acquiring a Torah scroll for the community, and serving as its leader all the days of his life. And so that the children do not grow up neglectful of Torah, he seeks out teachers for the village, tests them, and supports them in their service.

Through the influence of Reb Yankev Leib Friedan, Prycko leases land to the Jews, gives them grazing grounds and stalls, and also gives them trade.

In addition to their meager trade, the Jews of the village also work a few Morgen[Ed1] of soil, raise cattle, and distinguish themselves as farmers. Again the false hope of normalization, peace, and tranquility of home awakens in them.

I remember the communal matzah baking, when I was still a little boy. All the Jews of the village participated. As if in a dream, the Seder nights pass before my eyes: reading the Haggadah, a guest in every home, a poor person from the neighboring village, reclining beside the family in fulfillment of the commandment "all who are hungry [let them come and eat]"… "We were slaves to Pharaoh in Egypt, and we built the store-cities…and we went out from there. …and here we are again in wretched exile. How long?..."Next year in Jerusalem!"

How we yearned for that homeland. How many tears flowed when we prayed to the Master of the Universe that "our eyes may witness Your return to Zion"—that the day would come when we would be farmers on our own earth in the Land of Israel, and not in this bitter exile, where we were like dung on the fields.

Many come to visit us from neighboring villages. Relatives forget to mock us as "hicks" when we make it known that village Jews do not differ from city Jews—their homes too are open to peddlers come from afar.

Holiday follows holiday, and joy follows joy. I remember the festival of Shavuot in the village, a true festival of spring. Houses were adorned in green, yards looked like forests, and the gentiles could not believe their eyes, seeing Jews rejoice on a land not their own. They lost no opportunity to bring this fact to the Jews' attention. This is the nature of Jewish joy: that it is always

Ed1   Unit of land measurement equal to .6309 acres.

diluted with sorrow. The Ukrainians "presented themselves" in the street in unruly mobs and the devils threw stones into Jewish homes.

Mourners sit with downcast eyes in the house of prayer. The benches are overturned, the men are barefoot, and the lapels of their clothing are torn. They bewail the destruction of the Temple. Sobs are heard from the women's section. Reb Yankev Leib Friedan, Z"L, opens up the book of Lamentations…

Emissaries come from Baron Rothschild, to see if the Jews of Lipica Gorna are truly farmers, bringing financial assistance with them. Help also comes from the American Jews. Cultural life returns to normal. Jewish children study in cheder. There are few Poles, and the big and beautiful school, built before World War I[Tr1], is without students, because the Ukrainians have proscribed it, and sought out different schools for themselves. In 1927, the Ukrainian national awakening begins, and they resume sending their children to the village schools.

The Poles return, remove their children from the common school, and set up a new one, which the Jewish children also attend. In practice, this is a Polish school comprised almost entirely of Jews. The Ukrainians see this as a betrayal and an act of complicity with the Polish enemy. Poverty and exploitation help to persuade the young Ukrainians that this is the case. An uprising against the Poles begins, accompanied by acts of provocation against the Jews. They begin to organize, establishing cooperatives, and the slogan of their boycott of Jewish goods is "Each to his Own." Their assembly hall becomes a center for propaganda against us.

The Days of Awe come, days of self-examination in matters between man and God, and between man and his neighbor. Leaders of prayer come from Rohatyn for the High Holidays, Reb Nechemye, or Reb Motsi (diminutive of Mordecai) the shochet (ritual slaughterer), and their affecting voices "break hearts." Jews who on ordinary days pull a plough, chop trees, and struggle for their subsistence, now come to understand the bitterness of their lot in wretched exile, where their honor is demeaned and their freedom stolen from them. And what is their plea to the Master of the Universe? Just a little peace and a piece of bread with salt. They never protest their difficult circumstances, and joyfully recite the blessing "Who brings forth bread from the earth." Who understood this blessing like we village-dwellers did? "Our Father, our King, fill our storehouses"—We repeat this prayer ceaselessly, because our situation deteriorates from day to day.

And for all the threats and persecution, the older generation never desists

Tr1 Text reads "World War II" but this makes little sense. I have assumed it is a mistake.

from their customs. "It is a mitzvah," my grandfather would say, "to begin building the sukkah on the eve of Yom Kippur." "Which sukkah?" I asked innocently. "The fallen sukkah of King David," he answered.

I still remember Simchat Torah at the house of Reb Eliezer Dorfman. The community acquired a new Torah scroll, so that it would not be without one. This was the only Torah scroll that survived the Bolshevik pogroms.

With what thrills of joy and love did we take note, we young people, of every letter of the Torah. How we rejoiced all through that night, singing Hebrew songs and feeling as though we were close to the Land of Israel, pioneers in one of its villages. That night many from Lipica Dolna joined our pioneer ranks, and a covenant was forged between the two Jewish settlements.

But our happiness is not long lived. The authorities disband the village council, which from 1928 has been dominated by the Ukrainians. The district governor chooses a Polish village headman and a Polish treasurer, against the will of the Ukrainians. The Ukrainians rebel, destroying public property, railroad tracks, and telephones, and they also burn private property and Polish farmsteads. A penal squad from the 51st battalion in Stanislawow, and a squad of young policemen from Poznan are activated in Lipica Gorna, at the village's expense, and these bands make use of the opportunity to pillage Jewish homes and assault Jews coming and going in the town. These are truly Days of Awe for us, in all senses of the word.

The winter goes and comes again and so too the fear and worry. Ukrainian youths go riotously through the village. One frosty night, their jackboots crunching the snow, they set fire to the house of Sara Poper, Z"L, and its four inhabitants are left naked, stripped of everything. In a few days, a "relief committee" is established to assist them. My mother, Z"L, Mrs. Matala Dorfman, and Mrs. Schweller organize a drive and gather new clothes, linens, beds, winter blankets, and so forth, and all of this is given as "secret gifts" so as not to injure, God forbid, the honor of the family. These were our "Yiddishe Mommas," their hands in everything, at all times and in all places: full partners in sorrow and worry, joy and festivity.

Some older children go to the surrounding cities to study in a gimnazjum. Their eyes are opened, and when they come home they will not keep quiet, and will not rest, and begin organizing the Jewish youth into Stam HaChalutz, HaShomer HaTzair, and Brit Trumpledor movements.[Tr2]

Tr2   These Zionist organizations can be translated as follows: "General Pioneers," "The Young Guardians," and "The Pact of Trumpledor." This last group is known familiarly as "Betar."

Among these founders, I recall Yechezkel Bratshpis, superlative in the study of Torah and many other activities. He was the one who brought the spirit of the pioneers to Lipica Gorna. He organized and handed on the activities of the K.K.L.[Tr3] and Keren Hayesod.[Tr4] A library was established, under the leadership of our dear friend Poper Z"L, who would neither rest nor be still till he had brought the whole young generation to read selected good books. His kind mother, Sara P., of blessed memory, after the restoration of her gutted house, offered us the use of it, and it became the site of our library, and our chapter of the HaShomer pioneers.

Many newspapers, in many languages, come to us every day. Pamphlets and all kinds of learning materials open our eyes and light for us the path we have chosen. Yechezkel Bratshpis, Z"L, does not rest on his laurels, but goes on to organize a drama club, into which he welcomes anyone who demonstrates even minimal singing ability. They put on a number of short plays from Jewish sources, and the proceeds go to the library, the movement, and to a reserve fund. Jewish youth from all around flock to Lipica Gorna, which is transformed into a spiritual and cultural center for the whole region. We establish strong ties with the nearby towns of Rohatyn and Brzezany. In summer and winter we hold meetings, joint hikes, and joint discussions on the future of Zionism and the aims of Jewish youth.

Can it be believed that in a village such as this many actually master the Hebrew language? Big and small alike sing Hebrew songs, and Hebrew poems and songs are well known to all the Jewish youth of the village. The chapter organizes a Hebrew club, and public lectures, led by Yechezkel, of blessed memory, on Jewish authors, and Jewish and Hebrew literature. The study of the Jewish histories of Graetz, Balaban, or Dubnow is required of all members.

The riots of 1929, and the news of them that comes to us through the Jewish press, cause us worry and dejection. We are all ready to join the struggle immediately, but the gates of Israel are locked. Illegal ships are returned and we are forced to wait until our hour comes, with prayers of peace for the Land and its Jews. Our mothers arrange a fundraising drive, serving both as donors and collectors.

In 1930, the first of our comrades go through kibbutz training. Our parents accompany us, filled with a joy mixed with fear. Will we be worthy? Will we make it? The skies of Europe are darkening. The black monster of the swastika is casting out its horror. What will happen? Will it come here too? What will become of us? Our hearts cannot possibly envision the events such as what

---

Tr3 "Keren Kayemet L'Yisrael": Jewish National Fund.

Tr4 "Foundation Fund."

actually came to be.

In 1933, Yankev Steinwurtzel (now Galili) is our first comrade to leave for Israel. His letters stir us, and the cry of "Come quickly, however you can," will not allow us to rest. After him, more of us immigrate to Israel.

A noisy train station, dear ones of all ages are singing, "We are going to the Land of Israel," but your heart cries, because you are being separated from those dear to you. Will you see them again? Tears of joy and sorrow intermingle. Hands press hands and hearts throb and plead, "Come, join us, for the enemy is at the gate!"

1933. Fascism rears its head. The madman proclaims his intention to conquer Europe, and the Jews above all else. The Jews of Lipica Gorna seem to set their worries aside and go on with their work in the fields, with the fattening of cattle, and with the bit of trade through which they eke out their living. The older children stay in the village, not wanting to abandon their parents. The war comes in an instant. The letters fall silent and the voices cease...

We are left adrift, bereft and lonely. We remain united with our dear ones, whose love and pleasantness never left them in life or death. Until the last of days we will remember the evil that the murderers did to us. We will remember our loved ones along with all the martyrs of Israel who were slaughtered without mercy and free of fault. Their blood cries out to all the world, and will not be still.

Jews in Lipica Gorna
By Ya'akov Glili (Steinwurtzel)

Translated by Binyamin Weiner - YB p. 360

I wish to summon memories of Lipica Gorna, the village where I was born and where I lived for twelve years. The name by which the village Jews were known is quite familiar: "Yishuvniks." If one wished to refer to another as a boor and ignoramus, it sufficed to call him "village boy" ("dorfs-yingl" in Yiddish.) There was some truth to this depiction, because most village Jews were terribly poor, and it was out of their arms' reach to bestow education upon their children. The distance from Jewish centers also exerted a negative influence, and when transportation was bad, these Jews could not allow themselves to send their children to the city. Besides, a child had to help his parents and at an early age was harnessed to the yoke of earning a living. Most were burdened with many children, and the traditional livelihoods of Jews in all places, and especially in the villages, did not allow for elevated lifestyles, let alone broad education.

Many leased taverns from the noblemen, or flour mills, or parcels of land. They also peddled all manner of haberdashery, maintained small shops, or traded in fowl and cattle. There were a few artisans scattered here and there, and some Jews even lived off tilling the land, but this was rare, since agriculture could not provide nearly as much as trade.

A few of the Jews who leased mills and property were quite wealthy. In the course of time, they even acquired their own mills and purchased their own property, though very few actually did this.

Despite their great poverty, the Jews spared no expense to provide their children with a little "Yiddishkeit." Several families would band together and bring a teacher from the city to teach the children the basic concepts of Tanach (Hebrew Bible), and teach them how to write a letter in Yiddish, and sometimes even in German. In the twenties, it was also customary to learn a little Hebrew, especially when the teacher was a young student who had been unable to complete his course of study for lack of funds.

In addition to the worries of livelihood and education, the Jews suffered further from a lack of security. There were schemes against Jewish property and plots against their lives. Often, bandits attacked the homes of village

Jews, robbing them and also setting the houses on fire, and the next day the Jews were without a cent or a roof over their heads. Even so, they could not go away to the city, lacking the means to do so. And so thousands of Jewish families lived in constant fear of tomorrow, worrying about security, livelihood, the fate of their children, and most of all the fate of their daughters, lest they be led astray, G-d forbid, to conversion.

According to the news that reached me, pertaining to the fate of these Jews in World War II, it seems that a portion of the village Jews were killed by Ukrainian hooligans even before the Nazi's systematic destruction began. Most were removed to the towns and placed in ghettos, and only a small number were able to hide in the forests, in bunkers, or here and there join the partisans, though the great number of these were murdered by the Banderowcy and only a few survived.

The picture I have drawn of Jewish village life portrays the reality that I knew in the village of Lipica Gorna. But on top of that, there was something special about this village that for several years served as a center for the surrounding towns. This was because of the founding of bubbling and seething Zionist pioneer youth movements. Thanks to them, the Jewish youth took on a new character. The charge was led by Stam Chalutz (General Pioneers), which was associated with the HaShomer HaTzair (Young Guardians) movement, and later by HaShomer HaTzair itself, led by older members of HaChalutz.

The youth began organizing in 1927/1928. A few young people, who detested the idle and stagnant life of the village, decided to found a Zionist youth organization. With the help of a friend from Podhajce, who happened to join the circle, they gave the village youth a chance to learn about Zionist issues, and founded a drama club that contributed to the independent cultural activities of the Jewish youth. With the proceeds from performances they founded a library and meeting hall that drew in scores of youth from a 40-kilometer radius. This was no small feat, considering the state of transportation in those days. In addition to plays, they held various benefits for Zionist funds, and memorials for men like Herzl, Trumpeldor, and so on. The village became a cornerstone, not just for the village youth, but for youth from surrounding towns as well. After the founding of Stam Chalutz, a group of youth broke off and started a chapter of Betar, but this contributed little to Zionist cultural activities, and none of its members immigrated to Israel. A Zionist meeting hall was established for the older youth, but its aims were hazy and unclear, and it did not last long.

At first, we had to struggle hard against old-fashioned beliefs, and the resistance of parents to sending their children to meetings of these organizations. But we triumphed over all these obstacles, with the help of people who saw the wisdom in supporting us. One of them was M. Schweller, the owner of a flour mill, who, though not a Zionist himself, still helped us as best he could. He was our shield and dear friend. I cannot possibly forget to mention my mother Rivkeh, Z"L, whose house was a meeting place for all the young people. At first my father stood to the side, but later he too helped us in all kinds of ways. Everyone who came to our house was received warmly, and though our voices rang out in debate late into the night, my mother, may her memory be blessed, did not disturb us at all. And mother Poper, who rented a room to our chapter, was just like her. With how much warmth and self-sacrifice did she worry over us, like a real mother? And when we went months without paying our rent, she would tell us laughingly, "So be it. If you don't have it, don't pay it." She even often lent us money to buy coal and firewood.

Apart from the regular activities, we read newspapers together in the chapter, and this was something of a novelty, because the newspaper had not previously been a regular guest in Jewish homes. But we also established more fundamental lessons in Zionist and socialist ideology. We were involved in every Zionist activity, beginning with collection work for the Jewish National Fund, and ending with the distribution of proceeds. In this service, we would wander far away, to the most remote villages, and were the first to bring something new to the village youth thirsting for activity. When there were congressional elections, Lipica Gorna became an election headquarters, and scores of youth would stream on horse or foot to the command center. All of these activities changed the nature of the youth of Lipica Gorna, and set them on the king's highway. Whoever was able began to attend secondary school in Rohatyn, but even in the village itself, the youth strove to acquire through independent study what they could not get in school.

I cannot record all the names of Lipica Gorna, and will recall only the few that contributed the most to the advancement of the youth. The Kornweitz family, one of whose sons, Yosef, Z"L, hid through the war in a bunker and was killed with his sister only a short time before liberation, served as a teacher for the children of Lipica Gorna, and began to spread Zionist ideology. And likewise, the writer of these lines was very much involved with the Jewish National Fund. Its beginnings in Lipica Gorna were humble, but with the rise of the youth movements it branched out and came to involve all the neighboring villages, until there was not a home without a J.N.F. contribution box. All the other young people also made their contributions to the youth organizations. The children of the Steinwurtzel, Kliger, Dorfman, and Fundik families played considerable roles in the Chalutz movement, being among the first to join, and they also immigrated to Israel in their turn. Most of the Chalutz members from Lipica Gorna went through training outside of Israel, but only some of them immigrated, whether legally or illegally. Two survived the war, and now live here in Israel. Most of them live on the kibbutzim of HaShomer HaTzair: Ramat HaShofet, Ma'arot, Ayn HaMiforets, Sharid, and K'far Meserik. The rest remained outside Israel, for lack of certificates or means to immigrate illegally. They were caught during the war, and put into the ghetto. Most of them did not want to abandon their parents, and perished with them…

I know that my brother Avraham stole out of the ghetto every week, went to the village, and brought back food for our parents, until he was caught by the Ukrainian Banderowcy. He was tortured cruelly for three days in the forest beside the village, until his soul departed, may his memory be blessed.

A small number of Jews from Lipica Gorna were able to hide in the forest, or in bunkers on Polish property. The Poles were a minority in the area and so were willing to help us, in contrast to the Ukrainians, who turned over any Jew they found to the German authorities. Thanks to the good relations that existed between Jewish and Ukrainian youth, there were never any murders in the village, but no help was offered either.

After the war, most of the survivors came to Israel, among them two daughters of the Schweller family, and only three immigrated to other lands.

Of the 25 families in Lipica Gorna, some 100 people or more, most perished in the Rohatyn ghetto. Today there are some 15 people from Lipica Gorna in Israel, and in addition, a few individuals from surrounding villages such as Lipica Dolna and others. All the immigrants from Lipica Gorna have integrated into the work and creative life of Israel.

It pains me greatly that such a small remnant remains of these deeply rooted Jews, all good Zionists, who with purity of heart believed in immigration and the building of Israel. Let these pages be a monument to the thousands of Jewish families who lived in the thousands of villages of Galicia, scattered among the Gentiles, their hearts simple and warm Jewish hearts. Whenever someone contested their views, they responded with understanding, and they devoted themselves to the cause of redeeming the Land of Israel and redeeming themselves.

May their memory be bound up in the life and the building of Israel.

The Rohatyn
Association

The Organization of Survivors of Rohatyn
By Zvi Skolnick, Tel Aviv

Translated by Binyamin Weiner - YB p. 363

About the Organization

Among the immigrants who came here when the State of Israel was established, there were many from Rohatyn and its vicinity. They have scattered throughout the land and have begun putting their lives back together after the terrible Shoah that befell the Nation of Israel during World War II.

In 1949, as a result of the efforts of organization member Zvi Fenster (Felker) and the writer of these lines, a decision was made to establish in Israel an organization of survivors from Rohatyn and its vicinity. The organization came into being, and the list of residents drawn up in Israel made it clear that there were some 200 survivors from Rohatyn and its vicinity here. At the start, the organization's regular activities extended only to the organization of yearly commemorations of the martyrs of our city, and to the dispensing of moral and financial support to those in need.

In addition, we undertook the following activities:

On Tuesday on the eight of Tammuz 5720 (5 July, 1960), we took sacks of earth from the three graves of our martyrs in Rohatyn, brought to Israel by the family of Dr. Avraham Sterzer, for burial in the cemetery of Kiryat-Shaul. (The grave can be found in block 4, zone 2, row 25, grave 19, between the graves of Natan Ben-Yaakov and Strinov.)

On the initiative of member Yehoshua Spiegel, the family names of the martyrs of Rohatyn were inscribed above the individual names on a parchment scroll by a sofer (religious scribes). In a special ceremony held on 20 July, 1961, the seventh of Iyar 5721, the scroll was placed in the memorial to the martyrs of Rohatyn on Mount Zion, in the presence of several score members of the organization.

In 1959, the board of the Survivors of Rohatyn and its Vicinity decided to bring out a book to perpetuate the memory of our city's Jews, who were devoured by the Nazis, to serve as an eternal light to their pure souls and as a tombstone on the unmarked graves of those whose dust was scattered in all directions. It was clear to the members of the committee from the start that the matter was enmeshed in difficulties,

397

such as the gathering of material, the raising of funds, and so forth. From 1959 to 1962, individuals from among the descendants of Rohatyn worked diligently to compile material, solicit essays of recollection, raise financial resources, and accomplish extensive organizational work. Their labor was crowned with success by the publication of this book.

***

In the name of the board of the Organization of Survivors of Rohatyn and its Vicinity, I express our deep gratitude to the son of our city Yehoshua Pinchas Spiegel, son of Rabbi Avraham-David Spiegel, may he rest in peace, for his efforts in bringing about the book "Rohatyn—The Life of the City and its Destruction."

In his work—which began with collecting material, raising money, establishing ties between survivors of our city in Israel and other lands, directing the composition of essays, soliciting sketches and essays of local color, and gathering photographs, and ended with the delivery of all of these materials to the editor and the printer—he was persistent and diligent. Despite the difficulties that stood in his way, he kept on until he reached the long-awaited goal.

This book of witness will be a candle to the souls of the community of Rohatyn and its vicinity. May the memory of those who were consumed by the German murderers be blessed.

Son of our city—congratulations!

> With esteem and appreciation,
> Dr. Avraham Sterzer
> President of the Organization

Commemoration held in 1961 in Israel. A. Milstein, Y. Green, Rabbi Dr. Nurok, Cantor Gelbstein, Dr. Yechiel Ben Nun, Yehoshua Spiegel.

Israeli Rohatyn Society meeting of expatriates from Rohatyn and its environs.

Grina Sterzer, her husband Dr. Abraham Sterzer, their son Menashe and Yehoshua Spiegel on the occasion of interring sacks of earth from the mass graves of the 1942 akcja and 1943 Judenrein. Mrs. Sterzer took the earth with her in 1945 upon leaving Rohatyn.

Israeli Rohatyn Society meeting of expatriates from Rohatyn and its environs.

Rohatyn Society in the U.S.A., Dr. Y. Lewenter and his wife Cyla (Bandler); Dr. Golda Fisher Joslyn and her husband Maynard Joslyn; Yehoshua Henne and his wife Gusi (Berlinger); Dr. Jack Faust and his wife Hedda (Waldinger); Zev (William) Halpern and his wife Rozia (Rosette) Faust Halpern. The surviving remnant.

In this caption, we designate for special praise (three of them); they are Dr. Yitzhak Lewenter, Dr. Golda Fisher, and Yehoshua (Sam) Henne (here on his visit to the USA), because, thanks to their contributions, this book could be published.

Additionally, we single out for praise the expatriate of our town, Rachel Straulicht (Sambor), who discovered owners of the many photos and edited them for this book.

Rohatyn Society in Israel dedicating a Memorial Plaque to those who perished in Rohatyn and its environs, in the Holocaust Chamber (Marteif HaShoah) on Mt. Zion.

English
Section

Rohatyn: A World Is Gone with the Wind
By Dr. Jack Faust

YB English Section, p. 7

I am writing this article for the benefit of the younger generation of "Rohatyner" who read and understand only English and consequently are not in a position to know what this book is all about.

This book commemorates the lives of our kinfolk who were all so inhumanely killed by the Nazis.

I will not dwell, however, upon the sickening subject of Nazi savagery of which everybody has heard, but instead will relate a page of the history of our town, as it was prior to World War II. It might give our second and third generation of "Rohatyners" in America an idea about our background and the life their parents and grandparents lived before they came to these shores, and perhaps help them to understand us better.

We all came from a town in eastern Galicia, called Rohatyn, not far from two great cities, Lwow and Stanislau (Stanislawow). In Yiddish abbreviation it was called "R'teen."

The name Rohatyn is derived from the Ukrainian word "Roh" which means a horn. The horn of an elk was the official emblem of our town, which was referred to in olden days as the Royal Free Town of Rohatyn. History has it that our town was founded in the year 1185, which is about 50 years before the English got their Magna Carta, and about the time of Moses Maimonides, one of the greatest Jewish philosophers. Now that we have the proper historical perspective, we will turn back to the life of the Jewish community in Rohatyn. Jews lived in Rohatyn for hundreds of years, practically from its very inception, as bits of information in various Polish and Ukrainian annals tell us.

It is interesting to note that in the days of the false Messiah, Sabbatai Zvi, there was a large and thriving Jewish community which prided itself on being among the most ardent followers of the "saviour." That is why the Rohatyner Jews were called the "Shabse Tzvinekes" by the residents of the surrounding towns.

Our town must have been built according to well-laid engineering plans. No hodgepodge of streets and little huts as in most of the towns in Poland and

Russia, but wide straight streets around a big square in the very center of the town. Facing the square were multi-storied brick houses and two monumental-looking churches, one Polish, the other Ukrainian. I particularly liked the two picturesque fountains on each side of the square, where people used to gather at all times of the day to fetch and drink water or just to "exchange news."

A helicopter view would have shown the beautiful scenery around the town, colorful fields, forests, a river, an extinct volcano known as the "Devil's Mountain," and the long, straight line of a well-kept highway, known as the "Emperor's Road." The "Kaiser Road," as some called it, was part of the main artery of roads in Galicia, which connected our town through Lemberg with the cities of Western Europe, and through Stanislawow with the bigger towns of east-south Russia. There was another connecting road, running north, which connected our town through Tarnopol with northeastern Europe.

No wonder Rohatyn became a center of business, which won it in the old days the status of a "Royal Free Town" and drew many merchants and farmers from all the surrounding towns and villages. As the Seat of County Administration (Starostwo) Rohatyn had under its jurisdiction over one hundred towns and villages, such as Bursztyn, Bukaczowce, Bolszowce, Stratyn, Knihynicze and many others. On a Wednesday, the day of the weekly fair, one could not find a place to park ones horse and buggy because all the municipal and private parking lots were filled to capacity.

Prior to World War I life in our town, characterized by the gaiety and conviviality of its people, was pleasant and easy. There were daily walks on the pleasant streets of the town, particularly the one leading to the railroad depot, called the "Koleiufka." All the streets in Rohatyn were lined with trees, but this one had a double line of trees, which made it a favored place for promenading. This was our "course," where one could see everybody, relatives and friends, have dates with boy or girl friends and walk and talk late into the night. These walks, which were a daily ritual in our town, are among the more pleasant memories I have of Rohatyn, but what made Rohatyn lively was its progressive youth.

Rohatyn's young people were well educated and well aware of what was going on in the wide world outside our town. There were two high schools, both coed, and a number of libraries, well stocked with books in different languages. One could always find a copy of a famous work of world literature, either in its original language or in translation.

There was a movie in town and I remember seeing "Quo Vadis," "The Last Days of Pompeii," and the "Exodus of the Children of Israel," a sort of "Ten Commandments," way back before World War I. There were theatrical performances, either by professional theater ensembles or amateur groups, of which there were a number in town. The amateur groups were usually composed of members of social and political clubs, like the "Eretz Israel Verein," which sponsored many a show in Rohatyn.

I remember particularly a performance called the "Shechite," (the Massacre) given before World War I, in which Pater, Bernstein, Wald, Meyer Lewenter and Miss Beder and Toni Loew participated. Meyer Lewenter, a brother of our Dr. I. Lewenter, gave a performance as a Shadchan which was long the talk of the town; it was simply unsurpassed by any professional comedian.

The First World War

All this "pastoral" life came abruptly to an end in August 1914, when the war broke out. Within a few weeks Rohatyn was invaded by the Russian Army, first looted completely and then burnt to the ground. Whoever could run away fled in panic before the Cossacks reached the town, but many remained and suffered hunger and privation. The Russians did not like the Jewish people and treated them as "Austrian spies." Consequently, before they were forced out by the returning Austrian-German army, they dragged away as hostages to Russia all the male Jewish population, old and young. Before they left, they also burned down the few Jewish houses that were left in the southern section of the town, called the "new town," first taking away anything they could lay their hands on.

The only adult men left in town were the Dayanim (religious judges); both the elder Henne (who has a son, Sam, living in Bayonne, New Jersey) and the younger, Spiegel (whose son Yehoshua lives in Israel). Both men led a group of terrified women and children who were running frantically in all directions away from the burning houses and flying bullets.

I remember that night of horror: the town on fire, street skirmishes between the retreating Russians and the advancing Austrian soldiers, and us, four little boys, my brothers Leo, Mundzio and Kalman and myself, walking the streets of Rohatyn. In the confusion which gripped the town we became separated from our mother and didn't know where to hide, so we walked the whole night, the streets a desert of ruins of burned houses, with no human beings anywhere.

Because of hunger, lack of shelter and the presence of the decaying bodies of dead soldiers, lying for days in the streets, an epidemic broke out and took hundreds of lives. First dysentery, then typhoid and then cholera. I remember people walking and then suddenly keeling over and other people running away from them. I lost my grandmother Rose and my beautiful little sister Goldele within 15 minutes of each other. When we ran to help our grandmother I heard my mother's cry, "Goldele is dead."

Town carts finally came and carted away the bodies and threw them into a pit, Jews and non-Jews together. There was no help, no doctors, no medications, no food, no water, except contaminated water. We lived from scraps of food found at army camps, and chunks of ice which we found in one cellar of a burned house. We all got sick too, but managed to survive by sucking ice chunks.

With the advancing Austrian army things came slowly to almost normal. People started coming back from Vienna and Prague and, what was most important, our male population came back from exile in Russia. I shall never forget the joy, the singing and dancing in the streets, when wives saw their husbands and mothers their sons. My father also came back on a short furlough from the Austrian Army, after having been wounded in one of the battles with the Russian Army.

Soon life began pulsating again in Rohatyn. Some houses were rebuilt, businesses were established, and we youngsters went back to school. It was a bit queer for me to sit among school children, because in the meantime I had "graduated" to the position of the man of the house, supporter of a family of six at the ripe age of 13. But giving up the status of a grown-up had its compensations. First, it meant being together with other teenagers. Second, I had to put on the uniform and cap which high-school boys in Austrian days were obliged to wear, and this made me look as elegant as an Austrian officer.

Things went well for a while, and soon we had our clubs and organizations functioning and new ones being formed. Of great influence was the newly-formed HaShomer, a sort of boy and girl scout organization, strongly oriented toward Israel. Originally we had a few kvutzot for high school students only, but the idea of the HaShomer caught on so fast that soon we had to open the doors to all Jewish boys and girls and to form more than a dozen "civilian" kvutzot.

My fondest memories of my youth go back to those years. Being together with a large group of young people and having a lot in common with each other meant a lot to us. Studying together, learning Hebrew, Jewish history, Jewish and Hebrew songs, created for us a world of special interest. True friendship blossomed among the Shomrim and Shomrot in these kvutzot and even today, when one meets a fellow Shomer in America or in Israel, there is nothing that can express our feelings of joy and happiness in seeing each other again.

Peace Came with a Bang

All these good times ended in 1918 when "peace" came. To us in Rohatyn peace came with a big bang. There soon was fighting again, but this time between the Ukrainians and Poles, both of whom wanted possession of the town. When the Ukrainians took over, they treated us fairly; when the Poles took over, they treated the Jews like second-class citizens. The goodwill of the Ukrainians was particularly demonstrated when the Petlura hordes, also Ukrainians but from across the Russian border, threatened to wipe out the entire Jewish population in town, as they did in other towns of Galicia.

The Ukrainians gave us permission to organize a militia and even supplied us with rifles and machine guns to defend ourselves. Almost overnight a self-defense group was organized, formed by Jewish ex-soldiers and members of the HaShomer, all under the command of Captain David Tuerkel. In those days we were proud to wear a blue-white armband with the Star of David, while patrolling the streets of Rohatyn. All of us were ready to fight and protect our families with our lives when the alert was sounded that Petlura's Cossacks were already in Bursztyn. Fortunately, the town's military authorities, with Professor Borys as commanding officer (he taught us mathematics in high school), rode out to Bursztyn to forewarn the Petlurowces to bypass Rohatyn because there was a hot reception waiting for them in town. They took his advice and our town was spared the fate of other towns like Bukaczowce, where the Petlura Cossacks maimed and killed many of our people.

Soon the Poles took over and we became Polish citizens, after having been Austrian citizens most of our lives and Ukrainian citizens in between. To us, Polish rule (or rather misrule) meant one good thing – it opened a window to the West and gave us a chance to renew contact with America. I shall never forget the first letters that arrived from America after a silence of five years. The first food packages and money that we received were actually lifesavers. Soon clothes packages began to arrive and we began to look like human beings again.

However, the good days did not last long. In 1920 the Russians came back again, this time as Bolsheviks, which meant Communists in those days. They promised us everything: equality before law and freedom from oppression, but started their rule by taking away everything they could lay their hands on, from the poor as well as from the rich. Again we had to suffer hunger and privation because there was no chance to earn a living or a possibility of getting any food. The Communists fed us with propaganda, meetings twice a day in the center of the town, and free newspapers. No wonder we considered it a great relief when the Poles came back, although we knew what to expect from them. At least there was a chance again to get help from America and to plead for an affidavit.

Many of our people left Rohatyn in 1920, soon after the Bolsheviks left. Our people emigrated wherever they could, a great number to America, some to Canada, South America and even to South Africa and, of course, to Palestine. The flower of our youth went to Palestine as chalutzim. Our Shomer organization suffered so much from this exodus to Palestine that soon afterwards, depleted of most of its members, it fell apart. Unfortunately, many had to remain in Poland …

Jewish community organizations did a lot in those days to make life a bit easier for those that could not leave the town. With the help of the Joint Distribution Committee the local Jewish Council (the Kahal) opened soup kitchens, where children of all ages got three meals a day. Food packages and clothes were distributed to needy families and some families were put on steady relief. Relatives from America helped to put us on our feet again, and their money helped to open up business and trade and to rebuild our houses again.

Slowly everything became normal again. The new houses which were coming up in town gave Rohatyn a new look. The houses were bigger and roomier and were all equipped with electric lights, lending Rohatyn the appearance of a modern, progressive town. Even the streets became lively again, with a semblance of the good old pre-war days. Jewish youth organizations became active again and by the joint efforts of the Eretz Israel Verein and ex-Shomrim produced a play, called "The Jewish King Lear." This was a sure sign of a "comeback" of social life, as evidenced by the fact that practically every Jewish family in town attended that performance. The show was followed by a dance, and the proceeds of the big affair were designated for the erection of a Jewish National House in town.

We needed a Jewish Center very badly. Most of our communal affairs, meetings, lectures, play rehearsals and weddings had to take place in the Municipal Bath building (in bood). Every day of the week there was some special activity going on in the Bath building, but on Friday the building had to be relinquished to bathers. Going to the Turkish bath on Friday was a weekly ritual, which few wanted to miss, not only because they needed a work-out on the hot benches, followed by a dip in the pool (the mikveh), but also because it was a chance to meet friends and exchange news. It was quite lively on a Friday in the Public Bath, and everyone had a lot of fun. For one thing, it made us forget what was going on in the outside world and on the streets, ruled by the Poles.

Life under the Poles

With anti-Semitism rampant all over Poland, Jews encountered discrimination in every field. Jews could get no job in government or private industry. All doors were closed to them, regardless of ability or qualifications for the job. There were quite a few Jews in Rohatyn who held positions in the Court, in the Income Tax Department and in County and Town Hall offices, but they were all squeezed out and replaced by Poles. Jewish shopkeepers and tradesmen were assessed with such exorbitantly high taxes that they could barely make a living. Many had to close their shops because it was impossible to carry on, and joined the jobless, walking the streets and looking for something to do but finding nothing. More and more people became dependent on help from America, and a letter from America with money was virtually the only source of income.

The Jewish youth were particularly badly hit. Finding themselves barred from colleges in Poland, they had to seek admission to colleges abroad, although few could afford it. However, they went, working hard at any job they could find in order to finish their college education. I was one of the first to go to Prague in Czechoslovakia, to study chemical engineering, although there was a Polytechnic Institute right in Lemberg. Although I passed the entrance examination with the highest marks I was turned down, only because of religion.

When I came back to Rohatyn in 1928 as a graduate chemical engineer, I found myself, like other Jewish fellows in town, and many thousands all over Poland, an "unwanted and superfluous Jew." The situation became hopeless and Jewish youth was restless, if not desperate. There were no cases of juvenile delinquency, but there was a trend to do something radical, and many of us older fellows were afraid youngsters would fall into the clutches of Communism. Fortunately, there were strong Jewish national organizations in town to take care of the younger fellows and to help keep them out of reach of the Communist soul catchers.

Among the new youth organizations was the HaNoar HaIvri, where gifted Jewish boys and girls found an outlet for their desire to be active. Boys demanding more direct action found a place in the Brit Trumpeldor Organization, which was inspired by Zev Jabotinsky, founder of the Revisionist Zionist Organization. For the older fellows inspired by the positive thinking of Zev Jabotinsky, there was the HaZohar. The HaZohar took in everybody, young and old, single and married people, and soon became one of the most active and strongest organizations in Rohatyn. Those who went in for sports and athletics were active in the Maccabee Jewish Soccer Club. Rohatyner

411

boys excelled in all kinds of athletics just like American boys and perhaps a bit more.

Under the capable leadership of their captain, Joseph Kartin (now a resident of Haifa), the Maccabee team became so proficient that they could take on any big league soccer club and come out on top. Many a soccer game was won by the Maccabee club, and Rohatyner Jews and non-Jews were very proud of their local team. The record has it that the local Polish team lost many a game to the Maccabees. Woe unto any local hooligan anti-Semite who dared molest any Jewish girl or boy in town! These boys could, and many times did, return better than they got.

The last affair that I attended in Rohatyn was a play, *Dos Groise Gevins*, by Sholem Aleichem. I organized the amateur group, directed the play and saw to it that the proceeds of the show and dance went to three favorite charities of mine, the Auxilium Academicum Judaicum, which helped out many Rohatyner college boys studying abroad, the WIZO, a Zionist Women's Organization, and the fund to build a Jewish Center.

Shortly afterwards, on a Sunday, I took my last walk on the Rohatyner course. I did not have to go to anyone's home to say good-bye, because everybody was, as usual, on the promenade.

I stopped at a house near the Sokol, where my life-long friend, Sam Spiegel, lived, married to Felka Schwarz. Half-jokingly I asked Sam why there were no children in the family. He answered seriously: "There is no future for Jewish children in Poland, what's the use of having them?" I reprimanded him for expressing such defeatist ideas, but Sam had a strong foreboding of what was coming, and he was right. When the Germans and the stormtroopers took over Rohatyn, the fate of our people was sealed. The whole Jewish population was massacred and only a handful escaped.

Jewish Rohatyn, where our kinfolk lived for centuries, was utterly destroyed, by the greatest devastation any people every suffered. To us, who survived by the grace of G-d, it is a lost world, gone with the evil wind. We carry on and attend to our daily tasks, but there is a pain and bitterness in our hearts which only those who suffered directly can understand.

There is no forgiving the murder of our parents, brothers, sisters, relatives and friends. We shall always remember our dearest as long as we live, and their memories will be holy in our hearts and minds. It is my fervent hope that our children and grandchildren will always remember their kinfolk who died as martyrs for Kiddush Hashem. Let us hope that this Yizkor Book, written in memory of Jewish Rohatyn, will help us remember the loved ones we lost.

Faust family picture taken at the Faust home in honor of Jack's engagement to Hedda Waldinger in 1931. Standing from left: Bertha Faust, Max Faust, Kalman Faust, Miriam Rothen Faust, Leon Faust, cousin Rachel Gelbert, and Cylia Blech Faust. Sitting from left: Jack Faust, Hedda Waldinger, David Faust and Devorah Loew Faust. Pictures of relatives hang on the wall behind them.

Shmuel Kartin and his wife Chanah (Widerker).

Joseph Wald (Vald) and his family.

Zosia Altbauer, Jetka Schafel.

Dr. Michal Gold.

Moshe Freiwald, Miriam Eiberhar.

A World That Was
By Dr. Golda Fisher

YB English Section, p. 18

No one lives forever! Individuals come and individuals go. Some have fulfilled a purpose in life and others have gone unnoticed. Some had much to offer, but were never given a chance, while others lived a long life with no aim or purpose. No one will ever fully understand the mystery of it all, and very few if any, of those who succeed us, will fully understand the agony and suffering of the millions of Jews whose dreams and hopes were so tragically cut short.

Those Jews who were born on the American continent, and have led a more or less protected life, have never fully known the sting of anti-Semitism or the frustrations of a hopeless future. Some may even feel "superior" because "it did not happen to them." Yet I, who have spent half of my life in Europe and half of it in America, can assure our future offspring, in America or in Israel, that the people of Rohatyn had fine men and women with high aspirations and brilliant intellects, with many wonderful ideas and ideals and with many inspired dreams of a brighter and more beautiful future in a friendlier world.

The intellectual life of Rohatyn was centered around the gimnazjum, which stood majestically in the center of our little town. Next to it was the other important structure, the town church. To us Jews, who comprised a majority of this town of 10,000 people, the fence around the church furnished a backdrop for a convenient meeting place. Here, in front of the fence, the Jewish youth gathered, discussing their problems, planning their future or whistling at us girls passing by.

If one stood there long enough, one could meet almost anyone in town and, since there were very few telephones in those days, it was an easy way to make dates, exchange books, plan meetings or just talk about a hopeless future. For even before the war and the ghastly slaughter to come, the future looked so very hopeless to most of the youths leaning against that fence!

Some of us, like myself, were fortunate enough to have the opportunity of studying abroad. It was not easy to be accepted at foreign universities, and its cost was prohibitive for most of our people with their meager incomes. To be accepted in Poland was almost out of the question. There was a

415

"numerus clausus" for medicine and its related fields at all Polish universities. Some Jews who were privileged to attend a Polish university were permitted to study law, but to the majority, only philosophy was open, with the dubious outlook of what one could do with it later. For how many Jewish teachers would Poland choose to employ? And so many a time, as I would pass these boys along the fence, graduated or about to graduate from gimnazjum, my heart would sink, knowing how little life had to offer them. After all, a girl can always get married and raise a family – but a man? To what avail were scholastic attainments or fine personality or good looks? Unless he had good connections or money to go abroad, his fate was sealed.

To follow in one's father's footsteps was rarely desirable. Most of our fathers were shopkeepers or artisans and could hardly eke out a living for themselves. The few who were professionals could hardly accept their sons as associates, and only the few well-to-do merchants could absorb their sons into their businesses. Consequently, at the important turn of life, when the boy became a man, he had only two alternatives: to keep his ideals and sacrifice his future or to "sell" himself in order to attain a profession. For it was obvious in our day that there was no need for any more merchants or artisans, and Jews were just not given a chance to be anything else. They even had very little chance to migrate, as Palestine was closed by the British and America was accessible only to those few who had relatives willing to serve as guarantors. Even for the latter there were many years of anxious waiting, as the Polish quota was a small one.

To "sell" oneself meant to get "hooked" or engaged, not to your childhood sweetheart or the girl of your dreams, but to that "lucky" girl whose parents had saved and slaved all their lives to scrape enough money together for a dowry. That dowry would either buy the young man a business, or, preferably, send him to a university abroad. It was a hard test of character for the young men, for many of them must have been tempted to desert their betrothed at the end of their studies and marry either the girls they always wanted or ones they met while studying abroad. I must say the majority came through with "flying colors" as they buried their beautiful dreams in order to fulfill their obligations. How lucky were the few boys whose parents could make the sacrifice to send their sons abroad without commitments, and how uniquely lucky was I that my father thought as much of his daughter as of his son. Thus I was given the chance to go abroad to study medicine and not "sold" to some potential doctor. I should explain here that, although Polish Jews were barred from studying medicine in Poland, they were allowed to study abroad. Then, provided they could pass a rigid licensing examination, they were permitted to practice in Poland. This regulation, understandably, closed the medical profession to all but the exceptionally brilliant. To the generous decision of my father to send his daughter to medical school in Vienna, I feel I owe my life.

My lovely younger sister Ania was not old enough to receive the same chance as I. With her rare beauty, her brilliant intellect, her charming personality, what a contribution she could have made! And I think sadly of several girlfriends who might have had the same opportunity as I if only their fathers had the wisdom and foresight of my parents. Particularly I think of Mina Mandel, whose father Lipa was a wise man but who chose to marry her off instead of sending her abroad.

Others of my girlfriends who finished "matura" had little choice, for they had little means. I feel particularly for Helka Landau, strikingly beautiful and so eager to "drink from the cup of life." And Lonka Holder, with her great charm and wisdom and her constant, friendly smile. And what about all other girls who never had a chance to go even to high school? I knew them all in our Zionist organization, which was the only hope for a better future and which gave some substance and meaning to our existence.

We were mere children when we were drawn into the movement. Little did we know that Israel would really take shape in our lifetime. To all of us Israel was a reason to exist, something to work for, and our Zionist meetings were our Scout Clubs and country clubs, social dances, summer camps and, most of all, a place to keep all of us out of trouble. Whoever heard then of juvenile delinquents? We had too much to do and to plan for, so much work to do to bring our ideals to fulfillment.

We must have matured very fast, for our discussions were on lofty planes. We covered Jewish and Zionist history and world politics. Between the ages of fourteen and sixteen years my brother and I, with other friends, organized Zionist chapters of HaNoar HaIvri and Keren Kayemet L'Yisrael (J.N.F.) and even assumed leadership. Naturally, we had our fun too! What wonderful community singing and dancing and what beautiful hikes! No, we did not need chaperones and our parents did not need to worry. Neither did any of the shy girls or boys need to worry about "girl meeting boy" or getting a date. We were all in it together, through thick and through thin, and someday we were all going to build a better world. Only it did not happen that way! Very few really saw their dream come true with a Jewish State born and with it the rebirth of Jewish dignity. The majority were thrown to the wolves of human cruelty, beastly sadism while a world of "fine people" looked on and remained aloof.

Gone are the many synagogues and the many people who walked so humbly under G-d. A great culture has been buried forever in Rohatyn, no less than in all the other cities. Gone also is the mysticism, the romanticism of the Hassidic group which I loved so dearly. How many children nowadays know the joy and exaltation of dancing with Hassidim and their Torahs on Simchat Torah? Never have I seen a jollier crowd at any dance anywhere. And to think that these men were just lost in the Talmud, plain fanatics, would be sheer nonsense. I still see their faces burning with desire for a better world, frantic at times and so warm and hopeful at others. Often I "traveled" with them into the higher spheres, exploring the stars and the heavens. So often, however, were they "down to earth," interested in that outside world which I, but alas! not they, was later to see. How beautiful and heartwarming were their tunes and melodies, expressing all they did not dare to express otherwise. And there were the "geniuses" among them, too: some who were fine scholars, others who were good teachers and others who had rare talents for something even as abstract as mathematics. How well I remember that tall Hassid with his long grey beard, solving mathematical problems for us students of the gimnazjum.

How much "richer" were we students of the gimnazjum, who kept our roots in the culture of our forefathers, filling our hearts and minds with their great heritage. How hard must it have been for the few "assimilated," those who preferred the ranks of the Polish intelligentsia, to accept their final horrible fate. What a pity that the few Jewish professors we had were so insecure in their positions that they never dared to be one of us. Some of them were as despicable and corrupt as our non-Jewish professors, forcing Jewish parents to give bribes to enable their children to enter the gimnazjum or to pass their examinations, particularly the "matura."

An Englishman once said to me that every country has the kind of Jews it deserves. How very true! Yet Poland did not even deserve the kind of Jews it had in return for the kind of treatment it gave them. There should have been many thieves and many more cheats. Stealing from the government was a "mitzvah" and cheating at examinations was almost a "must." While a non-Jew had to be terribly dull not to pass, a Jew had to be exceedingly bright to pass without cheating or bribery. Many a professor thought nothing of acquiring merchandise at a store belonging to the parents of a pupil and never paying for it. If a bill was sent, the pupil was sure to flunk out. I'll never forget the courage of my dear father, who went to the house of the mathematics teacher to demand money or the return of his merchandise. My brother was a mathematical "genius" in those days and there was no chance of his failure. So many years have passed and I still bitterly resent the "bleeding" of Jewish parents for good marks for their children. Can you then imagine the sweet joy and the exaltation when, on the morning after "matura" (graduation from high school), our Jewish orchestra (The Faust brothers) would awaken you with the joyous tunes of Jewish melodies? I do not think that any serenade ever sounded sweeter. And yet, how many of those who finished gimnazjum ever had a chance for further education?

Yes, the Fausts played at "maturas," and they played at the weddings. They played after the Yom Kippur fast and on any occasion when they might earn a zloty. One of them, who was our violin teacher, often told me about the adventures of his past. He had been in the great land of America and had a chance to marry a rich girl there, but he preferred to come home and to marry the girl he loved. He often wondered how wise it had been. Could he have foreseen his end? And what a hard job it was to teach kids like us all day and play at social functions all night! On Yom Kippur, when all of us would run home from synagogue after the Fast to rejoice with our families over the delicacies prepared for the occasion, the Fausts would run home to get their violins and go from house to house, playing happy tunes to wish those who could afford this "luxury" a happy New Year.

In spite of the usual faults of mankind, our people were a benevolent group. They always helped each other out and hardly ever did anyone really starve or go into bankruptcy. In no place have I ever seen so much money lending and borrowing so that some poor man could continue to make a living. No beggar was ever turned away and no one would ever go hungry on the Holy Sabbath or on a Holy Day. Seldom did we have a Friday evening without a stranger to share our meal, and it was my task, as a little girl, to watch at the window to see whether father was walking home with someone. On Saturdays I used to count the number of men he brought home for Kiddush. It was a good thing that our dear mother was a willing and happy hostess who was always prepared. During the week, too, most of our friends would pop in and out, to study or exchange books, etc., and our home was always an open one. From my mother I must have learned to have an open house for all our friends and visitors at all times and from my father I must have acquired the urge to travel. And from him, too, I learned the many beautiful songs, both Hebrew and Yiddish, which I cherish so much. My father had a beautiful voice, and when he was given the honor of chanting the prayers on the High Holidays, everybody in the synagogue used to rejoice. Most of all, we kids rejoiced, for as a token of appreciation, we used to receive a big basket of rare fruits, and so the High Holidays became doubly joyous for us.

Now all the synagogues are destroyed and all the Jewish homes taken over by people who hated us just as much as the Nazis, people who also participated in "heroically" capturing, torturing, and finally killing the frightened children, their horrified mothers, the weak and the old as well as the few survivors who had some strength after years of starvation but were hopelessly outnumbered. I have heard from some survivors that the hopelessness was even greater for those survivors whose entire famlies were wiped out, leaving no one to remember them. May this book be a consolation to them and a testimonial that the names and sufferings of their loved ones are not forgotten and live imperishably in our memories. If when the end came, my parents and my sister found some consolation in the fact that my brother and I were safe in another land, I am grateful.

But how can we, the survivors, ever find consolation? Perhaps some comfort can be found in the hope that out of the shock produced by this monstrous Holocaust there will emerge such a revolution against man's inhumanity to man that future generations may never know the scourge of unreasoned hate and savage brutality.

Mina Mandel and Golda Fisher.

In Memoriam

By Morris Grant

YB English Section, p. 25

Memorials deal with death. There is nothing sadder than death. Death comes to all of us by the inevitable process of years or accident or violence. When the final day arrives, sometimes a summary is made by the remaining living. These are the questions they could ask. Did the deceased serve his country, his fellow man in some way? Did he ever bring joy to someone's heart? Did he help someone who was desperately in need? Did he do any good?

When we ask these questions about the people from our town we can truthfully answer in the affirmative. As we mourn the passing of our relatives and friends, let us discuss the good they did in their lives.

The Granowiter family: Nachman-Shlome, Berta, Tzvi, Azriel, and Ita.

We had many young people organized in Zionist organizations whose aim was the spiritual and physical preparation for immigration to Israel. The daily work in the Zionist organizations, which included rigid training in summer camps and on farms, created the hard core of the future sturdy citizens of Israel. It was

421

difficult to be an active member of a Zionist organization and at the same time attend the state gimnazjum. The school authorities and the local police kept a watchful eye and close vigil on Zionist "revolutionaries." The daily living habits of our young people made it hard for them to adjust to farm work. Their days were long and hard from sunrise to sunset and their work included manual labor as well as studies. They suffered but persevered. Some succeeded in reaching Eretz Yisrael and contributed to the building of the Jewish state, but most of them fell before they could reach their goal.

The people of Rohatyn always helped needy people, no matter where they came from. I can still see passing before my eyes the caravans of wagons of displaced people going by our town and asking for help. Our citizens formed committees, collected money and helped the needy. I remember how my father, who was on the committee, spent all his Sunday afternoons helping to take care of the poor and needy. The good deeds of our people were numerous. They gave of their time, effort and money without looking for recompense. Is it not therefore appropriate for us, the living, to pause and express our praise and admiration for these brave, good people, who were murdered without anyone coming to their help.

Shimek Teichman, Manke Straulicht (Shtrolicht), Nachman Rosenstein, Golde Fisher, Bentzion Freundlich.

422

A Diary of the Rohatyn Ghetto
By Rosa Halpern (Faust)

YB English Section, p. 27

June 24, 1941

This day will always be engraved in my memory. It was the beginning of the terror – the unending wailing of the sirens, screaming airplanes, bombs, fires, and above all, the fear of the unknown.

Wednesday: Unaccustomed silence. We don't hear the motors any more, nor bombs exploding. It is silent. I feel as if something is strangling me, something terrifying and powerful. It's so hard to keep from crying out. But who would hear? And who would help?

. . . . Thursday: They've come. On high horses, all of them tall, with clear but bitterly hard eyes. Without noise: only the plodding of the horses' feet sounded our knell.

. . . . Friday: All day long they are catching Jews to clean up the city. They are paid with the stick and the end of the rifle, with whatever they find at hand. Without consideration for gender, age or status.

Saturday: We're hungry. Someone brings news that they are giving out white bread. We run fast. Mother comes back happy. She was lucky. But her joy is soon spoiled. Someone is groaning on the stairs; it's father. He has been beaten. Father's story is interrupted by an inhuman shout. We run to the window. By the wall of the house opposite, behind the shul, Rabbi Teumim, Rabbi Spiegel, Amarant, Freiwald, Dr. Goldschlag and Rotbaum – all the officers of the Kehilah, are standing with their hands in the air. Local hooligans are standing opposite them and beating them as hard as they can. And at the same time they are shouting: "Now's the time to pay you back!"

My father stopped groaning and continued his story: "We were standing in line, quietly, without paying any attention to the provocations and insults. Suddenly one young fellow, practically a child, began to shout: `Jews to the fire!' That was a signal. Someone gave me a blow with a rifle butt, somebody else began to punch me and spit in my face, while a third urged me to bring the fiddle in order to play for the occasion. 'It's a big day today,' they laughed to each other."

Someone knocked at the door: "Give some soap, coffee and cocoa so that

423

we can ransom the hostages by the wall."

That's the way hell began.

In town everything was still chaotic. In their retreat the Russians had taken apart everything they could. Now the Jews had to clean up everything: the ruins after the bombardment, the broken windows, the broken wagons and autos. Every Jew, regardless of status, was taken to work. Jews who held official positions were required to hand over their keys and to resign. Shops were confiscated without appeal. Doctors, dentists, lawyers no longer waited for clients. For the Jews everything was closed and forbidden, even the right to go to the market.

The homes of the wealthier Jews were taken over by the army. They were given a half-hour's time to take themselves off. Every day Germans and Ukrainians fell on Jewish homes and took away any clothing or furniture they want. And woe to anyone who resisted.

September 5:   Advocate Alter and Professor Kartin have been arrested (to square private accounts). Mrs. Banner was beaten bloody by the barber across the street, in payment for many years of service and credit.

This month an order was published requiring the Jews to remain within the limits of the ghetto allotted them and to wear the degrading armband.

The Judenrat: In order to prevent the personal contact and the unending snatching of workers, as well as the robberies, the Jews elected a committee. Its members were mainly the former elected members of the Kehilah.

The Jewish workday began in different ways, depending on the demands of our rulers. In addition to organizing the work battalions, the Judenrat had to issue the special orders which marked the different days, as for example:

Fur-day: all Jews were ordered, within 24 hours and under the penalty of being shot, to hand over all women's and men's furs, children's sheepskins, and even fur collars.

Silver-day: In addition to the monetary contributions which all the German-Ukrainian officials demanded as bribes, all silverware had to be handed over, again with the threat that the failure to do so would mean an immediate death penalty.

The Judenrat became the spokesman for the Jews towards the outside world. It did everything it could to cancel the orders concerning the ghetto and the armbands, but nobody could do anything.

The removal to the ghetto took a few weeks. A lot of arguments and authority had to be used to move the Ukrainians and the Poles whose homes were now within the borders of the ghetto, though they received fine Jewish homes in return.

Sorrow, personal problems (who would live with whom?), and constant sensations such as the shooting of the wealthy Mr. Reiss, the tearing of the beards of elderly men and rabbis, the beating of Blech, the throwing of Rabbi Eliezer'l into the open privy, these were our daily portion.

It was dangerous to go out into the street, to remain at home, to go to sleep, just to live. The ghetto was filled with terror, tears and tragedy.

In January someone spread the news that a German auto with SS men had gone through the town. Engineers with maps and instruments were looking for a place for a new tile factory.

Afterwards, every day additional groups of men began to dig ditches. The town mayor himself personally directed the strenuous work. But the work went on at a slow pace. The snow, the frozen ground and the unfit workers didn't make it possible to attain the desired results.

In the freezing weather the Jews were ordered to undress half-naked and to work without a break. It became harder and harder to gather the contingent of workers that the Germans demanded. Workers returning from the forced labor did so beaten and sick. Finally they bribed the mayor not to be present at the work. The work gradually drew to a close. The engineers measured and calculated and the Jews prepared to build the tile factory.

Friday, March 20, 1942: From 6:30 in the morning we have been hearing people rushing about in various directions. Suddenly shouts and shooting. Mrs. Green comes running into our house and shouts: "Hide, they're shooting!" My cousin grabs her children and is the first into the cellar in the garden. Itche Hochberg's family follows them. They were so afraid that they nailed the door shut and we couldn't open it from the outside.

We run across the garden. From all sides we are warned from the windows to hide ourselves because they are shooting.

"Why?" Mrs. Katz asks me.

But without trying to answer I run to my parents' house. I barely have time to convince them to hide. There isn't much to decide: the cellar is without a bit of air. We wait ... We hear an order: "Come out!" Someone utters, "Sh'ma Yisrael ..." The others are struck dumb.

Amarant and other men had remained above. We hear blows and loud commands. Some women explain that their husbands are at work and the Germans answer: "Good."

They go away, after leaving a sign on the door, that the house is "Jew-free." We were saved from the first massacre, which continued until night. In the evening the snow was stained red ... Everywhere, in the streets and in the houses, dead people lay: men, women, young and old, children and infants.

That's how we made our acquaintance with the word akcja.

The first akcja in our town had been organized and planned to the least detail ... The ditches dug for the tile factory served as graves for three thousand Rohatyn Jews.

Gestapo men from Tarnopol had first surrounded the ghetto and then searched every house. Those trying to run away were shot.

People didn't believe what was in store for them; until the last moment they persisted in the illusion that they were being taken away to work camps. The Willig family stood in front of their house with a suitcase in hand and waited to be taken away. Sophia Schumer had wondered whether to take along her sewing machine and her Vienna diploma. Dr. Schumer-Teitelbaum had begged permission to be together with his little daughter. Permission was very generously given and both were shot with the same bullet.

The others were stood in rows, four abreast, and ordered to march towards the town square. When the whole group had gathered, they were ordered to kneel. The bestial game had begun.

Beards were plucked out. The unfortunate pharmacist, Lustig, had a pail of water put on his head and he was beaten with rifles. Then they remembered that doctors and dentists had the right to stand aside... They might still be needed... For some it was unfortunately too late. But Dr. Kreizler, Mrs. Katz, Rotbaum, the Freiwalds and some others who displayed enough energy and orientation managed to escape. Those chosen were separated and the others were loaded on trucks like beasts and carried away to destruction.

At the edge of the ditches the jewelry and the clothing of the victims were taken away. Then the shooting began. Dead and wounded fell into the graves. Some jumped in alive, hoping that they would be able to save themselves in that way.

There were some cases of people coming back. Among those who were buried alive and managed to return was the mother Leah Jupiter (Chana), who returned with frozen hands after she had lain in the ditch several hours. My best friend, Leah, had lain there as if she was fast asleep. Rega and Niusha (Nusia) Weintraub had been slightly wounded and had lain in the ditch calling for help. But no one was in a position to help them. The ditches were deep and they were unable to move under the weight of the dead bodies.

At night distracted mothers wandered about looking for their children. Men looked for their wives. Sometimes a live person was found among the corpses... Every house had its victims and had suffered the tragedy.

In the morning and for the next few days a group of Volksdeutsche (ethnic Germans born and/or living outside of Germany) rode about the ghetto gathering the furniture and other belongings of the murdered people.

In secret the Jews gathered the dead bodies and attempted to bring them to a Jewish grave. The order was to throw them into mass graves, to pour on gasoline and burn them!

The 20th of March 1942 – the first joint grave of Rohatyn Jewry.

The Death Of Chaimke

By Sylvia Lederman (formerly Sheva Weiler)

YB English Section, p. 32

Everyone of us who has remained alive after this terrible war asks himself: "Why was I chosen out of the entire family? For what was I rewarded? For what offense were they destroyed?

These questions will never find a reply.

Perhaps those who remained alive were left to remember those who perished so cruelly and to be able to tell the world how and why they died.

Whether we are alone or among friends, no matter about what we talk, the first or last subject will always be: Where did you save your life? Whom did you lose? The events we passed through follow us wherever we go. We are living with a past that can never be forgotten, with memories of family and relatives; we remember the dates of their births and the dates of their deaths. We often think that at least somebody has remained to mention their names, to cry, to light a candle on their memory day, to think about them always. But how many families perished entirely, without traces, without anyone remaining to recall their names, which are now forgotten for eternity? Families that lived in Rohatyn for so many years; children and grandchildren were born in this little town; the people used to help each other, they used to help the poor and the sick and suddenly they disappeared without a trace.

One of these many families was the Wiener family, who were my relatives. Hersh Wiener's wife, Rivka, was my mother's elder sister. I would like to describe the life and death of a Jewish family in Rohatyn.

There were two little houses near the old synagogue. In one of them lived Yidel Blotner with his wife and daughters; in the neighboring one – Hersh Wiener with his wife, his daughter Glikl and his son Chaim (Chaimke).

Yidel Blotner was my grandfather's brother. Both of Blotner's elder daughters, Esther and Gittel, belonged to the HaChalutz (the Pioneer). Thanks to that, they immigrated to Palestine prior to the outbreak of the war. The younger daughters, Tauba and Chawa, remained at home. All the sisters dreamed of meeting in Palestine. Unfortunately the war broke out and Tauba and Chawa were moved in the ghetto.

The Blotners were related to the Wieners and they used to live like one family. The houses were always full of girls and joy, and noisy like a beehive.

On the way home from school I used to call and play with Chaimke and to ask what the girls planned for the evening. That was how we lived until the war.

In the ghetto the Blotners were attached to another family and the Wieners were given one room near the electric station, where they lived with their daughter, Glikl, her husband and two children, their son Chaimke and Mr. Wiener's sister. Eight persons in one room were compelled to be satisfied without any right to complain. To whom … ? The food which they obtained with difficulty was divided among all and they lived from day to day; perhaps the next day would be better. My sister Roza and I often visited Aunt Wiener and tried to help them, sometimes bringing a hot dish for the children. Chaimke visited us often; we loved him like a brother.

Winter approached, with the troubles of lack of wood, lack of clothing, hunger. Uncle Weiner did everything he could to bring something home. His son-in-law helped him, since he came from Bursztyn (Burshtyn) and had some good friends among the farmers. It was dangerous for a Jew with a red beard to leave the ghetto for the village or market to buy some food, and he was often beaten or stoned.

I succeeded in "organizing" some flour and potatoes and mother decided to prepare pancakes to make a holiday for Chaimke, who liked them. Chaimke came to visit us. We resided at Yoina Nemeth's, which was quite far, but he came by side streets. Hot pancakes were spread on a plate.

"Aunt Gittel," Chaimke asked, "pancakes in the ghetto? Where did you get them?"

The child had tears in his eyes. He did not eat but gulped the food.

"You will be sick," mother said, "eat slowly."

But he couldn't; it was so long since he had eaten something tasteful.

"What a pity that Nuchem and Yidel haven't come," he said, remembering Glikl's children.

"You can bring them some," mother said.

Chaimke was happy. He sat for some time and described how his father tried several times to call on farmers he knew for some food, but had returned with empty hands because they were afraid to let him in.

"How long will it continue like this?" he wanted to know. "Will this war end soon? I would like to return to school. Why are we so mistreated, only because we are Jews?"

Chaimke was about twelve years old and could not understand. He asked questions to which we had no answers. He wanted so much to help his parents, his sister Glikl and her children. Nuchem was five years old and Yidel perhaps one year.

Evening approached. It was freezing cold outside. Chaim did not want to go home, but we had to take him because his parents would be worried. I gave him my sweater and warm gloves, a shawl and also woolen stockings, because his were torn. Chaimke thanked mother for the pancakes and promised to come again the next day. He took the dish for Glikl's children.

"When I grow up," he said, "I will take revenge." He did not know that this was his last visit and that there would be no tomorrow for him. He left happily and we escorted him to his house.

Glikl was thankful that she had something to give the children for supper and sighed: "How long are we supposed to suffer like this?"

On our way home we also called at the Teichmans, because Libcia was my best friend. Again we talked a little and I promised Libcia that we would meet tomorrow and perhaps go together to exchange something for food. That was my last meeting with Libcia.

With speedy steps we went home. Mother waited for us uneasily. We told her how thankful Glikl had been for the pancakes and that Chaimke would come the next day. We had decided to keep him with us if he agreed. We talked a little and called at the Nemeths to hear some news, as Yoine Nemeth often went to the Jewish Council to inquire about the ditches which had been prepared a few weeks before. These ditches were dug by the Rohatyn Jews and they worried us extremely. Some said they were for a brick factory, others said they were for shelters, and jokingly, we used to say that perhaps they were for ourselves, although nobody believed that this could be serious in the 20th century.

It became late, everybody went to bed. Nemeth and another neighbor had guard duty that night so we took off our clothing. We usually went to sleep dressed so as to be ready for escape if something happened. Very early in the morning I heard firing and jumped from bed towards the window. The Gestapo was dragging somebody by his beard, children were crying, and I shouted, "Mother, sister, let us escape, they are shooting and murdering."

It was cold outside, with high snow and frost – the 20th of March 1942. I ran to the toilet, my sister after me. We heard shooting, the steps of the Gestapo men, with their heavy military boots. My sister, who was always frightened, was crying and feverish.

"Stay here," I said, "and I will escape to …"

I did not succeed in finishing the sentence. I removed the yellow stripe from my sleeve and put it into my pocket. Dressed in my pajamas and wearing my woolen slippers, I ran in the direction of Kryska. I could not stay there to my regret and escaped from there towards Babince. I heard shouting, shooting, but I did not care. I was running as fast as I could. Near a forest at Kudcy I saw a little house far away. When I came near it, I fainted.

When I opened my eyes, a woman was standing by me and praying. She had dreamt that night that some trouble would come and that somebody would ask for help, and here I was. She had taken me into the house. I was completely frozen. She began to cook something. I looked through the frozen window and saw a Gestapo man and two Ukrainian policemen coming towards the house. I did not think too long and without saying anything to the woman jumped onto the stove and hid behind some bags which were lying there. After some time somebody knocked at the door. The woman had not even noticed that I had disappeared and called out, frightened.

"Who is knocking?"

"Police!" I heard. She opened the door. The policemen entered and asked her about a Jewess in a green coat. She did not know what to say.

"Look here," she showed them, "there is nobody here." I was lying on the stove, burning now after having frozen a little while before. My head hurt terribly. The policemen searched in the bed, under it, in the closet. They sat a while and then left. The woman remained alone with her grandchild in her arms, hardly knowing what to think. After some time, half alive, I freed myself from the rags. She cried out in astonishment:

"It is a miracle, a miracle of G-d!"

I passed the night in the stable, with the cattle, because she was afraid to keep me at home. Next day I was given her daughter's dress and I returned to town. According to her husband it appeared that all the Jews had been killed and I decided to return. How could I help it? I had left everyone in the ghetto.

I was walking slowly, with my head bent. Far away, near the Red School, I saw somebody coming closer. Tyla Nemeth, pale, with a parcel under arm, called quietly: "Sheva, Sheva! …"

"Tyla, are you alive?' I asked her.

"Yes," she replied. "Father was taken and thrown into the pit with an injured leg. He made himself appear dead but at night he freed himself of all the dead bodies over him went naked to a farmer acquaintance. In the morning the farmer came to the ghetto in order to fetch some clothing for him."

"Mother and sister, what happened to them?"

"They think you were killed"

"Are they alive?"

"Yes, your mother was standing in the cellar, behind the door. There was shooting but the bullet passed near the door. At the last moment your sister jumped into the toilet, where she sank up to her elbows. She cried for help during whole night and at dawn she was pulled out."

I did not ask anymore. I did not know whether to be happy or to cry. What difference did it make? The end was sure, sooner or later. As I came near the ghetto I recognized a frozen body. It was Margulies' son, with his hat frozen near his body. Then I noticed a big body in a fur. Mendel Hutter's father was lying in his son's winter coat, covered with blood, I had reached the vicinity of our house. From far I saw my cousin Anka bent over the earth. I did not see the body, but when I came near I heard her calling: "Sheva, look this is my mother." There was only a part of the head, with the hair frozen to the earth. Anka was crying and nearly mad, and we cried together.

When I entered the house I found Felker's mother lying on the floor. I stepped over the body and was inside the flat. My sister looked at mother, my mother at my sister.

"She is alive," she said. Mother did not even move, but said:

"Happy are the ones who have already met their fate. Nothing good awaits us."

"Mama, we must save our lives," I cried. "The Gestapo has already left, let us save ourselves, let us escape from the ghetto."

"G-d wants us to perish, we must perish!" Mother exclaimed. Sister did not speak. She only made some signs and showed me the wounds on her body and face. She was still terribly dirty from the toilet.

"Mama, Chaimke was to come yesterday to finish the pancakes," I said.

"That was before yesterday, do not go," she replied. "Perhaps they are not alive."

I did not wait too long and escaped from the house. It was quiet outside, like after a battle. Nobody was to be seen on the ghetto streets, which were splattered with blood. Passing by, I noticed a few dead bodies, but unfortunately I could not recognize them. I came near the Wiener's house, my heart beating strongly. Who knew what was waiting for me there! The door was open. I went into the house, the closet was open, everything was overturned, the furniture, old utensils, nothing was in its place. I began to cry, to call out, but nobody answered. I ran through the court, calling names, but in vain.

I remembered that uncle always used to say that if something happened he would hide himself in a stable belonging to a Polish woman living near the ghetto. I went in the direction of the railway station. It was not far and after some minutes I was there … When I knocked, a frightened woman's voice answered. She was afraid to let me in. I told her quietly that I was a relative of Wieners and she opened the door. I could tell from her face that something had happened. When I asked her if she knew something about Wiener she sighed, and I began to cry and to beg her to tell me the truth. Without speaking she took me by my hand and brought me to the stable. There were two bodies. Uncle

Hersh was lying stretched out on the ground and Chaimke lay near him with his head on his father's chest, as if his father wanted to continue pressing his son to himself. I was crying terribly.

"Chaim!" I repeated several times, but there was no reply. He was wearing the sweater and stockings I had given him two days ago. I could still hear his voice asking:

"Why are we so mistreated, only because we are Jews?"

He was still young and could not understand. When he was born he was given the name "Chaim" which means life.

The Polish woman was crying: "Such nice people and so cruelly murdered ..."

"What happened to my aunt, her daughter and the children?"

"They were apparently taken together with the others, as somebody saw them on the market assembled for shooting."

I looked again at the two innocent bodies and we left. I returned home. Here I found Anshel, Wiener's son-in-law, with his elder son. He had apparently run off in another direction and saved himself. The boy was very pale and frightened. He told us that his grandmother and mother were killed in a big grave and that grandfather and Chaimke were killed not far from the ghetto. He was only five years old, but he knew about everything.

We sat together, silent and miserable. Nobody said a word. Only Nuchem, the little boy, continued to ask questions and to tell how his father had kept his hands on his mouth and asked him not to cry, so that nobody would find them.

After a few hours we learned how many families had been taken away. Nemeth returned and told us more details. The Teichman family, Mrs. Mintz with her daughters, Dr. Lewenter's (Leventer's) whole family, Rabbi Elieser'l and family, Kowle, Margulies and his wife, Brailer and his family, the Hutter family, Messing's younger son, who was killed near the Judenrat, several members of the Weiler (Veiler) family, Dr. Goldschlag, Dr. Zlatkis, Reiss, Koenigsberg, Ania Engelberg and her mother, Rega and Nusia Weintraub and their parents, Mandel Lipa and his family, Tulcio Loev and wife and daughter, Beder Landau, Bohnen, Reiss and families. The majority of the ghetto population was dead.

The little group that remained no longer believed in miracles. We expected death every day. We no longer believed in a better tomorrow and only one problem remained: how to escape and to save our lives? This, of course, was not easy. So we suffered until the second pogrom, which took place on the Day of Atonement, when all were taken to the Belzec Crematorium to be burnt.

Deciding to escape from the ghetto, I parted from my mother and sister and left the ghetto on my birthday night, the 20th of November, in the hope that the war would soon be over and that some day I would return and perhaps find somebody.

But "Operation Judenfrei"[1] was finally completed, and in June 1943, my mother, my sister Roza and the few others who remained all perished.

This is how the Jews of Rohatyn were systematically destroyed and buried in one huge grave. We do not know where their bones are resting.

A holy duty is imposed upon us, the so very few who have miraculously remained alive, to remember the victims and the dates of their cruel death, and to tell of their suffering during the last short period of their lives.

---

1   Free of Jews, also called by the German Nazis "Judenrein."

How Rohatyn Died

By Dr. Abraham Sterzer

YB English Section, p. 40

The county seat of Rohatyn lay on the 70th kilometer of the Lemberg-Stanislawow highway. It was divided into two by a river, and it was surrounded on all sides by forests, fertile fields and pastures. Southeast of the town rose the majestic heights of the Czortowa Gora (Tshortova Gura) mountain, lonely and unconnected with any mountain chain and looking as if someone had lost it on the way.

The town had become famous for its fine fairs, which took place every Wednesday. Peasants from the more than one hundred neighboring villages would come to the fair on that day, to sell their produce and with the proceeds to buy what they needed in the town's stores, mainly manufactures, leather and ironware. The buyers and sellers were of course Jews.

In addition to the government and county offices, the tax offices, post office and police department, Rohatyn had two gimnazjums (a government Polish school and an autonomous Ukrainian school). There was also a handsome public school.

The town had 9,000 inhabitants, of whom 3,000 were Jews. Most of the Jews were well-off, with their own houses, shops, fields, forests and sawmills. Their grown-up children were sent to study in Lemberg, Cracow, Warsaw, and even abroad.

The Jewish community had two large synagogues and a number of smaller ones. Their religious life was led by the Rabbi and dayan. It also had a community president – a popular local citizen, and councilors. The Jews belonged to Zionist parties, religious and cultural organizations. There was also a young people's dramatic circle which presented performances in Yiddish. The income went for Zionist causes. There was also a private Hebrew school. A large part of the youth spoke Hebrew fluently.

Until the outbreak of World War II Rohatyn didn't stop building, since during the first war it had been almost completely burned down by the Russian army. In 1937-38 the Jewish population suffered a great deal because of attempts to drive them out of commerce. A Polish trade organization was formed, as well as a Polish commercial firm and an association of Ukrainian cooperatives. The Jews had no choice but to yield

435

and to look for other branches of trade.

The inhabitants of Rohatyn didn't remember a summer as fine as the one of 1939. The days were bright, with only a few rains; the markets were filled with fruit. During the summer months there were more guests than usual, friends and relatives from Lemberg, Stanislawow, Tarnopol and even from Cracow and Warsaw, coming to spend their vacations in Rohatyn. It seemed as if they all had decided together to leave big cities and to look for rest in our provincial town. Perhaps they were fleeing the big cities where everybody was occupied with politics because of Hitler's demands on the Corridor and the Free City of Danzig. Our peace had also been disturbed by current events. The newspapers carried bad news every day. From time to time the radio transmitted Hitler's war threats if Danzig was not jointed to the "Reich" and if the evils of the Versailles Treaty towards the German people were not corrected. These same speeches had special threats against "international Jewry," claiming that "the Jews were responsible for everything bad that had happened to the German people."

We all understood very well the meaning of these threats and told ourselves that they weren't only words. The annexations of Austria and Czechoslovakia proved that Hitler's threats had to be taken seriously.

It is therefore not surprising that the population was uneasy and nervous despite the pacifying government communiqués.

Jews were continuously asking themselves: "What are we waiting for?" There were, however, optimists of the older generation who had known the German in Kaiser Wilhelm's time. They remembered their culture and tact and didn't believe that the same Germans were capable of murdering or driving out Jews.

In any case, the roads out were already closed, even then. There was nowhere to flee. Only some rich people with foreign passports were able to leave. No country wanted to take in foreigners and especially Jews.

On the Polish-German borders the first camps were already in existence for Jews who had been driven out of Germany as aliens. Though they had once been Polish citizens, the Poles didn't want to recognize them, since they had been out of the country a long while, and didn't allow them to enter. The Polish Jews, of course, had to take on the burden of supporting these unfortunates.

Unrest grew from day to day. The non-Jewish population, however, was of a different opinion. The Poles were very hopeful. They blindly believed in the military potentiality of the Polish army and claimed that Hitler would have a hard nut to crack if he risked war. They believed that in the worse case the war would end with the loss of Danzig and the Corridor. In their naiveté they continued to believe that the Polish cavalry had a real role in the era of tanks and planes. The Polish government had also concluded a pact with England and they believed that England would come to their aid even before the German machine could begin to move.

The Ukrainians were still of another opinion. They believed that the war would come and that Germany would triumph. They were confident that the Germans would discriminate against the Jews and Poles and that they, the Ukrainians, would take over the property of both other groups. The Ukrainians knew that Germany would declare war not only against Poland but, eventually, also against the Soviet Union, and they hoped that after a German victory over the Soviet Union the Germans would set up a Ukrainian government. The Ukrainians didn't hide these beliefs and spoke about them out loud.

On the morning of September 1, 1939, the German army crossed Poland's western border and penetrated deep into Poland in three columns. The resistance of the Polish armed forces was a minimum one and was broken in the first battle. The enemy's military forces marched deeper into the country without any resistance. The government and the general staff had apparently not estimated the forces of the enemy and had not counted on such a powerful attack. All the defense lines were broken like threads.

The Ukrainians were the ones to rejoice in this in our neighborhood. They welcomed the downfall of the Polish regime with joy and prepared to take over when the Germans drew near. On the roads the Ukrainians shot at the retreating Polish forces. After three days of fighting Poland had de facto ceased to exist and anarchy reigned. It was only thanks to the energetic activities of the Jewish community, which had organized a self-defense organization, that the Jews were able to live through these terrible days of panic.

During the 15th, 16th and 17th of September the situation in the town became critical. The neighboring peasants, seeing that there was no longer any government or army, began to flow in masses into the town. Fortunately the local police had not left their posts, though the government itself had fled. The police realized the terrible situation that would be created if there were no government in place. They organized a defense unit and distributed arms to those who knew how to use them, and in that way saved the population from certain destruction.

But in the meantime something unexpected happened: instead of the German soldiers, the town was occupied by the Red Army.

Under Soviet Rule

The Jews felt as if they had been saved from destruction. The Poles, however, looked upon the Red Army as invaders since they would have preferred the Germans. The Ukrainians were split; the nationalists were disappointed because they had expected the Germans, who were supposed to drive out the Poles and give them Independent Ukraine. The poor peasant population, including the Ukrainians, however, were happy because with the arrival of the Soviet Army the peasants were told to divide the properties of the Polish landlords. They took the horses, the cattle, the pigs, grain and other property. In the course of three hours the landlords' courtyards were empty and bare. The property owners had fled to Lemberg during the first days of the war, since they were afraid to remain in the villages.

Most of the Polish Jews, except for a small group of Communist sympathizers, were afraid of the Soviet Union and Communism. Before their eyes were still the fresh memories of the Polish-Soviet Russian War of 1920. In addition, most Polish Jews were occupied in trade. Jewish workers, in general were very few.

But when on September 17, 1939, the Soviet Army entered the eastern regions instead of the Germans, the Jews without exception welcomed them as liberators and protectors against the Germans and the local population. The Jews welcomed the Soviet soldiers openly and the new power began to deal with the Jews with the same trust with which it dealt with its own brothers—the Ukrainians.

Jews were employed by the Soviet officials in the administration and even in the local militia. Jews went gladly to these tasks since there were very many unemployed craftsmen and intellectuals.

Meanwhile the reorganization of trade, industry and economy on a Soviet basis had begun. Cooperatives of shoemakers, tailors, tinsmiths, and bakers were organized. Each of these artels or cooperatives was headed by a leader with previous craft experience—in most cases a Jew. Raw materials were brought from Stanislawow, Lemberg and Tarnopol. In these cities, too, Jews played an important role as the most experienced craftsmen. The Jewish and non-Jewish workers in the artels worked under the guidance of Jewish directors. Control over the factories was in the hands of the Party, which again had greater trust in the Jews than in the non-Jews. The Party knew that we Jews didn't have any political aspirations and only wanted to work and live in peace. The Party also knew that behind the non-Jews there was an underground nationalistic organization which was carrying on sabotage against collectivization.

Under Soviet rule the number of Jews in Rohatyn almost doubled because of the large numbers of refugees from Germany. They included a large number of highly-educated intellectuals, who had once enjoyed good living conditions.

Now, however, they were poverty-stricken and had to sell the last remnants of their belongings. The government didn't have much trust in this category of citizens. First of all, the refugees didn't know the Ukrainian language. The Russians also knew that at the first opportunity these elements would gladly return to Germany. When passports were distributed, theirs were marked with a notice that they didn't have the right to move about freely throughout the country. Some of our local Jews, former traders, also received the same kind of passports, forbidding them to move outside the limits of Rohatyn.

War between Germany and Soviet Russia

The war broke out without noise or incident. The Russians were not panic-stricken and didn't lose their heads. From the first days of the war they moved in an organized fashion to draw deep into Russia. We thought they were only drawing back to the old border, but later it became clear that under the pressure of the German war machine the Russians were compelled to retreat as far as Stalingrad.

The Jews were gripped by panic and despair. Though they were very far from the Communist ideology they still would very much have preferred to remain under Soviet rule instead of falling into the hands of the Germans.

Many Jews wanted to flee with the Soviet Army. They did not, however, have their own means of transport. The Russians dissuaded us from fleeing, promising us that it wouldn't be long before they returned.

There was no choice but to remain. Flight with the Soviet Army was also very dangerous, since German planes flew freely in the skies and undisturbedly shot at and bombed the retreating soldiers and civilians.

The Soviet Army came back, but three years later, to find only six Jewish families. Nine thousand Jews of Rohatyn and the neighborhood had been destroyed in the suburbs and fields of the town.

The Germans Enter

On Wednesday, the sixth of July 1941, at six o'clock in the evening, the Soviet Army left Rohatyn without firing a shot. The German army marched in in their place. The non-Jewish population went out on the streets to welcome the long-awaited German army. No Jews, of course, were to be seen. They were hiding, frightened, in their homes.

The first night with the Germans passed quietly though tensely. In the morning the military town command arrived. The Jewish representatives were assembled and told to form a Judenrat. The local authorities hurried to issue an order commanding all Jews to wear armbands with the Shield of David.

Thursday and Friday passed relatively quietly though local hooligans ran wild. The Germans still did not intervene in Jewish affairs. They were front soldiers and had their own military affairs to occupy them. They only looked with equanimity at the independent actions of the non-Jews.

The First Black Saturday

Early Saturday morning, the ninth of July, 1941, a large number of young people from the neighboring villages and from Rohatyn itself were seen in the town, with nationalist emblems or armbands, and with sticks in their hands. This didn't presage anything good. Jews hadn't left their homes since Wednesday, not knowing what the Germans would do, whether they would allow us to breathe freely or whether hell would soon break out. The news from Lemberg and other cities was far from optimistic. Jews passing by accident had been caught, taken outside the city and shot.

About nine o'clock in the morning the Christian youths began to gather in the marketplace. From there they broke into the new part of town where most of the Jews lived. Some of the invaders also took positions by the houses in the marketplace. Terrible shouts and cries began to be heard. The attackers pulled the Jews out of their homes by force, beating them all the while. Everybody was panic-stricken. There was nowhere to flee since all the roads were blocked. Almost all the Jews were herded together by the synagogue. The plan was to drive them all in after taking away their valuables, to lock them in and then to set the building on fire.

Their plan, however, did not materialize this time. One of the doctors at the hospital, a refugee from Cracow, had accidentally met a German university colleague who was now a military doctor. The Jewish doctor knew that the plot was unofficial and asked his former colleague to intervene. The German actually did go to the higher authorities, who forbade further anti-Jewish actions. The Jews were allowed to go home, though of course without their rings and other valuables.

When the civilian authorities established themselves in the town they called together the representatives of the Jewish community: Shlomo Amarant, Dr. Goldstein, Eli Kreizler, Dr. Freiwald, Dr. Gotwort, Feivel Hochberg, Dr. Rosenstein, Michael Katz and some of the refugees. The Judenrat that was formed was supposed to represent the Jews towards the local authorities and the Gestapo in Stanislawow, and later in Tarnopol. It also had the task of moving the Jews into the ghetto. The Judenrat was also responsible for quiet in the ghetto, the carrying out of fines and contributions and other orders. This was understandably not an easy task, and a great responsibility.

To this very day I cannot understand the Jews who were members of the Judenrat and were active in it. They put themselves at the disposal of the Germans. I have the impression that they didn't grasp the Hitlerite aims. Perhaps they hoped that the Judenrat members and their families would escape danger and would not have to pay fines or go to the concentration camps.

These hopes proved illusory. In some towns the first to be hung were the Judenrat members, as in Lemberg, where on some charge the whole of the Judenrat was hung heads down in the street.

But I also marveled at the iron nerves of the Judenrat members. To sit and wait for the arrival of the Gestapo, or to be called to Gestapo headquarters, without knowing for what purpose or aim, was not a small display of courage.

The entrances to the ghetto were closed by gates, guarded by Jewish policemen.[1] These wore a leather armband on their left sleeve, with the words "Jewish Auxiliary Service." These armbands, meanwhile, protected the police from being taken away to labor camps. Jewish young men therefore were glad to join the ghetto police. There were times, however, when the armbands didn't protect the young people from death. In some of the actions and in the final liquidation the first to be shot were the Jewish police.

The ghetto wasn't able to absorb all the Jews of Rohatyn. Two families had to squeeze into each room. No one even spoke of a kitchen or other amenities. There was no place to put furniture, so that was left in the former homes, outside the ghetto. Jews were happy to find a corner for themselves and their children. This crowdedness led to extremely unsanitary conditions: the use of D.D.T. against lice and worms was not yet known. The ghetto became even more crowded when the Jews from the nearby villages were also forced in.

Life in the Ghetto

There was hunger in the ghetto from the very first months. Not all the Jews had something to sell. The Germans also forbade the peasants to have any contacts at all with the ghetto. Most Jews didn't have any Polish or German money, since we had been under Soviet rule from the 17th of September of July 1941. The Russian money we had lost all value. Whatever little the Jews had, had been taken by the Germans as obligatory contributions. Finally, the peasants didn't want to sell their goods for money, preferring to exchange

---

1 In 1943 the ghetto gates were guarded by Ukrainian policemen who were armed. The Jewish police were merely auxiliary and immaterial. (Donia Gold Shwarzstein)

them for men's and women's clothing.

The Jews were ready to do anything to save themselves from starvation and to give their children a bit of food. On the streets of the ghetto you could already see people swollen by hunger, and sick people, their faces dark as the earth. Despite this, we had to go to our work outside the ghetto – in the offices, stores, on roads and the railroad. Even the sick and hungry didn't receive either food or money for their work. People dreamed of a piece of bread or of a potato. And because of this the black market with the peasants flourished on the borders of the ghetto.

Sickness and Epidemics

The lack of food and the unsanitary living conditions and crowdedness made the ghetto prey to terrible sicknesses, especially dysentery and typhus. Lice flourished and filled the beds, the tables, and even the sidewalks. There wasn't any soap, nor any possibility to wash clothes or oneself. The inhabitants of the ghetto fell like flies. And there wasn't any help. The pharmacists on the Aryan side refused to sell the Jews any medicines.

The cemetery soon began to fill up. Jews died without count and without statistics. Weak by nature, they weren't sick for a long time. After two or three days of illness they just died. Wagons full were carried to the cemetery every day. People died without being wept over and mourned . It was hard to know what was preferable –to continue to live and suffer or the sooner the better to make an end of all the troubles.

The typhus epidemic reached its climax in the winter of 1942-43. At the demands of the authorities, the Judenrat opened a hospital with a limited number of beds, where the homeless and poor sick were brought. At one time, when the hospital was full, a Viennese Gestapo man, Hermann, entered the hospital, assembled the doctors, other workers and the nurses, shot the patients in their beds and then the personnel. Then he ordered the Judenrat to clear away the dead bodies and to open the hospital again.

Pessimists and Optimists in the Ghetto

When sorrow covered the inhabitants of the ghetto like a black cloud, when sickness had visited every house and family, when people walked about the ghetto with feet swollen by hunger, and when the Germans were celebrating victories on the Eastern front and Jews had lost their last hopes of salvation, all kinds of optimists, dreamers, Bible students, military strategists, historians and kabbalists began to appear.

Some of them held that the side winning at the beginning of the war soon consumed all its forces, coming to the conclusion weakened, and without military cadres, and thus loses the war. Others argued that because of her geographical and climatical position Russia was undefeatable. Her winters, autumns and springs were Russia's best defenses, they claimed. As an example they pointed to the history of Napoleon's defeat. Still others claimed that the Germans didn't have enough raw materials to carry on such a long and extended war.

The religious optimists and Bible students believed in a miracle of G-d. Days and nights they pored over the holy books looking for quotations prophesying terrible catastrophes for mankind, and especially for the Jews, in order to prove that some of the Jews would be saved.

These hopes for a miracle passed through the ghettoes and gave the Jews something with which to comfort themselves. For many it was the only ray of hope.

People began to follow the news from the front. Though the ghetto was closed and isolated from the outside world, news managed to penetrate. The news of the German defeats on the Eastern front was like medicine, and hopes for a miracle blossomed. The Hitlerite defeat in Stalingrad brought new life to the ghettoes, and aroused the hopes of liberation. People hoped that because of the defeat the Germans might stop murdering Jews; that they wouldn't have time or mind for it and would leave us in peace. What transpired, however, was completely different.

"Black Friday"
(March 20, 1942)

On this day seventy (70) per cent of the ghetto's inhabitants were murdered by the Germans and their helpers. The entire action took one day, from early morning to five o'clock in the evening. All the dead were buried in a mass grave behind the railroad station.

Without giving any reason the Germans had ordered the Rohatyn Jews to dig a big pit, 50 meters long and five meters in width and depth. We thought that the pit was needed for a tile factory. When the pit was finished work stopped and those who had worked on it forgot about it.

A little while later, when spirits in the ghetto had quieted down and there hadn't been any news of attacks from the neighborhood for some time, the Gestapo men came from Stanislawow, headed by Gestapo-General Krueger. They blockaded the entire ghetto and quietly entered. The Jews were peacefully sleeping. All of a sudden rifle butts began to bang on doors and windows and shouts were heard: "Jews, outside!"

With blows and curses the sleepy inhabitants were dragged to the market place. Nobody was spared – old people, women, children and the sick. All of them were driven into the cold and compelled to stand half-naked. This continued until 10 in the morning. Then they were all ordered to prostrate themselves on the ground, with faces to the earth. Anybody who looked up was immediately shot.

The captured Jews were then loaded on trucks, driven to the pits, and ordered to stand at the edge of the hole. Eight armed Germans shot at them and the dead bodies fell into the pit, together with the wounded and the unharmed. These were covered by another layer of bodies.

Before the shooting all the Jews were ordered to undress and to hand over any valuables they had. This continued until evening. When the church bells struck five, the shooting stopped, and the naked Jews who were still alive were told to go home. Three thousand adults and six hundred children were murdered and buried in the mass grave on that Friday.

A pretty eighteen-year-old girl, a refugee from Germany, was shot in both feet and had fallen into the grave. However, she had remained alive and didn't lose much blood. At night she managed with great effort to free herself and came back to the ghetto. By some chance the German police learned of this; they came to the ghetto and demanded of the Judenrat that she be handed over. She was shot on the spot.

Only 30 percent of Rohatyn's Jews had managed to hide in the cellars and attics. They thus succeeded in living a little while longer, until the second akcja six months later.

After the 20th of March 1942

The ghetto now was almost empty. People moved about confusedly for the first few days after the action, unable to grasp what had happened. Those who were left had lost their families, wives, husbands, children, mothers and fathers, and wandered about like a frightened flock of sheep. Everybody looked for relatives, friends or even acquaintances with whom they could live, or someone with whom they could mourn, though there were no longer any tears.

People wanted to be close to each other and new family relationships were established. It was very rare that a family had returned whole from the catastrophe.

The Germans began to fill up the empty ghetto again. They issued an order requiring all the Jews from the neighboring towns to leave their homes and to move to Rohatyn.

The Jews began to understand that if they wanted to hold out and not allow themselves to be caught again, they had to leave the ghetto and find hiding places on the Aryan side or build good hiding places in the ghetto itself, where they would be able to flee in the event of an "action." They had to be prepared to hide this way for forty-eight hours or more.

Every house began to build one or two such "bunkers" which could hold all the tenants. In time of need it was important that all the people in the house hid, because anyone found might be forced to reveal the hiding places.

The work on these bunkers took a long time, since a lot of precautions had to be taken. There was the problem of carrying out the excavated earth in a way that wouldn't attract attention The bunker had to have [concealed] ventilation, [but also prevent] so that a cough or the crying of a child not be heard outside. (Later there were cases when elderly or sick people were suffocated in the bunkers for lack of air.) For security the entrance of the bunker had to be as small and unnoticeable as possible.

The Germans knew about all this activity, and they therefore planned their "actions" in such a way that the inhabitants would be surrounded and caught in a net. In order to have warning against sudden attack every house began to arrange night watches. Whenever a suspicious sound was heard outside the ghetto the alarm was silently given, and everybody began to run to the bunkers. What with the children, the elderly people, the sick and the pregnant women, it was hard to disappear swiftly into the bunkers. More than once a bunker was discovered because of slowness. The danger remained once a group was in the bunker. The elderly people began to cough, the sick to groan, and the children to cry.

In order to prevent this, the elderly and the sick were quieted in some way and the children given injections of opiates. Sometimes these methods only led to an earlier death. When these methods didn't help and the child wasn't quiet, there was sometimes no other way out but to suffocate it. It was impossible to endanger the lives of a bunker full of people because of the crying of a child!

Once the bunkers were dug, there wasn't much desire to leave the ghetto walls and to try to save oneself on the Aryan side. It was easier to accept the bitter fate of dying in the ghetto or in the bunker than on the Aryan side where one faced the possibility of being handed over to the Germans. In their apathy Jews ceased to believe that they would live out the war. They felt that they were all sentenced to death.

It is interesting to point out that despite the difficult conditions in the ghetto no one died of heart disease or of nervous breakdown. There were very few cases of suicide. It seems that unconsciously the hope of living until Hitler's defeat continued to flicker.

Children and Old People in the Ghetto

In the Germans' general plan to murder all the Jews, the aged, the sick and the small children were the first victims. These were incapable of working and therefore "useless mouths."

When the Germans entered Lemberg they immediately murdered all the mentally ill in the hospital. In every "action" the murderers demanded of the Judenrat that the sick and the little children be handed over. There were also special "actions" against the sick and the children. It is true that in Rohatyn there were no such special "actions," since the Judenrat attempted to buy off the Germans whenever such an action was planned. But in any case, under ghetto conditions, the sick, the aged and the little children didn't have any privileged position. They were looked upon as hindrances by the younger people who wanted to plan rescue activities, to attempt to escape or to organize partisan groups, though no family, of course, agreed to abandon them These unfortunate souls couldn't meet the tempo required by conditions; they had to be helped along and this interfered with movement and decisions. The old and the sick knew the situation and were resigned to their fate.

There were cases where some sick or elderly people or a crying child led to the discovery of a bunker with 40 or 50 people, who thus lost their lives. Everybody loves his child, his old father or mother, but conditions were such that because of them whole families sometimes refused to go down to the hiding places, to run away to the woods or to hide with a friendly Christian, who in turn was afraid to take the risk of accepting whole families with children, or old and sick members.

The aged, the sick and the children in the ghetto had a special look of their own. Their eyes were sad, their cheeks deeply fallen, their lips without a smile. They dragged themselves about the ghetto, ragged, swollen by hunger and scarred by diseases. Children didn't play, only wandered about the ghetto, looking for something to eat. Most of the children seemed to be without age or face of their own.

Children of school age did understand their danger and conducted themselves like grown-ups in the hiding places. They knew how to hide in time of danger. It was much more difficult with the nursing children and sometimes drastic measures had to be used.

As for the youth, they had become hardened to their lives and despite the nightmare didn't forget how to love. There were marriages and new families were established. Even though everybody knew that it might be for only a short time nature demanded its own. Despite the terrible conditions some of the youths continued to meet, to dance, to sing and to play cards, though they knew that all this might be ended the next minute.

The Woman and Mother in the Ghetto

The older generation remembered the conduct of the German army during the First World War and thought that the Hitlerite occupation would act towards women in the same more or less humane and tolerant fashion. The women paid dearly for this illusion during the March "action." As soon as it became known that the Germans were dragging the Jews out of their houses, the men ran to hide and left the women and the little children at home, and most of these were killed. Among the three thousand adults who were slaughtered on that day there was a large proportion of women.

The woman in the ghetto had to worry about food for her family and to go to work on the Aryan side together with the men. She had to work hard at home, to carry water from the well or pump, to wash clothes, to cook and to watch the children. At forced labor she had to exert herself in order not to fall behind the men. During an "action" the woman had to think of herself, her husband and her children, to see that she had food in the bunker for the whole family, diapers for the infants, water, and even a rubber sucker for the baby so that it would be quiet and not betray the hiding place.

At times of epidemic she often lay in bed with her children, sometimes without anybody even to give her a drink of water. Her husband was often either already dead or at work on the Aryan side.

Long observations showed that women conducted themselves better than the men during "actions," and didn't become hysterical. They were more prepared to make sacrifices for the family. In many cases their behavior, their mental stability, straight thinking and healthy common sense helped save their families from danger.

The Ghetto, the Ghetto People, and the Christians Outside

In general we can say that the Rohatyn ghetto appeared clean. The Jews themselves tried to keep it clean in order not to give the Germans any excuse for repressive actions. The Judenrat also did whatever it could and even assigned special people to keep the ghetto clean and orderly.

The wealthier Jews were dressed decently and cleanly. The opposite, however, was true of the poorer population, whose appearance was a very sad one; they were ragged, barefoot, dirty, unshaven, hungry and swollen. Their eyes were sunk deep in their sockets. Nothing bothered them anymore. They didn't even care about the news from the front, and their main interest was how to come into possession of a piece of bread, not only in order to still their hunger but also to ease the unending pain in the stomach and intestines. They were resigned to the fact that there was no salvation for them. The religious Jews among them stopped praying to G-d. If they could, they would rather have complained of his having deserted them.

The Jew seemed like a strange animal when he was on the Aryan side, and that is the way the Christian populace acted towards him when he marched through the Christian streets on his way to work every day. The Jew was afraid of the open street and felt himself helpless there and insecure. He felt surer and more secure in the ghetto, among his people.

The Christians looked upon the Jews marching to work as upon a gray mass, or dark shadows, still alive but long since sentenced to death.

The Jews had a friend in Rohatyn—a Dr. Runge, who shared their suffering and wanted to help them. He very often came to the ghetto, to treat the sick, to comfort them with the hope that the Germans wouldn't win the war. But on the other hand there was Dr. Melnik, whose house was in the ghetto and who had remained there with the special permission of the authorities. He was the only Christian among the thousands of Jews and from his windows he had a good opportunity to observe the sufferings and unhappiness of the ghetto inhabitants he hated so much.

1942, The Second "Action" in the Rohatyn Ghetto

Rosh Hashanah 1942, before dawn. All the inhabitants of the ghetto were sunk in sleep. The Gestapo, together with the local gendarmerie and the Ukrainian auxiliary police blocked all the exits from the ghetto. The armed band was led by Obersturmführer Miller and Hermann (both from Vienna). They entered the ghetto, called out the Judenrat and ordered all the Jews to present themselves and to be ready for the transport that would leave from the railway station. Freight cars were already waiting. With the help of the Jewish police the Judenrat had to conduct the Gestapo from house to house, and to help them assemble all the Jews of the ghetto. Even more, the Jewish police had to help the Gestapo uncover all the hiding places to drive all the Jews to the ghetto square and to bring them to the station.

Thanks to the attention of the Jewish police and the people on watch during the night, it had become known to the ghetto that a large group of Gestapo men had come from Tarnopol. The ghetto was aroused and warned to remain close to the bunkers. This time the Jews were better prepared. Every house already had its buried bunker under the floor, in a closet or cellar.

In the course of the action it became clear that not all the bunkers were properly prepared with all the necessary conditions to maintain the people for a whole day.

The Germans and their helpers went from house to house and searched carefully in all the corners and under the floors, since they found hardly anyone in the rooms. Despite all the precautions about 500 people were dragged out of the bunkers. Those who tried to escape were shot on the spot. The same fate was accorded the aged, the sick and others not fit for the transport.

When a bunker was discovered the Germans sent in a Jewish policeman to collect all the valuables and then to drive out all the people inside. The Germans themselves were afraid of being killed if they went into the bunkers.

Sometimes gendarmes uncovered bunkers but were bribed and closed them up again and went away. This, however, could only be done when they were alone, and not accompanied by a Gestapo man.

At five in the evening the akcja was complete. The captured Jews were escorted to the railway station and from there carried to Beljitz (Belzec). Some of them managed to jump out of the train during the night and to make their way back to the ghetto. Many of those who escaped in this way were later killed by the Christian population.

After the Second "Action"

After the second "action" the ghetto looked like a dead city. Only a few lonely and mournful individuals made their way through the empty streets.

Some days of mourning passed and life slowly went back to normal. The daily cares again began to absorb those who were still alive. Once again they began to go to work outside the ghetto, to look for food and to think of improving the bunkers which had not been discovered. The autumn was passing and winter was close. These were the last days of the year in the ghetto and also the hardest. Men were hungry and sick to the bone and stiff with cold. They didn't have shoes for their feet or a piece of wood to heat the rooms.

Meanwhile the Germans began to bring together Jews from various places where they had been permitted to remain for various reasons. Jews from the neighboring villages and towns were driven into the ghetto, which again became full. The empty streets were lively again and the houses were occupied once more. This concentration of Jews in the Rohatyn ghetto again didn't presage anything good. Everybody understood that another "action" was being prepared. Since there was nowhere else to look for help all hopes were placed in the bunkers and people began to work feverishly to make them stronger. A few began to look for escape on the Aryan side, but without hopes. They knew that the Christian only had one aim: to take from the Jew his last belongings and then to drive him out (if he didn't kill him himself). There were others who sneaked out of the ghetto and went to friendly peasants. People were afraid to go to the woods since they didn't have any arms. Only large groups, capable of protecting themselves against attacks and of obtaining food, dared go to the forest.

The Judenrat went to the Gestapo headquarters in Tarnopol very often and took along various presents in the hopes of learning their future plans for the remaining Jews. They were sure that an "action" was coming, but they didn't know when and what form it would take. Would it last for one day only or for several days? These trips were very expensive but the members of the Judenrat were personally interested in them, since their own fates were at stake. If the third "action" would take only some of the Jews, the Judenrat would continue to exist and they would be able to save themselves and their families. But if the whole ghetto was liquidated, then the Judenrat itself would no longer be needed.

The Third "Action"

On Tuesday morning, the eighth of December 1942, the Gestapo from Tarnopol together with the gendarmerie (as in former "actions") surrounded the ghetto and closed all the exits. Suddenly the Jews learned from the Jewish police of the new "action." There was hardly time to get out of bed and run to the bunkers since the Germans had come into the ghetto very swiftly. As usual the Jewish auxiliary police had to go along with the Germans and to help them uncover the hiding Jews. Many sick people didn't succeed in hiding, and they were immediately shot or taken to the Ghetto square.

By five in the evening the Germans had succeeded in gathering more than 2,000 Jews, who were led by armed escort to the railway station and from there in freight cars to Beljitz (Belzec).

This time many small children died in the bunkers because of the too-large doses of opiates they had been given. Most of the bunkers also didn't have enough air and some children simply suffocated. But even in this there was a terrible comfort: it was better for the children to have died in their sleep, instead of being shot by the Germans.

The German Defeat at Stalingrad

We had already known of the German defeat at Stalingrad in December 1942. At the beginning of February 1943 the German army at Stalingrad surrendered officially. The ghetto was stirred by the news. There was great joy. The hungry and sick almost forgot their own troubles; it seemed as if the Germans were already defeated and that the world was coming back to itself once more.

In truth the defeat behind Stalingrad was only the beginning of the end of the Hitlerites. But it was not yet the end, nor the end of our tragedy. On the contrary, our condition became even more tragic. The Gestapo's demands became harsher. The trips to Tarnopol with money, gold and jewelry became more frequent. The local gendarmerie also became harsher in their demands. The Christian population was waiting for the moment when the last of us would no longer remain alive, so that there would be no live witnesses to their sins against the Jews.

Resignation soon reigned again. Thoughts of flight from the ghetto in order to find some place where one could live out the short time that probably remained before the German defeat increased. Others again began to strengthen their bunkers so that they could wait there until the end of the war.

Spring 1943

The warm, sunny and pleasant spring of 1943 brought good news of the continued German defeats on the Eastern front. This wasn't really very much of a comfort for us since the slow and systematic retreat of the Wehrmacht couldn't help us. We needed a sudden breakdown of the whole Hitlerite regime or a breakthrough on all fronts. But this good news lifted our morale and gave us the hope and strength to support us in the nightmare-like days. With greater energy we took ourselves to reinforcing the bunkers or thinking of escaping to the Aryan side if an occasion came. The ghetto inhabitants came out of the gray and grimy houses into the sun. It was a pleasure to warm oneself in the sun, to catch a little nap. Hunger and weakness didn't leave thought for dreams, but in sleep one could still hope. They dreamed of the good days that had passed, of human freedom or of the future which was slowly, so slowly coming.

But there was also bad news from the nearby and more distant Jewish communities which were being steadily destroyed and evacuated. Lemberg was almost completely empty of Jews.

The Murder in the Cellar

In nearby woods, the peasants discovered a bunker where Jews were hiding. They informed the gendarmerie who immediately came and shot all the hiding Jews. Only one man managed to escape. But on the way to Rohatyn he was attacked by peasants who wanted to hand him over to the

Germans. He had no alternative but to fire at them and one of the peasants was shot in the foot. The others fled and he dragged himself to Rohatyn and lost himself in the ghetto.

The wounded peasant reported the incident to the Rohatyn gendarmerie who demanded of the Judenrat that they turn the Jew over. However, they couldn't find him, since they didn't know who he was. The gendarmerie ordered that if he were not handed over within two hours the Judenrat would have to hand over 20 other Jews as hostages. Negotiations didn't help: the gendarmes remained adamant. The Judenrat were afraid that the gendarmes would inform the Tarnopol Gestapo who might decide to liquidate the entire ghetto. Since the gendarmes hadn't specified which 20 it had to be, the Judenrat ordered the Jewish police to pick out some sick and aged people who were close to death. Twenty such Jews were selected and given to the gendarmes, who led them all down into a cellar. Seven gendarmes placed them along the wall and shot at them till they were dead. When they were convinced that all were dead they ordered the bodies cleared and carried to the cemetery. (I was present when the dead bodies were carried out of the cellar.) Under the hill of dead bodies there was one Jew who had been saved by a miracle. He got up, left the cellar and went home. We felt that we had got off easy; the Gestapo would have demanded more.

May - June 1943

In the months of May and June we began to hear that all the surrounding places had been completely emptied of Jews. Now it was sure that the fate of the Rohatyn Jews was sealed and that our days were numbered. We began to become accustomed to the thought of the coming end. We often talked of approaching death as of a natural and inevitable event. We began to sell everything which still remained from former times and began to buy food to still our hunger. In some houses there were parties, with food and drink and song. There wasn't any music since the Faust family musicians were no longer with us. Only David Faust, with his wife and daughter, Rosa, were still alive.

On Shavuot, June 5, 1943[2], the Gestapo came to Rohatyn from Lemberg. They surrounded the ghetto and took away the remaining Jewish population. About two o'clock past midnight, 18 kilometers away from the town I heard the bang of the machine guns. The Germans were killing the last inhabitants of the Rohatyn ghetto.

An hour before the Gestapo's entry into the ghetto, I, together with my

---

2   The actual date was June 6, 1943. (Donia Gold Shwarzstein)

family, had left my home and stolen away to a Ukrainian acquaintance. The next morning I sent the peasant to find out what had happened to the ghetto. When he came back he told us that the ghetto no longer existed. The streets were empty. Someone might still be in the bunkers but nobody knew. Before the last action there were about three thousand (3,000) Jews in the Rohatyn ghetto.

"Oh that my head were waters, And mine eyes a fountain of tears, and I may weep day and night for the slain of the daughter of my people."
(Jeremiah, 9, 1)

Stone memorial on Mt. Zion in Jerusalem dedicated to the memory of Jews from Rohatyn and its environs who perished.

453

Martyrs

We Will Remember...

We will remember our brothers and sisters who perished, may G-d avenge their deaths, the martyred community of Rohatyn, its youth, its elderly, its men, women and infants, who were put to death by the most heinous persecutor of Israel of all generations, and who were never granted a proper Jewish burial.

We will remember all of our city's Jews and the Jews of our city's surroundings, together with all the martyred Jews of Poland and Europe, the vibrant life they led, the brave acts they performed, their learned people, their artists, merchants and intellectuals who kept alive the legacy of the House of Israel in Exile and who placed Zion at the pinnacle of their joy. May this book be the everlasting monument over their unknown graves until the last generation.

Below are the names of the saintly souls of Rohatyn and the surrounding area who were massacred, Z"L, in the time of World War II[1]:

Aiberhar (Eiberhar), Meir, Basie, Mirtzi, Meila, Feige, Yisrael and their
    relatives
Akselrad, Zvi, Keyla, Mordechai
Akselrad, Chaim and his family
Akselrad, Michael
Akselrad, Fishel, Roza and children
Allerhand, Zev and his family
Altbauer (Altboier), Raizel, Shimon-Yitzhak and children
Alter, Dr. and his wife
Altman, Freyda, Yisroel
Altman, Malka, Klara, Yitzhak, Yosef
Altman, Matzie
Altman, Yosef, Reizel
Auerbach (Oyerbach), Bunim, Tzila (Cyla)
Auerbach (Oyerbach), Shlomo, Uri, Leytzie

---

1   Ed: In most cases, I have tried to render the names in the prevalent Yiddish pronunciation, some in parentheses.

Bader (or Beder), Yehoshua, Yisrael
Bader, Shlomo, Chaya, Yaakov, Hirsch
Bader, Leyzer, his wife, Shaul, Chana, Yehoshua and his family
Bader, Gershon and his family
Bader, Shmuel and his family
Band, Moshe
Baner, Fishel, Yisroel-Eli, Risha, her husband and children, Shalom, Bronka
Baner, Malka
Baner, Moshe, Yuta, Chaya, Frida, Gitel, Miriam, Mindel (from Stryj)
Baner, Sarah, Chaim
Baum, Chana, Chava
Becker, Noach and his family
Beidof, Dudka, Hirsh and their families
Beigel, Yisrael-Mendel, Sarah, Chaya, Yonatan, Rachel
Blasenheim, Miriam, Mordechai
Blasenheim, Moshe, Shoshana, Yitzhak, Cyla, Chaim, Nachum, Aharon
Blech, Shmuel, Roza, Bina, Salka, Vilus (Wiluś)
Blei, Beyla, Hirsh-Ber (from Czortkow) and family
Bloch, Eliezer, Rivka and children
Blautstein (Bloitshteyn), Chana, Tzila, Chaim
Blotner, Sarah
Blotner, Yosef-Yehuda, Purya, Tova, Chana
Blum, Roza, Motel, Klara and his sister
Blumenreich, Tzvi
Bohnen (Bonen), Moshe, Charna, Aryeh, Mina, Sarah, Pepa, Nachum
Bokser, Tova
Bomrind (Baumrind), Naphtali, Maltzie, Leybisch
Bomze, Avraham, Pola (Tenenbaum), Lonka
Borak, Zvi and his family
Brandstein, Esther, Meir, Malka, Reizel
Branstein (Brenstein), Meir, his wife and their families
Branzweig, Esther Malka (Schmorak)
Bratshpis, Aryeh, Chaya, Feyga, Sheindel
Bratshpis, Meir and his family
Bratshpis, Yaakov and his family
Bratshpis, Yecheskel, his wife, Yehuda, Feyge, Elimelech
Bratshpis, Yichezkel (Lipica)
Breiter, Zev, Tzipora, Sasha
Brik, Eli, Rachel, Baltzia
Bring (Bering), Yitzhak, Esther and two children

Busgang, Aryeh-Yehuda, Pesya, Rachel, Shoshana, Yehoshua, Avraham
Busgang, Dov, Shaindel, Hanya
Busgang, Leib
Busgang, Rivka
Busgang, Tzila (Cyla), Yehoshua
Chaimovich, Chayim
Doler, Oskar and his family
Doler, Yitzhak and his family
Durst, Alter, Leybisch
Duv, Selka, Sarel
Ehrlich, Leytzie (Leah), Benzion, Sarah, Moshe, Chaya, Shoime (Shlomo),
    Nachum
Eichenstein, Nuni, Gisa, Ronka
Eisen, Moshe, David and their families
Eliezer, Rabbi, affectionately called Rebbe Reb Leizerl, his wife, Pinchas,
    Bracha, Yaakov, Chava, Nechama
Etner, Yehoshua and his family
Faust, Alter, Devora, Sheva, Yaakov, Vilush (Wiluś), Dudek, Bunya, Yudel,
    Etka
Faust, David, Devora, Kalman
Faust, Itzik-Hirsh, Feiga, Naftali and his family
Faust, Leib, Tzila, Karol, Kuba, Fridzie
Faust, Mordechai-Shmuel, Feiga, Dolek
Faust, Yaakov, Sara, Roza, Moshe
Feld, Devora, Sara, Maks
Feld, Elka, Michael, Munio, Klara, Adela
Feldberg, Yehuda-Zvi
Felker, Chava, Shalom (Brandstein), Shaindel, Leah
Fenster, Mirtzi, Yenti, Yichezkiel
Fenster, Moshe, his wife, Yitzhak, Chaya, Yoel
Fidelbogen, Yosef and his family
Fisher, Yoel, Esther, Chana
Flank, Beyla, Avraham
Frage, Feigah, Tzizi, David, Hinda, Leitzi, Roza
Frage, Yaakov, his wife, Mindel (or Mendel)
Freindlich (Freundlich), Mendel, Chava
Freiwald, Chanoch, Sheva, Yishaya, Moshe, Lipa and their families
Fried (or Freid), Nisan and his family
Fried, David and his family
Furman, Sara, Lea

Gan, Ezriel, Brantzi and children
Gartin, Zelig and his family
Gelber, Yose, Rozia, Mundik, Izio
Gire, Yudel, his wife, Lavi, Shiki, Vovi, Duvidl, Naphtali, Brana
Gleicher, Yisroel, Sheindl and children
Glotzer, Tova, Miko, Munio, Izydor
Gold, Dr. Michal
Gold, Michael, Sobel, Chana, Feiga; Genia, her husband and their children
Gold, Yitzhak, his wife Chava Schafel Gold, his sons Michal and Mayer
Gold, Schmuel, his wife Hinda, his sons Schmerl and Moshe, daughters
    Chana and Rachel (Rozia)
Goldhaber, Naphtali, Gitel, Yaakov, Genya, Sala, Gershon
Goldschlag, Avraham-Zvi and his family
Goldschlag, Dr. and his family
Goldworm, Dov, Yechezkel
Gotlieb, Hirsh and his family
Gotlieb, Leib, Sheintzi, Hildis, Freyda, Moshe, Dina, Breina, Tzipa and
    their families
Gotlieb, Natan, Cyla and one child
Gotswort, Fani
Gotwort, Zvi and his family
Granowiter, Nachman, Shlomo Bila, Zvi, Ezriel, Ita (Weksler)
Green, Yisrael-Leib, Girel-Frida, Esther, Feiga
Grinzeid, Nechemiah and his family
Gutenplan, Batya
Gutman, Aharon, Sartzi (Sarah), Bronia, Mordechai
Haber, Avromtzie (Avraham) and his family
Haber, Feige
Haber, Michael, Genia, Yitzhak, Nusia
Hader, Moshe, Elka
Hakin, Yosef, Nachum-Hirsh, Sheva, Golda, Reizel, Yeshaya-Leib,
    Avraham
Haller, Leah
Halpern, David, Klara
Halpern, Motel, Tzvi, Yehoshua, Chana
Hamer, Yehuda
Handschuh (Handshoi), Shlomo, Glikl, Nachum, Yehuda
Has (or Haz), Miriam, Mordechai
Hauptman (Hoiptman), Yishaya and his family
Hauser (Hoiser), Nachman, Rivka, Dora (Band) and her son Yona

Hausman (Hoisman), Ephraim, Sarah-Feiga and children
Henne, Yichezkel, Gentzie, Simcha (sons of Rabbi Meir Shmuel
    Henne, Z"L)
Hirshhaut (Hirshhoit), Yehuda, Zvi and their families
Hochberg, Dovid and his family
Hochman, Eizik, and his family: Chana, Leib, Rivka; Eliezer and his family
Hochman, Matis and his family
Hochwald (Hochvald), Sara, Hirsch, Horen, Yona, Maltzie and children
Holder, Zvi, his wife, Lonka
Holz, Esther, Yitzhak, Yosef, Rozia, Shmuel and their families
Holz, Zusha, Golda, Zelko, Hirsh Leib, Yizkhak (Izi)
Horn, Dovidkie, Bronka and children
Horn, Yona, Maltzie and children
Horshovski (Horszowski), Feivel, Zosia, Berta
Horwitz (Horowitz), Avraham, Pearl
Huter, Chaim and his family
Kamerling, Yaakov-Moshe, Chaya-Yuta, Tzila, Yitzhak-Eliahu, Uri-Noach,
    Zvi, Shlomo
Kaminker, Aharon, Mirtzi, Yosef
Kanfer, Efraim, Esther, Uri, Etka, Yisrael, Malka
Karpen, Natan, Shmuel-Leib and his wife Fruma
Kartin, Aba and his family
Kartin, Menio, Brunya
Kartin, Moshe-Leib, Blima, Yaakov, Lipa
Kartin, Shmuel, Chana (Widerker)
Kartin, Uri, Neshi, Gusta, Salka
Kasten, Shmuel-Mordechai and his family
Katz, Maltzie, Shlomo, Chana
Katz, Michael, Tzipora, Genia, Moshe, Mendel, Elihu
Katz, Yosef, Ve'itzi-Dina, Chaim, Asher
Kaufman (Koifman), Michael and his family
Kaufman (Koifman), Michael, Sara, Antshel; Gitel, her husband, three
    children
Keinfeld, Avraham, Roza, David, Frida, Mundek
Keyzel (or Kizel), Zalman, his wife, Mordechai, Michael
Kirschen, Buni, Mintzia and their family
Kirschen, Buni, Mintzia and their relatives
Kirschenbaum (Kirschenboim), Leybisch, Chuna, Yuta, Gitel, Rivka
Klarnet, David, Sima and their families
Klarnet, Simcha and his family

Klarnet, Yosef, Golda, Meir, Tova, Gogi, Sender, Tzipi and their children
Klein, Sara, Yosef
Kleinberg, Dr. and his family
Klirsfeld, Hinda
Klomberg, Devora, Pepka
Koenigsberg, Shiltzie and his family
Koenigsberg, Yichezkie and his family
Koenigsberg, Reb Avraham-Tzvi and family
Kohn (Cohen), Chaya, Veibush, Munio and their children
Kohn, Yosef, Vitzia-Dina, Chaim Asher
Kornblau (Kornbloi), Fani, Tosia (Schmorak)
Kornweitz, Menachem-Mendel, Mina, Yosef, Chana, Regina
Kornweitz-Parnes, Dr. Izydor, attorney
Kovler, Moshe-Leib, Esther, Chaim, Malka, Binyamin, Heni
Krand, Adela and her family
Kreizler, Filo and his family
Kreizler, Fishel and his family
Kreizler, Shlomi and his family
Kreizler, Zev, Raizel (Weisberg) and her son
Krig, Leib, Berel, Soshi (Zosi), Feiga
Kronenberg, Golda
Kupferstock, Malka, Moshe, Esther, Tova, Chaim
Laks, Yosef (HaCohen), Drezyi, Basie (Bashi), Chaya, Sara, Yehuda, Uri,
    Feivish
Landau, Shalom, Zushia-Yaakov, Roiza, Yehoshua, Rivtzie, Beyla, Zvi and
    their families
Landau, Shlomo and his family
Langer, Regina, Moshe, Malka, Tzila, Rozia
Langer, Shlomo, the Revered Rabbi and his wife, Yehuda-Tzvi, Tuvia, Uri,
    Avraham, Yisroel
Laufer, Binyamin
Laufer, Binyamin and his family
Leinwand, Blima (Spiegel), Elza, Yechiel-Michel, Yitzhak
Lev, Litman and his family
Lev, Naftali and his family
Lev, Zev and his family
Lewenter (Leventer), Avraham-Alter (HaCohen), Malka, Meir-aryeh and his
    family; Moshe-Nachman, Esther-Rachel, Zusman-Pinchas, Mordechai
    Tzvi, Yona (Tova)-Rivka and her family; Refael, Mordechai-Lewenter,
    Moshe (Marcel), son of Dr. Yitzhak and Tzila Lewenter

Libling, David, Tunka and two children
Libling, Tonka and her two sons
Lichtgarn, Yaakov and his family
Lieder (Lider), Alter and family
Lieder, Michael, Chaya
Lieder, Yisroel, Esther
Lilien, Mordechai and his family
Lipschitz, Yehoshua, Alta and their families
Losberg, Tzirel
Mandel, Lipa, Puli, Itke, Avraham, Mina, Chemvah
Manhart, Dr. Berel and his family
Mantel, Yishaya and his family
Mantenberg, Nachum and his family
Margolis, Esther and her family
Margolis, Uri, Hinda and his two sons
Mark, Elisha, Brina and children
Martzes, Chana, Kalman, Leybisch, Yitzhak, Yisroel
Mauer (Moier), Pinchas and his family
Mauer, Sara, Eliezer, Tova, Fridzia and her daughter
Mauer, Yitke
Melman, Yitzhak and his family
Menkes, Leybisch, Yosef and family
Menkes, Yitzhak, Gitel
Mesing, Elihu and his family
Mesing, Moshe-Leib, Mintzie
Mesing, Uri, Rachel, Kreindel, Chava, Esther-Gitel, Eliezer
Mesing, Yehuda-Zvi and his family
Met, David, Kayla and their relatives
Milstein, Benzion, Sala, Tonya
Mitman, Marina
Mondschein, Dolek, Kuba and their families
Moshel, Dvora, Chemlana
Nagelberg, Szymek and his wife Hela Wald Nagelberg
Nashofer, Leybisch, Henya and children
Nemet, Yona and family
Neutaler, Avraham, Tzila, Yuta, Yisroel, Zigmunt, Etel, Rivka
Pantzer, Yehoshua, Golda (Dunya)
Pantzer, Yihoshua, Yosef, Buni
Pikholz, Frida, Yehuda, Henye
Pizom, Avraham and family

Podhortzer, Moshe-Leib and his family
Poper, Sara, Avraham
Preis, Moshe, Ginze and children
Preser, Hirsch, Yuta and their families
Pundik, Alter, Michael, Toni, Leibla and their families
Rauch (Roich), Nechemiah, Uri and his family
Rauch, Raizel, Michael, Dov, Freida
Rauch, Uri and his family
Ravitsch (Rawicz), Shmuel, Yenti
Reichbach, Shlomo-Mendel, Esther, Rachel-Leah, Hug'i, Salka, Chana,
    Malka
Reischer, Gitel
Reiss, Tzvi, Rachel, Rozia, Salka, Meir, Leib and their relatives
Relis, Yisroel, Dunk and her child
Rokach (or Rokeach), Brana, Mechel, David and children
Rosenbach, Sima, Rachel, Beilah
Rosenberg, Pinchas, Veitzie, Feiga, Refael, Zvi, Uri, Mani
Rosenstein, Aba and his family
Rosenstein, Meir and his family
Roter, David, Gitel (Spiegel), Yitzi and children (from Kozowa)
Rotrauber (Rotroiber), Yishaya, Leitzie, Mundek
Schafer, Esther and her family
Schafer, Leib, Sara; Tzvi and his family; Eidel, Chantzie, Feiga, Rivtzie and
    their families
Schames, Yehuda, Breina, Michael, Buntzie
Scharer, Shmuel, Shaindel, Izi, Buski
Schechter, Mordechai (the Shochet), Esther, Moshe, Brantzie, Aharon,
    Yihoshua, Uri, Chaim, Chaya, Tzvi
Schechter, Sara, Perel, Blima, Rachel, Tzvi, Shlomo (family of the Shochet
    Mordechai)
Schechter, Yehuda
Schechter, Zvi
Schein, Yitzhak, Rivka, Soshi, Mani, Moshe, Kavi (grandchildren of Rabbi
    Kavi, may he rest in peace)
Schmorak, Dr. Zev, Berta, Fani
Schmorak, Dr. Eliezer
Schnap, Zelig, Avraham, Moshe, Yosef and children
Schnaps, Yisroel, Eltzie, Avraham
Schnee (Schnei), Leybisch, Veitzi-Liba, Zev, Golda and their families
Schneekraut (Schneikroit) Moshe and his family

Schneekraut, Moshe, Kuta
Schneekraut, Tsharna-Chaya and children
Schneekraut, Yaakov-Yona, Raizel, Avraham, Uri, Yitzhak, Rivka
Scholer, Zev and his family
Schor, Binyamin and his family
Schor, Yaakov-leib and his family
Schreiber, Uri, Michael, Yaakov, Chana
Schreier, Yehuda, Toiva and children
Schulster, Shmuel and his family
Schwadron, Zvi and his family
Schwartz, Zvi, Klara and son
Schweller, Moshe, Toiva, Edmond, Chana, Tamar and their relatives
Schwerer, Chaim-David
Segel (Siegel), Shichna and his family
Skolnick, Chaim, Frida, Amalia
Skolnick, Natan and his family
Skolnick, Shlomo and his family
Skolnick, Yitzhak, Ruth
Skolnick, Yulek (Julek), Chana, Dzunia
Spiegel, Naftali, Rachel, Shmuel, Klara
Spiegel, Pinchas, Maltzie, Tosia, Izi
Spiegel, Rabbi Avraham-David, Chana-Tova, Chaya, Yisroel, Chaytzie,
    Yuti, Yaakov-Meshulam, Yenti, Chana-Tova, Raizel, Veytche-Rivka
Spiegel, Shmuel, attorney, Fela, Hilda
Shtuzer (Stuzer), Moshe, Bracha
Sini-Fuks, David, Beyla, Daniel
Sofer, Sara
Springer, Zusha, Rachel
Stein, Moshe and his wife; Malvina, Lusia and her husband (Halpern)
Steinmetz, Wolf, Feiga, Mintza, Esther
Steinwurzel, Yosef, Rivka, Maltzi, Avraham-Aharon, Yitzhak,
    Yocheved-Yuntzi, Avraham, Buska
Storch, Moshe and his family
Streichler, Esther, Dov, Moshe, Chaim, Zusha-Leib, Tzvi
Straulicht (Shtrolicht), Uri and his family
Straulicht (Shtrolicht), Yaakov, Pepa and children
Straulicht (Shtrolicht), Yaakov, Pnina, Chana
Straulicht (Shtrolicht), Yehoshua-Falik, Shlomo-Yishayahu, Raizel, Pepa,
    Fishel
Straulicht (Shtrolicht), Zisel, her daughter Pesiya, and her grandchild

Eliezer
Stryjer, Brina, Yosef, Sofer, Sara
Stshelisker (Strzelisker), Rivka, Chayim Leah, Yishayahu, Shmuel-Yehuda,
	Nachum, Devora, Shlomo (from Brzezany)
Tabak, Moshe, Beyla, Tzipora, Malka, Yaakov
Tabak, Yaakov, Mariam, Shifra, Yenti, Chayke
Tannenbaum (Tannenboim), Malka, Leah, Pepka
Teich, Kopel, Tzvi and their families
Teichman (Szymek), Shimon, Malka and child
Teichman, Avraham, Chaya, Hanzel, Yitzhak
Teichman, Ben Zion, Sara
Teichman, Shaul, Reizi-Mariam, Brontzie, Avraham, Klara, Shmuel, Esther,
	Libtzie
Teichman, Shimon, Sara
Teichman, Yosef and his family
Teitel, Ayzik and his family
Teitel, Fishel, Yoel and their mother
Teitel, Shlomo, his in-law David and his granddaughter
Teumim, Rabbi Mordechai-Lipa, his wife, two of their daughters, and son
Top, Avraham, Sara, Mirtzi, Tosia
Top, Puli, David and Zosha and their families
Tunkel, Chava, her sons and Yudel Komurin
Tuerkel, David, Shaindel (Schleicher)
Wachtel, Leib, Golda and children
Wachtel, Yosef, Freida and children
Wagschal, Tzirel
Wald, Meir, Yachtzie, Yosef, Klara, Hela
Wald, Yosef, Ava, Frydzio, Meir, Yulia, Yosef, Klara, Hela, Wilhelm, Sala,
	Hela, Andzia
Walker, Tzvi and his family
Watreich, Moshe, Anshel, Shlomo, Shimi, Leib, Beila, Munisch (Moonish)
	and their families
Weich, Michael and his family
Weidman, Avraham, Chaya, Zofia, Aryeh, Tzila
Weidman, Avraham, Shaindel, Reizel
Weiler, Chaim
Weiler, Gita, Roza
Weiler, Meir, Bluma and children
Weiler, Mendel and his family
Weiler, Motel and his family

Weiler, Shmuel, his wife and children
Weinreich, Michel, Esther, Hudel, Balcia, Rozia and their families
Weinstock, Ephraim, Yuta, Leah, Naftali, Avraham-Eliezer, Matis (from Chodorow)
Weinstock, Leah, Uri, Yisrael
Weinstock, Sheur, Devora-Eidel, Perel, Roza, Hudel, Esther, Breina (from Knihynicze)
Weinstock, Yitzhak
Weintraub (Weintroib), Golda, Moshe (Morris/Maurice), Berta, Herman (Tzvi), Chaya and her husband; Rega, Nusia, Lipa and his wife
Weisberg, Chayim-Hirsh, Sheindel
Weisbraun (Weisbroin), Moshe, David, Ben Zion, Berel, Shmuel and their relatives
Weisbraun (Weisbroin), Moshe, Dvora
Weisman, Moshe, Hentzie and children
Weiss, David, Fruma, Yitka, Eliezer, Gitel, Moshe, Yaakov, Yisrael
Weiss, Yehuda-Tzvi, Leah, Elza, Rivka, Meir
Wider (Wieder), Yaakov, Sima, Chaya, Michla, Sara, Chana, Wolf, Bluma
Widerker, Yosef, Sara, Chana, Moshe
Wildman, Avraham, Chana
Wiener, Zvi, Rivka, Chaim
Willig, Giza, Sheva and two children and Tzvi
Willig, Mordechai, Rivka
Willig, Zev and his family
Wind, Menachem Mendel, Sara, Yaakov, Rivka, Moshe
Wind, Tzvi, Rivka, Chaim
Windreich, Tzipa
Yoresh, Aba, Raizel
Yoresh, Gitel and her family
Yozef, Devora, Doba (Dova)
Yufeiner (Jupeiner), Shmuel, Tova, Zalman
Yupiter, (Jupiter), Chayim, David, Chana, Manya, Leah, Avraham, Yehuda Tzvi
Yupiter, Moshe, Mirel, Leah, Libtzie, Yisroel-Hirsch, Hilda
Yuta, Chaya, Frida, Gitel, Miriam, Mindel (from Stryj)
Zaler, Sender, Gogi and children
Zeif, Mordechai, Michael (Reichbach), Sara, Chaya, Yafa, Yosef, Shlomo (Zider)
Zider, Moshe, Sorel, Esther, Bluma
Zider, Note, Chaniya, Aharon, Leah

Zilber, Golda, Duntzia
Zilber, Maks, Rozia and children
Zilber, Yosef and his family
Zin, Avraham-Leib and his relatives
Zin, Yitzhak, Rachel, Yisrael, Chaya Roza, Golda, Yehuda, Yirachmiel,
    Shlomo
Zlatkis, Chaim, Izio and their family
Zlatkis, Dr. Veivush and his family
Zlatkis, Izi and his family
Zonenschein, Feivish, Sara, Chanina
Zucker, Litman, Michael, Shlomo
Zukerkandel, Moshe, Blima (Blau), Yitzhak, Aharon (Borenfeld), Breintzi

PART II

Israeli Society holds memorial. March 20, 1982, Kiryat Shaul, Israel.

Rohatyn in the Mirror of Memory
By Donia Gold Shwarzstein

W hat is a town visited 50 years later, its streets ghostly and empty of its former life, its buildings overgrown with additions obscuring old contours of houses, outlines of streets and lanes? Is it the same place? It is not.

Where is that place and how can it be found? Only in the memories and the recorded images and words of its surviving expatriates.

Can we recapture the town, its flavor, its accents, its typical words in its everyday life?

Where is the rhomboid shaft of light in the entranceway that comes in from the open door and breaks on the corridor wall – as it did on warm days of summer?

Where are the jeweled fields, flowers amid the grass and grain under the sunny sky?

The scenes that flicker in the mind. The scenes that still flicker in photographs, evoking so much that can be brought out into today's light. Not all the frames of all the films comprising the manifold lives of the town will be returned, but one mirror set together, set like pieces of mosaic will be put whole again. The fragmented, shattered mirror of the town's world will be a surface reflecting the images of the living town: connected frames capturing individuals, families, comrades, friends arm in arm, swimmers at the river, children playing beside the flower beds in the town square, Kolejowka, with strollers right beside us and strolling couples in the distance in the narrowing lane between the massive fruit-laden chestnut trees ... the town will spring to life through images of photos yet to be retrieved, through tales yet to be retold, through letters and diaries yet to be brought out of private drawers, through archives yet to be researched, through poems yet to be made known and read: it will sing with the echoes of all the voices once heard, of all the voices still ringing in our ears ...

Those who will gaze at the mirror of the town will come away knowing from whence they came, will know what are the misunderstood strains of meaning of words heard from their parents or grandparents ... such will be the fabric of the town mirrored in its images and words ...

The Yizkor book augmented, expanded in a pageantry of images, in plain sight for viewers to see together, is unlike a book which is only a single solitary experience. The town, hidden behind the cloud of dark events will spring to its former life. There is more than the Yizkor book delivered. There is so much more.

Walk the streets of Rohatyn now and the sights clash with the images of the once living town. The present is a ghost and bears no resemblance to the vitality and bustle and joy of variegated bounding life.

The pageantry and mosaic of Rohatyn can be reconstructed in the mirror of chips and pieces to bring its verve and beauty to life. Don't seek it in the geographic location. You will find it transposed into a new framework and place, a mirror in images, words and movement on the canvas of its recreated life, in this volume and others which may come.

Kaddish in Rohatyn

June 10 - 11, 1998

Opening Address

To the assembly of local population and Jews coming from Israel, USA, and Europe

By Freda Kamerling Perl, Member of Organizing Committee, Israel

June 10, 1998
Dear friends and fellow Rohatyner,

Fifty years have passed since we left our homeland, and so my Ukrainian language is not as good as it used to be. I would like to start by quoting the Polish-Jewish poet, Stanislaw Jerzy Lec, who wrote in one of his aphorisms: "People think that tears come only in times of sadness, but I think one tends to cry also in the face of sublimity ..."

Standing here today looking around me, I see people whom we've never met before, people with different customs, a different language, a different faith – all here to share with us an immense grief. Is this not that sublime moment the poet talks about, which constrains our throat and brings tears to our eyes? It is a shame that such moments did not take place back then, but let us hope they may become a part of our future.

First let me address the young, who were not yet born when the war took place, or were too little then to have any memories of it. No doubt you find it hard to believe that such horrors did indeed take place. It was not done in the name of any religion or faith – not pagan, not Islamic, not Christian, which command to 'love thy enemy.' This was the work of the devil.

You may have wondered why it happened. As far as one can answer, it was the result of one thing only: pure hatred, which logic cannot grasp. In looking for a logical reason, we may say it happened because our people had no country to call their own. I find an affirmation of this view within your own literature. During my visit last year I was given a book you must all be familiar with: the story of the Rohatyn heroine Roxolana. The motto of the seventh chapter says: "Many dark paths lead to unknown gates, for those who have no homeland." Many peoples have walked across those roads but never succeeded in crossing the gate and therefore vanished from history. Our people have made it along the bloodshed road, but managed to pass through the gate and were resurrected.

Finally, I would like to thank you all for being here today. We shall return home, but the stones and the monuments will remain here on your soil. We ask you to cherish these sacred places. Every nation has it better and lesser persons. Don't let the latter destroy the memorials. Allow the victims lying under the rocks to rest in peace till the Day of Judgment – as both we and you believe.

Those of you, who will be passing by, stop for a moment, pick a wildflower and lay it down on the stones. Raise your eyes to heaven in prayer: may we never let such a tragedy happen again on our land.

If all around the world people would make that wish, it would be a step towards the ideal of the prophet: "Nation shall not lift up sword against nation, neither shall they learn war and none shall make them afraid."[1]

(Delivered in Ukrainian in Rohatyn, June 10, 1998, at the Memorial Services dedicated to those who perished in the Holocaust in Rohatyn and vicinity.)

---

1   Isaiah 2:4

Elegy
Fifty-five Years After the Destruction of the Ghetto of Rohatyn
By Rabbi Yoel Ben-Nun, of Israel

B"H
June 10, 1998[1]

To my grandfather, Reb Yoel Fisher
To my grandmother, Esther Fisher nee Shatshlisker
To my aunt, Chana Fisher
To all the holy martyrs of Rohatyn and its surrounding area who are
buried in the mass grave in Rohatyn
May the Almighty avenge their death!

How do I begin this elegy? Everything about it evokes gloom, every memory is black. The houses that have remained are desolate as are the synagogues - all memories of the community in its glory. Stories of the slaughter, the ghastly murder in the pits, the mass grave. All are well known but nevertheless appalling. Even after 55 years have passed, it is still difficult to deliver an elegy.

But - if we could have said just one sentence to our holy loved ones who had been killed and to those who were on their way to being murdered, before their souls arose to the heavens, this is what we would have said: The accursed - the wicked - have not succeeded in eradicating Jews and Judaism from the world! You have continuity - perpetuity - descendents who remember and will never forget you. In the Land of Israel there is a Jewish state, where children are born and raised—grandchildren and great-grandchildren of the holy martyrs of Rohatyn and all the other communities that were destroyed. This is our great revenge: the continuation of Jewish life, the continuation of memory, the command—never to forget—which is engraved with a steel pen on our hearts. It is this that proves daily our victory and the defeat of the wicked!

I am sure you would have died more peacefully if we could have told you this directly a moment before you passed away. And it is therefore that we are here at this meeting after 55 years to say this to the ears of heaven and earth, to the sun and the stars, to the ears of the dead who are buried, to the ears of the neighbors who have survived and to the ears of the descendents who are alive and following in their path, that they will not be forgotten.

Rest in peace dear brothers who are buried here in this mass grave, you have continuity - alive and kicking, remembering and not forgetting, raising the Jewish flag on high, remembering Rohatyn and the other Jewish communities - and building Jerusalem.

Giving Testimony at the Gravesite of March 20, 1942

By Sabina Wind Fox

Translated from Yiddish by Donia Gold Shwarzstein

Sabina Wind Fox at March 20, 1942 Monument
June 10, 1998

At this place where we are standing now, on the 20th of March 1942, 3,500 Jews of the community of Rohatyn and vicinity were murdered and were buried here in two mass graves.

It was a cold day; the frost and white snow were stained with Jewish blood. It started at seven o'clock in the morning, and was called "akcja." People were taken out of homes and gathered in the lot of the town square in the center of the town. They were ordered to lie on the ground with their faces down, while two trucks, loaded with people, went back and forth, transferring them to the mass graves.

The graves were previously dug. Every day the Judenrat sent 40 people

480

to dig them, and an engineer was constantly taking measurements, so the people thought that they were preparing trenches for air defense. It was done in such a shrewd and psychologically influential way, that we did not know the horrible truth.

On the way to the graves a few people jumped off the trucks, but they were shot at. The trucks could not reach the graves - the road was steep and the people were made to run, and many were killed because they tried to run away. In the graves, not everyone died. There were a few individuals who told of how some were lying at the edges of the graves, pretending to be dead, and at night they came out.

I remember that one of them was Yona Nemeth, and the wife of the lawyer Barban – Yoyne Nemeth. Raysa Stryjer told me that after the akcja she went to see the graves with many other people, and the graves were moving. One woman in the open grave cried to her: "Stryjerowa, I am not wounded, get me out of here, I am Zlata Kenigsberg." People did not react because of sightseers. Wagons with whitewash arrived to the place, and lye was poured over the people in the graves who turned their heads to the other side, as they were still alive. The next day more lye was poured, and also on the days after, and the graves sank down.

After this akcja, there remained 500 Jews in the ghetto of Rohatyn, who later perished in yet another akcja.

After the liberation on the 28th of July 1944, a few of us Jews survived; and the first steps we took were to the graves. We saw that high grass grew over the graves, and they sank lower than the surface of the ground.

Now we stand here, after 57 years, thanks to the Rohatyn Organization in Israel, along with the municipality of Rohatyn, which helped us to set the gravestones and contributed half a hectare of land for that purpose.

These gravestones are a memorial for our families, and for all the Jews of Rohatyn and vicinity. I hope that the local people will keep them up and that they will be taken care of, and that every person who passes by will look, and stop to think about what and where a wild and blind hatred brought on such a barbarian tragedy, and that such a disaster and crime will never exist again in the world.

We Come in Silence
By Donia Gold Shwarzstein

June 10, 1998[1]

W̲e come in silence - to speak to our dead - the voice of the children of
the Rohatyn ghetto

We come in silence. We have come to hold a memorial service for our
dead.

We have come to pay our respects to you, our loved ones. We have come
to speak silently with you, our loved ones, you who are buried in this ground,
in and around this town. Our hearts are broken; our minds are stunned by
what happened here. We are mute. We commune in silence with our dead.

Though you are interred here, we have never left you behind; we carry you
with us in our sleep and in our waking hours. You and we are never apart. We
never expected to set foot here, on this ground. But out of love and respect
for you, whom we have lost here, we have come to acknowledge you in this
place and to commune with you here.

It is here that you taught us our first words. It is here that you taught us
names of birds, insects, flowers. It is here that we children played. Of my
playmates, none survived - I only recall the name of Beata.

In 1943, inside this prison ghetto the children secretly still tried to go
to school, to a hidden school. In the last days before the Judenrein in the
menacing shadow of the forbidden exit gates, one rare quiet day, they played
their last hopscotch - rejoicing in the beauty of the spring sun. (This was the
only day the Gestapo did not show up in the ghetto for live target practice.)
Innocent children believed, trusted, loved and hoped.

A child in the Terezin Ghetto wrote, just before he was killed:

"I was once a little child,
Three years ago,
That child who longed for other worlds.

---

1 Delivered (as required by Israeli Rohatyn Committee) in Ukrainian before a mixed
audience of Jews returning to hold a memorial and local population.

But now I am no more a child
For I have learned to hate.
I am a grown-up person now,
I have known fear."

"But anyway, I still believe I only sleep today,
That I'll wake up, a child again, and start to laugh and play.
I'll go back to childhood sweet like a briar rose,
Like a bell that wakes us from a dream." (Hanus Hachenberg, IX. 1944)

On that last Shavuot, June 6, 55 years ago, we did not decorate the houses with green branches, as we used to; we did not sing songs. The play stopped. We died. And it was here that the ground either swallowed us up or spat us out; those of us who survived ... it spat us out orphaned to flee far into the distance.

After that Judenrein, the Jew still alive was without a community; he knew there was no more community. The Jew in hiding, on the run, was in a cosmic void - a loneliness, a despair not to be expressed ...

We have come now to this place to close a broken circle. We have come just briefly to commune with you who are buried in this town, just briefly to pierce that loneliness ... We have come to acknowledge you in love, to speak of your goodness and to say Kaddish.

Poem

By Chaya Rosen, USA, Member of Faust Klezmer Family

June 10, 1998

Crawling out of their hiding place
A hole dug deep in a Polish forest
They escorted two children
Blinded by the light of day not seen for 18 months

My brother seven and sister age three were gently consoled
Don't be afraid it won't hurt

Expecting an onslaught of bullets in the forest
My starved and deprived of all hope
Father and mother were hailed by
Russians announcing that it was all over

What a strange notion
That it was all over

In a land fertilized by human char
Hallowed heaps of bones that used to be
Lives uprooted overturned stumbled over
Not liberated

My parents and their two children made their way out of this place
Which had once been called home

Marching bands did not herald their freedom
Victory songs were not heard
No medals were pinned
No martyrs were mourned and their nightmares never ceased

Poem

Crossing three continents
They carried their satchels, children and pride
Handing us their legacy it would become mine
I am the daughter of survivors

At four I sat on my mother's lap
Watching her serve small sandwiches and tea
To a sobbing circle of women bemoaning
Failed efforts to save their babies who'd been thrown to the fires

Quietly I heard their voices
In seven languages they whispered their stories of slaughter
By the time I was seven I desperately wanted to fix things
But I didn't know how so I vowed that I would never stop listening
At fourteen I decided to shut it all out
Ashamed I spent most of my time trying to disguise my isolation and pain
Then I discovered my Faust family musicians
The Klezmorim photo from here in Rohatyn

Faces of my grandfather
David Faust his father and brothers
Jewish musicians dressed in black
Bearded men peered out of the photo

What were they doing to my heart?
Why were they beckoning me calling me out by my old forgotten name?

They spoke without moving their lips
I understood them with my soul
They knew me
We were connected

By the time I reached my mother's age
The age she was when she flew past flying bullets
With bare feet she raced across these frozen fields
Marked by black booted Gestapo

Climbing over barbed wire that ripped her flesh
She fought her way out of holes in the ground
Stealing stale potato peelings
Grasping on to her children
By the time I reached this age
The sounds of the Klezmer music returned
Their old melodies echo and reverberate
Taking me where words cannot

Creating sparks - Holy sparks
Reviving a renaissance of Jewish spirit and passion
Evoking feelings felt deeply
Fixing me evolving and repairing you

In dozens of new ways
Their joyful music swings and cries
Beckoning healing
Reminding us of who we used to be

Compelling me to return to this place Rohatyn
To touch the walls that held the Mezuzot
My Grandfather's frail fingers
Fixed upon the wall

You who pass through this town
Know that a descendant like me
Mourns and returns
To resound a lifelong promise and lament

I'll rip my cloth tear out my hair return to Rohatyn and howl like a dog
To restate the following vow
From generation to generation we must look upon ourselves
As if we personally passed through sacred sites such as this one here in
Rohatyn

Letter to Fishel Kirschen
Read at the 1943 Monument During the Memorial

Translated by Donia Gold Shwarzstein

Bensheim [Germany, Displaced Persons' Camp], May 2, 1947

D ear Friend Fishel,
Today I received your letter of March 30 and I'm answering all of you at once. I have long awaited such a letter. I thought that you already know the fate of your parents, you, Fischer and Kartin and Hader and others. After all, Rohatyn people received letters from you and no doubt they reported to you and to all the others. But it appears that this is not so. So it is my fate to bring the Job-like news to all remaining survivors of Rohatyn. On March 20, 1942, 4,500 Rohatyn and other Jews perished. This was the first pogrom [akcja] in our town. Your parents survived that. They lived in Fischer's store, because your house was outside the ghetto and Fischer's house was on the boundary. The Fischers and Kartins also survived. On that day I lost my parents and one brother. Two brothers escaped with their lives and the three of us remained. Yom Kippur 1942 was the second akcja in Rohatyn. After they murdered the Rohatyn [Jews], they threw Knihynicze [Jews] into the ghetto (the ghetto existed from the first day of July 1941). The akcja lasted two days. Ukrainians and Volksdeutsche were helping. On the second day they destroyed the Fischers' house. This was committed by the shoemaker Wlodek, the youngest, with a Gestapo. They took away your parents and the Fischers and the Stsheliskers (Strzeliskers). That day they deported your father to Belzec, Rawa Ruska. Your mother ran away from the [collection] place and lived until the third akcja, that is until December 8, 1942, at which time they deported her to Belzec, and she did not return. Old Fischer jumped from the train in Psary and returned to the ghetto. On the same day (Yom Kippur) they took Stsheliker and Shayke to [forced] labor from the collection point, and they did not perish that day. Hanka Fischer was then in Podwysokie and she too remained alive. On Yom Kippur perished Fischer's mother and Mrs. Stshelisker. Old Stshelisker fell ill with typhus and soon died. Shayke was a [Jewish] policeman and perished during the liquidation of June 6, 1943. Yoel Fischer was in the Judenrat until March 20, 1942. He perished during the

487

liquidation, and [they] are buried in the Doller's cegelnia (brick factory) behind the Klasztor (Monastery-Hospital). Hanka Fischer was in Podwysokie together with the refugee dentist from Bistritz (Bystrzyca). After the liquidation of the ghetto she had to run away from there. Ukrainians captured her at a train station and they shot her. The Kartins conducted themselves with dignity. None of them served in the Judenrat. Lipa was in the [Jewish] police force, but he left it even before March 20. They built under their house a powerful bunker, known by the name Sevastopol; it was considered a place in which you could stay many years of the war. They excavated and moved hundreds of tons of soil into Melnik's garden. That is how they were lost; Melnik lived in the ghetto and he gave them away. They joined with the Messings; they built several rooms underground; they installed a supply of water, a sewer and electricity. They stored provisions for years and waited. They all perished June 6, 1943. Herman Weissbraun was also in this bunker, and he alone remained alive. He is now in America. Lipa and M.L. Kartin are buried in the ruins. All others they took to the cegelnia mass grave, where in 15 graves they buried approximately 3,500 Jews. You may ask how were there so many Jews in Rohatyn? Well, Rohatyn had several thousand refugees from the West from 1939, besides that they brought to Rohatyn [Jews] from Knihynicze, Bursztyn, Bolszowce, Bukaczowce, Chodorow and hundreds of those who jumped from trains, the "jumpers." G-d knows from where else [they came], so that overall in Rohatyn they ground up 12,000 Jews.

Sender Pasweg was mobilized into the Polish Army in 1939, and from then on there is no news - he is probably not alive. Is Dolek Pasweg in Palestine? The Paswegs perished in March [1942]. They lived by the Melmans in Nowe Miasto [New Town]. Pasweg's house remained intact, and also Fischer's house. Your house was smashed to a pulp. Schmilko Holz was with me in the forest. Binyamin Laufer was shot. In one of the raids on them (a whole group was there) in those months, his colleagues struck him. It appears he was mentally ill. Granowitter, Herman, perished with his mother, June 6, in the liquidation. His brother Izio died in the camp in Zborow. He registered well. He worked in a German Arbeitsamt, he stole documents, so that he may be able to leave with Aryan documents. He was given away by the sister of Yumka [pronounced Yoomka] Kowler, when she was caught in Cracow.

And now Fishel, a few words about us Rohatyn people. I see that you know that I was in the police, but out of graciousness you do not want to write about it. Yes, I was. When the Germans arrived the Ukrainians created the ghetto, the Judenrat, and the entire apparatus. We judged that this will last a short time, that it will end well, and on the initiative of Dr. Goldschlag and Zlatkis they invited umpteen of us young people, in order to create with them a police, so that power does not fall into the wrong hands. In the Judenrat were Amarant, Dr. Goldschlag, Dr. Zlatkis, Beidaff David, Skolnick Chaim, Fischer Yoel, Messing Ire, Auerbach Shimon, Beigel. In the police were Ettner, Haskel, Rotrauber, Yudel, Lipa Kartin, Weissbraun H, and Meyer (the Chief [of police]), Glotzer, Salomon, Faust Wilus [pronounced Viloos], Kinstler Salek Granowitter Herman and I. This is how it was until March 20, 1942. At that time Zlatkis, Goldschlag, Beidaff, Ettner and others perished. At that point the rest quit [the police] and so did I. After that things were different. All towns provided people to the Judenrat and to the police. And it was a veritable Tower of Babel. In the Spring of 1943, I went to the forest together with my brothers and my present wife. In the forest there were many [Jews], I think around a thousand Jews. From the forest returned: my brother, Moine (Chuny perished in the forest), my wife, I and some man by the name of Gabriel Grunberg, and Kuba Glotzer, the son of Meyer Glotzer. In July 1944 to Rohatyn returned around 30 persons, but those hid out by farmers, in cellars. Several perished later in the Red Army. Of those who survived, the following are here in Germany: (Oziasz) Glotzer, and two daughters. In Rychbach, Poland, there are Leybisch (Aryeh) [Blech] and Moishe Blech (Moshe Nas'hofer), Zin Markus, Süsser, Mrs. Metek (or Melek), cousin of M. Metek (or Melek), Mrs. Stryjer, Gutstein Munko and a few Jews from the surrounding villages, such as Lipica (the Schwellers, the Hausers). You can see from this that very few remained [alive here]. On the other hand, many returned from Russia, for instance the Mondscheins, Poldek and Ludwig, the Hollers Moishy, Yosale, the Halperns, Wolek [pronounced Volek], and Izio. Also living here now are Sabina Wind Fox, Ciucia [pronounced Tsiootsia] Tenenbaum, Rozia Faust, all three hid out in Rohatyn, (sister Lola Mark).

No signature

Stamped with logo of Society of the Rohatiner in Israel

489

Return To Hell 55 Years Later
Surreal And Overwhelming
by Donia Gold Shwarzstein

Fifty Jewish expatriates made their first solemn journey, in June 1998, to Rohatyn, a small town in the Western Ukraine, 50 kilometers southeast of Lwow. Rohatyn was the concentration ghetto for several towns, e.g. Bukaczowce, Bolszowce, Bursztyn, Knihynicze and nearly 100 villages.

The contingent of "pilgrims" from three continents numbered ten survivors and six pre-war expatriates. The others were second and third generation descendants. They came to say the first Kaddish at the mass graves[1] fifty-five years after the destruction of the ghetto. They also came to witness the dedication of memorial gravestones and of a plaque attesting to 600 years of Jewish communal life in Rohatyn affixed to the former Judenrat building. The Israeli Rohatyn group, with the cooperation of the local Mayor and district representatives, laid the groundwork for the occasion.

Rohatyn, 1998. Dedication of monument of Judenrein June 6, 1943.

The arrivals gathered in parties of two, three or more; only two people from the U.S. traveled alone. Adult children accompanied a parent; this was their gift of love to the parent. Members of the extended Faust family of klezmer fame came to honor their grandparents, who went "al kiddush hashem" during the extermination (the "Judenrein" akcja). They also came to touch the erstwhile grandeur of their patriarch grandfather. The deracinated heirs came to touch they roots.

At first, a return to the western Ukraine was unthinkable! Survivors, who left in 1945, the images of akcjas still fresh in their minds, were in the grip of trauma: "Shattering sights and sounds await us. Our Jewish town awaits us ... a killing ground ... from which there is no escaping ... and we are on the way there? The mere thought seized us with terror and cut off breath. Return to that Hell where death stalked us well past the fall of Hitler? What sane person would do that?"

Yet as soon as we arrived, we found ourselves whisked off to City Hall. For two hours we were feted, welcomed by officials, reporters, cameras, and local onlookers, greeted almost as if we were returning triumphantly to our hometown. Town politicians and clergy were fully represented. Their speeches reverberated in a tongue whose echoes were long ago silenced in our consciousness! An unheard chorus storming into our introverted spirit. To those of us who remembered the insurrection in the countryside - some of us barely escaped with our lives in 1945 - this opening session was surreal!

The official speeches, the gestures of eager hospitality, the air of festivity were jarring, at odds with our state of mind. I drew away into silence, into a private space. I was not there, I was in mourning, engaged in painful memory, loss and deep-seated grief.

For years, I had doggedly consigned that cursed time of 1941-1945 to

Rohatyn, 1998. At 1942 Memorial.

another plane of consciousness, as though by this device the inexpressible evil could be stopped from contaminating the postwar world! But in 1998, once the memorial service was proposed, the long suppressed inner need to stand at the graves was compelling, and the reality of the place had to be faced. I felt my heart would break if I didn't go! Once there, standing in those places of origin, we were all in the palpable presence of our loved ones and felt affirmed by the encounter. Those of us who as children in 1945 were severed from family and everything familiar, for years had to deal with shadows of memories, becoming tormented shadows ourselves. For us it was difficult to come back, but it was also difficult to leave!

Before setting out on this "reunion", we expected a quiet communal service and time for private grief. But it was not to be so.

Three separate memorial dedications crammed into one day, were followed by just one day of private pilgrimage. At each of the mass graves, speeches or recitations were delivered by Ukrainian clergy, a Roman Catholic priest (in Polish), government representatives, as well as a recitation by a school child and a poetry reading by a Ukrainian woman. The 50 Jewish mourners were also joined by local citizens, including children. Some came out of curiosity, others out of sympathy. A few could be seen wiping away a tear.

Eulogies given by our people, delivered in beautiful local Yiddish, Hebrew, English, Ukrainian, and Polish, recounted the horrors of the past and poured out words of love and sorrow about the families and the community we lost and our unswerving promise to remember. The rabbi of Ivano Frankivsk (Stanislawow) spoke movingly about Jewish hassidic roots in the Ukraine and thankfully noted that at last there was a Minyan (quorum for prayer), and Kaddish could be said for these martyrs. Israeli flags fluttering in the wind, candles in Magen David formation were lit. After Kaddish and K'eyl Molei Rachamim ("Merciful G-d"), we linked hands and sang Ani Maamin ("I believe"). For a moment we were a community in spirit, unintruded upon by being watched by spectators. The letter of Rabbi Yechiel Ben-Nun from Israel (grandson of Rabbi Fisher of Rohatyn), read in Ukrainian at the gravesite, addressed the dead by contrasting past and present: "...the Jewish culture was not destroyed, we are developing the State of Israel..., you have a good shift" taking up your task, "rest in peace in your common graves. We shall never forget you."

Only one voice, that of a newly-discovered survivor found living in the Ukraine, dared speak of and warn against revising the story of the Ukrainian role in the history of the period. However, he immediately followed this by giving due praise to the righteous Ukrainians, who rescued him in a concentration camp.

At the mass graves of June 6, 1943, one curiosity seeker yanked my sleeve and told me of his connection to the massacres. His father was one of the gravediggers, he told me - all of whom were rewarded afterwards by the SS with a feast of food and drink. He didn't refrain from painting the gory details! On another occasion, after I had given a eulogy in Ukrainian, a middle-aged woman approached me and exclaimed, "But you are like us! You are just like us!" It must have come as a revelation to her that I looked astonishingly like they did, and yet I was from that Nazi-instituted ghetto in Rohatyn!

The distance between the time when Jews resided in the area and the present had grown so great that the local historian, the Deputy Mayor[2], felt compelled to deliver a capsule sketch of "a proud 5000-year-old Jewish history," of Jewish life in Galicia, and specifically, of Jewish life and contributions in Rohatyn. He emphasized, as did other local speakers, the once "peaceful coexistence of Ukrainians and Jews." As educator, he emphatically decried "anti-Semitism in all its manifestations."

By referring to Cain and Abel, the Roman Catholic priest raised the question of the accountability of the perpetrators. He concluded that only the Almighty would know the answer. He said his parishioners were disquieted when asked to speak of those ill-fated days.

The first of two Greek Orthodox priests to address us asked the Jewish people to accept the heartfelt sympathy of the Ukrainians on the loss of the "guiltless victims" at the hands of German Nazis. The second priest thanked the Jewish community for inviting him and his co-religionists to take part in this memorial to honor the victims.

References were also made to the Bible and the Jews: "The Jews are the chosen people..." These words rang like haunting echoes of past sermons, when identical phrases were invoked as epithets against us! One speaker stated that "the Jews are as numerous as stars in the heavens and sand in the sea"; is that the perception? He asserted "and they have the right to live." One clergyman concluded his address by wishing all nations in the region [of Israel] "peaceful skies."

The local officials repeatedly called for friendship and cooperation between Israel and the Ukraine.

The words and the welcome mat contrasted with 54 years ago. It was as though someone had rewritten a familiar play. Was there some kind of spell at work? Are the days of the Messiah imminent? Somehow, the present scene reflected in the mirror of the past, obeyed other laws, tore at the contours of past experience, wrenched perspectives! Today we are God's children, 54 years ago we were the despised and a threat to mankind!

In addition to finding the survivor Boris Arsen from Ivano Frankivsk (Stanislawow) in the Ukraine, news of our return rewarded us with the amazing discovery that two Jewish children had survived. A five-month-

2   He enumerated Jewish buildings now in public use.

old girl had been taken under the protective wing of a single Polish woman. She survived in Poland. The other child survived in the Ukraine, raised a family and is still living there, albeit in extreme poverty and need.[3] These were heartwarming discoveries and brought about an amazing reunion! Never in a million years would any of us fathom that a Jewish child would find cover in the heartland of 1940's Ukrainian nationalism. Her biography is a story of unbelievable harshness. I discovered this survivor by way of a Ukrainian woman, who came to greet me. The most touching moment came when I met the daughter of the surviving Jewish child.

Entering the Ukraine of 1998, especially the major cities, is like

Plaque on wall of former Judenrat building at the edge of what was the Rohatyn ghetto from 1941 until 1943. The Judenrein was on Shavuot (June 6) 1943.

leaving the West behind and entering a destitute Austria of the 19th century. Though the land is still beautiful, the towns are ravaged. In this once fertile "breadbasket" of Europe, poverty is rampant. The plight of children moved one of our group to make a contribution to the orphanage housed in the former Judenrat building. People sympathetically lament the conditions in the Ukraine, but oh, how I wish that the Jews of these towns and hamlets had become poor and had remained alive!

Once a provincial town with a cosmopolitan orientation in fashion, education and commerce, the present Rohatyn stands in sharp contrast to the Rohatyn of our day. Its streets and sidewalks are now eroded by decay. The town looks withered, tawny, lethargic; it was unrecognizable. As one of

3   Please see chapter entitled, "Three Rohatyn Survivors We Discovered in Rohatyn in 1998."

us who left in the early 30's remarked, "They have turned the town into a village." Gone is the 1930's cosmopolitan aspect - witness the photos of women of the 1930's elegantly dressed, complete with hat and gloves. Gone also is the pageantry of Ukrainians and Poles in their Sunday best promenading from the Kosciol and Tzerkve churches. Gone is the vivid mix of three different cultures, each distinctive; each living, working, celebrating side by side and each a full-scale community.

Gone are all three synagogues; only a cornerstone stump of the large synagogue, which couldn't be dislodged when a half-paved road was built in its path, stubbornly remains. Gone are all the Jewish communal buildings, which were witness to Jewish life in prewar times. Some desecrated Jewish burial stones, from 1941 used as pavement, were retrieved from the streets and returned to the cemetery by the present Deputy Mayor. The ghetto was burned down when fires were set and grenades were thrown to smoke out the Jews in the bunkers during the Judenrein (final liquidation of the ghetto). The cemeteries, like the Jerusalem of Lamentations, lie desecrated, devastated and abandoned.[4]

At the concluding ceremony, our spokeswoman from Israel made an appeal to the Ukrainian community to preserve the mass graves and monuments, to protect them against vandalism. She quoted a motto from the book about the local 16th century heroine Roxolana, who was captured by the Turks in Rohatyn in 1529, but later was installed as the Sultan's favorite wife. The epigraph states: "Many dark roads lead to unknown gates those people, who have no country of their own."[5] To the young local people in the audience, who might wonder if such evil as the Holocaust really took place and who knew little about the Jews, she offered one rational explanation for the plight of the Jews throughout the ages. She said, "The Jews were persecuted, because they too, until the creation of the State of Israel, were a people without a country."

Subsequent ruminations

Agata Tuszynska in her book on Poland Lost Landscapes records following the tracks of Jewish life in towns described in Isaac Bashevis Singer's novels. She says "in the little Jewish towns there are traces, there is a sense of something missing, the erasure of a certain important element of prewar daily life." I wonder, would the older Ukrainians with a memory of Jewish life in Rohatyn also say that there is something missing, something

---

4   The restoration still needs investment and work.

5   Approximate translation.

495

gone from the warp and woof of life in their Ukrainian Rohatyn? Would they also sense that dynamic interlocking pieces of the clockwork of that prewar civilization are missing?

Rohatyn, Ukraine. Memorial stone on mass graves site of March 20, 1942 akcja, in which 3,600 Jews were annihilated, including 600 children.

Memorial stone on mass graves site of June 6 (Shavuot), 1943 Judenrein akcja. During the 3 day liquidation of the ghetto, bunkers were turned into craters by grenades.

Update of Condition of Jewish Monuments in Rohatyn and of the Town in May, 2003

Israeli and US Rohatyn Societies' Efforts

by Donia Gold Shwarzstein

The Israeli Rohatyn Society made three trips to Rohatyn to lay the groundwork for the memorial, to put up memorial stones (designed by Zahava Tal, daughter of Mr. and Mrs. Acht of Rohatyn) on the mass graves, to clean up and secure the two Jewish cemeteries, and finally, to provide for the care and maintenance of those sites. The year following the Memorial Service care was provided by the Deputy Mayor, high school principal, together with school children. The Israeli Rohatyn Society provided for the fencing in of both the old and new cemeteries, the buttressing of the old cemetery retaining wall (to prevent bone leaching), as well as for the erection of signs at the entrance to each. According to reports I received from the Israeli Society, an international Jewish group subsequently modified the fence of the new cemetery in strict observance of Jewish law. The maintenance of these sites is still dependent on local Ukrainian work and good will. At the outset, maintenance was supported by a modest stipend from the Israeli Rohatyn Society.

Since 2000, both the Rohatyn Society in Israel and in the US began to lose their key people, their moving spirits. Remaining leaders of the Israeli Society worried about the long-term care of the mass grave monuments and the cemeteries. Their Society's funds were nearly exhausted in the last two years. They expressed the hope that the work of maintaining those sacred sites would somehow continue.

The Town of Rohatyn since 1998

Since that memorial in 1998, the town of Rohatyn has dressed up for tourists. The town square, the town square centerpiece of Rohatyn, as well the streets and sewer/water infrastructure in the center have been rebuilt from below the ground up.

During the German Nazi era the Rohatyn town square was the infamous German creation – the Umschlagplatz – the collection point for Rohatyn Jews to be taken to their mass graves. That is where I found myself on that fateful March 20, 1942. Every surviving Jew of Rohatyn remembers or has recorded that Umschlagplatz.

The town square has gone through several re-creations. During the Polish reign, it was a park with flowerbeds and benches, a place for young children and families; in 1944, it was the site of obelisks dedicated to Soviet soldiers, "Heroes of the Soviet Socialist Republic," who died fighting the Banderowcy;[1] in 1998 it was a brooding forest of unrelieved grimness, where aged peasants huddled on a bench in its deep shadows.

Since the reconstruction of Rohatyn, with funds obtained from Kiev by the indefatigable Mayor, the town square is dominated by a tall female figure, a

beauteous statue of Roxolana, who was abducted by the Turks, but succeeded in becoming the reigning monarch of the conquering Turks. Roxolana is Rohatyn's Ukrainian folk heroine, whose history is distant enough in time to arouse no contention, nor evoke painful memories for any ethnic group there.

Rohatyn in 2003 has a world-class tourist brochure and features the Jewish mass grave monuments among its sights. Its target population consists of the post-World War II Ukrainian expatriates and Jews in search of roots. Rohatyn's Ukrainian pride is its 17th-century painted wooden church. This historic church is situated right across the river from where the ghetto stood, from which on June 6, 1943 (during the Judenrein) desperate Jews fled across the bridge, being felled by pursuing shots just steps from its entrance. The new Rohatyn map, unlike the 1943 Nazi period map unwittingly handed to us in 1998, does not have the glaringly vacant space where the ghetto was "liquidated" in June 1943.

Alas, the pride of Rohatyn Jews, the big synagogue, whose interior was ornamented with beautiful paintings, no longer exists – only its crude relic stump stubbornly protrudes in the path of a now dusty side street!

In 1945, after war's end, survivors sped from the Rohatyn area to Poland as soon as the Four Powers' Agreement afforded lawful westward passage in freight trains. And from there, taking risks to life and limb, survivors continued their flight across the Iron Curtain to the West.

In 1998, we, the handful of Jewish mourners, returned to Rohatyn. We received a welcoming reception from the Mayor, his family, the County officials, the clergy (also from a local childhood friend of mine), and a small group of local onlookers. That was a stark contrast to our plight during the Nazi period, as well as the time of our departure in 1945.

In 1998, and in 1999 when three delegates went to Rohatyn to complete the work of enclosing the cemeteries and putting monuments and signs in place, our group stayed at the Mayor's and his neighbor's home. The Mayor,

1 The Soviets subsequently resettled large numbers of the local population.

his wife, and children were hospitable and gracious. The Mayor and Deputy Mayor kept watch over the cemetery improvements and the monuments' erection that our Israeli Society initiated. The Deputy Mayor put in effort to have school children in the summer of 1998 and 1999 tend the mass grave sites, plant flowers around them.

I am looking at the shining Rohatyn tourist brochure, with its ancient historic church, as well as the panoramic photo of the so-called New (Jewish) Cemetery, both recently sent from Rohatyn to Freda Kamerling Perl in Israel and forwarded to me. I feel such an ache – Rohatyn's beautiful synagogue is irretrievably lost!

Though we unavoidably had to face the scenes of our devastation, we survivors are grateful to the Israeli Rohatyn Society that they set in motion and saw through to fruition the Memorial services in Rohatyn.

In Memoriam

Letter from beyond the Grave
By Genia Messing

Translated from Polish by Donia Gold Shwarzstein

Rohatyn, 24th January, 1943

My Dear Beloved Sister and One and Only Brother!

We have begun the fifth calendar year of war, of a horrific war, a war that will be unique in the historical annals of mankind.

The outbreak of the Polish-German war brought us an upheaval similar to that of other nationalities, however the second war, and afterwards the arrival of the Germans, brought us the extermination of Jews altogether, and of Polish Jewry in particular.

My Dear Ones, I want to describe to you in miniature, condensed, our nightmarish past.

The arrival of the Germans evoked among us, Jews, a terror, a panic-stricken terror, because we knew what means they used with respect to Jews. But we did not imagine how far they went in their savage sadism. Already in the first week they drove a crowd of Jews into the big synagogue, and there the worst scenes played themselves out. At twelve o'clock came to us a Ukrainian militiaman with the order that in five minutes' time everything living, everyone who's alive, take all provisions and head for the synagogue. We knew, more or less, what awaited us. In any case, one thing was certain, the men were in the greatest danger - that is what we all thought. We hid Father and Luzer in the attic. This was a very flimsy, inadequate hiding place. We prayed to G-d that he should not abandon them in this difficult moment.

Mother was sick, she was lying in bed, and beside her was Karola; Grandmother was in her room. Having packed provisions into a backpack, I put it on my back, a kerchief on my head - I removed the ring from my finger and gave it to Karola - I went into the room, to take a last look at my sweet mother, for I was certain that they will shoot us all there. I couldn't utter a word to Karola, because tears were choking me terribly.

I looked around at our dear home, and with one glance said goodbye to it. With what a terrible feeling I left home. I joined the group of people from our street. My body bent under the somewhat for me excessive weight.

And the Ukrainian militia guard beat us so terribly with his rifle that it was impossible to take a step forward. He kept screaming constantly "Wio, hajta, skoro, skoro."[1] and with every word, he struck us with his rifle butt.

In this way we crossed the entire town. When we arrived at the synagogue, they separated us from the men; they took our provisions, stood us against the wall and told us to wait. No one stood guard beside us. At this point one woman started shouting: "We have gone through terrible Jewish troubles here for a dreadful butchery [to come]. Let us say prayers in preparation for death."

When the first words of prayer were uttered, a German arrived and ordered us to disperse. The men, however, remained in the synagogue. There they tied the rabbi to the large candelabrum - blood was running from his head, that is how terribly they beat him. They ordered him to sing, to deliver a speech. Each of his words was accompanied by a punch. Not only did they beat him, they tormented everybody.

On returning home, I learned that they will set the synagogue on fire with the people inside. Just imagine what was going on in the Jewish streets! Women collected gold, silver, money, and in this way they succeeded in rescuing 600 Jews from a terrible death. This was the Germans' greeting to us.

After some time they demanded from us contributions; they issued an order to put on a white band on the right arm.

Four weeks after this reception, their plan for the Jewish quarter was unveiled. We had to vacate our house and move to another street. We moved three times, and for five days we had no roof over our heads.

The worst thing was that Mother was bedridden. My poor, distressed mother wept whole days. Father slept near me on the floor, Luzer by a friend, and I with Karola in some kind of terribly dirty kitchen, where fleas ate us steadily.

In the end we got an apartment by the Family Kartin! We lived seven months in relative peace. Father worked in the Kahal (Jewish Community Council), Luzer was a Jewish policeman, and I with Karola took care of housekeeping. Mother was quite weakened; she didn't get off the bed.

This way passed the winter, which was quite hard for us; we didn't have enough money, and everything was priced very high (high cost of living). Yet somehow we staved off misery. In truth, Father looked very bad, but this was more because his spirit was suffering, more from the distress than from that diet. We waited for spring with great longing; we set our hopes on it - we believed that it would bring us a change for the better.

---

1   "Hajta, wista wio," is the way in Polish and Ukrainian a horse is being ordered to get moving, "skoro, skoro," means fast, fast.

But unfortunately, the first day of spring announced our great disaster. A horrible pogrom[2] took place in our town.

The 20th of March was mad, echoing Chmielnicki's (Chmielniszczyzna) bloodbath—in the course of eight hours, it swallowed two and one-half thousand Jews[3]. March 20th will be written in our history in letters of blood.

My Dear, do you know what the word pogrom signifies? Do you know how much sadism, cannibalism, barbarism and savagery this word contains?

No, most certainly, no, because it cannot be defined in words, for the phrases will be empty, they will fail. One has to go through a pogrom to describe it. Unfortunately, we are that unhappy generation, whose lot it is to be subject to pogroms uninterruptedly.

March 20th started beautifully. That morning the sun rose early to warm with its golden rays this human valley of tears, which was frozen and permeated with ice and chill. Birds chirped cheerfully in the air. No one had a presentiment that within a few minutes such a savage tragedy will run rampant in the town. At 7:00 in the morning I went down to the storeroom to feed the chickens – all of a sudden a shot was fired. I didn't know what this signified, but before I could collect my thoughts, a second was fired, then a third, and the next. Barely able to breathe, I rushed into the room.

Father stood in his tallis and prayed. I tore the tallis from him and rushed him from the room to go into hiding. Luzer at that time was already at his post. All the men in the building were already in the hideout when one woman fell dead on the street at the hands of the criminals. After this happened even the women went into hiding. Only I and Karola remained at Mother's bedside; we couldn't leave her alone, and it seemed to us that she would not be able to climb up into the attic.

But at the last minute, when they already led people from our neighbors' house, we grabbed Mother and hid together with the rest of our building's residents.

My Dear Ones! You cannot imagine what was happening. They surrounded the Jewish quarter from all sides; there was no possibility of escaping. Masses of people treaded along the streets, led by the Germans, by Ukrainian Militiamen and young Ukrainians. Everything that was alive had its say – everyone tried to fulfill his great civic duty and deliver a few Jews to the slaughter.

They drove them all forward toward the town square. Outside raged a

---

2   The German Nazis referred to them with the antiseptic word Aktion; in Polish akcja.
3   Three and one-half thousand were annihilated on March 20, 1942.

dreadful wind, it howled and wailed as though it wanted to express its great pain and protest against the insane surge of killings. Along the streets moved ill-fated mothers, holding their darling children in their arms. Unfortunate Jewish mothers - how many waking nights you spent at your babies' cribs, how much suffering you went though until you raised them; how your heart rejoiced when you heard the first chirrup. Mothers, fathers, with what care you assisted your sons in starting to learn Chumash - and your joy knew no end at their bar mitzvah! On the 20th of March you yourselves had to lead your treasures to the massacre.

On the town square, in the deep snow, they deposited the human mass, heads earthward; they mistreated them so terribly that some begged for the bullet. What shattering shrieks and screams tore from the little ones' chests. The older ones didn't weep, their dull gaze turned to the ground; they awaited their terrible end.

You Barbarians, how could you look on, laugh and rejoice, when so many beautiful children - children who just an hour ago clung in their warm beds to their mother's heart, so many beautiful healthy boys and girls, who were just blossoming - were being tortured. Are you completely devoid of all feeling? Did you never possess your own family and hearth?

At the outskirts of town they prepared two huge graves, which were dug by Jews. Many a Jew prepared the grave for himself and his family. From the town square they drove the people in autos to the graves, so as to end the life of two and one-half thousand.

Mothers implored that they should first kill them and afterwards their children. But the sadists didn't want to grant their plea. Our Luzer was driven away in the last transport. All day he lay in that terrible weather and frost, beaten, broken; he got a bullet near the grave before evening.

Earth, how could you absorb this many young sacrifices! Why did you not oppose? Why did you not refuse asylum space to so many young people? Did you also accept this act? Did you also join the savage criminals and help them in this deed. You swallowed in big draughts the young, healthy, and so innocently spilled blood.

And when it was already too much drink (to saturation), you gave it back, forming small streams of Jewish blood.

My Dear Ones, are you imagining what went on here at home? There was no end to our fierce despair. We placed on the altar of suffering and torment of our people such an exquisite sacrifice - we gave our brother, handsome, wise and bursting with life. Fate played on us such a terrible trick, for it seemed to be the intended irony of fate that our brother, just before his brutal death, grew so manly and good looking. Our heart had to be of iron, since it did not burst. To lose such a wonderful brother and yet go on living - that became a natural thing.

Amid this terrible suffering, began a beautiful spring. But not for us. The sun did not shine for us; nor did the birds chirp cheerfully for us. In our hearts was a deep pain and limitless longing. The only variation in our gray life was our excursion to the graves, to our beloved unfortunate victims. Here we could cry our fill, scream out from within our terrible pain. We tore ourselves with difficulty from the cold grave to come back to our dismal ghetto.

Misfortune, which was our lot, followed one upon the other in rapid succession, and we fell into an uncontrollable despair, in which we constantly existed. Not quite six months after the pogrom, a typhoid epidemic broke out in the ghetto. Our father became ill right at the beginning. He was sick four days and died. In the last two days he was completely unconscious.

My Dear, are you picturing what we were going through? I stood at Father's bed for hours; I shouted and called to him – I wanted that he at least look at me one more time. But it was in vain. Father didn't hear and didn't see; he just stared into the distance with blank eyes, snored with an open mouth, and jerked his arms and legs.

Oh G-d, this was just something so terrible - to stand and look on how such a dear being ends and not to be able to help him. My poor mother was lying beside him in bed, observing all this. Oh, what must have gone on then in her ailing heart! Father passed away so lightly, so blissfully; just before giving up his spirit, he heaved a deep sigh; he let the cane fall and finished life. He was so wondrous, so majestic, that I looked the whole time at his soulful face. This picture will remain forever in my memory.

My Dears, do you remember Father's beautiful hands? They were so marvelous and aristocratic on his deathbed. They didn't let us look for long at our dear Father; soon they took him away and buried him in a dark grave next to Grandfather. The son didn't say Kaddish at the Father's grave, for he already rested an eternal sleep in this massive grave.

Broken in spirit, we returned from the cemetery home, where our sick mother lay suffering terribly. We sat seven days of penance in a state of profound pain and inconsolable grief. My sick mother's condition became markedly worse. She became swollen. It was so hard for her to move, to sit up. Oh, how terribly she suffered. A wound opened in her belly, from which flowed endless fluid. Her suffering went over her strength, but it didn't have to last much longer, because four weeks after Father's death we experienced the second pogrom.

This was on Yom Kippur. That was a terrible holiday for us. You know very well how this day affects people's disposition, and especially us, for our wounds were still so fresh. We couldn't find a place for ourselves. A dreadful pain tore the heart in shreds. We were not allowed to cry or say anything out of our concern for Mother.

Early in the morning on Yom Kippur, not far from our house, a car drove up with men in green uniforms. We knew at once what their arrival announced. We jumped out of bed in our nightgowns; Mother drove us from the room, so we would go into hiding. But there was no talk of her coming with us, for she was then already in agony, yet completely clear thinking.

And we, grown wild, mean – I have no words to describe our low moral state - we did what Mother ordered. We left her behind in bed and went into hiding. What do you think of us? I know, we deserve your contempt, but perhaps the time will come when you will understand us. That pogrom lasted two days. You can't imagine what it's like to sit on a scorching day in a dark underground hole, nearly without any access to air, without food. How much of our strength it took, when every few seconds we heard the steps of those criminals above our heads. Our hearts beat with hammer blows when they were already beside our bunker, and it was solely thanks to the good fortune of fate that they did not find us out. My pen is too poor to describe all this to you. But were I able to do so, you would still not comprehend it. To sit and to listen intently if a shot isn't fired upstairs - for that is where our dear Mother was lying - and when we didn't hear one, we were sure, that we will still find her alive. But though the murderers didn't kill her, our unfortunate Mother died of dreadful fright.

My Dear Ones, can you imagine what I went through, when I slipped out of the bunker, flew like a madwoman to Mother to hug her, and found instead only a dead and icy body. Believe me, My Dear Ones, I couldn't even shed one tear. Only a wild, dull scream escaped my chest. For this was really something awful. For six whole years, we never left our sick mother in the room, but in the last hours of her life, we did! She ended like a dog, not having her closest people beside her, not having anyone to turn to with her last wish. I couldn't dwell on Mother for long, because the enemy continually raged outside. The next day, when it was possible to leave the hiding place and go to the apartment, we found an empty bed. They took Mother to the common grave. This was so terrible. I think you know what meaning a mother's grave has for children. But we couldn't help ourselves, we couldn't do anything. Before we could collect our senses, the third pogrom started. Again the bunker,[4] again the fear, the alarm. And so continually, continually, our life is a chain of terrible suffering and frightful panic. We survived terrible things. If a year before somebody had written about a utopia,[5]

4   Bunkers were constructed to escape capture during akcja.

5   As used here, an imaginary world, but not visionary and ideal, with an imagined political and social system.

dealing with the subject of our Jewish reality, he would have been accused of fantastic, implausible inventions; or he would have been thought degenerate, belonging altogether to a different epoch. To live in a period of such a high flowering of culture and civilization and to undergo such terrible cataclysms, is an abnormal thing.

To proclaim progress on one hand, and on the other hand to murder innocent people, unarmed women and children – this will remain an incomprehensible matter.

Our gigantic enemy wanted to completely wipe the Jewish nation off the world arena. He may have succeeded by about 60 percent, but he will not destroy it entirely. We are the only people in the world, who, despite many nations repeatedly conspiring against us, continue to exist and will exist until mankind's last days!

Eternity is imbedded in the psyche of our nation. Israel has survived all nations, which once were lying in wait to bring about its extinction, and Israel will also survive this dark wave of murders of its sons.

Be well. When good times return for our Jewish people, may it be our good fortune to meet face to face, and for me to relate to you the sad history of Polish Jewry.

Genia

I am entrusting this letter to a Polish family, which, in the event of our death, will mail it to you after the war. After you receive this letter, I beg you, reward them generously.

My Dear Family, only today, that is, in the fourth month [of the year][6] I am delivering this letter. When I wrote this letter, I didn't believe that we would be alive until this season! But what do we have from that: the war is already approaching its end; we know that its end will be wonderful, but, unfortunately, we have little chance of surviving it. The enemy rages on, he's going mad, he's in a hurry to finish us off. We need a big miracle, for terrible days are coming for us. We are among the few localities left where a handful of Jews are still around.

My Dear Ones, do you have any idea what goes on in our hearts? The war will end, and yet they keep on murdering us so terribly. One would wish so to survive the war, and to tell you all that has happened. Only we will no longer be human. We will be without hearts, without even minimal feelings; we will be wild people, people from the [dark, lawless] Middle Ages.

We stand helpless, unable to do anything. No one wants to reach out a hand of friendship. Everything turned its face away from us, and most of all our Great G-d abandoned us to be prey to fate. There are moments, when we envy our Luzer and our parents. But so what, nobody asks us anything; they are doing with us whatever pleases them.

Be well,
Genia

Friday, 6:00 o'clock, April 11, 1943.

Deposited by Nat Gutenplan at Yad Vashem, I. D. : Yud Daled-Vav Shin, Snif Tel Aviv, #Mem - 2694/156.

Written in Polish by Genia Messing, referred to in the Yizkor Book as Esther-Gittel.

---

6   The Rohatyn ghetto was liquidated on Shavuot, June 6, 1943.

Dr. Michal Gold

By Donia Gold Shwarzstein

On the steps of Charles U. Medical Faculty in Prague.

Dr. Michal Gold of Rohatyn received his medical degree in 1934 at the Medical Faculty of the German University, a part of the Charles-Ferdinand University in Prague. After completing his studies, he was unable to practice medicine in Poland. Besides quota restrictions in the number of Jews allowed to enter a Polish medical school, Jews who obtained their medical degree abroad faced restrictions in being admitted to the two-year course required to have their medical degrees accredited in Poland. In a letter of May 26, 2001 from Dr. Sterzer of Ramat Gan, now deceased, I learned that he, Dr. Gold and Dr. Teichman, were not admitted to the two-year program required, while their Gentile colleague was admitted immediately. Drs. Sterzer and Gold were employed as physicians from 1939 until 1941, under Soviet occupation. At that time Dr. Gold was appointed Public Health administrator. Dr. Teichman, who received his medical degree in France, immigrated to the USA, where he practiced medicine.

Dr. Gold was a genteel, refined gentleman. He was beloved by his large circle of friends. According to Dr. Sterzer, "Dr. Gold was supposed to marry the daughter of Rohatyn advocate Goldschlag. The girl was very beautiful and a trained singer. Her name was Doda. Unfortunately they did not live to fulfill this goal."

Dr. Gold was blond and fair-haired. On March 20, 1942, in the first akcja, Dr. Gold was at the outskirts of the town, far from the ghetto. The Gestapo would not have known that he was a Jew, but one local individual informed on him and had him shot.

Mrs. Freda Kamerling Perl from the village of Zolczow provided this brief written account of Dr. Gold's dedication as a physician and of his humanity.

"Dr. Gold, was my sainted brother's friend. I knew him because in 1935, when my mother fell ill with ulcers – which in those days was considered a serious illness – Dr. Gold came to us every other day in order to administer injections. Our entire family awaited his arrival with enthusiasm, especially the children, for he had a winning personality and he loved joking with them. My father praised his modest ways, for he never allowed us to pick him up from the train station, or to take him there. He always went to the train station on foot." On a previous occasion, when we met in person she told me that his service was rendered free of charge.

A Neighbor's Recollection of Dr. Michal Gold

"I remember the family Gold from my earliest youth. We lived on the same street, Slowackiego, in the town of Rohatyn, and only four houses separated from the Gold house. I remember every member of the family, but especially their younger son Michal. He was young, quite a handsome man, blond. He finished his medical studies abroad, since in Poland admission to medical school and the practice of medicine were greatly restricted for Jews.

There were five children in our family, and so it frequently happened that one of us was ill. Mocio (Mordechai) Teichman used to be our family doctor but after he married an American and emigrated to the U.S., Michal Gold was the only one who came by to treat our family.

A disastrous accident occurred when my younger brother Milek cleaned the stable for the cows and stuck the rake through his boot. Blood burst out through the boot. No one thought there would be serious consequences. Not a single member of my family was at home, and so they (whoever was present) washed his wound with petroleum.

A few days later Milek got high fever; he didn't want to eat. Dr. Michal Gold came by and asked: 'What happened?' At that point everyone remembered that blood had burst through the boot. Michal immediately sent a prescription for medicine to the apothecary. He suspected that this is tetanus, and as a rule an injection must be given without delay, or else the consequences are very dire. The injection was too late, and a severe reaction set in. After the injection my brother's body was in a tremor; he became swollen. This lasted several hours. Mother fainted and fell from her bed, because she couldn't bear the frightening outlook. Just then my brother came to and said that he feels better.

Michal Gold continued to come several times a day, and he did all this without compensation. All he was concerned about is to be there in case he was needed. These days there aren't many people like he. May his memory never perish."

More
Memoirs

My Journey to My Place of Birth

By Freda Kamerling Perl, Bat Yam, Israel

September 1992

My journey to my place of birth can be described in the words of the greatest French author, Marcel Proust: *À la recherche du temps perdu*... One cannot detach oneself from childhood memories, and this is of course a well-known human characteristic – the desire to see the place we came from, and maybe the desire to see what it looks like in our absence.

I distinctly wanted to step once again on that same ground on which I used to run barefoot, playing hide-and-seek as a child; on those dirt roads where I hurried day by day to the train station on my way to school in Rohatyn; to get another glimpse of those green flourishing fields where I used to dream my childhood dreams.

We left my place of birth with no looking back, leaving no trace or sign of our presence behind. And here I am now, alive, with an Israeli passport which intrigues the clerk in the airport of Lwow, who calls out to his colleague: Hey, look, an Israeli passport!

And the woman dwelling on the land that used to belong to us, who had already managed to build a house where our old house used to stand, is alarmed – is my coming a sign of my intention to reclaim that which belongs to me, to my family...

It was not easy to get my family's consent to such an "adventure." The state of interior security was not encouraging, but I was lucky – the villager who was my host (a righteous man in Sodom) arrived at the airport with his son, in a car, and after my two-day stay drove me back to the airport. In fact, I was hardly ever on my own, and therefore I couldn't affirm nor contradict whatever was written in the press.

I came to Lwow from Warsaw in a 55 minute Euroflot, and if it hadn't been for the melancholic thoughts that came to my mind, I could have felt like any other tourist on his way from Paris to Amsterdam. Naturally, that was not the case. I was tense and the agony started gnawing at me as we left Lwow (where I had never been before).

We started among the green fields and the forests – the thought that in that same landscape that horrible tragedy of our people, our dearest, took place, gave me no rest. I did not cry. Neither was I able to say a word. I broke into

517

tears only later on, on the last day, sitting alone in my room, writing postcard after postcard...

While we were driving through Bobrka Stare Siolo, Strzelisko, Podkamien, Czercze I couldn't help thinking that the houses we passed by, the streets we walked through were once filled with Jews, who gave those towns their essence. And now – not a sign, not a trace of all those people of those days!

We went into Rohatyn from Slowackiego Street (if I remember correctly) through the Polish monastery, which used to stand by Matylda's Photo Studio. I recognized the street on the spot. It was there where my friends—Sabina Wind Fox and Lusia Segal—used to live. We stopped at the rynek. I moved out of the street feeling strange, as if I were dreaming. I looked around—the same buildings, the same kamienice, but it all seemed much smaller, as if partially sunk in the ground.

I went for a walk from Preis's house. I went into Krotka alleyway where I lived with the Rotraubs as a student na stancji [as a boarder]. The stores of Reiss, Bohnen and Kleinwachs were still there. On the other side of the street I didn't recognize any names. Then I turned to Mickiewicz [Street] heading for the Babincie [neighborhood]. The view had hardly changed; only the trees had become thicker and it felt like everything was swelling with green—perhaps trying to hide something ...

I tried to recall how Rohatyn looked 51 years ago, when, as a little girl, I came from my village to visit the town, which then seemed like a metropolis. The noise, the commotion, not necessarily signs of good life—no, life was hard and sweaty, but it was life!

I waited for a miracle to happen, for the sudden appearance of someone from that period, or at least for a voice to be heard out of all those voices that filled the town back then. But it was all in vain. No miracle occurred – it was all gone for good. What I was looking for wasn't there to find.

I went to a building I thought to be the synagogue. The building was being redecorated for some social event. It was Sunday, and it was clear that some construction work was going on, but there was no one to ask whether that was truly the synagogue, and what was being built there instead.

My village had changed. As an accidental tourist I might have admired changes: a paved road instead of a dirt road, water installation instead of wells, electricity instead of oil lamps, gas for heating; not one thatched roof (strzechy) hut, pleasant accommodations (though without indoor lavatory), modern furniture; there is plenty to eat and food is no longer served in a clay bowl for everyone to eat from with wooden cups.

During private conversations one could admit that all this so-called "wealth" is the remains of the former Soviet regime. Nothing remains as a reminder of the German presence, and questions about those times are constantly answered with the same phrase: "Don't ask, don't ask."

On my way back home I was bothered with the thought that perhaps we are obligated to do something to prevent the final erasure of our existence there. I know that tombstones and monuments are being erected on top of mass graves in various towns. Maybe we ought to do the same…

The Circle of Life, Zolczow-Rohatyn
By Freda Kamerling Perl

It was June 10, 1998, a beautiful summer day. There we stood together, about 50 of us, survivors of the small town of Rohatyn, who'd come from the U.S., Europe and Israel. We were gathered together around the memorial stones we'd erected to commemorate the Jews of Rohatyn and the region murdered by the Germans. The second of Nissan, according to the Hebrew calendar, was the day they'd liquidated the Rohatyn ghetto, 13,500 Jews from Rohatyn, the region, and those refugees who'd fled from Western Poland after the outbreak of war between Germany and Poland.

It's an old saying, that what goes around, comes around, and my circle begins in the village of Zolczow, near Rohatyn, where I was born, like Mother and Grandma before me. Most of the villagers were Ukrainian peasants - about 200 households. There were 10 Polish families, and when I was a little girl, only seven Jewish families. By the time World War II broke out, their number had dwindled to three, ours, my aunt's family, and one other.

I was the fourth of eight children: Tzila (Cyla), Ze'ev (Wolcio), Zvi (Hersh), myself, Sonya (Sheindel), Shlomo, Yitzhak (Itzio) and Yair. My parents had a farm, but although on our neighbors' farms the whole family worked, even the toddlers, we used hired hands. Our parents wanted us to have an education, and sent us to school.

Every Sabbath we held the minyan in our house and the Torah scroll was kept there permanently. We could hold the minyan thanks to the addition of men who lived in the neighboring villages, like Danilcze and Ujazd. At holiday-time we held services in Lipica (Lipitza) Gorna, a village near ours, because they had more Jews.

There was very little conflict between us and our Ukrainian neighbors, because we didn't have a store or an inn, so they weren't suspicious of us. The peasants usually bought on credit, and being mostly illiterate, they had no idea what they were signing for. They thought, and sometimes with good reason, that the Jewish storekeepers were adding to their tally.

The one quarrel I remember was over land. There was a disputed path between our land and our Ukrainian neighbor's. During spring ploughing, our neighbor always shaved off a few inches to his advantage so that in the end, the path was wholly on our land. Grandfather wasn't about to put up with that, and the quarrel burst out every year, but Dad (who didn't bother about trifles), let it be. I should add that these land disputes were common among the villagers themselves, the resulting court cases making a fine living for lawyers.

It was because we'd lived together peaceably, that until after the end of the war, I'd thought that our villagers would remember all our family had done for them, and not harm them.

When we were little we all played together, Jews and Ukrainians, and as happens among kids, the game would end in a quarrel. We were pretty evenly matched. The gentiles would yell, "dirty Jew," and we would yell right back, "Ukrainian thief, drunkard, murderer." But if Fedya, the village bully appeared, we'd run off to Mother to complain. Her reply was always the same, "Then don't play with them," and I'd answer, "But Mummy, who'm I going to play with then?"

The family wasn't big enough to organize group games, and if we stayed mad at the other kids, then we'd not be able to make a fire in the fields with them and roast potatoes that tasted like Paradise.

I have to admit that I was often jealous of the gentile children. They had defined tasks to do both at home and in the fields, whereas all our parents demanded of us were high grades and good behavior.

And how we envied them their Christmas tree, and how we begged our parents to let us look at it, at least. But when Pesach (Passover) came, it was our turn to impress the others with our matzot that we distributed as gifts.

When I was 10, I finished the village school and went to school in Rohatyn, riding on the train every day. Since that day, I've always looked on Rohatyn as the town of my youth. Mother was delighted that I'd stopped mixing with "shiksas and shkutzim," and was associating with Jewish girls.

I finished 10th grade at that school. When the Soviets entered that part of Poland, they created a Workers Youth High School. I worked as a secretary in a grain warehouse in the mornings and went to school in afternoon. My matriculation certificate is dated June 26, 1941, five days after war broke out between Germany and the USSR. I'll speak little of the years 1939-45, my return to Poland and until I immigrated to Israel in 1957, but I will touch on a few events because they're branded in my memory.

First of all there's September 1, 1939, Friday and a beautiful day such as only a Polish fall day can be. I was standing by the gate of the local council where they'd posted notices of the outbreak of war. On them they'd also written, "Since Creation, the Pole cannot be brother to the German." I wasn't afraid then, but that day and that poster have stuck in my mind ever since. Perhaps it was because, although I knew nothing of war, I somehow felt that this war would be different.

When war broke out my parents didn't panic. They remembered the German soldiers of 1914 who gave chocolate to the children, and how a German soldier had saved my sister's life by taking from her a live grenade she'd been playing with. A family council determined that my three brothers, my sister Sonia and myself should leave home, should cross over into Russia, until it was all over. We were sure that the USSR was mighty, would crush the Germans in a few days, or at the most weeks, and then we'd come home.

My sister Tzila, who was married and a mother, stayed at her home in Chodorow (Hodorov), and my two younger brothers, Yitzhak and Yair, then 13 and 10, stayed with my parents. Before we even crossed the border, we had company. German planes strafed us from above, and on the ground the government orders kept us moving east. That temporary flight across the border lasted four years, in the "October Light" kolhoz in Saratov, a province near the Kazakh border.

All three of my brothers served in the Red Army. Zev fought his way from the siege of Stalingrad to Berlin, came home without a scratch on him and covered in ribbons and medals. Zvi fell at Stalingrad and Shlomo at Leningrad. And there are still those today who say that Jews never smelled gunpowder …

In 1957, I immigrated to Israel and Rohatyn was resurrected. I met friends, as well as an older generation who'd left Rohatyn before the outbreak of war. They had established the Rohatyn Emigrants Association, which every year commemorates the liquidation of the ghetto on the second of Nissan. We'd also meet to swap memories, stories and jokes.

Once the war had ended I swore that I'd revisit the scenes of my youth, but that didn't happen until Perestroika. In the meantime, the only reply to the letters I'd sent was that all the remaining members of my family had perished.

I learned from another source that a local Ukrainian had murdered my father and brother Yair. The son of a local peasant had hidden them but his brother committed the murder. Justice overtook that man when the Soviets drove out the Germans. He was tried and shot for that and other murders.

This news stiffened my resolve, but I returned to Zolchow only in 1992. According to the Israeli press, personal security in the Ukraine was none too great, but despite my family's protests, I decided to go on what was certainly an adventure. I called it "Looking for Memories of Things Past" in homage to Proust's great novel.

I flew from Warsaw to Lwow in an Aeroflot that looked as though it had been bought at a flea market.

In Lwow, Stepan Horiszni and his son were waiting for me. They drove me to Zolczow, and brought me back three days later. On the way we passed town after town like Bobrka, Strzelisko or Nowe Siolo, towns once rich in Jewish life and today they're "Judenrein."

Rohatyn is on the way to Zolczow. We drove in via Slowacki (Slovatsky) Street where my friends Sabina Wind Fox and Lucia Segal used to live. We stopped in the town square, the town center. I got out of the car with the weird feeling I was dreaming. I looked around - the same houses, the same kamienice (tall houses), but everything looked smaller and uglier.

I walked about from Preis' house to Kirschen's, then Kreizler's, Rotrow's and on. I walked into Mickewicza towards Babince, where my school was. I tried to remember the way Rohatyn looked 51 years ago when I'd come to what seemed to me to be the big city. There was noise, crowds, and not necessarily signs of the good life - no, it was a hard life, sweat and hard work, but we lived then …I hoped a miracle would happen that suddenly I'd see someone from those days or that at least I'd hear a sound like those that filled the air then, but in vain. No miracle. It was all gone without a trace. I didn't find what I'd lost.

I went to where the Great Synagogue of Rohatyn had stood formerly. At the beginning and the end of the school year we students would gather there for services. The rabbi would bless us and say a special prayer for the state president and the prime minister. In 1992 all that was left of the synagogue was a skeleton, which I recognized by its arched windows. In 1996, nothing was left at all …

Zolczow had also changed. A casual tourist should have marveled at the changes wrought by the villagers who'd "liberated" materials for some of them during the Soviet regime. Instead of a dirt track there was now a paved road, piped water replaced wells, electricity instead of oil lamps and gas for cooking and heating. There's not even one home with the traditional thatched straw (strzecha) roof, but pretty cottages, still with outside privies.

No signs remain of the German occupation, and when I asked, I was told time and time again, "Don't ask, don't ask … " On the second day I went to the place where my father and brother are buried. It was raining (kapusniaczek) and my tears mingled with the raindrops. In the middle of a field covered with shoulder-high grass and a few late-blooming summer flowers, there is a grove of bushes and trees where the villagers also buried their diseased animals … I spread flowers given me by the woman who lived in what had once been our home. That was my Yizkor for my father and brother.

While I was there, I saw that the Soviets had erected two memorial stones on the mass graves of those slaughtered by the Nazis. On them was the legend: "In Memory of the victims of fascism," without saying that these were Jews. Seeing this I had the idea that we ourselves should erect memorial stones with an inscription that identified the victims as Jews.

I brought the idea to our association, and after much discussion pro and con, it was adopted. In 1994 we contacted the authorities in Rohatyn. We worked with them on the project for four years, which culminated in the ceremony with which I began this account. When we sang together the Kaddish and the "Ani Maamin" I closed the circle that I call Zolczow-Rohatyn.

The Village Of Perenowka (Perenoovka)

By Jacob Hornstein[1]

Perenowka was three kilometers from the center of Rohatyn. It was surrounded by very well-planned potato fields and vegetable gardens. In the center of all the gardens was a brook of refreshing water. All around there were apple, cherry and pear orchards. It was very hard to overcome the temptation to help oneself to all the delicious fruit.

We came here mainly to enjoy the beauty of the fields, the spring water and the swarms of the birds. But above all we had meetings and discussions of Israel, the kibbutz movement and Chalutziut. In Rohatyn about 4 to 7 youth movements were in existence, which tried to propagandize and attract youth to the Chalutziut. It was a real fight for the souls of our youth to bring them to the Socialist Labor Zionist movement.

I was a member of HaShomer HaTzair. Later we had a split in the movement and I parted to HaNoar HaTzioni.

Perenowka in the spring of the year was also an island with a multitude of storks landing on the straw roofs of the farmers' houses. The spring water - its freshness is still in my nostrils, its taste is still on my lips. Perenowka was a place where our leaders recited poems, read stories to us and provided facts about Israel and the Yishuv (the Jewish population there).

All in all, Perenowka was a meeting place for lovers, but for our youth eager to chart a new course, it was, above all, a place to get more information about their future.

Perenowka was an island of beauty where our oppressed souls could breathe freely and concentrate on a better future.

---

1 Recollections written down by Jacob Hornstein of Brookline, MA. Mr. Hornstein left Rohatyn in 1931 for Chalutziut in Palestine and after marrying Judith Korem moved to the USA, where he raised a family. Deceased 2008, Z"L.

The Story of the Faust Kapela
(Also called Faust Klezmorim)
By Rosette Faust Halpern

In front, seated from left to right: Grandfather Moishe Faust and Granduncle Wolf Zimbter (a scholar in Jewish scriptures); Standing from right to left: the four Faust brothers, David Faust playing the violin (Kapellmeister after Grandfather retired), Yitzhak Hersh Faust playing the flute, Yankel Faust playing the trumpet; On the far left: Mordechai Shmiel Faust playing the clarinet; In the center: the "Badchan," guests and some members of the family. (Photo courtesy of Alex Feller.)

The traditional instrumentalists among the Jews of Eastern Europe were called in Yiddish Klezmorim. The name Klezmer is derived from the Hebrew words Kle, which means instrument, and Zemer, which means song. In short, they were "instrument singers."

My father was a traditional musician, a Klezmer, and so were his three brothers. His father, grandfather and great-grandfather, from generation to generation, for about 200 years, were Klezmorim. They were known throughout Galicia as the "Faust Kapela." The first violinist was the "Kapellmeister," the leader. After my grandfather Moishe Faust retired, my father, David Faust, the oldest son in the family, who played first violin, became the Kapellmeister.

Grandfather taught each of his sons to play a different instrument. Yitzhak Hersh, the second son, played the flute. The third son, Mordechai Samuel, played the clarinet; Jacob (called Yankel), the youngest, played the trumpet.

The discipline in the Kapela was very strict; everybody had to learn to read and play from notes. This rule was a "sine qua non." One could improvise a tune on occasion, but he had to write it down on paper, in musical notation. That is how my grandfather Moishe became a composer. His improvisations at weddings became popular and famous all over Galicia. In connection with this statement, there is a story of how the picture of the Faust family musicians, taken in 1912 in the town of Rohatyn (Poland), found its way into the Jewish daily newspaper in New York, the Jewish Daily Forward.

My brother, Jack Faust, gave the following information to me:

It began with a package of sheet music, which grandfather Moishe Faust composed and sent to his friend, Hersch Gross, in New York. He, in turn, showed it to the music critic of the Forward, and then to Abe Kaplan, the editor of the Forward. Impressed with the caliber and finesse of the music, they cabled instructions to their reporter, on assignment in Vienna, to visit Rohatyn and photograph the composer and his Kapela. That is how the picture appeared in 1912 in the illustrated edition of the Forward.

When the Jewish Museum on Fifth Avenue in New York produced an exhibit of pre-war cultural life of Jews in Poland, they included the Forward photo of the Faust Kapela. It is interesting to notice the difference between the two generations featured in the picture. The older generation members are strictly Orthodox in dress and appearance. The younger, the four sons, are in vested suits, according to the style of the time. Members of the older generation were educated in Jewish Scriptures, were considered scholars, and were respected by the Orthodox community. Very often the Kapela incorporated songs with religious services: on welcoming the Jewish New Year, at the conclusion of the Sabbath, and on other occasions.

A few survivors still remember the melodies that lifted the spirit of the community. Some tunes (Nigunim) taken from religious prayers, with the addition of a definite rhythm, became so popular that it was commonly said, "a wedding without the Faust Kapela is not worth attending!" To the delight of many newlyweds, the Hungarian "Rakoczy March," incorporated in the repertoire of the Kapela, became the wedding march.

After the wedding ceremony, guests listened to a special potpourri of traditional Jewish music called in Yiddish "Zum Tish" (at the table). This was the time Jewish traditional musicians had a chance to show off their skill and art of playing. The compositions played were usually based on liturgical melodies and Jewish folk music. This was also a special time to honor parents and important members of the brides and groom's family. My father, the Kapellmeister, with great gusto, skillfully supplied the appropriate music and requisite accolades.

In actuality, the main family income came from private music lessons given to the children of the Polish officials, as well as a large number of high school students. During World War II grateful parents of students returned numerous favors, including supplying the Faust family with food, which in many instances became their main sustenance, staving off hunger. Among the beneficent individuals was a woman whose children had been my father's students. This woman was also instrumental in my surviving the Holocaust.

1999 Speech: Reflections on the Implications of the Holocaust

The pivotal event in both the history of the Jewish people and of my own family in particular

By Marta Wohl, Daughter of Herman Wohl of Rohatyn and his wife, Bertha Wohl, of Bursztyn

Sixteen years ago, on April 9, 1983, my father attended the Yom Hashoah Commemoration in this synagogue. In July of that year my father and my mom came to visit me in California, and, under a full moon in the Yosemite Valley, we started what was supposed to be a series of audiotape recordings of his story. It was both the first and the last recording. My father passed away in November of that same year. He followed his brother, Moine, who died 15 months earlier, and who, along with my mother, Bertha, survived in the ghettoes and forests of the Ukraine, what was then Eastern Poland. I would like to dedicate this speech to both of them, and bring their spirits into the room with us tonight.

Tonight I want to share with you the trip that my mother, my brother and I took last June to Rohatyn, my father's hometown, a small town in Western Ukraine about 45 miles from Lwow, and to Bursztyn, my mother's hometown, an even smaller town near Rohatyn. But our journey actually started much earlier than last June.

In the past ten years, many, many Jews have gone back to cities and towns all across Eastern Europe and Russia, to reconnect with their lost roots. And many Jews have had just as strong a feeling that they would never want to go back. Initially, my mother was one of those. "Why go back? What's there? Not even graves, no houses, no Jews left – for what? And who wants to give even a penny to those anti-Semites?" I could certainly understand my mother's point of view. And yet, as we all know, although there was massive collaboration by Poles and Ukrainians in the destruction of Polish Jewry, there were also righteous Gentiles, who put themselves and their families at great risk, by helping the local Jewish population during the War. And one of those righteous Gentiles is Anton Malinowski, who helped my parents survive in the forests for over 18 months, and with whom my parents had stayed in touch for over 50 years. Anton, a farmer now living in Western Poland, went with his son-in-law to Israel, to try to meet my mother, but his letter of intent reached my mother when she returned from Israel, so they never met [there]. A second letter from Anton, with a picture of him at Yad Vashem and a plea for her to come to Poland while they were both still alive, convinced my mother to go. So, in August of 1994, my mother and I spent an amazing week in Warsaw and Cracow, meeting Anton Malinowski and his daughter's family, and making a deep, soulful connection to this family, a family that we have revisited and are in regular contact with to this day.

But what about Rohatyn? And Bursztyn? The door to the past had been cracked open with this visit – could it open fully? No, my mother said. She wasn't ready to go back to the Ukraine. It was too lawless, too backward, too dangerously anti-Semitic there. Even Anton advised us against going. I've never pressed my mom on these issues. I believe that this kind of journey is something you have to want to do, not be talked into doing.

Two years later, my mother read in the Together newspaper[1], put out by the American Gathering of Jewish Holocaust Survivors, that a group of Rohatyners were considering returning as a group. Rohatyn was a county seat, and was the site of a ghetto, where many of the remaining Jews from over 100 outlying towns and villages, including Bursztyn, had been gathered. Two actions by the Germans, in March of 1942 and June 1943, had killed over 12,000 Jews, and two mass graves existed there. A preliminary trip by two Rohatyners found one gravesite filled with garbage and old bones; the other site was being used by farmers. The cemeteries were in ruin. This prompted negotiations by the Israeli Rohatyn group with the local Mayor and district representatives for over a year and a half, to get the sites cleaned and to get access to the farmer's land, in order to build memorial gravestones at each site. A plaque was also affixed to the former Judenrat building in the town itself.

So, in June of 1998, a group of 60 people, survivors and their families, second and third generation, from Israel, the United States, England and Poland made the journey back to Rohatyn to dedicate these gravestones. My mother, my brother, Martin Wohl, and I were three among this group.

We arrived in Lwow, for a 3-day visit, after spending two days in Warsaw. On a stiflingly hot day, we endured Ukrainian border control bureaucracy and registered at the Grand Hotel, an older hotel in the city's center. It had been restored to some of its former majesty, with beautiful rugs and tapestried walls, but lacking in most of the conveniences we, as Westerners, were accustomed to, especially in one critical area – air conditioning! So as if to

---

1   A Tribute to My Jewish Rescuers of Rohatyn, Donia Gold Shwarzstein, Together, August 1996, p. 29.

set the scene, we were "challashing" (near fainting) as soon as we got there!

That afternoon our guide took us on a tour of old town Lwow. According to Talmudic teaching, "We do not see things as they are. We see them as we are." And as I am second generation, I saw Lwow as what it is now, not what it once was. To me, Lwow was a somewhat dilapidated but still beautiful city. The survivors, however, were shocked at its shabby condition. Once considered one of the jewels of Eastern Europe, and home to a thriving vibrant Jewish community, the second largest in Poland, they couldn't get over the decay they perceived. I was also busy looking at the Ukrainians with the same feeling I had had four years ago in Poland, and 25 years before that in Berlin – a mixture of fear, suspiciousness, distrust and outright hatred – a blanket emotion that didn't distinguish between ally and anti-Semite, between people of conscience and rapacious, eager collaborators. These were my first feelings upon stepping into what I considered the "belly of the beast."

We went to the site of the former ghetto of Lwow, but couldn't depart our bus, as the heat of the day erupted into a violent thunderstorm. From rain-drenched bus windows I strained to see a solitary boulder commemorating the murder of 135,000 Jews murdered in Lwow. One boulder.

Later that night, as the air cooled, my brother and I strolled outside our hotel, where people were sitting on park benches, playing chess, socializing and dancing to outdoor bands. I observed a culture stepped back in time, so different from the fast-paced, high-tech world I lived in. I could not deny them the same humanity that had been denied to the Jewish people during the reign of terror. I thought of the next day, our day at Rohatyn, with a mixture of dread and anticipation.

The bus to Rohatyn carrying the American contingent left early the next morning. I was saddled with cameras and video cameras, determined to be a "daughter" at the ceremony, but also determined to document the events as much as possible. The ride to Rohatyn was also a trip back through time. People in horse-drawn wagons jostled past us on the poorly maintained roads, and lush fields with farmers using hand tools were evident. The beauty of the countryside was a surprise to me, and a strange counterpart to the knowledge of the terror that I also knew its past to hold.

As we arrived in Rohatyn I heard one of the survivors cry out – "This is not our Rohatyn." That feeling of non-recognition of something being so basically wrong and missing, would persist for most of the survivors. As reported by <u>Donia Shwarzstein</u> in a Together article[2]:

2   Return to "Hell" Surreal and Overwhelming-Rohatyn 55 Years Later, Donia Gold

"Once a provincial town with a cosmopolitan orientation in fashion, education and commerce, the present Rohatyn stands in sharp contrast to the Rohatyn of our day. Its streets and sidewalks are now eroded by decay. The town looks withered, tawny, lethargic, unrecognizable. As one who left in the early 30s remarked, 'They have turned the town into a village.' Gone are all three synagogues; only a cornerstone stump which couldn't be dislodged when a half-paved road was built in its path stubbornly remains. Gone are all the Jewish communal buildings which were witness to Jewish life in prewar times."

As soon as we arrived, we were whisked off to City Hall, where we were met by the Mayor, elected officials, clergy, reporters and local onlookers. Although these gestures of eager hospitality and acknowledgment helped with a sense of safety and protection in a potentially hostile environment, it was also the beginning of a surreal atmosphere that continued the entire day. We were greeted almost as if we were triumphant survivors returning home from war—and yet this was the place from which the survivors had barely escaped with their lives! A series of speeches in Ukrainian, translated into English by our guide, welcomed us and informed us of the day's agenda. While people politely listened to the speeches, I saw survivors gather themselves into private spaces of painful memory, loss, and deep-seated grief. In the midst of the programmed speeches, an Israeli survivor stood up and started speaking in Hebrew. Immediately, the smiling town officials shot nervous glances at each other – were these Jews going to go along with the "program" or was there anger that couldn't be contained? There were murmurings from the audience. But what came forth was not anger, but a reminder to my generation – that Rohatyn is not just the site of cemeteries and mass graves, but a place where our ancestors lived for 600 years as a vital part of the culture of this town. Rohatyn is not only where our families were murdered. It was also a place where our families had lived.

Under police escort, we rode in our buses to the first memorial site, a huge field on the outskirts of town. This was where my father's parents and his brother Zisha were killed. The Rabbi of Stanislawow led us in the Kaddish. Israeli flags fluttered in the wind; Yahrzeit candles were lit. The blistering heat increased the intensity of the moment, as if palpable waves of heat carried the stirred spirits of our dead ancestors. We linked hands and sang "Ani Maamin." Outside of our group, those present included town officials, Russian Orthodox clergy, and Ukrainian peasants. Speaking in Ukrainian, Polish, Yiddish, Hebrew and English, eulogies and testimony were given by our people,

Shwarzstein, Together, January 1999, p. 24.

recounting the horrors of the past, "pouring out words of love and sorrow for the families and community that was lost and affirming our unswerving promise to remember."

Holding my camera, I shook with sobs as a woman recounted in Yiddish how they were rounded up, laid face down in the marketplace, dragged to the ditches, which they [the Germans] had forced the Jews to dig for weeks, and shot people into the ditches. They wanted to save on ammunition, so they lined up five people and shot one bullet through them. This meant that many people were buried half-alive in the graves. This heaving mass of humanity rendered the ground red with blood for weeks; they had to pour lime onto the entire area in an attempt to contain it. Later they made the Judenrat pay for the ammunition.

As the ceremony ended, my brother and I slowly walked up to the crest of the hill, closer to where the actual massacre occurred. We looked at the peaceful, bucolic scene, with no hint of its terrible history. A few Ukrainian women had witnessed the ceremony from this vantage point. My brother, through gestures, tried somehow to communicate to those women that our grandparents were buried here. Realizing the absurdity and futility of the situation, he said to me, "I guess I just don't know the international symbol for our grandparents were murdered here." We both dissolved into the kind of hysterical laughter that serves as a release for unbearable feelings of grief and sorrow, rage and loss.

We then went to the second memorial site, where my mother's parents and her sister, Shaindl, had been killed. It was a much smaller site, enclosed by surrounding hills, and yet many more Jews had been killed here. I couldn't imagine how 8,000 bodies could even be buried here. I was surprised, yet proud to hear the main testimony - someone was reading a letter that my father had written after the war, while he was in a displaced person's camp in Bensheim, Germany, to a Rohatyner in Israel. In it he described as much as he could remember what had happened to the Jews of Rohatyn, as a community and individually.

At each site the memorial gravestones referred to "the brutal killing of the Jews by the German Nazis from 1941-1944." No Ukrainian publicly acknowledged any of their people's complicity, and only one survivor spoke of and warned against revising the Ukrainian participation in the history of this period.

In the afternoon, my mother, brother and I went to search for the site of my father's house, and the house next door, where my mother's family lived in the ghetto, which is how my parents met (but that's another story). Although unsure of herself, my mother eventually found the place, by the river. The

Germans had burned the original homes to the ground during the war[3], to smoke out any Jews that still might have remained there. As I looked at the river, and the large back yard, and the houses, I thought about the stories of survival that my father often told me while growing up. "The river that ran red with blood" – here was the river; the different bunkers that my parents hid in – here was the yard. I was acquiring a canvas of sensory memories to re-envision the narratives I'd been told all my life. I listened to the sounds of roosters, the flowing river, I looked at the old man living in the house that was built on my father's property. I tried to see, hear, smell, sense extra hard, extra carefully – to be as close to being in my parents' environment as I could ever experience. Another piece of the circle of healing was complete.

The third day was the day of private pilgrimage. We hired a driver and set off to Bursztyn, my mother's hometown, near Rohatyn. We saw the sign for the town, drove on the main road, and my mother did not recognize anything. Within minutes we saw the sign indicating we were leaving Bursztyn! Quickly, we made a U-turn. After a discussion with some locals, it became clear to my mom that a whole new town, new Bursztyn, had been built. We eventually found old Bursztyn, but most of its landmarks were gone. Not only had all signs of Jewish life vanished, but even the palace, which housed Poland's only princess, was gone. We couldn't find my mother's house, nor even access the road it was on. My mother was in a state of disorientation and shock, and we had to urge her to press on, that we had come this far and this was our one chance at finding any part of her former life. We finally found a church she recognized, and a neighbor invited us in for conversation and tea. By chance, we talked to another woman on the street, who got into our car and took us to the local community center. My mother's face lit up as she discovered her old school next door. The woman then took us to the real find in Bursztyn, the old Jewish cemetery. Amid overgrown weeds, goats and geese, about 100 stones, beautifully chiseled with Hebrew letters and drawings, still stood. My mother said her grandfather was buried there. We walked quietly through the field of stones, feeling the connection to those we did not know, but whose history and blood was intertwined with ours. And we were grateful for the good fortune of meeting the woman who could lead us to this treasure.

We decided to visit Rohatyn once again. My brother suggested that we go back to the mass graves, and quietly, without the hoopla of the previous day, say Kaddish. My mother and I agreed, and we met up with some friends in another car. Together we went back to each site and made our peace with the restless

---

3   See German Nazi map of Rohatyn after the Judenrein of June 6, 1943 – where the ghetto had stood is a blank space.

souls we sought to soothe. This still communion was one of the most profound moments of our trip.

Cecilia Klein writes: "A survivor will go to a funeral and cry not for the deceased, but for the ones never buried." At the mass graves in Rohatyn, the Jews were never buried, not with stars of David, tombstones, or any reference to their Jewish identify. Even in death, their identity was denied to them. Everything that made them individuals was taken from them.

But even in death, and even after 55 years, and despite all their enemies' efforts, we were there to affirm their identity. They are our loved ones, our mothers and fathers, our sisters and brothers, our extended family, our ancestors, our community. We were there to acknowledge and mourn those we lost, and the many others for whom no one was there to mourn.

I found an alternate Kaddish prayer that addresses the sanctification of each person's name, and, on that last day in Rohatyn, in a quiet moment, I read it, and dedicated it to the unnamed dead in those graves:

Each of us has a name given by the source of life and given by our parents.
Each of us has a name given by the mountains and given by our walls
Each of us has a name given by the stars and given by our neighbors
Each of us has a name given by our sins and given by our longing
Each of us has a name given by our enemies and given by our love
Let us sing the soul in every name and the name of every soul,
Let us sing the soul in every name the sacred name of every soul
As we bless the source of life so are we blessed.

The journey to Rohatyn continued the process of transformation for myself, my mother and my brother. I respect the courage it takes for all survivors to face their past, and I am deeply honored to bear witness with you.

Annihilation of Rohatyn

As Recounted by Sabina Wind Fox on January 3, 1986

Translated from Yiddish by Donia Gold Shwarzstein

The annihilation of the town Rohatyn - however much we may speak about it, however much we may tell of the enormity of the brutality – words cannot convey what happened. For when it started – no one knew it would be like this – no one believed.

To us came from Central Poland a lot of refugees, who ran away because the Germans came there; and they didn't tell of any such killing – for if they had, all would have fled with the Russians, for there was still time – but no one believed that there would be such a catastrophe. It started in the first days, as soon as they [the Germans] arrived; they [the Ukrainians] put in jail the young people, who were rumored to belong to the Communist party, and in jail they tortured them terribly. Dr. Alter, who was known to be "left leaning" – they locked him up and beat him and they tortured her [his wife] for two weeks. In other towns they even put all those people to death.

Right after that in the morning they got hold of all the Jewish youth—the girls were put to sweep all the roads, to cut the grass in the park, to clean the barracks that the Russians abandoned. The gentiles were instructed—this was on placards – that it is forbidden to sell anything to a Jew, or to bring anything – and the Jews who had nothing, were right away going hungry.

And by Kudrik, the Greek Orthodox priest … the entire Ukrainian Intelligentsia gathered there – they met to fix the ghetto boundaries; and at the same time they decided who would be in the Judenrat. Chosen were Dr. Goldschlag, Amarant, and several other men - I will recall the rest of the names a little later… Jews were supposed to turn to the Judenrat with problems, and the Judenrat was supposed to settle everything. Within just a few weeks they made the ghetto, which after repeated akcjas [roundups, deportations and mass killings] grew smaller and smaller. Periodically they also brought in Jews from the vicinity, from the villages, from the smaller towns, such as Knihynicze, Stratyn; and later, after the first liquidation and the second liquidation [of the smaller towns in Rohatyn district]… and when they liquidated the Bolszowce and Chodorow Jewish community, whoever remained alive there came [was transferred] to our ghetto.

The first akcja on the 20th of March, 1942 - quite early in the morning they surrounded the ghetto, they ordered all the people to come out of their houses, everyone ... they ordered people to fall into double file lines and led them to the town square, that is the lot in the center of town; and the people remained lying with their faces to the ground (... Why? Maybe because there wasn't enough room ...); they had altogether two open trucks – to transport them to the mass graves ... which the Jews had been digging for a period of two months; the Judenrat received an order to furnish 40 men for this project. It was then whispered among the gentiles that the Jews are digging their own graves, but the Jews kept consoling themselves that these were defense trenches against cannons, because a German engineer was present throughout the dig and regularly checked the measurements with great precision. On the very last day of the dig, when the Jewish men were still working there, they began to drive the Jewish people to those big dugouts. It was very cold then, there was a bitter frost and snow. So the people lay frozen; nobody of them [those who were driven from their homes] understood yet, that they should have gone into hiding; no one had yet built any bunkers; no one yet understood that they must plan for survival.

And on that day they murdered 3,500 Jews. There were also many Jewish refugees among the murdered, not only local Jews. And the akcja started quite early ... a car arrived with Gestapo. First off the Gestapo went into Bojczuk's [pronounced Boychuk] restaurant to get drunk. And later they began – and the Ukrainians helped seize the Jews - and they loaded the people on the trucks and drove them to the two massive dugouts. Few escaped from the graves - even those who were wounded were buried, children were thrown in alive -one fell on top of the other. The few who escaped and remained alive gave this account: first the Germans picked three men; they told them that they will stay alive, but they must strip [collect the people's] the people of clothing, money, gold teeth; two large cases were filled.

The akcja came to an end toward night.

The next day some of the people who remained alive went to the graves to look. Mrs. Stryjer told me that buried beneath bodies were people, who were still alive and were begging to be pulled out; but the gentiles stood around and didn't allow it. One girl they rescued from the mound of bodies – she was a refugee - they carried her home on a bed sheet – her feet were shot through with bullets – but she died in the evening. Mrs. Stryjer recalled that one man told her that one person called out from the grave: "Jaroslave Koenigsberg, schlepptmicharous" (please, pullmeout)." Buttheycouldn't. The Ukrainians standing at the graves did not let them.

Then wagons with lye were brought in. Lye was poured over the people in the graves, so the local gentiles would be protected from disease. As the lye was poured, some still jerked their heads away. But those who brought the lye kept pouring it on the graves. The graves sank deeper and deeper, below the level of the ground around the graves. On the graves high grasses began to grow.

That day, March 20, 1942, I went out of the ghetto in order to pay taxes – they asked me to do a favor. The bathhouse had belonged both to the Jews and to the gentiles. It was now located inside the ghetto. A Jewish barber still worked in the bathhouse, and he begged me to go in his stead to pay the bathhouse tax. So that day, early in the morning, I went to the County Hall (Rada Powiatowa). For that reason I was outside the ghetto on March 20th, and therefore I could have escaped and not returned to the ghetto. On leaving the County Hall – this was close to the Ukrainian gimnazjum (high school) - I heard the Ukrainian youths shouting to the Gestapo, "Beat them!" I understood at once that this meant "Beat the Jews," so I began to run back into the ghetto. That morning I was supposed to do sewing by a gentile woman - she lived in a house where Kowler used to live. Just as I started to cut across the small street near the synagogue on the way there, I saw them lead Jewish girls at gunpoint. The gentiles, to whom I was running, were sitting in their house in a state of fear, now and then looking out the window to see what was going on. I kept running to them like a madwoman; as I was running, one of that family grabbed me and pulled me out (of the street) by my ears. While I was running, two Ukrainians pursued me. Ekstein's sister, lying hidden in the gentiles' cellar, observed one Ukrainian in hot pursuit behind me. She saw that all he had to do was stretch out his arm and he would have grabbed me. But just at that moment Mrs. Winter crossed his path, and she was the one they seized. When the gentile (where I was supposed to sew) wanted to drive me from his house, I wanted to go back to the ghetto, but it was no longer possible. The boundary of the ghetto was sealed off. So I remained there; I hid in the outhouse. But I knew that I could not stay there for long – if members of the family came in, they would see me there. The house once belonged to Kreizler; it was near the Jewish market stalls. I discovered a Jewish boy hiding in the outhouse. He was a child of one of the Shochtim. He ran away from the Umschlagplatz. He gave me a full account of what was happening in the ghetto: "And they came and they drove all the Jews from their houses; they ordered them to take with them their best possessions, and then they made them lie face down on the town square." He fled from there. But the boy was unable to tolerate the bitter cold of that day; he didn't want to remain in the outhouse. He wanted to leave in the worst way, but I held on to him, for I knew if he took one step, we would be discovered. I also knew, however, that we could not remain there.

A gentile man was splitting wood with his daughter in that courtyard. He came into the outhouse. He saw us, and he drove us out. A bit later he let us back in, and I was promising him all kinds of rewards for allowing us to hide. In spite of that, he went to the woman of the house and reported us to her. Her husband at the time worked for the Landeskommissar. She told the man, "I know nothing." So the man couldn't drive us out then. But when he finished work, he drove us out on his own time. Later, when I was in the forest after the liquidation of the ghetto, I told Rozka Glancberg (Glanzberg) about this incident, and Rozka, who worked for that woman as a maid at that time, told me that the woman did not want to drive us out. In those days Jews wanted to work for a gentile family in hope of some kind of safety. The man drove us out at about 1:30 in the afternoon. It was our luck that at that hour there was no shooting, while all the Jews were lying on the Umschlagplatz. I set out for the Umschlagplatz. The gentiles were looking out from all the houses and they saw me with this little boy. Just then instead of continuing to walk, I began to think, "I will go with the backyards of the houses ringing the town square." I did that, and there was a kind of neglected apartment, in which Lipschitz kept kerosene and benzene, and as I opened the door, a gentile came out and told me, "I can't keep you here; crawl in somewhere." The courtyard was cluttered with all kinds of junk and with barrels. I crawled into a thing in which people relieved themselves ... I hid there with the little boy. No sooner did we get in there, and the akcja started again in full force: more shooting, more killing. Two more boys escaped from the Umschlagplatz and hid in one of the containers not far from us. They had to be close by, because I heard the Ukrainian young men searching for them and I overheard them talk among themselves "When we catch them, the Germans won't need to do anything to them." And I already heard their breathing. The gentile who told us to crawl in somewhere must have been watching us as we crawled into the hiding place, and he told them, "I don't believe anyone is here, search there, further up." They left the courtyard. Later, in about two hours, the gentile woman brought a dry sack to spread out beneath us, she brought a covered tea kettle with hot coals, so that we could get warm, and she brought pieces of bread. When such kindness is shown a Jew at a time when he is worth nothing—that is not something to forget. But I was as if turned to stone (unable to speak)—I believed that no Jew was left alive; I thought that even if I stay alive, to whom will I turn? In the evening the boy left. He said he's going. He told me later, that he first went to the gentile family and they gave him food. I did not go out yet. I lay there a whole night, even though the gentile came at night and told me, "I see that the Jews who survived are already back in the ghetto, and I see smoke rising from the chimneys. Go there." He thought that I wanted to go, but I didn't go. Only at about 10:00 in the morning the next day did I run out. In the snow there were shattered brains. When I didn't see smoke rising from our chimney, I knew that Mother was not there. On coming back, I met two of my brothers. One hid out in a house in which we used to live, the Akster house; it used to belong to Yuzkevich (Juzkiewicz/Juszkewicz), a gentile; my brother hid in the groundwork [foundation], on which a house was to be built. The second brother worked with another fellow in the Sokol; the Sokol watchman hid them. And now we began to sit and wait, hoping that Mother would return, hoping that perhaps some people returning from where they hid during the akcja might have seen her. The talk was that there were rare cases that people returned. It was very rare, very rare that someone returned from the graves, in those cases when a layer of bodies did not cover them, or in cases when they were at the edge of the grave … then they might return. In those cases they might have crawled out at night.

In the first days, as soon as the Germans arrived, Ukrainians went to Jewish homes and took the Jewish youths that were employed by the Soviets or belonged to the parties, the Communist party, and put them in prison. They imprisoned young men, and among them was Dr. Alter. The females were incarcerated separately. They came to search for my brother. They came to look for my brother, and he wasn't home. So they wanted to take another brother, who was an invalid. So I said, I'll go instead, and my little sister said, she's also going. My mother was careful; she had the youngest brother follow us to see where we were being taken. They took us immediately to prison. There I saw the two Glancberg sisters, Henie Kinstler and a few more girls; they told us that they had been sitting there for one and one half days. Then we heard beatings and loud screams – that is how hard they beat the men. They didn't give us any food, and that is how we sat. The next day what they brought us… At noon I took a look, and there was a window with bars, and the military were in the yard; a great deal of hay and straw was strewn about in the yard, and the Jewish men were already working there. They were ordered to gather the hay. In the yard I spotted a father and his young son working there. The Kinstler girl, who was in the prison, began to yell to her brother "Meilach!" But this was strictly forbidden. The Ukrainians were standing guard. One of the guards led away the father—because the father had glanced in the direction of the window. When I saw this, I knew already whom I was up against. I saw things are very bad, because I was thrown together with leaders of the Komsomol, with Communist youth. I took a look at the window, and there was my mother. She pushed into my hands a few pairs of warm socks; she thrust into my hand some food. I said, "What has happened, you are not

540

allowed to stand here." She said, "You don't worry—I can stand here." And she told me how things stood. When she came to the jail, they didn't want to let her in at the gate. The prison was heavily guarded. So my mother went to the Weisbergs, got some brooms, she took a feather duster, and she came to the gate and said, "I work here." So they let her in. Inside she went to high-ranking Germans, and sent each of them to check on the innocent girls in prison, and she tried to do something to have them released. One of the men came and consoled us, but then came a German high officer who said to her, "The innocent always suffer." And so it went on until she came to the windows, and then the gentile standing guard wouldn't let her come near, but she promised him she would teach him German. The fellow then said, "I have a book, I don't need you." But she didn't look at the book; she at once began teaching him German: "Zug, Guten Morgen, Zug, Luft." Right away he learned a few words. Then she told him that he didn't have to look at her when she spoke. In this the way she stood at the window and consoled us. At home there was still one brother and an aunt. When Mother saw that it was nearly evening and we were still not released, she went to the priest Kudrik; there she saw the entire Ukrainian intelligentsia seated at his table. My mother thought she'd turn to him as a neighbor - she didn't know that the entire Ukrainian intelligentsia would be gathered there. They sat there and contemplated what to do. They were making the plan of the ghetto. But mother kept on talking, "They have arrested all, and they did nothing wrong. They are quiet girls, but they came and they took them ..." And those seated made no reply. They listened; they only listened. Then they informed her that today there will be a Judenrat, and the Judenrat will take care of all issues that Jews have with the authorities. "We have already decided," they said. "The Judenrat will consist of Dr. Goldschlag, Amarant (and a few more people, but at the moment I cannot recall their names)." And those men didn't know yet that they had been chosen to be on the Judenrat. My mother was the first to report it to them. The Judenrat immediately called a meeting and began to intervene on behalf of those who were imprisoned. The Ukrainians released us immediately - myself with my sister; they released us that very night. The others sat in prison for one more week in terrible fear. I'll never forget the faces of our neighbors when we came home; we saw the fear in the eyes of the Jews; we saw how all of them experienced the worry and the suffering that we went through; no one knew what terrible things tomorrow would bring. And worst of all, no one could believe that it would come to such a terrible disaster.

Rebbe Reb' 'Leizer'l and Rebbe Reb' Shloimele
By Donia Gold Shwarzstein

From the time I was very young, I remember the names of Rebbe Reb' 'Leizer'l and Rebbe Reb' Shloimele spoken with great warmth and quiet affection.

One Sabbath day, when I was about five years old (just before the war), my grandfather took me by the hand into his world. When we reached our destination, we turned into a deep front yard. The yard was alive with girls running about playing games with vocal merriment. At the end of the yard we climbed a flight of stairs. On the second floor the entrance opened up to reveal long white tables, Hassidim seated, their attention turned to the head of the table, engrossed in listening and in hushed communication. My Zayde had brought me "tsum Rebbens Tisch" (to his saintly Rebbe's table). Rebbe Reb 'Leizer'l's was a sacred space in the world of ordinary Jewish folk. There on the Sabbath and on Holy Days my grandfather, like others, found his inspiration and refuge.

Rebbe Reb' 'Leizer'l and Rebbe Reb' Shloimele were revered men whose quiet, humble piety infused the world of their followers with tranquility, buoyed the life of a large stratum of the community and filtered into all of our town.

This visit to Rebbe Reb' 'Leizer'l is indelibly embedded in my visual memory and has persevered in spite of the passage of years and the overwhelming horrific events that overshadowed all existence.

The World of the Pious in the Ghetto
Early Spring 1943
By Donia Gold Shwarzstein

Even under siege, privation, and stalking death, Hassidim didn't flinch; in the very clutch of the enemy they continued their devotion to teaching, study and prayer.

In early spring, 1943, in the ghetto, my mother gave me intricate directions and sent me to a clandestine school. I set out to a destination I did not know, weaving in and out between sheds, hidden passages, back alleys, always watching my rear and surveying a 360 degree angle to spot a Gestapo, should he suddenly appear, all the time paying no heed to heart-stopping terror. At the end of this terrifying race to outrun the Devil, I came smack upon a long, enclosed, curtain-draped veranda. Could this be it? There was no sound. I took the three stairs up, hesitatingly opened the door, and to my amazement before me sat two rows of young boys in Hassidic garb and their Hassidic Melamdim (religious teachers). A few boys momentarily turned their heads, looked surprised, but just as quickly resumed their study. Their space suspended in serenity eclipsed the surrounding war zone.

I had entered the world of the Cheder in the ghetto. This was not a school for me, and I quickly beat a retreat.

How astonishing, how courageous the sight - the orderly proceeding of concerted religious instruction of Jewish boys. In the jailer's very grasp, in the days approaching the final akcja (total annihilation), they continued without complaint their devotion to their faith. Unforgettable! To our great sorrow, their lives were snuffed out. To my knowledge, none of them survived.

In Remembrance of Refugees who Found a Haven in Rohatyn, 1939 - 1941
by Donia Gold Shwarzstein

The refugees lived among us briefly. Hopefully a number survived. But many may have perished without a name or record. For a short time they were part of our Rohatyn community and contributed to its rhythm and life – this is in their memory. The following are two families I remember.

As Imposing as Hollywood Stars

Our home became particularly lively: a new presence was introduced, a childless couple in their mid-thirties, so different from any seen before. I was taken with their elegance, aristocratic handsomeness and grace. They were tall, stately. They befriended me and actually took time with me. They occupied our living room, which was turned over to them as part of the effort to extend hospitality to the refugee contingent, which came to our town in 1939-1940. I was fascinated with a large impressive thing, large – it stood on their night stand. This thing had an elaborate face, with two dials and the large face with many stopping points, in fact two different "waves." That thing, a radio, the likes of which I had never seen, emitted communiqués in all kinds of voices and languages. That was exciting. I asked questions and they gladly explained. It was exciting to come in contact with the wider world. This was the first time I heard French, Spanish, English and all the central European languages, and I delighted in guessing from which capital the particular communiqué was coming. They were constantly tuned in to the radio.

As I recall, word was that this cultured and cosmopolitan couple, a husband and wife, were no less than the stars of the Bucharest Yiddish Theater. It was hard to associate such elegant, high fashion magazine figures with the Yiddish language and theater. Yiddish in my experience was above all the everyday lingua franca, particularly of the older generation, and in my limited purview, a provincial phenomenon. I was only seven years old. And these are my memories.

We had to pass through their bedroom on the way to and from our bedroom, but we were discreet and considerate, and they were at all times, it seemed, acclimated and unruffled by their circumstances.

And then they integrated into the life of the town with a celebrated event that drew the entire Jewish town into it. Their presence enlivened and enlarged the spirit of the town.

This was different. This was not just going in the afternoon to the Sokol, sitting in seats with mother, and viewing a film starring Shirley Temple or Deanna Durbin. This was a new perspective, a larger lens.

The big event was the performance of a Yiddish play this couple put on in our town with amateur actors. The play was either Dos Gevins (The Jackpot) or Der Oytzer (The Treasure). The performance was a festive occasion held in the Sokol, to which a large part of the Jewish population, including my parents and grandmother, turned out. As the play opened, I remember the hushed darkened theatre, the lighted stage. It was awe inspiring. Since the directors of the play lived in our house, I was the child actor playing the part of a boy. I remember seeing my parents and grandmother seated in the first row; quite a privileged position. I recall, toward the end of the play, my part was to crouch down in the cemetery scene and to yawn convincingly. During that scene, my parents became quite agitated - I could hear their stirring and whispering – they were very worried that I was dragged into this play sleepy and exhausted: "Dos Kind is meed" (the child is tired).

My Parents' Social Life - Contacts from Work, 1940-1941

The second refugee family I remember with fondness was a young couple with a baby. The young woman had an unassuming, gentle charm – her lovely beauty recalled Lilli Palmer. The husband seemed to have a slightly receding hairline, but good-looking in his own way. They were genteel in their demeanor. They were devoted new parents who hovered over their baby, whose bassinet was almost always nearby. Their harmonious home was a pleasant place to visit. Even though I had nothing to contribute to the conversations, I sat as an avid observer; I looked forward to those visits. Part of the conversation between my father and the gentleman concerned work. They were both employed at the flour mill, to my knowledge, my town's sole industry. Having a government job under the Soviet system was at times a matter of technical skill, but often just a matter of chance; such a job provided a measure of safety in preventing deportation to Siberia; and most of all, at a time when all property was nationalized, it was a great boon in being able to provide for one's family.

A Miracle Discovered. In 2008, in search of Rohatyn refugees on the e-mail hub Allgenerations, I received a reply from Halina Frankl. She turned out to be the refugee baby.

Halina's Family's Story and Ordeal

"Mother was born in Oswiecim as Helena Juker. She was one of eight children. She and her two brothers were the only survivors. In 1939 she married my father, Joseph Ber Gelbard (born in Czestochowa). My father was an attorney, and had an office in Bielsko-Biala. Both my parents were fluent in the German language.

Upon the arrival of the German army, my parents fled east to Soviet-occupied Poland. I was born in 1940 in Krzemieniec. Some time after my birth my family ended up in Rohatyn. From July 1941 until November 1941 we were in the Rohatyn ghetto."

In Rohatyn Right after the German Invasion - as Related to Halina

Ukrainians rounded up Jewish males, including Halina's father, and locked them in the large synagogue. They poured kerosene and threatened to set the synagogue on fire. Her father, apprehended not yet fully clothed, seated himself next to a window so he could break out in case of fire.

Her mother had kept a pillowcase full of dry challah to feed the baby. One Ukrainian grabbed the pillowcase from her and took it away. Her mother, quite angry, speaking in German, appealed to the German army officer nearby to get her challah back for her. Near the synagogue was a stockpile of food. She said to the officer: "Don't you have small children at home that you have to feed? That Ukrainian was a Communist under the Soviets, but now he passes himself off as a Volksdeutscher." The German officer recovered her food for the baby. He asked: "What else do you need?" Still angry, she said, "I only want the challah for the baby, nothing else." He slipped a bar of chocolate between her and the baby. He then asked her, "Where is your husband?" She answered, "They took him to the synagogue."

In the synagogue the Rabbi had a noose around his neck and stood on tiptoe. If he slipped, he'd be dead. The synagogue was not set on fire. This was either because the fire department warned the Ukrainians that the flames would engulf the surrounding residential neighborhood, or, perhaps, because the German officer stopped it. He released all the men from the synagogue.

After Rohatyn. "Some time in 1941, my family fled Rohatyn. From 1941 until February 1943, my parents and I stayed with Father's parents in the Warsaw ghetto. During roundups and actions my parents found hideouts in the ghetto, and at no time did they wear the yellow star. There, somehow, my mother obtained from a priest outside of Warsaw a new identification as Miss Ida Kaczinska. After the death of my grandparents in February 1943, six weeks before the ghetto uprising, we escaped from the ghetto, and moved into the city on Jerozolimska Avenue. I was smuggled out of the ghetto by being thrown over the ghetto wall in a cushion. Father then worked as a railway bookkeeper.

"In May 1943, my father was arrested and put in Pawiak Prison. He was kept in detention in that area outside of Warsaw until the end of the war, at which time he was shot by the AK partisans.

"After my father was arrested, my mother arranged for me to stay with a Polish family in [the village] of Blonie. On one of her visits to me in April 1944, my mother was arrested. She was taken to Grodzisk Prison and then to Pawiak Prison. Two days before the Warsaw uprising, she was taken to Germany to Ravensbruck [Concentration Camp] and from there to Neubrandenburg [Concentration Camp].

"[After liberation] my mother searched for me; she found me with another Polish family and took me back, although my caregiver did not want to give me up.

"In 1949 my mother married Joseph Altberg. We lived in Wroclaw until February 1957, when we immigrated to Israel. In 1967 I moved to Canada. I got married in 1973 and I have two children. My mother died in 1977."

How Baby Halina Was Saved - in Her Mother's Words[1]

With the help of a Polish acquaintance acting as intermediary - Mrs. Alicja Mizia, who lived in the courtyard of Jerozolimska Avenue - I handed over my daughter to the custody of her acquaintance, Mrs. Maria Klawinska, who lived in the village of Blonie, near Grodzisk.

Since my daughter had Semitic features - she has brown hair with dark eyes – and since Blonie was a village where everyone knew everyone, and everyone knew exactly how many children each family had, Mrs. Klawinska did not dare keep my child in her house. She kept the child hidden in a locked storeroom, which was located next to the kitchen; she was the only one who had the key. This storeroom was small and windowless. Only at night was the child brought out through the kitchen and exposed to air. The child was very fearful and

instinctively sat quietly in the storeroom - it knew very well that it must not cry. The child was trained like a dog.

As I lived on Aryan identification papers from February 1943 until spring 1944, I traveled from time to time to Blonie to see the child. I had to

1 Translated from German by Donia Gold Shwarzstein.

witness how my child grew progressively paler, more undernourished, more and more fearful. Unfortunately I had no way to change my child's living conditions. I was happy that Mrs. Klawinska, in spite the danger to her own life, was willing to continue to keep my child.

This situation lasted until March 1944; at that point neighbors began to get suspicious that Mrs. Klawinska was keeping Jews in hiding. Therefore she was forced to transfer the baby to her sister, whose name, unfortunately, I cannot recall. Her sister lived in Wlochy, near Warsaw.

I knew nothing of this, and when in April 1944, I came to Blonie to visit my child at Mrs. Klawinska's, I was arrested on suspicion of being Jewish and put in the Grodzisk Prison.

From that time on I lost all contact with my child. In 1945, after liberation, when I returned to Warsaw, I immediately set out to Blonie to find out where my child was. From Blonie I traveled to Wlochy, to Mrs. Klawinska's sister. But I didn't find my child there either. I finally learned that my child did not remain for long in Wlochy, even though, as I then learned, there the child was also kept hidden from the outside world. In spite of that, neighbors "smelled Jews." Mrs. Klawinska's sister, whose name, as I mentioned before, I cannot recall, transferred the child to another sister, who lived in the village of Laski. This second sister, whose name unfortunately I also cannot recall, and who lived on the outskirts of her village, kept my child in a hiding place behind a wardrobe, locked away from the outside world.

My daughter's rescuer told me that she was also very afraid of her neighbors and she did not dare have the child stay in her room. Only at night did she take the child out of her hiding place; she kept her in her room for 2-3 hours, and, at that opportunity she also fed her warm food.

In 1945 my child was nearly five years old, but she was in wretched condition. She was small, thin, pale, and could move only with difficulty; she was very anxious and afraid to speak out loud. It took a long time before the child got used to me as her mother. Only after some time, only after being surrounded by a mother's warmth for quite a while, did she gradually begin to speak and to move more freely.

Refugees in Rohatyn - Halina's parents

Three Rohatyn Survivors Discovered in Rohatyn in 1998

- Boris Arsen (formerly Axelrod/Akselrod), now deceased, came to the 1998 Yizkor Service from Ivano Frankivsk. He delivered a speech at the Service in Rohatyn. Boris Arsen survived concentration camps. After his liberation, he returned to Rohatyn and subsequently settled in Ivano Frankivsk.

In 2004 he published his memoir in Ukrainian entitled Moya Hirka Pravda (My Bitter Truth).

- A five-month-old infant named Anna was raised by her Polish protectress. Anna is the daughter of Doda Goldschlag and granddaughter of Rohatyn advocate Dr. Goldschlag. Anna's family did not survive. She grew up in the Cracow area, became a physician and raised a family.

- Mariya Vasilivna, the girl who survived in a Rohatyn area village, at the age of eight wandered out of the ghetto during the Judenrein akcja. She was found crying beside a village church by a Ukrainian man. A childless Ukrainian couple took her in. As a child she worked as a cowherd. Later she worked on a collective farm and in a medical clinic in Rohatyn. Her Jewish family did not survive. She has raised a family of her own. Some time after the 1998 Memorial in Rohatyn her economic situation improved due to the efforts of several attendees at the Memorial.

1999 visit to Boris Arsen's home in Ivano Frankivsk. Around the table left to right: Freda Kamerling Perl, Mrs. Arsen, Boris Arsen, next to Fischel Kirshen, on Right, Boris Arsen's son.

Biographies
of
Contributors

Most of the contributors of articles to the Yizkor Book of Rohatyn lived in Israel. The following were in the U.S.A.: Dr. Jack Faust, Dr. Golda Fischer Joslyn, Morris Grant (Granowiter), Rosa (Rosette) Halpern (nee Faust), Sheva Lederman (nee Weiler). Their articles appeared in the 62-page section of the Yizkor Book. Dr. Abraham Sterzer lived in Israel, but his article (not identical) appeared in both the Hebrew/Yiddish book and in the 62-page English language section of the book.

Zev Barban (Hebrew: Baraban)[1]

Translated by Rabbi Mordecai Goldzweig

Zev Barban was born in Rohatyn, in Eastern Galicia, (10/10/1900) to his father, Yaacov (a postal clerk under the Austrian regime) - his family name was composed of the initials of a Jew of several generations ago, well-known in his day, "Bar Rabbi Nachum or Bar Rabi Natan" – to his mother, Leah, from the family Small. He was a student in school under the tutelage of Raphael Soferman (later one of the senior secondary school teachers in Herzliya, Tel Aviv) and in one of the public secondary schools in Poland. In the fall of 1914 he fled with his family to Vienna because of the Russian invasion. There he finished his secondary education in German and joined the Zionist Youth Scouting group, HaShomer, which after some time became the educational-political movement, HaShomer HaTzair. In 1917 he was drafted into the Austrian Army. He served there with the rank of officer candidate. With the crumbling of the Augsburg reign and of the military, in October 1918 he returned with his parents to Rohatyn, which had become [first] the Ukraine and afterwards Poland. There he founded the Shomer HaTzair nucleus group, which he headed up.

At the end of the summer of 1920 he left with the first stream of the Third Aliyah, with a group of Rohatyn friends. On November 21, 1920, after three months of wandering, they arrived in the Land [of Israel]. In 1921 in Tel Aviv, together with Meir Ya'ari (who was previously with him in HaShomer in Vienna), Richard Weintraub, Yehoshua Hanich, Leibel, and the Leiter sisters and others, he participated in the founding of Kibbutz HaShomer HaTzair, Kiryat Anavim, Herzliya.

In 1925, he joined the founders of the Dramatic Studio and the workers'

1 Encyclopedia Le'Chalutzei Hayishuv U'Bonav, Vol V, pp. 2096-7, (YIVO) Institute for Jewish Research, New York. Segments of Encyclopedia article about Barban were translated from Hebrew by Donia Gold Shwarzstein..

theater Ohel. From then on he became a permanent member of the Ohel Troupe; there he weathered all the difficulties and tribulations of creating the theatre. He contributed to shaping the character of the theatre and played important roles in its best performances.

Among the key roles he played, it is important to mention Yaacov in "Jacob and Rachel" (Moshe Halevy, 1928), HaMelech Tzidkiyahu in "Yirmiyahu" (Halevy, 1929), Disraeli in "Disraeli, A Play in Four Acts" (Parker, Louis N.), Simcha Meir Ashkenazi in "Brothers Ashkenazi" (Israel Joshua Singer, 1936), the painter in "The Doctor's Dilemma" (George Bernard Shaw), Rabbi Akiva in "Bar Kochba" (Shmuel Abramski), the Baron in "The Lower Depths" (Maxim Gorky), Senator Langdon in "Deep Roots" (Arnaud D'Usseau and James Gow), Edmond in "King Lear" (Shakespeare). At the time of the guest appearance of Elizabeth Bergner, he took the part of one of the investigators in the Inquisition in the play "Saint Joan" (George Bernard Shaw).

He married Devorah (his partner in the Ohel Troupe), the daughter of Pinchas Kastelanitz from Smolin. There is a separate article about her in the volume.

He was known as one of the good announcers of the Land [of Israel] in folkloric performances and in village and town festive celebrations. He led and gave stage directions for many performances of the youth movement and in schools. He led many Festival of Weeks celebrations in the Haifa schools and many Purim Festivals in the season of Ad-Lo-Yada Carnivals in towns around Tel Aviv. He was stage director of plays for Haganah evening programs during the time of the underground. He performed in evening readings for the Jewish Brigade during World War II and later in army camps and in infirmaries of the Israel Defense Forces during the time of the War of Independence.

In 1933 - 34 he took part in the Ohel tour of Western and Eastern Europe and in the 1950s in Western Europe.

David and Esther Blaustein (Yid. Blustein)
As written down in Polish by Sabina Wind Fox

Translated by Donia Gold Shwarzstein

Esther was the daughter of Yidel Sofer Blotner; her mother was Ponja (pron. Ponya). Esther Blotner had four sisters. Her oldest sister, Sarah, married Aharon Gutman. They had two children - Bronia, born 1918, and Mordechai "Motl", born 1921. This entire family perished in the Shoah. The second sister was Tauba (Yid. Touba). The third sister, Chava (Chawa), who married Chaim Blaustein, David's brother, had a small child. All of them perished in the akcjas in Rohatyn. The fourth sister, Gitel, was married to

Moshe Mandelberg in Israel. They had three children: Michael, Yoel, Bruria (pron. Broorya). Gitel and Moshe are no longer alive.

Esther Blotner came to Israel first, David Blaustein followed. They married and had two sons: Yehuda and Chanan (pron. Hanan). A butcher by trade, he supplied hotels and large establishments. David Blaustein was a member of the Rohatyn Association. David's sister Cipa (pron. Tzipa), her husband and small child perished in Rohatyn in the Shoah.

Cyla (Tzila) and Aryeh Blech
By Donia Gold Shwarzstein

Cyla and Aryeh Blech were married in Rohatyn before the Nazi persecution. Before the war, the Blechs were economically comfortable. They, together with others, survived the liquidation akcja in 1943 in one of the fortified bunkers in the Rohatyn ghetto. Ultimately the Germans destroyed the bunker with grenades and fire. The ghetto liquidation lasted several days. For Mr. and Mrs. Blech, survival came at a high cost.

The Blechs were in Rohatyn after liberation. From there they left for Western Poland, pursuant to territory and population exchanges established by the Four Powers agreements. The Blechs lived in Reichenbach (Dzierzoniow) for a period of time and, together with his brother Moshe Nas'hofer, made a living from a delicatessen shop. While there, Aryeh and Cyla Blech, for several weeks, gave me room and board. In the 1950s the Blechs made aliyah to Israel and settled in Tel Aviv. They raised their son there and earned a living in the grocery business.

On my visit to Israel in the 1980s, they hosted a reunion in their apartment for me and a number of Rohatyn survivors, thus ending a 40-year separation. Mr. Blech passed away in the early 1990s. Mr. and Mrs. Blech have a son, daughter-in-law and three granddaughters.

At this point, both husband and wife have passed away.

Yitzchak Bomze
As recorded in Polish by Sabina Wind Fox

Translated by Donia Gold Shwarzstein

Yitzchak's parents were named Baruch and Scheindel (pron. Shayndl). He had two sisters, Lonka and Bronia and a brother, Abraham.

Yitzchak Bomze arrived in Israel in 1925. His passport read Yitzchak Avivi. At first he was a Chalutz in the Kibbutz Beit Alfa. After leaving the Kibbutz, he lived in N've-Chaim, near Chedera (Hedera), where he made a modest living from a buffet-type restaurant.

He had two sons, Baruch and Shlomo. One son was a chauffeur, and the other made a career in the military.

Jacob Faust
By Elie Faust-Levy (his daughter)

Jacob Faust, a research chemist, author and journalist, was the eldest son of David and Dora (Loew), the family who led the much-loved "Faust Kapela" (Klezmorim) of Rohatyn. Educated at the University of Cracow and the Deutsche Technische Hochschule of Prague, he emigrated to the U.S. in 1931 after marrying Hedda Krig Waldinger, a Stanislawow-born American citizen whom he met when she returned to Poland to visit her family. Once in the US, he became active in the Federation of Polish Jews in America; a foreign correspondent for several dailies in Poland, among them Chwila (pron. Khvila); and in the American Jewish Congress, where as Chairman of the boycott Committee in the late '30s and early '40s he organized efforts to alert the U.S. public and government to the Holocaust.

Head of the Research and Development lab of L. Sonneborn & Sons from 1935-65, he held numerous patents in the U.S., Canada, among them pioneering work on vitamin E.

He died in 1983 at the age of 81, survived by his son, daughter, and three grandchildren. He is listed in the Biographical Encyclopaedia of American Jews (1935); American Men of Science ('55); and Who's Who in World Jewry ('55 and '65). Many of his numerous articles on Jewish life are in the archives of the YIVO Institute for Jewish Research in New York City.

Autobiography of Rosette Faust Halpern
New Jersey, January 2002

The family Faust lived in Rohatyn for several generations. I was born to Deborah and David Faust, as the youngest of six. Named Roza, I was called Rozia. I attended elementary school, while at the same time taking two Hebrew school classes after hours. During the Soviet occupation, I attended the Ukrainian high school; this became a life-saving preparation for my survival.

At the time of the ghetto period I was helped by Ukrainian friends to escape to the nearby village of Skomorhy. I left the ghetto under the assumed name of Darka Wasilkiewitz, and worked as a companion to a paralyzed wife of a priest. Recognized, I returned to the ghetto. Liberated—reborn, I joined my beloved Willie in Uzbekistan, Asia. We married, we returned to Poland and settled in Reichenbach, Silesia. Always committed to Zionism, we organized HaNoar HaTzioni, a most successful chapter. With the chapter recruited by the Jewish Agency, we landed in France. There, among other things, I was active with WIZO locating Jewish orphans, who were then conveyed to Israel.

While carrying out assignments there, I had time to attend the school of Guerre L'Avinge, where I met the great masters of fashion design.

At this time, I was helped to locate my big brothers. Upon their insistence that the family reunite, my brothers arranged our passage to the U.S., with the stipulation that in time we would settle in Israel.

To appease my guilt for not going to Israel, I became active and worked diligently with the local Hadassah, moving from chairman to president. I felt redeemed when our chapter was recognized by Hadassah in Israel. I also served as president of the Essex chapter of Friends of Brandeis University and continue to be an officer there.

It was at this time that I registered at the F.I.T. (Fashion Institute of Technology), where I earned a degree in Fashion Design. I worked as a free-lance designer while attending to my most sacred role as a mother to our only son David, our pride and joy.

Our son David, an established dentist, father of two adorable daughters, made our happiness complete. Unfortunately, our happiness did not last. On April 17, 1999, I lost my precious husband, the love of my life. My husband, William Halpern, had a law degree from Poland, but studied in the U.S. engineering, which became his career.

Now I try to find a cause to live for. I keep busy. I am referred to as a "professional volunteer" for Jewish causes.

Golda Fisher Joslyn
Letter to Jacob Faust

D r. Golda Fisher Joslyn's biography in her own words, in a letter addressed to Jacob Faust, brother of Rosette Faust Halpern. Ms. Halpern graciously provided the letter, which had been intended for her husband, William Halpern. As Ms. Halpern explains, Golda Fisher and William Halpern graduated together from gimnazjum in Rohatyn and "kept [a] very friendly relationship due to their Zionist involvements.

Mrs. Maynard A. Joslyn
1317 Spruce Street
Berkeley 9, California

April 15, 1955

Dear Jacob:

You folks were very sweet to write that card. My husband read it and said: "tell your friends you're not so nice and not so young anymore." Of course, that is his way of teasing me, particularly when "Galizianer" are involved. His parents came from Russia & he always thought Galizianer were horrible until the Lewenters visited us from New York & he liked them very much. Claire Messing also stayed with me for a few weeks. She is now in Los Angeles. Her brother Max and Granowitter (Moses) are in Miami Beach, Florida. As you probably know, the Lewenters are in N.Y.C. where he is practicing.

As for myself, I went through a million adventures from Vienna, via Holland and England to the USA. Somehow I managed to study 2 yrs. in England and 3 yrs, in the USA and graduated medicine in 1943. Then I decided to see the US before settling down, so I specialized in different parts of the country until I settled in California. You may know that my parents perished in Rohatyn almost 6 mo. before liberation. My brother went to Israel and has been teaching in Haifa for 16 yrs. now, so—I was all alone in this country and on my own. Eight yrs. ago I met & married my husband, a typical American Colonel (he was 4 years in the Pacific in charge of food supplies for the US army in China, New Zealand & Australia).

Actually, he is the "genius" and should be in the "Who's Who," but he refused, so he is only in the non-Jewish one. He has been Professor of the California University for over 20 yrs., of all things, in agriculture. He is a biochemist, food technologist & electrical engineer and is one of the original discoverers of frozen foods, dehydrated foods, etc. In 1951, we were both guests of State of Israel for 6 months, because they wanted Maynard to revise their food production. We had a magnificent time, were looked after by Weizman, Ben Gurion, the army and a bunch of scientists, farmers, and manufacturers. I managed to help the Medical Association and am still working for them here. While in Israel, I saw Izio Hadar (wife & 2 children), Rozka Hader (husband & 2 children), Dov Kirschen (wife & girls) & of course my brother (wife & 3 children). Jozek Kartin is also supposed to be there, but I did not get to see him.

Here we own a very lovely huge home, & probably because of it are forever entertaining. Since Maynard & I have friends in all corners of the earth, we constantly have people "drop in," lately particularly from Israel. Maynard, besides his busy profession, is doing very well as a "converted" Zionist; he is president of the Technion here and Vice President of the Z.O.A.

Me—I am a "verbrennte Zionistin," so I am unofficial Israeli consul out here, lecturer for Hadassah & other Jewish org. & representative of the Israel Medical Association. I also run the house (with help), have a part-time practice & work in hospitals.

(Personal parts of the letter are omitted)

Dr. Fisher Joslyn died childless. Her brother Rabbi Yoel Ben Nun lives in Israel.

The following was obtained from the Alameda Contra Costa Medical Association, California. Dr. Golda Fisher (Fischer), a practicing pediatrician, retired from medical practice in 1980. She died on August 6, 1992. She was a member of the Association and a member of the Contra Costa Board of Health. She graduated Medical University of South Carolina, Charleston, 1943.

Her obituary appeared in the now defunct Oakland Tribute (Alameda Newspaper Group). Maynard A. Joslyn's obituary appears on November 29, 1984. He was listed in the Who's Who.

A number of newspaper notices announced her speaking to a Unitarian Church in Oakland, to Mira Vista Parents Association, and to Hadassah. Articles also expound on the culinary arts.

She spearheaded the formation of the American Physicians Fellowship or Friends of Israel Medical Association of the West Coast.

Autobiography of Sabina Wind Fox
Translated from Polish by Donia Gold Shwarzstein

I was born in 1919 in the village of Kozary near Bukaczowce. I finished seven grades elementary school. After finishing seven grades, I took a sewing course during the day, and went to gimnazjum at night, earning a high school diploma (matura).

I was a member of the Shomer Ha'Tza'ir Zionist Organization. I survived the Shoah in and around Rohatyn. From my entire family only my brother Milek and I survived. Except for the two of us, all perished in the Shoah: my parents, two brothers, Kopel and Moshe, and a sister Ginia. Of the entire extended family on both my parents' sides, uncles, aunts, cousins, all perished in the Shoah.

After the war I went to Poland, and after that to Germany. I married in 1946 in Germany, and in 1947 we made our way to Israel on Haportzim, an illegal ship. My husband and I have two children and three grandchildren.

Josef Juzef (pron. Yuzef)
As recorded in Polish by Sabina Wind Fox
Translated by Donia Gold Shwarzstein

In Rohatyn this was the last family of Spanish (Sefardi) origin. Mr. Juzef was born in 1914. In Rohatyn, he belonged to the Zionist organization Gordonia. He worked in Mr. Skolnick's print shop. He came to Israel in 1949-1950. There he resided in Pardes Chana, where he established a print shop; this brought him a great deal of business and a good livelihood.

David Kartin
As recorded by Sabina Wind Fox
Translated by Donia Gold Shwarzstein

David Kartin was born in 1911 in the village of Zalanow. He died just a few years ago. In 1936, he made aliyah to Israel, together with his father and two sisters. His sister Leah Holder lives in Netanya.

David Kartin belonged to the Rohatyn Association in Israel. His brother, Shmuel (Shmil) Kartin, remained in Rohatyn. In 1940 his brother married Chana Widerker. Both were killed in the akcjas in the Shoah.

Dov Kirschen
By Sabina Wind Fox
Translated from Polish by Donia Gold Shwarzstein

He was born in 1912 and died in 1998 in Israel. Mr. Kirschen's parents, Abraham and Mina, owned in the center of Rohatyn a multi-story building and hotel and ran a tavern on the ground floor.

Dov completed gimnazjum in Rohatyn in 1934 and left to continue his studies in Palestine (Israel) and England. He worked in Haifa as engineer, specializing in petroleum refining.

Throughout his life in Israel he lived in Haifa with his wife and only daughter. He also had a brother Fishel (Fiszel), who was very active in the Rohatyn Association.

Fishel Kirschen
As recorded by Sabina Wind Fox
Translated by Donia Gold Shwarzstein

Fishel Kirschen, brother of Dov Kirschen, made aliyah in 1937. He received his higher education in Israel. He was an officer in the IDF. After retiring from the military, he established a business for insulating buildings against noise.

While president of the Association of Rohatyn and Vicinity in Israel during the 1990's, he and the Association's steering committee, consisting of Freda Kamerling Perl, Sabina Wind Fox and Z. Fenster, were instrumental in establishing cooperation with the Rohatyn administration in the Ukraine and bringing about the memorial service in 1998, setting up memorial monuments and restoring the cemeteries. He and his committee were indefatigable in activating the Jewish survivors from the Rohatyn area worldwide in pursuing and achieving those goals. He recently died in his home near Tel Aviv. His wife predeceased him. Fishel Kirschen is survived by two children.

Anna Kornbluh
Provided by Freda Kamerling Perl

Anna Kornbluh was born on March 9, 1909, in the town of Rohatyn, in Eastern Galicia, as the daughter of Tonia and Moshe Schweller. She studied and resided for many years in the capital city of Eastern Galicia Lwow, which until World War II was part of Poland; today it is known as Lviv and belongs to the Ukrainian Republic.

Anna Kornbluh was imprisoned in the ghetto of Rohatyn until its liquidation. Her mother was murdered in the massive akcja which took place in this ghetto on March 20, 1942. Anna with her husband and father succeeded in surviving the liquidation of the ghetto of Rohatyn in June 1943. Her father was killed in Rohatyn by Ukrainians in April 1945, after the end of German occupation but a month before the war ended. Her husband, Joseph Kornbluh, who was a telecommunications engineer and served as Director General of an ORT professional school for Holocaust survivors in post-war Germany, died there in a road accident in 1947.

Anna Kornbluh immigrated to Tel Aviv, Israel in 1950.

Sylvia Lederman (née Sheva Weiler)
by Donia Gold Shwarzstein

Sylvia Lederman of Rohatyn lost her father early in life. She supported her mother and family by working as buyer and bookkeeper in a bookshop in Rohatyn. During the Nazi occupation she succeeded in escaping from the Rohatyn ghetto. Using Aryan papers with an assumed name, she boarded a train to Germany and landed there in a monastery. She spent the rest of the Hitler period there. After liberation, she remained in West Germany in a Displaced Persons camp. There she met her husband Irving Lederman, originally from Lodz, Poland. They married and immigrated to New York City, where he worked as cutter and manager in a garment factory and, for a period of time, she as seamstress. They were members of the Rohatyn and Lodz societies and had a rich social life. After Irving's death in the 1990's, she continued to live in New York. In 1996 the Ledermans held a reception in their home, as part of an effort to assist the Rohatyn Association of Israel in preparing for restoration of Jewish graves in the Ukraine. The guest of the reception was Freda Kamerling Perl from Israel, delegated to meet with members of the U.S. society of Rohatyn expatriates.

Sylvia Lederman was related to Anna Kornbluh and Dov Schmorak, the Israeli diplomat who was from the Rohatyn area, where he survived the Hitler period. Sylvia died in New York in 2008, leaving the legacy of her autobiography, entitled Sheva. She requested that it be published posthumously by Syracuse University Press.

Dr. and Mrs. Isaac (Yitzhak) Lewenter (pron. Leventer)

By Donia Gold Shwarzstein

It is impossible to record Dr. Lewenter's biography, what little of it can now be reconstructed, without first and foremost thinking about his and his wife's separation from their one and only young teen or preteen son in 1939 and their subsequent separate fates.

In Rohatyn Dr. Lewenter was a successful and prominent physician. Mrs. Lewenter was active in the community. She organized a summer camp for poor Jewish children. She provided for refreshments out of her own pocket. As related by the Rohatyner Lorka Mark Lang, she and her friend Donia Amarant were volunteer counselors in the camp. They took the children on outings into the countryside.

According to entries in the New York Medical Association directory, Dr. Isaac Lewenter of Rohatyn got his medical degree in 1922 from the Medical Department of Jan Kazimierz University in Lwow (Uniwersytet Jana Kazimierza, Wydzial Lekarski) in Poland, in a country which restricted to a very few the admission of Jews to medical school. In 1939 the Lewenters embarked on a pleasure trip to witness the U.S. World's Fair, leaving behind their one and only son in a summer camp. World War II broke out and Poland was quickly overrun by the Nazis. The parents could no longer return to Poland, and they were not destined to be reunited with the son. In the ghetto, their son reported daily for the mandated labor detail. To our knowledge, he perished in the Rohatyn ghetto in the Judenrein of June 6, 1943.

At some point, Dr. and Mrs. Lewenter settled at 575 West End Avenue in Manhattan, New York City, where he practiced family medicine. Among his patients were Rohatyn expatriates, such as the Gutenplan family. Dr. Lewenter is listed in 1968-69 as Assistant Adjunct at and on the staff of Beth Israel Hospital. Not much of the Lewenters' life in the US could be reconstructed sixty years later. It was said that after Dr. Lewenter retired, the couple settled in Israel, some said on the West Coast. Where they lived out their last days is not clear.

In New York Dr. Lewenter was a member and officer of the Rohatyner Young Men's Society founded in 1894. (The society has cemetery plots in Queens, NY, in Mt. Hebron and Mt. Zion.)

Anschel Milstein
As recorded in Polish by Sabina Wind Fox
Translated by Donia Gold Shwarzstein

Before leaving Rohatyn in 1924, Anschel Milstein was employed four years by a Polish locksmith. In Rohatyn, he was a member of Poalei Zion.

His father, Nachman, was a melamed. His mother's name was Alta. Nachman and Alta Milstein had a daughter, Perel (Pearl), and two sons, Zvi and Anschel. Nachman Milstein had a brother by the name of Noach, who was also a melamed.

In Israel Anschel Milstein lived in Ramat Gan, where he had a locksmith's shop. In Israel, he was active in the Association of Rohatyn expatriates.

Rachel and Moshe Nashofer (pron. Moshe Nas'hofer)
By Sabina Wind Fox
Translated from Polish by Donia Gold Shwarzstein

Rachel Nashofer (nee Bal) was born in 1918 in the village of Lipica Dolna. She had two brothers, Moshe Yosef, Abram Yitzchak, and a sister Genia. Once the Rohatyn ghetto was established, they were driven into the ghetto.

In the December 6, 1942 akcja, they were being deported to Belzec by train. Rachel begged her brothers to jump from the train, but they didn't want to. Rachel jumped off near Chodorow (Hodorow). Her cousin Bernard Kessler and Abraham Haber also jumped. Rachel and her cousin Kessler survived the war in the cellar of the Rada Powiatowa (the District Council building).[1] They survived under terrible conditions, suffering hunger and thirst, but Mr. Haber died there. The custodian was responsible for saving the people in the hideout in the cellar.

Moshe Nashofer was born in 1906. Before the war he was engaged in egg export. His first wife, Elza, perished in 1943 after the last akcja. Moshe survived in the forest together with his little son Bumek.

After liberation, in 1946, Rachel Bal and Moshe Nashofer married. They had a daughter, Tzipora, who is married and has three sons. From Rohatyn the Nashofers went to Dzierzoniow (Reichenbach) in Lower Silesia, where he and his brother Aryeh Blech and sister-in-law Tzila (Cyla) opened a delicatessen store.

Moshe, Rachel, son Bumek and daughter Tzipora made aliyah in 1950.

---

1 The bunker in the Rada Powiatowa was in the cellar. Thirteen Jews were hidden there in terrible conditions of squalor and lacking food. The custodian Bordovey, who knew about them, was helping them. But he was unable to supply sufficient food. All but two survived; Mr. Haber died of starvation and the young volunteer Juzio Stryjer died trying to forage for food for the group (p. 321 in original Yizkor Book).

They lived all the time in Haifa and ran a grocery, in which both husband and wife worked. Their daughter Tzipora lived in Haifa with her husband and children. Bumek died in 1999, leaving his wife Chaya and children. Moshe Nashofer died in 1991 in Israel.

Herman (Zvi) Skolnick
By Michael Skolnick, Brooklyn, NY (his son)
Supplemented by Sabina Wind Fox

Herman (Zvi) Skolnick was born in 1920 and died in April 2000. Until 1939, he lived in the small town of Rohatyn with his father Chaim (Haim), stepmother and brothers. His mother died in 1929, when he was just nine. Chaim Skolnick, who was one of the successful businessmen in Rohatyn, employed Jewish workers and provided them the rare opportunity to learn a trade. Chaim Skolnick owned a printing press and got work orders from all over Poland. He was listed in a business directory under the Aryanized name Joachim Skolnick, which proved good for business. Herman Skolnick had two older brothers and one stepbrother. His brother Julek (Yoolek) was an officer in the Polish army; his brother Isaac (Ajzik) worked in their father's print shop. Brother Isaac and his wife Rozia's daughter Dzidzia, a young child, miraculously survived the Holocaust. She was placed in an orphanage in Israel. From there she migrated to South Africa, where she raised a family. She had two sons, one or both of whom moved to the U.S.A.

Herman was in a Displaced Person Camp in Bavaria. In 1948 he made aliyah (went to Israel). He and Zvi Fenster were the prime movers in organizing the Rohatyn Society in Israel. In Israel Herman Skolnick worked for the Israeli police force. In the 1960's he emigrated to New York. In New York he married and had a son, Michael.

In New York he was very active in the Rohatyn Young Men's Benevolent Association. He often spoke of growing up in Rohatyn and of the friends he made there. In the waning years of the association, Herman Skolnick kept the spirit of the association alive. He used to bring the survivors together for meetings and celebrations. He was also a moving spirit in supporting the efforts of the Israeli Society to rehabilitate the Rohatyn Jewish cemeteries, mark the mass graves there and honor the martyrs of the Shoah in Rohatyn in 1998. Since his death in 2000 his dedication to the now-dwindling Rohatyn expatriate community is sorely missed. He is survived by his wife, a retired teacher, and son, a social worker.

Yehoshua P. Spiegel (1914-2001)
Editor of the Rohatyn Yizkor Book
By Sabina Wind Fox

Translated from Yiddish by Donia Gold Shwarzstein

Born in Rohatyn, Yehoshua Pinchas Spiegel was the editor of the Rohatyn Yizkor Book, Rohatyn, the Town That Perished. He contributed significant articles to the book. The successors of the Rohatyn community owe him a debt of gratitude. Yehoshua P. Spiegel was married to Hadassah Bard (in Yiddish Barad; currently in English Barth).

Yehoshua P. Spiegel, son of the last dayan of the town, was a descendant of devout Jews and a line of rabbis of the Rohatyn Jewish community. As a young man he joined the modern Zionist youth movement HaShomer HaTzair, and it was rumored that for this reason his father was not appointed to the position of rabbi of the town.

While he was still in Rohatyn, in deference to his father, the beloved dayan of Rohatyn, Yehoshua continued to keep his head covered by wearing a cap. In Rohatyn he prepared for aliyah to Israel by working as a printing trade apprentice in the Teichman print shop. Despite working as a printer, he continued to dress in a professional manner and not as a worker. Before going on aliyah, he went on Hachshara. That is where he met his future wife Hadassah. After making aliyah, he first settled on a kibbutz. Throughout his years in Israel, he worked on Al HaMishmar, a publication of the Kibbutz Artzi movement, where he began as a typesetter.

After a number of years, Yehoshua Pinchas Spiegel turned his attention again to religious subjects and wrote a number of books, among them 'Rishpei Torah, Al Chamisha Chumshei Torah and Mishloach Manot.

His father would have seen the hand of G-d in his aliyah.[1] The dayan and his family remained in Rohatyn and perished in the Holocaust. Unsuspecting of what was going on in the first akcja, they were taken by the Gestapo from their home. They survived the first akcja, but perished in the end.

In the 1980's Yehoshua Spiegel retired and moved into a retirement community in Ra'anana. He was the ba'al tefilah there and was very well liked. He exhibited a talent for painting.

He died in the summer of 2001 at the age of 87. He was survived by his wife and children, two daughters and one son, a physician, all living in Israel.

Sabina Wind Fox, her husband, Mr. Fishel Kirschen and Donia Gold Shwarzstein paid a visit to Yehoshua and Hadassah Spiegel in Ra'anana. At

---

1 Refer to The Young Dayan, Yizkor Book, pps. 166-169.

that time Mr. Spiegel gave his blessing to Donia to have the Yizkor Book translated into English, to be published in book form, as well as to expand the book to include additional material, as well as a photo montage of Rohatyn.

The Yehoshua Spiegels at home in Israel, 1986.

Dr. Natan Spiegel (born 1905)
Professor of Ancient Western Literature and Philosophy

Dr. Spiegel was the uncle of Yehoshua Spiegel, the editor of the Rohatyn Yizkor Book. He lived in Jerusalem.

In Rohatyn, his father had a small factory in his home, in which he produced uniform insignia for the military, insignia for town officials and gimnazjum students. His mother was bent over from overwork, his siblings suffered ill health.

As a young child, Dr. Spiegel was deeply influenced by his beloved teacher, Nachum Milstein. He studied in the Polish gimnazjum in Rohatyn. In 1925, after completing secondary school, he studied philosophy in Lwow. Before the outbreak of the war and until the end of the Soviet occupation in 1941, he taught in a gimnazjum in Kalusz.

He survived World War II in the Soviet Union. After the liberation of Rohatyn by the Soviet Army, he wrote to Rohatyn to inquire about the fate of his family. On December 16, 1944, the town mayor Stolarczuk (Stolarchook) wrote him that "all your family was killed."

In 1946 he returned to Western Poland, and in 1947 he made aliyah to Israel. He authored books on ancient Greek and Roman literature.

Autobiography of Dr. Abraham Sterzer
Written in Ramat Gan, Israel, on August 27, 2001
Translated from German by Donia Gold Shwarzstein

I, Dr. Abraham Sterzer, was born in Doliniany, near Rohatyn, on June 26, 1904. In 1909 my father moved to Strzeliska, where he was a farm leaseholder. I attended school in Strzeliska. I graduated with a high school diploma from the secondary school in Rohatyn. I studied medicine at the Medical Faculty of the German University in Prague (Charles-Ferdinand University in Prague, consisting of the combined Czech and German Universities), and received my medical degree there.

When World War II broke out, the Soviets came to our area. During their occupation I headed the Polyclinic in Rohatyn. After a period of two years the Russians left and the Germans marched in.

The Germans immediately set up a ghetto (Jewish quarter) in Rohatyn. On March 20, 1942, the Germans shot 3,000 Jews, among them 600 children. One and one-half years later, just before the final liquidation of the ghetto, a former Ukrainian patient of mine secretly came into the ghetto and took with him into the forest my wife and child and myself. He rescued my life and that of my wife and 3-year-old son. We survived the war with that Ukrainian. After the war ended, my family and I migrated to Reichenbach (aka Dzierżoniow), Lower Silesia, Poland, where I was engaged in the hospital for two years. After that we migrated to Bad Reichenhall in Germany. There we lived in a Displaced Persons Camp of five thousand Jews. I practiced medicine in the camp hospital. Two years later, after Ben Gurion declared the establishment of the Jewish state, my family and I went to Israel. I arrived in Israel on November 28, and a few days later joined the staff of the general hospital and worked as doctor until my retirement in June 1972. I have been retired since 1972.

Mrs. Grina Sterzer, nee Faust
By Dr. A. Sterzer
Translated from German by Donia Gold Shwarzstein

Grina (pron. Greena) Faust Sterzer was born in Rohatyn in December 1908. She attended elementary school and secondary school in Rohatyn. I got to know her in high school. We married in 1938. My wife's father was a merchant and owner of two brick factories. After the liquidation of the ghetto, she survived the Nazi occupation in the woods together with me and our two-year-old son. We were together in Reichenbach, Bad Reichenhall, and from 1948 in Israel. We had one son. She died suddenly on January 6, 1997.

[Ed. Note: The Sterzer's son Menashe Sterzer had a professional interest in the subject of youth delinquency in immigrant societies. His PhD dissertation at the Justus Liebig University in Giessen, Germany, 1974, was entitled "Chief Causes of Youth Criminality."]

Leah Teichman Ring
As recorded by Sabina Wind Fox
Translated from Polish by Donia Gold Shwarzstein

Lonka (Leah) was born in 1910. Her parents were Shimon and Sarah. Her parents owned a print shop. Her older sister Bluma (pron. Blooma) left for Israel a long time before World War II. Her brother Mordechai (aka Motio), a physician, left for America and remained there.

Leah belonged to ShomerHaTzair. In Rohatyn, she organized the WIZO, as well as Gan Ivrit, a pre-kindergarten.

Lonka studied pedagogy to become a teacher. In 1938 she landed in Israel. Throughout the years there she taught school (40 years) in Kibbutz Eyn-Hamifratz. She married Israel Ring, who hailed from Berlin. They had two sons and six grandchildren. Their sons also settled on Kibbutzim.

In 1998 she began to paint and produced astonishingly good work. At first she painted from sketches, later she painted nature scenes from her imagination. Her husband organized a permanent exhibit of her work, which has received critical acclaim. She wrote an autobiography, which has not yet been published.

Chaya Weissberg-Weinreich
As recorded by Sabina Wind Fox
Translated from Polish by Donia Gold Shwarzstein

In 1940 Chaya Weissberg-Weinreich married a Russian Jew and left for Russia, where she survived the war. Her father Baruch, also nicknamed Boortzia (Bórcia), was by trade a saddle and mattress maker. His two sons, Michael and Betzalel, helped in his business. His other daughters were Esther, Adela, and Rajzel. All, except for Chaja (Haya), perished in the Shoah.

Marcus Zin (Polish Cin, born 1903)

In 1945, while traveling from Stanislawow to Rohatyn, he survived a truck accident, which claimed many lives. From Rohatyn he migrated to Western Poland, he then fled to West Germany. He married while still in Germany. He made aliyah between 1946 and 1948. There he is survived by his wife and children.

Leah Zuch (pron. Tzookh)

As recorded by Sabina Wind Fox

Translated from Polish by Donia Gold Shwarzstein

L eah, also knows as Lonka, was the daughter of Akiva Wagschall (Wakszal) and Cirit (Tzirit). Akiva Wagschall was the gabbai in the synagogue. The family was held in high regard. They were a family devoted to Zionism. Upon finishing her university studies, well before World War II, Leah made aliyah to Israel. Her sister, Salka, also settled in Israel. Their father lived to do the same.

Leah Zuch lived in Tel Aviv. She had two daughters. Leah Zuch was engaged in the business of employment of women in domestic work.

Regina Hader Rock

By Donia Gold Shwarzstein

R egina was the author of "From Hiding Place to Hiding Place." Marvin Rock, her only son, contributed this photo of his mother Regina Hader Rock on March 6, 1995. Marvin Rock was born in the Displaced Persons Camp Eschwege, Germany. He writes: "This picture was taken in Eschwege. My mother is pregnant in this picture."

568

APPENDIX

New Jewish Cemetery, 1998.

Photographs from Rohatyn Society Visits

Willam Halpern seeing off group bound for Rohatyn, 1998.

Left to Right: Mr. Jacob Hornstein seen off at JFK by friend, Herman Skolnick and William Halpern, 1998.

Reception in Rohatyn Town Hall, 1998.

Part of visiting group, Rohatyn, 1998.

Chaya Rosen reciting poem at 1943 Memorial Monement, Rohatyn, 1998.

At 1942 Memorial, Rohatyn, 1998.

Rohatyn, 1998. Kuba Glotzer and friends in their Red School classroom.

Day of Yizkor in Rohatyn, Rohatyner group walking from Town Hall toward rynek on way to dinner.

June 10, 1998, Memorial day in Rohatyn - Rohatyn expatriates at dinner.

Rohatyn, 1998. Dedication of monument of Judenrein June 6, 1943.

Rohatyn, 1998. At 1942 Memorial.

Rohatyn, Ukraine. Memorial stone on mass gravesite of March 20, 1942 akcja, in which 3,600 Jews were annihilated, including 600 children.

Plaque on wall of former Judenrat building at the edge of what was the Rohatyn ghetto from 1941 until 1943. The Judenrein was on Shavuot (June 6) 1943.

Memorial stone on mass graves site of June 6 (Shavuot), 1943 Judenrein akcja. During the 3 day liquidation of the ghetto, bunkers were turned into craters by grenades.

Emissaries of Israeli and US Rohatyner Societies at 1942 Memorial, Rohatyn, 1999.

Local friend points to unmovable foundation stone of large synagogue, Rohatyn, 1999.

Fishel Kirshen praying at Old Cemetery, Rohatyn, 1999.

Old Cemetery Retaining Wall constructed at behest of Rohatyn Societies, Rohatyn, 1999.

Sign at both Rohatyn Jewish cemeteries; a part of reconstruction projects of Rohatyn Societies, Rohatyn, 1999

New Cemetery gravestones recently brought back from roads, Rohatyn, 1999.

Letter from Society of the Rohatiner in Israel

ארגון יוצאי רוהטין והסביבה
בישראל
**Society of the Rohatiner
IN ISRAEL**

August 1999

To our fellow Rohatiners,

We would like to inform you that between July 17 and 27 a delegation of our society visited Rohatin in order to finalize the project of perpetuating the memory of our holy brothers in the town of their burial. The 3 delegants were: Fishl Kirschen and Frida Perl (Kamerling) from Israel and Donia Schwartzstein (Gold) from the United States.

We were glad to find all the sites we set up last year in good shape and even attended to by the locals, without any need for encouragement on our behalf. The sites are clean, a pavement leading to them from the street was built, flowers were planted, and in the coming fall, trees will be planted in order to mark the borders of the sites. All of these tasks are the work of the deputy mayor, Mr. Mihcael Worobetz, to whom we owe our deepest gratitude and respect.

THE MUNICIPALITY OF ROHATYN, ON ITS OWN INITIATIVE, HAS CONSTRACTED STEPS IN THE OLD CEMETRY, FOR

In visiting Rohatin this time we had in fact two goals: THE CONVINIENCE OF

1. To receive the orders from last year and expand some of them. THE VISITORS.

2. To find a solution for the providing of protection and care to the sites.

Thanks to the generous donation of our town member, Mr. Yakob Hornstein, we were able to expand and initiate more work in the field of preserving the two cemeteries in Rohatin. Two major achievements have been made up till now:

a. In the **old cemetery** we have built an aesthetic concrete wall which supports the hill on which the cemetery lies, and prevents it from falling apart, from the opening of graves and the scattering around of skeletons, especially in the rain season and during the melting of snow in the spring.

b. Ih the **new cememtery** we have built a metal net in order to prevent erosion resulting from constructions in the area. Moreover, a hedge will be planted along the fences of the two cemeteries to strengthen them.

In the area of the two cemeteries we have set up two large granite signs, two meters high each, with a concrete foundation, both engraved with the inscription: "The Jewish cemetery whose tombstones were uprooted brutally by the German Nazis". In the old cemetery we added the sentence – "one of the oldest cemeteries in the Ukraine".

In the new cemetery we decided to gather the tombstones (tombstone ruins, to be more accurate) which are uncovered from time to time during construction work in the town.

c. The **preservation** problem - No legislation has yet been made in this issue in the
   Ukraine. We solved the problem temporarily by assigning the task of looking after the
   sites to Mr. Worobetz, in return for $200 per year.

We would like to add that the rabi of the Jewish community in Stanislavov, Mr. Koleshnik,
had promised to visit the place from time to time and keep an eye on it's condition.
And finally, we would like to take the opportunity and enclose Testimony Forms provided to
us by the Yad Va-Shem Institute. These forms are dedicated to the memory of the holocaust
victims. They should be filled in in capital letters, in English only (no other language is
required). Please attach to the forms a sum of $20: $10 to cover the expenses of mailing the
forms back to Yad Va-Shem, and another $10 for current expenses related to the orders made
in Rohatin. The checks should be for the Society of Rohatiners in Israel.

Please send the forms and the checks to the following address:

Fishl Kirschen
34 Yehonatan st.
Tsahala
Tel Aviv 69081
Israel

Happy New Year !

On behalf of the society,

F. Kirschen, Chairman

Rohatyn Town Council Resolution

Rohatyn People's Town Council
Committee to Implement Resolution #23
February 1997, Rohatyn
Resolution concerning the Perpetuation of the Memory of the Victims of War and of Political Repression on the terrain of the town,

In order to implement the resolution/ordinance of the Rohatyn County Administration promulgated on the 19th of October of 1996, No. 361, "About the commemoration of the victims of war and of political repression in the territory of county", and pursuant to the petition of the Jewish citizens who left Rohatyn, situated within the District of Ivano-Frankov:

Be It Resolved:

1. To fulfill the request of Jewish expatriates of Rohatyn and environs living in Israel and North America, to properly perpetuate the memory of Jewish citizens, who perished at the hands of German Nazis between the years 1942 and 1944.

2. To affix a memorial plaque on the facade of the building of the school dormitory (formerly the "Judenrat") from the side of Kociubinski Street in the Ukrainian, Hebrew and English languages.

3. To place memorial stones on the sites where Jewish citizens lay buried, carried out in accordance with the artist's drawing/design and dimensions:

    a.   Near the country road Rohatyn-Putiatynce past the Babince cemetery;
    b.   On the territory of the communal property not far from the former hospital/Polish Monastery (Klasztor)

4. To carry out improvements, to the extent that they are indispensable, in order to complete the proposed project, so that it be consistent with the architecture of the town.

5. To request from the Director of the Rohatyn Department of Public Works (Citizen H. Janko) to section off a space of 0,04 hectares in the area where Jewish victims are buried, for the purpose of placing there a "memorial stone". It is necessary to fence in that section and to clean it up.

6. The agency responsible for communal property (citizen S. Cemcuk), and the agency responsible for road construction (citizen Y. Charyn) and the Department of Public Works (citizen W. Yanko) - are obligated by March 15, 1997 to clean up and put in order the burial sites of the Jews, murdered by the fascists in the years of World War II.

7. All expenses connected with the perpetuation of the memory of the Jewish citizens will be borne by the Rohatyn Association in Israel and North America.

    Chairman of Implementation Committee, W. Husak
    Secretary   H. Baznik

Glossary

Admor (pl. Admorim) An acronym for "Adonainu, Morainu, VeRabbeinu" ("Our Master, Our Teacher, and Our Rebbe"). This is an honorific title given to scholarly leaders of a Jewish community.

Agudah aka World Agudat Israel A global organization founded in 1912 by many leading Orthodox rabbis at a conference in Katowice to promote the ideals of Orthodox Judaism.

Akcja Literally, "action" in Polish. An akcja was basically any action to destroy Jews. In ghettos, Jews were rounded up and then killed or deported to death camps.

Al Kiddush Hashem See "Kiddush Hashem"

Aleph-Beis/Aleph-Bet The Hebrew alphabet.

Aliyah Literally, "going up" in Hebrew. There are two primary usages of this term: 1) People who "make aliyah" leave their homes to settle in Israel. 2) When a person is called to witness the reading of the Torah during a prayer service, they are called up for an "aliyah."

Aryan identity card An identity card issued during World War II that identified holders as Aryan.

Avodah Literally, "service" in Hebrew. Used here, it refers to a central prayer recited while standing during any service.

Ba'al(ei) tefilah (lot) The leader(s) of a prayer service, sometimes a cantor.

Ba'al Shem Tov/Besht Rabbi Yisroel (Israel) ben Eliezer (August 27, 1698 - May 22, 1760). Considered to be the founder of Hassidic Judaism.

Banderowcy Followers of Stepan Bandera. A faction of the
(pronounced Organization of Ukrainian nationalists which
Banderovtsy) cooperated with the SS and killed thousands of Poles and
Jews between 1941 and 1944. After liberation of the area
by the Soviet Army in 1944 this Ukrainian movement
carried on its fight from the underground.

Beit Midrash/ A study hall, sometimes attached to a synagogue.
Beit HaMidrash/
Beis Medresh

Betar A Zionist movement founded in 1923 in Riga, Latvia by
Ze'ev Jabotinsky. The name "Betar" is an abbreviation
of "Brit Yosef Trumpeldor," meaning "The Covenant of
Trumpeldor."

Bnai Zion Foundation Formed in 1908, Bnai Zion was formed to help the Zionist
Congress in the work of obtaining for the Jewish people a
legally secured, publicly assured national home in
Palestine.

Boikes Shoes.

Brit Trumpeldor See Betar.

Brit aka Brit Milah Ritual circumcision.

Brit HaChayal Literally, "soldier's covenant" in Hebrew, an association
of Jewish Polish army reserves founded in 1932 in Radom,
Poland. They were inspired by Ze'ev Jabotinsky, who had
founded the Jewish Legion for the British in WWI, openly
trained Jews in self-defense and toured Poland in the 1930's
to convince Jews to move to Palestine.

Bund A secular socialist party founded in Vilna in 1897. It sought
to unite all Jewish workers and achieve recognition for
Jews as a nation with a legal minority status.

Cabala/Cabbalah See Kabbalah.

Capote (or Kapote) Literally, a "kaftan" in Yiddish. A long black coat worn in
Eastern Europe and now worn by some Hassidic men.

Cech Literally, "guild" in Czech and Polish.

Chalutz Literally, "pioneer" in Hebrew. Popularly, Jewish immigrants to Palestine after 1917 who worked in agriculture and forestry. For the movement Chalutz, see Hachalutz.

Chalutziut Literally, "pioneering" in Hebrew.

Chanukah Eight-day Jewish holiday celebrating the rededication of the Temple of Jerusalem in 165 BC.

Chayot HaKodesh Literally, "living beings" in Hebrew. Referred to in mystical writings and Kabbalah as angels. Sometimes associated with the 12 tribes who are to be re-united in the future.

Chazan The Hebrew term for cantor. A professional ba'al tefilah, often hired by a congregation for his skill, knowledge and voice.

Cheder Literally, "room" in Hebrew. A Jewish religious school for young children; mostly boys.

Chesed Elyon Literally, "Kindness of the Most High" in Hebrew.

Chevra Kadisha An organization of Jewish men and women who see to it that the bodies of Jews are prepared for burial according to Jewish law.

Cholent A traditional Jewish stew simmered overnight, for 12 hours or more, and eaten for lunch on the Sabbath.

Chovevey Zion Literally, "lovers of Zion" in Hebrew. Refers to religious, apolitical organizations that are now considered the forerunners and foundation-builders of modern Zionism. Many of these first groups were established after pogroms in Eastern European countries in the early 1880s, with the aim to promote Jewish immigration to the Land of Israel, then a part of Ottoman Empire, and advance Jewish settlement there, particularly agricultural. Baron Edmond de Rothschild responded by supporting massive land purchases and underwriting Jewish agricultural settlement in Eretz Yisrael in the late 19th century.

Chumash One of the Hebrew names for the five books of Moses, the Pentateuch or the Torah.

Commandment See Mitzvah.

Council on Four Lands (in Hebrew, "Va'ad Arba Aratzos") A government-sanctioned central body of self-governing Jewish authority in Poland from 1580 to 1764. Delegates came from the "four lands"; Greater Poland, Little Poland, Ruthenia and Volhynia and met regularly to discuss taxation and other issues important to the Jewish community.

Daf Yomi The practice of studying one specific page of Talmud each day, allowing for all participants to complete the study of the entire Talmud in one 7 1/2 year cycle. It was initiated by Rabbi Meir Shapiro, the rabbi of Lublin between the world wars, and is still practiced by Jews around the world today.

Darshan A preacher who would interpret or explicate scripture.

Dayan Literally, "judge" in Hebrew. A dayan is an officer of a Beit Din, a religious court of law.

Etrog(im)/Esrog(im) Literally, "citron(s)" in Hebrew. This fruit is used in rituals during the Jewish holiday of Sukkot.

Fiakernik A driver of a horse-drawn, passenger carriage.

Final akcja Literally, "final action" in Polish. This referred to the liquidation of the ghetto Jews and the destruction of the ghetto. In Rohatyn, the date was June 6, 1943.

Frankist Follower of Jacob Frank, an 18th-Century Jewish religious leader who claimed to be the reincarnation of the self-proclaimed messiah, Sabbatai Zvi.

Galicia/Galizien Polish/German word for Eastern and Western Galicia that was part of Poland before WW II.

Gaon An honorific title given to a notable rabbi.

Gemara From the Aramaic word "gemar", literally, "to study." This rabbinic commentary, analysis and debate of the Mishna forms the basis of Jewish law. There are two versions; one published around 350-400 BCE in Israel in Hebrew and one published around 500 CE in Babylonia in Aramaic.

General-gouvernement A German term referring to parts of Poland occupied by Nazi Germany which Hitler wanted make "as German as Rhineland." In August 1941, Eastern Galicia (including Rohatyn), which until then was occupied by the Soviet Union, was added by Hitler to the Generalgouvernement.

Gestapo A contraction of the German words, "Geheime Staatspolizei," it was the official secret police of the SS and had the authority to investigate acts of treason and espionage. In 1936, it was empowered to operate without judicial oversight and to set up and administer concentration amps.

Gimnazjum (Polish) (Gimnazja) A type of school(s) in parts of Europe providing secondary education.

Gemilas Chesed Literally, "giving kindness" in Hebrew.

Gordonia Gordonia was a Zionist pioneering youth movement, based largely on the ideology of A. D. Gordon. Its stated principles were the "building up of the homeland, education of members in humanistic values, the creation of a working nation, the renaissance of Hebrew culture, and self-labor (avodah atsmit)." For articles on Gordon and Gordonia, see Encyclopedia Judaica, Jerusalem (1972), Volume 7, pp. 790-794, and pps. 805-6.

Gutte Voch Literally, "good week" in Yiddish. A common greeting between Jews after the Sabbath.

HaChalutz Literally, "the pioneer," in Hebrew; a Zionist association formed in 1918 by Joseph Trumpeldor.

Hachshara Literally, "preparation" in Hebrew. Refers to training in agricultural and other skills necessary for founding or contributing to farms and settlements in Israel.

HaKibbutz HaArtzi In 1927, United Kibbutz Movement was established. Several HaShomer HaTzair kibbutzim banded together to form HaKibbutz HaArtzi. In 1936, HaKibbutz HaArtzi founded its own political party, the Socialist League of Palestine.

Halacha/Halachot In Hebrew, Jewish law(s).

Halachic Per Halacha.

Hallerczyki An independent Polish army created in 1918 by General Jozef Haller on behalf of the Polish National Committee. Also known as the Blue Army, it eventually had over 100,000 soldiers. The Hallerczyki wreaked pogroms against Jewish communities in Eastern Galicia.

Halicz Before Lwow developed and became more important, Halicz was the capital of Red Ruthenia. The district of Halicz included the town of Rohatyn and surrounding communities.

HaNoar HaTzioni Literally, "Zionist Youth" in Hebrew, it is a youth movement established in 1926.

HaNoar HaIvri Literally, "Hebrew Youth" in Hebrew, it was a youth movement. In the years 1931-32, the HaNoar HaIvri, HaShomer HaLeumi and Herzliya movements united with the HaNoar HaTzioni.

HaShomer HaTzair Socialist-Zionist youth movement founded in 1913.

Hassidism/ Hassid From Chesed, the Hebrew word for kindness. Religious movement started in Eastern Europe in the 18th Century by the Ba'al Shem Tov as a reaction to what was seen as an overemphasis on academia. He taught his followers that one may achieve divine service through faith, prayer and spirituality.

Hassidut Piety, from the Hebrew word for kindness, Chesed.

Haskalah Enlightenment or education, from Sechel, the Hebrew word for intellect or mind. The term refers to an 18th-Century Jewish enlightenment movement.

HaTechia Literally, "revival" or "rebirth." A Zionist organization.

Hatikvah Literally, "the hope" in Hebrew. The poem Hatikvah was written in 1878 and was adopted as the text for the national anthem of the State of Israel.

Havdalah Literally, "distinction" in Hebrew. A prayer said at the close of the Sabbath or festivals to identify the distinction between holy and secular times.

Herzl, Theodor (May 2, 1860–July 3, 1904) Considered the father of modern Zionism.

Hitachdut A Zionist youth movement.

Holy Sheloh/Yeshaye Horowitz (1565 - 1630) A rabbi and mystic best known for his work "Shnei Luchot Habrit."

Hoshanah Rabbah The seventh day of Sukkot; a day with distinct rituals and traditions. See Sukkot.

Huppah The portable canopy beneath which the couple stands while the wedding ceremony is performed. The term ḥuppah may also refer to the wedding ceremony itself.

Judendirektion Literally, "Directorate for Jews" in German. It was responsible for managing Jewish affairs in Galicia.

Judenrat Literally, "Council of Jews" in German. Administrative bodies that the Germans required Jews to form in the German occupied Poland.

Judenrein Literally, "clean of Jews" in German. See Final akcja

Jüdische Ordnungspolizei The Jewish police, which reported to the Judenrat.

Kabbalah An esoteric theosophy based on the Torah and developed between the 7th and 18th centuries.

Kahal The local governing body of a European Jewish community administering religious, legal and communal affairs.

Kamienice Polish for "houses."

KKL/Keren Kayemet L'Yisrael A fund created in 1901 to develop the land of Israel.

Kashrut The state of being kosher.

Kehilah (Kehilot) Jewish community(ies).

Ketubah Marriage contract.

Kiddush Prayer made over wine before drinking.

Kiddush HaShem Literally, "sanctification of G-d's name" in Hebrew. Any action by a Jew that brings honor, respect, and glory to G-d. The ultimate act of Kiddush Hashem is when a Jew sacrifices his life rather than transgress G-d's cardinal sins (i.e., idolatry, incest, adultery, murder).

Kimcha D'Pis'cha Literally, "flour for Passover" in Aramaic. A Talmudic requirement to provide flour to the poor before Passover. In lieu of this, communities collect monies for the poor at this time of year.

Kippa Hebrew term for small head covering worn by a male. In Yiddish and English, known as a yarmulka.

Klezmer (Klezmorim) A Yiddish word derived from the Hebrew words "klei," meaning vessel and "zemer" meaning "song." It is a music and musical tradition of Jewish folk music played for weddings and other occasions.

Kloiz (Kloizen) A Yiddish word for a synagogue established by or for like-minded people.

Korban Mincha Siddur A standard prayer book designed for use by women. It includes Yiddish translations for all of the prayers, some commentaries as well as sections on Jewish law.

Kreishauptman Literally, "circuit commander" in German. The circuit was an administrative subdivision of the District in the Generalgouvernement territories.

Kultusrat Literally, "education council" in German. The supreme organ of the Jewish community; covering all areas of culture, education, social affairs, security, etc. The council of the Rohatyn Jewish community was in service between 1904 and 1910.

Kvitel A Yiddish word meaning "a little message." Refers to anonymous written prayers or wishes given to rabbis or placed into cracks of the Western Wall in Jerusalem.

Lag B'Omer A holiday celebrated on the 33rd day of the Omer.

Lamed Vav Names of 2 Hebrew letters whose cumulative value is the numerological equivalent of 36. According to Talmudic tradition, the world needs thirty-six righteous people to exist.

L'Chaim Literally, "to life" in Hebrew. A popular toast at Jewish celebrations.

Landeskommissar A German term for the head of administration for a particular county.

Lemberg German name for city also known as Lwow (Polish), Lvov (Polish), and Lviv (Ukrainian).

Likutei Amarim (also known as Tanya) Written by Rabbi Schneur Zalman of Liadi (1745-1812), it is a seminal document in both the study of Hassidic thought and of Kabbalah.

Lokal Meeting place in Polish.

L'shona ha-bo-oh b'Yerushalayim Literally, "to the next year in Jerusalem" in Hebrew. A prayer said at various times that reflects the hope that Jews will soon return to their land.

Lviv/Lvov/Lwow see Lemberg above.

Maayan Tahor A volume written by Rabbi Moshe Teitelbaum, a portion of which appears to have been included in the Korban Mincha Siddur (see above).

Maccabi The reference here is to the Jewish sports organisation that traces its roots to clubs formed in Eastern and Central Euopre in the 1890's.

Machzor(im) A prayer book used for holidays that incorporates additional prayers specific to that day.

Maot Chitim Literally "money for wheat" in Aramaic. See Kimcha D'Pis'cha.

Marszalek The presiding officer or speaker of the sejm (Polish parliament), or the speaker of the sejmik, the district or regional congress.

Maskil(im) Proponent(s) of Haskalah (see Haskalah).

Matura High school graduation, usually with a diploma

Matzah (Matzot) Unleavened bread; the only kind of bread allowed on Passover.

Mazel Tov Literally, "good luck" in Hebrew.

Megilla (Megillot) Literally, "scroll(s)" in Aramaic. Usage here refers to the Scroll of Esther, part of the "writings" in the Old Testament, which is read during the holiday of Purim.

Melamed (Melamdim) See HaMelamed above.

Menachem Av Av is the fifth month on the Hebrew calendar. On the 9th day, Jews fast in commemoration of the destruction of both temples. The word "menachem" means "consoling" as the balance of the month focuses on consolation.

Mezuzah (Mezuzot) Hand-written parchment scroll(s) affixed to the doorpost(s) of a house. Also often used in reference to the case which holds the scroll.

Mikveh A ritual bath for purification.

Mincha The second prayer service of each day.

Minyan A group of 10 (traditionally men) required to say certain prayers.

Mirkevet Hamishne Written by Rabbi David Moshe Avraham (ancestor of Yehoshua Spiegel), completed in 1740, published 1895 in Lwow. It is a comprehensive commentary, with original interpretations and harmonization between modern rulings and Talmudic opinions. These are fundamental clarifications of the Mechilta (running commentary on portions of Exodus) by Rabbi Yishmael, 90-135 CE, that show the author's knowledge of ancient and medieval Rabbinic literature.

Mishnah/Mishne (Mishnayot) The first major redaction of Jewish oral law, it reflects debates between 70-200 CE by the group of rabbinic sages known as the Tannaim. It was published by Yehudah Hanassi about 210 A.C.E.

Misnaged (Misnagdim)/ Mitnaged (Mitnagdim) Literally "opponents" in Hebrew. In the 18th Century, a group of Ashkenazi religious Jews opposed the rise and spread of early Hassidic Judaism and became known as Misnagdim.

Mitzvah One of the 613 commandments in the Torah. Colloquially, refers to a "good deed."

Mitzvah haba-ah be-aveiro Doing one mitzvah while transgressing another.

Mizrachi Religious Zionist organization founded in 1902.

Mohel One authorized to perform the brit milah (ritual circumcision).

Musaf Additional prayers recited on the Sabbath and festivals.

Ne'ila Prayer service recited only on Yom Kippur.

Ohel Ohel Theatre (Ohel Tent Theatre), theatrical company of the Jewish Labor Federation, founded in Palestine in 1925.

Olah During the existence of the Temple, several kinds of offerings were brought. The Olah offering was entirely consumed by fire. When the Torah was translated into Ancient Greek, they translated Olah as holocaustos (burnt).

Omer The period of time between Passover and Shavuot. Each day is counted.

Orach Chaim Originally, a section of Rabbi Jacob ben Asher's Arba'ah Turim, it now is a general reference to mitzvot set to be performed at certain times, days, weeks, months, or years.

Oy Gevalt Yiddish exclamation, "Oh, woe is me."

Pańszczyzna Literally, "corvee" in Polish (unpaid labor required by a feudal lord).

Glossary

Parnass (Parnassim) Leader(s) of the Jewish community.

Phylacteries A pair of black leather boxes containing scrolls of parchment inscribed with 4 biblical verses; traditionally worn on the forehead and left arm during morning weekday prayers. In Hebrew, Tefillin.

Pirkei Avot Literally, "Chapters of our fathers," it is often referred to as "Ethics of our fathers," as this tractate of the Mishnah primarily features ethical maxims, advice and insights.

Poalei Zion Literally "Workers of Zion" in Hebrew. Started in the Russian Empire in the early 1900's, this Marxist Zionist organization established branches around the world.

Podwodne Obligation of the towns and villages to provide horse-drawn carriages for the king, his court, and the officials who were travelling in the name of the authorities as well as for the armed forces.

Pogrom An organized massacre, especially of Jews

Pri Megadim A commentary on various Jewish texts written by Joseph ben Meir Teumim of Lwow in the 18th Century.

Protekcja Literally "favoritism" in Polish (pronounced "protekseeya").

Purim A festive Jewish holiday commemorating the events featured in the Book of Esther.

Rashi Acronym for Rabbi Shlomo Yitzhaki (1040-1105). His comprehensive commentaries on the Tanach and the Talmud are staples of Jewish learning.

Rav Hebrew and Aramaic word for rabbi.

Reb Honorary title like Mr., used when addressing an elderly Jewish male.

Rebbe Yiddish word for rabbi.

Rebbetzin A rabbi's wife.

Red Ruthenia "Czerwona Rus," a province that included the area that later became Galicia.

Ringplatz Literally, "ringside seat" in German. Used colloquially to describe a central town square.

Rynek "Town square" in Polish.

Sabbatean(s) Follower(s) of Sabbatai Zvi. See Sabbatai Zvi.

Sabbatai Zvi A 17th-Century rabbi and Kabbalist who asserted that he was the Messiah. His followers were called Sabbateans.

Safa Brura Literally, "clear language" in Hebrew. There were Safa Brura societies which promoted the learning of Hebrew and were influential in promoting aliyah.

Sanacja Literally, "purification" in Polish. A broad political movement from 1926 to 1939 which was against corruption in government.

Sefer Torah Literally, "book(s) of Torah" in Hebrew. A scroll or scrolls
(Sifrei Torah) hand lettered by a professional sofer (scribe) on parchment.

Segula (Segulot) Remedy(ies) and/or protective measures issued by Admor Yehudah Zvi Brandwein, founder of Stratyn Hassidic dynasty.

Sejm (pron. Saym) Polish National Parliament.

Sejmik District parliament.

Selekcja Literally, "selection" in Polish. Process used in
(pron. Selektsia) concentration camps and ghettos to select inmates for death, forced labor, or other purposes.

Shabbetzvinikes/ Followers or those thought to be followers of Sabbatai Zvi
Shabse Tzvinekes

Shabbat/Shabbos Hebrew/Yiddish word for the Sabbath.

Shabbos B'Reishis The Sabbath during which Genesis is read. This occurs in the Fall after Sukkot.

Shabbos Shuva Literally, "Sabbath of repentance" in Hebrew. It is the Sabbath which falls between Rosh Hashanah and Yom Kippur.

Shadchan Marriage matchmaker.

Shammes/Shamash Yiddish/Hebrew word for the caretaker at a synagogue. Also, the 9th candle which is used to light and "watch over" the other Chanukah candles.

Shavuot/Shavuos Pilgrimage festival which is celebrated 1 day in Israel and 2 days outside of Israel.

Shechina One of several names for G-d.

Sheygetz (Shkutzim) Gentile man (men).

Shidach (pron. Shidakh) (Shiduchim) Proposed male or female match(es) for marriage.

Shiksa Gentile woman.

Shlita Acronym for Sheyihye L'orach Yamim Tovim, literally, "may he have long, good days" in Hebrew. A blessing.

Sh'ma Yisrael The first words of a seminal Hebrew prayer recited during all services, upon waking, before bed and before dying.

Shemoneh Esrei Literally, "eighteen" for the original 18 blessing included in this prayer which is central to all Jewish services.

Shoah Hebrew word for the Holocaust.

Shochet (Shochtim) One(s) authorized to perform the ritual slaughter of animals.

Shofar Instrument made from an animal's horn that is blown on various occasions including Rosh Hashanah.

Shomer (Shomrim) Literally, "watcher(s)" in Hebrew. Usage here generally refers to Zionist groups.

Shri Acronym for Shem Rosha Yirkav, literally, "may the name of the evil one rot" in Hebrew. A curse.

Shtadlan A Yiddish word for one who intercedes with the authorities on behalf of Jewish community.

Shtele(s) Yiddish for market stall(s) or job(s).

Shtetl Yiddish for small town(s).

Shtibel (Shtiblach) Yiddish for little house(s). Often used in reference to small synagogues, especially Hassidic.

Shtreimel Wide-brimmed, often fur-lined hat worn by some Hassidim.

Shul Yiddish for synagogue and place of study. Derived from the German word for school.

Siddur (Siddurim) Daily prayer book(s).

Simchat Torah Jewish holiday that celebrates the receiving of the Torah on Mt. Sinai. It is a one-day holiday that follows Sukkot.

Sochaczki Polish word for free trade fair for meat imported by peasants from the surrounding villages.

Sofer Literally, "scribe" in Hebrew. One who is authorized to pen Torah scrolls, tefillin, mezuzot, etc.

Sokoł A fitness or training center sometimes used as a clubhouse or auditorium.

SS Abbreviation for Schutzstaffel. The SS, under Heinrich Himmler, was responsible for many of the crimes against humanity perpetrated by the Nazis during the World War II.

Stam-Tsioni Literally, "plain Zionist," a Zionist organization.

Starosta In Poland, a district administrator.

Sukkah Hebrew word for the booth in which Jews eat or sleep during Sukkot in commemoration of the temporary dwellings the Israelites lived in during their journey in the desert.

Sukkot Jewish pilgrimage holiday which takes place during the fall harvest, and commemorates the Biblical journey from Egypt to Israel.

Szos A Polish term referring to taxes on paved roads.

Ta'amei Hamikra Special signs or marks which identify the tones to be used when chanting each word of Hebrew Bible as part of a service.

Tach V'Tat Yiddish term for the pogroms of the Khmelnytsky (Chmielnicki) Uprising in 1648-49 during which Jewish Ukrainian communities were devastated.

Tallit or Tallis A rectangular prayer shawl, with fringes at the corners.

Talmid Chacham (pron. Khakham), Yid. Talmid Chochom Honorific title given to one well versed in Jewish law.

Talmud Composed of the Mishnah and the Gemara which comprise the body of Jewish oral and rabbinic law; presented in the form of debate and discussion.

Talmud Torah Community-supported Jewish elementary school for teaching children Torah and other religious studies.

Tanach The Jewish Bible.

Tanya An early work of Hassidic Judaism, written by Rabbi Schneur Zalman of Liadi, the founder of Chabad, in 1797 CE.

Tarbut association A network of secular, Zionist, Hebrew-language schools.

Tefillin See Phylacteries.

Tishah B'Av A fast day on the ninth day of the month of Av which commemorates the destruction of the First and Second Temples.

Tichye Literally, "so you shall live" in Hebrew. A blessing.

Torah The first five (and most important) books of the Hebrew Bible. Also known as the Pentateuch.

Torah reader The one who chants a portion of the Torah during a service.

Tosafot Medieval commentaries on the Talmud.

Treif meat Term for any meat that isn't certified as kosher.

Tzaddik(im) Literally, "righteous one(s)" in Hebrew. In Hassidism, it refers to the spiritual leader of a Hassidic community.

Tzayg Slang for ready-made suits. Perhaps from the German zeug (stuff, material).

Va'ad Governing council. In Rohatyn, it consisted of Parnassim, who, while Rohatyn was a crown town, had their election approved by the Voivode, Tuvim (notables) and members of executive committees

Va'ad Gelila (Va'adei Gelilot)/Va'ad Hagalil Jewish district council(s).

Verein In Yiddish, association.

Vice Starosta In Poland, a deputy district administrator.

Voivode In Poland, a provincial governor.

Weekly portion The portion of the Torah read in a given week.

Wio! (Pron. Viyo) In Polish & Ukrainian, a command to horses to get moving, to proceed.

WIZO Women's International Zionist Organization.

Yahrzeit In Yiddish, the anniversary of a person's death.

Yiddishkeit Literally, "Jewishness" in Yiddish. The Jewish way of life as expressed in the practices of the traditional Jewish religion and its customs. The term has a warm ring for the Ashkenazi Jew, denoting the positive aspects of Jewish habits.

Yishuv The Palestine Jewish settlement or community (before the establishment of the State of Israel).

Yishuvnik A member of the Yeshuv.

Yom Tov In Hebrew, Holy Day or holiday.

Yoreh Deah A section of Rabbi Jacob ben Asher's compilation of halacha, Arba'ah Turim.

Zemiros (Yiddish) or Hymns sung around the table on Shabbat and holidays.
Zemirot (Heb.)

Zionist A Jew who wishes to move to Israel.

Zloty Polish currency.

Zohar Literally, "splendor" in Hebrew. Widely considered the most important work of Kabbalah, it is a mystical commentary on the Torah.

Z"L In Hebrew, "Zikhrono LiVrocho" - May his/her memory be for a blessing.

Timeline
World War II & the Holocaust in Rohatyn

September 1, 1939	War breaks out
August 23, 1939	Molotov Ribbentrop Non-Aggression Pact signed
September 1939	Rohatyn occupied by Soviet Union
June 1941	Hitler attacks Soviet Union
July 1941	Rohatyn occupied by German Blitzkieg
July 3, 1941	Ukrainian militia formed
July 6 or July 12, 1941	Beating of Jews by Ukrainian militia
	Jewish males locked in synagogue
August 1, 1941	Eastern Galicia comes under control of Generalgouvernement
	Rohatyn becomes regional town
	Jewish ghetto established in Rohatyn
	Local Ukrainian elite appoint specific Jews to Judenrat
	Jews ordered to wear yellow Star of David
November 1941	Rohatyn becomes a sub-district under (Stanislau) Stanislawow
	Gestapo Chief Asbach moved to Brzezany
December 1941	Fur & jewelry decrees. Jew must surrendered all to government
Winter 1941	Judenrat orders 150 laborers to assemble to dig large pits
March 20, 1942	Akcja: Gestapo & Ukrainian militia round up Jews; 3,600 killed
May 1, 1942	Perimeter of ghetto reduced
	Hunger & typhus epidemic
September 21, 1942 [Yom Kippur]	Yom Kippur Akcja - Gestapo from Tarnopol carry out action
October 1942	Jews from satellite towns driven into Rohatyn ghetto
December 8, 1942	Akcja – 1250 Jews deported to Belzec
	Ghetto hermetically locked, under armed guard
	Jews seek hiding places in underground bunkers
May 15, 1943	Secret meeting in ghetto to prepare for armed struggle
June 6 - June 9, 1943 [Shavuot]	Judenrein Akcja - total annihilation; ghetto leveled; small survivor group flees to the woods
July 24, 1944	Rohatyn liberated by Soviet army

Index

In honor of those who perished

www.ingramcontent.com/pod-product-compliance
Lightning Source LLC
Chambersburg PA
CBHW021843090426
42811CB00033B/2123/J